THE
BEAUTIFUL DRIBBLING GAME

The Scottish F.A. Challenge Cup
in the
19th Century

by

Stewart Mathers

The Beautiful Dribbling Game

ISBN: 978-0-9956998-0-9

———

ACKNOWLEDGEMENTS

To the numerous librarians across the length and breadth of Scotland who fetched countless items from their archives for my perusal.

To the proof readers – Alex, Hannah, James, Jim D, Jim W, Leanne & Murray

To Steve Bartrick (http://www.ancestryimages.com) for permission to use his image of Pictorial World's "Football Match at Dumbarton: Dumbarton v Queen's Park" engraving as the basis of the book's front cover.

DEDICATION

To my late father Alf.

---

iv

PREFACE

I began my Scottish F.A. Challenge Cup and League research as a hobby back in the late 70s. My original aim was to create the definitive reference for all matches played in these national football competitions.

Since then there have been several commendable publications covering these topics [I]. These enabled me to establish that the completeness and level of accuracy of my 19th Century Scottish F.A. Challenge Cup seasons results collection was second to none. This therefore became the subject of this book.

During my predominantly newspaper based research, I came across a number of interesting match reports and articles, not all relating to cup matches. These I scribbled down for my private collection. To both capture the era, and eliminate many historically reported inaccuracies, I decided to include these.

With the help of the online British Newspaper Archive [II] and ProQuest [III] websites I have been able to retrospectively find the original references to a large percentage of these reports and articles, with the others most likely coming from other regional newspapers of that time [IV].

[I] - Scottish Cup 1873-1986 John Byrne   ISBN 0946531 331
    Breedon Book of Scottish Football Records Gordon Smailes   ISBN 1 85983 020 X
    The Complete Scottish F.A. Cup Results Book 1873-2012 Alex Graham   ISBN 978-1-86223-250-1
    Scottish Football Historical Results Volume 1 1873-1900 Brian McColl   ISBN 978-1-326-04836-5

[II] - http://www.britishnewspaperarchive.co.uk

[III] - http://www.proquest.com [The Scotsman Digital Archive]

[IV] - most probable, but not limited to:-
    Airdrie and Coatbridge Advertiser, Arbroath Herald, Ardrossan and Saltcoats Herald, Ayr Observer, Ayr Advertiser, Ayrshire Argus & Express, Ayrshire Post, Dumbarton Herald, Dumfries and Galloway Standard, Evening News & Star, Evening Times, Galloway Advertiser and Wigtownshire Free Press, Glasgow News, Hamilton Advertiser, Helensburgh and Gareloch Times, Helensburgh News, Kilmarnock Herald, Kilmarnock Standard, Lennox Herald, Moffat News and Times, Paisley Daily Express, Paisley and Renfrewshire Gazette, Paisley Herald and Renfrewshire Advertiser, Perthshire Advertiser, Scottish Athletic Journal, Scottish Referee, Scottish Sport, Scottish Umpire, Stirling Journal, Stirling Observer & Stirling Reporter.

NOTES

Many cup ties in the early years of the competition ended with the losing clubs protesting against the result for a variety of reasons, however paltry. These were subsequently discussed at the next Association Committee Meeting and either upheld or dismissed. This book provides details of almost all of the upheld ones and some of the more unusual dismissals.

I encountered many conflicting or erroneous score lines in the newspapers. Most of the former were with matches in which there had been one or more disputed goals during play. In some instances the score lines even appeared to differ according to the allegiance of the reporter. A good example of this is the West End v Govan tie of October 1876. Where there have been discrepancies, I have tended to go with the result for which there was a local match report available or, barring that, the most commonly reported score line.

For most seasons, the early rounds of the cup competition were played on a regional basis. This information is captured in this book and, with few exceptions, the ties are ordered as per the original draws.

Cup ties with an unknown date are marked with a +. The dates given for these are the most probable ones based on other matches played around that time by the teams involved.

Ties whose first match was played on a venue opposite to the draw are denoted with a **v*** *versus*. I would like to highlight that prior to 1880 the choice of ground for the first match in a tie was decided by the toss of a coin.

ABBREVIATIONS

The following abbreviations are used in this book:

Abbreviation	Word or Phrase
abd.	Abandoned
dbd	Disbanded
5th K.R.V.	5th Kirkcudbrightshire Rifle Volunteers
F.S.	Final Stage
4th V.B.S.R.	4th Volunteer Battalion Scottish Rifles
Kilmarnock C&FC	Kilmarnock Cricket & Football Club
npl	Not played
P.S.	Preliminary Stage
prot.	Protested
Q.C.	Qualifying Cup
Q.O.S. Wanderers	Queen of the South Wanderers
R.R.V.	Renfrewhire Rifle Volunteers
scr.	Scratched
S.F.A.C.M.	Scottish Football Association Committee Meeting
S.F.A.A.G.M.	Scottish Football Association Annual General Meeting
2nd A.R.V.	2nd Ayrshire Rifle Volunteers
6th G.R.V.	6th Galloway Rifle Volunteers
10th D.R.V.	10th Dumbartonshire Rifle Volunteers
3rd Edinburgh R.V.	3rd Edinburgh Rifle Volunteers
3rd L.R.V.	3rd Lanarkshire Rifle Volunteers
w/o	Walkover

CONTENTS

FRIENDLY MATCHES

1869-1873

29th May 1869

Friendly **Hamilton Gymnasium v Queen's Park**

HAMILTON GYMNASIUM versus QUEEN'S PARK FOOTBALL CLUB – A match was played between the above Clubs, on the ground of the former, on Saturday the 29th ult., when the latter were the winners by four goals and nine touches down.

Ref 1869001

Footnote

If the ball crossed the goal-line wide of the goal, touches (touchdowns or rouges) counted. See Early Laws of the Game 1863 – Law 7. Later to be replaced by the corner kick.

7th August 1869

Friendly **Queen's Park v Hamilton Gymnasium**

HAMILTON GYMNASIUM versus QUEEN'S PARK FOOT-BALL CLUB – A return match was played between the above clubs, on Saturday last, on the ground of the latter, when Queen's Park Foot-Ball Club was again victorious by two goals.

Ref 1869002

23rd June 1870

Friendly **Queen's Park v Airdrie**

QUEEN'S PARK against AIRDRIE – A match – fourteen a side – was played between these clubs on the recreation grounds of the South Side Park on Thursday night, and was witnessed by a large and respectable assemblage of spectators, who evinced much interest in the contest. The game was played according to the London Association rules, which bid fair to become erelong the standard throughout the country, the disallowance of hacking, tripping and other objectionable features of the Rugby play favourably distinguishing them. The same rules, we may mention, were adopted in the great International match between England and Scotland, recently played in London. The match of Thursday night, although keenly contested and reflecting much credit on both clubs, cannot be described as a close one, the superiority of the Queen's Park being conspicuous throughout. Indeed, this club is steadily earning a claim to the title invincible, it never having, as we understand, in all the various matches it has played, lost a single goal or suffered even to the extent of a "touch." On this occasion the game, which occupied one and a half hours, placed four goals to their credit, against nothing, notwithstanding the really good kicking and untiring vigour of the gentlemen from Airdrie, who, in point of physique and individual ability, were all that could be desired. The match was played throughout with great spirit and in perfect good temper, notwithstanding a high average number of falls.

Ref 1870001

9th July 1870

Friendly **Queen's Park v Drummond**

DRUMMOND v QUEEN'S PARK – A match, 18 aside, played according to the association rules, took place in the Queen's Park on Saturday, between the above clubs, which resulted in favour of the Queen's Park by 1 goal and a touch down.

Ref 1870002

20ᵗʰ September 1870
Friendly   **Airdrie v Queen's Park**
QUEEN'S PARK v AIRDRIE. This match – ten a side – was played on the ground of the latter at Airdrie, on Tuesday afternoon, according to the association rules, the Queen's Park, winning by three touches down.
Ref 1870003

24th September 1870
Friendly   **Hamilton Gymnasium v Queen's Park**
QUEEN'S PARK v HAMILTON GYMNASIUM – This match was played on the field of the latter, at Hamilton, on Saturday, with fifteen a side, according to the association rules. During the game, which lasted one hour and a-half, the Queen's Park succeeded in placing four goals to their credit, notwithstanding the persevering play exhibited by the members of the Gymnasium.
Ref 1870004

29ᵗʰ October 1870
Friendly   **Queen's Park v Hamilton Gymnasium**
QUEEN'S PARK FOOTBALL CLUB v. HAMILTON GYMNASIUM – This match (14 of the former against 18 of the latter) was played in the Queen's Park on Saturday afternoon. The play, which lasted one hour, was throughout in favour of the Queen's Park Club, who succeeded in taking three goals.
Ref 1870005

15ᵗʰ March 1873
Friendly   **Clydesdale v Granville**
This match took place on the fine ground of the Clydesdale, Kinning Park on Saturday. Matches between clubs adhering to the rules of the Football Association are few and far between in Scotland, as the clubs are yet small in numbers compared to those who prefer the Rugby style of play; but slowly and surely the beautiful dribbling game is beginning to be appreciated in Glasgow, where there are now several clubs who directly support the Association. The ground, which was somewhat soft owing to the heavy sleet showers of the previous day, was otherwise in good condition for the game, which commenced at four o'clock, but in consequence of the coldness of the afternoon very few spectators were present. The captain of the Clydesdale, who won the toss, elected to play with the wind in favour of his team, the Granville having it in their faces during the whole of the first round. For a short time both teams played pretty evenly together, but steadily and surely the Clydesdale gained ground, and a splendid run brought them in front of the Granville fortress, where a long and severe scrimmage occurred, out of which the ball was sent to the feet of Mr M'Arly by Mr Campbell, and the former, taking advantage of its position, had a straight shot at goal, but before it came to the tape Mr Ker took it in hand, and, by a fine drop kick, freed his goal from danger. After another scrimmage, this time near the centre of the ground, a splendid run by the Granville forwards, headed by Messrs Broadfoot, Keay, Kinloch, and Rae, brought the ball well in front of the

Clydesdale fortress where several long shots were made by Messrs Raeburn, Hetherington, and Malcolm, but without effect, the back play of the latter being most effective all through the match. For a little the ball was kept pretty evenly between the two strongholds, till successful manoeuvre by Messrs M'Pherson, Webster, Anderson, and Taylor brought it out from quite a shoal of open feet, and by a splendid piece of combined dribbling, landed it once more in front of the Granville goal, where the former finished up with a shot at the fortress. After this the ball was repeatedly kicked off from the Granville corner flag, but the latter players ably succeeded, just as half time was called, in raising the siege. On entering the second round of the game, the Granville, this time with the wind at their backs, soon drove their opponent before them, and landed the leather in front of the Clydesdale goal, where it remained for a considerable time, and several of the players made attempts to reduce the stronghold – the first shot of the match being made by Mr Broadfoot, whose arrow like kick, had it not been finely repelled by Mr McNab, would have brought dismay to the side and the Clydesdale. In turn the ball was as often, if not oftener, sent over the Clydesdale line than was the case with the Granville in the first round; and nothing could have saved play of the backs and half backs, among whom were the captain, Messrs Swan and W. Wilson. At the end of an hour and a half's play (the ball by this time showing signs of decay, and had previously deceived several of the players), the game was declared drawn, neither side having won a goal. The Clydesdale wanted two of their best players on the occasion, Messrs Gibb and Hendry. Sutrs- Clydesdale - Messrs M'Nab, goal; W.Wilson, Sinclair, backs; Taylor, M'Arly, Anderson, M'Pherson, J.Wilson, and Webster forwards. Granville – Messrs Ker, goal, Neil, Raeburn (captain), backs; Mackay, Hetherington, half backs; Kinloch, fly kick; Broadfoot, Malcom, Keay, Lyon, and Rae, forwards.
Ref 1873001

12th April 1873
Friendly   Dumbarton v Jamestown
This match was played on the ground of the former on Saturday the 12th. There was a large number of spectators. The ball was kicked off by the Jamestonians and kept well in Dumbarton quarters the first half of the game. A very fine run was made by one of the Dumbarton half backs, which might have resulted in a goal had the ball been well directed. On changing sides the play was alivened by the introduction of a lighter ball, the first being most evidently for Rugby playing. After some very hot playing, and as the game drew to a close, the Jamestown men managed to pass the ball between the goal posts, however the umpires decided, as the ball had not been thrown straight in from touch, that the goal was not legally won, on this the game stands drawn.
Ref 1873101

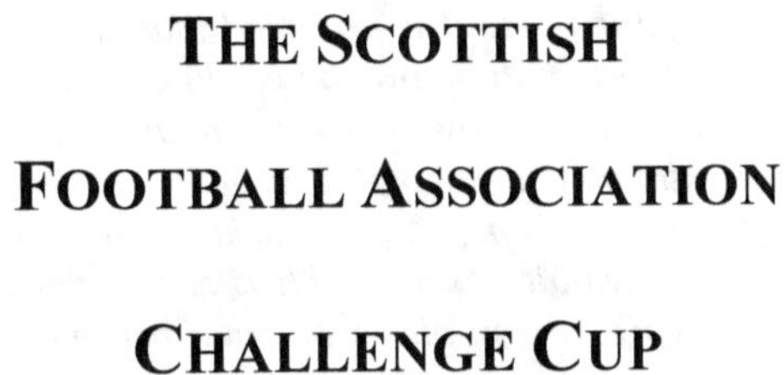

THE SCOTTISH

FOOTBALL ASSOCIATION

CHALLENGE CUP

Following a meeting of the Queen's Park committee on 8th February 1873, their secretary Mr. Archibald Rae wrote to the Scottish clubs proposing a Scotch Cup for competition among Scotch clubs the following season.

Representatives of the Clydesdale, Dumbreck, Eastern, Granville, Queen's Park, Rovers, 3rd Lanarkshire Rifle Volunteers and Vale of Leven football clubs attended the historic meeting, on 13th March 1873, held at the Dewar's Temperance Hotel, in Bridge Street, Glasgow.

There it was agreed to start a cup competition and to form themselves into "The Scottish Football Association" for the promotion of football under Association rules. This was announced later in the newspapers as:

"A national society for prosecuting the favourite game of football has been formed under the title of "Scottish National Football Association." The committee is composed of the leading members of various clubs, and it is provided that all clubs in Scotland playing according to the rules of the association may be eligible for membership, and that the annual meetings shall be held in Glasgow. The rules in question are admirably framed, and stipulate that the maximum length of the ground shall be 200 yards, and the maximum breadth 100 yards. "Tripping" and "hacking" will not be allowed, nor will players be permitted to wear any nails, except such as are driven in flush with the leather - the same prohibition applying to iron plates or gutta percha on the soles or heels of the boots." [I]

The Association Challenge Cup trophy and eleven badges were purchased in 1874 for the sum of 56 pounds 12s 11d. The trophy was made by Messrs. George Edward & Sons with the design of ornamentation taken from a sketch by William Ralston [II]. This depicted one of the Scottish players dribbling during their first official international match against England at Hamilton Crescent on 30th November 1872.

[I] *– Glasgow Herald 19th May 1873*
[II] *– Published in the The Graphic 14th December 1872*

Footnote
Incredibly, the goalless result of the first Scotland v England match was not to be repeated until their 87th meeting, on 25th April 1970, at Hampden Park.

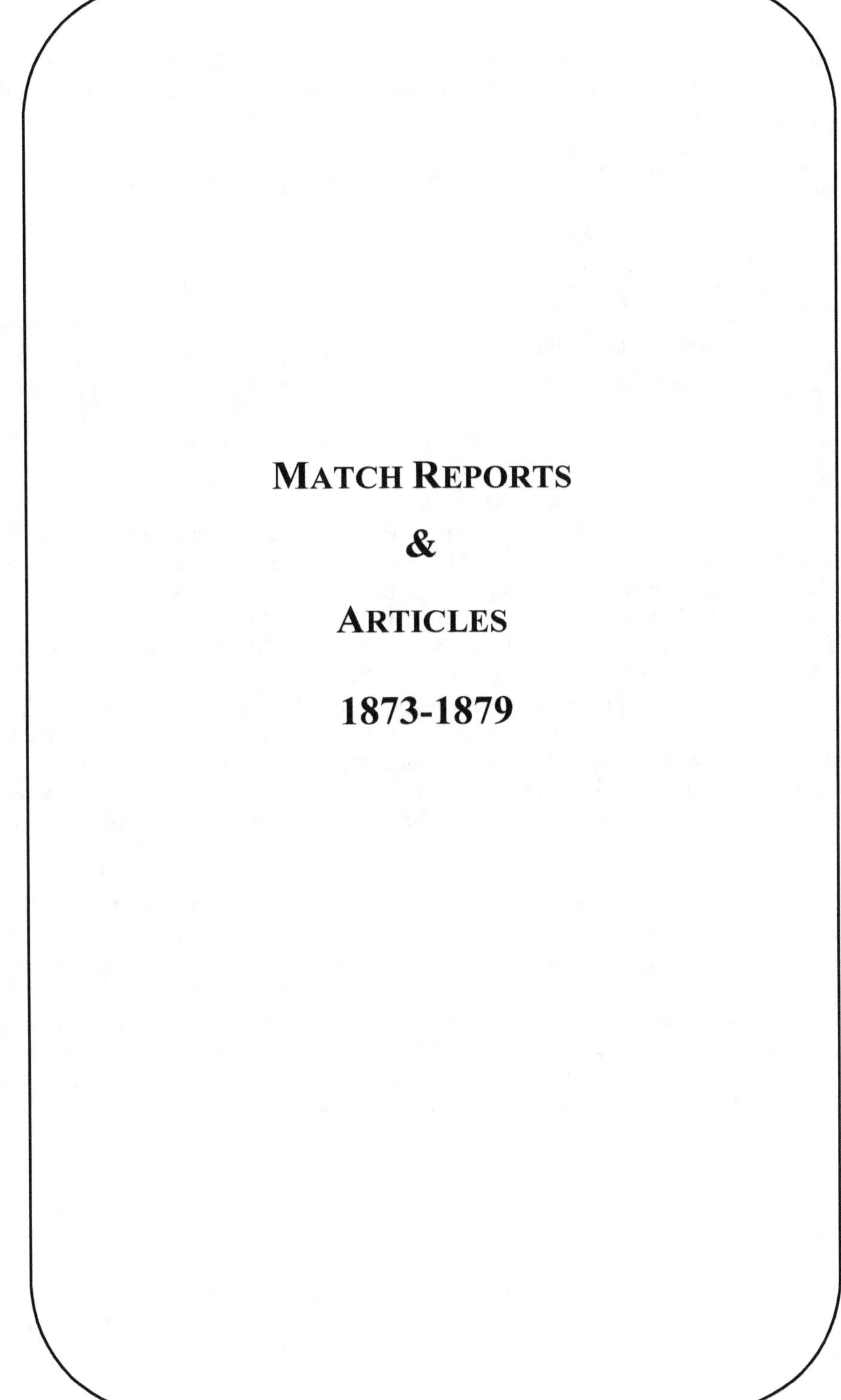

MATCH REPORTS

&

ARTICLES

1873-1879

9th + October 1873
First Ties Draw   **Scottish Football Association Challenge Cup**
S.F.A.C.M. [Reported 10th Oct]. The committee have drawn the first ties in the competition for this trophy, to be contended for during the season of 1873-4 for the first time. The drawing resulted thus: -

> 3d Lanark Rifle Volunteers – Play Southern
> Kilmarnock - Play Renton
> Dumbarton – Play Vale of Leven
> Rovers – Play Eastern
> Dumbreck – Play Queen's Park
> Blythswood – Play Western
> Alexandra – Play Callander
> Granville – Play Clydesdale

Ref 1873002

18th October 1873
First Tie   **Alexandra Athletic 2-0 Callander**
On Saturday afternoon these clubs played their first tie for the Scottish Football Association Cup, on the ground of the Alexandra, Cumbernauld Road. The sides were:-
Callander - Goal-keeper, Picken; backs, Connal and Clark; half-backs, Ross and Easdon; forwards, A. Macfarlane, Davidson, Macbeth, Corbett and Miller.
Alexandra - Goal-keeper, W. M'Kilroy; backs, Ritchie and M'Kinnon; half-backs, Ware and Laing; forwards, M'Arthur, Harvie, Hastie, Dick, M'Whinie and P. Kinnear.
The Callander won the toss but having wind and ground in their favour, elected to give the kick off to the Alexandra. Play for a time was good, but despite all their efforts, the Callander men were pressed hard home by their opponents several times. At the end of about twenty minutes, Dick of the Alexandra dribbled the ball for the centre and cleverly secured a goal for his party. Sides were then changed. Some pretty good exchanges ensued, but though the Callander men frequently invaded the territory of the Alexandra, they were unable to secure the much-coveted honour of kicking goal, which after a spirited struggle, for a second time fell to the latter, thanks to M'Arthur. After a pause, the game was renewed, and till time was called was kept up with great energy - neither side, however gaining a victory. The Alexandra club, which thus won the tie, most unquestionably owe their success to the superior manner in which they were marshalled. Their opponents manoeuvred at times very badly and were in many movements quite out-distanced by the younger club, which has only been a very short time in existence. Should the Alexandra improve at the rate it has done for the past few weeks, it may safely be expected to again distinguish itself before the close of the season.
Ref 1873003

18th October 1873
First Tie   **Renton 2-0 Kilmarnock**
This match, the first tie for the Association Cup, took place on the Queen's Park, Glasgow, on Saturday last, and after an hour and a half of stiff play, resulted in favour of the Dumbartonshire players by two goals. The play on both sides was rather wild at first but improved greatly before the game closed. It should be mentioned that the

Kilmarnock were one short of their proper number.
Ref 1873004

18th October 1873
First Tie   **Eastern 4-0 Rovers**

Played on the Flesher's Haugh, Green, for the Scottish Football Association Cup (Tie), and results in favour of the Eastern by four goals to none. The first was gained by P. Andrews, who made a run at goal, and with his usual activity carried the ball through. The Rovers tried hard to retrieve themselves, but after the ball had been carried down field a few minutes of furious play by the Eastern managed to secure a goal, the decisive kick being met by D. Stewart. The ball was soon active again and a short scrimmage ended in front of the Rovers goal, the Eastern forwards pressing them very hard. A goal ultimately taken by P. Andrews. Sides again being changed, with some very earnest and economical play a goal was taken by J. Blackwater.
Ref 1873004

25th October 1873
First Tie   **Western 0-1 Blythswood**

This match one of the ties for the Association Challenge Cup, was played on the Western ground on Saturday. The first half of the game was very evenly contested, but the second was rather in favour of the Blythswood. Within a few minutes to time the ball, being about the centre of the field, was played well forward by Mr J. Phillips, and by his and Messrs Smith, McPhee and Gibb's efforts brought it in front of the Western's goal, when Mr Gibb made a splendid shot, and sent the ball under the tape. The match thus ended in favour of the Blythswood by one goal to none. For the Western Messrs Campbell and R. M. Liddell rendered valuable service, as did also Messrs J. Phillips, Wright, and Davidson for the Blythswood.
Ref 1873005

25th October 1873
First Tie   **Queen's Park 7-0 Dumbreck**

CHALLENGE CUP COMPETITION – Queen's Park v. Dumbreck - This match between these clubs, in the first tie for this cup, was played on Saturday, on Hampden Park, Mount Florida, Cathcart Road the new private ground of the former club. The ball was kicked off at four o'clock, and it was very speedily made evident that the game was all in favour of the Queen's Park Club. Just fifteen minutes after the kick off, the first goal was scored for the Queen's Park by A. Broadfoot; and other six fell in rapid succession before the powerful play of the senior club. The goals were taken by Mr Lawrie, two, Mr W MacKinnon, two, Mr M'Neill, two, and Mr Broadfoot, one. The match ended in favour of the Queen's Park by seven goals to none. Teams – Dumbreck – Kennedy, goal, Gardner and M'Niven, backs, Dunn, flykick, J.R. Turnbull (captain) M'Leish, Gibson, Greenalade, Ferguson, Walker and M'Naught, forwards. Queen's Park – Neill, goal, Taylor and Campbell, backs, Thomson and Ker, half backs; Leckie, M'Neill, Angus, M'Kinnon, Wm MacKinnon, Lawrie, and Broadfoot, forwards.
Ref 1873006

25th October 1873

First Tie   **Clydesdale 6-0 Granville**

The first tie between the Clydesdale and Granville Football Clubs for the Association Cup was played at Kinning Park on Saturday afternoon. A lively interest was felt in the match by players in the west, and consequently, although the weather was decidedly uncomfortable, a number of spectators were present all through the game. The ground was soft and sloppy, and mishaps to the players were unusually numerous. The Clydesdale team was, all round, perhaps, the best which could be got together in the west, and although it was generally believed that the match would end in their favour, the result – six goals by the Clydesdale against none – was an undoubted surprise. The elevens were:- Clydesdale, - T. Anderson, W. Gibb, J. Laing, A. Raeburn, J. Macpherson, and G.F. Webster (forwards); J. Stanley (captain) and D. Wotherspoon (half backs), J.P. Tennant and W. Wilson (backs), and J. Macnab (goal.) Granville – R. Hetherington, W. Malcom, W.S. Rae, T. Keay, T. Donald, and Norval (forwards); J. Mackay and T. Highet (half backs); J. Finlayson and R.C. Kinloch (backs), and Barr (goal.). Play commenced shortly before four o'clock, and was continued with great energy for an hour and a-half. Shortly after the ball was kicked off, a splendid run was made by the Clydesdale forwards, and the goal-keeper having missed the ball, it was nearly sent through, but by an effort, the Granville saved the goal. After another fine run, however, Anderson succeeded in kicking a goal for the Clydesdale. Ends having been changed, the Granville for some time were kept closely pent up in their own ground, and after a tough struggle, a shot at goal by Webster sent the ball through below the tape. A few minutes later another goal was smartly secured by Macpherson, and in a short time Raeburn had the same honour. The ends having been changed, another fine run by the Clydesdale forwards brought the ball into dangerous proximity to the Granville goal, and the ball was eventually dribbled up and sent through the tape by Macpherson. Although all through the Granville did their utmost to avert defeat, the game continued painfully one-sided, and after a brief tussle, Macpherson scored another goal for his party. At this stage the play of the Granville visibly improved, but their opponents likewise redoubled their exertions. Macpherson followed up a fine run by the forwards, by again kicking the ball low between the posts. For the Clydesdale, the whole of the forwards played conspicuously well, and for the backs, Wotherspoon and W. Wilson did excellently what little they had to do. For the Granville's the players who most distinguished themselves were T. Highet, Finlayson, Kinloch, and Keay.

Ref 1873007

25th October 1873

Friendly   **Dumbarton 0-3 Vale of Leven**

The Vale won the toss, and elected to play with the sun in their favour. Dumbarton kicked off at 3.30 and the ball was immediately returned to their own quarters, where it was kept by the scientific play of the Vale men up till half-time. When this was called no goal had fallen to either side, but the Dumbarton goal had a few narrow escapes. Ends were changed, and play had not lasted five minutes when George M'Gregor cleverly scored a goal for the Leven. The ball had not been in motion ten minutes when a second goal was secured by the same man. Some very stiff play now took place, the Dumbarton men making desperate efforts to prevent a third goal being taken. In this, however, they were not successful, for shortly before time was called a third goal was secured by John

M'Gowan, and finally, when time being called, the ball was close to the Dumbarton citadel. The play of every member of the Vale side was all that could be desired, while the Dumbarton men undoubtedly deserve great credit for the noble stand they made during the game. This match was looked forward to with great interest, and over 1000 spectators were on the ground.
Ref 1873006

15th November 1873
Second Tie Replay   Clydesdale 0-0 3rd Lanarkshire R.V.
In consequence of the contest between these clubs for the Association Cup ending in a tie on the previous Saturday, after a spiritedly-contested game, much interest was manifested in the second match, which also took place at Kinning Park, in presence of about 500 spectators. Although the committee of the Clydesdale had adopted the sensible plan of having the touch-line roped off, so great was the excitement towards the close of the game that the ground was invaded on several occasions by excited spectators. As was the case in the previous tussle, darkness came on before the finish, and although the game continued till time was called, both teams found themselves in the same position as they did a week ago.
Ref 1873009

... Play was commenced a little after three o'clock by the Clydesdale kicking off, and was continued for about an hour and a-half. So equally matched are the clubs that once more the game resulted in a tie, neither succeeding in securing a goal. The play throughout was really excellent, and at times the excitement of both spectators and players rose to an extraordinary pitch.
... There seems no other course left but that the tie will again be played off, and it is to be hoped on that occasion the time for commencing play will be earlier in the day, as towards the close of the game on Saturday darkness completely hid the players and ball from the spectators.
Ref 1873010

22nd November 1873
Second Tie   Queen's Park 1a0 Eastern
... The ball was to have been kicked off at three o'clock, but owing to the late arrival of the Eastern captain the kick-off was not taken till twenty minutes after the hour. This was unfortunate, as it necessitated the stoppage of play, owing to darkness, ten minutes before the expiry of time.
Ref 1873011

22nd November 1873
Second Tie   Renton 0-0 Dumbarton
A match was played on Saturday between these clubs, on the ground of the former. Renton won the toss, and elected to play against the wind. The ball was kicked off at 3.30, and remained in neutral quarters till ends were changed. After this there was some very keen play, but both sides were about equally matched. When time was called the ball was in the middle of the field – the game ending in a draw. Being for the Association

Cup, it will require to be played over again next Saturday. A large crowd witnessed the match.
Ref 1873012

29ᵗʰ November 1873
Second Tie Replay   Renton 1-0 Dumbarton
Renton won the toss and elected to play with the wind. Dumbarton kicked off at 2.50, and the ball was immediately returned by the Renton backs, and a run was made right up to the goal defended by Dumbarton, where some good play was shown on both sides. Ultimately the ball was brought back to neutral ground where it remained until half time was called. The ball was then kicked off by Renton, and brought onto Dumbarton quarters by the Renton forwards, who showed good play; but it was gallantly repelled by the Dumbarton backs and half-backs, who after the lapse of a quarter of an hour succeeded in kicking it back to the middle of the field. It then became evident that the Renton team meant something for with a good run by the forwards the ball was brought to within ten yards of the Dumbarton citadel, where a fierce struggle took place for some time, but by a gallant rush of the Renton team it was finally kicked through. The Renton Club is thus in the third tie.
Ref 1873013

20ᵗʰ December 1873
Third Tie   Clydesdale 4a0 v Blythswood
BLYTHSWOOD v CLYDESDALE - This match, for the Association Cup (third ties), took place in Kinning Park on Saturday, and resulted in an easy victory for the latter club by four goals to nothing. Owing to the unfavourable weather, very few spectators were present. The game commenced about three o'clock. The Blythswood were successful in winning the toss, and this necessitated their opponents to play against a strong gusty wind which blew across the ground during the whole of the game. At the outset the Blythswood, with the wind in their favour, kept the ball pretty well in the centre, and on two or three occasions threatened the Clydesdale goal with danger, and the goal-keeper of the latter club had to kick off frequently in front. The back play of the Clydesdale, however, was equal to the occasion, and little anxiety was manifested as to the ultimate safety of the latter's fortress. In about half-an-hour after the game began, in spite of the wind and the steady forward play of one or two of the Blythswood forwards, including Messrs W. Phillips and Bruce, a splendid rush by the whole of the Clydesdale forwards was too much for the younger club, and Mr Gibb, by a fine steady shot, scored the maiden goal for the Clydesdale. On ends being changed, the latter club made another fine charge, and so well was the ball middled by the half-backs and backs, that another goal was soon kicked by Mr A. Taylor. Shortly after this the third goal was kicked at the upper end by Mr J. Wilson ; but this was rather a lucky one, as the ball struck the hand of the Blythswood goal-keeper before it went under the tape. Shortly before time was called, and when the spectators could scarcely distinguish the players, another goal was successfully kicked by Mr A. Taylor, the ball being finely centred by Messrs Gibb, Gardner, Wilson, and Hendry. After this goal the umpires agreed to cease play as the light was very bad, leaving the Clydesdale victorious by four goals to none.
Ref 1873014

21st March 1874

Final Tie   **Queen's Park 2-0 Clydesdale**

The competition for the Scottish Football Association Challenge Cup, between the above two clubs, was played on Hampden Park, Glasgow, on Saturday, in presence of nearly 2000 spectators. The fact that this is the first time that these clubs have met on the football ground in opposition to each other, increased the interest felt in the match. The Clydesdale winning the toss, chose to play with the strong wind in their favour. The ball was kicked off by Thomson (Queen's Park) at 3.45. In spite of the wind the Queen's Park managed by a splendid piece of dribbling on the part of Weir, to run the ball up to their opponents' goal, where they had several shots, though nothing definite was obtained. Half-time was called without any advantage being gained by either. The Queen's Park on having the wind in their favour, came away in grand style and W. Mackinnon, by excellent dribbling, managed to send the ball under the tape. The play was now fast and furious, but the Queen's Park in ten minutes added another goal, kicked by Leckie. No other event of note took place during the remainder of the game. For the Queen's Park the play of W. M'Kinnon, Weir, Campbell, and Taylor was particularly good. For the Clydesdale, Anderson, M'Pherson, Kennedy, and Wotherspoon rendered their club good service. The handsome silver Challenge Cup, valued at about £50, now therefore becomes the property of the Queen's Park Club. The teams were :-

 Queen's Park - Dickson, goal; Taylor, Neill, backs; Campbell, Thomson (captain), half-backs; Leckie, Weir, A. M'Kinnon, W. M'Kinnon, M'Neill, Laurie, forwards.

Clydesdale - Gardner (captain), goal; Wotherspoon, M'Arly, backs; Raeburn, Henry, half-backs; Anderson, Lang, M'Pherson, Gibb, Kennedy, Wilson, forwards.

Ref 1873015

26th March 1874

Miscellaneous   **Vale of Leven's Record**

Vale of Leven – During the season just closed this club but played seven matches, in which they took ten goals and lost one.

Ref 1873016

23rd August 1874
Miscellaneous   **Fatal Accident at a Foot-ball Match**
Robert Atherley, shoemaker, 19 years of age, residing in Alexandria, died on Sunday afternoon from the effects of a kick received on the stomach, while engaged in a football match between the Alexandria Junior Club and, the Renton Club, on Saturday in the Public Play Ground, Alexandria. Yesterday, a post-mortem examination was made by Dr Carnachan, who found that death had been caused by rupture of the stomach. The authorities are investigating the case.
Ref 1873017

17th October 1874
First Tie   **Dumbarton 2-0 Arthurlie**
Played at Dumbarton and resulted in favour of the Dumbarton side by two goals to none. The game was keenly contested by both sides, but from the beginning the Dumbarton team had the play in their favour, their goalkeeper never handling the leather throughout the whole game.
*Ref 1874001**

Footnote
Result given as a 3-0 win for Dumbarton in the 1875 S.F.A. Annual

---

17th October 1874
First Tie   **Kilmarnock 4-0 Vale of Leven Rovers**
This match one of the first ties for the Association Challenge Cup, was played on the ground of the Kilmarnock and resulted in favour of the Kilmarnock by four goals to nothing. These goals were kicked by Messrs Frank Reid and J.B. Wilson (simultaneously), D. Brown, J. Wallace, and D. Sturrock. The forwards of the Kilmarnock played very well, as did those of the Rovers, but the back play of the Kilmarnock was far too strong for them.
Ref 1874002

24th October 1874
First Tie Replay   **Hamilton 0-0 Rovers**
This tie which was played on 17th inst., and resulted in a draw, was again contested on Saturday, on South Avenue, Hamilton, and resulted again in a draw, no goals being obtained by either club. Messrs Morton and Cassells had some fine runs for the Hamilton, and once or twice placed the Rovers' goal in danger, but the latter, who played well together, had the best of the game throughout and pressed their opponents to play a defensive game, especially after half-time.
Ref 1874003

Footnote
Hamilton later scratched to Rovers.

24th October 1874
First Tie   **Clydesdale 0-0 Vale of Leven**
Played on the ground of the former, Kinning Park, in presence of a large number of spectators, and resulted in a draw. Before commencing play the Clydesdale formally protested against J. Ferguson playing on the ground that he was a professional [runner], although it was replied that he usually wrought in the Vale of Leven from one year's end to the other, and that there was no objection made to him when he played in the international match. The play was very equal on both sides; and within a short space as five minutes both goals were threatened. The Vale men were unfortunate in the matter of touching the ball with their hands, their opponents at an early stage claiming no fewer than six free kicks off to one claimed by the Vale of Leven. The latter club won the toss, but at the end of the three quarters of an hour no goal was gained on either side. The same result was declared at the close of the match. It would be invidious and unfair to single out names, for both teams individually and collectively, played well.
Ref 1874003

The tie for the Association Challenge Cup was played off between the above clubs on the ground of the former at Kinning Park, and resulted in a draw, neither side obtaining a goal. Throughout the whole of the game the play was very equally balanced, the ball being run up from one end of the field to the other every few minutes. During the last quarter of an hour the play became fast and furious, both sides working with great determination. The back play of the Clydesdale was very strong, but it was counterbalanced by the good collective play of the Vale forwards.
Ref 1874005

S.F.A.C.M. [Reported 9th Nov]. Vale of Leven have been disqualified.
Ref 1874006

24th October 1874
First Tie   **Dumbreck 5-1 Alexandra Athletic**
This contest, for the Scottish Football Association cup, took place on the ground of the former at Ibroxhill, and resulted in favour of the Dumbreck by five goals to one. The Athletic won the toss, and preferred playing with the wind and ground in their favour. The ball was kicked off at four P.M., and after some fine play on both sides, the forwards of the home team proved too much for their opponents, and at 4.20 a goal was got in favour of the Dumbreck, being propelled through by one of their own men. Sides having been changed, the forwards of the Dumbreck made a fine run towards their opponents' goal, and by some good passing, the ball was kicked under the tape by Mr Watt, to the credit of the Dumbreck ; time 4:23. The Athletics now settled down to their work, and Messrs M'Arthur [forward] after some excellent play took possession of the ball, carrying it to within a short distance of the Dumbreck goal, when, on its being centered to Mr Hastie, that gentleman kicked for goal, the ball being returned by Mr Turnbull [goal keeper] only to rebound from Mr Hastie through the goal, making one for the Athletics; time, 5.58. The other three goals for the Dumbreck were taken by Mr M'Leish. Great improvement was observable in the general play of the Dumbreck, and special notice is due to Mr Service for his splendid play at half back, and to Messrs M'Leish, Wardle, Walter Forbes, and Ferguson for their brilliant forward play. In the Athletics Mr Laing [half-back] and Messrs Naghorn, Hastie, and M'Arthur [forwards] deserve great

credit for their play.
Ref 1874007

November 1874
Second Tie Draw   **Scottish Football Association Challenge Cup**
S.F.A.C.M. [Reported 9th Nov]. Second Tie draw:-

> Queen's Park against West End
> Clydesdale against Dumbreck
> 3d LRV against Standard
> Eastern against Kilmarnock
> Dumbarton against Rangers
> Renton against Helensburgh
> Rovers or Hamilton bye

Ref 1874006

28th November 1874
Second Tie   **Standard 0-2 3rd Lanarkshire R.V.**
The game resulted in a victory for the 3d by two goals to nothing and some good play was shown by both sides despite the very unfavourable condition of the ground. Within five minutes from half-time the Volunteers secured their first goal by a neat kick from A. Lang from the corner flag. In about twenty minutes after this, during which time the 3d had been pressing their opponents rather severely, a beautiful shot from D. Reid was the means of securing for them the second goal. Nothing further happened to either side after this, and the game ended with the result indicated above.
Ref 1874008

12th December 1874
Second Tie Replay   **Dumbarton 1-0 Rangers**
The Dumbarton Club took a goal shortly after the game commenced. The ball, however, went over instead of under the tape, and a dispute arose. The referee belonging to the Dumbarton claimed it, but was protested against, he being in the centre of the field at the time, and could not see whether the ball went over or under the tape. The Rangers had the best of the play throughout the game.
*Ref 1874009**

6th March 1875
Fourth Tie   **Dumbarton 0-1 Renton**
This match, one of the ties in the fourth drawing of the cup competition, was played at Dumbarton, and resulted in favour of Renton by one goal and a disputed one to nothing. The match excited considerable interest, and was witnessed by a large crowd.
Ref 1874010

27th March 1875
Fourth Tie Replay   **Queen's Park 2-2 Clydesdale**

These two clubs met again in friendly rivalry on Saturday afternoon, the scene of the contest being Hampden Park. There was an immense attendance of spectators, who watched the progress of the game with great interest. A strong breeze blew from the north west, and somewhat interfered with fine play, but altogether little fault was to be found with the display. With one or two exceptions the teams were similar to those which met on Kinning Park on the Saturday previous. First honours were scored in favour of the Clydesdale by Anderson, who kicked the ball in beautifully from the corner. Sides being changed, the Queen's Park gained the advantage formerly enjoyed by their opponents of a favourable wind, and at once beamed them into the down territory, speedily securing a goal well kicked by one of the M'Kinnon. Honours were thus balanced, but the Clydesdale were soon again placed in the lead, and again by Anderson, who sent the ball through from the centre. On changing positions for the third time, Highet succeeded in following Anderson's example, and, on time being called, so the match ended - in a draw.

Ref 1874011

10th April 1875
Final Tie   **Queen's Park 3-0 Renton**

The day was fine, the ground in excellent order, and a very large number of spectators witnessed the match. The team took the field at a quarter to four. The Renton had a decided advantage in point of weight. The Renton captain won the toss, and elected to play with the advantage of a slight breeze, although this was counteracted to some extent by having to play with the sun in their faces. During the first half of the game no goals were taken by either side, although the Renton had rather the best of the play. A change of ends at half-time gave the wind to the Queen's Park and they at once took the ball up to their opponents' territory. They made no score, however, until within a quarter of an hour from time, when a corner kick by Weir landed the ball in front of the Renton goal, and M'Kinnon played it through. Five minues only elapsed when another goal was placed to the credit of the home team, the ball being dribbled by M'Neill and passed to Highet, who put it through. A third was taken shortly before time from a fine shot by N. M'Kinnon. The match all through was an exceptionally rough one; charging, which seems to be the speciality of the Renton men, being indulged in to a great extent. For the Queen's Park, the most prominent were Taylor and Phillips as backs, and Highet, A. M'Kinnon, and N. M'Kinnon as forwards ; while Kennedy, a back, and Brown and M'Crae as forwards, work hard for the other side.

Ref 1874012

2nd September 1875
Miscellaneous　　　　　**S.F.A. Annual General Meeting**
SCOTTISH FOOTBALL ASSOCIATION - The annual general meeting of this Association was held on Wednesday evening in Dewar's Hotel, Bridge Street, Glasgow – Mr A. M'Bride (Vale of Leven Club) in the chair. The secretary's and treasurer's reports showed the Association to be in a flourishing condition. Thirty-three local and provincial clubs were represented. Mr A. M'Bride (Vale of Leven Club) was appointed president; Mr R. M. Liddell (Western Club) honorary treasurer; Mr William Dick, 73 Whitevale Street, Glasgow (Alexandra Athletic) honorary secretary. The following clubs were elected to send a representative to committee:- 3d L.R.V. Club, Clydesdale, Rangers, Drumpellier, Hamilton, Havelock, Queen's Park, Eastern, Dumbreck, 1st L.R.V., Renton, Rovers.
Ref 1875001

21st September 1875
Miscellaneous　　　　　**First Tie Draw**
SCOTTISH FOOTBALL ASSOCIATION – At a committee meeting, held in Dewar's Hotel, Glasgow, last night, the first ties for the Challenge Cup were drawn. As many as forty nine clubs entered, showing an increase of twenty-four on last year. The following is the result of the drawing :- Heart of Midlothian against 3d E.R.V., Dumbarton against Lennox, Renton against Alclutha, Vale of Leven Rovers against Vale of Leven, Star of Leven against Helensburgh, Clydesdale against Eastern, 3d L.R.V. against Havelock, Western against Caledonian, West End against Partick, Queen's Park jun., against Renton Thistle, Dumbreck against Vale of Leven Rovers, Glasgow Towerhill against Lancelot, Rovers against Oxford, Ramblers against Northern, Alexandra Athletic against Queen's Park, Telegraphists against St. Andrews, Sandyford against 23d R.R.V., Rangers against 1st L.R.V., Hamilton against Airdrie, Levern against Arthurlie, Drumpellier against Barrhead, Ardrossan against Mauchline, Kilbirnie against Ayr Thistle, Kilmarnock against Ayr Eglinton, Edinburgh Thistle, a bye. The ties must be played off on 23d October at the latest.
Ref 1875002

Cup Competition Rules
6. The names of the Clubs entered for Competition shall be placed by the Committee in one lot, or in lots, according to their districts; and shall be drawn from such lot, or lots, in couples at a time. These couples shall compete with each other, and the names of the winning Clubs shall be placed in a lot, or lots, drawn in couples, and compete as in the first tie, and so on until the final tie is played; when the winning Club shall hold the Cup for the current year.
7. In the event of a Club getting a "bye" in any of the drawings, the Committee, at the next drawing, shall first draw a Club to play against it from the lot, and then proceed in drawing couples *Vide* Rule 6.
Ref 1875003

Footnote
As Sandyford were drawn in the Glasgow District region in all of their future cup matches, there is a likelihood that they were placed in the Renfrewshire district for the First Ties ballot. Rangers likewise appear to have been placed in the Lanarkshire district.

16th October 1875
First Tie   **Queen's Park 3-0 Alexandra Athletic**
Queen's Park won the toss and chose to defend the east goal. First goal was won five minutes after the off by splendid kick from Wm. M'Kinnon. Another goal was scored for Queen's Park fifteen minutes after half time, by a good high kick of Heriot's. A corner kick from H. M'Neill went through the goal, but was fouled, for which a free kick one foot from the goal line was given and resulted in another goal being scored for Queen's Park.
Ref 1875004

16th October 1875
First Tie   **Heart of Midlothian 0-0 3rd Edinburgh R.V.**
The first tie for the Association Cup between teams of the above clubs took place on Saturday in Craigmount Park, lent by Mr Syme. The game was divided into two periods of forty-five. The Volunteers having won the toss, chose the north or upper goal. During the first period the Volunteers pressed their opponents goal, which, however, they stoutly defended, though several good shots were made by D. Hogg and J. Wood, none of which took effect until half-time and the ends were changed. Again the Volunteers pressed their opponents hard, and until time was up the ball seldom left the latter's part of the ground, with the exception of a run or two which Mitchell got, though he had not got far past the centre flag when he lost it, and the ball was quickly passed up towards the Mid-Lothian goal. Nothing of much importance occurred for some time until Wilkinson getting the ball dribbled it up to near the goal, then shot but unluckily the ball struck the tape and rolled over it. Shortly after this time was called, the match ending in a draw, neither side gaining a goal.
For the Mid-Lothian, T. Purdie (captain), D. M'Beath and G. Mitchell played well, as did T. Fraser, J. Shaw, and D. Hogg for the Volunteers.
Ref 1875004

26th October 1875
Second Tie Draw   **Regional Placements**
S.F.A.C.M. [26th Oct].
Kilmarnock (Ayrshire) placed in the Glasgow & Suburbs region.
Drumpellier (Lanarkshire) placed in the Edinburgh region.

30th October 1875

Second Tie   **3rd Lanarkshire R.V. 0-1 Rangers**

3rd Lanark protested that Rangers kicked off both halves.

Footnote

Rangers may have fallen foul of the change to Law 3 in season 1875-76 which stated :-

"Ends shall only be changed at half-time. After a goal is won, the losing side shall kick-off, but after a change of ends at half-time, the ball shall be kicked off by the opposite side from that which originally did so ..."
Ref 1875003

Prior to this, ends were changed after every goal and only at half-time if the match was goal-less.

13th November 1875

Second Tie Replay   **Rangers 1a2 3rd Lanarkshire R.V.**

This match, the only one of consequence played in Glasgow, took place on the ground of the Rangers, Burnbank, which was in anything but condition. The Volunteers wanted a couple of their usual team. The first goal was scored by the Rangers through a clever run by M. M'Neil, but the Volunteers were not very long in equalising matters by forcing the ball through after a scrimmage, and eventually a second goal was registered for them, the ball touching the leg of one of the Rangers' backs. Darkness set in before time was up, and play was eventually stopped. The Rangers intend lodging a protest about one of the goals.
Ref 1875006

This was the only game of any consequence which took place in Glasgow, and it was stopped before time was up, after the Rangers had a lot of kicks from the 3d L.R.V. corner flag. The Rangers' captain protested against the crowd invading the ground, which will be laid before the Association.
Ref 1875007

S.F.A.C.M. [16th Nov]. The protest of the Rangers was not sustained.
Ref 1875008

6th November 1875

Second Tie   **Kilbirnie 0-0 Mauchline**

These two clubs met on Saturday, at Bridgend Ground, Kilbirnie, to play off their tie in the second draw for the Association Cup. From the start to the finish the game was a most exciting one. The strangers falling to the upper goal played the first half of the game with a slight advantage, and pressed their opponents very hard for some time; but the latter defended their goal in a skillful manner, and after a good deal of hard work they worked the ball into Mauchline territory, where they succeeded in keeping it for a considerable time. Several runs were made for the goal, and after some hard pressing a goal was claimed for the home team, which was, however, disputed. After half-time the game grew more exciting. Some capital play was shown by both sides, and the game ended in a disputed goal for Kilbirnie, which will be referred to the association for

settlement.
Ref 1875009

Footnote
Kilbirnie scratched after the committee didn't decide in their favour.

6th November 1875
Second Tie   **Thistle (Edinburgh) 0a0 3rd Edinburgh R.V.**
A match between the above clubs took place in the Meadows. The ball was kicked off by the Thistle, but nothing of importance took place until time was called. Ends were changed, and after about twenty minutes play, rain began to come down so heavily that the game was stopped. Conspicuous among the Thistle were M'Intosh and M'Neil; while for the Volunteers, Stewart and Stenhouse played well.
Ref 1875010

27th November 1875
Third Tie   **Vale of Leven 6-0 Mauchline**
Issues between the Vale of Leven and the Mauchline Clubs were tried on the Victoria Park, thanks to the courtesy of the 3d L.R.V. Club. The Vale of Leven, having had the ball at their feet, played it, and so effectively that they managed to shoot their ball six times under their opponents' tape, while their antagonists were not equal to returning the compliment once.
Ref 1875011

27th November 1875
Third Tie   **Rovers 4-0 3rd Edinburgh R.V.**
The above clubs played off their cup tie, which resulted in favour of the former club by four goals to nothing. The play all through was chiefly confined to the Edinburgh's territory. At 3.15 the ball was kicked off by the captain of the Edinburgh team, putting it well down to his opponent's goal, where for about ten minutes it was kept, until one of the backs of the Rovers kicked it up the field, where their forwards got it, and managed to carry it up to the goal of their opponent, through which it was put from out a maul. The other three goals were taken after half-time, one of them having been put through by one of Edinburgh's backs from off his head, W. Peden's kick from the corner flag being well judged for the mouth of goal.
Ref 1875012

18th December 1875
Fourth Tie   **Vale of Leven 2a0 Rovers**
The Rovers met the Vale of Leven at Alexandria. The Vale won the toss and elected to play with a slight wind in their favour. Shortly after the kick-off the ball was brought to dangerous proximity to the strangers' goal, but their backs succeeded in freeing the citadel, and after some fast play on some neutral ground, the ball was again in front. The Rovers kicked out in self defence, but at this early period of the game it became evident they were over-matched. Again and again was their goal seriously threatened, but, by a

run of fortuitous accidents, remained intact. The Rovers made several runs, which showed that their knowledge of "passing" was good but the half backs of the Vale were ready to meet them, until a combined effort, they got behind the half-backs through the backs, and made a long shot at the Leven goal, which was only saved by Wood cleverly throwing the ball over the crossbar. The corner-kick resulted in nothing, and half-time was called with no result. Ends being changed, the Vale team returned the offensive, and brought the ball down the field in splendid style, but fortune seemed to be against them, for the ball still would go on the wrong side of the post. At last, however, after a scrimmage, it did go through, and once having found the way, it was not long till it was successful in another attempt. Darkness had now began to set in, and the ball was becoming all but invisible, and it was agreed to stop the game in favour of the Vale by two goals to none. The Vale forwards played their usual fast "passing" game, but they often lost their advantage when in front of the goal by being too eager. The strangers' forwards played very unselfishly, and "passed" beautifully, but were, with one or two exceptions, slow.

Ref 1875013

15th January 1876
Fifth Tie Replay   Dumbarton 1-1 3rd Lanarkshire R.V.
At Alexandria …So overjoyed were the Lanark team at what they had accomplished that one or two of them actually tumbled somersaults on the dirty grass, and embraced each other lovingly.

*Ref 1875014**

22nd January 1876
Fifth Tie 2nd Replay   3rd Lanarkshire R.V. 3-0 Dumbarton
The cup tie between these two clubs - which in the two previous meetings was left undecided, each club scoring one goal - was by permission of the Scottish Football Association, again contested on the ground of the 3d L.R.V., Cathkin Park, on Saturday. There was a large turn-out of spectators. The ground was not in very favourable order, being hard and slippery. The Volunteers had the best of the game throughout, and scored three goals, one against and two with the wind, against nothing.

Ref 1875015

25th September 1876
Miscellaneous   **Hibernian Football Club Refused Admission**
The Hibernia, a club in connection with the Young Men's Catholic Association in Edinburgh, has also joined the East of Scotland Association this season, and promise to be an acquisition to the district. They are entered along with the other clubs in the district above mentioned for the East of Scotland Challenge Cup, and though their application for admission to the Scottish Football Association has been refused, it is anticipated that the petition which the other Edinburgh clubs are getting up in their favour will result in the committee altering their former resolution.
Ref 1876001

25th September 1876
First Tie   **Dunfermline v Heart of Midlothian**
In Edinburgh and East of Scotland district, the Heart of Mid-Lothian, owing to deficiency of membership, has scratched to Dunfermline.
Ref 1876001

30th September 1876
First Tie   **St Andrew's (Kilmarnock) 1-1 Ayr Eglinton**
Footnote
Ayr Eglinton subsequently scratched to St Andrew's due to their forthcoming amalgamation with Ayr Academy to form Ayr Academicals on Thursday October 19th.

30th September 1876
First Tie   **Parkgrove 0-2 Lancefield**
Played on the ground of the latter [Parkgrove], and resulted in favour of the Lancefield by two goals to none. The goals were kicked by M'Callum and Jeffrey.
Ref 1876003

30th September 1876
First Tie   **Northern 12-0 Telegraphists**
Played at Hyde Park. Northern scorers - Cunningham 5, Cray 3 Christie 2, McIntyre 1, Arthur 1.

7th October 1876
First Tie   **Clydesdale 6-0 Craigpark**
This match was played off on Saturday at Titwood Park, and after a very one sided game resulted in the Clydesdale team obtaining six goals to none. One or two of the Craigpark men showed good form but want of a combined effort prevented them having a single shot at the opponent's goal.
Ref 1876004

7th October 1876
First Tie   **Eastern 2-0 Alexandra Athletic**
Protested owing to no referee being present. Match declared void.
*Ref 1876005**

21st October 1876
Second Tie   **St Clement 2-1 St Andrew's (Edinburgh)**
These clubs met at Kirkcaldy, on the ground of the local club, to compete in the second stage for the Association Challenge Cup. In the first "half" no goals were taken, but the play was considerably in favour of the Dundee team, and several opportunities of scoring were not taken advantage of. In the second period the spectators were treated to an excellent exhibition of the game. Play became fast and exciting, the ball being taken merrily from goal to goal. Out of the *melee* in front of the St Clement goal the ball bounded off one their players and under the tape. This reverse caused the Dundee men to play with increased spirit, and the leather was soon brought up to the St Andrew's stronghold, which Sharp succeeded in reducing. This goal was objected to, but was allowed by the umpire. Shortly after Stiven had a nice run up the left wing, and middling the ball to M'Lennan the latter sent it through. "No side" was soon thereafter called, Dundee winning by two goals to one.
Ref 1876006

21st October 1876
Second Tie   **Star of Leven 0-4 Dumbarton**
Played at Alexandria on Saturday and resulted in favour of Dumbarton by two goals and two disputed ones to none.
Ref 1876007

21st October 1876
Second Tie   **Busby 1-0 23rd Renfrewshire R. V.**
S.F.A.C.M. [Reported 30th Oct]. The committee of the Scottish Association have dismissed the protest lodged by the 23d R.R.V. about the goal taken by the Busby team in the match on the 21st instant.
Ref 1876008

21st October 1876
Second Tie   **West End 2-2 Govan**
Two reports:-
Played on the ground of the former, Avenue Park Cowlairs, and resulted in a tie, each club scoring two goals. The Govan club scored a third goal, but it was disputed and eventually disallowed by the referee.
*Ref 1876009**

Played at Avenue Park, Cowlairs, and after a well contested game resulted in favour of the Govan by three goals to two.
*Ref 1876010**

28th October 1876
Second Tie Replay   **Govan 0-1 West End**
Two reports:-
Played at Fairfield Park, ground of former and resulted in a draw, one goal each being scored by both Clubs.
*Ref 1876011**

Played at Fairfield Park, and after some very fast play resulted in favour of the West End by 1 goal to 0.
*Ref 1876012**

28th October 1876
Second Tie   **Q.O.S. Wanderers 0-4 Girvan**
On Saturday a match was played between the Girvan Club and the Queen of the South Wanderers, Dumfries, on the Race Park here (at Newton-Stewart about equi-distant from Dumfries and Girvan) - eleven aside - for the Association's Silver Cup. The game lasted for an hour and a half, and the goals were pitched at 150 yards. When time was called up Girvan counted four goals to nothing. The captain of the Dumfries team played well, as did two or three others, but on the whole he was poorly backed, while the Girvan men played well together and won cleverly, some fine spurts of kicking and running being witnessed. Mr K. M'Houle acted as umpire for Girvan, and Sergt. Walsh, 3rd W.R.V., for Dumfries, and Mr J. McCreath was referee. The match was witnessed by a large number of spectators, the game not being common here. The utmost good humour prevailed, although there was an occasional hitch now and again, and an appeal to the umpires. The weather was splendid.
*Ref 1876013**

11th November 1876
Third Tie   **St Clement 1-2 Northern**
The third cup tie between these clubs was played on Saturday on the Magdalen Green. The ground was covered with snow to the depth of six or seven inches, and consequently the play was inferior to what it would have been under more favourable circumstances. In addition, L M'Lennan, the captain of the Dundee team, was unable to play, and the home club was thereby considerably weakened. The St Clement won the toss, and chose to play with the wind in their favour. At 2.25 the Northern kicked off, and following well up, the ball was brought unpleasantly near the St Clement goal, and for some time play was principally confined to the territory of the St Clement. Dundee managed to break away with the ball once or twice, but all attempts on their opponents' stronghold proved fruitless. About twenty minutes after starting, Glasgow succeeded in scoring the first goal. Until half-time no more goals were taken. During the second period the game was somewhat more equalised, St Clement playing pluckily to redeem their fallen fortress, and succeeded several times in bringing the ball up to the goal of the Northern. On one of these occasions Smith shot at goal, but the ball rebounded from the goalkeeper, and the opportunity was lost. The ball again travelled towards the Dundee goal, and from a free kick in favour of the Northern, the ball was passed under the tape, and thus the second goal was secured for Glasgow. After this some keen and closely contested struggles took place; gradually the St Clement wrought their way up the field, and out

of a scrimmage, they succeeded in shooting the ball between the posts. In about ten minutes afterwards time was called. The match thus ended in favour of the Northern by two goals to one. The passing play of the Northern was superior to that of the St Clement. For the strangers, White and Powrie played well, while for the home team Smith and Stiven showed the advantage. The half back and back play was also excellent. The following are the names of the St Clement team - Goal, D. R. Stewart; backs, J. M'Lennan and J. Hay; half-backs, C. Duff and J. Westwater; forwards, W. Swan, F. Sharp, R. Lunan, W. Robertson, J.P. Smith, and A. Stiven.
Ref 1876014

18th November 1876
Third Tie   **Edinburgh Swifts 1-1 West End**
West End disqualified for not playing Swifts in accordance with the Rules.
*Ref 1876015**

9th December 1876
Fourth Tie   **Ayr Thistle 1-1 Partick**
S.F.A.C.M. [Dec 12th]. The match played on Saturday last between the Ayr Thistle and Partick Clubs has been declared in favour of the local players by the Committee of the Association, on the ground that, by the desire of the Partick, the match was not played at the time at which it should have been. The Thistle have been drawn against the Glasgow Lancefield.
*Ref 1876016**

15th December 1876
Miscellaneous   **Scottish Football Annual**
It is satisfactory to learn that the issue of last year's Scottish Football Annual proved such a success that the honorary secretary of the Scottish Football Association (Mr W. Dick) has been encouraged to continue his little venture, and to nearly double its size. The Annual for the coming season contains a complete list of Association Clubs (now numbering in Scotland 68, with names and addresses of secretaries, colours, &c. Remarks on the leading Scotch players, results of matches, and a deal of information useful to football players go to make up the remainder of the work. It is well printed, neatly got up in scarlet cloth, and as it is published at the modest price of 6d., it is thus placed within the reach of the majority of players.
Ref 1876019

30th December 1876
Fifth Tie   **Queen's Park 1-2 Vale of Leven**
This game notwithstanding the condition of the ground, caused by heavy rain, was one of the fastest ever played on the Queen's Park ground. For the first time since the formation of Queen's Park in 1867, they on Saturday sustained a defeat from a Scotch club, and that too, in an Association tie. The Vale of Leven, which has gained this coveted honour, has been for the last three years considered the most dangerous rivals of the Queen's Park in the west, but their former efforts only resulted in their defeat, the

last tie between the two clubs last year ending in a victory for the Queen's Park by two goals to one.

On Saturday, however, the result was vice versa. The Queen's Park captain Mr J. Taylor, chose to play from the east goal, with the slight fall of the ground in his favour. The ball was kicked off at 2.30pm, and for a short time the Vale's forwards by their swiftness ran the ball well into their opponent's territory; but the Queen's Park settling down to work, soon caused them to play on the defensive. About twenty minutes after the kick-off, Highet brought down the ball, but while centring it, he was collared, and the ball kicked out. The throw in placed the ball right in front of the Vale of Leven goal, it was spooned, and while coming down was headed through. After the kick-off the game still continued in favour of the Queen's Park, but the splendid back of the Vale of Leven rendered all efforts at scoring ineffectual. The forward play of Baird, Ferguson and M'Dougall for the Vale of Leven succeeded several times in freeing their goal. With the change of ends at half time a change in the play also took place. After the kick off the Vale of Leven men were soon at their opponents' goal, and a long shot by M'Intyre (back) when kicked out by Dickson rebounded into touch off M'Dougall. Dickson kicked off, but the fine forward play of the Vale, aided by backing up, still kept the ball at the Queen's Park goal. About twenty minutes after the kick-off, Baird of the Vale of Leven succeeded in sending the ball through by a good screw kick just as it was going into touch.

After the kick-off Weir for the Queen's Park, had a fine run up the right side, causing M'Intyre to kick out. The throw in did not succeed, and again the Queen's Park had to play on the defensive. The side forwards several times succeeded in relieving their goal, but the ball was soon returned. About fifteen minutes before time, Baird and Ferguson brought the ball down to the Queen's Park goal, and a fine centre caused Dickson to throw the ball out, but it was returned and thrown out again, when Baird dropped the second goal for the Vale of Leven amidst great excitement. Nothing further particular occurred excepting a fine run by Weir and Smith for the Queen's Park, the ball being kicked out as Smith was centring; time being shortly afterwards called, just as the Vale had worked the ball well into their opponent's ground.

Teams:-

Queen's Park:- J. Dickson, goalkeeper; J.J. Taylor (captain) and R.W. Neill, backs; C. Campbell and I. Phillips, half-backs; W. Mackinnon, A.L. Senior, J.B. Weir, H. M'Neill, T. Highet and Tod or Smith forwards.

Vale of Leven:- W.G. Wood, goalkeeper; A. Michie and A. M'Intyre, backs; W. Jamieson and A. M'Lintock, half-backs; J. Ferguson (captain), J. Baird, J. M'Gregor, R. Paton, D. Lindsay and J. M'Dougall, forwards.

We understand a protest has been lodged by the Queen's Park regarding the second goal taken by the Vale of Leven, as it is alleged a foul was declared before the ball went through.

Ref 1876018

1877
Miscellaneous   **Protest Ruling**
Protests and appeals must be formerly intimated to the referee and to the competing Club before the Club protesting leaves the ground on which the match has been played, and must be lodged with the Secretary of the Association within three days thereafter.
*Ref 1877001**

11th September 1877
Miscellaneous   **Applications**
S.F.A.C.M. Applications from 44 clubs for admission into the Association were considered. The following 36 were duly admitted :- Alexandria, Albatross (Barrowfield), Avondale, Ailsa, Blackfriars, Catrine, Clyde, Clifton and Strathfillan, Glenkilloch, Hurlford, John Elder, Kilmarnock Football and Cricket Club, Kilmaronock Thistle, Kelvinbank, Maybole Thistle, Mount Vernon, Greenock Morton, Newmains, Our Boys, Oxford, Pollockshaws, Petershill, Pollockshields, Port-Glasgow, Rosslyn, 17th R.R.V., Shaftesbury, Strathclyde, Shaughraun, Stonefield, Tarbolton, Uddingston, Vale of Calder, Waverley and Winton.
Ref 1877002

22nd September 1877
Miscellaneous   **Fatal Football Accident**
On Saturday Week, a boy aged 11 years, named R. Devine, son of James Devine, near Cathcart, while engaged in the game of football twisted his leg by missing a kick which he made at the ball. The lad did not inform his parents of the mishap till he was forced to leave his work, at Netherlee Printworks, on Tuesday in great distress. On a medical man being called in, the youth was ordered to the Glasgow Royal Infirmary, where he was taken on Friday evening last, and had his leg amputated. He died eight hours after being admitted.
Ref 1877003

29th September 1877
First Tie   **10th D.R.V. (Kirkintilloch) 1-0 Star of Leven**
Played at Kirkintilloch, and ended as it commenced, with a dispute. The 10th took one goal, and the Star maintain that they are entitled to another - the cause of the dispute.
The outcome was decided in favour of the 10th DRV, who are held to have won the tie.
We understand that the ground upon which the committee based their decision was the refusal of the Star to accept the decision given by the referee.
Ref 1877004

29th September 1877
First Tie   **Shaughraun 1-2 Clifton and Strathfillan**
Played on Saturday on the ground of the former in Lochmill. During the first half of the game no goals were taken by either side, and at half-time both teams agreed to stop 10 minutes for refreshments. On play being resumed, the strangers succeeded in scoring two goals against one for the home team, and time was called at 11 minutes from the commitment out of the second half, while the ball was in close proximity to the strangers' goal. The Shaughraun protested against the Clifton and Strathfillan claiming the tie on the ground that they had still 11 minutes to play when time was called. The Association will have to decide the matter.
Ref 1877005

Footnote
Protest not sustained.

29th September 1877
First Tie   **Girvan 0-6 Mauchline**
On Saturday last the Mauchline football club (having drawn the Girvan Club in the first tie for the Scottish Association Cup, and losing the toss) played at Girvan, the result of which was an easy win for the Mauchline team by 6 goals to nothing which were all got in the first half.
*Ref 1877006**

6th October 1877
First Tie Replay   **Tarbolton 1-3 Maybole Carrick**
These clubs met on the ground of Tarbolton on Saturday, the game resulting in favour of the Carrick by three goals to one. The strangers kicked off, and succeeded in scoring within the first three minutes. The Tarbolton kicked off, and, after a piece of "give and take" play they obtained a goal, to which the Carrick Umpire dissented, but the Referee decided in their favour. After change of ends the Carrick had several good runs, and obtained other two goals. The home team played well, but the combined play of the strangers told upon their opponents.
*Ref 1877007**

6th October 1877
First Tie   **Rangers 13-0 Possilpark**
Played at Kinning Park, and resulted in favour of the Rangers by 13 goals to nothing. The Possilpark, whose back play is very heavy were expected to render a good account of themselves, but the passing tactics of the Rangers' forwards proved too much for them. The game has progressed but five minutes when Marshall in conjunction with M'Neill succeeded in lowering their colours. This was immediately followed by a second goal from the feet of J. Watson, a third by a shot from Bickitts, who was in good form at half-back; another by P. Campbell; and a fifth shortly before half-time taken by this same clever player. At change of ends the Possilpark wrought hard, but to no purpose, the game becoming one-sided, another eight goals being credited to the Rangers, three of which were kicked by the brothers Campbell, two by Hill, and one each by Marshall,

Watson and M'Neill. A few of the Possilpark showed good individual play, but have yet much to learn in the way of passing. Their captain played well at back.
Ref 1877008

6th October 1877
First Tie   **Q.O.S. Wanderers 6-0 Stranraer**
A tie for the Association Cup was played at Newton-Stewart on Saturday afternoon between the Wanderers of Dumfries, (Captain Alfred Ward) and the Stranraer Club (Captain J. C. Matthews). The match was a very unequal one, the Dumfries team evidently having had far more practice than their opponent, and displayed a greater amount of skill throughout the game. When time was up the Wanderers had scored six goals to nothing. The latter part of the game was conducted under very disadvantageous circumstances, a dense fog having settled down, which prevented the ball from being seen.
*Ref 1877009**

13th October 1877
Friendly   **Ayr Thistle v Kilbirnie**
Ayr Thistle hosted Kilbirnie in a friendly the week before their cup tie. Result:- Ayr Thistle 0, Kilbirnie 1.
*Ref 1877010**

18th October 1877
English Cup   **Queen's Park Withdrawal**
The Queen's Park Club, Glasgow, has sent a notice of withdrawal from the competition for the English Cup.
Ref 1877011

20th October 1877
Second Tie   **23rd Renfrewshire R.V. 0-1 Thornliebank**
Played at Cathcart, ground of the latter [23rd R.R.V.], and resulted in favour of Thornliebank by one goal to none.
Ref 1877012

20th October 1877
Second Tie   **Arthurlie (Barrhead) 1-0 17th R.R.V. (Lochwinnoch)**
This cup tie match was played on Saturday at Dunterlie Park, Barrhead, and resulted, after a close game, in favour of the Arthurlie by one goal.
Ref 1877036

10th November 1877.
Third Tie   **Rangers 13-0 Uddingston**
For the third round draw, Rangers were placed in the Lanarkshire region having been in the Glasgow & Suburbs section for the first two rounds.
*Ref 1877013**

17th November 1877
Third Tie Replay   **Drumpellier 0-0 Glengowan**
Two conflicting reports were submitted for this match. One gave Drumpellier a one nil victory. The score was regarded as 0-0, and being a second draw between the two teams meant that both qualified for the next round.
*Ref 1877014**

1st December 1877
Fourth Tie   **Thornliebank 1-2 Hibernian**
Two conflicting reports:
"Played on the ground of the latter [Thornliebank], resulting in favour of the strangers by two goals to none."
Ref 1877015

"Played at Pollockshaws and resulted in a win for the Hibernians by two goals to one."
Ref 1877015

Thornliebank protested they [Hibernians] scored a disputed goal. The SFA declared the match a draw and ordered a replay.
*Ref 1877017**

S.F.A.C.M. [4th Dec]. The match between the Hibernian [Edinburgh] and the Thornliebank on Saturday last was declared a draw.
Ref 1877018

8th December 1877
Fourth Tie   **Hibernian 2-2 Thornliebank**
Played off on the ground of the [Edinburgh] Association, Mayfield Park, and as in the first match resulted in a draw, both clubs scoring two goals.
Ref 1877019

1st December 1877
Fourth Tie   **Barrhead 0a0 Partick**
This match was brought to a stop after 25 minutes play by an accident happening to John Currie, a baker, one of the Partick team, getting one of his legs broken.
*Ref 1877020**

1ˢᵗ December 1877
Fourth Tie   **Rangers 0-0 Vale of Leven**
… Immediately before half-time a throw-in gave M'Farlane a chance, but it was stopped by Watt. On change of sides the Rangers immediately assumed the offensive and gave their opponents hard times. Twice in quick succession M'Neil, well backed up by Hill, came away down the right side, and, dodging the backs, made fine shot. For some time the Rangers had the best of a fast game, and looked very dangerous, the brothers Campbell making some fine runs. This was followed by some give-and-take play till about fifteen minutes before time, when darkness began to make the game somewhat risky for the backs. The superior stamina of the Dumbarton men now began to manifest itself, and, they put on the work for Vallance and his co-defenders in fine style. Throw in near goal and shots, however, were all well parried till about two minutes before time, when the ball was put out near the Rangers goal. Paton, for the Vale, threw the ball into play, and after slight scrimmage in the centre, Baird, who was lying well out, got the leather, and made a shot which struck the post, and went spinning through the goal. Immediately on this taking place it transpired that the umpire of the Rangers had claimed the throw in taken by Paton for his club, and it appears that the referee was considering the claim when Baird obtained the goal. The referee subsequently sustained the claim of the Rangers, and accordingly anything that took place after the throw-in by Paton was invalid. The consequence was that the goal was disallowed. The crowd breaking in immediately on time being called converted the field into a perfect quagmire.
Ref 1877015

S.F.A.C.M. [4ᵗʰ Dec]. A communication from the Vale of Leven Club was read, claiming that as they scored a goal against the Rangers on Saturday they are entitled to be declared winners of the cup tie. After some discussions the committee decided that the goal claimed by the Vale could not be allowed.
Ref 1877022

19ᵗʰ December 1877
Miscellaneous   **Football Accident**
At Kilbirnie. Football accident on Wednesday night, a boy about 12 years of age, name Miller while playing at football, at Glengarnock, had his leg broken below the knee. He was attended by Dr. Ferguson.
*Ref 1877023**

22ⁿᵈ December 1877
Miscellaneous   **Football Accident**
While a match at football was being played between Shotts and 2nd Queen's Park, Glasgow, James Patterson, one of the Shotts forwards, got his leg broken below the knee by coming in contact with one of the opposition's forwards. He was conveyed home attended by Dr Caldwell.
*Ref 1877024**

29th December 1877
Fifth Tie   **Renton 2-0 Thornliebank**
Renton goalkeeper only handled the leather once.
*Ref 1877025**

5th January 1878
Fifth Tie   **Beith 0-4 3rd Lanarkshire R.V.**
These teams on Saturday last, met here on Netherhill Field, in presence of about 1000 spectators, to decide their fifth tie for the Scottish Association Challenge Cup, the match resulting in the defeat of the home team by four goals to none. The game was one of the coarsest ever witnessed in Beith, in fact, the play of the strangers was disgraceful. Not only did they indulge in heavy charging, but in tripping, playing out of place, and continually claiming "throw in" when they knew perfectly well they had no right to the ball. For these manly acts the Glasgow men received great applause in the shape of hissing from the spectators, who could not refrain from showing their indignation, so ungentlemanly was their conduct towards the Beith team. The match looked more like a fight than a game of football. The strangers were by far the strongest team and took advantage of this by commencing heavy charging at the very start, consequently the home team, although showing more science of the game, was overpowered by the strength of their opponents. The kick off took place a few minutes after 3 o'clock p.m., the strangers playing downhill. For the first quarter of an hour the game was pretty evenly contested, the home team having a corner kick which all but secured a goal. Shortly after this a goal was scored by the Volunteers. The ball being kicked off the home team, despite having charges made on them, with judicious passing brought the leather well up the field. A foul occurring about 20 yards from goal, a free kick was the penalty. Edmonstone placed the ball well in and it was headed by M'Guire, the ball shaving the goal post. On the leather being set in motion, the strangers were at their old game and were successful in disabling one of the home backs who had to leave the field. Shortly after this by a heavy charge one of the home backs was rendered worthless for the remainder of the game. Half time was called with no more goals being taken. With only nine men the second half was gallantly contested by the home team, and only three more goals were got, one of which was headed through by one of the home backs. The goal of the strangers had two narrow escapes in this half, the ball striking the post on one occasion, and just missing on another. Although defeated, the home team certainly did not disgrace themselves.
*Ref 1877026**

12th January 1878
Sixth Tie   **South Western 1-0 3rd Lanarkshire R.V.**
This cup tie came off on the ground of the latter at Copeland Road, Govan. When time was called the South-Western were the winners by one goal to nothing. We understand the 3d L.R.V. have protested against this result, having, as they allege, taken two disputed goals.
Ref 1877027

19th January 1878
Sixth Tie Replay   **South Western 1-2 3rd Lanarkshire R.V.**
The protested cup-tie match between these clubs was played on the ground of the latter [South Western], Copeland Road, Govan in presence of the largest crowd that had ever gathered at a football match in the district. Feeling ran high and the partisans of both teams were strongly represented. During the first half of the game the Volunteers, with a slight breeze in their favour, were unable to score, but many tries were made at the goal of their opponents, which were either not directed with judgment or missed the mark by a few inches. The play throughout, however, on both sides, was coarse. Indiscriminate charging and strong kicking being the features of the game, which, but for a partial observance of association rules, might have passed rather under the exciting and mauling characteristics of Rugby play. Two or three good runs on both sides were, however, made. The game ended in favour of the 3d L.R.V.
Ref 1877028

This tie, which was won by the South-Western on Saturday the 12th inst. By one goal to nothing, was, owing to a protest lodged with the Association to the effect that the spectators interfered with the game, played over again in Copeland Park, Govan. A very exciting game was the result, and, at the termination the Volunteers were declared the winners by two goals to one.
Ref 1877029

Before play began the South Western protested to the effect that they had won the match on the previous Saturday and that the decision gave against them by the Association Committee was unjust, inasmuch as one of the members who voted against them was one of the players in the match itself; and secondly, that one of the witnesses against them also voted for the adverse decision.
*Ref 1877030**

16th February 1878
Seventh Tie   **Renton 1-3 3rd Lanarkshire R.V**
The cup-tie contest betwixt the above clubs came off at Renton, on Saturday last, in a storm of wind and rain, which, however, did not prevent a crowd of 2000 gathering around the ropes, to witness the last round of the association cup ties, barring of course, the final. The ground was a perfect quagmire, and the ball heavy and difficult to play. The Volunteers faced the wind and rain, and were soon called on to defend their goal from the repeated attacks of the Renton forwards, who forced the playing until Hunter, by a fine piece of tackling, brought the ball from the goal mouth, and sent it into midfield, where a fine display of passing by the Volunteers transferred the play into Renton territory, when M'Arthur neatly placed the ball at the disposal of M'Crimmond, who piloted his way along the left wing, and crossed in front of goal, where M'Intyre was waiting, and swiftly sent it through. Wallace making a desperate effort to catch it. After securing a corner kick, Renton made a vigorous assault, and some hot work took place in the immediate vicinity of the Volunteers' goal, when Hunter made a capital run up the field and centred well, but M'Arthur was first on the ball, and soon Wallace was called on to intercept a couple of smart shots from the feet of the Rentonians, who were taxing to the utmost the defensive powers of the Volunteers, Kennedy and Hunter coming in for the lion's share of the work. At length the siege was relieved, and a smart run by

Kaye was lost by the ball going harmlessly past the Renton lines, but it was soon at the other end of the field, and a couple of fruitless corner kicks fell to the Renton. A splendid run by Hunter, junior, followed, who kept the ball at his feet, until he gave it the parting shot, which M'Kay caught and kicked out, and the ball remained in neutral ground till half time was called, after a very fast game.

In the second half, Renton ran the ball well up into the strangers' ground, but its stay was only temporary. The play was quickly removed to the Renton goal, which was beset on all sides by the redcoats. Shot after shot was levelled in vain, the Renton backs playing a strong defensive game, and repelling every attack in a fine style, until a hand against the 3rd, relieved the siege, and gave M'Crimmon a fine run who centred well, but the parting shot was caught by Wallace, and Miller had a good opportunity on the right wing, which he lost by sending the ball into touch.

The nature of the ground was beginning to tell on the players. Renton were perceptibly "staying" better than their opponents, and amid great cheering, brought the ball against wind and rain right in front of goal, and shot it through amid the greatest enthusiasm which was speedily changed into hooting and groaning as the referee decided "no goal," on the plea of "offside." A brilliant display of passing on the part of the Volunteers brought the ball again in front of the Renton goal, which fell from a smart attack by the red coats.

M'Crimmon, who had been playing magnificently for his team, again worked his way through the backs and was dangerously near goal before he was fairly tackled, and the ball sent down once more to the Renton goal which was reduced for the second time after a sharp scrimmage. Three minutes later a long shot was parried by M'Kay, only to be sent through before he recovered himself, the game ending in favour of the Volunteers by three goals to one. The "final tie" will thus be played between the visitors in this case, and the Vale of Leven, on the 9th prox., in Glasgow.
Ref 1877031

Footnote
Match protested. No reason yet found during research. Possibly due to Renton's disallowed goal.

9th March 1878
Seventh Tie Replay   Renton 1-1 3rd Lanarkshire R.V.
Notwithstanding the very unfavourable character of the weather on Saturday – heavy rain falling all afternoon – several somewhat important matches were played. In the list was the second meeting between the 3rd L.R.V. and the Renton in the contest for the Association Cup. The result was a drawn game, one goal being scored by each team. That of the Volunteers, got just on the call of time, was protested against, but allowed by the referee. In accordance with the instructions of the Association Committee, play was continued for another half hour, but no more scoring took place.
Ref 1877032

16th March 1878
Seventh Tie Secnd Rply 3rd Lanarkshire R.V. 1-0 Renton
The undecided cup tie between the 3d L.R.V. and Renton Clubs was played off at Cathkin Park. At the conclusion of the game it was found that the Volunteers had won by one goal to none.
Ref 1877033

30th March 1878
Final Tie   **Vale of Leven 1-0 3rd Lanarkshire R.V.**

The final tie for the Scottish Football Association Cup was played on Saturday in Hampden Park, Glasgow, between the Vale of Leven and the Glasgow 3d L.R.V., in presence of ten thousand spectators. In the first half the Vale scored a goal. Nothing more was done, and the cup fell to the Vale of Leven, who won it last year. The match was very severe, several of the players being hurt. The Vale of Leven play on the 13th April in London the Wanderers, who have won the English cup for three years in succession.
Ref 1877034

13th Apr 1878
Friendly   **Wanderers v Vale of Leven**

On Saturday, the first match played between the most famous of the English Association football clubs, the Wanderers, and the Vale of Leven, took place at Kennington Oval, London. As the Wanderers for three years in succession have won the English Association Challenge Cup, and the Vale of Leven have twice in succession carried off the Scottish Cup, the trial of strength between the two teams was looked forward to with very great interest. Unfortunately the weather which promised well in the morning turned out very badly. Play had lasted only a few minutes when the rain began to fall, and for the remainder of the game it kept on without intermission, coming down at times very heavily. Before the game was over the ground was terribly soft and slippery, it being really remarkable how the men kept their footing and carried on the game at the pace they did. The attendance was good for a London ground, and the game was watched with intense interest, every piece of good play meeting with its reward in the shape of loud applause, and nearly all the spectators kept their places to the finish in spite of the drenching rain.

… Play began at half-past three, the Vale of Leven having lost the toss for choice of goals kicked off.

… The ground by this time was in very bad condition. A great run by the Vale of Leven ended in a corner kick from "hands." Another fine attack by the Vale of Leven followed, however, and a third goal was kicked by Ferguson. The goalkeeper got the ball, but slipped down and let it go through the posts. After this nothing of consequence took place, and the call of time left the Vale of Leven with a brilliant victory by three goals to one.
Ref 1877035

3rd September 1878
Miscellaneous   **Proposed Rule Changes**
S.F.A.A.G.M. The meeting then took into consideration the proposal of the Alexandra Athletic Club, that "When the ball is in touch a player of the opposite side to that which kicked it out shall throw it from the point on the boundary line where it left the ground (in any direction the thrower may choose). The ball must be thrown at least six yards, and shall be in play when thrown in, but the player throwing it shall not play it until it has been played by another player." It was pleaded that this would tend to a greater of assimilation with the rules of the clubs in the sister kingdom, while on the other hand it was contended that there was no necessity for the alteration, and that it would destroy the arrangements of the clubs for this year. On a division the proposal was negatived by a large majority. Another proposal was made by the Caledonian Club to have no jumping allowed during the game, and to have this practice put in the same category as tripping and hacking. It was agreed that the jumping objected to should be that of jumping at a player; but the previous question was moved, as the adoption of the new proposal would lead to a great amount of trouble, and as it was impossible for a football player to keep on his feet throughout the game. It would also give the umpire a greater amount of work, and lead to disputes. On a vote, it was agreed by 37 to 36 to adopt the proposal.
Ref 1878002

On the motion of Mr Dick, of the Alexandra Club, it was proposed "that when the ball is in touch, a player of the opposite side to that which kicked it out shall throw it from the point on the boundary line where it left the ground, in any direction the thrower may choose. The ball must be thrown at least six yards, and shall be in play when thrown in, but the player throwing it shall not play it until it has been played by another player". Mr Young, of the South-Western, moved the previous question, which was adopted by a large majority.

It was a matter of regret that the business before the committee during the year was principally the consideration of protested cup ties. Some of these disputes arose through the carelessness of club secretaries, sometimes through misunderstandings, sometimes through quibbles about the rules, but more especially through the action of biased umpires. In the interests of the national game, it was to be hoped that this subject would receive the serious attention of club committees, so that the utmost care might be exercised in the selection of individuals, to, fill the important position of umpire at the matches during the coming season.
Ref 1878003

September 1878
First Tie   **Port Glasgow v Pollockshaws Athletic**
Pollockshaws Athletic disbanded prior to the competition starting giving the Port Glasgow a bye.

21st September 1878
First Tie   **Barrhead 2-0 Wellington Park**
Two reports:-
This tie was played at Parkhouse, Barrhead, on Saturday, and resulted in favour of the home team by one goal and one disputed to none.
Ref 1878004

Resulted in favour of the Barrhead by two goals to nothing.
Ref 1878005

Played at Parkhouse, the ground of the latter [Barrhead], on Saturday. After some close play the game resulted in a victory for the Barrhead players by 1 goal to nothing. During the game repeated rifle bullets from the direction of the Nitshill targets, went whirring through the air inside the enclosure, much to the consternation and danger of the spectators and players.
Ref 1878006

28th September 1878
First Tie   **Falkirk 2-0 Campsie Glen**
The above tie was played at Randyford on Saturday last, in the presence of a large turn-out of spectators, and resulted in a win for the Falkirk team by two goals to none. The home team having won the toss, kicked off at 3.45, the forwards at once taking up the ball to their opponent's goal, and smartly passing it through, scoring the first goal one minute after the kick off. During the rest of the game some excellent playing was shown by both sides. A little before time was called the home team showed their superiority by taking the ball up the whole of the field, and by some clever passing, sent it through the goal, thus winning the match by two goals to none. The home team played well together. The following are the players:- Falkirk - R. Peddie (captain), W. Peddie, left; John Taylor, W. Gentleman, centre; James Neill, James Ferguson, right; W. Geddes, half-back; George Richardson, half-back; D. M'Millan and R. Service, backs; William Carmichael, goal. Campsie Glen - J. M'Farlane (captain), C. Reid, left; A. Stirling, J. Murray, centre; J. M'Kay, M. Dalton, right; T. Rodger and J. Murray, half backs; T. Reid and G. Gray, backs; W. Brown, goal.
Ref 1878007

Other report:
Played at Falkirk. Falkirk 1 goal and 1 disputed goal to Campsie Glen nothing.
Ref 1878008

28th September 1878
First Tie   **Newmains 0-12 Upper Clydesdale**
Played at Newmains and after a very pleasant game resulted in an easy victory for the Upper Clydesdale by twelve goals to none; kicked by G. Williamson, W. Muir, and R. Colthart 3 each, A. Colthart, R. Crystal and A. Williamson 1 each.
*Ref 1878009**

28th September 1878
First Tie   **Lanemark 2-2 Kilmarnock Athletic**
Played at New Cumnock and resulted in a draw - each team securing two goals. The Lanemark team showed a decided improvement on last year's form, being very speedy, and displaying their usual sharpness in "heading tactics". The Athletics were not fully represented, and in consequence did not manage to take full advantage of their opportunities.
*Ref 1878010**

28th September 1878
First Tie   **Kilmarnock 0-2 Kilbirnie**
As was expected, the home team were defeated though the Kilbirnie had fully the advantage of the play, and got two goals to none, Kilmarnock had many chances to score, but played bad at goal. Rather a large and noisy party came from Kilbirnie, and by their enthusiasm kept the spectators in good humour.
*Ref 1878011**

28th September 1878
First Tie   **Mauchline v Maybole Carrick**
"Through unforeseen circumstances, the Maybole Carrick were unable to play, and scratched in favour of Mauchline."
*Ref 1878012**

October 1878
Miscellaneous   **Football Accident**
On Saturday afternoon while a match was being played between the Kilmaurs football club and the Galston Blue Bell club, a young man named James Steele met with a rather severe accident, whereby his collarbone was fractured, caused by coming in collision with a fellow player. He was speedily attended by Dr. Buchan, and is progressing favourably.
*Ref 1878013**

5th October 1878
First Tie   **Clifton and Strathfillan 0-1 Vale of Teith**
Doune - The Vale of Teith Club although that a very late institution, have contrived in their matches so far, to give an excellent account of themselves. Last year their play was characterised by considerable science, conjoined to a determination and pluck that rather astonished some of their more weighty neighbours. Having joined the Association, their first tie for the Cup was against the Clifton at Strathfillan (Tyndrum Club).
The Doune men, after a pleasant run by rail, reached Tyndrum early in the afternoon. The field for the contest was about a mile from the station, and getting to the ground, the preliminaries were quickly settled.
At kick off the play commenced with great spirit, albeit a shade roughish. The home team experienced greatest difficulty in holding their own against the persistent efforts of the Doune forwards, more than one of them kicking handsomely. The Tyndrum goal was

seldom out of danger, the ball always there or thereabouts. The Tyndrum lads wrought well and hard, although at times they got rather bunchy and crowded for effective play. The kicking and running on both sides were considered much above the average of provincial clubs, and looked well for future work. On time being called it was found that the Doune team were the winners by one goal and a disputed one to nothing on the part of the Tyndrum. The run home of our men by rail was quite an enjoyable one after their work.
*Ref 1878014**

8th October 1878
Second Ties   Cup Drawings
Upper Clydesdale got a bye in their draw and were placed in the Dumbartonshire draw.

Footnote
Arbroath were drawn against St Clement. The two teams played out a no scoring draw at Baxter Park, Dundee on the 12th October. There is no mention of this being a cup match. The tie is recorded as St Clement having scratched.

19th October 1878
Second Tie   Portland 4-1 Thornliebank
The Portland having got the bye in their county in the drawing for the second tie, were placed in the Renfrewshire division and drawn against Thornliebank. The match was played on Hamilton Park; and notwithstanding the rough play of their opponents, the Portland were victorious by 4 goals to 1.
*Ref 1878015**

19th October 1878
Miscellaneous   Charging
In a reference to "charging" one reader writes:-
Happily the "accidents" that happened at football matches in Kilmarnock have not been attended with fatal results; but although we have been thus fortunate, there have been many sad instances of the terrible danger incurred by this practice at other places. Last season almost every week the newspapers had to record one or more fatal football accidents, and with scarcely an exception these were as a result of "charging".
*Ref 1878016**

19th October 1878
Second Tie   Hibernian 3a0 3rd Edinburgh Rifle Volunteers
After the third kick-off the Hibernians lost no time in again getting near their opponent's goal, and managed by some capital passing play to give the ball to Rourke's custody, and he scored the third goal, sending the leather neatly between the posts. A fourth goal soon after followed for the Hibs, but the referee disallowed it owing to one of their men having played offside. At this point [30mins] W. Hume and Shaw, of the 3rd Edinburgh R.V., retired - the first spitting blood and the second lame, and it was decided to abandon the match in favour of the Hibernian - who had three goals to nothing. A mixed friendly

game was thereafter played until full-time.
Ref 1878017

26th October 1878
Second Tie   **Cree Rovers 0-3 Q.O.S. Wanderers**
An Association cup tie was played between the above clubs on the afternoon of Saturday last on the ground of the former, near Kirroughtrie. The match created a great deal of excitement, and there was a large concourse of spectators of both sexes, notwithstanding the price of admission to the field was threepence for male visitors, the ladies being allowed free access. The Rovers got the kick-off, and a very exciting game of an hour's duration followed. The Wanderers, however, notwithstanding the plucky play of a number of the Rovers, succeeded in scoring three goals to nothing - although on two occasions it was only by dint of bad luck the Rovers were prevented from scoring.
*Ref 1878018**

26th October 1878
Second Tie   **Glengowan 2a1 Airdrie**
Played at Airdrie - the game throughout was characterised by such brutality that the referee had to put a stop to it. In the first half Glengowan score two goals, and in the latter portion of the game Airdrie contrived to score a goal. This seems to have exasperated the Glengowan players, who resorted to "charging" and two of the Airdrie players got themselves seriously injured, one having his collar-bone broken, and another his leg seriously bruised. The game was abruptly put an end to.
Ref 1878019

Played at Glengowan, Caldercruix, and resulted in a victory for Glengowan by two goals to one.
Ref 1878001

HORSE-PLAY AT FOOTBALL
In a football match in the Airdrie district on Saturday one of the "teams" behaved, it is said, with such unexampled brutality that the game was stopped by the referee. One player had his collar bone broken and another was seriously injured. The Procurator-Fiscal should be able to find a remedy for such fun.
Ref 1878037

S.F.A.C.M. [29th Oct]. The Glengowan Club for playing a rough game and indulging in unnecessary charging while playing a cup tie with Airdrie, were disqualified from taking part in the competition for the season.
Ref 1878020

FOOTBALL BRUTALITY
Sir – I beg to contradict the report in your Monday's issue of the football match – Glengowan v Airdrie – as your correspondent seems to know nothing whatsoever about it. The game was played at Caldercruix, not Airdrie, as stated by your correspondent, and no injury happened any of the Airdrie players in the slightest. The game was stopped on account of one of the Airdrie players brutally kicking one of the Glengowan players on the stomach, which led to a dispute, and on the referee asking us to resume play the

Airdrie Club refused, when the referee decided in favour of the Glengowan. I may add that one of our players had to retire before we had played ten minutes on account of rough play, which was brutal in the extreme. On no occasion have we been subjected to anything like it, as it is quite away from Association rules, and on no account would we play them again unless before a committee from the Association. Your inserting the above in your columns will oblige – I am &c.,
 JAMES GLEN, Secy., Glengowan Football Club
Ref 1878021

Footnote
Despite Glengowan being disqualified, Airdrie were not reinstated.

9th November 1878
Third Tie   **Heart of Midlothian 2-1 Arbroath**
Arbroath losing the toss, had to journey to Edinburgh to meet the Heart of Midlothian at Powburn.
*Ref 1878022**

Footnote
Up until 1880 with the exception of the final tie, clubs had to toss for choice of ground. Should one of the two clubs, drawn against each other, have a private ground, then the match had to be played on that ground. The definition of a 'private' ground was also extended to that of a 'public' ground made private for a match.

4th November 1878
Miscellaneous   **Football by Electric Light**
Some 20,000 people assembled in the vicinity of Hampden Park, on Monday night to witness a football match played under the rays of the electric light.
*Ref 1878023**

7th November 1878
Miscellaneous   **Football by Electric Light**
The match at football by electric light, held in Springvale Park, Midton Road, Ayr, last Thursday evening, attracted upwards of 1000 spectators, notwithstanding that the weather was showery and disagreeable. It was attempted to light the field by three lights - a great central light equal to 6000 candles at the far end of the field, and one lesser light at each corner of the field adjoining Midton Road. Each lantern was placed on the top of a sort of tower about 20 feet in height. Three portable engines were employed to work the electric machines. At first the lights worked satisfactorily. The large field was well flooded with a brilliant glare of light, though the shadows interplay between the gleams from the different lanterns destroyed the unity of the effect. Where the light shone it was so pure and bright that the colours in a tartan shawl could all be distinguished as clearly as in daylight. As a spectacle the match was very interesting and picturesque - reminding one of a pantomimic exhibition on a large scale - the agile figures of the players flitting about amidst the lights and shadows with as rapid action and as keen rivalry as in broad daylight. We are informed by some of the players that they had quite a sufficiency of

light for the game. The Ayr players had a disadvantage in the first half of playing with their faces towards the glare of the great centre light, which shone right into their goal, and illuminated the houses far beyond with a light almost equal to that of noon-day. This great light gave the best impression of the electric light of any that we have seen. It seemed less ghastly in its brilliance than the one exhibited in Ayr two months ago. This was no doubt partly owing to the character of the reflectors used. The game was well contested, but the Glasgow University team (which included 2 or 3 Queen's Park players) proved rather heavy for the Ayr Academicals, and scored three goals, while the local players were only able to secure one. Shortly after half-time the rain began to come down heavily, which had the effect of making the belts of the engines slip, and the current of the electricity thus being broken, the lights went out one after the other, and the game could not be finished. There can be no doubt that with more favourable weather the exhibition would have been more successful.
*Ref 1878024**

8th November 1878
Miscellaneous   **Football by Electric Light**
A football match between the Kilmarnock and Portland Clubs was played on the ground of the former, Rugby Park, by electric light on Friday evening last. The novelty of the display - this being the first occasion on which the electric light has been shown in Kilmarnock - attracted an immense crowd of spectators. The lighting apparatus was the same as that used at Ayr on the previous evening - supplied by Mr E. Paterson, electric engineer, London, and consisting of three lights, one affording an illumination power of 6000 candles, and the others 1200 candles each. The exhibition, though not free from defects previously experienced, was considered the most successful of the present series of experiments. The largest of the three lights continued very steady during the whole game, but the others were somewhat intermittent and unreliable, apparently on account of the engines. The evening was fine, with bright moonlight, but in the intervals between the streaks of electric light there were deep shadows, in which the movements of the players were with difficulty followed. The game was rather a rough one and two of the Kilmarnock team were disabled before it was half through. The result was a victory for the Portland by three goals to none.
*Ref 1878025**

16th November 1878
Third Tie   **Partick 1-2 Thistle (Glasgow)**
The Partick evidently took their opponents too cheap in having several 2nd eleven in the team, and got beaten by two goals to one.
*Ref 1878026**

30th November 1878
Fourth Tie   **Thistle (Glasgow) 2-1 Stonelaw**
S.F.A.C.M. [10th Dec]. Protests in connection with the fourth ties were considered. In the case of the Stonelaw v Thistle the latter club was disqualified for having played with three gentlemen not members of their club, and who had previously taken part in cup

ties. As a consequence Partick was reinstated.
Ref 1878027

30th November 1878
Fourth Tie   **Helensburgh 2-1 Heart of Midlothian**
The champion Association club of the East of Scotland having lost the toss, had to journey to Helensburgh to play off the tie with Helensburgh. The game was very fast, remarkable for rough play, and was played from beginning to end under protest, Helensburgh objecting to the referee brought by the Heart from a neutral club in Glasgow, and insisting on playing with a referee chosen by themselves. Pullen scored for the Heart in the first half, while the first goal got by Helensburgh in the second half was disputed on the ground of the player being offside. Close on time Helensburgh scored a goal.
Ref 1878028

S.F.A.C.M. [10th Dec]. The Heart of Mid-Lothian, it may be remembered, played this club [Helensburgh] under protest all though on the 30th ult., and the Sub-Committee of the Association so far sustained the objection as to reorder the match to be played a new, but at Helensburgh again - a decision which the Heart did not consider fair. At a full committee meeting in Glasgow, the Heart of Mid-Lothian were disqualified for not acting up to the Sub-Committee's decision, and to be considered as having scratched to Helensburgh.
Ref 1878029

30th November 1878
Fourth Tie   **Renfrew 0-4 3rd Lanark Rifle Volunteers**
Played at Renfrew, and resulted in a win for the strangers by four goals to none. The volunteers had the advantage of the ground, and goals were scored in the first half by Kay (2) and M' Donald. On changing ends, Renfrew played up much better, and occasionally got well within range; but their shots were somewhat erratic, while one or two assaults were frustrated, by the Lanark backs. Before time was called, J. Hunter, with a clever back-kick, placed the fourth goal to the credit of the Lanark team.
*Ref 1878030**

21st December 1878
Friendly   **Hibernian v Helensburgh**
The majority of the Scotch Rugby and Association clubs had declared their matches off previous to Saturday, owing to the weather, but with probably more valour than discretion the above clubs agreed to meet to play off their tie [Fifth Round]. The Helensburgh men arrived in the forenoon, and by half-past two several hundred spectators had assembled on the ground of the Hibernians at Powderhall, but after stripping and entering the playing ground the Helensburgh men refused to play, the reason assigned being the condition of the ground. A friendly match was proposed, but this the adherents of the green stripes would not hear of, and sides between the Hibernians were formed and play engaged in, but it does not call for details.
Hibernian 'A' 6 Hibernian 'B' 2.

Ref 1878031

19ᵗʰ April 1879
Final Tie　　　　　　**Vale of Leven 1-1 Rangers**
This final tie was played at Hampden Park, in presence of one of the largest assemblies ever present at a football match. The game proved of the most exciting description. Playing with the wind in their favour Rangers soon threatened the Vale citadel, and in twelve minutes Struthers finished with a shot which took effect - an appeal for "off side" being disallowed. A little later the same player scored again, but on appeal the goal was disallowed. Nothing further occurred up to the change of ends, when the play for some time was pretty even, each end in turn being assaulted. Towards the close, however, the Vale penned their opponents, and after a long-sustained assault the Rangers' citadel was reduced - the ball, out of a loose scrimmage, rolling slowly through. Only a minute or two remained, and the match ended in a draw - one goal each.
*Ref 1878032**

[Feb 1884] It will be remembered in 1879 the Rangers and the Vale of Leven fought the final tie, the game ending in a draw; or was said to have been a draw, though the Rangers protested they had won. The Association, however, upheld the decision of the referee, and ordered the game to be played over again on the following Saturday. The Rangers asked the Vale for further time, as some of their players had been injured in the previous game, but the Vale insisted on the Rangers obeying the orders of the Association, and playing the tie on the time appointed. The Rangers declined, and did not put in an appearance, and the Vale, claiming the cup, were awarded it by the Association.
Ref 1878033

26ᵗʰ April 1879
Final Tie Replay　　　　**Vale of Leven v Rangers**
The Vale of Leven team put in an appearance at Hampden Park on Saturday afternoon presumably with the expectation that the Rangers would be there to meet them. In the present state of matters, however, the Rangers, as was anticipated, did not come forward, and the Vale men left the ground. The dispute will be settled by the committee of the association at a meeting to-morrow evening.
Ref 1878034

S.F.A. Annual Meeting 29ᵗʰ Apr. In reference to the dispute regarding the decision in the final Cup-tie contest, a letter was read from the secretary of the Rangers stating that representatives would be present to ask an explanation. Mr W.S. Vallance spoke at considerable length as to the refusal of the committee to consider their protest. He referred to the protest which was lodged by the Vale of Leven in the similar match last year, and thought that if it was entertained and discussed, Rangers' protest this year should have been treated in like manner. The matter was based upon one man being "off side," but it was peculiar that the umpires could not name the man who was "off side." Mr Watt pointed out that admitting a man was "off side," there was an infringement of the rules by the Vale of Leven in the ball having been kicked off from goal and not from the place where the man was said to be "off side." He further stated that he heard one of the umpires tell a Vale of Leven player that it was only five minutes from time, and he would ask if it was possible for the gentlemen who were acting as judges to be imbued

with the neutral spirit which should exist at a final Cup tie? (Applause and hisses.) A member of the Rangers Club moved that the protest should be considered at this meeting, but the Chairman (Mr Hamilton) ruled that it was incompetent. Mr R.B. Colquhoun submitted to the meeting that the protest lodged by the Rangers was in reality no protest at all, as the point was decided by their rules. This view had been taken by the committee, and he could not see how anyone could look at the point at issue in any other light. As to informing one of the players how long the game had yet to last, he said that it was quite a common, and he did not consider it a wrong practice, and on the occasion under review he would just mention that he was asked similar inquiries by those on the Rangers side. He emphatically denied that he had had any bets on the issue, and he had been assured by the others who were judging along with him that they were in a similar position. (Applause.) The subject was then allowed to drop, the Chairman remarking that the Rangers, if they wished, might bring the matter before the new committee.
Ref 1878035

29th April 1879
S.F.A.   **Annual Meeting**
At the annual meeting of the Scottish Football Association, held in Glasgow on Tuesday evening, Mr Allan stated that the sum at the credit of the Association was now £850, 10s. Mr Dick, the secretary, in his report stated that the position of the society was most gratifying, there now being 126 clubs on the roll. Both in the town and country the cup competitions had provoked an amount of ill-feeling between certain clubs, which was as uncalled for as it was disgraceful. This jealousy would require to be watched, or it might prove to be the ruin of the game. Attention was called in the report to the desirableness of having an assimilation of the rules of the game, which could only be done by the formation of a National Football Association.
Ref 1878036

Footnote
From an initial S.F.A. membership of just 16 clubs in the 1873-74 season, numbers increased rapidly as see below from the reported membership figures:

1st Sep 1875	**50**	-- --- 1876	**68**	-- Sep 1877	**91**
3rd Sep 1878	**116**	29th Apr 1879	**126**	28th Apr 1880	**140**
24th Aug 1881	**136**	27th Apr 1881	**144**	26th Apr 1882	**128**

26th August 1879
First Ties   **Cup Ballot**
S.F.A.C.M. The first ties ballot included:-

Kilmarnock Athletic v Ayr Thistle

Footnote
Although it didn't appear in first ties published in newspaper reports, Kilmarnock were drawn against Ayr Academicals.

Research, based on various reports, supports that Ayr Academicals likely amalgamated with Ayr Thistle, to form Ayr Football Club, at the "Annual Meeting of Ayr Football Club" held at the Assembly Rooms on Monday, April 7th 1879. Coincidentally, or not, a "Mr F. Henry" was appointed vice-captain with an "F. Henry" having played for Ayr Thistle in their 9-0 cup defeat from Vale of Leven in 1877.

Ayr Academicals were themselves the product of a previous amalgamation between Ayr Eglinton and Ayr Academy on Thursday, October 19th 1876.

The drawings for the first ties of the following 1880-81 season were no better with:-

Hurlford v Ayr Thistle

20th September 1879
First Tie   **Arbroath 5-1 Our Boys (Dundee)**
This the first match of the season was played between these clubs in a field near Elliot on Saturday. The weather was fine, and the game was witnessed by a large crowd of spectators. The Our Boys won the toss, and chose to play with the wind at their backs. The Arbroath captain kicked off, and the ball was soon returned by the Dundee forwards. Milne, the Arbroath goal-keeper, proved equal to the occasion, and some fine play took place. The Arbroath men came away with a rush, and after a hard struggle the captain succeeded in getting the ball through, a feat that excited much applause. The Our Boys then kicked off, and soon got into their opponents' territory, but with no effect. The Arbroath forwards again getting the leather were soon up to the goal, Alexander making a second goal. After this period the Arbroath was severely pressed, and Our Boys secured their first goal by a fine shot. No change took place till time was called. The Dundee captain kicked off against the wind, but the ball being well returned, the Arbroath, forwards were soon on the leather… Nothing came of this move, the ball going behind. The Our Boys' goal-keeper kicking off, Alexander secured it, but it came off one of Our Boys' players, which resulted in a corner kick. The same player kicking the ball, it went under the bar out of the goalkeeper's hands, thus making the third goal for Arbroath. The ball being kicked from the centre, the strangers came away with a rush, but it was of no avail; Devlin, getting the ball, made a dash down the field, putting it through, and securing the fourth goal for Arbroath. Shortly after Hannah, by a good long shot obtained a fifth goal. This event finished the match, as time was called not long after. For Arbroath the following played well – Milne, goal; Devlin and Cromar as backs; Scott, Bruce, Mill, and Alexander, forwards. For Our Boys – Butter, Westwater, Wilson, Moore, Baxter, and Gorthy.
Ref 1879003

20th September 1879
First Tie   **Barrhead 0-5 Renfrew**
Played at Parhouse, Barrhead. In the first half of the game the play was evenly balanced, no goals being scored; but in the latter part the Renfrew team secured five goals to none for the Barrhead. During the play several rifle bullets came whizzing over the heads of the players and spectators from the Nitshill targets, much to the astonishment and danger of the onlookers and players.
*Ref 1879001**

Rifle Match   **19th R.R.V., Nitshill v. 16th R.R.V., Thornliebank**
A match took place between these companies on Saturday at Nitshill range. Conditions – 10 men a-side, all to count; distances, 200, 500, and 600 yards; seven rounds at each; any position. The day was very unfavourable for shooting. A strong, gusty wind from the left front made good scoring difficult. The total scores were – 19th R.R.V., 675; 16th R.R.V., 644. Majority for Nitshill, 31.
Ref 1879002

20th September 1879
First Tie   **Stranraer 2-0 Cree Rovers**
The first tie between the Stranraer and Cree Rovers (Newton Stewart) football clubs in the contest for the Scottish Football Association Cup was played off here on Saturday last. The match, which took place in a field belonging to Mr John Cowan, Aird, began shortly after three o'clock and was witnessed by a good number of spectators. The Stranraer Captain won the toss and chose to play with a slight wind in his favour. During the whole of the first half of the game the Stranraer players pushed the Cree Rovers hard, and three times the ball was put through the Rovers' goal, but owing to disputes arising in all three cases the referee could not decide on any of the goals, and therefore none of them were counted. At half time ends were changed, but though the Cree Rovers had then the wind in their favour the play was decidedly in favour of Stranraer. From a free kick got by Stranraer the ball was kicked well into the Cree Rovers' goal, and M'Guigan in attempting to keep the ball out touched it, when it bounced through between the posts, thus counting as a goal for Stranraer. A short time after this a scrimmage took place at the Rovers' goal, and George Porteous managed to get the ball through, thus gaining another to the credit of Stranraer. No gain being taken on either was from this time till the finish, the match thus ended in favour of Stranraer by two goals to none.
*Ref 1879004**

25th September 1879
Committee Meeting   **First Ties Protests & Admissions**
The committee met on Thursday night for the consideration of several protests in connection with the first ties – Mr D. Hamilton, vice-president, in the chair. In the protest of the Star of Leven against Jamestown the referee's decision was sustained. Consideration of the protest of the Alclutha against Helensburgh was delayed. In the protest of the Vale of Leven against Dumbarton the referee's decision was sustained – viz., Dumbarton won by four goals to three – but considerable discussion took place

regarding the rough play and unseemly conduct of two of the Dumbarton team. After evidence from some of the committee who were present, the committee debarred one of the back players in the Dumbarton team from taking part in any future cup ties or matches played under the auspices of the association. In the protests of the Irvine and Cumnock clubs the committee decided that the match be played on Saturday first. The following new clubs were admitted to the membership of the association:- High School, Glasgow; Plain[s] Blue Bells, Airdrie; Cartside, Bellshill, Barrhead Rangers, Stewarton, and Strathmore, Dundee.

Ref 1879019

27th September 1879

First Tie Replay   **Kilmaronock Thistle 0-8 Renton**

This match was played at Kilmaronock, the teams having met at Renton a week ago, when the game ended in a draw. It was entirely reversed on Saturday, when from the outset Renton played a hard and fast game, scoring eight goals, and the home team none. Kilmaronock wanted two of their best men.

Ref 1879005

27th September 1879

First Tie   **Campsie Glen 4-1 Milngavie Thistle**

These two Stirlingshire clubs met on the ground of the former at Lennoxtown, and after a hotly-contested game, in which the Campsie Glen had much the best of the play, victory rested with them by four goals to one. Shortly after half-time, when each club had scored one goal, a dispute arose, which resulted in the Milngavie team leaving the field. After a time, however, they returned, and agreed to play the game out. From this point the Campsie Glen had it much their own way, and by some smart play added another three goals to their score within fifteen minutes from commencement. Some very good play was shown by individual members of both teams.

Ref 1879005

Footnote

Game replayed after protest upheld on the grounds of the pitch not being roped off.

27th September 1879

First Tie   **Falkirk 4-2 Grasshoppers**

This match came off on Saturday last on the ground of the former at Randyford. Owing to this being the first draw for the association cup, great interest was manifested by the large number of spectators who appeared on the ground - there being about 400. The home team won the toss, and played off with a little wind in their favour, pressing the strangers' goal so hard, evidently determined that their first essay for the cup would be a success. After some hard playing on the part of both clubs, half-time was called with one goal, and a disputed one to the credit of Falkirk. The ends now being changed, the wind by this time blowing stronger than the first half, was more favourable to Bonnybridge, who, taking advantage of this, played with vigour, seemingly resolved to retrieve lost honours; but the "bairns" showed an impregnable front, and having pressed their opponents' goal pretty hard for about half-an-hour, were successful in placing other

two goals to their credit. Towards the end of the game play was getting very loose on the part of the home team, for which they paid dearly by Bonnybridge securing two goals. For the Falkirk team Leishman, A. Ferguson, and Johnstone played well; while James Richardson, as back, was always on the spot, and saved many dangerous attacks. The Bonnybridge team played well, the only name worthy of mention being Paterson (back) who appeared to be in rare form and kicked well.
Ref 1879007

27th September 1879
First Tie   **Catrine 0-2 Hurlford**
At the start Hurlford went rapidly at it and for a time seemed to be going to have play all their own way, but having settled down the play was more equal, and was carried on with the best of feeling, at the same time with the greatest determination to win by both sides, on a whole were highly pleased with the match, if we exempt the playing of Banks, one of the Hurlford backs, who in his over-anxiety seemed neither to regard tripping nor striking out with his fists, as unfair in the game, and which decidedly got him into bad favour with the onlookers. We think it is a pity that one man should mar the harmony of what ought to be carried on in a completely friendly spirit, however fast.
*Ref 1879008**

11th October 1879
Second Tie   **Whitefield 3-1 Northern**
S.F.A.C.M. [21st Oct]. To be played over, on account of the cross-bar being under the specified height.
Ref 1879009

25th October 1879
Second Tie Replay   **Northern v Whitefield**
This match should have taken place on Saturday, but the Whitefield at the last moment scratched in favour of the Northern. The Northern will therefore meet the Pollockshields Athletic in the third round.
Ref 1879010

21st October 1879
Second Tie   **Protests**
S.F.A.C.M. The following are the decisions in the various protests:- ... Kilmarnock Athletic v. Kilbirnie, protest of Athletic not sustained; Stewarton v. Ladywell. After hearing the evidence of referee, protest dismissed; Beith v. Portland, referee's decision sustained; Airdrie v. Cambuslang, protest dismissed; Bellshill v. Excelsior, protest not sustained; Milton of Campsie v. Campsie Glen, protest dismissed, referee's decision sustained; Jordanhill v. John Elder, the protest sustained.
Ref 1879009

18th October 1879

Second Tie   **Heart of Midlothian 3-2 Brunswick**

The failure of the Heart to have a ball delayed the start till late, and the match was finished almost in darkness, and made the result somewhat unsatisfactory. The Brunswick won the toss, and preferred the dry end, the lower part, which had been undergoing alteration, being partly under water. Purdie kicked off, and the ball travelled to Brunswick goal. Some good back-play ensued before the forwards got the ball, and the game became more open. After about half-an-hour's play, Alexander scored first goal for Heart out of a scrimmage. Up till the end of half time the Brunswick had the best of play. Stewart equalised matters by scoring a goal for the Brunswick. A few minutes after, Reid left his post and allowed A. M'Neill, by a splendid shot, to score the second goal for the Brunswick. In the second half the Heart got a second goal out of a scrimmage, while third was disputed, on the ground of the ball having been fouled. The last goal was got in darkness, and was scored for the Heart by one of the Brunswick "heading" it through his own goal. The match thus ended in a win for the Heart by four goals (one disputed) to two.

Ref 1879011

1st November 1879

Third Tie   **Arbroath 6-1 Strathmore (Dundee)**

This match was played on the Arbroath ground, near Elliot Station, on Saturday. The Arbroath kicked off against the wind, and after some fine play, secured three goals during the first forty-five. The Arbroath had the wind during the second forty-five, and again secured three goals, while the Strathmore made their only one almost at the close. The result was as under:- Arbroath, 6; Strathmore, 1. Owing to the weather the number of spectators was not as large as usual.

Ref 1879012

1st November 1879

Third Tie   **Jamestown 5-1 Lennox**

S.F.A.C.M. [11th Nov]. In the protest of Lennox v Jamestown, the committee elicited that R. Paton, who acted as referee in the match with the Star of Leven and Jamestown, was a member of the Jamestown club at the time, consequently the Jamestown club was disqualified. The Committee decided that the Star of Leven should play the 10th D.R.V. on Saturday first, the winner to play the Lennox.

Fourth Ties Draw

3d L.R.V. or [Glasgow] University v Star of Leven, Kirkintilloch or Lennox

Ref 1879013

1st November 1879

Third Tie   **Heart of Midlothian v Hibernian**

This important Cup Tie was to have been played on the ground of the Heart of Midlothian at Powderhall, but owing to a dispute with the lessee, had to be postponed till Saturday next. About twelve o'clock the Heart, to the number of forty, took possession of the ground and the various money boxes, but about two o'clock the

manager with a posse of policemen rejected those present from the ground and money boxes.
Ref 1879014

8th November 1879
Third Tie   **Heart of Midlothian v Hibernian**
This important Cup tie was announced to be played at Mayfield, but through a dispute as to the time of starting the above two clubs did not meet. The Heart team turned up about one o'clock and kicked the ball through the goal, while the Hibernians appeared shortly after three and also kicked the ball through. As both teams claimed the match, the matter will now be left for decision with the committee of the Scottish Football Association.
Ref 1879015

S.F.A.C.M. [11th Nov]. The dispute was regarding the hour at which the game was to start, and the Committee decided that the match should be played on Saturday first, on the ground of the Hibernians.
Ref 1879016

15th November 1879
Third Tie   **Hibernian 2-1 Heart of Midlothian**
The match between these clubs, for the Scottish Association Cup tie, took place at Mayfield, Edinburgh, on Saturday. Doubts were entertained as to whether the Hearts, after the dispute which occurred between them, would meet the Hibernians; and the latter club for the purpose, as they advertised, of not disappointing the public who might come out to witness a game at football, made an engagement with the Glasgow South-Western in the event of the Hearts not coming forward. The Hearts, however, came up to time, and, after a very rough and noisy game, the referee gave a decision in favour of the Hibernians by two goals to one. The Hearts entered a protest, because, as they allege, the bar of the goal posts was three inches too high. This will require to be decided by the Association.
Ref 1879017

12th November 1879
Miscellaneous   **A Scotch Team Crossing the Atlantic**
It has been an open secret for some time past that a team of Scottish football players is being organised for a tour on the other side of the Atlantic. The arrangements have already been pretty fully gone into, and everything now seems plain sailing. As probably intended, the team will leave for America in the month of April next, and the tour, which will extend over two or possibly three months, will embrace the most of the principal towns of Canada and the U.S.. Mr Wm. Dick the indefatigable secretary of the Scottish Football Association, who has left nothing undone to ensure the success of this new departure in the history of football, will likely go out with the team. The arrangements in connection with the tour, which fall to be made on the other side of the Atlantic, are being attended to by Mr. D.K. Brown, the editor of a Toronto newspaper, and a football enthusiast. In communication to the Secretary of the Scottish Association, of date October 31, Mr. Brown predicts for the visitors a warm reception in America, where the game of football is making considerable progress. The following crack players have, we

believe, volunteered to serve on the proposed Transatlantic team:- Goalkeepers - Messrs N.C. M'Donald, Alexandra Athletic and Glasgow University; Robert Gardner, Clydesdale. Backs - Thomas Vallance, Rangers; William Somers, Queen's Park; W.S. Thomson, Queen's Park and University. Half-backs - Hugh M'Intyre, Rangers; David Davidson, jun., Queen's Park; A. M'Lintock, Vale of Leven. Forwards - J.B. Weir, Queen's Park; W. Struthers, Rangers; John Smith, M.A. Edinburgh University; W.W. Beveridge, Glasgow University, John Ferguson, Vale of Leven; John Campbell, South-Western; Peter Campbell, Rangers. Mr Harry M'Neil, the well-known captain of the Queen's Park, will also probably number one of the players who go out to do battle with our American cousins.

Ref 1879018

15th November 1879

Fourth Tie　　　　　　　　**Kirkintilloch Athletic 5-2 Star of Leven**

The Jamestown having been disqualified in their cup-tie competitions, these two clubs met at Kirkintilloch to decide who should play off with the Lennox. During the first half each team scored one goal, but on change of ends the Athletics pulled better together and completely overpowered their opponents. The smart play of Gourlay and Dunsmore on the right, ably seconded by M'Andrew at the back, was most effective. The goalkeeper of the Star had hard work, but in the end his charge succumbed four times. The strangers, for whom Docherty and Forbes did good work, added one more to their score, the game thus resulting in favour of the Athletics by five goals to two.

Ref 1879017

15th November 1879

Friendly　　　　　　　　**Renfrew v Pollockshields Athletic**

These two clubs, which are drawn against one another in the fourth tie for the Association Cup, met at Renfrew on Saturday. Owing to no referee turning up, the captains of the teams decided to play a friendly game for one hour. No goals were taken in the first half. In the second half the Pollockshields Athletic warmed up slightly, and scored three goals in rapid succession. A little later one of the Pollockshields Athletic backs missed his kick, owing to the slippery state of the ground, and his mishap was at once taken advantage of, and a goal scored by the home team. At the end of the game a corner kick which fell to the Renfrew was well placed by Douglas, and a goal was scored just after time was called. It was therefore disallowed. The game thus ended in favour of the Pollockshields Athletic by three goals to one. These teams meet in the Cup ties at Pollok Park next Saturday.

Ref 1879017

Footnote

This non-cup tie related friendly proved to be a good indicator for the cup tie itself, which was won by the Pollockshields Athletic by 2 goals to 1.

22nd November 1879

Fourth Tie   **Kilbirnie 1a1 Hurlford**

The game was stopped by the referee after half-an-hour's play in the second part owing to darkness having set in, and thus ended in a draw - one goal each.

*Ref 1879021**

2nd December 1879

Fourth Tie   **Kirkintilloch Athletic's Three Fourth Tie Matches**

S.F.A.C.M. [2nd Dec]. The results of the fourth ties in the cup contest were stated to be as follows: - South-Western beat Arbroath, four goals to none, Pollockshields beat Renfrew, two goals to one. Dumbarton beat Clyde, 11 goals to none, Kirkintilloch beat Start of Leven, five goals to two; Kirkintilloch beat Lennox, six goals to two; 3d L.R.V. beat Kirkintilloch, five goals to one; Rob Roy beat ....

Ref 1879022

Footnote

These additional matches were due to the disqualification of Jamestown arising from their tie against Lennox. Lennox, Kirkintilloch Athletic and Star of Leven were thus reinstated - hence their retrospective ties albeit in the "Fourth Ties".

20th December 1879

Fifth Tie   **Thornliebank 12-0 Rob Roy**

At Deacon's Bank. Thornliebank kicked off, and had soon the ball in the strangers' quarter, but they spiritedly repelled the attack. The Thornliebank forwards got on the ball and soon scored a neat goal. When half-time was called they had four goals to their credit. Fortune now seemed to have deserted the strangers, and despite a well sustained defence the ball slipped through their goal occasionally, and at the call of time their colours had been lowered no less than 12 times, they having failed to score. From the first Thornliebank showed their superiority. The whole of the forwards played with their wonted skill and dash. The tackling of the half-backs, and accurate kicking of the backs showed up splendidly. The Rob Roy men were badly represented - their team including five Second Eleven men.

*Ref 1879023**

20th December 1879

Fifth Tie   **Parkgrove 0-1 South Western**

A pretty evenly contested game was played by these clubs at Trinidad Park. In the first half the South-Western obtained a goal, and in the earlier portion of the game they had generally the best of it. Their opponents, however, played better in the concluding half, and made strenuous and well-directed efforts to score, pressing the South-Western players very hard sometimes. On one occasion there was a lively scrimmage in front of the South Western goal, and the Parkgrove players contended that they put the ball through. This is denied by the other side, and the referee not being near enough to say how the matter really was, the point has not yet been decided. The game at the end stood this way - the South Western had made one goal and the Parkgrove claimed this disputed goal.

Ref 1879024

S.F.A.C.M. [23rd Dec]. A protest was considered from the Park Grove Club, and the committee decided that the match, Parkgrove v. South Western be played over again on Saturday first.
Ref 1879025

27th December 1879
Fifth Tie Replay   Parkgrove 2-3 South Western
These clubs again met at Govan on Saturday to play off their draw in the cup ties. During the first half the South-Western, favoured by a strong gale, pressed their opponents pretty closely. Once or twice the Parkgrove team managed to get the ball well down the field, but nothing resulted in any of the different occasions. Fully ten minutes after the kick-off Miller, for the South-Western, scored the first goal; a second as cleverly made shortly afterwards, and before half-time the South-Western succeeded in placing a third to their credit. On positions being changed the Parkgrove, with the wind in their favour, secured two goals - the first being obtained by Watson, whose play all through was very fine. Towards the close the play became somewhat exciting, but nothing further resulted, and the game thus ended in favour of the South-Western by three goals to two. The weather the whole time the game was in progress was of the most miserable description, a violent gale of wind, accompanied by a drenching rain, rendering play well nigh impossible.
Ref 1879026

27th December 1879
Sixth Tie   Thornliebank 0a2 3rd Lanarkshire R.V
At Thornliebank. This match was started by the home team kicking off up the hill in a perfect storm of wind and rain, which had reduced the ground almost to a puddle; the soil, being clayey, rendered anything like accurate kicking almost utterly impossible. After some hard runs up and down the field the volunteers succeeded in placing two goals to their credit. When the game had been about thirty-five minutes old the teams, by mutual consent, agreed to postpone the match till Saturday first, when it will be decided on Cathkin Park ; and a tough fight may be expected, the Thornliebank showing up very creditably against their older opponents while the game lasted.
Ref 1879027

21st February 1880
Final Tie   Queen's Park 3-0 Thornliebank
The Queen's Park team defeated the Thornliebank Club in the final tie for the challenge cup of the association by three goals to none. The match was played on Cathkin Park before a pretty fair assemblage, but outside the field there was a much larger gathering, thousands refusing to pay fancy prices for the privilege of seeing an ordinary football match and enjoying the comforts of a deal board seat on a wet, dirty afternoon. Rain fell heavily before the match began, and it kept on during the play in the first half of the game. But those allowed to stand in the mud at a shilling a-head or privileged to sit on the deal boards at double the price looked happy and satisfied enough so long as the play was exciting and "the enemy's fortress threatened." Play began by the Thornliebank representatives kicking off. In a short time the ball was close to the visitors' goal, and

Ker fired to score, but failed. A number of corner kicks were secured by the Queen's Park Club, but the ball could not be induced to go through. Ker made a clear run down the field and shot for goal, but the attempt was a failure. A great deal of kicking-out was indulged in, the play being against the Thornliebank Eleven. Thirty-five minutes had elapsed before a goal was got, the Queen's Park scoring from a tussle near the suburban players' goal; and in other ten minutes - just as half-time was up - a second goal fell to their lot. In second half of the game both sides played vigorously, and clever runs were made by the forwards, but time was almost up before another goal was scored, the Queen's Park players again proving too much for their opponents. The result of the very stubbornly contested match was Queen's Park three goals; Thornliebank none. The strangers played with great vigour, but they could not defeat the superior tactics pursued by their opponents, who exhibited some fine play in dodging and passing on the ball. Teams:-

Queen's Park :- Goal, John Graham; backs, W.S. Somers, R.W. Neil; half-backs, C. Campbell, D. Davidson; forwards, J. Richmond, J.B. Weir, T. Highet, George Ker, J. Kay, H. M'Neil (captain).

Thornliebank :- Goal, J. Cadden; backs, J. Jamieson, W. Marshall; half-backs, A. Henderson, W. M'Fetridge; forwards, A. Clark, A. Brannan, W. Anderson (captain), D. Wham, T. Brannan, A.S. Hutton.

Ref 1879028

28ᵗʰ April 1880

S.F.A.   **Annual General Meeting**

The annual general meeting of the Scottish Football Association was held last night in the Lesser Trades' Hall, Glasgow – Mr D. Hamilton, vice-president, in the chair. There was a large attendance of representatives from the different clubs.

THE LATE SECRETARY

Before proceeding to the business of the meeting, the CHAIRMAN referred to feeling terms to the almost irreparable loss football players had sustained by the death of the secretary of the association – Mr Wm. Dick. His name is widely known, not only in Scotland, where Mr Dick was so much loved, but also in England and upon the Continent. He was sure Mr Dick's name would be cherished and respected by all who knew him for the work he had done. (Applause.) He proposed that they record in their minutes an expression of the loss the association had sustained in the death of Mr Dick, and that an extract be sent to his mother in her bereavement. (Applause.)

MR JAMES A. ALLAN seconded the motion, which was cordially agreed to.

Ref 1879029 gh29ap80

Footnote

Mr Dick was only 29 years old. A benefit match between Clapham Rovers, the holders of the English Challenge Cup and the Queens's Park was arranged with proceeds going to Mr Dick's bereaved mother.

15ᵗʰ May – Queen's Park 3-2 Clapham Rovers at Hampden Park.

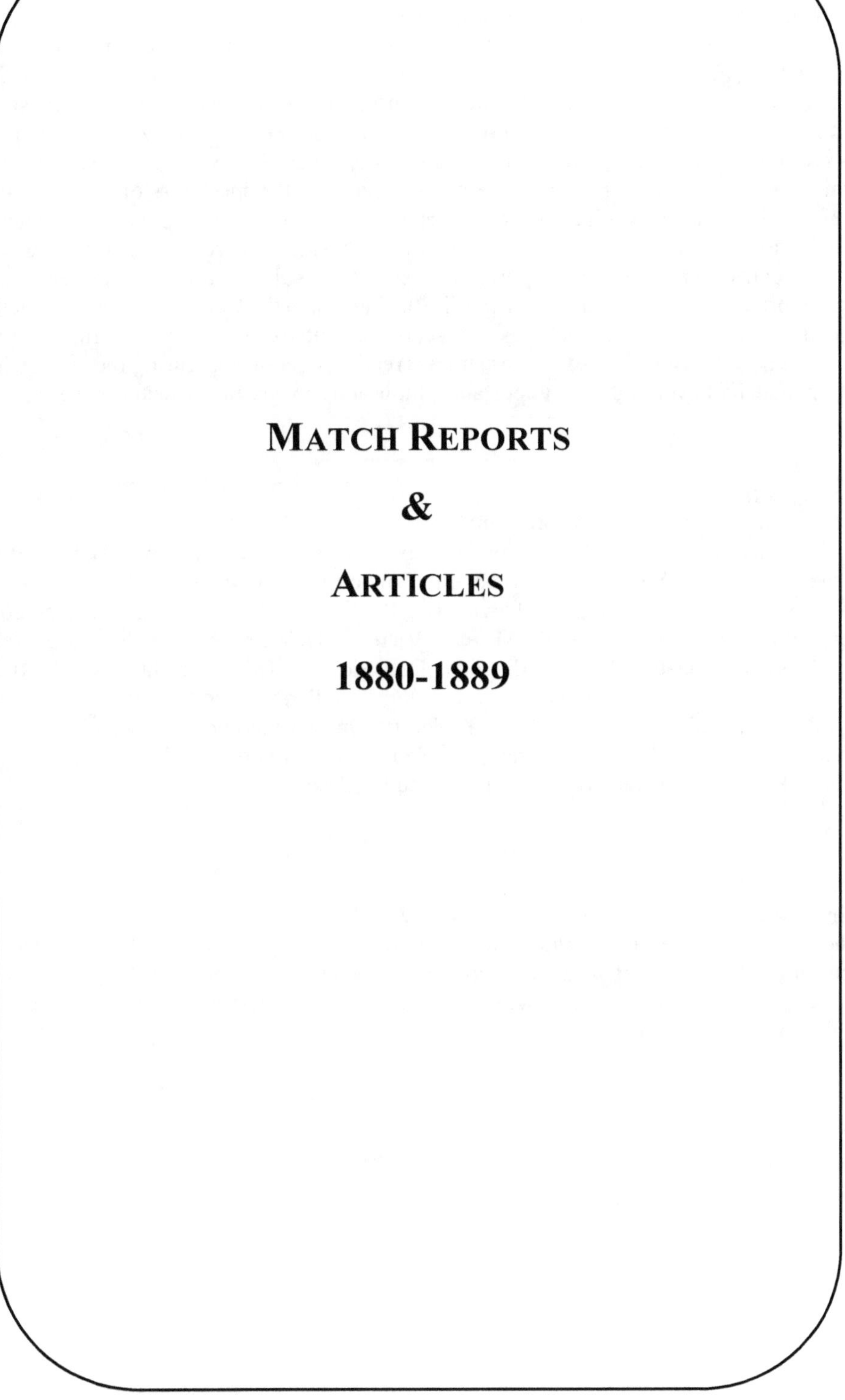

Match Reports

&

Articles

1880-1889

1880

Miscellaneous   **Honour to Queen's Park**

In 1870 the Association game was little known in Scotland, the only Club then playing it were the Queen's Park Club of Glasgow. To this Club the honour must be accorded of instituting the Game in its present form in our country - not merely by the enthusiasm with which the members of that Club conspicuously entered into every arrangement for its promotion, but more, perhaps, by the skill it displayed on the field. By the manner in which the Queen's Park players presented the Game to the spectators of their matches, they succeeded in awakening a general interest in it by the public, and a desire to engage in it by all lovers of manly sports. Thus in a very short time there arose in Glasgow, and in its vicinity, various Clubs playing the Association Rules; and these also being soon able to present a good appearance in public, the interest in the Game has been so widened and deepened throughout the West of Scotland, that to old and young the Football grounds have become the great resorts for recreative sight-seeing during the season, and in any match of even ordinary importance, thousands congregate to witness the play.
*Ref 1880001**

24th August 1880

S.F.A.C.M.   **Admissions**

On Tuesday evening the following twenty-seven clubs were admitted as members of the General Football Association:- Maxwell (Pollockshields), Pilgrims, Partick Thistle, Ingram, Cowlairs, Lancefield, Shawlands Athletic, Windsor, Rankinston, Abercorn, Johnstone, Johnstone Rovers, St. Mirrens, Victoria (Helensburgh), Airdriehill, Lanark, Tollcross, Uddingston, Bridge of Allan, Dunkeld, 5th Kirkcudbright R.V., Oakfield (Greenock), Campsie Athletic, Central (Campsie), Royal Albert (Larkhall), Coylton "Coila," and Pollock (Pollockshields). The committee recommend that clubs in the vicinity should avoid fixing Saturday, 11th September, for cup-tie matches on account of the cricket match between the Australians and Clydesdale.
Ref 1880038

4th September 1880

First Round   **Grasshoppers 1-2 Milton of Campsie**

The above clubs met for the first time at Bonnybridge, in presence of a large number of spectators. Play was not so good as formerly, owing to the length of the grass, which was a great hindrance to both teams. The Milton had the best of the game throughout, which finished in their favour by two goals to one.
*Ref 1880002**

11th September 1880

First Round   **Lenzie v Thistle Athletic**

Thistle Athletic failed to appear.
*Ref 1880003**

11th September 1880
First Round　　　　　　　**Lennox 1-2 Helensburgh**
S.F.A.C.M. [21st Sep]. Owing to an irregularity in the appointment of a referee the match was declared null and void.
*Ref 1880004**

11th September 1880
First Round　　　　　　　**Stranraer 3-0 Q.O.S. Wanderers**
A match between these two clubs took place in a field at Rephad on Saturday last in presence of a large number of spectators. The Reformatory flute band was in attendance, and played at intervals during the game. The captain of the Stranraer team having won the toss for choice of goal chose to play with the wind in his favour. The Dumfries men kicked off the ball, but it was soon taken possession of by the Stranraer team, who ran it down the field and managed within a short time from the start to put it through their opponent's goal amidst the cheers of the spectators. The Stranraer team took two other goals during the first half of the game. At half-time ends were changed, and Stranraer started the ball with the wind against them. They several times looked like scoring, but failed mainly owing to the back play of Beattie and Burns, the latter of whom played a capital game throughout. No goals were taken in the second half, and the match thus ended in favour of Stranraer by three goals to none.
*Ref 1880005**

11th September 1880
First Round　　　　　　　**Rangers 4-1 Govan**
The officers and sailors of the Russian yacht Livadia, to the number of 250, have intimated to the Rangers their intention of being present at Kinning Park to-day to witness the Cup-tie, Rangers v. Govan.
Ref 1880006

11th+ September 1880
First Round　　　　　　　**Rankinston v Maybole**
S.F.A.C.M. [21st Sep]. The [Maybole] protest in regard to the match Maybole v Rankinston was sustained, as the ground was not roped in, wherein the spectators interfered, was ordered to be played again. On account of the rough play of the Rankinston, it was agreed that the association should appoint a referee who would report.
*Ref 1880007**

11th September 1880
First Round　　　　　　　**Whitefield 1-1 Athole**
S.F.A.C.M. [21st Sep]. Owing to an irregularity in the appointment of a referee the match was declared null and void.
Ref 1880008

18th September 1880
First Round   **Kilmarnock v Stewarton Cunninghame**
This cup tie should have been played off on the Rugby Park, on Saturday, but the Stevenston team failed to turn up (the home team waiting on them for upwards of two hours), and the Kilmarnock got a bye.
*Ref 1880011**

18th September 1880
First Round   **Auchinleck Boswell 1-7 Cumnock**
.... however about two minutes after the kick off, the colours of the Auchinleck were lowered for the first time by a splendid header from Morrison. Another goal was added to the score about a quarter of an hour afterward, from a free kick about a dozen yards in front of the goal. A slight disagreement took place even although the referee had given a foul. Had number thirteen of the cup competition rules not been infringed by the want of flags for the umpires and referee, this quarrel would have been avoided, and it certainly showed bad policy on the part of the Auchinleck to go against the referee's decision seeing that they and they alone were to blame for the want of the said flags.
*Ref 1880009**

18th September 1880
First Round   **Coupar Angus 4-1 Strathmore (Dundee)**
These clubs met at Coupar Angus on Saturday to play off the first tie for the Scottish Football Association cup, in a field belonging to Mr Grant, Pleasance, before a large concourse of spectators. The Coupar Angus Captain won the toss, and elected to play with the sun at his back. During the first half the Coupar Angus, by combined play, succeeded in scoring four goals, against one taken by their opponents. In the second half the play was more equal, neither side obtaining a goal. The play of Blair at goal and Duncan at half-back for Coupar Angus, and the forward play of Smart and Henry for the Strathmore were much admired. The match thus ended in a victory for the Coupar Angus by four goals to one. The following were the teams:-
Coupar Angus - Goal, A. Blair; backs, L. M'Farlane and G. Robertson; half-backs, W. Duncan and W. Davidson ; forwards, Davidson, Chalmers, Mitchell, Gilzean, Clark and Anderson.
Strathmore - Goal, G. M'Lean; backs, S. M'Lean and McNaughton; half-backs, Cook and Porter; forwards, Petrie, Hedger, Howie, Harris, Smart, and Henry.
Ref 1880010

2nd October 1880
Second Round   **Excelsior 2-3 Airdrie**
Played on the Airdrie cricket ground, resulting in favour of the Airdrie by three goals to two.
Ref 1880012

2nd October 1880

Second Round   **Coupar Angus 1-2 Arbroath**

A match for the second tie for the Association Cup was played at Coupar Angus on Saturday. After a keen contest the game resulted in favour of the Arbroath by 2 goals to 1, and a disputed goal claimed by the Arbroath Club.

Ref 1880013

2nd October 1880

Second Round   **Kilbirnie 3a0 Kilmarnock Athletic**

Kilbirnie already one goal up ….. but after some good "headwork" Durrock did the needful, scoring the second point for the home team. Shortly after this, the Athletic made a bold effort to score, and the cry of "off-side" was raised, but they played on, and the ball came off the home keeper and went through. The strangers claimed a goal but the referee decided against them, and after much unseemly squabbling, they left the field refusing to abide by the decision. The home team remained and put the ball through the posts lately occupied by the Athletic, and time was called by the referee, with three goals to the credit of Kilbirnie. The game was unpleasant up till the incident referred to and would likely have been contested to the end, but for the interference of some of the Kilmarnock spectators who urged the Athletic to leave the field. We believe the Athletic team have lodged a protest against the decision of the referee.

*Ref 1880014**

S.F.A.C.M. [12th Oct]. Match declared null and void by the committee and a replay ordered.

*Ref 1880015**

9th October 1880

Second Round   **5th K.R.V. 4-3 Stranraer**

A match between these two clubs took place on the ground of the former at Palmerston grounds, Maxwelltown, on Saturday last. The captain of the 5th K.R.V. won the toss, and chose to play down the hill with the wind in his favour. The Stranraer team started the ball, and in the first ten minutes they were successful in scoring a goal. Unfortunately for the Stranraer team one of their half-backs (Bell) got himself hurt soon after the game began, and they were under the disadvantage of playing with a man short. The 5th K.R.V. near the end of the first half scored their first goal, and when half-time was called the sides remained equal with one goal each. The Maxwelltown team at half time started the ball against the wind, and their play was in all respects inferior to that of Stranraer, but were more successful in scoring, and on time being called they had managed to secure 4 goals, while Stranraer had 3. The match thus ended in favour of the 5th K.R.V. by one goal.

*Ref 1880016**

23rd October 1880

Third Round   **Mauchline 2-1 Kilmarnock**

"The Kilmarnock allege that time was called too soon, and for this and other reasons they have protested." In Mauchline it was generally thought the contest would be a

walkover. There would be between 200 and 300 persons present, which included a few "Mauchline Belles" - rather pleasant looking mortals, though, as is usual everywhere, a little "home outrageous". The game was contested, for a cup tie, in a very pleasant manner, with nothing of an annoying sort, "long to be remembered," about it, if we except the pleasant smiles of the fair sex glorying over the success of Mauchline.
*Ref 1880017**

S.F.A.C.M. [2nd Nov]. The protest Kilmarnock against Mauchline was sustained on account of the referee's connection with the Mauchline club being considered too intimate to qualify for the position, and the match is to be played over again at Mauchline on Saturday next.
Ref 1880018

6th November 1880
Third Round Replay   Mauchline 3a3 Kilmarnock
The game finished in darkness after 60 minutes at 3-3. Mauchline protested that Kilmarnock turned up late but not upheld. Kilmarnock arrived about 3 o'clock due to the heavy roads caused by the torrential rain. The players were drenched at the time they arrived.
*Ref 1880019**

23rd October 1880
Third Round   Cowlairs 2-1 Alexandra Athletic
S.F.A.C.M. [2nd Nov]. The protest Alexandra Athletics against Cowlairs, was sustained on account of one of the Cowlairs being not considered a *bona fide* member, and the match was declared off, and to be played again on Saturday next at Cowlairs.
Ref 1880018

23rd October 1880
Third Round   Arbroath 2-1 Rob Roy
The opening match for the season of the Arbroath Club came off on Saturday in the new park secured at Gayfield. The Club with which they joined issue was the Rob Roy of Callander, the members of which team were decidedly superior in weight to their antagonists. The park, which is in close proximity to the town, has been thoroughly cleaned, fenced, and enclosed. The weather was excellent and the turn-out of spectators large. These Clubs are the only two that are still in the ties for the Scottish Football Association Cup in the East of Scotland, and considerable interest was manifested in the struggle for supremacy. The Arbroath Captain won the toss, and chose to play down the slight incline on the ground. The Rob Roy kicked off, and the ball being well returned play began in mid-field, where it was kept for a considerable time, until J. Scott secured the ball, and by a fine run down the field ended up by a clever shot from the right, which went spinning through amidst great cheering and waving of hats. This early success augured well for the home team. This put the Rob Roy on their metal, and on the ball being kicked off they made determined efforts to score, but the goalkeeper was always equal to the occasion. A splendid rush, however, by the strangers' forwards equalised the game. The Arbroath replied by scoring another goal from the foot of Hogg just before half-time was called. The Arbroath in turn then kicked off, and the game now assumed

a very fast character. Splendid runs were made by both teams, and scrimmages in front of each goal were very frequent, but no more scoring took place. When time was called the Arbroath were declared victors by two goals to one after one of the fastest games played in Arbroath, the play throughout being of a very high character. The Arbroath Club will now be in the fourth tie for the Scotch cup. The following are the names of the teams :- Arbroath - Goal, J. Milne; backs, J.W. Baird, D. Williamson; half-backs, D. Guild, D. Bruce; forwards, W. Alexander, J. Christie, W. Hogg, J. Robertson; centres, J. Scott, W. Mann. Callander - Goal, A. M'Intyre; backs, D. M'Martin, J. M'Laren; half-backs, A. Wilson, G. Collier; forwards, A. Robertson, A. Reid, A. Ferguson, J. M'Donald; centres, W. Buchanan, D. M'Gregor, Captain. W. Dow, acted as umpire for the Callander team, and D. Duncan for the Arbroath. R.W. Neill, Queen's Park, was referee.
*Ref 1880020**

The Arbroath wore striped guernseys while the Callandar wore Rob Roy tartan.
Ref 1880021

23rd October 1880
Third Round   Falkirk 1-6 Dumbarton
The Dumbarton team being one of the crack teams of Scotland, there was a large turn-out of spectators. Falkirk won the toss, and had the wind and sun at their backs for the first half, but the grand back play of the strangers kept the ball well up in the home ground; and it was not long before the home team's goal was taken. After the kick-off from mid-field, Dumbarton again pressed the home team; and after a stubborn defence by the backs and goal-keeper, scored again. A third goal was taken before half-time. After change of ends, the strangers were successful in scoring other four goals, but one was disallowed on account of off-side, and the home team secured one - the strangers winning by 6 to 1.
Ref 1880022

30th October 1880
Third Round   Cartside 4-3 Yoker
The above teams met at Over-Johnstone. The Yoker having won the toss, chose to play with a strong wind in their favour, and in the first five minutes scored two goals. From this to the call of half-time the Yoker had the best of the play, and succeeded in scoring again. On ends being changed, the play was of a give and take nature for the first fifteen minutes; but after that the Cartside pressed the strangers, and were successful in lowering their colours four times. The game thus ended in favour of the Cartside by four goals to three.
*Ref 1880024**

S.F.A.C.M. [2nd Nov]. The protest Yoker against Cartside, was declared drawn on account of dubiety of one of the goals secured by Cartside after darkness had set in; the match to be played on Saturday next at Yoker.
Ref 1880018

23rd October 1880
Third Round   **Queen's Park 8-1 Pilgrims**
Played at Hampden Park before a good attendance. The Queen's Park team were not looking very sprightly after their Sheffield excursion, and for a long time played rather loosely, the Pilgrims making several runs on their goal. Indeed, once or twice M'Callum had to use his hands pretty smartly to prevent the ball going through, the spectators cheering the plucky play of the Pilgrims, many of whom, it may be stated, are old members of the late Parkgrove (Govan) Club. That they were but novices at the game the members of the Queen's Park eleven found out by the pressing play of their opponents. After 30 minutes kicking up and down the field, however, Anderson kicked a goal for the Queen's Park, repeating this success in ten minutes by adding another, and M'Neil finished the first half of the match by popping through a third. The fourth goal was secured by the Queen's Park immediately after the kick-off, and a fifth was taken from a runner kick, Gow "heading" the ball through. Smith scored the sixth goal, and from a scrimmage, Anderson added the seventh, and Smith, shortly after, the eighth. At this point Godwin made a clever run for the Pilgrims, and, guiding the ball well, sent it between the Queen's Park posts amid applause. The young club got no more, however, and the tie ended in the defeat of the Pilgrims by 8 goals to 1. The thrashing was a severe one, but the Pilgrims nevertheless made an excellent show. Godwin as a forward playing with rare judgment, and dodging some of his stronger opponents very cleverly. M'Intosh, at back, supported the young club well; and, indeed, all round the Pilgrims played a good game, and with some practice will yet show in some advantage in big matches.
Ref 1880026

13th November 1880
Fourth Round   **Arthurlie 4-3 South Western**
Arthurlie report:- These clubs met on Dunterlie Park, the ground of the Arthurlie. To decide their tie for the Scottish Cup. The match was not commenced till about fifteen minutes after the advertised time. The South-Western kicked off, and after some neat play obtained a corner kick, from which they registered their first goal. Shortly after the ball being again set in motion the strangers claimed a foul, about which there was some disputing, during which the ball was kicked off and put through the Arthurlie's goal, and on appeal being made to the referee a goal was given. This was rather discouraging to the home team, who, now set to work, and in ten minutes had two goals to their credit, thus equalising matters. From this up till half-time no further scoring took place. On change of ends it seemed as if the Arthurlie were going to have things pretty much their own way, four corner kicks falling to them in close succession, but the South-Western forwards getting away had a clear run the whole length of the field, and eluding the backs succeeded in registering another goal, giving them a total of three to two. Shortly after the kick off, Clark of the Arthurlie, getting the ball well at his toe had a magnificent run, which resulted in his scoring a third goal for the Arthurlie. With matters again equal, the South-Western set the leather in motion ; but again the Arthurlie were at it, and after some fine passing secured a fourth goal. From this till call of time no further scoring took place, the match ending in favour of the Arthurlie by four goals to three. This was the most exciting game which has been played at Dunterlie Park this year. According to another correspondent:- "During the last half hour the play was carried on in total

darkness, and the home team again and again claimed to have scored, and every run, no matter where it finished, was hailed with shouts of goal by the spectators. It was now impossible to follow with accuracy the course of the game, the referee in his efforts to do justice being met by oaths and threats of personal violence, and the home team's friends in their enthusiasm looking after the strangers' goalkeeper and paying unasked and unwanted attention to their backs. The matter has been submitted to the Association Committee in the form of a protest."
Ref 1880027

S.F.A.C.M. [23rd Nov]. A protest by the South-Western against the Arthurlie was considered, and the match between these clubs was ordered to be played over again.
Ref 1880028

27th November 1880
Fourth Round Replay   Arthurlie 2-1 South Western
Played at Dunterlie Park, Barrhead, in presence of about 2000 spectators, Play was commenced at 2.30P.M., the strangers choosing to kick off with a favourable wind. In the first half of the game the play was pretty even, but nothing decisive occurred. On exchanging ends the Arthurlie showed their superiority over their opponents by scoring first, but by determined efforts on the part of the strangers matters were speedily equalised by their scoring a goal also. Up till time was called nothing further took place, but it was agreed to extend the play for half an hour to enable the game to be decided, the result being in favour of Arthurlie, who added another goal to their previous one, making a win for the home players by two goals to one.
*Ref 1880033**

23rd November 1880
Fourth Round   Clarkston v Mauchline
S.F.A.C.M. [23rd Nov]. It was resolved that the undecided tie between the Clarkston and Mauchline should be played at Mauchline.
Ref 1880029

Clarkston telegraphed that game will be played.
Ref 1880030

27th November 1880
Fixtures today: Mauchline v Clarkston at Mauchline
Ref 1880031

27th November 1880
Friendly   Bathgate v Clarkston
Played at Bathgate, and resulted in an easy win for the Clarkston team by five goals to none.
Ref 1880032

Footnote
Despite agreeing to play the match with Mauchline it looks like Clarkston may have taken umbrage in having to travel away despite being the first drawn in the ballot.

27th November 1880
Friendly   **Clydesdale 2-0 Drumpellier**
Since the Clydesdale retired from the cup drawings, it has fallen into obscurity. Years ago it used to be in the mouth of every enthusiast; now it is only on very rare occasions you hear its name mentioned. If the members of the present team are anxious to revive its historic greatness, let them come to the front as they did in the rosy days of Gardner and Wotherspoon. The clubs they play now are only second-rate, and all the ingenuity they possess has to be brought into play in order to beat them. Between the Clydesdale and Drumpellier clubs there is a very strong bond of friendship, and the game on Saturday partook more of a social gathering than a football match. The game was pleasant, and when all was over the Clydesdale were declared winners by two goals to none.
Ref 1880034

Footnote
The Clydesdale Football Club were part of the Clydesdale Cricket Club and came about *"more for the purpose of keeping members together during the winter months* [1]*"* Despite being founder members of the S.F.A. and losing to Queen's Park in the first Scottish Cup final in 1874, their demise was rapid, scratching in the First Round ties each season from 1878-79 through to their last 'appearance' in 1881-82. On 11th September 1880, whilst most of the First Round ties were being played, the "18 of Clydesdale" were engaged in day two of their drawn cricket match against the touring Australian side at Titwood. A G.M. Wilson who scored 16 runs for the "Eighteen" was presumably the same G.M. Wilson who played at back against Queen's Park in the 1874-75 season's Fourth Tie.
[1] *– Ref 1880035*

26th March 1881
Final   **Dumbarton 1-2 Queen's Park**
The final tussle of the season for the Scottish Football Challenge Cup came off on Saturday afternoon on Kinning Park. The contesting clubs were the Queen's Park and Dumbarton; and at the close of a stubbornly-fought game victory rested with the former by two goals to one. By this, the latest of a very long series of the most signal successes, the Queen's Park became the holders of the Challenge Cup for the third year in succession, re-asserting at the same time their undisputed claim to be recognised as the premier football club in Scotland. The interest felt in the result of Saturday's contest was the most intense. Not for several years has a match played in the City, or indeed in Scotland, created such a lively and widespread commotion in the ranks of that large and increasing section of the community who patronise outdoor sports. It was *par excellence* the match of a period extending considerably farther back than the season now drawing to a close. In the Dumbarton team it was believed the Queen's Park would find antagonists worthy of their steel, and the really fine public appearances made of late by both clubs tended of course to strengthen this conviction. It was hardly to be wondered at, therefore, when, in addition to this tension of public feeling, there was the strong incentive to outdoor exercise of the most seasonable weather, that the turnout of spectators at Kinning Park should have been very large. Never, perhaps on any previous occasion has there been such a concourse of people within the boundaries of the little

burgh. More than an hour before the match was announced to begin the seething crowd of city-pent people began to sway westwards. Every thoroughfare leading to Kinning Park had its quota of pedestrians; trains and tramway cars were largely taken advantage of, while hansoms, cabs, and other vehicles also helped to expedite the general exodus. Half an hour before play commenced the grand stand was fully freighted, and the management were reluctantly compelled to "refuse money" from all late comers. By the same time the standing-space around the ropes, even at a shilling a head, was more than comfortably filled. It had however, to submit to a much greater utilisation. Every inch of ground was valuable, and the crowd packing itself into the smallest possible compass, after the fashion peculiar to an eager and a good-natured gathering, made some parts of the park even more valuable than the most exacting management could have ventured to hope. Outside the park the press was equally great. Every point of vantage within several hundred yards was taken advantage of by men and boys of all ages, of whom it may be said that, while their interest in the match was too marked to be doubted, they were evidently resolved to get their amusement more cheaply than their neighbours. One could not but remark the cool audacity of some of these individuals. For instance, a band of thirty or forty took up their quarters on the roof of a church session-house immediately overlooking the park, and haughtily declined the repeated and well-meant attentions of a couple of policemen. A numerically stronger contingent took possession of the waggons of a mineral train on the railway line to the south of the football field. They were speedily reinforced, and every waggon had soon its living freight. In this state of matters the train was set in motion, but the passengers were apparently in no way alarmed, and they stuck manually to their waggons. The result was that the train was in the end brought to a standstill at the part of the line adapted for witnessing the proceedings which afterwards took place than that in which it originally stood. The officials gave up the attempt to dislodge their unwelcome passengers, who remained masters of the situation. In all directions the crowd asserted itself by its overwhelming numbers. Whichever way one looked, there was the same unbroken wave of human faces - eager, watchful, pre-occupied. Play was announced to begin at half-past three, and at that time the crowd of people in and around the park must have numbered close upon 20,000. ... Play was begun by the Dumbarton representatives kicking off. The Queen's Park, who promptly returned the leather, soon received a corner kick, but nothing resulted, the ball after repeated attempts to score being sent over the bar. The play continued dangerously near the Dumbarton goal, and another corner kick soon fell to the lot of the Queen's Park. They again, failed to make anything of it. Ker soon after this got on to the leather, and passing it to Anderson, that player in trying to score sent it over the cross bar. By a splendid bit of passing, Brown and M'Kinnon of the Dumbarton team carried the ball to the other end of the field, from which, however, it was speedily returned to the Dumbarton territory by Watson, who played throughout admirably. Following this a good run was got for Dumbarton, and some very fine play near the Queen's Park posts ensued. Harry M'Neil then succeeded in getting away with the leather, and ran it smartly to the other end, where, however, it was at once kicked out of play. Soon afterwards, and within fifteen minutes of the start, Kay from a long shot put the ball between the Dumbarton posts. Loud cheering greeted this achievement. On resuming the Dumbarton players gave a better account of themselves. Twice in rapid succession M'Callum, the goal-keeper for the Queen's Park, had to use his hands. A foul was given afterwards in mid-field against Dumbarton, but the Queen's Park made

nothing of the advantage. After a while the Dumbarton goal was again threatened, but the ball was shot past the posts. Both teams had by this time settled down to their level best play, and the Dumbarton men, ten minutes after the first goal had been taken by the Queen's Park, equalised matters, Brown sending the ball between the posts. There was again loud cheering. Nothing further was accomplished in the first half of the game, the play towards the close being of a give-and-take description, and both goal-keepers were repeatedly required to defend their positions. On play being resumed in the second half the Dumbarton and the Queen's Park goals were threatened the one after the other. M'Callum's saving powers were a second time called into action. Securing a corner kick, the Queen's Park retaliated with an attack on the Dumbarton uprights. The ball was, however, carried to the other end of the field, and it was some few minutes afterwards - a quarter of an hour from the commencement of the second half of the game - that Kay took the second goal for the Queen's Park. From this till the end of the game the play was in favour of the Queen's Park. No further scoring, however, took place, and the result of the match was thus, as stated above - Queen's Park, 2; Dumbarton, 1. At the close of the game the captain of the Dumbarton team lodged a protest against the result, on the ground that the crowd had interfered with the play.
Ref 1880036

9th April 1881
Final   **Queen's Park 3-1 Dumbarton**
The final tie for the possession of the Scottish Association Challenge Cup was played on Saturday on Kinning Park. It will be remembered that teams representing the Queen's Park and Dumbarton Clubs met in the final tie on the same ground a fortnight ago, and after a stubbornly contested game the Queen's Park players were declared the victors by two goals to one. At the conclusion of the match, however, a protest against that decision was lodged on behalf of the Dumbarton players on the ground that a number of spectators broke into the field towards the close of the game and interfered with the play. The association at a subsequent meeting sustained this protest and Saturday's fixture was the result. It was quite evident that preparations of an extensive nature had been made for the better accommodation of spectators, and precautions were also taken to prevent the crowd interfering with the play, as they did at the previous match. At the corners of the field, which proved to be the weak points a fortnight ago, strong wooden barricades were placed, while in addition to the regular stand on the north side, temporary erections were put up along the east and south sides. The extra accommodation thus provided was filled with spectators about an hour before the advertised time of kicking-off. At the time of commencing people were standing round the ropes four and five deep. The weather on Saturday left nothing to be desired as far as spectators were concerned, although it can scarcely be doubted that the players would have preferred a cooler day for so hard a match. Victory again rested with the local men, who won the match by three goals to one - a result which cannot but be satisfactory to the majority of football players, as it proves that they are still able to maintain their position as the premier club.
Ref 1880037

23rd August 1881
First Round Draw   Largs Mystery
Footnote
The draw for the First Round included the following ties in the Ayrshire region:

Largs v Girvan
Kilmarnock v Largs Athletic

Neither Largs nor Girvan appeared in the Second Round draw suggesting that they either disbanded or scratched. This is highly plausible in the case of Girvan, as they had scratched in the previous two seasons in the First Round and were never to appear in the cup drawings again. The situation with Largs is somewhat different. A Largs Athletic made their first appearance in the Cup this season, and with no other Largs club reportedly playing in Ayrshire at this time, it is probable then that Largs was an erroneous mix up with Largs Athletic.

10th September 1881
First Round   St Bernard's 1-0 Heart of Midlothian
Teams from these clubs played their tie match for the Scottish Cup on Saturday, at the Royal Gymnasium. The event drew together a large number of people. The game was, of course, played under the Association code. It was splendidly contested throughout, and now and again loud applause was elicited from the spectators by bits of good play. Both goals were several times in imminent danger, but no advantage was gained until about the close, when one of the Stockbridge lads, by a well-directed kick, brought down the Hearts' fortress - a result which was followed by ringing cheers all around the ground. As nothing more of a decisive character happened, the St Bernard's team were left victors. For about the last quarter of an hour, St Bernard's lost the services of one of their players, who had met with an accident.
Ref 1881001

10th September 1881
First Round   Annfield 1-1 Eastern Athletic
EASTERN ATHLETIC v ANNFIELD (CUP TIE) - Played on the ground of the latter, and resulted in their favour by two goals to one.
ANNFIELD v EASTERN ATHLETIC (CUP TIE) - Played on the ground of the Annfield, and resulted in a draw - one goal each.
Ref 1881002

17th September 1881
First Round   Queen's Park 14-0 Caledonian (Glasgow)
A crowd of several hundred spectators was attracted to Hampden Park to witness what was expected to turn out a good match. The Queen's Park mustered a pretty strong team, as will be seen from the names which follow, and the opposition club, although not by any means one of the first or even second order, was expected to show some good play. As it turned out, however, they were thoroughly overmatched, so much so that the game

was altogether one-sided and anything but interesting. As the result of the hour and half's play the Queen's Park scored 14 goals, while the Caledonian did not succeed in getting a single one; in fact, they only once really endangered their opponent's goal. Five of the goals were taken in the first half and the nine came in rapid succession in the second, only about a minute elapsing between some of them. It goes without saying that the merits of Thomson, who kept the Queen's Park posts, were not tested. Watson, who, with A. Holms, played back, was quite in his old form, doing some really good work for his team. Gow, half-back, did fairly well. Of the forwards, Kerr, Anderson, Fraser, Brock, and Allan played a fine game, some good passing being exhibited.
Ref 1881003

17th September 1881
First Round   **Paisley Athletic 6-1 Port Glasgow Athletic**
One of the backs (Whitehill) got his leg slightly bruised by falling on the ropes, which would not have occurred if the ropes had been removed back from the touch line, instead of being placed almost directly above the lines.
*Ref 1881004**

17th September 1881
First Round   **5th K.R.V. 3-2 Moffat**
The tie between these clubs for the Associations Cup was played at Maxwelltown on Saturday. When time was up each time had scored two goals, and it was agreed to play an extra half-hour, when 5th K.R.V. scored another goal, and won the tie by three goals to two.
*Ref 1881005**

20th September 1881
Second Round   **Admissions**
S.F.A.C.M. Two new clubs – namely, the Vale of Leven Hibernians and the Stewarton [Cunninghame] – were admitted to the membership roll, while the Dunblane Wanderers (omitted in first round) were included in the ties.
Ref 1881006

S.F.A.C.M. Another letter from the Dunkeld, who were admitted into the Association immediately after the [27th April] General Meeting but whose right to compete in the Cup Competition had been overlooked was also considered and on the motion of Mr Hamilton seconded by Mr Wallace (Beith) it was agreed to allow them to take part in the second round.
Ref 1881007

Footnote

Dunblane Wanderers, and not Dunkeld, were admitted into the Second Round as Dunkeld had already participated in the first round ballot having been admitted to the S.F.A. the previous season. This looks like an error by the secretary in the S.F.A. minutes. The following First Round result was given in the Perthshire region:

> Dunkeld a bye – Rob Roy scratched.

Ref 1881006

The following ties were published in the Second Round:

> Dunblane v. Vale of Teith
> Dunkeld v. Coupar Angus

Ref 1881006

However, it was Rob Roy who played against Coupar Angus. A penned amendment to the results in the S.F.A. minutes had both Dunkeld and Rob Roy with byes.

17ᵗʰ September 1881

First Round   **Bridge of Allan 1-1 Thistle Athletic**

These clubs met on the ground of the Bridge of Allan club on Saturday last to decide their tie in the first round of the Scottish Association Cup Competition. There was a good turn-out of spectators. The Thistle captain having won the toss kicked off the ball, and both teams started with determination. During the first half, the home team, though having the best of the game, could only score once. In the second half, the home team having to play with ten men, one of the players having to retire hurt, the strangers put the ball through the goal fifteen minutes before time was called. It was agreed to play half-an-hour extra, but neither side could gain any advantage. The match thus resulted, after a very fast and exciting game, in a draw – one goal each.

Ref 1881006

20ᵗʰ September 1881

Second Round   **Stirlingshire Region Results & Cup Draw**

S.F.A.C.M. Results of First Round ties:-

STIRLINGSHIRE

Falkirk beat King's Park, Stirling, by three goals to none.
Strathblane beat Dunipace by seven goals to none.
Milton of Campsie beat Southfield by three goals to none.
Grasshoppers a bye – Central, Campsie dissolved.
Bridge of Allan v Thistle Athletic, two drawn games.
Lenzie a bye – Campsie Athletics dissolved.

"The drawings for the second round:- "

STIRLINGSHIRE

Grasshoppers v. Falkirk.
Milton of Campsie v. Lenzie.
Bridge of Allan v. Strathblane.
Thistle Athletics, a bye.
Ref 1881008

Footnote

Despite the Second Round draw, Thistle Athletic and Bridge of Allan played off their First Round tie. Research to date is summarised as follows:
- No reference has been found to a cup tie between Bridge of Allan and Thistle Athletic prior to September 17th.
- The extra time match of September 17th was played at Bridge of Allan. This reflects the home advantage they gained from being drawn first in the cup tie ballot and therefore supports this as being the first match. Thus the 'two drawn games' reason for the original Second Round drawings, made on September 20th, may have been a mistake.
- The match on October 1st was played at Milngavie, in line with a first replay.

1st October 1881

First Round Replay   Thistle Athletic 8-0 Bridge of Allan

The cup tie between the Milngavie and Bridge of Allan, played on the ground of the former, resulted in the defeat of the Bridge of Allan by 8 goals to nothing. The strangers played two men short.
Ref 1881010

1st October 1881

Second Round   Partick Thistle 3-1 Pilgrims

S.F.A.C.M. [11th Oct]. Protest sustained on ground of enclosure not properly roped and staked.
*Ref 1881011**

1st October 1881

Second Round   Cambuslang 6-2 Airdrieonians

Played on the ground of the former at Westburn Green, Cambuslang, and resulted in their favour by six goals to two. The visitors played with nine men.
Ref 1881010

1st October 1881
Second Round   **Airdrie 1-1 Airdriehill**
S.F.A.C.M. [11th Oct]. Airdrie and Airdriehill were ordered to play over again.
Ref 1881013

4th October 1881
Second Round   **Cartvale Draw Omission**
A meeting of the Business Committee was held in these rooms at one o'clock on Tuesday the 4th Oct for the purpose of considering what should be done with the Cartvale who were omitted in the second round of the Cup drawings. The Secy stated to those present which included J W Hamilton - who occupied the chair - Messrs R Broome, Devlin, Young, Paton and Stoddart that he had been in correspondence with the Johnstone, who had received a bye, endeavouring to get them to meet the Cartvale, but as they considered it unconstitutional to play a club which had not been drawn along with the others, the only course open to the committee was to give both clubs a bye, and this they instructed the Secy to do.
Ref 1881014

8th October 1881
Second Round   **Thistle Athletic 3-2 Strathblane**
S.F.A.C.M. [11th Oct]. Strathblane in their protest evinced many charges against the Thistle of Milngavie and also against the Referee whose 'imperfect' knowledge of the Rules of the game was the chief occasion of the protest. Mr M'Culloch who acted as referee was summoned to the Committee who felt satisfied that all of his decisions had been fair and honest and on the motion of W. Browne seconded by Mr Wallace (3d LRV) it was unanimously agreed to hold the deposit fee and dismiss the protest.
Ref 1881015

8th October 1881
Second Round   **Harp (Dundee) 1-1 Our Boys (Dundee)**
At Tayside Park, the grounds of the Harp, the above clubs met to play off their tie for the Scottish Association Cup. Both clubs having a good name in the North of Scotland, a very large number of spectators turned out to witness the game. Each club scored a goal, and the match ended in a draw.
Ref 1881016

S.F.A.C.M. [11th Oct]. Protested. To be played "again" at Harp if improvements can be made to the length of their enclosure.
*Ref 1881017**

15th October 1881
Second Round Replay   **Our Boys (Dundee) v Harp (Dundee)**
This match came off on Saturday afternoon at Clepington on the ground of Our Boys, and resulted in their favour by five goals to two.
Ref 1881018

8th October 1881
Second Round   **Lugar Boswell 3-1 Annbank**
Annbank ought to learn how to conduct themselves before appearing in public to play at football, especially their captain, who instead of keeping his men in order, tried all he could to keep up the strife, in swearing and shouting, at which a great many of the spectators left the field saying it was shameful.
*Ref 1881019**

8th October 1881
Second Round   **Milton of Campsie 3-1 Lenzie**
S.F.A.C.M. [11th Oct]. Protest that the field was a stubble one. Ordered to meet again on a better ground or failing that at Lenzie.
*Ref 1881020**

8th October 1881
Second Round   **Wellington Park 3-4 Kilbarchan**
Wellington protested on the grounds that the colours of the competing clubs were alike, causing confusion; but the committee, while repelling the objection, did not order the 10s. deposited to be forfeited.
*Ref 1881021**

22nd October 1881
Third Round   **Partick 1-2 South Western**
These clubs met at Whiteinch, Partick, to play off their Cup tie. Allison, the South-Western skipper, having won the toss, elected to play with the wind at his back, and thus aided, his team were from the start the aggressors. M'Cartney did the needful for his side when the game was about four minutes old, and although after this the shots and chances were many a considerable interval elapsed before goal No. 2 was scored from the foot of Copeland. Play continued up till half-time wholly in Partick territory, numerous corner kicks being well taken by Cairns, but the score was not increased. On change of ends the Partick team were confident in their ability to be at evens with their rivals; but Heggie and Campbell at back were in brilliant form, and, being well guarded by the half-backs, the goal remained intact. Wylie and Erskine, on the right wing, put in some good work for the Govan club. Indeed, had the centre not been weakened by the transference of Copeland to the half-back, they must have scored against the hurricane. About twenty minutes from time the resolute efforts of the Partick forwards were rewarded by a well-got goal. From this till call of time the South-Western line of defence remained unbroken; and although their forwards still made frequent incursions to the Partick goal mouth, no other point was added, the match thus ending in favour of the South-Western by two goals to one. For the South-Western, Erskine and Wylie, in the front, played a pretty game; and Heggie, at back, surpassed all his former efforts. Urie (forward) and Smith (back) did good service for the Partick.
Ref 1881022

S.F.A.C.M. [1st Nov]. Partick claimed a goal, and draw; remitted for further consideration.

Ref 1881023

Footnote
Later upheld and replay ordered.

5th November 1881

Third Round Replay   South Western 1a0 Partick

These teams met at Copeland Park, Govan, on Saturday afternoon, to play off the undecided cup tie, when the game came to an early and unsatisfactory end by the Partick men leaving the field before half-time was up, after a disputed goal had been awarded to the South Western by the umpire. After the game was commenced, the teams appeared to be pretty well matched, but the play was, if anything, rather rough, and there was a dispute or two previous to the one that led to the stoppage of the match. When half-time was about up, the ball was thrown in, and the South-Western men getting it well in amongst them, ran it close to the Partick goal, and after a little scrimmage it was kicked up to between the posts and stopped by the goalkeeper, who crouched down and caught it with his hands. The South-Western held that it had been caught inside the line of the posts and claimed a goal, while Partick alleged that the ball had been thrown out legitimately by their goalkeeper. The umpire, however, decided that the ball had been stopped inside the goal, and, to use a legal phrase, sustained the claim of the South-Western. This neither satisfied the Partick team nor their friends outside the ropes. The play ceased, and in a few minutes the Partick men left the field, followed shortly afterwards by their opponents. The spectators now commenced to make a good deal of noise, and a portion of them went straight to the gatekeeper and demanded that their money should be returned. The gatekeeper made for the club-house, in front of which all the people had now gathered, some clamouring for their money, and others insisting that the game should go on. One gentleman in the club-house called upon a single policeman to clear away the crowd, but the officer stood quietly by, and listened with evident unconcern to the remarks passed by the more outspoken ones, which were never at any time either threatening or much out of place. It was at length announced that the South-Western were willing to finish the game, but by this time the Partick team were preparing to go away. The 2d Pilgrims then entered the field, and played for some time with the South-Western, but the most of the spectators moved off on finding the original match was not to be finished. The matter will be brought before the Association.

Ref 1881024

22nd October 1881

Third Round   Stranraer 4a1 Q.O.S. Wanderers

Stranraer won the toss, and chose to play with a strong wind in their favour, which was very strong throughout the game. The Queen of the South Wanderers started the ball against the wind, but it was soon taken possession of by the Stranraer backs, and, playing it to their forwards, who were eager to score and not calculating the strength of the wind, sent it over the bar. This was repeated later, but a good shot from J. M'Quiston registered the first goal for Stranraer. The Wanderers playing a good defensive game, it was very difficult for Stranraer to score, and a shot crossing the goal line gave Wanderers a free kick. The goalkeeper, unable to send the ball any distance against the wind, played it to one of the backs (M'Millan); but S. Carrath being on the spot managed to put the ball

between the uprights. The play was of a give-and-take nature, and very fast, but a splendid shot from H. M'Keand sent the ball again through the posts. The ball again started from the centre was soon returned to the Stranraer forwards, who travelled with it very fast, but were checked by Burns who played a good game for the Wanderers. Half-time being nearly up, the home team were making an attempt to score, and from a throw in the ball was again sent between the posts by W. Mackie, making the fourth goal for Stranraer. On changing ends the Wanderers played with great determination to equalise matters, but by the splendid back play of Stranraer were unsuccessful in scoring for nearly half an hour. On obtaining their first goal they gained courage, and several fine shots were made, but took no effect R M'Caig playing splendid at goal. Stranraer forwards played well against the wind, and some fine runs were made on the left wing by J. M'Kinstrey and W. Mackie, the former being the most conspicuous. About seven minutes before call of time a dispute arose as the Wanderers' right wing player threw in the ball in an angle into the mouth of the Stranraer goal. One of the Stranraer half-backs claimed a foul throw in; but the Wanderers played on, put the ball through the posts, and claimed a goal. The umpires could not agree, and the referee's decision, which is final, was that the ball be brought back and thrown in. The Wanderers would not agree to this, and left the field. The game thus ended in favour of Stranraer by four goals to one.
*Ref 1881025**

22nd October 1881
Third Round　　　　　**Kilmarnock 2a0 Kilbirnie**
For nearly half an hour neither side could gain the advantage, when the Kilmarnock score a second goal from the foot of Hay. After it had been scored the Kilbirnie umpire disputed a previous throw-in, and though the referee (Harkness of the Rangers) decided against the Kilbirnie, the umpire would not allow the men to play on although to the onlookers they appeared ready and willing to do so - and for some time they left the field amid the disapprobation of the onlookers. The matter will, it is said, come before the Association.
*Ref 1881026**

S.F.A.C.M. [1st Nov]. Infringement of rule 5 not sustained.
Score allowed to stand.
Ref 1881023

22nd October 1881
Third Round　　　　　**Cambuslang 4-2 West Benhar**
S.F.A.C.M. [1st Nov]. Protested. The spectators encroached on the ground sustained.
Ref 1881023

29th October 1881
Third Round　　　　　**Partick Thistle 2-0 Petershill**
S.F.A.C.M. [1st Nov]. Protest - on ground that enclosure was not properly kept, and some horses broke in and stopped play for some time; to be played over.
Ref 1881023

29th October 1881
Third Round　　　　　**Kilbarchan 2-1 Johnstone**
Played at Whitlands Park, Kilbarchan, in presence of a large field of spectators, and after a very well contested game, resulted in Kilbarchan obtaining one goal and one disputed to one goal for the Johnstone. The Johnstone team lodged a protest against the result.
Ref 1881029

S.F.A.C.M. [1st Nov]. Protest on ground of spectators encroaching on the pitch sustained.
Ref 1881023

5th November 1881
Third Round Replay　　　**Kilbarchan 2-2 Johnstone**
Last Saturday's match having been declared null and void by the Association, the above teams met again at Whitlands. Johnstone was the first to score, but the home team within five minutes from their reverse made matters equal. During the second half the play was very keen, each side securing a goal. After the hour-and-half had been played the teams agreed to play other 20 minutes, but although each side played with great determination no further scoring was made, and the game thus ended a draw.
Ref 1881024

12th November 1881
Third Round 2nd Reply　　**Johnstone 3-0 Kilbarchan**
Played at Carbank Park, Johnstone. Owing to this being the third time that the above teams met in the third round, considerable interest was manifested in the game, and there was a large turn-out of spectators. The game resulted in favour of Johnstone by three goals to none.
Ref 1881032

19th November 1881
Fourth Round　　　　　**Glasgow University 4-5 Cartvale**
The third goal scored by the Cartvale was smartly held by Ness in front of goal, when to the astonishment of his team, the referee immediately decided that the ball was through, the ball having, in fact, been held two feet out from goal.
*Ref 1881033**

19th November 1881
Fourth Round　　　　　**Queen's Park 3-1 Johnstone**
Shortly after kick-off, Harry M'Neill met with an accident, his jaw-bone having been dislocated and he retired from the contest. ... Harry M'Neill is a great favourite with football players, and regret is expressed that even for a time he should be disabled from appearing along with the Queen's Park team.
Ref 1881034

3rd December 1881
Fifth Round   **Clyde 4-5 Cartvale**
Clyde started the match with only ten men. By the time they had their full complement of players they were losing by two goals to nil.
*Ref 1881035**

3rd December 1881
Fifth Round   **South Western 1-2 Rangers**
… In the second half the play resembled that of the first 40 minutes of the previous half, and it was not till the Rangers got a throw-in on the left wing near their opponents' goal that they scored again. On the ground that the ball was not thrown in straight the South Western players protested, but the goal was allowed. No other change took place, and the Rangers won by two goals to one. The captain of the Southern team, however, again protested against their second goal before leaving the field, and the matter will likely come before the committee of the Association.
Ref 1881036

S.F.A.C.M. [13th Dec]. The Secretary then submitted a protest from South Western against Rangers whose second and winning point it was alleged was scored from a throw in which was far from straight. Several members of the Committee who were present admitted that the ball was considerably off the straight and with this evidence before them the Committee agreed to sustain protest. Permission was granted to play the match on 24th seeing the Rangers had arranged an important fixture for the 17th inst. [Ancients v. Modern]
Ref 1881037

17th December 1881
Challenge Match   **Rangers - Moderns v Ancients**
A match between the present players of the Rangers and the eleven of 1875 was played on Kinning Park. The weather was very unfavourable, and there was consequently a poor turnout of spectators. With the exception of three members all the old players were present, and contrary to expectations the veterans succeeded in making a draw – three goals each.
Ref 1881038

24th December 1881
Fifth Round   **Rangers 4-0 South Western**
Played on the ground of the former at Kinning Park, Glasgow. A fair number of spectators were present. The game resulted in favour of the Rangers by 4 goals to 0.
Ref 1881039

3rd December 1881
Fifth Round   **Hibernian 2-6 Dumbarton**
S.F.A.C.M. [13th Dec]. The following is a copy of the protest lodged with the Association Committee by the Edinburgh Hibernians, a perusal of which, should it fail to sustain, may at least amuse our readers.

Catholic Institute,

Edinburgh, Dec 4th 1881

TO THE SECT. S.F.A.
SIR, - while apologising to your committee for any trouble we may cause in desiring its protection and at the same time expressing our insuperable objection to complaining without good cause. We beg on behalf of the Edinburgh Hibernians to protest against Saturday's Cup Tie being determined in favour of Dumbarton. Believing your committee to be the legitimate guardians of fair play and becoming conduct on the field and the most competent judges of what is right and what is wrong of what is honest and that which is opposed to all sentiment of Trust and shall submit in a brief manner the grounds upon which our protest is founded in hope that this may receive careful consideration at your hands. The moment the Dumbarton entered the field they objected to Mr Thomson acting as referee and protested in a very decided manner to that gentleman's presence. Thus the game began with recriminations and the abusive and demonstrative attitude at once assumed by the Dumbarton Umpire was such that beyond a doubt he intimidated the Referee and disgusted our Umpire and players so much that the former declined to have deliberate falsehoods forced upon him which the latter seeing that all hopes for fair play were abandoned by Mr Whelagan allowed the visitors to do pretty much as they pleased until call of time. We hold that Mr Thomson was either grossly ignorant of the rules, or decided unjustly against us. Four different times were the Dumbarton players at as being undoubtedly offside and as many times did thus score. While our players stood and drew the attention of the Umpires to these facts. We cannot believe that the referee was acting conscientiously, but in error when he decided the 2nd and 4th goals as fair goals those being especially noticeably and we trust he will have the courage to admit at your meeting that his position was rendered very doubtful and that the Dumbarton Umpire surrogated to himself the duty of deciding one way or another the second cause for complaint is the fact that a money bet on the result of the game was contracted by the Dumbarton Umpire I think it is superfluous for me to point out to your committee that is a secy right. Such conduct as this is pregnant with many evils and is sufficient to cover his decisions with suspicion and his honesty and impartiality with doubt or discredit. What I have most affirmed cannot be contradicted as the gentleman (Mr M'Donald) who made the bet can verify the statement. The next ground for complaint is that Mr M'Pherson played for Dumbarton (of the Vale of Leven F.C.) on Saturday and we have got to learn what he not already played in a Cup Tie or that he is a bonafide member of the Dumbarton. We ask in Justice that your committee decide that the Tie be played over again on Saturday next or when arranged that Referee and Two Umpires be appointed by the Association Referees and Umpires who will not be deferred from a faithful performance of the duties required of them - I remain, obediently Yours,
TOM O'REILLY

The committee sustained the protest on the first grounds only.
*Ref 1881040**

7th January 1882
Sixth Round   **Queen's Park 15-0 Shotts**
The cup tie was played on Hampden Park, before, considering the disagreeable weather, a very fair attendance of spectators. It was thought the members of the country club would show considerable advantage in their play with the Queen's Park, as during the season they had defeated several well-known teams. The show they made on Saturday, however, would not have been their true form, as from first to last they were overpowered, and failed to score at all. Before close of half-time the Queen's Park had run up nine goals, and when time was called they had added six to that number, the game resulting in a win for the Glasgow club by fifteen goals to none.
Ref 1881041

A couple of hundred enthusiasts went out to Hampden Park on Saturday to see the senior club for once in a way get someone to make them warm up a bit. Ten minutes were all that were necessary to show that the Shotts could not play football. They kept their goal clear for that length of time, and then G. Ker began the scoring. I must not forget to say that the Shotts lost the toss and had the strong wind and the sleet showers in their faces; but, when it came to the turn of the Queen's Park to have these adverse influences against them, the accumulation of goals went on all the same, until they finally amounted to fifteen, while the Shotts got none at all. Geordie Ker was in rare form, three goals being placed to his credit; Johnny Kay, however, who played the best game of the day, has four notches to his name; "Daddy" Anderson's total of scores is the same as Ker's; Harrower, who is a great acquisition to the Queen's Park, and who will ere long be quite as good as his companion Ker, took two goals, and Allan one; the other two went through out of scrummaging in front of the goal. It will thus be seen that the game was a very one-sided character, the visitors not making a semblance of a fight. This was the only Association match of any consequence played on Saturday.
Ref 1881042

28th January 1882
Sixth Round   **Dumbarton 2-1 Rangers**
Time was called with the ball in touch a few yards from the Rangers' goal line. A protest was lodged on behalf of the Rangers with the referee on the ground that he had stopped the game five minutes too soon; but he, on the other hand, maintained that the teams had played the full time.

S.F.A.C.M. [31st Jan]. A meeting of the committee the protest of the Rangers against Dumbarton was held to be good after presentation of conclusive evidence.
*Ref 1881043**

4th February 1882
Sixth Round Replay   **Dumbarton 5-1 Rangers**
The football match of last Saturday between the Dumbarton and Rangers, ended as most people, we feel sure, desired it should end, in a bad beating for the Rangers. On the

previous Saturday the Dumbarton men won in the most honourable manner a hard fought game by two goals to one. A stupid or a designing referee for whom the clubs were in no way responsible called "time" four or five minutes before the proper time, and although the Association was responsible for their referee and might have been reasonably expected to uphold his *ipse dixit*, yet they resolved, upon the protest of the Rangers, that the match should be played over. Not only so, but the injustice was further seen in allowing the Rangers to alter their team, presumably with the view of strengthening it and making a better fight and possibly vanquishing their opponents. The Rangers, however, must now be sorry for their action, for instead of an honourable defeat they have had to succumb to a very hard drubbing which will not easily be forgotten.
*Ref 1881044**

18th February 1882
Seventh Round   Dumbarton 11-2 Cartvale
Played at Dumbarton in the semi-final round of the cup ties. The wind blew a gale, and occasional showers of rain made things rather uncomfortable for both players and spectators. Dumbarton lost the toss, and the strangers, with the strong wind at their backs, were soon over the home lines. From the goal kick Meikleham, Brown, and Lindsay got possession, and carried the ball through the opposing backs, A. Kennedy scoring the first goal for Dumbarton within a couple of minutes from the commencement of the game. The Cartvale men made a home attack on the Dumbarton goal, but are long, mainly through the exertions of P. Miller and Lang, the ball was again in the vicinity of their citadel, and Lindsay had little difficulty in adding goal No. 2. The same player shortly added a third goal. The Dumbarton were soon again pressing the strangers, but the forwards broke away and by a lot of long passing carried the leather over the home lines. The kick-out was well returned, and Fulton scored the first goal for the Cartvale. Before half-time Lindsay and Meikleham had added another goal to the Dumbarton score, making a total of 5 to 1. The game was now virtually won, as it was impossible for the strangers to make up their lee-way in the face of the strong wind. They, however, played a much better game in the second half than in the first, and succeeded in adding another to their score. For Dumbarton, Meikleham scored two goals in the second half, Lindsay 1, M'Aulay 1, Lang 1, and Brown 1, which brought their total up to 11 goals, against 2 for the strangers.
Ref 1881045

26th April 1882
S.F.A.   Annual General Meeting
The annual general business meeting of the Scottish Football Association was held in the Lesser Trades' Hall last night – Mr J. Wallace, Beith presiding. There was a large attendance. The secretary read the annual report, which bore that, compared with last year, there was a decrease in membership. From a variety of causes no fewer than 37 clubs were forced to dissolve, but applications in the early part of the season were received from 25 clubs. There were, however, 128 clubs on the roll, which the committee considered very gratifying.   The report further stated that the Challenge Cup competitions of the season had been quite as interesting as those of former years. A short discussion took place regard to an alleged infringement of the rules of the association by

the committee during the past season. It was intimately agreed, on the motion of Mr M'Bride (Vale of Leven), seconded by Mr Slater, to adopt the report, with a caution to the committee in future not to alter any of the existing rules, unless with the consent of a meeting of the association. The statement submitted by the treasurer showed a balance of £173 0s 2d. The income for the year amounted to £1028 12s 10d, and the expenditure to £359 15s 7d. Notwithstanding, the exceptionally good season, the statement showed a deficiency on the year's working of fully £21. A long discussion took place about the lavish expenditure; and in reply to Mr Paton (Dumbarton) a detailed account of the expenditure connected with the Welsh International Match was submitted, the figures for that fixture being :- Income, £113 3s 10d ; expenditure, £124 7s 3d. Exception was also taken to the expenditure connected with the English International, and the income for which amounted to £525 15s 8d, and the expenditure to £178 2s 5d. Mr M'Bride (Vale of Leven) said one of his objects in attending the meeting was to look into the financial statement. He was connected with the association several years ago, and at that time he thought the expenses were far too high. When an expenditure of some £50 or £90 was then incurred in connection with International fixtures the figures were looked upon with a degree of horror, but now nothing was apparently thought of an expenditure of £178 2s 5d. The disbursements, indeed, were so heavy that even with two large "gates" there was a net deficit for the year of fully £20. What would it be next year, he continued, when instead of those matches being played in Glasgow, the association had to send two teams to England? It was time the matter was inquired into, and an end put to the constantly increasing insinuations thrown in the teeth of football players, viz. – "What is your association? Way, you draw "gate" after "gate" and spend it in champagne, cigars and Sunday-driving." (Applause). Mr Petrie (Northern) said he was a member of the committee four years ago, and at that time the association had about £700 at its credit. That sum, however, had been gradually lessened to the present paltry amount. After several members had given strong expressions of opinion with regard to the conduct of the committee, Mr M'Killop (Cartvale) proposed that, while adopting the treasurer's report, the meeting severely censures the committee for their lavish expenditure during the year, and regrets that the balance was not £200 instead of £20 to the debt of the association. Mr Nicholson (Vale of Leven) seconded the motion, which was unanimously agreed to.

Ref 1881046

9th September 1882

First Round   **Queen's Park 12-1 Thistle**

Played on Hampden Park, and resulted in an easy win for the Queen's Park by twelve goals to one. From the outset it was evident that the junior eleven was overmatched, and when the Queen's Park once got the leather through they scored rapidly. At the end of the first half the score stood - Queen's Park, eight goals; Thistle, one. In the second half the Queen's Park who played well together, took other four goals. The Thistle, though suffering such a severe defeat, were not by any means hemmed in, and clever runs by the forwards were occasionally made into the Queen's Park ground. The back play of the home side was, however, steady, and the leather was invariably returned to the forwards. The back defence of the Thistle was also strong, although the goal keeping was at times faulty.

Ref 1882001

9th September 1882

First Round   **Our Boys (Dundee) 5-1 Hibernian (Dundee)**

These Clubs having been drawn against each other in the first round of the Scottish Cup tie competition, they met on Saturday afternoon on the ground of the latter at West Craigie. Our Boys having won the toss decided upon playing with the wind at their backs, and it was quite apparent shortly after the game started that the junior team would have no chance against their more experienced opponents. Any incursions made by them into Our Boys' territory were of such an isolated nature, not being supported by the back players, that there was little or no chance of them scoring. However, by a piece of good luck they succeeded in sending in a shot from the right wing, which just went under the tape out of reach of the Our Boys' goalkeeper. The game was a very pleasant and enjoyable one throughout, and ended in a victory for Our Boys by four goals, the scores were Hibernians, one and Our Boys, five goals.

Ref 1882002

9th September 1882

First Round   **Angus 1-2 Balgay**

The football season was commenced in Forfar on Saturday afternoon by a match between teams representing these clubs, played under Association rules on a field over the farm of Bankhead. The strangers secured a goal in the first 45 minutes. The Angus took the first goal in the second forty five minutes, and near the end of the game the Balgay succeeded in adding another to their score.

*Ref 1882003**

Towards the end of the match the Balgay succeeded in passing the ball though the lines, but as the goal posts were accidentally knocked down at the time a dispute ensued, when the referee decided that it was not a legitimate goal. Being the first match played in the district this season, considerable interest was manifested in the game.

Ref 1882004

9th September 1882
Miscellaneous   **Edinburgh Football Calendar**
A very neat calendar has just been issued by Mr F Wad, secretary to the Edinburgh
Football Association, giving the rules of the game, along with the results of the challenge
competitions during last season.
*Ref 1882005**

9th September 1882
First Round   **Clippens 2-3 Glenpatrick**
Played at Old Moss Park, the ground of the former. A well-contested game resulted in
favour of the Glenpatrick, who throughout played a good passing game, by three goals
to two.
Ref 1882006

16th September 1882
First Round   **Coupar Angus 1-3 Dunblane**
Played at Coupar-Angus, for the Association first cup tie. Six goals were made - 3 by
Dunblane, 1 by Coupar-Angus, and two were disputed. Majority for Dunblane 2.
*Ref 1882007**

16th September 1882
First Round   **Drumpellier 4-3 Clarkston**
S.F.A.C.M. [19th Sep]. Several protests in connection with the first round were
considered. That of Clarkston against Drumpellier, which was based on the fact that the
ground was not the regulation size, was sustained, and the tie to be played over again on
Saturday first.
Ref 1882008

16th September 1882
First Round   **Johnstone Athletic 0-3 Cartvale**
Played at Mossbank Park, the ground of the former, in presence of a large number of
visitors, and after a hard contest resulted in a victory for the Cartvale by three goals to
none. The splendid play of M'Millan, the Athletic goalkeeper, prevented his team from
suffering a much heavier defeat.
Ref 1882009

30th September 1882
Second Round   **3rd Lanarkshire R. V. 2-0 Clyde**
… Ends having been changed, the Clyde were the first to show in a nice combined run,
and for a time matters did not look particularly bright for the home team. However, the
ball was got out of danger, and coming to Stewart he got full possession of it, and eluding
Pollock, passed to Marshall, who put it over the bar. Close play now ensued, both sides
making desperate efforts to score, but none were successful. A run now took place
between M'Clure, Andrews, and Strong, in which M'Clure was conspicuous by a clever

bit of dribbling, finishing up with a splendid shot which just grazed the bar. The Volunteers now carried the ball well up the field, and Marshall passing to Scobie, a scrummage ensued before the Clyde posts, the ball ultimately going under. On the leather being kicked off, play remained in the mid field for some time, and Bowie getting on the leather, made off for the "3rds" goal, passing half-backs and backs, and finished a splendid run by scoring for the Clyde, the home team appealing to the referee, on the ground that the ball had been fouled, but the point was disallowed. Time was called soon afterwards, the game thus ending in favour of the Volunteers by two goals to none. A protest has been lodged by the Clyde on the ground that the referee is a member of the 3rd L.R.V.
Ref 1882010

S.F.A.C.M. [4th Oct]. The following protests were sustained, and the matches ordered to be played over on Saturday first:- The Clyde against 3d L.R.V., ...
Ref 1882011

30th September 1882
Second Round   Dumbarton 8-0 King's Park
These two teams met at Boghead, Dumbarton, to play off the tie in the second round for the Association Cup. The ground was in excellent condition, but a strong wind was blowing, which was the means of deteriorating from the play. Dumbarton won the toss, and ere a few seconds were over, the spectators, who were numerous, were called upon to greet the success of the home team. The strangers did all in their power to save their colours from falling, especially the goalkeeper and the backs, who played an excellent game, and to whose agility alone is due the fact that the hitherto unknown team did not suffer a much more decisive defeat. As it was, however, the Stirling men were very easily defeated. Four goals were placed at the credit of the Dumbarton team in the first half, which was exclusively in favour of that team. In the second part, however, the strangers showed better pluck, but with no greater results, as the Dumbarton succeeded in adding other four to their score - the match thus ending in favour of Dumbarton by eight goals to none.
Ref 1882012

30th September 1882
Second Round   Partick Thistle 14-2 Mavisbank
At Jordanvale Park. Half-time Partick Thistle 10 Mavisbank 0.

30th September 1882
Second Round   Cowlairs 13-0 Apsley
At Gourlay Park, Springburn, in presence of a good turn-out of spectators. After the kick-off the strangers brought the ball well down to the home goal, but it was smartly returned, and from a neat centre Weir headed the first goal for the Cowlairs. In ten minutes the Cowlairs had scored another two goals. before half-time the home team had added other five goals to their credit, and at the call of time the score stood, Cowlairs, thirteen goals; Apsley, nothing.
Ref 1882013

30ᵗʰ September 1882
Second Round   Southfield 1-14 Renton
Played at Slamannan, the ground of the Southfield, and resulted in the total defeat of the home team by 14 goals to 1. The ground was of the most primitive description, there being neither touchline nor ropes. The Renton soon made themselves at home, and the forwards, all playing a passing game, were always in the Southfield ground. They scored 6 goals in the first and 8 in the second half.
Ref 1882014

30ᵗʰ September 1882
Second Round   Vale of Leven 16-0 Milngavie
This game was played at Alexandria on Saturday, and resulted in an easy win for the Vale by 16 goals to 0. The strangers to all appearances home had little practice, and there was a great deal of want of combined play among the forwards. Their defence at goal was very poor. They sustained the defeat with great coolness.
Ref 1882012

30ᵗʰ September 1882
Second Round   Sir John Maxwell 5-3 Port Glasgow Athletic
Played at Norwood Park, Pollock, Pollockshaws, the ground of the former, and resulted in their favour by five goals and three disputed to three goals.
Also:
Played at Pollockshaws, resulted in a draw - 3 goals each.
Ref 1882013

S.F.A.C.M. [4ᵗʰ Oct]. The following protests were sustained, ... and the Port-Glasgow against the Sir John Maxwell.
Ref 1882011

7ᵗʰ October 1882
Second Round   Sir John Maxwell 2-6 Port Glasgow Athletic
Over at Haggs Castle the Sir John Maxwell have a nice piece of ground, and on Saturday the Port Glasgow were playing on it, and they appeared to know more about the ground than the occupants of it did, as at the end the strangers were four goals to the good.
Ref 1882017

7ᵗʰ October 1882
Second Round Replay   Cartvale 1-3 Arthurlie
Another protested tie – that between the Arthurlie and Cartvale – was placed beyond the tribunal of dispute, as the former won by three goals to one. I was not aware at the time of writing last week that the Arthurlie were going to protest, but it appears one of the Cartvale players had taken part in the first round for a Lanarkshire club, and as that is against the rules the Arthurlie gained their protest. No doubt it was rather hard on the Busby men to have to play the game again after winning it, but the fault was their own and, indeed, they ought to feel grateful to the S.F.A. for allowing them to compete at all,

as I have known clubs who were guilty of a similar demeanour thrown out of the competition. The Arthurlie should not have lost last Saturday's match, as they are a long way better players than the Cartvale, whom they evidently held too cheap, and the consequence was they got thrashed. However, on Saturday they made amends for previous shortcomings by playing up brilliantly. I have seen a gentleman who was at the game, and he tells me the Barrhead men never let a chance pass them. The game was exceedingly rough, and the spectators behaved in the most disreputable manner.
Ref 1882017

30th September 1882
Second Round   Partick 2-1 Pilgrims
The tie between the Pilgrims and Partick should have been played on the former's field, but, being without one, the game had to be decided on the latter's ground, which was well patronised. The game was exceedingly well contested, the play on each side being very clever, and at the close there was only the difference of goal between the two, and that difference was in favour of the home players, who scored in all two goals against one got by the Pilgrims, whose play was highly meritorious, considering they have no ground to practice on. The Partick team has a lot of young supple players doing service this season, and as all of them are closely attached to each other in friendship, there is hope that the dismal cloud which has hung so long over the Partick will be dispelled.
Ref 1882019

30th September 1882
Second Round   Queen's Park 3-2 Rangers
The most interesting football contest in the west was that at Hampden Park between these teams, the object being to get into the third round for the cup. The play, which lasted an hour and a half, was generally disappointing. Again and again the ball was kicked off the field; there was repeated foul play, and of aimless shots there were not a few. The Rangers kicked off, with the wind. From the east goal, and ten minutes after the first goal was had by the Queen's Park out of a scrimmage. Under similar circumstances the Rangers, ten minutes later, succeeded in equalising matters. Having been driven back by the Queen's men, the leather was returned by a blind kick through the goal, no less to the surprise of the goalkeeper than the spectators, and at half-time the Rangers had two goals and the Queen's Park one. In the second half the Queen's Park obtained two more goals - the one out of a free kick had for a foul, and the other out of a scrimmage. The Queen's Park thus won by three goals to two. The new throw-in rule, both hands being overhead, was in vogue on this occasion for the first time.
Ref 1882020

S.F.A.C.M. [4th Oct]. See Second Round Protests below.
Ref 1882011

4th October 1882

Miscellaneous   **Second Round Protests**

S.F.A.C.M. The protest by the Rangers against last Saturday's match being decided in favour of Queen's Park, was, after discussion, not sustained. The protest by the Arbroath Club against Dunblane was similarly dealt with. The following protests were sustained, and the matches ordered to be played over on Saturday first:- The Clyde against 3d L.R.V., the Arthurlie against the Cartvale, and the Port-Glasgow against the Sir John Maxwell.

Ref 1882011

7th October 1882

Second Round   **Aberdeen 1-4 Harp (Dundee)**

Conflicting reports:-

These teams met on Saturday at Aberdeen, and after a fast and exciting game, victory resulted for the Harp by four goals to one. For the first twenty minutes the play was of a give-and-take description. After this the Harp began to gain ground, and by some fine passing worked the ball down to the Aberdeen's goal, when play of most exciting description took place, the ball being sent in time after time; but the coolness of the Aberdeen's goalkeeper prevented any scoring. Shortly afterwards the Harp again returned to the attack, and managed to score their first goal. Shortly before half-time the Harp added another point to their score. On change of ends the Aberdeen tried hard to retrieve their loss, and were so far unsuccessful, for getting the ball they made a splendid run down the field, when they scored their first and only goal. About twenty minutes before the finish the Harp scored their third goal out of a scrimmage, and shortly before time scored their fourth goal, a pleasant game thus terminating in favour of the Harp.

Ref 1882021 (Dundee Report)

The captain of the home team having won the toss, elected to play with the wind, and the Dundee leader kicked off. The ball had but been more than a minute in play when the Harp running it up into the home team's ground got it close to their goal and it passed between the posts. They claimed a goal, but it was disputed and the umpire disallowed it. For some time after the ball was knocked about the field pretty lovely, being in each end of the ground alternatively. The teams, it was evident, were equally matched and for a considerable time, although several corner kicks were claimed and played, no advantage was gained by either side. At last the Dundee men got the ball well in front of their opponents posts, and, after some fine play on the part of both teams the Harp succeeded in putting it through, scoring the first goal of the day. Both goals were several times severely assaulted after this, but nothing further was scored during the first half. In the second period the play was pretty much of the same character, the ball being at one time in the Aberdeen's territory and then in that of their antagonists, and then both goals were more than once in danger. At one period the play of the Dundee men seemed to be getting rather demoralised, and the home team keenly and promptly took advantage of every opportunity which presented itself. Getting the ball from the half-backs, on one occasion the forwards of the home team carried it in fine style to within easy reach of the Dundee goal, and after dribbling it beautifully for some distance, Lethlan got it very easily between the posts and scored. Both teams had now scored a goal to their credit. A minute after the ball was put in play it was again kicked up to the Harp's goal, and

another point was nearly scored. Thereafter the ball was sent into the Aberdeen territory, and the Harp, getting the benefit of a free kick, claimed a goal; but it was disputed. After a "squabble", it was agreed that the ball should be thrown free into the air from a point a few yards distant from the Aberdeen goal, and, this being done, the strangers got hold of the ball, and added another goal to their score. On being kicked off anew, the ball was kept for a minute or two about the middle of the ground; but the Harp forward again secure it, and, passing it through their opponents, again succeeded in placing it between the posts. Time was shortly afterwards called, and the match accordingly resulted in a win for the Dundee team by three goals to one.
Ref 1882022 (Aberdeen Report)

Footnote
The discrepancy in scores appears to be centred on Harp's first goal for which no dispute is mentioned in the *Dundee* report. In the *Aberdeen* report, however, it states that the "umpire disallowed it". This is presumably the Aberdeen umpire, but this report makes no mention of the referee's decision.

7ᵗʰ October 1882
Second Round   **Addiewell 0-14 Heart of Midlothian**
This tie in the second round of the Scottish Cup was played at West Calder, resulted in an easy victory for the "Heart" by 14 goals to nothing.
Ref 1882023

7ᵗʰ October 1882
Second Round   **West Benhar 10-1 Shotts**
SHOTTS v BENHAR (ASSOCIATION CUP TIE) – These clubs met in the second round of the cup tie, on the ground of the latter, at Harthill. Shotts suffered defeat by 10 goals to 1.
Ref 1882023

21ˢᵗ October 1882
Third Round   **Falkirk 2-2 Renton**
This, the 3d round of the ties for the Scottish Football Association Cup, and which has caused not a little excitement among the enthusiasts of the game in the district for the past week, came off on Saturday last on the ground of the former at Blinkbonny. The weather was most unfavourable for football, rain falling during the greater portion of the game. Notwithstanding this drawback, upwards of 400 spectators lined the ropes, being the largest number that has ever mustered on the Falkirk ground to witness a game at football. Renton set the leather a-rolling, they having lost the toss, and for the first 15 minutes or so were busy round the home goal, three corner kicks falling to their lot; but although they were pretty well placed nothing came of them. The home team, however, gathering themselves together, by some good combined play, transferred the scene of operations to the other end, and although they had some good chances, they like their opponents, were unable to score. Runs and counter runs formed the main feature of the game in the remaining part of the first half, both goals being assailed in turn, and up to the end of half-time neither side gained any decided advantage. In the second half the

home team set the ball in motion with the ground against them, and the play for the first 20 minutes was of a give and take nature, when Renton, by a long shot, succeeded in lowering the Falkirk colours. Nothing daunted by this reverse, the home team strove hard to equalise matters, and ere a short time had elapsed the left wing broke through the strangers, and A. Ferguson, by a neat centre, gave Sanderson a chance of scoring, which he availed himself of amid loud cheering. Falkirk centre forwards then getting possession of the leather from the kick-off, parted with it to the left wing, who again took it up to the front of goal, where W. Gibson shot goal two amidst still greater cheering. Nothing of further note took place till within 15 minutes of time when a scrimmage took place at the home goal, out of which the Renton players alleged the ball went through, the umpires differing however. An appeal was made to the referee, who gave a goal. Falkirk disputed this point and lodged a protest, which was considered by the committee of the association on Wednesday night. The committee decided to have the game played over at Renton today, this game being considered a draw.
Ref 1882024

21ˢᵗ October 1882
Third Round   Arthurlie 1-0 Thornliebank
This match between the above clubs in the third round of the cup ties for the Scottish Association cup was played at Barrhead in presence of over 3000 spectators. Owing to the heavy rain before the game commenced the ground was rendered very soft, and good passing play was almost impossible. The Arthurlie won by one goal to none.
Ref 1882025

S.F.A.C.M. [25ᵗʰ Oct]. Protest on the grounds that the ball was of oval (or rugby) shape and was more than 28 inches in circumference "an extremely paltry excuse".
*Ref 1882026**

28ᵗʰ October 1882
Third Round Replay   Arthurlie 0-0 Thornliebank
Several undecided and protested Cup tie matches were played on Saturday. The chief of these was the one between Arthurlie and Thornliebank, which was played at Barrhead. The latter, who were on the losing side in the last match, protested, on the ground that the ball was not fit for playing with, and their protest being sustained, both met again on Saturday. Feeling ran very high, as it always does when these clubs meet, and the play, I regret to say, was a little too coarse at times. Some blame Thornliebank, and others the Arthurlie, so under these circumstances it is best to hold both responsible. No points were scored by either team...
Ref 1882027

S.F.A.C.M. [1ˢᵗ Nov]. The following are the draws for the fourth round:-
Vale of Teith v. Hurlford, Hibernians v. Partick, Edinburgh University v. Vale of Leven, Arthurlie or Thornliebank v. Queen of the South Wanderers, Glasgow University v. Partick Thistle, Cambuslang v. Queen's Park, Renton v. Lugar Boswell, Dunblane v. 3ʳᵈ L.R.V., Kilmarnock Athletic v. Abercorn, Johnstone v. Pollockshields Athletic, Dumbarton a bye.

In the event of a draw again taking place between Thornliebank and Arthurlie, the latter

will play Queen of the South Wanderers at Barrhead, and the Thornliebank the Dumbarton at Thornliebank.
Ref 1882028

S.F.A. Business Meeting [2nd Nov]. There was an unusually full attendance. Among the protests considered was one by the Arthurlie, who took exception to the committee's decision on the ground that a quorum was not present when the protest from the Thornliebank against the Arthurlie was being considered. The committee refused to go back on their decision, and ordered the clubs to play the tie over again at Thornliebank.
Ref 1882028

4th November 1882
Third Round 2nd Replay Thornliebank 0-0 Arthurlie
The third contest in the third round for the Scottish Association Cup between the above Clubs was played on the ground of the Thornliebank. Despite a very showery day, there was an attendance of about 3000 spectators. The ground was in wretched condition, and during the play quite a gale of wind blew over the field. The Thornliebank kicked off the ball, both teams setting hard at work. Notwithstanding that the Arthurlie had a stiff hill to contend with in the first half of the play, they worked hard and kept their own against their opponents. Ends were exchanged without either side scoring, and in the second half of the game, as in the first half, the play continued to be pretty evenly balanced, the game ending in a draw, neither side securing a goal.
Ref 1882029

21st October 1882
Third Round   Lugar Boswell 6-0 Pollock
This game was played at Rosebank Park, Lugar. The strangers turned up with ten men, and had to play a man short for the first half hour. The game from beginning to end was very much one-sided, Lugar registering five goals in the first half and three in the second, but two of the latter were disallowed, the game thus ending in favour of Lugar by six goals to nothing.
*Ref 1882030**

2nd December 1882
Fifth Round   Hibernian 3-4 Arthurlie
These clubs played in the fifth round of the Scottish Cup Tie at Easter Road, Edinburgh. During the first half a loose, rough game was played, the Arthurlie securing three goals and the Hibernians two. The latter part of the second half was played in semi-darkness. A few minutes before time was called the home team got a third goal, and immediately afterwards the west men took the ball up the field, and secured their fourth goal. At the finish the score remained unaltered, the Arthurlie being thus the victors by four goals to three.
Ref 1882031

The match, which resulted in a win for the strangers by four goals to three, was finished in semi-darkness; the ball being invisible to the spectators round the ropes.
Ref 1882032

S.F.A.C.M. [12th Dec]. Protest on two grounds - that one of the goals scored being offside, therefore the match was a draw; and also, that the Arthurlie indulged in considerable rough play.

Protest sustained and neutral ground ordered for replay.
*Ref 1882033**

23rd December 1882
Fifth Round Replay   Arthurlie 6-0 Hibernian
This protested cup tie was played on neutral ground, the Rangers having granted the use of Kinning Park for that purpose. There was a good turn-out of spectators, a considerable proportion of whom hailed from the Barrhead and Edinburgh. Both clubs played well, but the Arthurlie had the best of the game, and at the call of time had scored six goals, while their opponents failed to obtain a single point. From a clever piece of passing the Barrhead players sent the leather under the bar in less than a minute after kick-off. The Hibernians, who played against a strong wind with the sun in their eyes, were repeatedly in front of their opponents' goal, but all their efforts to score were frustrated by the Arthurlie backs. The Arthurlie, on the other hand, made good use of their opportunities, and added other three goals before half time was called. In the second half the same ill-success attended the efforts of the Edinburgh club. The Arthurlie took three additional goals, one of which was disputed, leaving them victors by six goals to none.
Ref 1882039

3rd February 1883
Sixth Round   Kilmarnock Athletic 1-2 Arthurlie
The Arthurlie were making determined efforts to make matters equal when "Baker" broke away, and - followed by his forwards - got to midfield - some good passing landing the ball to the left side. This run seemed to be too fast for the referee, and he was in mid-field when Catterson headed the ball to the centre - Clark meeting it and handily putting it between the posts. It was held - and claimed by the Arthurlie players - that the ball was a yard over the line when Catterson headed it, but the referee being out of position, the goal was given to the Arthurlie by that official - the Athletic protesting.

S.F.A.C.M. [6th Feb]. At an Association meeting on Tuesday night, a protest having been lodged by the Athletic - the faulty goal was thrown, and the teams ordered to play over on Cathkin Park on Saturday first.
*Ref 1882034**

24th February 1883
Semi-final   Dumbarton 1-0 Pollockshields Athletic
At Hampden Park. About five minutes from time a long shot was raised high into the Pollockshields goal. Roxburgh, standing near his left post, stopped the ball with both hands, and, dropping at his feet, Holm and he scrimmaged it safely outside the post. Dumbarton claimed a goal, and after a consultation between the umpires, who disagreed, the referee, Mr Sydney Broadfoot (Lenzie), allowed the point. A scene of great excitement followed, the crowd calling on the Shields players not to play. Had they taken this advice they would have put themselves out of court, but they wisely finished the

game and lodged a protest. There cannot be the slightest doubt that the ball never went through the posts. Our reporter happened to be standing at the Pollockshields goal at the time, and can positively declare such to be the fact. Mr Broadfoot is unquestionably wrong in his decision. He is a gentleman of well known probity, and one that would not give a verdict he honestly did not believe to be correct. In this case, however, he is utterly wrong, and an injustice has been done the Pollockshields Athletic club. The game then according to the decision of the referee, resulted in a win for Dumbarton by one goal to none.
*Ref 1882035**

The Dumbarton have done a graceful act, and one that might be expected from a club of their high standing. They have relieved the committee of the Scottish Association of all further trouble in the matter of the protest of Pollockshields Athletic against the result of the recent cup tie played between the clubs by requesting that the game should be considered a draw. Under these circumstances the tie will be played over again at Boghead, Dumbarton on March 17th. Both clubs have asked that Mr Broadfoot should again act as referee.
*Ref 1882036**

7th April 1883
Final Replay   **Dumbarton 2-1 Vale of Leven**
The undecided final cup tie for possession of the Association Challenge Cup was played on Saturday on Hampden Park, with the result that the trophy this year, for the first time since its institution in 1874, goes to Dumbarton. The Vale and Dumbarton, it will be remembered, played a drawn game on Hampden Park, a week ago, when each club scored two goals. On Saturday the contest was resumed, and at call of time the score stood :- Dumbarton, two goals; Vale of Leven, one. As on the first day's game, there was an immense concourse of spectators present, the attendance being calculated at 15,000. The grand stand and three extemporised erections were filled long before the game commenced, and late-comers had to content themselves with only passing glimpses of the play over their neighbours' shoulders. Independent of the interesting nature of the game, the weather was in itself a great inducement for the big gathering. A genial temperature prevailed, the sun being of summer warmth, which made the outing a most pleasant one for everybody. The objectionable forms which for the accommodation of the large crowd had been placed in front of the grand stand a week ago were removed and three others substituted. These, however, were placed in such a position as not to interfere or inconvenience the occupants of the stand, who thus witnessed the game with some degree of comfort.
Ref 1882038

11th August 1883

Miscellaneous   Novelty in Football

A new feature in football north of the Forth was introduced here by Our Boys Football Club on their ground at West Craigie Park, Dundee, in a game of five-a-side, on Saturday. The novelty drew a very large concourse of spectators. The interest being greatly aided by the leading local clubs as well as strangers sending teams to try their abilities in the new game. The Our Boys as an inducement for clubs to enter for this new contest offered as prizes five handsome gold badges as a first prize, five silver ones as second, and a football as a third.

Ref 1883001

18th August 1883

The final heats in the five-a-side competitions introduced by Our Boys Football Club were played off on Saturday at West Craigie Park in presence of a large concourse of spectators. From the merits of the teams left to play it was expected some very exciting and hard contested games would ensue, and the admirers of the game were not disappointed in the expectations.

... A dispute arose as to the decision of the referee about one minute before the call of time in regard to a foul claimed, and the Strathmore, on the decision being given against them, left the field, giving Our Boys 3 the third prize. The two teams left to play off for the gold and silver badges were Our Boys 2 and Perseverance, and the Boys proved victors by 5 goals to nothing. Both teams received a well-deserved cheer from the spectators for their hard won victories. Mr W.E. Buchan, the President of Our Boys F.C., presented the winning teams with their prizes on the ground, and complimented them on their success.

Ref 1883002

25th August 1883

Friendly   Arbroath v South Western

This match came off on the ground of Arbroath at Gayfield on Saturday afternoon. Both sides were in fine form, and the play was sustained with increasing energy to the close. Glasgow was the first to score, having made a goal in three minutes after starting. This was all that was accomplished during the first heat, although the goalkeepers had their work to do. In the second forty Glasgow soon secured a second goal, after which there was for a space nothing but hard work. At length Arbroath goaled the ball very easily, the Glasgow keeper having gone too far from his post to assist his party. The result was thus - Glasgow, 2; Arbroath, 1.

Ref 1883003

28th August 1883

Miscellaneous   Fatal Termination of the Football Accident at Arbroath

We regret to announce that this accident, to which we referred briefly on Monday, has terminated fatally, death taking place at 6a.m. yesterday. The deceased was a young man named James Gordon, flaxdresser, residing in Howard Street, aged 23. He was unmarried. He was an experienced player, and on this occasion was selected by the Arbroath as their goalkeeper. The accident occurred at the close of the match, time having been called, when the ball was close up at the Arbroath goal, and an effort was being made by the Glasgow team to add to their score. Gordon was in the act of endeavouring to catch the ball with his hands, so was standing upright, at the moment when he got a blow in the stomach, but whether with a foot or any other part he was unable to say. He fell down, and had to be driven home. Dr Low was his medical attendant, but Dr Anderson was also called for consultation. Their efforts, however, were unavailing, and after three nights' agonising pain, he died, as already stated at 6a.m. yesterday morning. Yesterday this sad event was the all-engrossing subject of conversation in Arbroath, where great interest is taken in the game.

Death was caused by rupture of the liver.

Ref 1883004

6th September 1883

Miscellaneous   **Football House in Springvale Park Broken Into**

The burgh police have just succeeded in tracing a serious case of housebreaking by boys at Springvale Park, Ayr. The Police received word that on Tuesday night [4th Sep] the football home had been broken into and entirely cleared of its contents, including about a dozen jerseys, 6 pairs of white knickerbockers, four pairs of "pants", several pairs of boots, &c. Quite a little band of boy thieves seem to have been concerned in the theft, two of whom, John M'Kane and John Dickson, both boys of fourteen, have just been apprehended. Four jerseys and a pair of pants were found concealed in a hedge near the Commonhead Industrial School, while a pair of boots were found in the possession of M'Kane. On Monday the three young lads, John M'Kane, John Dickson and Francis M'Inally, were charged with the offence. They all pleaded guilty, and were sentenced to 10 days imprisonment each, and afterwards to be sent to a reformatory for five years.

Ref 1883005

8th September 1883

First Round   **Clippens 3-2 Johnstone Athletic**

These teams met at Old Moss Park, Clippens. During the first half the Clippens played with the wind in their favour and succeeded in scoring three goals to one for the Athletic. In the second half the Athletic only managed to add one goal, the play during this half was very rough, and at the conclusion of the game, which resulted in favour of the Clippens by three goals to two. The Athletic lodged a protest, on the ground of the Clippens having played with tacketed boot.

S.F.A.C.M. [18th Sep]. Protest not sustained.

*Ref 1883006**

8th September 1883

First Round   **Kilmarnock Athletic v Beith**

These teams having been drawn together in the first round of the Scottish Cup, were ordered by the Association to play off their game on Holm Quarry on Saturday. On Thursday night the Athletic received a letter from the Beith secretary stating that they would play off the tie as arranged. Bills were accordingly printed, and the match advertised. A goodly number of spectators turned out to see the game, and the Athletic players were all dressed ready for starting. The Beith team, however, failed to turn up,

and, strange to say, sent no word to that effect. the home team were rather in a dilemma, and sent a deputation to the Rugby field in the neighbourhood, where a practice game between the first and second of the Kilmarnock was going on, asking if they would agree to fill up the gap, but they politely declined. A scratch team was afterwards got up, and play carried on for about an hour.
Ref 1883007

8th September 1883
First Round   **Partick Thistle v Pilgrims**
At the last moment the Pilgrims' arrangements fell through but they turned up at Partick, and with the aid of some strangers played a friendly game resulting in a win for the Partick Thistle by eleven goals to one.
Ref 1883007

8th September 1883
First Round   **Renton 2-1 Dumbarton**
S.F.A.C.M. [18th Sep]. The most important protest of the lot was that of Dumbarton against Renton. It was on two grounds - first, that the ground was five yards short; and secondly, that the crowd encroached on the field of play. The former ground, was not entertained on a division by 15 to 3, and the latter, after the evidence of the referee and both umpires had been led, met with the same fate, and the committee decided that the Dumbarton be thrown out, and Renton awarded the tie, by 14 to 3. The committee by 14 to 4 also decided to withhold the deposit.
Ref 1883009

8th September 1883
First Round   **Partick 0-8 Queen's Park**
The circumstances under which this tie was played on Saturday last were of remarkable description. Muir Park, Partick, the scene of operations, was on Saturday in a state utterly unfit for football. It lay almost entirely under water, or, more properly speaking, the surface was a sea of mud, in which the players floundered and rolled for an hour and a half. The scene presented many amusing features, and the various mishaps were greeted with roars of laughter by a crowd numbering fully four thousand.
Long before the game was concluded the players presented a pitiable appearance, being wet through, and covered with dirty black mud from head to foot. (Queen's Park protested before the start of the match owing to conditions but won comfortably 8-0).
*Ref 1883010**

8th September 1883
First Round   **Q.O.S. Wanderers 7-7 5th K.R.V.**
A first tie took place at Nunholm North between the South of Scotland Wanderers and the 5th K.R.V. (Maxwelltown.) In the first half of time the Wanderers had five goals to their opponents' two, and on commencing the second half added another; but, as if confident of victory, they rather slackened their efforts, while the 5th K.R.V. made desperate exertions to retrieve their position, and within eight minutes of time being

called had made four goals more. The Wanderers, however, made another goal, and seemed as if certain to win, but just on the point of time being called, the 5th put through the ball, and both teams being seven, the contest ended in a draw.
*Ref 1883011**

8th September 1883
First Round   **Kilbarchan 3-4 Paisley Athletic**
The referee was disgracefully set upon by the followers of the latter club [Kilbarchan], and but for the interference of the police he would have been very badly treated.
Ref 1883012

8th September 1883
First Round   **Annbank 1-3 Mauchline**
Our football players complain bitterly of their treatment at Annbank on Saturday. Being present, I can vouch for the facts. It was the old story of the visitors being stoned out of the place. Brave, noble, generous Annbank! The gallant policemen as usual became invisible about the time their services were needed. For myself, had I not skillfully ducked a particular brick, I fear I would not have been troubled for a time at least with the annuls of the city.
*Ref 1883013**

8th September 1883
First Round   **Portland v Stewarton Cunninghame**
Stewarton came in for a bye, because the Portland Athletic players are no more.
Ref 1883012

8th September 1883
First Round   **Maybole 0-4 Cumnock**
Footnote
Despite playing on the 8th September the S.F.A. believed the result to have been a draw and thus had "Cumnock or Maybole" having a bye in the Second Round drawings and also instructed the tie to be played off on 22nd September.

8th September 1883
First Round   **Vale of Leven 12-0 Levendale**
At Alexandria. The Levendale is a most promising young team (the most of the players being in their teens), but on Saturday their experienced and powerful opponents proved too much for them. Till the close of the first half the play continued much in favour of the Vale, by which time they had scored nine goals. With the aid of the breeze, the Levendale showed up well, but were unable to score, while their opponents added other three to their total, thus winning their first tie by twelve goals to none.
*Ref 1883015**

8th September 1883
First Round   **Glenpatrick v Bute Rangers**
S.F.A.C.M. [18th Sep]. The Bute Rangers claimed their tie with the Glenpatrick on account of the latter's failing to meet them on the 8th Sep at Glenpatrick, after the Rangers had travelled all the way from Rothesay to fulfil their engagement. Several communications from both clubs were read & Mr Wallace moved and Mr Harrison seconded that the Glenpatrick be disqualified & the tie awarded to the Bute Rangers. This was unanimously carried.
Ref 1883016

8th September 1883
First Round   **Edina 2-1 Kinleith**
Ended abruptly before full time was played by the Kinleith leaving the ground just after Edina got their second.
*Ref 1883017**

S.F.A.C.M. [18th Sep]. The Kinleith protested against the Edina on several grounds, principally that the referee was a member of the first named club. After hearing the evidence of the referee in question and the secretary of the Edina, Mr Wallace moved and Mr Harrison seconded that the match be declared null & void. Mr M'Culloch moved and Mr Devlin seconded an amendment that the Kinleith be thrown out but Mr Wallace's motion was carried by a majority of 14 to 5 whereupon Mr Stevenson moved that the game be played on the same ground on Saturday first with half an hour extra in case of a draw, but Mr Wallace moved and Mr Crerar seconded an amendment that both clubs be disqualified but the amendment was rejected by 14 votes to 4.
Ref 1883016

22nd September 1883
First Round Replay   **Edina 4-0 Kinleith**
These teams replayed at Mayfield in the Scottish Cup tie. Edina, four goals; Kinleith, nil. Kinleith played with nine men.
Ref 1883018

15th September 1883
First Round   **King's Park 11-0 Lenzie**
This tie in the first round, which was looked upon as the most important one in the county, was played on Gowanbank Park, the ground of King's Park, before a good turn out of spectators. The local clubs practiced hard of late for this encounter, as Lenzie on the last time of meeting were the victors by 2 goals to 1. The tie, however, lacked all interest by Lenzie turning up two men short, the game from first to last being a complete farce, the King's Park having matters all their own way, and eventually winning by the score of eleven goals to nothing. Indeed, so one sided was the game, that the strangers were only once over the home team's lines. The game was started by the Lenzie kick-off at five minutes past 4 o'clock. The home team at once commenced a fusillade on the visitor's stronghold, but so bad was the shooting that twenty minutes had nearly elapsed before Miller drew first blood by hammering a clever ball through. The ball was no sooner kicked off, then, Laidlaw scored a second goal with a splendid shot. Half time

found the score standing King's Park 5 Lenzie 0. The second half was almost a repeat of the first, but the home team's forwards played with greater dash, and when time was called had added another six goals. No fewer than 11 goals were scored by the home team, but the peculiarities of the new offside rule, coupled with the strangers playing only one back, ensured five of them to be disallowed.
*Ref 1883019**

15th September 1883
First Round Replay   Strathmore (Arbroath) 1-1 Balgay
These clubs met on the ground of Arbroath at Gayfield Park on Saturday afternoon to play off their undecided cup tie. The Balgay Captain winning the toss chose to defend the east goal. The ball having been set in motion by the Strathmore centre, it was immediately run down to the Balgay goal, where shot after shot was put in, but to no purpose, until Munro for the Strathmore by a splendid kick succeeded in scoring the first goal. This put the Balgay on their mettle, as on the ball being kicked off they run it down to Strathmore territory, when Lorimer for the Balgay equalled matters. No more scoring took place on either side during the first half. On ends being changed the play became very fast, the ball travelling from one end of the field to the other but the Strathmore by some good combined play carried the ball down to their antagonist's citadel, when Hogg scored another goal for the Strathmore, which, however, was disallowed. Another disputed goal was shortly made by the Strathmore and time being up both teams left the field, the cup tie still remaining undecided, the matter is to be left to the decision of the committee of the Scottish Football Association.
*Ref 1883020**

S.F.A.C.M. [18th Sep]. Balgay and Strathmore (Arbroath) tie having twice ended in a draw, both clubs were put into the hat.
Ref 1883009

15th September 1883
First Round   Dunfermline 1-13 St Bernard's
8th Sep. Dunfermline, who were drawn against the St Bernard's, have been allowed an extra day –viz., till the 15th – owing to their sports taking place on the 8th.
Ref 1883022

15th Sep. Played at Dunfermline on Saturday, for the Scottish Football Association Challenge cup. The game was very one-sided, and from the outset the strangers had it all their own way, scoring in quick succession. At the close the St Bernard's were victorious by 13 goals to 1.
Ref 1883023

15th September 1883
First Round Replay   Hibernian (Dundee) 3-4 Perseverance
The above teams met on Saturday on the ground of Our Boys, West Craigie Park, to play off their undecided cup tie match. The game was of give and take character throughout, but ultimately victory rested with the Perseverance by four goals to three.
Ref 1883024

22nd September 1883
First Round Replay   Tollcross 4-3 Airdrie
Played on the ground of the former at Wellshot Park, Shettleston. The ball was set in motion by the Tollcross, and after a very fast game the score at half-time stood - Airdrie, 2; Tollcross, 1. On change of ends the game became faster and faster, and at call of time the game stood - Airdrie, 3; Tollcross, 3 - making the game a draw. An extra half-hour had to be played, and at the end of half-time the score still remained the same. On change of ends the Tollcross scored the only goal in this half, and were thus left masters of the field amidst great cheering and excitement, by four goals to three.
Ref 1883025

29th September 1883
Second Round   Thornliebank 14a0 Bute Rangers
The Thornliebank had little difficulty in defeating the Bute Rangers by 14 goals to none, and the game was brought to a close by mutual arrangement 15 minutes before time. The Bute club look a likely lot, but want a lot of training and drilling up.
Ref 1883026

29th September 1883
Second Round   Kilmarnock 3-0 Hurlford
In the second half the play changed like magic from passing and dribbling to charging and hacking. The game certainly became dangerous for about half-an-hour. It would be hard to say which of the two were superior at this class of game, but the Kilmarnock scored another two goals, M'Laughland and Wark giving the finishing touch on each occasion.
*Ref 1883027**

29th September 1883
Second Round   Strathmore (Dundee) 3-1 Balgay
These clubs met in the second round of the Scottish Cup ties on the ground of the former at Magdalen Yard Road on Saturday, before a limited number of spectators. From the fact that the Strathmore on the preceding Saturday in the first round of the County Cup tie won by nine goals to love, very little interest was manifested in the game. The Balgay (with their team slightly altered) started the ball with the wind in their favour, and ran it well up into the Strathmore's ground, but it was very soon transferred to their territory. Soon after this the Balgay came away with a rush, and succeeded in scoring the first and only goal. On the ball being again started from midfield, some play of a give-and-take nature took place, until a nice run on the left wing of the Strathmore brought the ball into

close proximity to the Balgay's goal, when, from a good centre from the left wing, Petrie headed it through, thus equalising the score. After this and until call of time some play of an objectionable nature was imported into the game, but notwithstanding this the Strathmore succeeded in scoring other two goals, the Balgay failing to score. The game ended in favour of the ground club by 3 goals to 1.
Ref 1883028

29th September 1883
Second Round   Newcastleton 1-4 Heart of Midlothian
The Scottish Association was I believe, misinformed as to the whereabouts of Newcastleton, it being stated to the committee that it was somewhere near Edinburgh, or they would scarcely have asked the Heart of Mid Lothian to journey 150 miles so early in the competition to play a cup tie. It is not surprising that the Hearts grumbled at what they believed unnecessary expense. However, they came out of it with flying colours, winning by four goals to one. Their team was not up to its full strength.
Ref 1883026

20th October 1883
Third Round   Thornliebank 1-0 Kilmarnock
S.F.A.C.M. [30th Oct]. The Kilmarnock won their Scottish tie protest - the referee "funking" [smoking], and of course the association had no alternative but to declare the game as if never had happened, the teams being ordered to play over at Thornliebank.
Ref 1883030

20th October 1883
Third Round   Greenock Morton 1-2 Kilmarnock Athletic
The Athletic were favoured with the news so late as last Saturday that the Greenock had protested their game. In this case, the referee had the pluck to stick to his colours, but this did not seem to suit the S.A. [Scottish Association], and, having constituted the Kilmarnock club's captain referee for the moment, he was found to suit admirably. Result - Greenock claimed a foul, the referee sent by the S.A. didn't see it, but the captain of the opposition admitted seeing a foul, and for his honesty the S.A. pilfers a goal from the Athletic, and sends them back to Greenock! Unparalleled conclusion, without reason, without precedent and in the interest of justice, let us hope never to be repeated. It seems strange that the protest was listened to at all, seeing that the protesting team did not comply with the rules and lodge it with the referee on the ground. This is just another proof, however, that a Kilmarnock club stands at a great disadvantage in the matter of protested games and there can be no doubt but that had the circumstances been vice versa, the Morton would not have had to play the Athletic twice ere meeting the Cambuslang.
Ref 1883031

27th October 1883

Third Round Replay   Harp (Dundee) 2-1 Arbroath

These teams played off their tie in the third round of the Scottish cup ties at Arbroath on the previous Saturday, which resulted in a draw - one goal each. Both teams met again on Saturday, and an attendance of fully 5000 spectators witnessed one of the hardest games ever played in the North of Scotland. The Harp kicked off, and with a combined rush soon swarmed round the Arbroath goal and shot after shot was repelled in grand style by Milne, the Arbroath custodian. The Arbroath forwards, getting possession of the sphere, and playing in good form, carried the ball well into the Harp territory, but Darcy at back interposed, and relieved the home goal. The Harp forwards, getting possession of the leather, stormed off for the Arbroath goal, and, playing their usual close passing game, cleared all opposition, M'Mahon scoring the first goal for the home team amidst tremendous applause. The game now became very fast and exciting, and shortly before half-time Rock scored the second point for the home team. On change of sides the Arbroath trying to redeem their lost ground, played with terrific dash, but the stubborn defence of the Harp back division was so good that once only were the Arbroath able to break through - the game therefore resulting in a win for the Harp by two goals to one. Teams:-

Arbroath - J. Milne, goal; Christie and O'Kane, backs; Bruce, Milne and Guild, half-backs; Robertson, Stirling, Wm Mann (captain), Tucket and Fleming, forwards.

Harp - McTaggart, goal; Darcy and Kilmartin, backs; Holm and Darcy, half-backs; Rock, Reilly, M'Mahon, M'Girl, Merry and Phin, forwards. J. Smith Umpire.

Ref 1883032

10th November 1883

Fourth Round   Battlefield v Edinburgh University

Edinburgh University scratched owing to their inability to get up a team to come through to Glasgow.

Ref 1883033

23rd February 1884

Final   Queen's Park v Vale of Leven

22nd February. The Vale of Leven have approached the Queen's Park in order to try and affect a postponement of the final tie, which is to be played tomorrow. The reason given is that a near relative of Forbes died this week, which would prevent him playing. The Queen's Park, owing to their numerous arrangements, were compelled to decline to grant the request; neither would the Business Committee of the Association interfere. While everybody will sympathise with Forbes, it is hardly the thing to postpone a well-advertised match because one man may be absent. It is not improbable, however, Forbes will take part in tomorrow's game.

Ref 1883034

The final tie between the Queen's Park, Glasgow, and the Vale of Leven for the Scottish Football Association Cup, which was to have been played at Glasgow this afternoon, has been declared off, owing to the inability of the latter to raise a sufficiently good team. The probability is that the Vale, not being able to play their tie on the day appointed by the Association, will be declared out of the match, in which case the trophy will go to

the Queen's Park.
Ref 1883035

As the Vale of Leven was unable to play the Queen's Park in the final tie for the Scottish Challenge Cup on Saturday, the Queen's Park met the 3d L.R.V. at Cathkin Park. About 4000 spectators attended. In the first half the Queen's scored thrice, and in the second once, thus winning the match by four goals to nothing. The 3d L.R.V. towards the close pressed their opponents severely, but were unable to score.
Ref 1883036

S.F.A.C.M. [1st Mar]. The Association Challenge Cup. - A meeting of the Scottish Football Association was held in the rooms, Carlton Place, on Saturday night Mr T Lawrie presiding. After discussion it was agreed to award the Queen's Park the Challenge Cup in respect that the Vale of Leven failed to meet them on the day set apart by the Association for playing off the final tie.
Ref 1883037

29th March 1884

English Cup Final   Queen's Park v Blackburn Rovers

The final tie for the cup between these well known clubs came off at Kennington Oval, London, before an immense turnout of spectators, variously estimated at 12,000 to 15,000. The remarkable success of the crack Scottish Club in the whole series of cup matches up till now gave the event quite an International importance, their defeat of Aston Villa, who were considered their strongest opponents, making them favourites for the final. Thrice the present clubs have met without the Queen's Park being able to get the better of their opponents, though on two occasions the Scotsmen played ten men part of the game. A stiff contest was, therefore, anticipated and, after a hard fight, the Lancashire club gained the winning points, and the English challenge cup, by two goals to one. At the beginning of the match it looked as if the Queen's Park would have matters all their own way, as in the first fifteen minutes they succeeded in putting the ball twice through the Rovers' goal. In each case, however, the score was disallowed by the referee, but the decisions did not meet with general approval, the feeling with regard to the first point especially being that it was quite legitimate. This disheartened the Scotchmen completely, and for the rest of the match there was a great lack of spirit in their play. At half-time the score was two to one in favour of the Rovers, Brown and Forest having done the needful for them, and Christie for the strangers. No further score was made, and the cup remains in Blackburn for another year. What is noticeable is that the English challenge cup has been played by sixteen Scotsmen out of the twenty two – five of the Rovers being imports from Scotland.
Ref 1883038

Footnote

Blackburn Rovers again beat Queen's Park in the final the following season. Scottish Clubs last competed in the English F.A. Challenge Cup in season 1886-87. At the Annual Meeting of the S.F.A. on the 10th May 1887 it was agreed "That clubs belonging to this association shall not be members of any other national association."
Ref 1886034

26th August 1884
First Round Draw
East End (Dundee) – a bye

5th September 1884
The East End, it seems will not have the walk over to the second round of the Scottish Cup competition that the results of the drawings indicated. By an overlook of the Committee, the Coupar Angus Club were left out of the Association, and the odd place fell to the East End, who consequently were published as having received a bye. The mistake has been promptly rectified, however, and the East End will have to fight their way to the second round with the Coupar Angus. The Madeira Park team [East End] have choice of ground, so that the contest, which takes place on 13th inst., will be played in Dundee.
Ref 1884034

13th September 1884
First Round   East End 8-1 Coupar Angus
The tie that fell to be played off in the first round of the Scottish Cup ties between the above Clubs came off on Saturday on the ground of the Strathmore F.C. at Rollo's Pier in presence of a pretty large number of spectators. The ball was started shortly after four o'clock by the Coupar Angus, and, being well followed up, play was confined to the goal of the East End for some time, and then the Coupar Angus were successful in scoring for the first and only time during the game. After this the forward play was anything but combined on either side. The East End, however, scored two goals before the close of half-time. In the second period there was a marked improvement in the East End forward play, and a corresponding falling off in the play of the strangers – the match resulting in a win for the East End by 8 goals to 1.
Ref 1884001

13th September 1884
First Round   West End v Perseverance
This match was fixed to take place on Our Boys' Park at West Craigie, but the Perseverance not putting in an appearance, the West End enjoyed a walk over.
Ref 1884035

13th September 1884
First Round   Wishaw Swifts 2-1 Dykehead
S.F.A.C.M. [23rd Sep]. Dykehead protested that the ground was too short.
*Ref 1884002**

13th September 1884
First Round   Aberfeldy Breadalbane v Vale of Teith
Played at Aberfeldy on Saturday. The Vale lodged a protest as to ground, &c., and Aberfeldy offered a bye, which was accepted.
Ref 1884003

13th September 1884
First Round   **Volunteer Athletic 1-4 Vale of Nith**
During the game the utmost good feeling prevailed and at the close the home team cheered the victors.
*Ref 1884004**

13th September 1884
First Round   **Cartvale 12-1 Greenock Rangers**
Cartvale scorers :- Donohue 1, Calderwood 4, M'Fall 2, Dunbar 3, Wyllie 1, Barnet 1.
*Ref 1884005**

13th September 1884
First Round   **Thornhill 0-13 Q.O.S. Wanderers**
Queen of the South Wanderers scorers :- W- Halliday 3, Patterson 2, Hastings 1, Armstrong 3, Farish 3, Dun 1.
*Ref 1884006**

13th September 1884
First Round   **Abercorn 3-4 Greenock Morton**
S.F.A.C.M. [23rd Sep]. Protested – registration.
Ref 1884007

27th September 1884
First Round Replay   **Abercorn 2-2 Greenock Morton**
S.F.A.C.M. [30th Sep]. The Morton and Abercorn having been drawn twice in the cup tie the ballot was again resorted to. The result was that the Abercorn was drawn against Arthurlie, the Morton securing a bye.

Original draw on 23rd Sep:-
    Arthurlie v Morton or Abercorn
Ref 1884009

13th September 1884
First Round   **St Mirren 4-3 Neilston**
S.F.A.C.M. [23rd Sep]. Protested – registration.
Ref 1884007

23rd September 1884
Miscellaneous   **Professionalism**
S.F.A.C.M. The question of professionalism was brought under the notice of the committee, and a sub-committee was appointed to inquire into the question, and report to the committee later on. A bye-law was also passed that each club engaged in a cup tie shall, after conclusion of the game, hand the names of its players to the umpire of the winning team who shall forward them to the secretary of the association.
*Ref 1884008**

20th September 1884
First Round   **Kilmarnock 6-1 Hurlford**
S.F.A.C.M. [23rd Sep]. Protested – registration.
Ref 1884007

27th September 1884
First Round Replay   **Hurlford 3-1 Kilmarnock**
S.F.A.C.M. [30th Sep]. The protest from the Kilmarnock against the Hurlford was sustained, and the latter was disqualified for not having their team registered.
Ref 1884009

23rd September 1884
Miscellaneous   **First Round Protests**
S.F.A.C.M. The protests by Bo'ness against Hibernians, Partick Thistle against 3d L.R.V., Rock against Yoker, and Clyde against Cowlairs, were dismissed.
Ref 1884007

4th October 1884
Second Round   **Yoker 17-0 Tayavalla**
The Tayavalla journeyed to Yoker on Saturday to play the team of that ilk. The game, which calls for no special comment, was entirely in the hands of the local team who overcame their opponents to the tune of 17 goals to none.
*Ref 1884012**

4th October 1884
Second Round   **Thornliebank 1-0 Port Glasgow Athletic**
S.F.A.C.M. [14th Oct]. A protest by the Port-Glasgow Athletic against the Thornliebank on the ground that one of the players was not registered in time was sustained, and the match was fixed to be played at Port-Glasgow on Saturday.
*Ref 1884014**

4th October 1884
Second Round   **Dunfermline 1-11 Heart of Midlothian**
S.F.A.C.M. [21st Oct]. The first business taken up was the consideration of the Dunfermline against the Heart of Midlothian which was based on the ground that the latter played professionals in the cup tie between the clubs. This particular protest took nearly three hours to consider. A number of witnesses were examined at great length, including M'Nee, late of Cartvale and Maxwell, late of Arthurlie, who were the men charged with being professionals. Mr M'Killop (president) made a long speech, strongly denouncing professionalism. He pointed out its evils, and urged the necessity of purging association football from an evil which was calculated to ruin it. His speech had evidently been carefully prepared. His facts were lucidly put, and the revelations he made showing the ground professionalism had already gained were listened to with marked attention by the committee. The Cartvale, to which Mr. M'Killop belongs, had also a

protest against the Heart of Midlothian, which alleged that the Edinburgh Club had induced some of its players to desert by offers of money or employment, their wages being made up to a certain sum. Mr Turner, on behalf of the Heart of Midlothian, read a mandatory protest against the whole proceedings. Mr Smith, the treasurer of the club, produced his accounts, and he was severely cross-examined regarding them. M'Nee next appeared before the committee, and his examination lasted over half-an-hour. He denied that he received any money for playing football. Maxwell the other player, also underwent a searching examination. Mr Wilson, the secretary of the Cartvale, gave evidence. Calderwood, a member of the club, who had played for a time with the Hearts, but who had afterwards returned to his own club, gave evidence against the Edinburgh Club. Before the committee came to a decision, Mr Turner, on behalf of the Heart of Midlothian, replied on the whole case. Mr M'Killop, as a member of the Cartvale Club, left the room during the latter part of the proceedings. The committee, after having carefully considered the whole question, decided to suspend both M'Nee and Maxwell for two years from playing for any club in any match, and also expelled the Heart of Midlothian Club from the Association. They awarded the tie to the Dunfermline. The committee made their decision applicable to cup ties only. The Heart's can, therefore, play their friendly matches.
*Ref 1884015**

Footnote
Hearts appealed in November but this was rejected. They were re-admitted later.

4th October 1884
Second Round   **West Benhar 9-1 Shettleston**
At Harthill, the ground of the former, in the presence of spectators whose conduct throughout the match was most unseemly. The Benhar have earned an unenviable notoriety for rough play, and on Saturday there was a further exhibition. One of the Shotts backs had to be carried off the field so dangerously hurt that the doctor had to be called in. The Shotts were much lighter than their opponents, and were fairly frightened out of the match, losing by nine goals to one. Protest was raised by Shotts against West Benhar for alleged intimidation by the crowd and rough play. After the evidence of the referees was taken, the clubs were ordered to play over again at Airdrie.
*Ref 1884033**

11th October 1884
Second Round Replay   **East End 2a5 Strathmore (Dundee)**
These Clubs, who drew their other match a week ago, met on Saturday at the East End's ground in their tie in the second round of the Scottish Cup competition. The East End began the game with quite a hurricane blowing at their backs, and being also favoured by the incline of the ground, this had the effect from the first constraining the Strathmore to play on the defensive almost continuously in dangerous proximity to their goalposts during the first period. By dint of hard defensive play, and the difficulty the attacking party had in shooting anything like accurately owing to the wind, the Strathmore colours only fell twice during the period. Favoured by the gale in the second half, the Strathmore took up the attack, and before two-thirds of the stipulated time had elapsed had scored

five times. Meanwhile a deluge of rain had descended, completely saturating the players, and the East End evidently seeing the hopelessness of maintaining a contest with the odds so much against them called a parley, and ultimately abandoned the match while yet twenty minutes remained of the statutory time. The Strathmore will therefore take part in the third round.
Ref 1884016

25th October 1884
Third Round   Queen's Park 2-3 Battlefield
The Association Challenge Cup tie was played off at Hampden Park, and resulted in the quite unexpected defeat of the premier club by three goals to two. The rain made the ground very heavy, and falls were pretty frequent during the match, but despite this fact some fast play was shown by the forwards on both sides. The Battlefield forward division were, however, better organised than their opponents, and showed themselves quicker on the ball when in front of goal. When time was called the score stood - Battlefield, three goals; Queen's Park two. The result created quite a sensation among the spectators, who turned out pretty fairly, notwithstanding the heavy rain. The Battlefield have, therefore, the honour of defeating the Queen's Park for the first time on their new ground. The home team were well represented, while the Battlefield wanted two of their regular eleven.
Ref 1884017

25th October 1884
Third Round   St Mirren 1-0 Renfrew
Rather curiously the Renfrew umpire a few minutes before time protested to the referee that he had stopped the game in the first half some four minutes or so before time, though he was certain when ends were changed that the time had been all right, and had agreed with the referee when he gave his ruling to that effect.
*Ref 1884018**

S.F.A.C.M. [4th Nov]. The Renfrew protest against St Mirren was sustained on the ground that the full time had not been played, and the clubs were ordered to play again at Paisley on Saturday.
Ref 1884019

8th November 1884
Third Round Replay   St Mirren 3a0 Renfrew
This tie was played at West March, and resulted in favour of the Saints by three goals to nothing. The Renfrew kicked off, but were well held in check during the whole of the half by the Saints, they scoring two goals. The Renfrew soon refused to play the second half [due to the inclement weather], and the Saints kicked a further ball through the goal, and the referee awarded them the game.
Ref 1884020

S.F.A.C.M. [11th Nov]. The protest of Renfrew against the St Mirren was sustained, and the game ordered to be played at Paisley on Thursday first.
Ref 1884021

13th November 1884
Third Round 2nd Rply   St Mirren 6-3 Renfrew
Yesterday, for the third time within the past three weeks, the St Mirren and the Renfrew met in the third round of the Scottish Cup competition. The result of a hard game was a victory for the St Mirren by six goals to three. Of the St Mirren's front rank Johnstone and Harper did all the work, the former having three goals to his credit, and Marshall was best at back. M'Dougal, Rassine, and Whyte played well for Renfrew. Like the preceding two matches, the game of yesterday was played at Paisley.
Ref 1884022

25th October 1884
Third Round   Dean Park 2-2 Dumbarton Athletic
Dean Park protested over a registration irregularity. Match replayed at Govan on Dean Park's ground.
*Ref 1884023**

25th October 1884
Miscellaneous   Fatal Football Accident
On Tuesday the authorities at Airdrie received information to the effect that a young man named William M'Ginlay (23), a smelter at Newton Steel Works, and residing at French-land, Tollcross, has died from the effects of a charge or kick which he received while playing at football on a field on the farm of Bogleshole, Carmyle. The deceased, it appears, had played for nearly an hour after receiving a charge on the lower part of the belly, and had subsequently adjourned with the others to a public-house, and had been quite merry in their company. He died, however, shortly after going home. Dr Scott, Tollcross, states that death was caused by rupture of the bowels caused by a kick.
Ref 1884024

29th October 1884
Miscellaneous   The Scottish Football Association and Professionalism
S.F.A.C.M. At a special meeting of the Scottish Association, the following rules about professionalism were passed:
1. A player is declared to be a professional when he receives any remuneration whatever, such as increased wages, or any sum, either directly or indirectly, over and above his reasonable expenses.
2. A club playing a professional player shall be declared a professional club, and expelled from this Association.
3. A member of any club belonging to this Association, or affiliated Association, can protest against any player on the ground of professionalism on depositing 10s.
4. Any club inducing a player, by promises of remuneration, as stated in by-law 1, to leave his club, shall be declared guilty of professionalism, and expelled from this Association.
5. Any club playing a cup tie or other match with a club which has been declared guilty of professionalism, shall be liable to be declared professional, and expelled from this Association.

6. The names of clubs and players declared professional shall be posted in the Association rooms, and intimated to the various clubs and affiliated Associations.

7. Any player who has played for a period of one month under the jurisdiction of any Association other than the Scottish Association cannot play in Scottish cup ties without the permission of this Association.

Recommendation - Any player receiving offers of remuneration from any club or individual is requested to intimate same to the secretary of this Association.
Ref 1884025

15th November 1884

Fourth Round   Arbroath 4-3 Rangers

This match was played at Gayfield, Arbroath, and the result was another of those surprises characteristic of the season, the favourite Glasgow club being defeated by four goals to three. At the outset the strangers seemed to have the game as they liked to take it. Ten minutes from the start Morton secured the first point of the match. Soon afterwards Gosland added a second, and the spectators were scarcely aware that play was resumed when Mackenzie lowered the colours of the home club for the third time. All now seemed lost for the Arbroath; but they speedily wakened up, and played with wonderful pluck. After some good runs they got the ball to the Rangers' goal, and out of a hot scrimmage Marshall sent it spinning through. Immediately afterwards the red jerseys again assumed the attack, and Fleming by a fine long shot put on a second goal. Early in the second half during which they put on a third half-back - Crawford cleverly eluded Chalmers and amidst great excitement the scores were made level. Some fierce play was now witnessed, both clubs maintaining a terrific pace; but while the Arbroath innermost line successfully withstood every onslaught, the citadel of the Rangers was, after some clever passing, captured for a fourth time. In the last 25 minutes the strangers made desperate efforts to make up their leeway, but all ended in failure, and the Arbroath secured a well won victory by four goals to three.
*Ref 1884026**

At the close of the match the Rangers took exception to the measurement of the ground, holding that it was not the required width. They measured it, and resolved to lodge a protest. The Arbroath, on the other hand, insist that the ground is of the requisite breadth, but they measure it diagonally to suit the angle at which it lies, while the Rangers insist on measuring it right across. At the close the referee seemed satisfied with the local measurement, but the matter may come up before the Association.
Ref 1884027

Rangers protested about the size of the pitch, having measured it to be only 49yds 2ft 1in wide, 11 in short of the minimum and sent a telegram back home after the match saying "beaten on a back green".
*Ref 1884028**

S.F.A.C.M. [25th Nov]. The protest of the Rangers against the Arbroath was dismissed by a majority of one.
Ref 1884029

S.F.A.C.M. [16th Dec]. The Rangers protest against Arbroath was re-opened, and the

protest sustained, the match to be played over on Saturday first, Arbroath having choice of ground.
Ref 1884030

20th December 1884
Fourth Round Replay   Arbroath 1-8 Rangers
This interesting match was caused by the Rangers having protested against the result of the previous match for the Scottish Cup, played a few weeks ago, and in which the Arbroath was the victor. The Rangers had the ground measured, and found that it was not of the statutory width. Their protest was ultimately sustained, and the match ordered to be played over again. At first it was feared that the Arbroath would not submit to this finding, but such was not the case, for they were quite willing to stake their reputation once more, and, that there might be no grounds for after disputes, set about altering their field to legal form and dimensions, the latter now being even in excess of requirements. The goals were also set square, and to accomplish this they had to secure a piece of additional ground. Under these altered circumstances the match came off on Saturday. There was a large attendance, when the inclemency of the weather was considered. The hour for commencing was fixed at 2.15, and shortly before that time Arbroath was on the ground. The Rangers arrived a few minutes later, and were received with groans and other marks of disapprobation. All being ready, the ball was kicked off by the Rangers and from the first the advantage seemed on their side. They kept the ball well up in the home territory, and in five minutes secured their first goal. This was disputed by the spectators as being off side, but the referee ruled it correct. Play then proceeded rapidly, and after some hot work and during a scrimmage in front of the goal the ball again eluded Milne's keen eye, and thus a second goal was scored. Thereafter the ball was kept well up at both ends, the goal keepers having an anxious time of it. Repeated corner kicks took place, and at length during a scrimmage after a corner kick, the Rangers again got the ball home, although this was inadvertently done through a misdirected kick by one of the home team. Be that as it may, when time was called, the Rangers were three and Arbroath nothing. Sides being changed, and after a short interval, the ball was kicked off by Arbroath. It was fouled, so Arbroath had a free kick. The ball was sent back by the Rangers' goalkeeper, only, however, to be returned by Fleming, and during a short and sharp scrimmage Crawford cleverly sent it between the posts. This result was received with tremendous applause, being all accomplished within one minute from the kick off. Thereafter the play, though animated and skillful, had no special features beyond the remarkable abilities of individual members on each side. After some fifteen minutes the Rangers scored again, and continued scoring until they put on five consecutive goals - the final result being Rangers, eight; Arbroath, one. The various stages of the play were received with shouts of approbation or the other thing according to the side which advantaged by it. But the Rangers may be said to have played the match under a fire of unceasing groans and hooting. This was ungenerously continued up till they were seated in the train, and as it steamed out of the station a final volley of groans were given by the large crowd of home sympathisers.
Ref 1884031

S.F.A.C.M. [6th Jan]. The Committee of this Association met last night. The first business considered was an appeal from the Arbroath Club against the decision come to in the matter of the Rangers' protest against Arbroath's ground, the Committee reversing

a judgment they had previously delivered. The Committee concluded not to consider the appeal.
Ref 1884037

15th November 1884

Fourth Round   **Annbank 5-2 Q.O.S. Wanderers**

Queen of the South Wanderers visited Annbank on Saturday to try conclusions with the village heroes, in the fourth round for the Scottish Cup. The ground was in a miserable condition, and the game was more of a test of strength than skill. In the first half the visitors were equal with their opponents, the score being 2 goals each. The second half, although stubbornly contested, ended in favour of the home team by 3 goals to 0. The visitors fairly broke down, and were quite unable to extricate themselves from the mud; but the home team seemed in their element; and showed superior staying powers. One of the spectators, whose sympathies were with the strangers, said "Lads, if ye had the staying powers, you could like them ower the back." The captain replied, "It's no the lack of staying powers that's wrong; if we hadna stayed sae lang in the mud, there would have been fewer goals against us." The Dumfries team have protested against the ground; but as the SFA already decided in a previous tie that the ground was suitable for football, their chance of gaining the protest is most unlikely. Annbank are anxiously waiting the result of the drawings for the fifth round, and should they be fortunate in having choice of ground, their chance is rosy.
*Ref 1884032**

27th December 1884

Sixth Round   **Battlefield v Cambuslang**

This cup tie should have been played at Kinning Park. The Battlefield, however did not appear. The Cambuslang went on to the field , kicked a goal, and claimed the match. No referee was present. On Saturday forenoon the Cambuslang received a telegram from the Battlefield stating that they would not play. Their excuse, it is understood, was owing to the hardness of the ground. A considerable crowd was present, and were much disappointed at the match not taking place.
Ref 1884036

S.F.A.C.M. [6th Jan]. In the protest of the Cambuslang against the Battlefield, the former claimed the tie, owing to the Battlefield not coming forward to play on December 27th. A rather lengthy correspondence, which had passed between the Clubs, was laid before the Association. The Committee were of opinion that the Battlefield were somewhat to blame for the contretemps that had taken place, and the Chairman admonished the Club in name of the Committee, who ordered the tie to be played on Saturday first at Cambuslang, instead of at Langside.
Ref 1884037

25th August 1885
Committee Meeting   Struck Off and New Clubs
The following clubs were struck off the roll for non-payment of their subscriptions :-
Cyrus, Deanpark, Kinning Park Athletic, Orchard, Possilpark, Springburn, Springburn
Hibernians, Clippens, Greenock Rovers, Johnstone Rovers, Kilbarchan, Lyle Athletic,
Paisley Athletic, Pollockshaws, Cunninghame, Kilmarnock Athletic, Airdrie,
Airdriehill, Chryston, Clarkston, Glengowan, Vale of Avon, Stenhousemuir,
Strathblane, Tayavalla, Lindertis, Perseverance, Newton-Stewart Athletic.
The following new clubs were admitted into the Association :- Alpha, Dunfermline
Athletic, Paisley Hibernians, Forfar Athletics, Union, Monkcastle, Cowdenbeath,
Southern Athletics, Oban, Broxburn Shamrock, Camelon, Bonhill, 10th L.R.V.,
Broughty, Aberdeen Rovers, Bon Accord, Westbourne, Avondale, Ayr Rovers,
Grahamston, Linthouse, St Peter's, Mearns Athletic, Helensburgh, Kirkintilloch
Athletics, Glencairn.
Ref 1885001

29th August 1885
Friendly   Aberdeen v Bon Accord
The Association Football Clubs in Scotland having, on account of the first round of the
ties for the Scottish Cup and gold badges, which takes place on September 12, to make
an earlier start than their Rugby friends, the above clubs began their season's work on
Saturday last. The Bon-Accord captain having lost the toss, the Aberdeen captain elected
to defend the west goal. The Bon-Accord kick-off was quickly returned, and the ball was
only once in the Aberdeen quarters during the first half of the game. At half-time the
Aberdeen had scored two goals. The second half was a repetition of the first, as the Bon-
Accord had again only one raid into their opponents' quarters. Two more goals were
added to the Aberdeen score in this half, and the game thus resulted in their favour by
four goals to love.
Ref 1885002

12th September 1885
First Round   Cambridge 3-1 Southern Athletic
S.F.A.C.M [22nd Sep]. Protested by Southern Athletic on the ground of "infringements
of the registration rule."
Ref 1885003

12th September 1885
First Round   Alpha 6-8 Cambuslang Hibernian
The Alpha played off their Scottish Cup Tie last Saturday with the Cambuslang
Hibernians. The weather was of the worst description, the ground being very soft, but
nevertheless a fair turn-out of spectators witnessed the match, which ended in a most
unexpected win for the wearers of the green by 8 goals to 6. The winners won the toss
and took good advantage of the wind, which blew a perfect hurricane during the whole
match. The advantage to the Hibernians aided them greatly, and they scored five goals
in the first half, the Alpha getting three against the wind. On the teams changing over it
was generally expected that the Alpha would easily get more goals, but chiefly owing to

good defence they could only bring their total to 6 - the Hibernians getting also 3. The match ended in their favour by 8 to 6. The winners played well all through, and certainly are to be proud of their victory. Moodie, Charters, Cassidy, Anderson, and Murray, were the only ones deserving mention on the losing side, the soft ground, no doubt preventing the others from showing anything like their usual play. The Cambuslang team was entertained to tea after the match, and a very enjoyable evening was spent.

Kyle of Cambuslang Hibernians scored 5 goals.
Ref 1885004

12th September 1885
First Round   East Stirlingshire 6-1 Campsie
Campsie played with 9 players.
*Ref 1885005**

12th September 1885
First Round   Helensburgh v Dumbarton Athletic
This match, which was fixed to take place on Saturday at Helensburgh, did not come off, owing to the Dumbarton men protesting to the goal posts being too high. The Helensburgh men offered to reduce the height, but the Dumbarton men refused to wait, owing to the boisterous and wet weather.
*Ref 1885006**

12th September 1885
First Round   Kirkintilloch Athletic 0-14 Renton
At Townhead Park, Kirkintilloch, in very inclement weather, resulting in favour of the Renton players by fourteen goals to none. Owing to the great inequality of the players, the match excited very little interest, though the Kirkintilloch players are said to have acquitted themselves fairly well.
Ref 1885007

12th September 1885
First Round   Clyde 1-0 Rangers
Seldom has the game been played under more disadvantageous circumstances. Heavy rain had fallen from an early hour in the morning, and the field, especially in the vicinity of the goals, was liquid mud and pools of water. Notwithstanding the nature of the weather between 1000 and 1500 spectators gathered round the ropes. The Rangers lost the toss, and kicked off in the teeth of a violent gale from the south. This, and the absence of Somerville, whose place was taken by Muir, heavily handicapped the visitors, and all through the first half the game was almost purely defensive on their part. Backed by the wind the Clyde men pressed their opponents home, and shortly after the play had commenced, Macfarlane shot the ball from the left wing of the forwards. Chalmers rushed out to save the goal, and at first there was an impression that he had succeeded in doing so, the Rangers being about to play on. The Clyde, however, placed the dispute in the hands of the referee - Mr Eglinton, of the Airdrieonians - who declined in favour of

the home team, the Rangers protesting. As the game advanced the wind began to tell upon the staying powers of the visitors, who rarely got the ball beyond the centre of the field. They were, however, successful in defending their goal. When the ends were changed the storm had lulled somewhat, and the Clyde men were able to make frequent assaults on the enemy's territory, but without gaining any material advantage. The blues became dispirited according as their opponents were elated, and, notwithstanding that the wind favoured them, failed to score, the match thus resulting in a win for the Clyde by one goal to nil. Mr Seaton acted as umpire for the Clyde, and Mr Watson for the Rangers. We understand that the Rangers lodged a protest on the ground that the ropes having given way, the spectators encroached on the field.
Ref 1885008

12th September 1885
First Round   **Heart of Midlothian 5-2 St Bernard's**
S.F.A.C.M. [22nd Sep]. For infringement of the registration rule, the St Bernard's protested against the Heart of Mid-Lothian. The Stockbridge club gained their protest, and the match will require to be played over again on Saturday, this time on the Saints' ground at Powderhall.
*Ref 1885009**

12th September 1885
First Round   **Johnstone 5-1 Greenock Rangers**
Played at Johnstone during a violent gale. Johnstone scored five goals against one by Greenock. The Greenock players left the field shortly after half-time in a drenching rain.
Ref 1885008

The Johnstone in spite of the rain remained on the field until call of time.
*Ref 1885011**

12th September 1885
First Round   **Lanemark 4-1 Monkcastle**
These clubs met on the ground of the former last Saturday to play their tie in the first round for the Scottish Association Cup. The day was a most unfavourable one, a high wind, accompanied by an almost incessant downpour of rain, lasting throughout the game. The home team won the toss, and elected to play with the wind in their favour, if it could be called so, as the wind was blowing nearly across the field. However, they took what advantage there was, and succeeded, by displaying good skill and cool determination, in putting three goals to their credit. In this part of the game, the whole of the home team play was done by their forwards, for the strangers only once succeeded in getting near the Lanemark goal. Just before calling time for the first half, Lanemark claimed another goal - a good shot being sent in, which was kicked out from under the bar, but the referee was too far back to give a decision. There were a great number of corner kicks in this half, but none of them were beneficial. Time at change of ends being called, the home team showed they were determined to keep what they had won, for after running the ball several times up to their adversaries' posts, it was sent through, off one of their opponents' legs. The ball being taken to midfield and set in motion, the strangers

ran it up, and, after a hot scrimmage, sent it through, thus putting one to their credit. No more goals were taken by either side. We think that with Barbour, Strahan, Broom, and Graham in the rear, and the forwards displaying such clever play as they did on Saturday, particularly the left wing, although the cleverest shot came from M'Ghee of the right, they will make it hard for their opponents in the next round. We admired the strangers for the way they conducted themselves. Losing teams very often show a little temper; such was not the case with Monkcastle.

*Ref 1885012**

S.F.A.C.M. [22nd Sep]. Match replayed after Monkcastle protested "for infringments of the registration rule".

Ref 1885003

12th September 1885
First Round   Harp (Dundee) 35-0 Rovers (Aberdeen)
This tie in the first round of the Scottish Cup attracted a large crowd to East Dock Street on Saturday afternoon. Although it was generally believed that the match would be pretty much a one sided one, yet some interest was manifested to see the play of the Northern team. The weather unfortunately was very unfavourable, and the Harp's ground, which is usually in fine condition, was heavy. The strangers were the first to enter the ropes and they met a cordial welcome from the spectators. They were quickly followed by the Harp men. The toss was won by the Aberdeen team, who elected to play to the north goal, and the ball was set agoing at 3.25. The kick-off at once placed the leather in dangerous proximity to the Aberdeen goal, and one minute after the start the first point was registered for the Harp by Murphy. The ball was hardly set in motion again when a second and third goal, both off Rock, were scored within three minutes of the opening. When the ball was started for the fourth time, the forwards of the home team ran away with it, but unfortunately carried it behind the goal. In consequence a free kick fell to the lot of the strangers, but nothing came of it, and a fourth goal was easily obtained for the Harp by Murray. Up to this time the Aberdeen men never had a look in at their opponents' goal, and indeed never had been out of their own territory; but they now put on a spurt, and endeavoured to get a hold of the ball. In this however, they failed, and the Harp men worked away very coolly, and from their kicks the strangers had repeated free kicks, but nothing came of any of them. The fifth goal for the home men was scored by Murray. Two "hands" in succession now fell to the Aberdeen players, and these were followed by a couple of corners for the Harp. Off the second corner the sixth goal was registered by Murphy, and within a minute afterwards the same player had the seventh point gained for his team by passing through the ball, which was cleverly placed by Murray. The next goal was very easily won, for no sooner had the leather been set rolling than Rock got hold of the ball, and in the most leisurely fashion imaginable took it to the goal and put it through. The ninth and tenth points were got very speedily by Darcy, jun., and Lees respectively. A period of very open and easy play followed, and a free kick by Anderson, the Aberdeen back, was at once repelled by the left wing of the Harp, and from a smart kick the ball struck the top bar of the goal and rebounded, but in a general scrimmage it was headed through the posts. The next three goals were got in as many minutes by Darcy, jun., M'Girl, and Neil. Murphy now obtained possession of the ball, actually walked past the Aberdeen with it, and cleverly passed it to Murray, who put it through

the uprights. The next goal was carried by M'Girl, and both teams were in the midst of a most exciting scrimmage when the whistle sounded half-time. The game at this time stood :- Harp, 16; Aberdeen Rovers, 0. The play up to this time had all been on the Aberdeen men's ground, and when sides were changed the majority of the spectators also changed their positions and assembled near the north goal, expecting that the play which had ruled the first part of the game would continue. To this they were not disappointed for scarcely had a beginning been set when the ball was driven right up to the goal, and with very little exertion put through by Murray. The remainder of the game was practically a walk over for the Harp. The Aberdeen men occasionally spurted, but without any good effect, and goal after goal was rapidly added to the large total of the home team. D'Arcy, jun., had five goals in quick succession, and Lees, M'Girl, Neill, and Murray were among the other scorers who contributed to increase the score. When time was sounded the score stood - Harp, 35; Aberdeen Rovers, 0. From the beginning it was believed that the game would be an easy win for the Harp, but no one expected that they would have been able to make such a score as they did. Never in any match in which the Harp has been engaged was such a total registered. When the same team beat the Broughty two years ago with a score of twenty odds, it was considered a big thrashing, but Saturday's work completely puts that performance in the shade. Aberdeen, it should be said, had only ten men in the field, and had thus an additional handicap to their much inferior experience to that of their opponents. M'Taggart, the home goalkeeper, was only called upon twice in the game to return the leather.
Scorers: D'Arcy Jun. (captain)10. McGirl 6, Murphy 5, Murray 4, Rock 3, Lees 3, Neill 3 D'Arcy Sen. 1
Ref 1885013

The Rovers' team is a young organisation, having previously only taken part in one match, that with the Bon-Accord, Aberdeen, and it only joined the Association for the first time this year. Their play with the exception of Anderson on the left, who at times, though perfectly unsupported, made an occasional brilliant run, was of a mediocre type. Their custodian especially gave a particularly weak-kneed exhibition of goalkeeping. The Harp had the game all their own way, as from start to finish it was only a question of walking up to their opponents' goal and putting through the leather. The strangers played a man short, but this fact could not have discounted the result to any appreciable extent.
Ref 1885014

12th September 1885
First Round   **Arbroath 36-0 Bon Accord**
The fixture of these Clubs in the first round of the Scottish Cup ties was played off on Saturday afternoon. The ballot gave the Bon-Accord the selection of ground, but they chose to come to Gayfield. The weather was unpleasant, and as a consequence the turn-out of spectators was not particularly large. At half-past three the teams faced each other - the maroons looking towards the west goal. The Aberdonians kicked off, and almost at once the ball was in their territory. A short scrimmage sent the leather out, but on being thrown in it was sent towards the strangers' goal, and Crawford administered the finishing kick, which secured the first point. This was the beginning of a one-sided game. The maroons, working in fine form, had everything their own way - the defence play of

the Bon-Accord being unworthy of that name. Goal after goal was notched, and at half time the score stood - Arbroath, 15; Bon-Accord, 0. Things looked no brighter for the strangers in the second half, all the action being practically in the vicinity of their goal posts, and when the whistle blew time the game stood thus - Arbroath, 36; Bon-Accord, 0.

Forty goals in all were scored, but four were disallowed by the referee for offside. Only once during the game did the colours of the maroons seem in danger of being lowered, but Collie saved. The play of the Aberdeen team all through, as can be imagined, was most mediocre, and as regards the individual work there was next to nothing worthy the least praise. The goals were taken as follows:- Petrie, 13; Munro, 7; Robertson, 6; Crawford, 6; Marshall, 2; Tackett, 2. The Arbroath team were:- Milne, goal; Salmond and Collie, backs; Milne and Rennie, half-backs; Robertson, Crawford, Petrie, Marshall, Tackett, and Munro, forwards. Milne the half-back, was captain for the day. It is believed that the score piled up by the maroons is unequalled in the annals of football.
Ref 1885013

Milne the active goalkeeper of the Arbroath, neither touched the ball with hand or foot during the match, but remained under the friendly shelter of an umbrella the whole time.
Ref 1885014

Footnote
Harp beat Arbroath 5-3 in the final of the Forfarshire Challenge Cup, on December 19th , to retain the trophy. This was the third year of the competition and the third year that the two clubs had been paired together in it. Harp lost to Arbroath 2-1 in the 1883-84 Final but won last season's Semi-final encounter 5-3 after a 2-2 draw.

22nd September 1885
Miscellaneous   **Notice of Motions**
S.F.A.C.M. [22nd Sep]. Notice of motions were given as follows:- " That the press be admitted to meeting; that clubs be disqualified when not correctly registered; that players registered before admitted are ineligible."
*Ref 1885017**

3rd October 1885
Second Round   **5th K.R.V. 3-1 Q.O.S. Wanderers**
This match was played at Palmerston, Dumfries on the ground of the Volunteers. A very exciting game resulted in a win for the 5th by three goals to one.
Ref 1885018

10th October 1885
Friendly   **5th K.R.V. 0-3 Q.O.S. Wanderers**
S.F.A.C.M. [13th Oct]. 5th K.R.V. had the services of Lockerbie of Lockerbie and M'Guigen of Newton-Stewart. Queen of the South Wanderers protested that they were not registered to 5th K.R.V.
*Ref 1885019**

17th October 1885

Second Round Replay   Q.O.S. Wanderers 4-3 5th K.R.V.

In consequence of a protest by the Wanderers having been sustained, this Scottish Cup tie was played over again on Saturday at Nunholm before a large turnout of spectators. An excellent game resulted in a win for the Wanderers by four goals to three.

Ref 1885020

3rd October 1885

Second Round   Dunblane 10-0 Dunfermline Athletic

At Kippenross Park, Dunblane, in the second round of the Scottish Cup ties. The weather was very disagreeable, rain prevailing during the greater part of the game, which greatly interfered with the play. Dunblane had it all their own way, scoring five goals in the first and five goals in the second portion, the game ending in their favour as above - by ten goals to nil.

*Ref 1885021**

10th October 1885

Second Round   Broughty 3-8 East End

Protested due to registration violation.

17th October 1885

Second Round Replay   Broughty 1-2 East End

Through the East End committing a flagrant violation of the registration rule, the Scottish Association, by way of punishment, made the offenders play the match over again on Saturday afternoon on the Broughty's ground at Forthill. The Broughty had one alteration in their team, while for the East End M'Intyre took the place of the malefactor. The weather was close and warm, and the ground a little slippery. There was a fair attendance of spectators. The turn of the coin falling in favour of the East End, they selected to play up the incline. The Broughty centre set the ball in motion, and after a fruitless run each way, operations were for some time kept up near the Broughty fortress, but through the strong defence it could not be taken. Duncan soon established peace at the Broughty citadel by making a splendid run nearly the whole length of the field. A vigorous attack was now kept up on the East End's stronghold. Duncan was the most conspicuous in the Broughty front line, and at this stage of the game he sent in a warm shot, which would have gone behind, but Reid was lying close on the uprights and caught it on his breast and put it through amidst loud cheering. The East End claimed offside, but the referee allowed the point. Feeling now ran high amongst the spectators, and appeals to the players to use brute force were frequently made. From this point of the game to the end of the first period the play was of a very even character, each goal being assailed in turn. Forrester missed some easy chances for the East End by his bad shooting. Once the Broughty looked like scoring again. They got the ball close on the goal line, and Mitchell could not get it away before he was surrounded by the fronts and compelled to fall on the ball. The Broughty fell on the top of him, and a terrific maul ensued, but gradually Mitchell crawled out from underneath his heavy human load and gave the ball to Simpson, who was not long in dispatching it up the field. At half-time the score stood – Broughty, 1 goal; East End, nil. The East End had now the incline in their favour, and were not long in showing that it was to be of some advantage to them,

but they lost many chances by rash shooting. Fully twenty minutes of the game had gone when Reilly, by a long, hard, and well directed shot, lowered the Broughty colours. The Broughty men had a faint look-in, but Simpson soon transferred the sphere to the other end, and several deadly shots were sent in by the East End fronts, but all of them were smartly repelled by the custodian or the heads of the full backs. The hard pressure now commenced to tell on the Broughty, and, although the East End were suffering from the effects of their Fast Day's trip, they were by far the freshest, and worked with grim determination to the end. The Broughty were pretty severely hemmed in, and the ball was kept crossing and recrossing the goal mouth in a manner utterly perplexing to the defenders. At last M'Intyre took advantage of their awkward state, and registered the second point for the East End. All the rest of the game the East End kept up almost constant bombardment, but could not get any more through. A fast, and sometimes rough game thus ended in a win for the visitors by 2 goals to 1. The Broughty never played a better game against the East End. The back division in particular showed grand defence, and was very difficult to pass. Some of the East End were evidently out of sorts, and did not play with their usual dash.
Ref 1885022

13th October 1885
Miscellaneous   **Drawings for Third Round**
S.F.A.C.M. There was a large attendance, and the crowd outside the building desirous to hear the result of the drawings was immense.
Ref 1885023

10th October 1885
Miscellaneous   **Football Death**
A melancholy accident happened at Dalmuir on Saturday last while a match was in progress between the Glen Rangers, Duntocher, and the Thistle Club, Dalmuir. A young man about 20 years of age, named T. Anderson (one of the Thistle players, and related about Bonnybridge), was charged by an opponent with considerable force. Every possible effort that was put forth to relieve him was unavailing, and he died in great agony about four o'clock on Sunday afternoon. He was buried on Wednesday in Falkirk Cemetery.

I am glad to hear that Bonnybridge has still some sympathy, but not Longcroft. It is very mean to learn that Longcroft will not give the 'Hoppers another day for their [Stirlingshire Cup] tie in consequence, and to show some respect for the unhappy youth who came to his fatal end. Don't play, 'Bridge, and I am certain the association will not come in the way.
Ref 1885024

17th October 1885
Miscellaneous   **Four-a-side Football Match at Perth**
On the Rangers' ground at Perth, between teams captained by Mr J. Pullar, Cowlairs; and Mr J. M'Rae of Perth Rangers. After an exciting game Mr M'Rae's team won by 2 goals to 1.
Ref 1885025

3rd October 1885
Second Round   **Kilmarnock 3-4 Hurlford**
A large concourse of spectators assembled to witness this tie between these old rivals at Rugby Park, the ground of the former. Kilmarnock won the toss, and elected to play with a strong wind and bright sun at their backs. Hurlford kicked off, and rushed down to the home goal, and nearly obtained a point, the ball sliding past the post. The kick off was collared by Smith, and after some splendid passing the Kilmarnock scored their first point, and shortly after obtained another. This looked rather dull for the strangers, but warming up to their work, and playing well together, Watson scored the first point for the team. The village heroes again returned with renewed vigour to the home fortress, and after some splendid play on behalf of the Kilmarnock the strangers scored again, from the foot of F. Goudie. This was all the scoring in the first half and the teams faced each other on equal terms. Some five minutes elapsed till Watson scored again for the Hurlford, and soon after another point, thus making them two goals in the majority. The play after this was of a give-and-take character till about five minutes from the finish Higgins scored again for the Kilmarnock. Soon after time was called, leaving the Hurlford victors by four goals to three. Protest by Kilmarnock on the grounds of a breach of registration was upheld.
*Ref 1885026**

17th October 1885
Second Round Replay   **Kilmarnock 1-1 Hurlford**
The crowd was very large. The game was furiously contested, and ended in a draw - one goal each.
*Ref 1885027**

24th October 1885
Second Round 2nd Rply Kilmarnock v Hurlford
The protest from the Kilmarnock against Hurlford having been dismissed at a business meeting of the S.F.A., the tie had to be played once more, and as it had to be played on neutral ground, Beresford Park was engaged for the occasion. As much interest had been taken in this tie, large numbers (many of whom had come by rail) congregated at the gate, but did not enter the field, owing to the rumour that Kilmarnock had not come, which turned out to be the case, their excuse being, it is said, that they had not received notice. The referee awarded the game to Hurlford. The strangers being anxious for a game, a team of the Ayr, composed of the 2d Eleven and others, consented to play, and a most enjoyable match followed. The score of the hour long game was 1-1.
*Ref 1885028**

31ˢᵗ October 1885
Second Round 2nd Rply Kilmarnock 1a1 Hurlford
In Springvale Park, Ayr, these two teams met for the third time in the second round for the Scottish Cup. In the first half neither managed to score, and the game was very uninteresting. In the second half both briskened up, and in the first 5 minutes both goals were in jeopardy. A dispute arose shortly afterwards; the Kilmarnock had taken a good run down the field, and the ball had gone over the touchline, and the Hurlford never thinking stopped play, but one of their opponents put the ball through the goal and claimed one. The Hurlford protested, but as usual in all protests came off second best. The whites made to leave the field, but better counsel prevailed, and for the next ten minutes the play was furious and unnecessarily rough, at the end of which time the Hurlford scored amidst great excitement. This caused several of the Kilmarnock team to lose their temper, and they began to use their fists rather freely. This had the effect of arousing the anger of the spectators, who jumped the ropes, and ended the game, which on the whole was in favour of the Hurlford. It was evident all through the game that a considerable amount of feeling existed between the opposing teams, caused on the part of the Hurlford by the most decidedly unfair treatment they have received at the hands of the association.
*Ref 1885029**

S.F.A.C.M. [3ʳᵈ Nov]. A long and animated discussion took place over the cross protests of Kilmarnock against Hurlford and vice versa. The clubs had been at cross purposes as to the ground in which the undecided tie should be played. The meeting seemed to be dissatisfied with the action taken by the Business Committee in the matter, and disapproval of that action by 12 votes to 8. On a further division on a motion that the game be replayed on the Hurlford ground against an amendment that the referee's decision as to a goal he had disallowed the Kilmarnock, but which he had subsequently admitted he had disallowed in error, ten voted on each side, and by the casting vote of the chairman the vote was carried. After still further discussion, in which some sympathy was expressed at the treatment Hurlford had received, it was decided that the game be replayed on the ground of Hurlford on Saturday first with an extra half hour to be played if necessary.
*Ref 1885030**

7ᵗʰ November 1885
Second Round 3rd Rply Hurlford 2-2 Kilmarnock
This undecided tie was played at Hurlford on Saturday. A protest was lodged on the field before the game commenced [by Kilmarnock]. The ground was soft, but no rain fell, Hurlford played with the wind and hill in their favour. Two thousand spectators were present. The feeling for the first 20 minutes' play was rather in favour of Hurlford, in which several glaring chances were missed. M'Knight shot badly at goal. Pressure continued at Kilmarnock goal, and in a scrimmage Porteus (Kilmarnock) miskicked the ball, and shot it through his own goal. Kilmarnock followed with a good ... but the goalkeeper repelled them. Again Hurlford returned to the attack, and kept the visiting backs busy. Richmond, the Kilmarnock goalkeeper, played in great form. Result at half time - Hurlford; 1 goal; Kilmarnock, nothing. At the start of the second half, from a pass by Walker, Smith scored for Kilmarnock. Pressure, on the part of the Hurlford, followed, and was continued for some time, Richmond still battering them out. Kilmarnock also

had an innings, without result. Again Hurlford pressed, and Battery scored from the left. Kilmarnock again scored from a scrimmage, and at the call of time the score was equal - two goals each. An additional half hour was played, but neither could gain a winning point, and the game ended again in a draw.

The following protest was lodged on the field previous to commencing the game:-

DEAR SIR - At a meeting of our committee held last night, the decision of the Scottish Football Association Committee re-protested Cup-tie, Kilmarnock & Hurlford, was fully considered, when it was unanimously agreed upon to ask the Association to reconsider their decision, as it is not in accordance with the "Cup Competition Rules."
1st. Rule 15, last sentence reads - "the question of interpretation of rules or laws of the game, an appeal may be made to the Committee of the Association, but the referee's decision must be acted on in the field, although under protest."
From the evidence which was brought before your committee, it was clearly proved and unanimously admitted, that the "laws of the game" had been misinterpreted by the referee, therefore it was plainly the duty of the committee to decide, according to the correct interpretation of the "laws of the game" by awarding a goal to the Kilmarnock. If the referee is considered competent, his decision must be acted upon; if incompetent, the game must be declared null and void, and replayed on the Kilmarnock ground.
2nd. Rule 16, first sentence and third clause - "Protests must be accompanied by a deposit of 10s."
The Hurlford representative who was in the room adjacent to the meeting, was asked by Mr M'Dowall to deposit 10s, but refused. Mr Halley (Partick Thistle), deposited the amount and the case was re-opened.
He considered that the action of Mr Halley was not in accordance with the spirit of this rule, and showed that he was actuated either by a spirit of partiality towards Hurlford, or antagonism towards Kilmarnock. We think that the duty of the committee is to settle disputes that come before them, and not to foster them by encouraging protests.
3rd. Rule 23 - "The committee of the Association shall have the power to add to the above rules as they from time to time may deem expedient, provided that they do not alter any rule adopted at the annual meeting."
We are extremely sorry that we have had to re-protest on this vexed subject but as a member of the committee, either through ignorance or partiality, have disregarded the rule adopted at the annual meeting, we have no alternative but to insist that the rules, as adopted by the Association, be strictly adhered to, and not altered to suit circumstances.
Kindly lay this protest before your General Committee at an early date, not that we lack confidence in the Business Committee's decision, but the vote of censure, passed on them by an extreme section of the General Committee, has placed them in an awkward position in the eyes of the football public. - I am, &c.
WM. MUNRO
John M'Dowall, Esq.,
Scottish Football Association.
*Ref 1885031**

14th November 1885

Second Round 4th Rply   Kilmarnock 1-5 Hurlford

These teams met on Rugby Park for the fifth time. The ground was in fair order, there was a large gathering of spectators. Hurlford had a heavy wind in their favour, and had the best of play for some time. Two or three chances were missed, but, latterly, M'Knight from the left scored a very clever goal. The other forwards disabling Richmond, a good run by Young and M'Pherson (Kilmarnock) was missed just at goal. Hurlford again returned to attack, but were confused when near the goal. "Sam" Goudie missed a good one from the left, and again Kilmarnock had a short innings. Hurlford, however, were not to be denied, and a long shot from a halfback put the Hurlford two goals up. Higgins had a neat run, but was put down to midfield by a hand at Kilmarnock's goal. Chance allowed it to escape. Continued play at home goal, and long and continued pressure repelled a fine run to the Hurlford goal, and the shot was missed a few yards from the goal. The Hurlford forwards did most of the playing, a fine shot by "Sam" Goudie being stopped by Richmond. Shortly after M'Knight got a third goal for Hurlford. Result at half-time - Hurlford, three; Kilmarnock, 0; The wind had fallen much, and the snow which fell at the beginning had cleared off. Higgins and Smith (Kilmarnock) had a neat run, but were repelled before they were dangerous. Still the Killie pressed. A pass from Higgins being collared by Dunn, the latter passed to Smith, who shot the ball through. After this, for some time, pressure was continued at the Hurlford goal, the home team playing in great form. Hurlford had now a look in, but the home backs sent them back. Kilmarnock were now showing the best play they have displayed in any of the five games, Higgins and Smith being most active, and the Hurlford backs were kept busy. A free kick made the Hurlford goal-keeper kick out for safety, but nothing came of the corner. Smith (Kilmarnock) had a clear goal, but Craig stepped in before him, and another corner came to nothing. Pressure at Hurlford end was relieved, and the ball was sent smartly down the field, and a fourth goal was scored for Hurlford. Some even play followed, but latterly a free kick in front of Kilmarnock goal gave Hurlford an opportunity of scoring further, A. Goudie doing the needful. As a contest the game was now over and both teams seemed to be well wound-up. In the last few minutes Kilmarnock made an effort to increase their score, but it was of no avail, and they were beaten by five goals to one. The Hurlford will play the Arthurlie in the third round on Saturday first.

*Ref 1885032**

14th November 1885

Fourth Round   3rd L.R.V. 3-2 Ayr

S.F.A.C.M. [24th Nov]. An idea seems to prevail all over the country that Glasgow clubs are to a certain extent favoured by the S.F.A., but the action of the committee in sustaining Ayr's protest against the 3rd Lanark will go a long way in dispelling an altogether erroneous impression. Ayr protested against the 3d Lanark on the following ground:- (1) That the referee on two occasions gave his decision before being appealed to by the umpires. (2) That the referee was not in a proper position to judge when he disallowed a goal scored by Ayr. (3) That the referee awarded a goal to the 3rd Lanark, when the ball was not through, he being at the time 30 or 40 yards from the goal-line. (4) That the 3rd Lanark umpire, contrary to all rules, coached the team, and claimed fouls before being appealed to by the players.

Beyond denying that their umpire coached the team, or appealed to the referee before being approached by the players, the 3rd Lanark had practically no defence to urge, and the case went to proof. The three former heads having reference to facts of play the evidence of the referee was sufficient to repel the objections. On the fourth point, however, it was proved conclusively that the 3rd Lanark umpire did coach the team, thereby placing himself in the position of a twelfth man. Mr. French committed an infringement of a well understood though unwritten law, and this view the Association adopted. On a division only three voted in support of the 3rd Lanark, and the match was ordered to be replayed at Ayr.

Ref 1885033

16th January 1886

Semi-Final   **3rd L.R.V. 0a4 Queen's Park**

These clubs having been drawn together in the sixth round of the Scottish Cup competition, met at Cathkin Park (ground of the 3d) to decide the tie. Much interest had been taken in the game, as both clubs were in the best of form, and had been playing splendidly all the season – particularly the Volunteers, who have of late been showing up exceptionally well, and aspiring determinedly to the high position they occupied some time ago. Some 3000 spectators were present. Unfortunately the weather was of the worst possible description for football. The ground was wet and slippery, and covered with snow, making really good play out of the question. To add to the general misery of the scene, snow fell pitilessly throughout, which, combined with the intense cold, made things rather disagreeable alike to players and spectators. Such atmospheric conditions were no doubt the cause of the limited attendance; and surprise was expressed by those who did turn out that instead of being postponed the match should have been gone on with. The Queen's Park had out their strongest eleven, including Harrower, who has been absent for some time. The Volunteers, however, were minus two of their usual eleven – Marshall and Weir. This to some extent demoralised them, but able substitutes were found in Connolly and A. Kennedy, an old 3d veteran. The Volunteers, having lost the toss, kicked off against a strong breeze, and after some play in their opponents' quarters, sent the ball behind. The Queen's Park, however, with the wind in their favour, soon transferred operations to the home ground, when a series of assaults were made on Collie's charge, but without effect. A swift ball from Christie's foot had a narrow escape of going through. M'Intyre and Johnstone had a break-away, but ended by sending the ball past. The game was shortly afterwards stopped in order to decide whether or not to go on, as the snow was falling mercilessly and seriously interrupting matters. Several of the players expressed a hearty desire to retire, and justly so but the spectators were decided in their manifestations to play on, which was done. Collie having kicked off, the Queen's brought the ball down again, and some exciting work was witnessed in home quarters, Hamilton, Christie, and Allan being conspicuous in the attack ; but the splendid defence of Tait, Rae, and Auld frustrated all efforts. Thomson, notwithstanding Marshall's absence, which he evidently felt severely, now exhibited some clever play. Several times he made in-roads, but was generally checked in time by the heavy odds against him. The Queen's Park however, were undoubtedly having the best of it – and, indeed, it was not to be wondered at, considering everything. The 3d back play, however, was capital, until Christie, having the ball passed to him, found an opening and headed through. From the kick-off it took all that the home backs could do to stave off the assaults mad on their fortress. Sommerville now showed up, sending in a beautiful low shot right into Collie's hands. A minute later he repeated the performance, this time with effect. Further on he scored again from a quick low shot, raising the total to three. Though in the minority the Volunteers were showing good defence, and occasionally attempted a run; but Watson and Arnott were too much for them. Hamilton, Lambie, and Harrower were exhibiting really fine play considering the ground. In several of their attempts to score they were all but successful. Christie required a lot of watching, and by his expertness proved very dangerous when near goal. From this up till half-time, with the exception of an occasional breakaway, operations were confined to the Volunteers' quarters. No further scoring, however, took place, the game standing – Queen's Park, three; 3d Lanark, none. The teams adjourned to the pavilion for shelter, and it was there seriously debated whether the match should be proceeded with, as both teams were benumbed with cold, and the snow was still falling fast. Indeed, several of the Volunteers were so knocked up that restoratives had to be applied, and rather than face up with a diminished team they decided not to go out. The Queen's Park, on the other hand, though not inclined to resume in such boisterous and disagreeable weather, were evidently anxious to finish off the match. The referee was appealed to repeatedly, and a long and spirited wrangle, in which high feeling was manifested on both sides, ended in the Queen's Park turning out in the field and kicking a goal. The spectators were much disappointed, and exhibited their wrath against the Volunteers in various ways. The protest of the 3d L.R.V. will be considered at a meeting of the Scottish Football Association this week. The tie will in all likelihood be played over again, as there must have been some misunderstanding in playing off the match on such a miserable day.

Ref 1885034

21ˢᵗ *January 1886*
Committee Meeting   Protest against Queen's Park
The protest lodged by the 3d Lanark R.V. against the Queen's Park was considered at a meeting of the Business Committee of the Scottish Football Association at Glasgow yesterday. The Volunteers protested on the ground that, owing to the snowstorm in which the match was played, several of their men were so benumbed with cold that they could not continue the game after half-time. The committee, after hearing the statements of both sides, decided to dismiss the protest. The Queen's Park therefore now play against either the Hibernians or Renton, who meet in the semi-final tie to-morrow. The Cambuslang also protested against the result of their tie with the Hibernians on the ground - first, that one of the goals should not have been allowed; and, secondly, that the match was not played on the day appointed. The committee also dismissed this protest as it was considered frivolous.

Ref 1885035

6ᵗʰ *February 1886*
Friendly   Rangers 2-10 Airdrieonians
Played at Kinning Park in presence of a large number of spectators. The ground was in wretched condition, being covered with at least two inches of snow. This probably gave the country team some advantage, but it does not account for the crushing defeat – ten goals to two – which the Rangers received.

Ref 1885036

1886
Miscellaneous   **Protests**
A protest cost 10 shillings. In cases where it was upheld, the money was returned else it was forfeited.
*Ref 1886001**

24-August 1886
Miscellaneous   **Membership Subscriptions**
S.F.A.C.M. The following clubs were struck off the roll for non-payment of subscription:- Cambridge, Dennistoun Athletic, Eastern, Granton, Pilgrims, Shawlands, 10th L.R.V., Mearns Athletic, Greenock Northern, Paisley Hibernians, Southern, Mauchline, Albion, Helensburgh, Levendale, Rock, Glencairn, Dykehead, West Benhar, Central, Angus, West End, Aberfeldy Breadalbane, Vale of Teith, Bon Accord, and Aberdeen Rovers. The following new clubs were admitted into the association :- Govan Athletic, Carrick, Blairvaddick, Kilbirnie, Kirkintilloch Harp, Duntocher, Vale of Leven Hibernians, Kirkintilloch Central, Mossend Swifts, Durhamtown Rangers, Broxburn Thistle, Airdriehill, Carfin Shamrock, Our Boys (Blairgowrie), Fair City Athletics, Erin Rovers, Caledonian Rangers, St Johnstone, Lochwinnoch, Orion (Aberdeen), Johnstone Harp, Pollockshaws, Slamannan, Vale of Bannock, Laurieston, Dundee Wanderers, Lindertis, Nithsdale and Vale of Annan, Armadale, Bellstane Birds, Burntisland Thistle. The Perthshire Association was also admitted.
Ref 1886002

Footnote
Consequent to their heavy defeats in the First Round of the Cup competition the previous season, neither Bon Accord nor Rovers payed their Association membership subscriptions. Both teams were still in existence as indicated below by their engagement in a season opening friendly.

11th September 1886
Friendly   **Rovers (Aberdeen) v Bon Accord**
The Rovers played their first match for the season with the Bon Accord on Saturday afternoon on the Links. The match ended in favour of the Rovers.
Ref 1886003

11th September 1886
First Round   **Aberdeen v East End**
The former telegraphed to Dundee early on Saturday forenoon to the effect that they had scratched to the East End.
Ref 1886004

11th September 1886
First Round   **Dundee Wanderers 2-7 Broughty**

This cup-tie, despite the rain, was played in Morgan Park. The attendance of spectators was thin at the start, but as the match went on a stream flowed in from West Craigie and by half-time the ground was well filled. A start was made by the home club kicking off, and although they had a strong south-westerly wind and the heavy rain rather against them, they kept the ball for some time in hostile lines. When about five minutes had elapsed, however, the Forthill team pulled themselves together, and playing with dash and determination made a rapid raid into the Wanderers' territory. Ovenstone repelled a deadly shot from the left, but the ball was promptly returned, and Graham sent it through amid cheers. At once returning, the Broughty sent the ball behind from a corner, but five minutes later a second goal was secured by Rae. After another fruitless corner to the Broughty, the Wanderers made a desperate effort to recover their leeway, but Evans fouled the ball, and the visitors making a fresh charge, carried the ground club's position a third time, Reid being the scorer on this occasion. The Wanderers alleged that the Broughty had claimed a hand off M'Mahon just before the leather was goaled, but the referee (Wynd, late West End), dismissed their plea. Enraged by these repeated reverses, the Wanderers made a dash on the west goal, and had a corner, but at the kick-off the Forthill fronts seized the sphere, and by some clever passing Graham again pierced the home armour, a fourth goal being thus hoisted for the visitors, amid hearty cheers. A hard attempt to retaliate was foiled for the time being by Lorimer, but the Morgan Park eleven promptly paid him another visit, and Milne getting the ball from Duncan, registered the first point for the home team just before half-time. By the time the second period was begun the wind had freshened considerably, and had veered more to the west - rain having gone off - and the partisans of the ground club anticipated that their pets would still pull the match out of the fire. The period was begun with a threatening incursion into Broughty ground, but the defence was superior to the attack, Elliot and Edmonds shining frequently; and a return visit was quickly paid to the home goal, which, after a corner, fell for the fifth time to a good shot by Reid. Again four goals to the bad, the Wanderers put forth all their strength, and forced their opponents to act on the defensive, but they were unable to get the leather through. When about ten minutes had expired the Broughty made a run west, during which the Wanderers claimed a foul, and before the referee (Wynd, late West End) blew his whistle Stewart picked up the ball. This led to an angry altercation with the referee, who had had several of his previous decisions questioned both by the Wanderers and a section of the crowd, and he now threw the whistle from him, and left the field. Ten minutes of a squabble followed, and then Christie (of the Forfar Athletic) having been induced to stand as referee, the match was resumed. After some further aggressive play on the part of the ground club, Duncan utilised an easy chance, and the score now stood two to five goals against the Wanderers. The Morgan Park men still kept up the pressure, but the play of their forwards in front of goal was very slack, and their shooting most erratic, which contrasted unfavourably with the brilliant defence of the whole back division of the Broughty. Henry managed once to send the ball past Lorimer [Broughty], but "offside" was given. Three minutes from the close the Broughty fronts made a splendid spurt, and amid enthusiastic cheers added two goals to their total, one being worked through from a corner, and thus won by seven goals to two. The result was wholly unexpected, but the Broughty fully deserved their victory. Their forward play in the first half and their defence in the second were

quite beyond the power of their opponents, only two or three of whom showed anything like form. Edmonds and Elliot, in particular, played a magnificent game all through. The contest at times was coarse and brutal. For instance, one of the Broughty had his nose deliberately struck and bled, while another was given a vicious kick on the side of the stomach, the ball at the time being some distance off. Teams:- Wanderers - Goal, Ovenstone; backs, M'Mahon and M'Intosh; half-backs, Langlands, Petrie, and Stewart; forwards, Henry, Evans, Millan, Guillan, and Duncan. Broughty - Goal, Lorimer; backs, Fleming and Elliot; half-backs, Forbes, Munro, and Edmunds; forwards, Anderson, Rae, Graham, Dargie, and Reid.
Ref 1886004

11th September 1886
First Round　　　　　　　**Port Glasgow Athletic 10-1 Johnstone Harp**
These teams met on Saturday afternoon at Clune Park, Port-Glasgow, in the first round of the Scottish Association Cup tie, the weather being very unfavourable for playing. The Athletics kicked off, and ten minutes from the start one of the centre forwards of the Johnstone team passed the ball to the right wing, and a smart low shot scored the first goal. The ball being again put into play, the Athletics at once assumed the aggressive in a very demonstrative manner. Brown, with a dashing run, carried the ball right up the field, and ran it between the posts. A minute or two later Cogan scored a second goal for the Athletics, and soon afterwards a third. Before half-time was reached Brown put on another goal for the home team. Johnstone kicked off in the second half, and made straight away for goal, but were intercepted, when Brown got well on to the ball, carried it along the wing, when he passed to the centre, and Neill scored for the Athletics. Neill a few minutes later took another goal. From this to the close the game was entirely in the hands of the home team, who added other four goals to their score, the game thus ending in victory for the Athletics by 10 goals to 1.
Ref 1886006

11th September 1886
First Round　　　　　　　**Arbroath 20-0 Orion**
Rain had fallen incessantly for five hours before the start of the game, and Gayfield Park was in a deplorable state. The match, though played in a downpour of rain, was witnessed by fully 500 spectators. The Aberdeen men had the advantage of the wind during the first period, but were unable to make such progress against their far more experienced opponents, the score at half-time standing 6 to 0 in favour of the home club. With the wind, and the heavy ground beginning to tell on the staying powers of the Orionians, the Arbroath were soon "piling it on," and ere the close of hostilities the rather large total of 20 goals stood against the "Granite City" men. The Orion is composed of men of fine physique, possessing considerable speed and a fair knowledge of the Association code, and with practice should develop into a good team. It is confidently expected that the Arbroath, to foster the game in the north, will give the Orion a visit before the end of the present season.
Ref 1886007
Footnote
Arbroath visited Orion on 9th April 1887 and won by 9 goals to 3.

11th September 1886
First Round   **Tollcross 0-3 Royal Albert**
S.F.A.C.M. [21st Sep]. Tollcross awarded tie against Royal Albert for non-registered player.
*Ref 1886008**

11th September 1886
First Round   **Pollockshields Athletic 2-1 St Andrew's (Pollockshields)**
S.F.A.C.M. [21st Sep]. Consequent upon the Pollockshields Athletics' ground not being properly chalked off when they played their tie with the St Andrews, the Committee decided that the match should played over again on Saturday first on the St Andrews field.
Ref 1886009

11th September 1886
First Round   **Dumbarton Athletic 8a0 Duntocher**
Played at Burnside, Dumbarton. The home team kicked off against the wind, and settling fairly down to work put on three goals before the change of ends. In the second half the Athletic men continued to keep the game in their own hands, and added goal after goal till 15 minutes from the close, when the Duntocher gave it up, and owned beaten, the score standing - Athletic, 8 goals; Duntocher, nil.
*Ref 1886010**

11th September 1886
First Round   **Vale of Leven Wanderers 6-3 Jamestown**
Played at Alexandria amid great excitement, the teams being well matched. At half-time each had registered two goals. In the second half the Wanderers showed more staying power, and at the close defeated Jamestown by 6 to 3.
Ref 1886006

S.F.A.C.M. [21st Sep]. The Jamestown protested against Vale of Leven Wanderers because one of the team, John Cummings, was a non-registered player. The Committee disqualified the Vale of Leven Wanderers and awarded the match to Jamestown.
Ref 1886009

11th September 1886
First Round   **Oban v Our Boys (Blairgowrie)**
S.F.A.C.M. [21st Sep]. Mr Christie said the Blairgowrie Our Boys were obliged to scratch to the Oban club, and he considered it was a hardship to the Our Boys, who could not travel to Oban and back in one day. He held that Our Boys should be placed in the Stirlingshire. The Committee decided to give the matter consideration at the annual meeting.
Ref 1886009

11th September 1886
First Round   **Greenock Rangers 3-4 1st Renfrewshire R.V.**
S.F.A.C.M. [21st Sep]. Greenock Rangers protested against the 1st RRV that two of the latter's players were not registered, and the Committee decided in favour of the Greenock Rangers.
Ref 1886009

11th September 1886
First Round   **Maybole v Lugar Boswell**
Match postponed owing to Maybole FC sports day which was cancelled due to inclement weather and rearranged for the following week come rain or shine. As a result Lugar Boswell were given a walkover.
*Ref 1886015**

11th September 1886
First Round   **St Mirren v Arthurlie**
These teams should have played their Scottish tie on the ground of the former on Saturday, but instead of doing so they engaged in a friendly game, and the St Mirren won by 3 goals to none. It appears that owing to the bad weather on Saturday morning the cup tie had been put off, and had been taken on again. Though there was some doubt as to whether the tie was to be played or not, both teams turned up. The Arthurlie objected to play the cup tie but were willing to play a friendly game; whilst the St Mirren insisted that the cup tie should be played. The Barrhead men, however, would play a friendly game only, and the St Mirren claimed the cup tie. After which both teams engaged in a friendly match.
Ref 1886006

18th September 1886
First Round   **St Mirren 5-3 Arthurlie**
Played on the ground of the former at Westmarch, Paisley, and a hard and exciting game ended in favour of the St Mirren by 5 goals to 3.
Ref 1886017

21st September 1886
Miscellaneous   **Second Round Draw**
S.F.A.C.M. The Dykehead were admitted into the Association, and to be allowed to take part in this season's ties.
Ref 1886009

2nd October 1886
Second Round   **Mossend Swifts 1-1 Hibernian**
Played at West Calder where the Mossend Swifts had only suffered one home defeat in 8 years.
*Ref 1886019**

2nd October 1886
Second Round **Newcastleton 1-5 Armadale**
The Armadale managed to dispose of the Newcastleton in the Scottish Cup to the tune of five goals to one. The forenoon was very wet, but cleared up at 1.45, the time fixed for kicking off. Armadale appeared promptly on the field, but only seven of the local team turned out. Mr M'Fadden, of the Hibernians, who acted as referee, did not allow the game to proceed until ten of the local team were on the field, the eleventh man turning up five minutes after kick-off. Newcastleton played up pluckily at first, but were far too light for the West Country men, who won as stated by five goals to one.
*Ref 1886020**

2nd October 1886
Second Round **Q.O.S. Wanderers 12-2 Vale of Nith**
.. resulted in favour of Wanderers by twelve goals to two. The Vale played one hour and a quarter with ten men, one of the men having been severely injured.
*Ref 1886021**

2nd October 1886
Second Round **Lugar Boswell 3-2 Dalry**
S.F.A.C.M. [12th Oct]. As to the protests, the first taken up was that of Dalry against Lugar Boswell on grounds which may be summarised as various. The referee, however, seemed to have been the chief delinquent. After some delicate questions had been put to that gentleman, and both umpires had been examined, the Committee upheld the protest by 11 votes to 9, and ordered the match to be played over again on the ground of the Lugar, the referee being held to be incompetent.
Ref 1886022

2nd October 1886
Second Round **Airdrieonians 3-2 Carfin Shamrock**
Played at Airdrie. The game was of a stubborn description, but in the end the Airdrie team won with a score of 3 goals to 2.
Ref 1886023

It seems the Airdrieonians are likely to be thrown out of the Scottish competition through having played a non-registered man, or one who had not been registered in full time. Sharp is the player's name. He was a Clyde player, but, for reasons best known to himself, left that club and joined Airdrieonians. This only occurred three weeks or so ago. It will stand hard with the Airdrieonians unless they can prove that Sharp was registered a month before the match was played
Ref 1886024
S.F.A.C.M. [12th Oct]. The Airdrieonians, who defeated the Carfin Shamrock, were disqualified on account of Sharp, of the Airdrieonians, not having been registered in time. The Committee decided that Sharp cannot play this season for any other club.
Ref 1886022

Shamrock reinstated.
Ref 1886026

The Carfin Shamrock have secured a bye in the third round of the Scottish, and mean to do the business. Of course Carfin is part of Motherwell and we are highly pleased to have a "Motherwell" club figuring among the cracks. I have heard that the Airdrieonians offered the Shamrock £15 to withdraw their protest but the "boys" refused the bribe with scorn. They thought the Scottish Cup and badge better than money. Go it Shamrock!
Ref 1886027

23rd October 1886
Third Round   Dumbarton v Tollcross
The Tollcross arrived minus three of their team, a scratch in favour of Dumbarton. Not to disappoint the spectators, the ground club supplied them with three substitutes. In the first half Dumbarton scored four times, the ball never going over Dumbarton's lines at all. Tollcross were the first to score in the second half, but the home team managed to put on other two goals, and thus won by six goals to one.
Ref 1886028

23rd October 1886
Third Round   Rangers 0-2 Cambuslang
Played at Kinning Park, Glasgow on Saturday. Four thousand present. Rangers kicked off, but Cambuslang pressed Rangers - Gourlay, Law and Buchannan having fruitless shots. On five minutes Plunderleith scored for Cambuslang. They continued to press, the ball going everywhere but through. Chalmers saved repeatedly. The Rangers made a short-lived attack, nothing resulting. Gourlay scored a second goal for Cambuslang - time, 33 minutes. Cambuslang scored a third goal, which was disallowed. Half-time result:- Cambuslang, 2; Rangers, 0. In the second period the game was very hard and exciting; the Rangers having improved in their play. Both goalkeepers were frequently called upon to clear their goals. After half an hour Cambuslang almost scored. A desperate struggle ensued. Heggie shortly afterwards nearly scored for the Rangers, Dunn saved grandly. Play was now even and rather rough, neither side scoring further. The match thus ended - Cambuslang, 2; Rangers , 0; The result created some surprise.
*Ref 1886029**

28th October 1886
Third Round Replay   Dunblane v East End
The East End were to have gone to Dunblane to settle the undecided question with the local Club there, but as it is impossible for the East End to get up anything like a team, the [East End] Committee have decided to scratch, so that Dunblane will go into the hat at the next drawing. Neither Spalding, Langlands, M'Laren, Ferguson, nor M'Intyre could get away, and perhaps it was just as wise to scratch as to contest the tie with a team so weakened.
Ref 1886030

4th December 1886
Fifth Round   **Harp (Dundee) v Dumbarton**
These clubs faced each other at East Dock Street in the fifth round of the Scottish Cup ties. The large crowd which assembled were rewarded by witnessing as hard and exciting a game as has been played on Dock Street this season. ... Towards the finish of the game, the Dumbarton infused increased vigour into their play, and had fully the best of the game, but no further scoring took place, and the referee's whistle shortly thereafter blew the call of time, when the scores stood drawn - two goals each.

"Onlooker" writes, with reference to last Saturday's Harp v Dumbarton game, that "at last the cat is out of the bag, and that the public now definitely know what many before suspected. It only remains to be seen whether the Dumbarton was aware that the match was advertised as a Cup-tie, and I think the Executive of the famous Western club should take the earliest opportunity of disclaiming all knowledge of such discreditable tactics. The Harp bungled the farce by not allowing the Dumbarton to win, but their object for this was the prospect of another big gate ... In conclusion I would ask the Harp's Executive what explanation have they to give to the public?"

"Honesty" has also a letter on the same subject. He writes - "If last Saturday's match was not a Cup-tie, then someone was guilty of fraud, and all the money drawn was got on false pretences, and the offender or offenders are liable to criminal proceedings."

"St Crispin," in the Dumbarton Herald, says:- The Harp conceived it better to scratch to our local cracks than undertake a journey to the Royal Burgh and sustain a certain defeat. While making this known to Dumbarton, the Harp authorities requested the "Sons of the Rock" to visit Juteopolis, and engage in a friendly game, and this accounts for the appearance of Dumbarton at East Dock Street. For financial reasons the Harp, however, thought fit to advertise the match as a Scottish Cup tie. I am glad the Dumbarton team are entirely free of blame.
Ref 1886031

8th January 1887
Sixth Round Replay   **Dumbarton 1-2 Hurlford**
Despite the very unfavourable weather conditions, these two crack clubs met on Boghead on Saturday to play off their undecided Scottish cup tie. Great interest was attached to this game, not only on account of the high standing of both clubs, but principally because the match would determine which would secure a place in the semi-final with the Queen's Park, which is to be played on Saturday first at Hampden Park Glasgow. The two clubs seem fated to meet each other in bad weather. It will be remembered that Hurlford on the 25th ult., the ground was in a fearful state, and Dumbarton then protested at the start on the condition of the field, but the game ending in a draw made the protest unnecessary. Owing to the heavy fall of snow last week, Boghead was very bad, notwithstanding that a number of the unemployed workman of Dumbarton had been engaged on Friday and Saturday carting the snow off the field. Dumbarton informed Hurlford of the unfit state of their field, but they determined to come and play, foul or fair weather. The ground was as hard as iron, and very slippery. Before commencing the game, Dumbarton lodged a protest with the referee on account of the unsuitableness of the ground. Dumbarton lost the toss, and M'Millan started the game. The ball was momentarily in the Dumbarton ground, but the home team at once took matters into their own hands, and commenced a hot and prolonged attack on the

Hurlford goal. First Robertson and Brown would canter up the field with the ball, but when it came to goal it either was headed away or else shot narrowly over the top. Madden then tried his little best, and nearly gained his point on several occasions, but through it would not go. Then the left wing would have a go at it, and this continued for fully thirty minutes, when Madden once more got on the ball, but not being in position to score himself, wisely entrusted the shot to Robertson, who scored a neat goal for Dumbarton. Hurlford were alive to their interests, however, and in a short space of time a determined rush for M'Aulay. Here a struggle ensued, and in the melee the ball was rushed though, and the game equalised. Half-time arrived without further scoring. Dumbarton on re-starting again, took the game in hand and started to press their opponents, but were very unlucky at goal. Shoot as they liked it could not be got through. W. Kerr, after ten minutes of the second half had gone, got injured, and had to retire, and Dumbarton were forced to continue the struggle minus one of their left wing forwards, which was a serious loss. Just after this Hurlford again came away with a dash, and with an open goal M'Knight had no difficulty in evading M'Aulay. This was their last chance, as Dumbarton continued to press them until the close of the game, but nothing but hard lines fell to their lot. No further scoring took place, and Hurlford were hailed the victors - but under protest - by two goals to one.
Ref 1886032

S.F.A.C.M. [11th Jan]. Yesterday afternoon a special meeting of the Committee of the Scottish Football Association was held in their rooms, 53 Waterloo Street, Mr Browne, the president, occupied the chair. The meeting was called to consider the protest made by Dumbarton against Hurlford, in their tie for the Scottish Cup. It will be remembered that when the clubs first met at Hurlford, the result was a draw - no goals being scored. Last Saturday the teams met at Dumbarton, when the match ended in a win for the Hurlford by 2 goals to 1. Dumbarton, however, protested on the ground that the field was in bad condition for play. This afternoon evidence was led pro and con before the committee. At the close the committee unanimously decided that the match be played over again at Dumbarton on Saturday first, and that in the event of a draw an extra half-hour be played.
Ref 1886033

10th May 1887
S.F.A.C.M.   **Cup Competition Rule Change**
On the motion of Mr Currie, of the Vale of Leven, it was agreed, in regard to the cup competition rules, that after the fourth round clubs drawing twice must play an extra half-hour on second day in order to finish the tie, and on neutral ground selected by the committee.
Ref 1886034

27th August 1887

First Round   Port Glasgow Athletic 11-0 Rangers (Greenock)

The first round of the Association cup ties was played on Saturday afternoon by these clubs at Clune Park, the number of spectators being very limited. The weather was too hot for football. From first to last the game was of a very one-sided nature. The Rangers being completely over-matched. Before the call of time in the first half the home team had secured six goals, while their opponents had failed to find an opening. In the second half the strangers, who showed a considerable lack of training, commenced to play with greater determination, Campbell at goal doing some excellent work. For some time he managed to keep out a lot of well-directed shots but about 15 minutes after play had been resumed, M'Millan took a seventh goal for the Athletic, Neill shortly afterwards put on another. M'Millan recorded a ninth, and also a tenth, and M'Laren finally put on an eleventh. A very one-sided game thus terminated in favour of Port-Glasgow by 11 goals to 0.

Ref 1887001

3rd September 1887

First Round   Hurlford v Annbank

The Annbank telegraphed at the hour of starting that they could not muster a team. Hurlford therefore claimed the game.

Ref 1887002

3rd September 1887

First Round   Ayr v Monkcastle

A report spreading that Allan and Auld (Third Lanark) were to play for the Monkcastle, and that the team was to be otherwise strengthened, led many to believe that the game would be a close one, especially as several of the Ayr first eleven were not expected to take part. No less than five second eleven had to take the field for Ayr, whose team was as follows:- Dunbar; Donnachie and M'Quinton; Dickie, Anderson, and Graham; Jack and Millar, Campbell, Ross, and Cunningham. In all cases the subs played well, and left scarcely anything to be desired. In the first half it appeared as if the strangers were about equal to holding their own, and some fast play was observable on both sides. The ball had scarcely been in motion a second until Allan found himself the centre of attraction, but Dickie rather took the shine out of him, and amidst ironical cheering the ball was driven well into the strangers' territory. In an almost incredible short space of time the fortress succumbed to the united onslaught of Miller and Campbell. Play was after this transferred to the other end, where a high shot eluded Dunbar. The equalising of the game was followed by, the usual mountebank performance of "Jay" & Co. That was the only time an opportunity afforded itself for such a display. The game after this was rendered unpleasant by a heavy fall of rain, and play fell off considerably. The referee had occasion during this half to stop the game and caution Campbell for rough play. The first half ended in favour of Ayr by 2 goals to 1. In the second half the strangers were seldom dangerous, and the home team managed to put together 4 points more, thus giving them the game by six goals to one. Seldom have we witnessed so many wounded as we did on Saturday. Donnachie was the first to go down, the result of an accident. Cunningham also suffered, but from the fact of his wound being evidently intentionally given, the crowd was somewhat loud in its sympathies. One of the strangers also got hurt, but the ways of Ayr folk are difficult to understand, and the manner in which his misfortune was received was scarcely sympathetic. It was not generally known that Monkcastle had scratched.

Smart practice by the Kilwinning boys wasn't it? They are drawn against Ayr, a rumour is spread that Allan is to play for them. People are led to believe that Allan is going to give up all offers to play for Glasgow clubs in Scottish cup ties, and pin his faith to the club of his native town, and that this club must be wonderfully improved when he takes such a course. The club arrives, there was a good gate, and there are few who imagine it is anything but a cup tie. They scratch before starting, however. Ayr consequently could not get on another fixture, and there was nothing for it but to have a friendly game with Monkcastle, or hand back the cash. It was a capital move, and left Allan and Auld free to play for other clubs.

I was glad to see the referee stop the game and caution the players on Saturday. It was what should be done oftener. I, however, did not see why Campbell was picked out; he appeared no worse than his opponent.

*Ref 1887003**

3rd September 1887
First Round   **Plains v Tollcross**
Tollcross failed to raise a team.
Ref 1887002

3rd September 1887
First Round   **Burntisland Thistle 4-2 Dunfermline Athletic**
S.F.A.C.M. [13th Sep]. Burntisland were disqualified on account of non-registration of players.
Ref 1887004

3rd September 1887
First Round   **Arbroath 18-0 Orion**
Played at Gayfield - the maroons commenced hostilities and a minute from the start forced a corner, from which they ultimately scored. Soon afterwards they again pressed, and added another point, S. Bouick heading the ball through. The Orion had a look in, but failed to break through the defence. Forcing the ball up the field the maroons again scored, S. Bouick doing the needful with a beautiful head shot. The Orion secured a corner, but sent the ball behind. Immediately afterwards their goalkeeper was called upon to negotiate a hard shot from J. Bouick, and succeeding in saving his charge in fine style. Arbroath made another attack on the Aberdeen goal, but the defence of the strangers proved equal to the emergency, the goalkeeper and right back distinguishing themselves. The maroons afterwards made a combined rush goalwards, when after smart play, Milne scored a beauty, which was followed immediately afterwards by another from the foot of Crawford. Doig was called out soon afterwards, and saved at the expense of a corner. Play continued in the strangers' territory and two goals fell to the Arbroath in rapid succession. Score at half-time stood 7-0. Arbroath now had the sun and wind in their favour, and put the ball through immediately after the start, but the point was ruled

off-side. After repeated attempts at goal, which were smartly warded off the goalkeeper, Penney found an opening, and scored the eighth point, the ninth following shortly afterwards from the foot of S. Bouick. Double figures were registered shortly afterwards by Collie from a free kick in front of goal and point 11 followed by Crawford. Goals followed in rapid succession and at the close the score stood 18-0. For the Orion Diack the goalkeeper, and Fettes the right back played a fine game. Arbroath played a good, though somewhat free-and-easy game.
*Ref 1887005**

3rd September 1887
First Round   **Vale of Leven v Kirkintilloch Harp**
Kirkintilloch Harp turned up in Alexandria to play Vale of Leven with only 7 players. Harp therefore agreed to scratch and played a friendly with 4 Vale men in their side. Vale won 9-2.
*Ref 1887006**

3rd September 1887
First Round   **Lindertis 1-2 Harp (Dundee)**
These teams met at Knowhead, Kirriemuir on Saturday afternoon in the first round of the Scottish Cup ties. There was a large turnout of spectators, a strong contingent being from Forfar. The Harp kicked off with the ground slope in their favour, and for a minute or two the ball was kept in home territory. The Kirriemarians then relieved themselves, and for a while confined the play to the neighbourhood of the Harp goal. Runs and counter runs followed, and then the green jerseys bore down on their opponent's goal, and kept the ball in dangerous proximity to the uprights until, from a fine kick by O'Kane, it was headed through by Mooney. For the remainder of the first half the play was rather uninteresting, but the Kirrie players held their own with their opponents. The Harp began well in the latter period, and soon added a second point. Murray giving the ball the necessary lift. The home team fell away for a little, and the Harp continued to press for some time. The play then assumed a more equal character, and towards the close of the game the Lindertis put on a spurt, and gave their opponents some trouble at their goal mouth. A minute or two before the call of time they secured a throw-in near the corner and the ball, touching one of the Dundee players, passed between the uprights. No further scoring took place, so the match ended - Harp, 2; Lindertis, 1.
Ref 1887007

S.F.A.C.M. [13th Sep]. Dundee Harp failed to register a man named [John] Mooney, and were disqualified.
Ref 1887008

3rd September 1887
First Round   **Grahamston 4-3 Redding Athletic**
S.F.A.C.M. [13th Sep]. Grahamston were disqualified on account of non-registration of players.
Ref 1887004

3rd September 1887
First Round　　　　　　**Broxburn Shamrock 0-4 Mossend Swifts**
S.F.A.C.M. [13th Sep]. Mossend Swifts were disqualified on account of non-registration of players.
Ref 1887004

3rd September 1887
First Round　　　　　　**Dunfermline 3-2 Lassodie**
S.F.A.C.M. [13th Sep]. Dunfermline was disqualified as the Secretary sent in his list of players for registration several days too late.
Ref 1887008

3rd September 1887
First Round　　　　　　**3rd Lanark Rifle Volunteers 1-2 Cowlairs**
S.F.A.C.M. [13th Sep]. The 3d Lanark protested against the Cowlairs, in so far that M'Leod, M'Pherson, and Robertson of the Cowlairs had played in Nottingham during the season 1886-87, and had not been reinstated into the Scottish Association before assisting the Cowlairs against the 3d Lanark. The 3d Lanark also protested against Calderwood on the ground of professionalism.

Mr Crerar, the 3d Lanark representative, held that as M'Leod and Robertson only returned from England ten days before the day in question they were under the jurisdiction of the English Association. He produced several letters from the Everton Football Club, which bore that the secretary of that Club had advertised in Scotch newspapers pledging itself to find the players employment. Calderwood answered the advertisement, and signed an agreement, at the instance of the Bootle secretary, to the following effect:- "I hereby agree to accept a situation from Mr Sim Jones for the next seven months at a rate of 27s per week."

The Chairman here mentioned that Mr Sim Jones was an enthusiastic football supporter of the Bootle Club.

Mr Crerar, proceeding with his evidence, read a letter from the Bootle F.C., which stated that Calderwood answered the advertisement appearing in the Scotch newspapers, and expressed the wish to go to Liverpool. He arrived at Liverpool, and the Bootle Club found him a situation. He kept this situation for only a few days, and agreed to return to Glasgow for his wife and family, requiring at the same time £5 to defray his expenses to Glasgow, and also to convey his wife, family, and himself to Liverpool. He never returned to Liverpool.

Mr Crerar further stated that he was led to believe that before leaving Liverpool Calderwood telegraphed to the Cowlairs Club that he would come back to Scotland if they sent him his railway fare, amounting to 15s. Mr Crerar emphatically said the Cowlairs had sent a Post Office order for that amount to Calderwood.

Mr Park, Lanarkshire, submitted that the Cowlairs Club, by sending an order for 15s, had infringed the rules regarding professionalism.

Mr Henderson, the Cowlairs' representative, being called into the meeting, said M'Leod played for Notts Forest against the Glasgow Rangers in Glasgow last April, but since then he had not played a single match for that club. M'Leod and Robertson played for a junior Club in Nottingham, that club not being in the English Association. That club certainly played for a cup, but the trophy had been presented by a newspaper. Mr Henderson admitted that Robertson and M'Leod were presently out of employment.

Mr Herd, secretary of the Bootle Club, deponed that Calderwood answered his advertisement for football players. Bootle was partly an amateur and partly a professional club.

Mr Currie, Vale of Leven, asked whether Calderwood would have been engaged if he could not play football?

Mr Herd - Certainly not.

At this stage Mr Crerar entered the room, and said that there was a very large hostile crowd outside, and he asked, for the safety of the witnesses, that policemen should be sent for. Several persons had jostled himself, and, in fact, no one could leave the building owing to the threats of those outside.

Messrs M'Leod, Robertson, M'Pherson, and Calderwood, were all cross-examined, the decision being that the charge against M'Leod, Robertson, and M'Pherson should be dismissed, but the Committee, after a long discussion, came to the decision that Calderwood was guilty of professionalism, and should therefore be suspended for two years. It was also unanimously carried that the 3d Lanark and Cowlairs should replay their tie on Saturday at Cathkin Park. The result was received outside with loud booing.
Ref 1887008

The SFA meeting closed at midnight after a sederunt of 5 hours.
Ref 1887013

3rd September 1887
First Round   **Aberdeen 4-9 Our Boys (Dundee)**
S.F.A.C.M. [13th Sep]. Our Boys' secretary having sent in the names for registration, the Christian names being wrong, the club was allowed to pass into the second round, as there had only been a mistake in the initials.
Ref 1887014

3rd September 1887
First Round   **Jamestown 3-2 Vale of Leven Hibernian**
At Jamestown, and was the hardest of all ties which took place in the Vale of Leven. After ten minutes play, the Hibernians sent the ball through. It was not until ten minutes from half time that M'Coll, for Jamestown, equalised from a judicious long shot. In the second half M'Coll again sent in a good shot. M'Millan added a third goal for Jamestown, and from a kick off one of the ground club the Hibernians secured a second goal. A hard game ended - Jamestown, 3 goals; Vale of Leven Hibernians, 2. The strangers have protested on the ground of rough play.
Ref 1887015

S.F.A.C.M. [13th Sep]. The Vale of Leven Hibs. protested against the Jamestown on the ground of rough play, the protest stating that the Hibs. had been treated more like beasts than human beings, one player having a wound seven inches long inflicted on his stomach. On the motion of Mr M'Fadden, Edinburgh Hibs., the tie was ordered to be replayed on Saturday at Alexandria. Hendry, the offending Jamestown player, was censured.

Ref 1887008

17ᵗʰ September 1887
First Round Replay   Vale of Leven Hibernian 2-2 Jamestown
Played at Alexandria. This was an undecided tie which, owing to rough play on the part of the Jamestown, the association decided should be replayed. There was a large crowd of spectators, and great excitement prevailed. The Hibs, set the ball in motion, and quickly besieged the Jamestown goal, securing two corners within a few minutes, but they were badly managed. Collins, one of the Jamestown backs, relieved the pressure, and sent the ball on to the forwards, but Munro kicked over the bar, and lost a fine chance. Again the Hibs. pressed Jamestown, but wild shooting in front of goal showed great want of judgment, at mid-field a hand was given against the Hibs., and the ball entrusted to Collins, who landed a beauty at the goal mouth, but the forwards were again unequal to the occasion. At half-time the game remained intact, no goals being registered. The second half was more exciting, but it was well on before the Hibs., relieved the monotony by securing the first point. A bit of fine play on the part of Jamestown forwards resulted in Munro equalising the game. Another goal was secured by Jamestown soon after, but during the last minutes of the game the Hibs., with great dash equalised, and the result stood 2 goals each.
Ref 1887019

24ᵗʰ September 1887
First Round 2ⁿᵈ Replay   Jamestown 3-1 Vale of Leven Hibernian
These teams met for the third time to decide their tie in the first round of the S.A. drawings. The game ended - Jamestown, 3; Vale of Leven Hibernians, 1. On Saturday evening, between 9 and 10 o'clock, while Mr Daniel Turner of Levenbank Terrace, Jamestown, who had acted as umpire for Jamestown in the cup tie between that team and the Vale of Leven Hibernian, was returning home from Alexandria Station, whether he had been escorting the referee at the match he was on the Jamestown Road set upon by two of the "Hibs" team, who struck him on the face, knocked him down, and brutally kicked him. Both eyes were quite closed, and from one side of the head to the other he was bruised. Dr M'Lelland attended Mr Turner yesterday (Sunday). The case is in the hands of the police.
Ref 1887020

In connection with the Cup tie which was played at Jamestown between the Jamestown and Vale of Leven Hibernian Clubs a fortnight ago, a letter was read from Mr Turner, the referee, who officiated at the match, in which he described the game as a brutal and uncivilised display of football; and mentioned that he had occasion to check two members of the Vale of Leven Hibernian team for rough play. The game, in his opinion, had more the appearance of a melee than a tie. He also accused the umpire of the "Hibs," with encouraging the players in ungentlemanly conduct instead of assisting him. He reported the two Hibernian players - Cannon and Conner - to the association. After discussion it was agreed to suspend Cannon and Conner for two months. M'Dowd was also suspended from acting as umpire during the remainder of the season.
Ref 1887021

13th September 1887
Miscellaneous   **Disqualifications**
S.F.A.C.M. The following clubs were disqualified on account of registration of players :- Mossend Swifts, Grahamston, Burntisland Thistle, Dunfermline, and Harp. The Pollockshields Athletic, Our Boys, and Lugar Boswell were before the meeting for the same offence, but in view of exceptional circumstances were not disqualified.
Ref 1887004

13th September 1887
Cup Drawings   **Shettleston Regional Protest**
S.F.A.C.M. A letter was read from the Shettleston protesting against being drawn in Lanarkshire, seeing their ground was within the municipal counties of Glasgow. Mr Sliman moved Mr Mackay seconded that Shettleston be reinstated seeing a mistake had been made and put in Glasgow in drawings.
Ref 1887018

24th September 1887
Second Round   **Alloa Athletic 0-1 Dunfermline Athletic**
S.F.A.C.M. [4th Oct]. Alloa Athletic protested against the Dunfermline Athletic, as one of the latter club's players had knobs on his boots, and as the player refused to take the boots off when requested. They also protested on the ground of rough play. Mr Mackay, of Northern, moved that the protest be dismissed, as the allegations had not been proved. The ten shillings were forfeited. Mr C. Campbell, of the Queen's Park, said it was very hard on players to be deprived of the use of knobs. He certainly objected to the English knobs, which were of the kind of spikes covered with leather. These knobs were very liable to do serious injury, but at the same time a small bar such as had been worn by the Dunfermline player was a great benefit to players and not dangerous. Ultimately, it was decided that bars worn should be no less than one and a half inches in length, and placed across the boot.
Ref 1887022

24th September 1887
Second Round   **Dumbarton 1-5 Vale of Leven**
When the players were leaving the field there was disgraceful melee, which cannot but be regretted by all interested in football. The players were surrounded, as is usually the case, by the people. At Boghead the situation is such as to greatly increase the crowd at the entrance and exit gates, and as the spectators leave the field there must necessarily be a great crowd at the gates and near the pavilion. During the game as we have already stated, Whitelaw, one of the Vale backs, struck a boy who had made a disagreeable observation to him. Incensed at this conduct, the crowd attacked Whitelaw, and several of the Vale players who went to his assistance were also roughly handled. The greatest excitement prevailed, and never before at Dumbarton has such a disgraceful affair been witnessed in connection with a football match. About three dozen spectators were using their hands, and some of them their walking sticks, very freely. Unfortunately, those desirous of rendering assistance, and the players in Dumbarton team were amongst those, were unable to cope with the disturbance, being on the outside of the crowd. Forbes owing to injuries on the head, was rendered unconscious for a time, and several of the

others were more or less injured. Latterly, by strenuous exertions, the players reached the pavilion. Those injured were carefully attended to and soon rallied, and were able to walk home. Several members of the committee of the Dumbarton Club were witnesses of the occurrences, but were helpless to avert it. They were, however, able to give such information to the burgh police authorities as will lead to the apprehension of the originators, and some of those who took a leading part in it. The incident in the course of the game, in which Whitelaw was the principal actor, will, it be said, be further heard. The police have arrested a blacksmith named George Burgess. He is charged with assaulting Forbes, the Vale of Leven back, and creating a disturbance.
Ref 1887020

24th September 1887
Second Round   Moffat 4-4 Q.O.S. Wanderers
In the first 10 minutes the Moffat captain (Niven) left the field with a dislocated shoulder.
*Ref 1887024**

24th September 1887
Second Round   Hurlford 9-1 Lugar Boswell
Lugar played with 10 men.
*Ref 1887025**

24th September 1887
Second Round   Renton 4-2 Dumbarton Athletic
S.F.A.C.M. [4th Oct]. A protest against Renton by the Dumbarton Athletics was next considered. The complaint was that the bars used by the Renton players were not according to the rules of the Association. The Athletics produced, amidst much laughter, a sketch of the Renton players' boots. The Chairman said that, while they admitted that the bars used by Renton were not very satisfactory, they could not move against Renton, as the Committee had only defined that night how the bars were to be placed. Mr Paul formally moved that the protest be dismissed. Agreed.
Ref 1887022

... deposit money was refunded the Athletics.
Ref 1887021

24th September 1887
Second Round   Lindertis 3-2 East End
Dundee East End protested against the Lindertis and stated the match ended 3-2 Lindertis. The referee agreed to by both teams from the Forfarshire Football Association unfortunately didn't turn up, and a gentleman who was understood to be a neutral was selected to act as referee, but as the game progressed the East End alleged that the referee Mr A Gray of Kirriemuir, cheered "with might and main" when the Lindertis scored. The East End also stated that the referee was under the influence of liquor. The other part of the protest was the field was a stubble one, and that there were no flags on the touchlines. The Lindertis admitted that there were no flags, but they said that all the rest

of East End's protest was false. Mr Gray, the referee, wrote that the field was a stubble one, that he was not drunk - (laughter) - and that he gave his decisions fair and square. As to the charge that he waved his hat when Lindertis scored, he said that he wore no hat on the day in question (laughter). The committee dismissed the protest and forfeited the 10s.
*Ref 1887028**

24th September 1887
Second Round   Redding Athletic 0-17 Camelon
CAMELON V REDDING ATHLETICS. These teams met on Saturday last on the ground of the latter before a good turnout of spectators, when a one-sided game resulted in the defeat of the Athletics by 17 goals to nil. From the kick-off Camelon had matters all their own way. W. Burns played half-back, while Dan Inglis played centre forward. The Athletics though playing a hard game, could not prevent Camelon from scoring, and at call of half-time the score stood 7 goals to nil. The Athletics started the ball for the second half, but it was soon returned, the half-backs playing a hard game, and a neat pass from J. Burns across to the right, Russell had no difficulty in scoring No. 8 three minutes from the start. Camelon still continued to press, and through a scrimmage in front of goal No. 9 was registered. Horne failed to stop a low shot from Brown, thus registering No. 10. Only once were the Athletics considered dangerous, when Maxwell and Henderson had a run down the field, the former sending the ball over the bar. From this to call of time Camelon kept up the siege in front of the goal, Brymer playing a good defence, but when the whistle sounded they had added other 7 goals, the game thus ending in an easy win for Camelon by 17 goals to nil. A. Balloch (E.S.) acted as referee.
Ref 1887029

15th October 1887
Third Round   St Bernard's v Dunfermline Athletic
The above teams should have met in the third round of the Scottish Cup tie, but for reasons best known to themselves, the Athletic scratched and invited the Saints to engage in a friendly game at Dunfermline.
St Bernard's won the friendly 2-1.
Ref 1887030

12th November 1887
Fourth Round Replay   St Mirren 2-2 Heart of Midlothian
Just as the referee was about to blow his whistle, a shot from a scrimmage again brought the teams on a level. The Hearts appealed against the goal, but the referee (Mr Kennedy, of the 3d L.R.V.) decided against them. The result of a fast, and at times very rough game was thus a draw - two goals
Ref 1887031

Heart of Midlothian unsuccessfully protested that the ball was kicked when time was up for St Mirren's second goal.
*Ref 1887032**

19th November 1887
Fourth Round 2nd Rply   Heart of Midlothian 2-2 St Mirren
At Merchiston (East Stirlingshire's Ground). Too dark to play an extra 30 minutes. St Mirren protested (unsuccessfully also) that McQueen of Hearts [half-back] fisted the ball out five times.
*Ref 1887033**

Footnote
This and similar incidents lead to the introduction of the penalty kick

---

26th November 1887
Fifth Round   Our Boys (Dundee) 4a1 Albion Rovers
At West Craigie, Dundee. Winning the toss, the strangers kicked off towards the south goal. Soon after being set in motion, the leather was brought into the Boys' territory, and a corner was given, but it was fruitless. After a run up to the north end, the leather was again brought back to the Boys' citadel, and it appeared as though the strangers were to score, but the ball went over the bar. The strangers were then pressed, and the ball was headed through by Chalmers. The Boys still continued to press for some time, but the ball ultimately went behind. The play for a while after this was pretty much of a give-and-take nature, but the Rovers ultimately got the ball into the Boys' lines. A corner was given, and the scores were equalised. In a short time after this Robertson got on the leather as the strangers were running it forward, carried it along to the north citadel and sent in a capital shot, but Hodson fisted out. The Boys sent in the leather again, but were unsuccessful in scoring. The Rovers then came south but did nothing, and the ball was again run up to the opposite end. The visitors got on to the ball again and brought it south, and this time they got a fruitless corner. The pressure having been relieved the Boys moved north, but the ball went behind. The Boys continued to press, but on centring the sphere Hodson fisted out. A fierce scrimmage ensued, and the strangers were in the act of getting away with the ball when Buttar sent the leather through, and the first half ended Our Boys, 2 goals; Albion Rovers, 1. The second portion of the game was on the whole rather tame. About a quarter of an hour from the finish Robertson collared the leather in front of his own goal and carried along the field. He passed to Moore, who sent in the ball, but the goalkeeper was equal to the occasion. Soon after this, however, Pearson managed to notch a third point for his side. Nothing further of any interest occurred until a few minutes from the finish, when a dispute arose on account of a foul which was claimed by the strangers, and which the referee refused. The men were requested to resume play, but the strangers declined. Two of the Boys then ran the ball along the field, and after centring it put it through, the referee giving them a point. The game thus ended – Our Boys, 4; Albion Rovers, 1.
Ref 1887034

4th February 1888
Final   Renton 6-1 Cambuslang
What is termed as the blue riband of Scottish Football was contested on neutral ground, Hampden Park, Glasgow. Cambuslang winning the toss, Renton kicked off, and play was open at the outset - McNee, for the Renton, getting away. Cambuslang next got a foul, but the advantage resulted in nothing. Cambuslang now, with the aid of wind

pressed, and got near the Renton goal, M'Coll relieving. Thereafter the Rentonians broke away, Semple and Jackson intervening, and Plenderleith and Gourlay taking up the running, the former was within an ace of scoring, Lindsay kicking out smartly. A brilliant attempt was then made by Renton, M'Nee and Campbell being conspicuous. In a twinkling Cambuslang forwards were sailing away for Lindsay's territory, a glaring miss by M'Kechnie aiding them in their course. Two abortive corners fell to Cambuslang, who were doing the most of the pressing. A magnificent effort was then made by Campbell on behalf of the Renton, that player running ¾ of the field, the ball, however, going over the lines. Kelly, for Renton, made an attempt to score, and soon afterwards Gourlay for Cambuslang, the efforts of both resulting in severe tussles at goal. The result of a determined onslaught by Renton was a goal in 16 minutes from the foot of M'Nee. No sooner was the ball set again in motion then M'Coll carried it up to the Cambuslang goal, the backs intervening cleverly. In a few seconds Cambuslang retaliated, and, but for a brilliant piece of goalkeeping by Lindsay, they would have scored on two occasions. Luck again saved the Renton goal. Shortly afterwards the Dumbartonshire players were busy at the Cambuslang citadel, a shot by M'Nee grazing the posts. A foul against the Renton a few yards from goal looked dangerous, Kelly eventually saving. Half-time was wearing on, and Renton pressed. They had three successive corners, and M'Callum smartly notched the second point for Renton seven minutes from the crossing over. On half time sounding, Cambuslang scored, amongst cheers. The first half thus ended - Renton 2; Cambuslang 1. Renton had the wind in the second period, and immediately on restarting M'Coll scored a third goal. Thereafter Cambuslang made a raid. Kelly, however, got possession of the leather, and Dunn's goal was soon in danger. From a throw-in the ball was put into Lindsay's hands, and though five Cambuslang forwards were instantly on him he saved amid loud cheers. The wind now told against Cambuslang, and Renton did most of the pressing, though the Cambuslang were now waking up, and Hannah and Kelso had frequently to do all they knew to stop the forwards. From a tremendous struggle at the Cambuslang goal M'Callum registered a fourth goal for his side, and three minutes later M'Callum a fifth. Cambuslang were now disheartened and a sixth goal was soon lost. Final score:- Renton 6; Cambuslang 1.
*Ref 1887035**

19ᵗʰ May 1888
Miscellaneous   Renton v West Bromwich Albion
This important fixture between the Scottish and English cup holders came off at Hampden Park, Glasgow, on Saturday before 6000 spectators. the weather was at the start was most oppressive, but when the game was fifteen minutes in progress a terrific thunderstorm, accompanied by a perfect deluge of rain, twice stopped play for several minutes. Indeed had it been an ordinary fixture it would in all probability have been postponed before half-an-hour had gone. Renton kicked off from the pavilion end, and at once got into Albion territory. The opening chapters of the game indicated a keen and close game. Renton first took up the pressing, the stalwart Roberts having to fist out from a stiff scrimmage. Then the Englishmen broke away in fine style, and made several dashing attempts to break through, but Renton's half-back line broke the attack. Renton generally did the persistent pressing, while the Albion indulged in fast gallops. Twenty minutes from the start, after sustaining a siege, Renton came away, and M'Callum scored, but the point was disallowed for off-side. However, five minutes later Renton

scored a legitimate point by M'Nee, after some pretty cross passing. At the half hour the storm caused a postponement for ten minutes, during which the field was flooded in some parts. On resuming and up till half-time the play was mostly in favour of Renton, but the footing was very treacherous. At half-time Renton were still leading. Strange to say, Renton had the wind in their favour both halves. The Albion were the first to be aggressive, and in five minutes equalised very softly. Then play was again stopped for some minutes owing to the severity of the downpour; and when it was resumed Renton took the upper hand, and M'Coll, who all through played with fine judgment, sent in a swift shot, which fairly beat Roberts. The Albion captain wanted to give it up, but Renton would not consent, and in spite of exceptionally severe rain, thunder, and lightening, the game was played out to the end. Renton had now the upper hand, and in spite of the slippery footing and the greasy condition of the ball, went at it with great earnestness and effect. M'Coll, with another daisy cutter, registered the third goal, and before the close J. Campbell beat Roberts with another. Four goals to one, at which total the score closed. Renton being hailed the world's champion.

West Bromwich Albion. - Goal, Roberts; backs, Green and Mason; half-backs, Timmins, Perry, and Horton; forwards - right, Basset and Woodall; centre, Baylisa; left, Wilson and Pearson.

Renton. - Goal, Lindsay ; backs, Hannah and A. M'Coll; half-backs, Kelso, Kelly, and M'Kechnie; forwards - right, M'Callum and H. Campbell; centre, J. Campbell ; left J. M'Coll and M'Nee.

Ref 1887036

2nd June 1888

Miscellaneous   **Renton v Preston North End**

These teams met on Hampden Park to take part in a match arranged as a testimonial to Mr Walter Arnot of the Queen's Park Club. Mr Arnot, after doing good service as a player, has determined to retire from the football world; and it was thought that if a game could be arranged between the Renton and Preston Clubs Mr Arnot's connection with the pastime would be fittingly brought to a close.

Renton, 4 goals, Preston North End, 2 goals.

Ref 1887037

1ˢᵗ September 1888
First Round   **Redding Athletic v Gairdoch**
Owing to two of the Redding Athletics men not turning up to face Gairdoch in their Scottish cup-tie, and as their 2ⁿᵈ XI. was off to play Laurieston 2ⁿᵈ XI., they could not get two registered men to fill up their places, so Redding scratched to Gairdoch and engaged in a friendly game. My old friend "Chick" Dearie and the centre-forward I mentioned last week (Smith) were the two players who failed to turn up. I am informed that a back was playing for Redding who has seen about *fifty* summers. I thought all members of football clubs who are that age had been relegated to the offices of an onerous character, but which do not require so much agility.

... Towards the close of the second half Ballantine kicked three corners against his own team, and the strangers took a goal off each, and just at the finish Honeyman, from a low swift shot, scored again for his side. Thus the Gairdoch won a hard game by 7 goals to the home team's 2. Mr Balloch, East Stirlingshire, was referee.
Ref 1888001

1ˢᵗ September 1888
First Round   **3rd Lanarkshire R.V. v Whitefield**
These teams met at Cathkin Park to play their Scottish Cup tie. Before the start, however, the Whitefield formally scratched, and a friendly game was played. Throughout the Volunteers had the best of the play, and scored twice in each half. But for the splendid defence of M'Culloch the Whitefield defeat would have been more severe. Result:- 3d L.R.V., 4 goals; Whitefield, 0 goals.
Ref 1888002

Whitefield turned up three men short and scratched. The Third put the ball through and claimed the tie. With the assistance of Burns and Morrison of the Third, the Whitefield played a friendly game, in which they were defeated by four goals to nil.
Ref 1888003

1ˢᵗ September 1888
First Round   **Paisley Athletic v Thornliebank**
These teams should have met at Paisley on Saturday, but the Athletic were unable to get up a team, and scratched to the Thornliebank.
Ref 1888002

1ˢᵗ September 1888
First Round   **Our Boys (Dundee) 5-4 East End**
These neighbouring clubs met to play their cup tie on West Craigie Park. Rain fell during the progress of the game, and the ground was somewhat soft. There was a large crowd of spectators round the ropes. For some time after the commencement the play was slow until a good shot was sent in by one of the Boys' forwards, which the East End goalkeeper deftly turned aside. The ball was kept in East End territory for a few minutes, after which their forwards essayed a run and sent in a good shot, which the Boys' custodian managed to clear. The West Craigie men responded by running the ball swiftly

towards the south goal, and for some time the play was principally confined to the neutral territory. The East End forwards now collared the leather, and ran it towards the north goal with a great rush, but the custodian managed to clear rather cleverly. A minute or two after this the home team by a well-placed shot succeeded in scoring the first goal of the match. Ten minutes afterwards the "wise men" managed to equalise, and up till the close of the first forty-five minutes the ground team had the best of the game, but no further scoring took place, and the period ended - one goal each. The second half was characterised more by sheer brutality than by the display of scientific football. Immediately after the restart both teams were conceded corner kicks, that of the East End being speedily converted into a goal. Both sides now had runs in turn, and ultimately the Boys also added a second point. For a few minutes after this more life was imparted into the game, and each team strove its utmost to notch a point. At this stage Moore got on to the ball, and had a brilliant run the entire length of the field, with the East End in hot pursuit, but, outdistancing all his opponents, he sent in a magnificent shot, which M'Intosh could not keep out. Soon after this the Boys scored a fourth point, and shortly thereafter a fifth goal was added. After this had been accomplished a regular *melee* took place on the field. Two of the home team had to retire injured, and soon afterwards other two of the players were engaged in a regular prize-fighting exhibition, inflicting and averting blows in a manner which would have done credit to professional pugilists. The combatants closed and rolled over, pounding away at each other with great vigour. They were, however, ultimately separated, and the teams engaged in a wordy wrangle in midfield, a number of them gesticulating wildly. After something like order had been restored the play was continued, and the East End scored two points in rapid succession. This was all the scoring, and the game ended - Our Boys, 5 goals; East End, 4 goals.
Ref 1888005

1st September 1888
First Round   **Slamannan 5-3 Grangemouth**
S.F.A.C.M. [11th Sep]. The Scottish Football Association met in Glasgow on Tuesday evening to hear protests from the first round of the cup ties, and to draw the ties for the second round. Grangemouth was the only club in Stirlingshire who protested; their cause of complaint being the unsuitable condition of the Slamannan ground. The protest was dismissed, and Grangemouth lost their 10s. I was rather surprised at Grangemouth protesting for the simple reason that they had the selecting of the ground, and decided that the match be played at Slamannan (their own ground of course not being ready for play).
Ref 1888006

1st September 1888
First Round   **Albion Rovers v Bellshill**
Bellshill were due to visit the Meadow. The Bellshill committee asked for a five o'clock kick-off but even then they failed to turn up by the appointed time. Albion Rovers awarded the tie.
*Ref 1888007**

1ˢᵗ September 1888
First Round   **Forfar Athletic 14-1 Lindertis**
These teams met on Station Park, Forfar, on Saturday, in the first round of the Scottish Cup Ties. The Lindertis kicked off uphill against the wind, and the ball was immediately returned and Lamont scored the Athletic's first point by neatly heading the ball through. In about ten minutes Cable had notched a second goal for the Athletic, and Dundas followed up with a third. The Athletic continued to have the game in hand, and added goal after goal until at half-time their total stood at 11, while the Kirriemuir record remained blank. In the second half the play was more equal, but the Athletic had decidedly the better of it, and added other three points. The Lindertis shortly after the start of the second period succeeded in scoring their first and only goal. The game therefore resulted - Forfar Athletic, 14 goals; Lindertis, 1.
Ref 1888005

1ˢᵗ September 1888
First Round   **Jamestown 1-6 Vale of Leven Hibernian**
At Jamestown. Last year when these teams met in their cup tie, it took three days to settle it. On this occasion the home players were chiefly young. In the first half the Hibernians scored twice, and in the second half they increased their total to six, while their opponents only gained one point.
Ref 1888003

S.F.A.C.M. [11ᵗʰ Sep]. Jamestown protested against the Vale of Leven Hibernians, on the ground that the latter was not a club. The chairman characterised this as a most absurd and uncalled for protest. It was summarily dismissed and Jamestown admonished.
Ref 1888010

1ˢᵗ September 1888
First Round   **Thornhill 2a2 Vale of Nith**
Played at Thornhill. From the first, the game was characterised by roughness. During the first part of the game the home team scored twice and the strangers once, and in the second no scoring was done until within ten minutes of time, when the Vale scored. Thornhill protested against this point, which the referee allowed; but in face of this the home team refused to take the decision, and consequently the referee and Vale players left the field. Before this however, the strangers lodged a protest on account of coarse play.
Ref 1888002

S.F.A.C.M. [11ᵗʰ Sep]. Considerable discussion ensued upon the protest of Vale of Nith (Dumfries) v Thornhill. According to the statements in the case, there seems to have been rough play on the part of the Thornhill and that the referee had been assaulted on the field. It was resolved that the tie should be replayed on the ground of Vale of Nith on Saturday first (15ᵗʰ Sep), and Marchbank suspended for six months, and Graham, M'Laren and A M'Creadie (all Thornhill players) for three months from all matches.
Ref 1888010

15th September 1888
First Round Replay   **Vale of Nith v Thornhill**
As a protest at the decision of the committee, the Thornhill failed to appear for the re-arranged match and Vale of Nith claimed the tie.
*Ref 1888013**

1st September 1888
First Round   **Kelvinside Athletic 16-0 Govan Athletic**
The Govan, losing the toss, kicked off, but the Kelvinside getting hold of the ball brought it up to their opponents' goal and scored. At half-time the home team led by 6 goals to 0. On the game resuming P. Stewart had a splendid run the greater part of the field and scored another goal. At this point two of the Govan men left the field, and the home team keeping up the pressure goal after goal was scored, the game ending Kelvinside, 16 goals; Govan Athletic, 0 goal.
Ref 1888002

1st September 1888
First Round   **Lanemark 7-0 Stevenston Thistle**
The Stevenston Thistle journeyed to Lanemark to play their first tie for the Scottish Cup. Unfortunately, only eight players turned up, three having deserted at the last moment. Three subs, were picked out of non-players that accompanied them. The Lanemark was victorious by 7 goals to 0. It will take a good team to beat Lanemark on their own ground should they turn out the same team.
*Ref 1888015**

1st September 1888
First Round   **Kilbarchan 0-1 Abercorn**
These clubs should have met on Saturday at Over-Johnstone in the first round of the Scottish Cup, but when the time arrived for starting the Kilbarchan refused to play on account of the state of the ground, and the Abercorn therefore kicked a goal and claimed the match.
Ref 1888002

1st September 1888
First Round   **Stewarton Cunninghame 4-3 Rosebank**
Protest made by Rosebank on the ground that there was a tree on the touchline, and it was also alleged there were numerous pools, and that a hedge ran along one of the touchlines. The referee thought the ground was quite playable; indeed, he considered the field was just an ordinary country field. The protest was dismissed.
*Ref 1888017**

1st September 1888
First Round   **Broxburn Shamrock 3-2 West Calder**
Void due to referee failing to appear.

8th September 1888
First Round   **Broxburn Shamrock v West Calder**
On September 8th Shamrock had at the last moment changed the field to Uphall, the Broxburn Sports Park not being available. West Calder team declared not got proper notice of change and declined to proceed to Uphall after arriving at Broxburn Sports Park.
*Ref 1888018**

S.F.A.C.M. [11th Sep]. The tie Broxburn Shamrock v West Calder was ordered to be played on Saturday at West Calder.
Ref 1888010

15th September 1888
First Round   **West Calder 2-1 Broxburn Shamrock**
This undecided Scottish Cup tie was played at West Calder. The Shamrock were the first to score, and the game then became fast. After this the Calder forwards were slack at goal. Davidson with a fine shot equalised, and at half-time the game stood one each. In the second half both teams strove hard to secure the winning point. After a nice run Jamieson scored. Result:- West Calder, two goals; Shamrock, one goal.
Ref 1888020

S.F.A.C.M. [17th Sep]. The West Calder claimed their having expenses for going to Broxburn to play the 'Shamrock' on the second occasion & stated they sustained the 'Shamrock''s share of the gate at West Calder until they got an answer. This claim was granted.
Ref 1888021

1st September 1888
First Round   **Annbank v Darnconner Britannia**
The kick off was fixed for 4.15pm, but the Darnconner wishing to start at 3pm instead, sent a messenger to Catrine to wire their intentions to Annbank. The messenger, however, seems to have been unacquainted with his duties, as he wired back to Darnconner that the kick-off was to be fixed for 3pm. The visiting team received the telegram in due course, and thought it was a reply from Annbank confirming the time of kick-off. When Darnconner arrived at the field a little before three o'clock there were no opponents to meet them, and after waiting half an hour in a drenching rain, they claimed the game and left the ground. Annbank appeared on the scene at the advertised time, 4.15pm, and finding that their opponents had fled, they went through the mask performance of kicking a goal (all off-side) and claimed the game. The referee, Mr William Miller, Kilmarnock, advised both teams to play the tie, but the Britannia refused.
*Ref 1888022**

The tie was ordered to be played at Annbank on Saturday first, kick-off 3.30pm (September 8th Annbank 5, Darnconner Britannia 1).
*Ref 1888023**

S.F.A.C.M. [12th Sep]. A protest against Annbank by Britannia was dismissed as informal.
Ref 1888010

7th September 1888
Miscellaneous   **Lenzie – Formation of a Senior Football Club**
At a meeting held in the club rooms, Alexander Terrace, on Friday, 7th inst., it was unanimously agreed to reform the senior club, which has been defunct for some time. The club promises to have a large membership, and they have secured as ground Craigmillar Park.
Ref 1888025

22nd September 1888
Second Round   **3rd Lanarkshire R.V. 8-0 Kelvinside Athletic**
This tie, which ought to have been played on Temple Park, was played on Cathkin Park, The Volunteers have been exceptionally lucky so far in the Scottish ties. Their opponents in the first round scratched, and this tie was considered almost a certainty. With the exception of one or two spasmodic attempts at the start, the Athletics were never in it, and retired defeated by eight goals to nil.
Ref 1888026

22nd September 1888
Second Round   **2nd Ayrshire R.V. 4-4 Maybole**
West End Park, Newmilns, was the scene of a most exciting game last Saturday, when the Maybole and Newmilns A.R.V, met in the second round of the Scottish Cup ties. Great interest was taken in the game, and a large gathering of spectators assembled. The Maybole kicked off and began business-like, a mis-kick of one of the home backs giving them a chance - which, however, came to nothing, the ball going behind. The A.R.V. now came away in good style, and getting within shooting distance, W. M'Cartney sent in a scorcher, which struck the post, but went behind. Continuing the pressure, the Newmilns team experienced hard lines in not scoring; but the defensive play of the strangers was good, and for some time their efforts were frustrated. At length, after about 20 minutes play, from a scrimmage in front of the Maybole goal, W. M'Cartney found an opening and put on the first goal for the Newmilns. The play from the kick-off became very fast, the Maybole team doing their utmost to equalise. Both sides were now playing with great determination, but neither seemed to gain any decided advantage. The strangers' front ultimately got away with a rush, and Barclay, the A.R.V. goal-keeper, was called on to save a swift shot. He caught it cleverly, but in kicking it out it struck against a player and went through. Half-time was shortly after called, with the score one goal each. On resuming play the home team settled down, and playing well together, had for some time the most of the play. From a good centre, Lawson scored the second point for Newmilns. Shortly after a third goal was scored by Young, and about 15 minutes from call of time Morton put through the fourth goal for the A.R.V. With only 15 minutes to go, it looked an easy win for the home team ; but the Maybole men now seemed to awake from their slumber, and to everybody's surprise completely took the upper hand and just romped round their opponents. Two goals were scored by them in about ten

minutes, and just before call of time they equalised the game amid the wildest excitement and to the consternation of the Newmilns team, who were all thunderstruck at the turn affairs had taken at the last minute. The game was pleasantly contested from beginning to end, and the spectators were very neutral, the strangers coming in for a fair share of the applause. The tie will be replayed at Maybole today.
*Ref 1888027**

22nd September 1888

Second Round   Arthurlie 3-2 Pollockshaws

S.F.A.C.M. [2nd Oct]. Pollockshaws protested against the Arthurlie on the grounds that the referee smoked his pipe contentedly during their Second Round match, and therefore could not blow his whistle at the proper time. The protest was dismissed amidst laughter, the referee stating that he only had a "draw" at half-time.
*Ref 1888028**

29th September 1888

Second Round Replay   King's Park 13-1 Slamannan

The above teams met on the former's ground to play off their undecided tie in the Second Round of the Scottish Cup. The home team had matters nearly all their own way, winning an uneventful game by 13 goals to 1. This is surely a big surprise to some, as the clubs played a drawn game at Slamannan the Saturday previous.
The strangers, who go in for "the long kick and rush" style of play, which takes well on their own ground, were nowhere in comparison to the King's Park. The Slamannan were inclined to be rough at times, the consequence being that two of the King's Park players were hurt, one of whom had to leave the field during the progress of the game. The whole of the King's Park forwards participated in the scoring. Gilchrist, Johnston and Merrilees each having 3 goals to their credit, while Ferguson had 2 and Bruce 1. The third goal taken by the King's Park was due to a mistake on the part of one of the Slamannan backs.
*Ref 1888029**

22nd September 1888

Second Round   Woodvale 3-2 1st Renfrewshire R.V.

S.F.A.C.M. [2nd Oct]. 1st RRV protested against Woodvale for playing their tie on ground of Thornliebank club. They contended that according to rules the match should have been played at Greenock seeing the Woodvale had no private ground of their own. After examining a posse from each club, it was decided to sustain the protest & order the tie to be replayed at Greenock on Saturday first.
Ref 1888030

6th October 1888

Second Round Replay   1st Renfrewshire R.V. v Woodvale

This tie was fixed to be played off at Academy Park, Greenock, when there was a large turn-out of spectators, but only eight of the Woodvale had put in an appearance about twenty minutes after the advertised time. The Woodvale having scratched, a friendly game was arranged between the two teams, the strangers getting supplied with two substitutes. The game was a very poor one, and resulted in a victory for the Volunteers

by 5 goals to nil.
*Ref 1888031**

29th September 1888
Second Round   Annbank 5-4 Hurlford
Hurlford protested against the Annbank on the ground that their players had been exposed on the field for fifteen minutes and also that Annbank played with irregular colours. The match was ordered to be replayed at Hurlford as it was proved that the Annbank violated the rules in playing with five different coloured jerseys. Annbank threw away a well-earned victory on the first occasion by adopting Jacob's uniform, which was said to be of many shades and colours. The Hurlford team were treated to showers of stones on leaving the village, and several members of the visiting club have received souvenirs of the game in the shape of nasty cuts and bruises. Annbank will require to be more careful or the SFA may proclaim their sacred plot Pebble Park.
*Ref 1888032**

6th October 1888
Second Round Replay   Hurlford 2-2 Annbank
This undecided Scottish tie was played at Hurlford in presence of 4000 spectators, The Annbank scored first after fifteen minutes' play, their success being greeted with loud cheering. The play waxed fast, and both goals were repeatedly attacked. The Hurlford custodian got several hot ones, but managed to clear. Annbank continued to have the upper hand, the Hurlford having to play all they could to keep them at bay. Towards the close of the first half Hurlford wakened up, but were again and again driven back bootless, Fitzsimmons, the Annbank goalkeeper, playing a superior game. In the beginning of the second half Hurlford equalised amidst tremendous excitement. The Annbank again forced the pace, and a shot from the right wing took effect. The home team put on a second goal about ten minutes from the close, a hard and exciting game ending in a draw - two goals each. Hurlford wished to play half an hour extra but their opponents refused.
*Ref 1888033**

13th October 1888
Second Round 2nd Rply   Annbank 2-3 Hurlford
These teams met for the third time in the second round of the Scottish Cup Ties. As will be remembered when they first met the Annbank were victorious by five goals to four, but the Hurlford protested, and the protest being sustained they had to meet again. The second game resulted in a draw, each team scoring two goals. On Saturday it was evident from the number of spectators who assembled in Pebble Park, Annbank, that considerable interest was taken in the game, there being a large attendance from Ayr. The game was not particularly noticeable for fine play, both teams indulging in heavy kicking. The first quarter of an hour was simply a series of fouls, the Annbank having, if anything, the best of play. Towards the end of the first half the home team managed to score, and though their opponents worked hard to equalise matters they failed. At the beginning of the second half the Annbank played with great dash, their efforts being rewarded by a second goal. The second half was well through when the Hurlford scored their first point; while shortly before the call of time they managed to equalise matters. An extra half-hour was then entered upon, and Hurlford hemmed in the Annbank almost

the whole of the first quarter, but could not notch a point. The second quarter was fiercely contested, and on one occasion, a shot was sent in to Dan, which he put out, but was immediately grassed, and while he and the Hurlford centre were embracing each other lying on the ground, the ball was shot through amid wild cheers of the Hurlford contingent. No more scoring took place and the result of the match was Hurlford 3 goals Annbank 2. It is needless to criticise the play of the teams, as they were too excited to play well, but the Annbank centre was a complete failure, and perhaps lost them the match.
*Ref 1888034**

13th October 1888
Third Round   3rd Lanarkshire R.V. 2-1 Queen's Park
Queen's Park protested against William Love, who played in the tie for the Volunteers, on the ground that he was ineligible having already played this season in the Cup tie for the Woodvale against the 1st RRV. The Third Lanark admitted that Love played for Woodvale in the Second round of the ties, but that the tie was declared null and void, and was replayed, Love not taking part. The Third Lanark had also asked the Business Committee whether they would sanction Love's playing in the tie against the Queen's, and they allowed the Volunteers to play him. After a deal of discussion, it was agreed to sustain the protest and the match to be replayed at Cathkin Park on the following Saturday.
*Ref 1888035**

13th October 1888
Third Round   Q.O.S Wanderers 11-1 Vale of Nith
The cup tie at Milldamhead, Dumfries, on Saturday, between the Vale o' Nith and Queen of the South Wanderers proved a bit of a farce. There was only one team in it from the start, the Wanderers winning much as they liked by 11 goals to 1. The Vale were handicapped by the absence of Larne and Dickson, but there is no denying the fact that they are streets behind the Cresswell Club. But for their clever goal-keeper the result would have been overwhelming. The Wanderers' back division played a game such as one seldom sees, and the manner in which they stopped the Vale forwards was even laughable at times. Corny and Harding were a bit frightened apparently at Carridice and their play was not to the same advantage as formerly. G. Halliday was tried on the left and proved an undoubted success. As has been already said Wood kept a splendid goal for the Vale and both backs (in whom the brunt of the work fell) were specially good. Mandell played both with his feet and his head as usual, and Robson was good on the right, but the others were mere stop-gaps.
Ref 1888036

13th October 1888
Third Round   **Uddingston v Glasgow University**
Played on the ground of the former. Owing to the inability of the University to bring together their registered team they scratched in favour of Uddingston, but a friendly game was played between the "villagers" and a scratch team from the college, the Uddingston winning four to none.
Ref 1888037

24th November 1888
Fifth Round   **Celtic 0-1 Clyde**
The Scottish tie between these teams was decided at Celtic Park before 8000 spectators. Play was fast and exciting. The Clyde attacked in the most determined manner, and in the first fifteen minutes had decidedly the best of the game. The soft ground upset the calculations of the ground men completely. Vigorously as the rival contestants assailed in turn, the defence could not be broken through. The home team steadied, and were now more frequently dangerous, M'Callum and Groves exhibited great dash up front. Chalmers saved magnificently. At this stage the players kept up the pace in the most approved fashion. At half-time the result was:- Clyde, one goal; Celtic, nil. The home team redoubled their efforts to score in the second half, but met with the most stubborn resistance. The Clyde still kept the game pretty open, and played up with surprising dash. The half-backs on both sides tackled superbly, and neutralised all dangerous incursions. Latterly the excitement was intense, and a brilliant game, considering the adverse circumstances, ended:- Clyde, one; Celtic, nothing.
Ref 1888038

S.F.A.C.M. [4th Dec]. The Celtic protested against the Clyde being awarded the cup tie played on 24th November because the ground was unplayable, and that for the last fifteen minutes the game was played in darkness. Mr Harrison, the referee, explained that the teams started to play a cup tie with the consent of both captains, that for the last eight minutes he could not follow the game, and that the game was late in starting, part of the delay being caused by several Clyde players having to remove bars from their boots. Mr Reid (Airdrieonians) moved that the protest should be sustained, and this was seconded by Mr J.B. Walker (Renfrewshire Association.) Mr Boag (Partick Thistle) proposed that the protest should be dismissed. Mr Graham (Renton) seconded. On a division the protest was sustained by 7 votes to 4, and the tie was ordered to be replayed on the ground of the Celtic on Saturday first.
Ref 1888039

8th December 1888
Fifth Round Replay   **Celtic 9-2 Clyde**
The protested Scottish Cup tie between these teams attracted nearly 9000 spectators to the Celtic Park. The Clyde won the toss, and Groves kicked off. The Clyde forwards, taking up the running, forced the ball behind. M'Callum executed a brilliant run up the right, and finished with a strong shot at goal, which, however, went wide. Play continued in favour of the home team, and, from a pass from the right, Maley headed a rather soft goal past Chalmers [Clyde]. Scarcely was the ball again in progress than M'Laren headed a second goal for his side. The Clyde men were next prominent, and Cherrie put a ball into Dunning's hands, which the custodian let through. The Clyde attacked

strongly, and within a minute thereafter Cherrie equalised with a splendidly judged shot. Tom Maley again scored, and the game stood at three goals to two in favour of Celtic on crossing over. The play opened in the second half with the Clyde attacking, but their career was brief, as Maley again dashed away on the left and added another goal. Gallacher, of the home team, though injured early in the first half, kept the field, but at this stage Hart, of the Clyde, was compelled to leave the field with his shoulder dislocated. The game abounded in hard knocks on either side, not directly attributed to roughness, but caused more by the fearless manner in which the rival teams contended for possession of the ball. Handicapped by the absence of their best back, the Clyde fell away a bit, and M'Callum headed a fifth goal, and Groves replied with a sixth - the best goal of the match. Another grand run by Groves, who played remarkably well, ended in the downfall of the visitors' goal for the seventh time. Time was drawing near, and gathering themselves together the Clyde made several vain attempts to score, but they were repulsed, and in the last few minutes the Celts rushed in a couple more goals, and thus won by nine goals to two.

Ref 1888040

24th November 1888
Fifth Round   3rd Lanarkshire R.V. 5-4 Abercorn
S.F.A.C.M. [4th Dec]. The Abercorn protested against the tie being awarded the 3d Lanark on the ground of darkness. Mr Watt, the referee, said he could follow the game, and he was of opinion that the match was finished in sufficiently good light. The delay in beginning the game was caused through his being late owing to the train. Mr Sliman moved, and Mr Boag seconded, that the protest should be dismissed. Mr J.B. Walker, seconded by Mr Williamson, moved that the protest should be sustained. By 7 to 3 this amendment was carried, and the tie ordered to be replayed on Cathkin Park on Saturday first.

Ref 1888039

1st December 1888
Fifth Round   Dumbarton 3-1 Mossend Swifts
S.F.A.C.M. [4th Dec]. Mossend Swifts protested against the Dumbarton on the ground that their men were treated by the Dumbarton in a disgraceful manner, being assaulted frequently during the game, and subjected to the most violent threats. The referee reported Madden (Dumbarton), and Ellis and Mackay (Swifts) for rough play. Mr Watt, after the referee had been heard, said this had been a brutal exhibition of the game on both sides. He moved that the protest should be sustained, and that the tie should be replayed on neutral ground with neutral umpires. Mr Robertson seconded. Mr Laing proposed that the protest be dismissed, and this was carried by 9 votes to 3, the deposit, however, being returned. It was resolved that Madden should be censured, and that Ellis and Mackey should be suspended for one month each because of their conduct.

Ref 1888039

2nd February 1889

Final   **3rd Lanarkshire R.V. 3-0 Celtic**

The final tie for the Scottish Cup was played between the 3d L.R.V. and the Celtic on Hampden Park. The attendance of spectators was a record one in the history of football in Scotland, there being, it is considered, 18,000 present. The money drawn at the gate was over £800, while £120 was taken at the stands, making a total of £920. The weather was most unfavourable, but notwithstanding large crowds began to wend their way to Crosshill even an hour and a half before at which it was advertised the match would begin. As we have said, a more unpropitious day, so far as weather was concerned, could not have been conceived. In the forenoon there were gusts of wind, accompanied by heavy showers of snow, which, however, were not of long durations. A thin coating of snow covered the field, and, in consideration of these facts, there were misgivings as to whether the game would be played. At eleven o'clock "the officials" paraded the field, and even went as far as playing a little game on the quiet, and decided that the ground was playable. As the day advanced the showers were heavier, and between two and three it fell in one continuous blinding shower. The decision to play the match having been come to, however, the people were admitted into the field, and they thronged in thousands. The time of waiting for the commencement of the game was most unpleasant, for the snow was driven along the field in violent gusts, and there was no shelter from the blast. But one topic was discussed. "Will the game be a cup tie?" was the question asked on all sides, and while uncertainty may have existed as to what would be the answer, everyone was agreed on the inadvisability of settling so important a match on such ground. A meeting of the association was carried hurriedly in the Q P pavilion, and it was decided, notwithstanding that the ground was by this time quite unplayable, that the cup tie should be played. Both teams played under protest, and it was understood that a friendly game only should be played. The Volunteers were the first [to] appear on the field and received a hearty cheer. They were followed immediately afterwards by the Celts, who came in for even greater cheers. Some amusement was caused by the teams engaging in snowballing each other.

Ref 1888043

Punctually at 3.15 the Third, having lost the toss, kicked off, and some exciting play immediately took place in front of the Third goal. A corner fell to the Celts, and M'Laren all but headed through the goal. The Celts were having decidedly the best of matters. The Third led by Marshall and Oswald, retaliated, but they could not get the ball past midfield. Downie was several times called upon to save his charge, which he did in excellent style. M'Callum put in a rare shot, which hit the cross-bar, and went over. Marshall and Oswald raised the hoped of the Third supporters until pulled up in clever fashion by M'Keown. A trip against M'Keown made the Third look dangerous for the first time during the contest, but M'Laren, with a good header, put the ball out of danger. Kelly was deservedly cheered for a splendid piece of play. The ball was taken to the Celtic goal by Hannah, who centred neatly to Oswald, jun., and the latter beat Kelly amid a scene of wild excitement. After this reverse the Celts played up with renewed vigour, and the Volunteers' goal had some marvellous escapes. A foul right in the Volunteers' goal-mouth looked as if the Celtic efforts would be rewarded, but do as they would they could not get the ball through the posts. Half-time arrived with the Celtic one down, although they had the best of the contest.

After a short interval the game was resumed, M'Callum being early prominent with a

dashing run on the right; while a foul still further equally as brilliant, and T. Kelly had some anxious moments, Some beautiful passing amongst the whole front rank of the Celts took place, and the ball was brought in front of Downie, but the forwards persisted in their close passing tactics, which, with the ground in such a condition, were practically of no use. Groves caused some excitement by one of his sensational runs, but the ground was against him, and he was deprived of the ball. The game continued very exciting, and after a clever run by the Third forwards, Oswald, jun., defeated Kelly a second time. The cheers which greeted his success were simply deafening. The Celts replied so feebly to this second reverse that the spectators realised that a Cup tie was not being played, and as snow began to fall heavily, hundreds left the field. The play after this calls for little description, the players being barely distinguishable, and, as far as could be seen, play was ruling at mid-field. Just before Mr Campbell blew his whistle the Third rushed the ball down and put on a third goal.
Ref 1888044

5ᵗʰ November 1889
S.F.A.C.M.   **The Final Tie to be Replayed**
Last night a special meeting of the Scottish Football Association Committee was held – Mr Slimman (Battlefield) presiding. The Chairman explained that the meeting was called in connection with the Celtic *v.* 3d L.R.V. cup tie. A document, signed on behalf of the 3d L.R.V. by Mr Brown, and on behalf of the Celtic by Mr Glass, agreeing before the teams stepped on the field last Saturday to play a friendly game only, on account of the unsuitablilty of the ground, and wishing the association to appoint another day for the playing of the tie, was read to the meeting. Mr Charles Campbell, the referee, explained that in the forenoon the officials inspected the ground, which was then in very good condition, and received unanimously that the gates should be opened to the public. About three o'clock, however, a severe snowstorm came on, and the representatives of both clubs pressed him very hard, stating that it was altogether out of the question to play a cup tie on such ground. He replied that the officials could not recognise any mutual agreement, and that the tie would have to be played under protest, which was done. The umpires (Messrs Harrison and Pask) corroborated Mr Campbell's statement, and further said that in some parts neither the goal line nor the touch line could be seen for the snow. Mr Campbell said the three officials were unanimous that Saturday last was not a day for playing a cup tie. Mr Reid (Airdrieonians) said that in the first place he would move that the association do not recognise any agreement between clubs, and that they simply consider the protest. This was unanimously agreed to. Mr Robertson (Queen of South Wanderers) then moved that, after what had been stated by the officials, the cup tie be replayed on Hampden Park on Saturday first. This was also unanimously agreed to, and Mr M'Culloch was chosen to act as umpire in place of Mr Harrison, who would be engaged at another match in Ayrshire. Mr Crerar, who now occupied the chair, said he wished it to be made known that he desired the price of admission to be sixpence. It was agreed, however, by 10 votes to 8, that the charge for admission be the same as last Saturday. This was all the business.
Ref 1888045

———————————

7th September 1889
First Round   **Vale of Athole v Crieff**
Owing to failure to raise a team by Crieff, Pitlochry [Vale of Athole] at the last moment obtained a bye in the first round.
Ref 1889001

7th September 1889
First Round   **Cowlairs 21-1 Victoria (Glasgow)**
At Cowlairs [Gourlay Park] the Cowlairs overwhelmed the Victoria by 21 goals to 1.
Ref 1889001

7th September 1889
First Round   **Celtic 0-0 Queen's Park**
The Celtic, having lost the toss, kicked off at 4.4, and the game was soon in motion. The Queen's were the first to make headway, but M'Keown saved grandly on more than one occasion. The Celts, led by Groves, retaliated but the ball was sent past. Sellar all but lowered the home colours with a good screw shot, but M'Laughlan turned the ball aside in grand style. Groves made off with one of his well known runs until Smellie stopped short his career. Twenty five minutes from the start Dunbar had the ball through, but Mr Sneddon declared it off-side, much to the disgust of the Celtic supporters. Some time was lost in keeping the ground clear, the crowd being so great that it was next to impossible to keep them off the field. Hamilton made a gallant attempt to capture the home citadel, but Kelly was playing such a great game as to be practically impossible. The Celtic now began to assert themselves in no uncertain manner, and the defensive tactics of the blazers were tested to the very utmost. At half-time neither team had scored. It was fully ten minutes before the game could be restarted, the ground being again encroached upon by the spectators to quite an alarming extent. A corner soon fell to the Queen's, but it was cleared. Hamilton had a good run in the centre, and M'Laughlan had to clear a good shot from his foot. The Celts' left wing replied with a telling run, Arnott having to save, but the ball eventually was sent behind again. J. Hamilton was to the fore with a good run and kick, but M'Laughlan, as on the previous occasion, proved equal to the task. At this point the spectators made their presence felt again, and the game had perforce to be stopped. A restart was ultimately made, and Sellar was soon conspicuous with one of his characteristic runs on the left. The breaks in on the part of the crowd now began to get serious, and the referee was compelled to declare it no Cup tie - with the consent, of course, of the opposing captains. This decision had no apparent effect on the teams who returned to the charge with renewed vigour. After a miskick by M'Keown, Sellar missed a rare chance by shooting over the bar. All interest in the game, however, appeared to have vanished, and the people streamed out of the grounds in thousands. No scoring whatever took place, and the game resulted in a draw.
Ref 1889002

7th September 1889
First Round   **Cambuslang St Brides v Airdrieonians**
S.F.A.C.M. [17th Sep]. The Cambuslang St Brides were, on the application of the Airdrieonians, censured for scratching to that club in the first round of the ties on the field, contrary to the rule, and were ordered to remit the gross half of the gate taken at the friendly game which was played.
Ref 1889003

Footnote
Result of friendly St Brides 1, Airdrieonians, 6.

7th September 1889
First Round   **Our Boys (Blairgowrie) 3a5 St Johnstone**
The Saints had a narrow escape in returning from Blairgowrie, the horses bolting on a bad piece of the road. Luckily, however, the driver, with the application of the brake and the assistance of two of the party, brought the noble four to a halt. The bridle slipping was the cause of the bolt. The Saints think that mile was done in record time, but still it was not fast enough to stop one of the players from getting down. Others were prepared to follow the example, but the horses were brought to a standstill.
Ref 1889004

S.F.A.C.M. [17th Sep]. A Mr Duncan sent a long letter to the Association, stating that in the match Our Boys (Blairgowrie) v St Johnstone a Mr Ovenstone, from Dundee, had acted as referee, and that he was not qualified for the office because previous to the match beginning he told the players on both sides to keep back ten yards from the ball. Throughout the game Mr Duncan asserted that Mr Ovenstone acted in a very partial manner, and that he was greatly to blame in the match being stopped fifteen minutes from time, when the St Johnstone were leading by 5 goals to 3. The Committee agreed to confirm the decision of the Sub-Committee, who had already discussed the subject.
Ref 1889005

Inassailable writes from Rattray, impeaching in forcible terms the conduct of the referee and the correctness of his decisions in the above match on Saturday. On the subject of the rough play, he understands "that he intends to report to the Association for rough play one of the Blairgowrie team, than whom there is no more gentlemanly player in Perthshire." In his opinion, the referee, if it had suit his plans, could have without compunction reported at least three players of the Perth team.
Ref 1889001

7th September 1889
First Round   **Clydebank v Vale of Leven Wanderers**
The above teams met on Saturday on the Hamilton Park Grounds, Clydebank. There was a very large turnout of spectators, but at the advertised time of starting the Clydebank found themselves short of four men, and the committee had no alternative but to make a present of the tie to the Wanderers. This created quite a stir among the spectators. A rush was made upon the treasurer, demanding the money back. Confusion and shouting prevailed, and ultimately checks were given to those desiring their money back, and

peace was restored. The teams played a friendly game and it was evident the Clydebank had underestimated their ability, Clydebank winning by 3 goals to 1.
Ref 1889007

7th September 1889
First Round   Ayr 16-0 Beith
At Somerset Park. Beith had their strongest team, which included Gilmour and Edminstone - two names well known in Ayrshire about a decade ago. Ayr had a slight wind in their favour during the initial portion, and score in two minutes from the start. Beith after this defended well, Lambie especially putting in some fine saving at the back, and it was nearly half-an-hour before the Ayr were able to increase their lead. After this, however, goals came thick and fast, and half-time found Ayr in majority of 8 goals to none. It was thought that, with the wind in their favour, Beith would show up better; but they rapidly tired, and Ayr had matters all their own way to the end. Final score Ayr, 16; Beith, 0. For Beith, Lambie at back was far and away the best man in the team. Arthur made his first appearance at back for Ayr, having retired for the last two seasons, but Saturday's play showed that he had lost none of his cunning and Ayr are lucky in having a couple of backs of the standing of Arthur and Sommerville, who have very few equals anywhere.
Some of the spectators at the game left Somerset Park in disgust, because they were unable to follow the scoring. It is expected that a scoring board will be erected for future matches.
*Ref 1889008**

7th September 1889
First Round   3rd Lanarkshire R.V. 3-2 Partick Thistle
At Cathkin Park – Scottish Cup tie. The Cupholders started against the wind, and by a smart piece of play scored the first in three minutes. Another ten minutes the Thistle equalised, but the Third again took the lead two minutes later. To the end of the first half the score remained unaltered. On resumption of hostilities the Thistle experienced very hard lines on two different occasions. The Cupholders came again and notched a third point softly. A quarter of an hour from time the Thistle captain was accidentally winded, and this incident formed an excuse for the crowd to flock on the field, where, despite the somewhat listless efforts of the police, they remained and prevented play for fifteen minutes.
Ref 1889027

EXTRAORDINARY SCENE ON A FOOTBALL FIELD

Before the conlusion of the tie between the 3rd L.R.V. and Partick Thistle on Saturday, while the 3rd were leading by three goals, the crowd broke through the ropes, putting a stop to the game. The disturbance was due to one of the Partick Thistle men receiving an injury, and lying down in front of his goal. One individual ran across the field, and was immediately followed by a large mob, chiefly composed of Partick Thistle supporters. The police rushed into the field to drive the mob back, but their efforts were unavailing. Several of the 3rd Lanark men received injuries at the hands of the crowd, but none of these were serious. The players then began to make their way to the pavilion,

but this was a matter of some difficulty, as the crowd surrounded them. Ultimately the pavilion was reached, and the game brought to a premature close. The Partick Thistle have protested against M'Farlane and Johnston playing.
Ref 1889028

Ultimately the ground was cleared and the game finished, the Thistle raising their score by a point well headed. The game finished in favour of the Third by three to two.
Ref 1889027

S.F.A.C.M. [17th Sep]. The Partick Thistle protested against Third Lanark regarding the decision of the tie. They held that it should not be awarded to the Third Lanark. The Partick Thistle stated that the spectators interfered with the players ; that Wm. Lapsley, of the Third Lanark, was a professional, he having in May last signed a professional form for the Sunderland Albion, and that he received his train fare, neither of which sums he had returned ; that Wm. Johnston, who also played for the Third, was a professional, he having received payment from the Sunderland Albion ; and that at least a majority of the Third Lanark players went to Sunderland after winning the Scottish Cup, and played the Sunderland Club, and received payment, and that they were professionals. The Third Lanark version of the story was that the match was stopped fourteen minutes from time through Proudfoot being injured. William Lapsley said he would return the money, while William Johnston said that he had signed the professional form, but refused to accept the money offered by the Sunderland. The Third Lanark Committee were in ignorance of their club having gone to Sunderland and played the Albion Club. Mr Lang, of the St Mirrens, who was referee, stated that he stopped the game the moment Proudfoot was injured. The game was not stopped because the spectators broke into the field. The match was stopped for eighteen minutes. The Association, after discussion, dismissed the first count, and as the players accused of professionalism had pursued a course similar to that of Groves, they could not interfere with them. The Chairman said – "We are coming to a happier age in football. Notwithstanding all the irritation we receive from England, I hope we will never be driven from the pathway which we are pursuing." The Business Committee then intimated to the two clubs concerned that the Partick Thistle's protest had been dismissed, and that the protest money was to be forfeited.
Ref 1889005

28th September 1889
Second Round   **Lugar Boswell 0-2 Ayr**
Ayr 2; Lugar 0; 1889 - At Lugar. Being minus Arthur and Sommerville at back many of the Ayr's supporters were quite prepared for defeat. During the first half, playing with the wind in their favour, Ayr only managed to score two goals; while the Lugar, though at times dangerous, failed to make any impression on Steel's charge. The game during the second half was of a rather "tousy" nature, the Ayr men playing a careful defence; while the scarlet clad "bhoys," by the force thrown into their play, showed plainly enough that they meant to win at all hazards, but science in this, as in all other cases, came out victorious. The Lugar men took their defeat very badly, and the Ayr umpire was severely assaulted by one of the players on entering the pavilion. The matter has been handed into the police, and the Association will also be asked to rule in the matter.
*Ref 1889009**

28th September 1889

Second Round   Lassodie 3-3 Cowdenbeath

S.F.A.C.M. [8th Oct]. The Cowdenbeath lodged a protest against the Lassodie on the ground that Lawson, one of the latter's team, played in the first round of the ties with the Dunfermline Athletic. Lassodie admitted the fact, and were disqualified for the cup competition, Lawson being suspended until 8th December.

Ref 1889010

28th September 1889

Second Round   Stevenston Thistle 3-2 Annbank

Annbank's protest was somewhat novel. They said that in the first half the Stevenston had the benefit of the sun and wind. The ball was often out of play, and a second ball was always supplied. In the second half the weather was as gusty, and another ball was not supplied. Time was thus lost. They held that the game should be played over because the Annbank scored a goal which was disallowed. The match ended Stevenston Thistle 3 Annbank 2. The Stevenston in their reply stated that Annbank said that when they got them into Annbank they would kick them out of the village. The referee who attended the cup tie stated that there was no ground for complaint, and the protest was accordingly dismissed and the protest money retained.

*Ref 1889011**

19th October 1889

Third Round   Wishaw Thistle 5-8 Linthouse

Played at Wishaw before a large crowd. The visitors started with the slope of the ground in their favour, and they had also the advantage of a strong wind which was blowing across the field. When half-time was called the score was 6 goals to 1 in favour of the Linthouse. The game which was of an unusually exciting nature, ended in the defeat of the Wishaw by 8 goals to 5.

Ref 1889012

19th October 1889

Third Round   Union (Dumbarton) 1-2 Cambuslang

S.F.A.C.M. [29th Oct]. Dumbarton Union protested against Cambuslang on the ground that the referee had allowed three minutes extra during which Cambuslang scored the winning goal on account of the delay in returning the ball when it went into touch. After discussion the protest was sustained by 8 votes to 7, and the tie ordered to be replayed at Cambuslang on Saturday first.

Ref 1889013

19th October 1889

Third Round   Northern 2-1 Carfin Shamrock

... Despite the favouring circumstances, the Northern proved too much for the visitors during the first half. When time was called, the score was – Northern, 2 goals; Carfin Shamrock, 1 goal. On restarting, Carfin began to press, and were having the best of it, when an unfortunate circumstance occurred which brought the tie to a sudden termination. Party feeling, which was very high during the first half, got the better of the

crowd, who broke through the ropes and engaged in a free fight. The referee and three or four of the Northern team were severely handled, and some of them seriously injured.
Ref 1889012

S.F.A.C.M. [29th Oct]. It was agreed, on the motion of the Chairman that the tie between the Northern and Carfin Shamrock be replayed on neutral ground. The game it will be remembered, was stopped a fortnight ago by the spectators encroaching on the ground of play.
Ref 1889013

19th October 1889
Third Round　　　　　　　**Lanemark 4-3 Ayr Athletic**
The Lanemark should see to the field being put in better order. The state of the touchline, which is a deep-cut line, is really dangerous.
*Ref 1889016**

19th October 1889
Third Round　　　　　　**Edinburgh University 1-9 Leith Athletic**
At Corstorphine. Notwithstanding their want of practice, the students showed considerable agility, their backs in particular being very prominent in saving the lines. Mills-Roberts put in some good work for the home team, but their forwards lacked the necessary combination in close quarters. Laurie had one of his speedy runs the extreme length of the field, but his parting shot missed by a few inches. For a time the Athletic fairly hemmed in their opponents, but the erratic shooting of their front lines spoiled many likely openings. Tired of acting on the defensive, the students took up the running and Forrest [Leith], in fisting out, slipped, and out of a scrimmage the ball was rushed through. M'Queen, after a beautiful run, centred to Clements, who fairly beat Roberts [E.U.], and thus placed the teams on level terms. The forward line of the Athletic had one of their famous dribbles, but Philipson got the leather out of danger. M'Queen had a tricky dribble through the entire team of students, winding up by beating Roberts, and thus gave Leith the lead. Half-time 1-2. The visitors pressed at the opening of the second half but the students offered good resistance. Laurie eventually scored the third goal for the Athletic. The Athletic had then matters much their own way, and two goals followed in quick succession by M, and H. M'Queen. The University became quite disorganised towards the close and the game finished Leith Ath. 9 Edinburgh University 1.
Ref 1889017

9th November 1889
Fourth Round　　　　　　**St Mirren 8-2 Lanemark**
After being drawn at home the Lanemark had the St Mirren guarantee them 15 pounds before they would consent to come to Paisley and forfeit their advantage. The Ayrshire team did well in accepting these terms, for if the match had been played at Lanemark the drawings would have been poor, and the result probably would not have been much different.
*Ref 1889018**

9th November 1889
Fourth Round   East End 3-2 Cambuslang
The Cambuslang were first on the ground, and, when their weight and physique was seen, it was felt that the East End had their work cut out for them. The "wise men" presented themselves at seventeen minutes to three o'clock, two minutes before the advertised time for kick-off, and were greeted with a cordial cheer from their friends. The referee (Mr Ness, of the Glasgow Rangers) was, however, not then present, and the teams, after waiting for twenty minutes, called upon Mr Watson, of the Dundee Strathmore, to act in Mr Ness's absence.
... three minutes before the close, while the excitement of the spectators was at its height, Longair, carried the ball South. A scrimmage ensued, and the gallant captain with a kick sure and swift, won the third point for the East End. This feat of Longair's was rewarded with great cheering and waving of hats and handkerchiefs.
The Cambuslang have lodged a protest on account of the late start, but they can scarcely expect that it will be sustained, seeing that the East End were on the ground before the advertised time for starting, and that the light was clear at close. The East End should certainly not be punished for the failure of the referee.
Ref 1889019

S.F.A.C.M. [19th Nov]. The protest of the Cambuslang against their tie being awarded to the Dundee East End was considered. The Cambuslang explained that the match was delayed at the start for want of a referee, and was as a consequence finished in darkness. The goal which gave the East End the lead was given just at the call of time, when it was a matter of great difficulty to make out the players. In addition, they objected to the referee who was a substitute for the official one, as he was a local man, and certain to be biased. In defence the East End stated that the match was delayed but for a few minutes and that they could not be taken to account for the official referee failing to appear. The Committee decided that the tie be replayed at Dundee on Saturday.
Ref 1889020

23rd November 1889
Fourth Round Replay   East End 3-2 Cambuslang
The match was played on Rollo's Pier, the ground of the Strathmore, which was in capital condition, and the weather being fine, the game was witnessed by about 5000 spectators. At 2.25 - or five minutes before the advertised time for the start - the strangers presented themselves on the field of combat, and their appearance was the signal for a good hearty groan, which of course, was indicative only of the great dissatisfaction felt in this quarter with the decision of the Association. The Pitkerro men turned out at the half-hour, and were greeted with a ringing cheer, but seven minutes were spent in an examination of the boots of the players, with the result that one of the East End was requested to change his "understandings."
Ref 1889021

16th November 1889
Fourth Round   Leith Athletic 4-1 Ayr
Five minutes had yet to go when to the astonishment of everybody on the field, the referee sounded the whistle, and the contest was at an end.
*Ref 1889022**

19th November 1889

Committee Meeting   The Queen of the South Wanderers Obliterated

The professional Sub-Committee of the Scottish Football Association had last night under consideration the protest lodged by the Moffat Club against the Queen of the South Wanderers on the ground of professionalism, and after hearing several witnesses from the implicated Club in regard to the specific charges tabled against them the previous week by the Moffat witnesses, they came to the decision to permanently disqualify and suspend the Wanderers as a Club, and also disqualified all the members of last year's Committee and team from ever taking official part in football. The decision virtually obliterates the Club.

Ref 1889025

30th November 1889

Fifth Round   Queen's Park 1-0 St Mirren

S.F.A.C.M. [10th Dec]. St Mirren protested against the Queen's Park being awarded the recent tie on the ground that the game was ten minutes late in starting owing to one of the Queen's players turning up late. They also maintain that the game was not finished till 1min. past four o'clock, at which time there was not sufficient light to follow the play, and that the game was stopped 1min 45secs before the expiration of the exact time, without making allowances for stoppages. The Queen's Park denied categorically the statements of the St Mirren. It was agreed by eight votes to three to hear the evidence. The referee (Mr Bishop) explained that it was not to dark when the game finished, that full time was played, and that no time was wasted sufficient to make allowances. After discussion, the protest was dismissed by nine votes to six.

Ref 1889023

6th June 1890

Miscellaneous   Q.O.S. Wanderers Sue Treasurer

SHERRIF HOPE, Dumfries, issued his decision on the Dumfries football scandal yesterday. The Queen of the South Wanderers Football Club sued their late treasurer for a balance of the funds alleged to be in his possession. The defender admitted having received the money, but averred that it had been disbursed in payment of players, and this being illegal, it was, he said, arranged that the payments should not pass through the books, but that the accounts should be made to balance by suppressing an equal amount of receipts. The Sheriff decides for the defender, and adds that the revelations are "very sad", as indications of the widespread deficiency in truth and honour among the class to which the football players and their friends in the town belong.

Ref 1889024

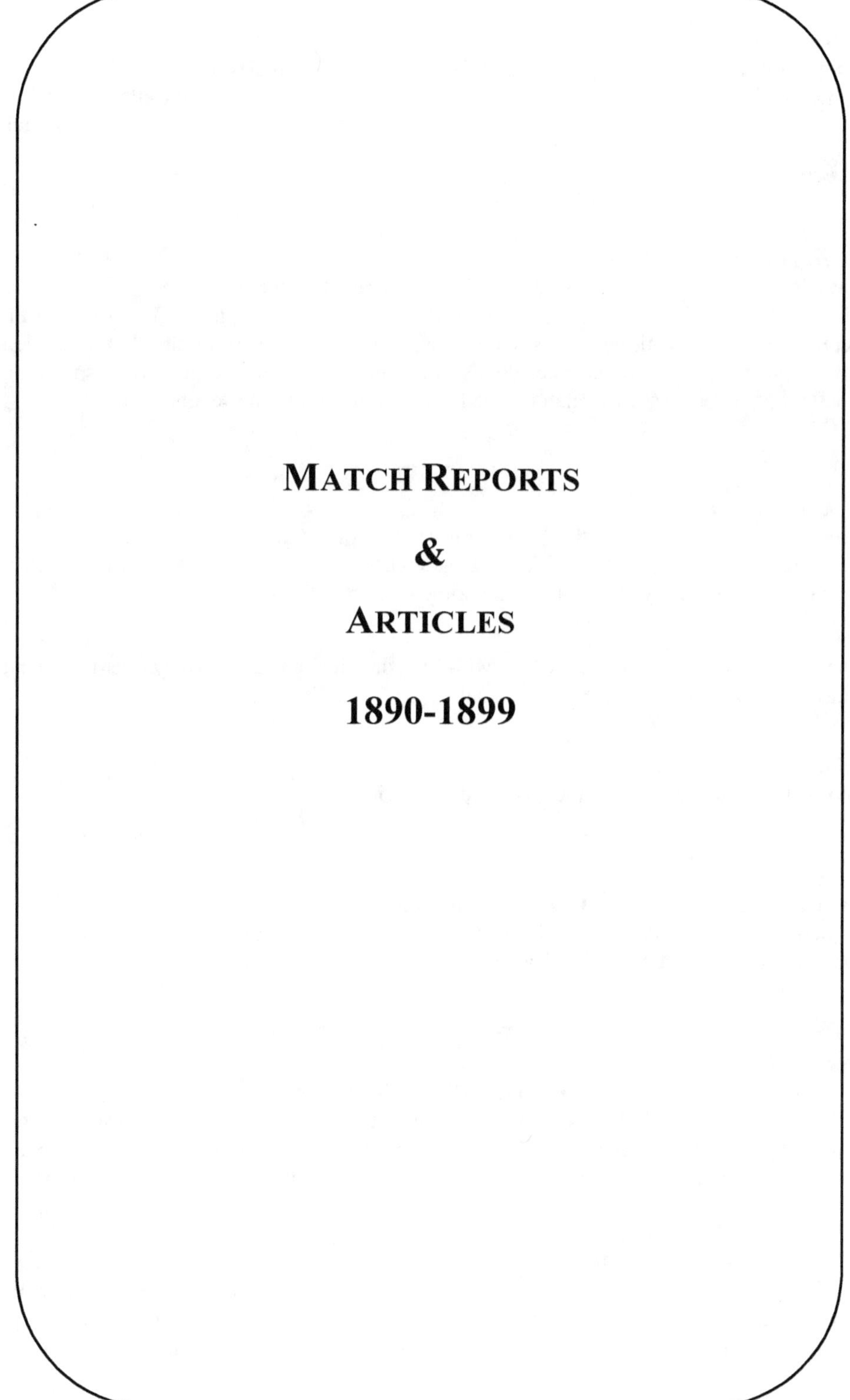

Match Reports

&

Articles

1890-1899

6th September 1890
First Round   **Rutherglen 6-0 Cambuslang St Brides**
At Lochgair. The strangers had to play a strong defence, and were not allowed once to score. The home team, although minus two of their best men, won the game by 6 goals to 0.
Ref 1890001

6th September 1890
First Round   **East End v Strathmore (Dundee)**
These old rivals should have met at Pitkerro Park on Saturday in the first round of the Scottish ties. After waiting a considerable time, and only four of the Strathmore players having put in an appearance, the money was handed back to the numerous spectators who had gathered to see the match. The East End thus enter the second round.
Ref 1890002

6th September 1890
First Round   **Mid-Annadale 15-1 Rising Thistle**
Mid Annandale (Lockerbie) v Rising Thistle (Lochmaben). This match was played at Lockerbie on Saturday and won by the home team by 16 goals to 1.
Ref 1890003

These teams met at Lockerbie, when Mid-Annadale had an easy victory over the Rising Thistle, a newly-formed club in Lochmaben, by 15 goals to 1.
Ref 1890001

Footnote
Score also reported as 15-0 and 17-1 and "majority of 14".

6th September 1890
First Round   **Dalry 5-2 Pollockshaws**
A member of the Pollockshaw Club, James Docherty, was suspended for three months for rough play in a cup tie with Dalry.
Ref 1890005

6th September 1890
First Round   **St Bernard's 7-0 Adventurers**
S.F.A.C.M. [16th Sep]. The Adventurers, Edinburgh lodged a protest against the result of the cup tie with the St Bernard's on the ground of professionalism, it being alleged that the latter club induced Ross, Dunfermline, to leave that town and join them on the promise of paying him a weekly wage for playing football. Before Ross had made up his mind to leave Dunfermline, it was alleged that he had been offered by the St Bernard's 10s a match and a job. Mr M'Dowall, secretary of the Association, said he had only received the protest that afternoon, and had telegraphed for representatives of both clubs to appear at that meeting. Mr M'Intosh, secretary of St Bernard's, who was called, stated that he had received too short notice for the case to go on that evening. It was decided

that the whole matter be remitted to the Professional Committee.
Ref 1890005

The following is the protest of the Adventurers in full:-
1st. That they induced Ross, of Dunfermline Athletic, to sever his connection with that Club and join theirs by promises of remuneration, and that they are at present paying him a weekly wage for playing football for them. Ross left Dunfermline, where he was employed as a cloth-lapper at a rate of 20s or so per week, and the St Bernard found him a job as a packer in a biscuit factory in Edinburgh, where the wages range from 15s to 18s, and expenses are considered higher than in Dunfermline. Before Ross had made up his mind to leave Dunfermline he told two of the officials of the Dunfermline Athletic that he had been offered 10s per match, and a job, and to others he said that he thought it too little to become a professional for. These parties we are prepared to bring forward as witnesses in support of our protest, or have their statements sworn to before a Magistrate. We may mention that Ross is at present enjoying a fortnight's holidays, having been allowed this by his new employers.
2nd. Ross was paid by the St Bernard a sum of 4s 6d for expenses when playing a trial match against the Raith Rovers on 9th August, when his expenses only amounted to 2s 6d.
Ref 1890007

SUSPENSION OF THE ST BERNARD'S – Quite a sensation was caused in Association circles in Edinburgh on Saturday when it became known that the St Bernard's, a club of the highest reputation, had been suspended for professionalism by the Professional and Business Committee of the Scottish Association. It was midnight on Friday ere the decision was arrived at. After examining Messrs Common [Secretary of Adventurers F.C.], Brown and Clark [Dunfermline Athletic], A.S. M'Intosh [secretary St Bernard's F.C.], W. Murray [Treasurer, St Bernard's], Ross [St Bernard's], and T. Paton [St Bernard's], the committee delivered the following finding:-
Having heard the evidence, examined the cash-books, and other documents produced, sustain the protest, and reinstate the Adventurers; find the St Bernard's guilty of professionalism under rule 11, Constitution and Rules, sub-sections b and g, and declare them suspended till 31st October; suspend the player James Ross till that date, and prohibit them from taking further part in football affairs in Scotland until said period expires. Ross, the player implicated, formerly belonged to the Dunfermline Athletic, and his suspension naturally gave rise to great jubilation in that town. In football circles generally, however, sympathy is felt for the St Bernard's who seem to have been severely dealt with. One result of the committee's decision is to bring nearer the legalising of professionalism, unless a more vigorous effort is made in the future to stamp out the secret professionalism which is stated to prevail in a number of the leading clubs in Scotland. As will be seen by the report in this column, the St Bernard's have adopted a new name till the 31st October – viz, "Edinburgh Saints."
Ref 1890008

6th September 1890
First Round　　　　　　　**Northern 5-0 Clydesdale**
S.F.A.C.M. [16th Sep]. A protest by the Clydesdale Club against the Northern for having played an illegible main in their cup tie was sustained. It was also decided that the player in question, J. Riddoch, be suspended for twelve months.
Ref 1890005

6th September 1890
First Round　　　　　　　**Carlton v Lugar Boswell**
GREENOCK CARLTON v LUGAR BOSWELL - The former scratched.
Ref 1890010

Footnote
Carlton and not Lugar appeared in the Second round draw. It is possible then that both sides actually scratched but Carlton were allowed through by the S.F.A.

6th September 1890
First Round　　　　　　　**St Johnstone 2a2 Coupar Angus**
These clubs met each other in the first round of the Scottish Cup ties on the St Johnstone Recreation Ground on Saturday. In the first period Coupar Angus scored two goals, but in the second half the Saints put on two points, the second of which was disputed and allowed by the referee, Mr Scott, of the Forfarshire Football Association, whereupon the game was stopped, and the Coupar Angus left the field determined to lodge a protest. According to the referee the game ended Coupar Angus, 2; St Johnstone, 2.
Ref 1890002

S.F.A.C.M. [16th Sep]. The protest of Coupar Angus against St Johnstone was dismissed on the ground that the secretary of the Association had not received notice of the protests within three days as provided by the rules.
Ref 1890005

6th September 1890
First Round　　　　　　　**Dumbarton 8-2 Smithston Hibernians**
Played at Boghead. The game should have been played on the ground of the latter, but as they had not a suitable pitch they had no alternative but come to Dumbarton. The home team opened the scoring about five minutes after the start, M'Naught making good use of a pass from Bell. Keeping up the pressure, Taylor was successful in getting another couple after some fine passing. The Hibs were playing with great dash, and scored two goals in quick succession. The home team got other two goals before half-time, the game then standing 5 to 2 in favour of Dumbarton. The play was not so fast in the second half, the strong sun telling very much on the men. The home team raised their total to 8. The Hibs, although they played hard for it, could not manage a point at all, the game ending - Dumbarton, 8, Smithston Hibs, 2.
Ref 1890001

6th September 1890
First Round   **Kilsyth Wanderers 2-1 Renton**
Contrary to all expectations, the Wanderers succeeded in pulling off their tie with Renton in the first round of the Scottish Cup, by defeating the crack team by 2 goals to 1 on their ground at Kilsyth. In their day the Wanderers have created one or two surprises, but this was the greatest of all, and of course, the jubilation of their supporters is very great.
Ref 1890014

S.F.A.C.M. [16th Sep]. The grounds of this protest were that the spectators encroached on the pitch, which was not properly roped off. One of the players being tripped by the crowd, and on account of playing a player under an assumed name. Mr Ferguson, the referee, said that the Renton players were frequently interfered with by the spectators, but the interference was not sufficient to cause him to stop the match. The Renton umpire said he saw the ball strike the spectators inside the line, but the ball was still played. When they were taking corner kicks his players were interfered with by the spectators. The Kilsyth Wanderers did not see any spectators at the spot where the man was said to have been tripped. There were only two or three spectators inside the ropes. It was decided, by a majority of twelve to eight, that the protest had not been formally lodged according to the rule.
Ref 1890015

6th September 1890
First Round   **Harp (Dundee) v Lochee**
The Lochee appeared at East Dock Street Park, but scratched on the ground, and agreed to play a friendly game. The Harp had the choice of goals, and set the Lochee men to face the sun. A spell of open goal to goal play having passed, Orchie drew first blood for the Harp, and Gowans shortly afterwards put on a third. After a bit of dashing play Heggie registered the only goal which fell to the strangers. Before half-time Brannon headed another point for the Harp, the scores then standing = Harp, 3; Lochee, 1. Early in the second period Ochie put the Harp another goal up. After this the play was mostly confined to the Lochee lines, with, however, an occasional raid on the Harp goal. The stripes defended gallantly, but near the close M'Culloch once more sent the ball home, and the game ended - Harp, 5 goals; Lochee, 1 goal.
Ref 1890002

Footnote
Later in the month Lochee changed their name to Lochee United and, in their first match under that guise, on the 27th September, lost 12-1 away to Broughty.

6th September 1890
First Round   **Dumbarton Union 12-1 Grasshoppers**
At Dumbarton. The home team were far too many for the visitors. The Grasshoppers managed to score the first point, and it was their last. At half time the game stood 5 to 1 in favour of Union. Adding 7 more goals in the second half, Union won by 12 goals to 1.
Ref 1890001

6ᵗʰ September 1890
First Round   **Burnbank Swifts 13-0 United Abstainers**
These teams met at Burnbank to play off their tie. Losing the toss, the Abstainers kicked off, and in a few minutes the Swifts had put on their first goal. From the kick off the visitors had a look in, but after this the Swifts settled down, and before half-time was called they had scored another 5. On crossing over, the Abstainers had a run into the Swift's territory, but were repulsed, and in a few minutes Burnbank again score, and continuing to press, they ran out winners by 13 to 0.
Ref 1890001

6ᵗʰ September 1890
First Round   **Cowdenbeath 10-1 Linlithgow Athletic**
This fixture was played at Cowdenbeath. The home team facing a strong sun, started the game up hill. Pressing hard for ten minutes they ultimately opened scoring from a shot which bounced between the posts from the leg of the Linlithgow back. Hostilities were kept up at both ends for twenty minutes, when Hughes, with a long shot put on a second point for Cowdenbeath. Two minutes from half-time Linlithgow scored a goal by a rather soft shot from Paxton. On change of ends the visitors played up well, despite sun and hill, but the vigour did not last long, and Cowdenbeath again took the game in hand, and towards the end the visitors were fairly out of it, goal after goal being sent in by the home eleven. Todd put on no fewer than five, whilst Hughes had two and Dow one. Result Cowdenbeath, ten goals; Linlithgow, one goal.
Ref 1890010

27ᵗʰ September 1890
Second Round   **5th K.R.V. 9a1 Mid-Annandale**
At Dumfries, 5th K.R.V. nine goals; Mid-Annandale (Lockerbie), one. Mr Cameron, of the Rangers, officiated as referee. One of his decisions was questioned by the Lockerbie men, and in consequence they left the field without finishing the game.
Ref 1890020

27ᵗʰ September 1890
Second Round   **Bo'ness v Bellstane Birds**
These teams should have met at Newtown, Bo-ness but the Birds failed to appear.
Ref 1890020

S.F.A.C.M. [7ᵗʰ Oct]. Bo'ness claimed their tie with against the Bellstane Birds, the latter having failed to play on the account of one of their players having been killed. Bo'ness however, withdrew their claim, and the tie was ordered to be played on Saturday first.
Ref 1890022

11ᵗʰ October 1890
Second Round   **Bo'ness 7-0 Bellstane Birds**
At Newtown, Bo'ness in the second round of the Scottish Cup. The Birds failed to appear a fortnight ago owing to the death of one of their players, and Bo'ness claimed the tie. Ultimately they withdrew their claim. Bo'ness were not at their full strength, while the Birds' team included only three of last year's eleven, and through the entire game they

played with only ten men. The home team, playing with the wind, put the ball through within ten minutes, and Hamilton shortly afterwards followed with a second. Bo'ness still kept up the pressure, and a shot was sent it. The ball striking the post, rebounded into play, and Robertson, of the Birds, inadvertently breasted it through his own goal. Scrimmages in front of goal resulted in Bo'ness raising their total to five goals in the first period, while the Birds were unable to score. The Ferry boys in the second half had occasionally a look in at Bo'ness goal, but during the greater part they had to act on the defensive. Hamilton and Weatherspoon each added a goal for the home team. Result:- Bo'ness seven goals; Birds, nil.
Ref 1890023

27th September 1890
Second Round   **Adventurers v Vale of Leven Wanderers**
These teams met at Slateford Road, Edinburgh. After seeing the park, which is an open one, the visitors gave the referee the following:- "The Vale of Leven Wanderers protest against the Adventurers for playing on a public park, and not roped." The Wanderers then left the field.
Ref 1890024

S.F.A.C.M. [7th Oct]. The Vale of Leven Wanderers objected to the Adventurers, because they considered their field a public park, and claimed the tie. The Adventurers denied the assertion, and referred the committee to their rent receipts. Further evidence was tendered, especially by Mr. Sneddon and Mr M'Culloch. The committee arrived at the conclusion that the Wanderers had no case, and they dismissed the protest unanimously, and awarded the tie to the Adventurers.
Ref 1890022

27th September 1890
Second Round   **Slamannan 5-2 Clydebank**
S.F.A.C.M. [7th Oct]. Clydebank's protest against Slamannan, on the ground that the goal-posts were not the required height, was, on the verification of the referee, sustained, the tie to be replayed at Clydebank.
Ref 1890026

27th September 1890
Second Round   **Burnbank Swifts 2-1 Stevenston Thistle**
...The Burnbank were now pressing and again scored, but the point was disallowed. Shortly after this the game was stopped owing to a mistake on the part of the referee blowing the whistle 12 minutes before time.
Ref 1890024

S.F.A.C.M. [7th Oct]. The Stevenston Thistle claimed their tie against Burnbank Swifts, on the ground that full time was not played. The fact was admitted by all parties, and the tie was ordered to be replayed at Burnbank on Saturday first.
Ref 1890022

27ᵗʰ September 1890
Second Round   **Inverness Caledonian v Lybster**
Lybster scratched to Caledonian (Inverness), owing to difficulty of visiting the ground of the latter.
Ref 1890020

27ᵗʰ September 1890
Second Round   **Broxburn 5-3 Clackmannan**
Owing to dissatisfaction in the Broxburn team at the last moment, there were many changes in it. Broxburn won the toss, and kicked off with a slight wind in their favour. The strangers defended well, and some time elapsed before Broxburn found an opening. This was soon followed with another point. Putting some dash into their own play, the strangers, in the face of the wind, got the ball well down, and beat Docherty. Broxburn added another point, and thus the first half ended. Clackmannan broke away on resuming, and Docherty, being out of his goal, could not regain it in time to save his charge, and a point had to be conceded. Broxburn bore down on their opponents, and A. Russell put in a good shot, which could not be saved. From the kick Clackmannan got well up, and again they followed with another point. From this the play got loose. The Broxburn were hovering near their opponents' goal when Ferguson sent in a fast shot which took effect. The game ended:- Broxburn, five goals; Clackmannan, three goals.
Ref 1890020

11ᵗʰ October 1890
Second Round   **Clydebank 5-2 Slamannan**
At Hamilton Park, Clydebank, before a large turnout of spectators, in dull and threatening weather, the above teams met to decide who should enter the third round. The home team kicked off uphill, and playing with great dash soon began to assert their supremacy by quickly scoring 3 goals. Play slackened down for a bit, and towards the end the visitors had the best of it, but were only successful on one occasion. The second half of the game was of a give-and-take nature, the visitors playing a hard and determined game. Clydebank put on number four, followed immediately after by one for the visitors. The home team then had one disallowed, and although only playing ten men augmented their total by one more, retiring winners by 5 goals to 2. Clydebank had not their full team, Barry and Gallacher being away, their places being taken by M'Innes and Leckie.
Ref 1890031

18ᵗʰ October 1890
Third Round   **Heart of Midlothian 3-0 Methlan Park**
This important tie, originally fixed by the Scottish Association to be played at Dumbarton, was, at the suggestion of Mr Sneddon [SFA president], decided at the recreation ground of the International Exhibition. The weather, though bitterly cold, was fine and in every way adapted for good football, and the enterprise of the Entertainments Committee was rewarded by an immense gate, variously estimated at from 9,000 to 10,000 spectators.
Ref 1890032

25th October 1890

Third Round Replay   Camelon 6-10 East Stirlingshire

Consequent on the drawn game the previous week these teams met at Victoria Park, Camelon, on Saturday, to decide as to which would enter the fourth round of the Scottish Cup ties. The attendance was not so large as on the previous Saturday, the wet weather, no doubt, preventing many from travelling to the Camelon enclosure. There would be close on 1500, however. Both teams were the same as on the previous Saturday. Camelon won the toss, and decide to attack the railway goal in the first half. A free kick immediately after the kick-off, enable Camelon to get well down to Mercer [ES], where they had a couple of throws. The play was mainly in the E.S. territory for the first ten minutes, though the goal was always kept clear. It was ten minutes ere Goodwin had his first goal kick, after which the game opened up. Johnston crossed the ball dangerously in front of goal, but it was cleared away. The Gorrie [C] had a try at the other end, which Mercer was lucky enough to stop. A couple of corners fell to Camelon ere the ball was got away, and it was taken to the other end, where Goodwin [C] in turn saved. Free kicks were given against both teams - one of which was for offside against Reid, who centred, and Alexander shot home. The ball was at both goals in quick succession, and then, after a sharp struggle, Carty [ES] opened the scoring twenty minutes after the start, Camelon had the first try afterwards, but it was wide. Johnston and Carty brought up the ball, and the former grazed the post. A corner fell to East Stirlingshire without result, and Camelon transferred the play to the other end, where Mercer saved a good shot from Fraser. He was not so successful, however, with a long return by Burns, which came into goal, M'Kechnie made a jump and let the ball roll under. Mercer made an attempt to save it, but only got part of the ball. This made the score equal. From this till half-time East Stirlingshire had the best of the play. A second goal was added by Howden after Goodwin had saved from the left. Five minutes from half-time Reid scored the third goal, and before half-time East Stirlingshire had a corner, from which Howden scored a fourth goal. The East Stirlingshire was thus in the lead by 4 goals to 1. The game was only three minutes old when some combined work by the East Stirlingshire left wing and centre resulted in Carty scoring with an oblique shot. The same player had a clear goal afterwards, but missed. After Camelon had sent the ball over their opponents' goal-line, another attack by East Stirlingshire culminated in Alexander scoring. With five goals of a lead, and likely to get more, it looked as if Camelon were to sustain a heavy defeat. Fifteen minutes from resuming, however, they received new energy, as from a drooping shot from the Camelon right, Ritchie, in attempting to return the ball, kicked it through his own goal. Five minutes afterwards a cross by Whyte bounded through off Fraser. This was putting a new complexion on the game, and Camelon were enjoined to "hurry up." Their next attack was repulsed, however, and East Stirlingshire quickly put on a couple of goals, both from long returns by Inch. The ball was kept at Camelon goal for a few minutes afterwards. Camelon repulsed their opponents, and the result of a scrimmage was that the fourth goal for Camelon was scored. Two minutes later Fraser sent the ball in from the left, and again it was scrimmaged through. The quick scoring raised the excitement to a great pitch. East Stirlingshire secured a ninth, then Camelon got their sixth goal, and Alexander finished the scoring by getting the tenth for his side.

Camelon were near scoring again just at the finish. Result - East Stirlingshire, 10 goals; Camelon, 6 goals. The referee was Mr Robertson, 5th K.R.V.
Ref 1890033

29th November 1890
Miscellaneous   **OLD MAN KILLED AT A FOOTBALL MATCH**
William Harvey, an old man, 86 years of age, and residing at 374 Great Eastern Road, Parkhead, Glasgow, died yesterday from injuries received the previous day. He had on the Saturday afternoon been looking on at a football match being played on a piece of vacant ground off Great Eastern Road. Apparently he got within the mark surrounding the ground occupied by the players, when David Smith, one of the players, on running after the ball, came against Harvey, throwing him to the ground and rendering him unconscious. The old man was carried home, but he never regained consciousness, and died at ten o'clock yesterday morning.
Ref 1890034

6th December 1890
Fifth Round Replay   Royal Albert 0a4 Celtic
At Larkhall, in presence of nearly 5000 spectators. The Celts scored the first point shortly after the commencement of the game, and keeping up the pressure soon added other two goals to their credit. The home team's play improved towards the close of the first half, but they failed to score. On change of ends play was more even, and each goal was corralled in turn. Ten minutes before time a slight accident occurred, and a "rush" by the spectators prevented the game being completed.
Ref 1890035

Celtic journeyed to Larkhall to meet Royal Albert. Latterly some rather disagreeable incidents happened, and twelve minutes before time the referee stopped play, the Celts leading by 4 to 0. Celtic claimed the match.
Ref 1890036

20th December 1890
Sixth Round   East Stirlingshire 1-3 Heart of Midlothian
... After 25 minutes had gone some grand play by the home forwards resulted in the equalising of the score. Play was keenly contested afterwards, and just before half-time Adams [the Hearts' back] fisted out the ball from under the bar. A free kick was given about a foot from the goal-line, but as a Rugby maul was formed the referee sounded his whistle, the score standing one goal each.
Ref 1890037

S.F.A.C.M. [6th Jan]. The Hearts complained of rough usage by the crowd at Bainsford, and it was agreed that no ties be played on the ground of the East Stirlingshire till 9th April.
Ref 1890039

20th December 1890

Sixth Round   **Dumbarton 3-0 Celtic**

At Boghead, Dumbarton, before a large crowd. The referee declared the ground playable, but both teams protested before starting play. Dowds kicked off, but Dumbarton carried the ball right down, and Mair banged it past Bell. M'Leod had then to save an attack of the Celtic forwards, which he did cleverly. Dowds looked like getting in, but he was given offside, and from the kick Bell missed an easy chance at the other end. The home forwards made a determined attack on the Celt's goal, and a second goal seemed imminent, but Bell cleared in the nick of time. Gallacher and Keir were both penalised for rough play. A free kick near Dumbarton's goal looked dangerous, but a "hand" off one of the greens neutralised the advantage. Dowds made a splendid try, but his shot was coolly met by Millar. Bell had a brilliant run all by himself, and put in a rare long shot which the Celt's custodian had some difficulty in getting rid of. M'Leod was then severely tested, but he did his work well, and in the twinkling the leather was over the Celt's lines. Half-time - Dumbarton, 1; Celtic, 0. Both teams restarted well and play ruled fast. Kelly tried one of his famous rushes, but Dumbarton's halves closed round him and dispossessed him of the ball. Dumbarton had many favourable chances, but were very slow to shoot. Muir at last made a good try from well out, and had the satisfaction of beating Bell a second time. Shortly after Reynolds got injured, and had to be carried off. Bell made a good run and, beating Gallacher and M'Keown, had no difficulty in sending the ball past his namesake. The same player headed another goal, and Galbraith slipped one in too, but both were disallowed. Dumbarton had most of the play towards the end of the game, but did not improve on their score. Shortly before time two or three score of spectators rushed on the field to stop the game, but the police and officials got them put off, and the game was finished. Result - Dumbarton, 3, Celtic, 0.
Ref 1890037

2nd June 1891

Miscellaneous   **International Board**

The International Board met in Glasgow last night [2nd] - Mr George Sneddon, president Scottish Association, in the chair. Representatives were present from England, Ireland and Wales. It was agreed that in future linesmen be appointed, whose duties shall be to decide when the ball is out of play, and which side has the throw-in. A proposal to the following effect was agreed to: - "If any player shall intentionally trip or hold an opposing player, or deliberately handle the ball within 12 yards from his own goal-line, the referee shall, on appeal, award the opposing side a penalty kick, to be taken from any point 12 yards from the goal-line. The ball shall be in play when the kick is taken, and a goal not be scored from the penalty kick"
Ref 1890040

6th June 1891

Miscellaneous   **First Ever Penalty Kick**

Airdrieonians v Royal Albert. These clubs contested the Airdrie Charity Cup final at Airdrie on Saturday. Over 2000 witnessed the game, which was well contested, though lacking scientific play. The Albert were fortunate in playing first with a stiff breeze, but only managed one goal - gained off a penalty kick taken [scored by James McLuggage] under the new law passed on Tuesday [June 2nd]. Airdrieonians were unfortunate in the second half, but the Albert were playing a fearless winning game, and scored another point with a fine shot by Bindall. The tie eventually ended in the Royalists' favour, the latter team winning by 2 goals to 0.

Ref 1890041

The two thousand who witnessed Saturday's final between Airdrieonians and Royal Albert likewise witnessed what is in all likelihood the first case of a referee granting a foul under the new law for tripping, holding, or handling the ball within twelve yards of goal. Mr Robertson (5th K.R.V.) was referee and decreed against one of the Airdrie backs soon after the start. That the new law was a puzzle to the players was evident, as all appeared to think they could stand in *front* of the ball as of old, but imagine the astonishment of both players and spectators when [James] Connor alone was left between the sticks, while his ten companions had to go six yards *behind* the ball along with the Royalists. In simple, the new law means that but two men settle such infringement, the kicker and opposing goalkeeper, and a goal is a moral certainty with half good management. The new penalty is most stringent, and referees will require to satisfy themselves that the law has been *wilfully* broken before bringing such penalty into force or we may hear of some "scenes" during the incoming season when cup ties are in full swing, and partisanship red hot.

 - Scottish Sport.

Ref 1890042

18ᵗʰ August 1891
Miscellaneous　　　　　　**Scottish FA Committee Meeting**
The secretary said that the Edinburgh Hibernians and the Dundee Wanderers had failed to pay their subscriptions. There were 18 clubs who had not sent in their money. Of the new clubs admitted, there were the Johnston Wanderers, of Forfarshire, and Our Boys, of Blairgowrie. The Wigtownshire and Southern Counties Associations were affiliated with the Scottish Football Association. The Dundee Our Boys asked to be admitted into the preliminary ties, as they had not got fixtures for those dates. They appreciated highly the honour which had been conferred upon them in placing them in the list of sixteen clubs exempted from taking part in the first four rounds.
Ref 1891001

5ᵗʰ September 1891
P.S. First Round　　　　　**Inverness Thistle v Wick Rovers**
S.F.A.C.M. [6ᵗʰ Oct]. Inverness Thistle asked that Wick Rovers, who had scratched late, be ordered to pay expenses incurred. Their request was acceded to.
Ref 1891002

5ᵗʰ September 1891
P.S. First Round　　　　　**Dalry v Catrine Thistle**
On Saturday afternoon Catrine Thistle Football Club journeyed to Dalry for the purpose of playing the first round in the cup tie, but the match did not come off on account of the non-appearance of the referee. A friendly match was played which resulted in favour of Catrine Thistle by 4 goals to 3.
Ref 1891003

P.S. First Round　　　　　**Dalry 5-0 Catrine Thistle**
These teams met at Townend Park, Dalry, on Saturday in the first round for the Scottish Cup, the previous Saturday's match having been declared void in consequence of a referee not being present. The game was a stoutly contested one, but the Dalry was playing a strong game and showed up a good deal better than their opponents. The game ended in favour of Dalry by 5 goals to nothing.
Ref 1891004

5ᵗʰ September 1891
P.S. First Round　　　　　**Q.O.S Wanderers 14-0 Douglas Rovers**
This match was played off at Cresswell Park on Saturday in very unsettled weather. The attendance of spectators too was not up to the average of a cup-tie day. The game began about ten minutes late, and the Wanderers at once assumed the upper hand, but for a long time the splendid goalkeeping of Penman kept them at bay. After repeated attacks, however, Shankland succeeded in lowering the Rovers' colours for the first time. With the exception of an occasional run up by the Rovers' forwards, which was easily checked, the Wanderers continued to have matters their own way, and Crosbie scored the second goal, while a third followed before half time, when the score was 3 goals to *nil* in favour of the Wanderers. On resuming, the Rovers for a time played up better, and Thomson was twice compelled to save. They were unable to maintain their improved form, however, and soon the Wanderers invaded their territory, and remained there until

the finish. Crosbie scored the fourth goal, and after two fruitless corners Shankland and Aitken rushed through the fifth. The collapse of the Rovers was now complete, and goal followed goal with great rapidity. Penman missed a shot from the left wing, and Kennedy, Borthwick, Craven and Shankland brought the total up to ten. The scoring now ceased for a time, but the Wanderers soon returned to the charge and Crosbie added two goals, while Craven and Shankland got one each. This was all the scoring, and the game ended: Wanderers, fourteen goals; Douglas Rovers nil. The game throughout was very one-sided, and but for the magnificent goal-keeping Penman, the Rovers would have had an even heavier defeat. Although they had the upper hand all through the game, the Wanderers were never called upon to exercise themselves greatly. Crosbie's shooting and placing were very fine, and the right wing seems at last to have been put into an efficient state. The Wanderers wore a badge of mourning on the arm out of respect to the memory of R. Burgess, who died on Saturday morning. He was a very promising player, and is much regretted in football circles in and around Dumfries.
Ref 1891005

5th September 1891

P.S. First Round   Johnstone 20-1 Greenock Abstainers

Played at Johnstone. A one-sided game throughout. The Johnstone played a fine combination game, a quality which was prominently absent in the strangers. Johnstone, 20 goals, Greenock Abstainers, 1.
Ref 1891006

5th September 1891

P.S. First Round   Ayr 12-0 Pollockshaws

These teams met on Somerset Park, Ayr. The weather was most unfavourable, rain falling heavily throughout the whole game. In the first half the Ayr scored two goals, while their opponents failed to register a point. In the second half Ayr had matters all their own way, adding other ten goals to their total, thus winning by 12 goals to 0.
Ref 1891006

5th September 1891

P.S. First Round   Arbroath 0a1 Brechin

The season opened on Gayfield Park, Arbroath, on Saturday with a match in the first round of the Scottish Cup ties. Brechin kicked off, and after some exciting play the first round ended Brechin, 1; Arbroath, 0. Ends being changed Arbroath had now the wind in their favour, but failed to derive any advantage from it. Their goalkeeper was kept employed, and did well, but it was at the other end where failure was. At length after a fine run up Arbroath sent in the ball and claimed a goal, but this was held by the referee to be offside, so was disallowed. This led to a dispute, and the Maroons have protested. In consequence there was no more play. The match being brought to a close before time. Brechin, 1; Arbroath, 0.
Ref 1891008

S.F.A.C.M. [15th Sep]. The Arbroath protested against the Brechin as the referee was a member of the Brechin Club. The referee, Mr Dalgetty, wrote that he disallowed

Arbroath a goal justifiably, and that three minutes from time the crowd broke in. The referee also reported that one of the Arbroath players, Henry Rennie, assaulted him by catching him by the throat. The referee said he had once been a member of the Brechin, but he was not a member at present. The game was a cup tie and not a friendly one. Mr Collie, Arbroath, said if it had not been for him the referee would have been half-killed. (Laughter) The Brechin referee left the ground seven minutes before time, but the Arbroath remained on the field. He admitted the referee was assaulted. It was ultimately decided that, as the game had not been finished, the tie be replayed on the ground of the Brechin Club.
Ref 1891009

15th September 1891
Miscellaneous　　　　　**Association Committee Meeting**
William Morgan, Monkcastle, and P. Maxwell, Kilmarnock Athletic, were censured for rough play. When they were formally censured by the chairman they smiled. The Chairman responded - "I think you have disappointed these gentlemen." (laughter)
*Ref 1891010**

26th September 1891
P.S. Second Round　　　　**Johnstone 4-7 Glasgow Thistle**
At Johnstone before a large crowd. The game was evenly contested, and was fast throughout. The Johnstone men played with great pluck, but the sloppy condition of the ground at goal lost them several goals. A few minutes after the second half started Mathieson, of the Thistle, met with an accident, and had to be assisted off the field. His temple was severely cut. The game ended - Glasgow Thistle, 7 goals, to 4 by the Johnstone.
Ref 1891011

26th September 1891
P.S. Second Round　　　　**East Stirlingshire 3a0 King's Park**
These teams met to decide their Scottish cup tie at Merchiston Park, Bainsford, on Saturday. A strong wind, amounting to almost a gale, blew from the west. Notwithstanding this, and the dull nature of the day, there was a large attendance of spectators. King's Park lost the toss and faced the breeze. They made little headway, and had to retire on their own goal. There play remained with little variation, and to add to the discomfort of the players and spectators heavy rain accompanied the wind soon after the start. The game was not long begun when a penalty kick was given against the K.P.. Johnston took the kick and sent the ball straight into M'Nab, who cleared at the expense of a corner. The game requires no detailed description, as it was mostly a series of corners, goal-kicks, and throws-in in King's Park territory. Only twice was the E.S. goal in danger - when M'Innes shot wide, and when Harley gave a corner. These were the only occasions the ball was over three-quarter field. Owing to an extra severe downpour the game was stopped 2 minutes before half-time, at the request of the captains of the teams. By that time, East Stirlingshire had scored three goals by Simpson, Reid and Johnston.

Ref 1891014

... and the players when they left the field looked more like a walking advertisement for somebody's soap as they appeared before they had a wash.
*Ref 1891015**

26ᵗʰ September 1891
P.S. Second Round   Royal Albert 6-6 Cowlairs
Lambie started the ball for the home team against a strong wind. Two minutes from start Burke scored for Cowlairs, and three minutes later the visitors put on other two points. The Royalists then played up, and Steel scored for them with a beauty. Continuing to press, the home team again scored. At half time the score stood - Cowlairs, 6; Royal Albert, 3. On change of ends the Royalists hemmed in their opponents, and six minutes from start scored fourth point. Keeping up pressure, they scored again, and eight minutes from finish equalised, and a splendid game finished in a draw - 6 goals each.
Ref 1891011

26ᵗʰ September 1891
P.S. Second Round   Broxburn Shamrock 6-4 Campsie
The Shamrock played with a high wind at their backs and pressed the Campsie very hardly in the first half, scoring five points, while the Campsie only managed to secure two. In the second half the rain came down in torrents, and the game had to be stopped for about ten minutes. On resuming, the Campsie had the best of the play, pressing the Shamrock continually, but the defence of the latter was splendid. The Campsie added two goals to their score, while the Shamrock added one, the game ending - Shamrock, 6; Campsie, 4.
Campsie protested against Broxburn Shamrock on the ground of severity of weather and it was ordered to be replayed at Broxburn on Saturday next.
Ref 1891011

3ʳᵈ October 1891
Miscellaneous   Annbank 4-0 Kilmarnock
These teams met in a charity match on the Rugby Park, Kilmarnock. The match was on behalf of the widow of an old supporter of the Kilmarnock, who was killed while returning home from a match between the clubs. A good deal of interest was evinced in the game, as besides the object of the match both teams are very popular with Kilmarnock folks.
Ref 1891016

13ᵗʰ Sep 1890. On Saturday night, shortly after nine o'clock, William Taylor, boot closer, residing at 7 Armour Street, Kilmarnock, was accidentally killed under very painful circumstance. A number of supporters of the Kilmarnock Club, including the deceased, accompanied the team to Annbank in brakes to witness the undecided Scottish cup tie between these two leading Ayrshire clubs. On the return journey a halt was made at the Holm Square, Kilmarnock, to let Taylor off. The deceased was lame, and walked with a crutch. He was riding in a brake, and got out all right, but unfortunately another brake

was following closely behind, and before Taylor could get clear he collided with one of the horses, with the result that the crutch was knocked out of his hand and he fell before the wheel, which passed over his chest. Death was almost instantaneous. The deceased, who was 43 years of age and married was employed in Messrs Clark & Son's factory.
Ref 1891017

24th October 1891
P.S. Third Round   Dunblane v Coupar Angus
These two teams should have met at Dunblane to play off their undecided Scottish tie. Dunblane received word at the last moment that Coupar could not raise a team. Dunblane thus gets into the fourth round without further opposition. Coupar Angus scratched as they were unable to raise a team.
Ref 1891018

7th November 1891
P.S. Fourth Round   Aberdeen 2-1 Dalmuir Thistle
At Chanonry in favourable weather, and in the presence of a large attendance of spectators. Both clubs were strongly represented, and an exciting game was anticipated. The visiting team came with a splendid reputation and were well received. Play opened in favour of the homesters, who conducted a smart attack on the Dalmuir citadel. Combining neatly, the Aberdeen fronts got round the opposing backs, but the parting effort went wide of the mark. The six yards' kick was secured by the locals, and by clever manipulation the leather was soon again in the vicinity of the strangers' goal. Two corners were secured, but both were abortive. Pulling themselves together the western men removed danger from their territory, and away they went to the other end. The home half-backs were eluded like a flash, and Ketchen and Wood were also given the slip. Down on Richie the Dalmuir forwards came and M'Lellan smartly shot the leather through and scored the first goal of the match. Long kicking between the backs characterised the play for some time, but gradually the game opened out, and some pretty passing was indulged in by the forwards of each team. The Chanonry eleven were having the best of matters, but performed miserably in front of goal, and threw away numerous chances. On the other hand, the strangers exhibited some clever passing, but the powerful play of Ketchen and Wood prevented them from scoring. Corners fell to Aberdeen, and the Dalmuir defence was sorely taxed, but the ball could not be got through, and at half-time the scores were :- Thistle, 1; Aberdeen, 0. Starting on the second period, both elevens played determinedly, and much enthusiasm prevailed round the ropes. Aberdeen received encouragement from all sides, and any bit of good play shown by the visitors was loudly cheered. The play of the home team improved as time wore on, and eagerly was the equalising point looked for. Whitehead put in a lot of beautiful work on the left, and Key in centre passed most unselfishly. After the visitors had been repulsed, the locals were granted a foul near their opponents' goal. The kick was well taken, and the backs being hustled, the ball was rushed through amid deafening cheers. Every member of the home team then wrought desperately in order to secure the winning point. For fully ten minutes the Dumbartonshire goal was hotly besieged, and had the shooting been less execrable, several goals must have been registered. Ineffectually the strangers tried to overcome the home defence, and then Key had the run of the day, passing all opposition,

and finishing by adding the winning point. Prolonged cheering greeted this performance. Play was hard till the finish, but no further scoring occurred. Result:- Aberdeen, 2; Thistle, 1. Mr J.R. Hunter, Montrose, acted as referee, and his decisions gave the utmost satisfaction. This is the first time in the history of the Aberdeen Club that they have reached the fifth round in the competition for the Scottish cup.
Ref 1891019

7th November 1891
P.S. Fourth Round   Annbank 8-2 Wishaw Thistle
Wishaw Thistle protested against the Annbank on the ground that the field was unsuitable and dangerous for playing. The Thistle stated that there was a quarry within a yard of the touch-line, while on the other side was an embankment which made it almost impossible to put the ball out of play. A Wishaw player was also accidentally charged over into the quarry, falling six feet. The protest was dismissed on a previous finding of the deputation of the Association who had pronounced the ground playable.
*Ref 1891020**

7th November 1891
P.S. Fourth Round   Cowlairs 9-3 5th K.R.V.
S.F.A.C.M. [17th Nov]. The 5th K.R.V. (Maxwelltown, Dumfries) protested against Cowlairs, on the ground that they had played Carson, whom they described as a professional. The Cowlairs replied giving a denial to the charge, and characterising the protest as a bogus affair. The CHAIRMAN, explaining that as this case was before the Glasgow Association in another form, suggested that the committee should await the decision of the affiliated body. Mr M'CULLOCH (Our Boys) thought this suggestion most extraordinary. He moved that the protest be considered now. The CHAIRMAN moved that consideration of the protest should be delayed until the Glasgow Association had come to a decision. Mr GILCHRIST (of the Glasgow Association) said that the case was very complicated, and the Glasgow Association were awaiting further evidence. Councillor W.G. Hay (Southern Counties Association), also favoured delay. He believed the 5th K.R.V. would be able to prove that Carson was a registered professional. By 17 to 8 it was agreed to proceed with the protest. Mr WILLIAM CRAIG, representing the 5th K.R.V., submitted documentary evidence that Diamond and Carson were both registered professional players, and had taken part in a match, Ardwick v Kirkmans Hulme, on September 16. They hoped, however, to have an affidavit on the subject. Mr HALLEY, of the Cowlairs, said telegrams had been received to the effect that no such club existed. Mr HINSHELWOOD, also of the Cowlairs, admitted having received a telegram on 18th September that Carson and Diamond had played in England, and warning the club against playing them. He could not say whether he had told Mr Halley, their match secretary, that he had received this telegram. The players, however, denied having played in England, and the committee considered their word as good as the telegram. In answer to Councillor Hay, the witness said the Cowlairs had not communicated with the Ardwick Club. Mr HARRISON (Ayrshire Association), in order to allow the 5th K.R.V. to produce the further evidence they expected, moved that the case be delayed. Mr PARK (Linthouse) seconded. Mr M'CULLOCH, on the ground that the committee had not sufficient evidence, proposed that the protest be dismissed. This

amendment failed to find a seconder, and Mr Harrison's motion was accordingly adopted unanimously. By a majority, it was agreed to as the Glasgow Association to allow the committee to have the benefit of the information in their possession. Wednesday, December 2, was fixed for the further consideration of the protest, and the secretary was instructed to summon Diamond and Carson to the meeting.
Ref 1891021

S.F.A.C.M. [2nd Dec]. Regarding the Carson and Diamond case, the meeting confirmed the standing of the Glasgow Association that the players named had agreed and played a match for Ardwick against a junior Manchester club on 16th September last. On the motion of Mr Campbell, seconded by Mr Baptie, Carson and Diamond were suspended from playing football in Scotland for 12 months. It was agreed that the tie between the 5th K.R.V. and Cowlairs be replayed at Springburn on Saturday first.
Ref 1891022

28th November 1891
F.S. First Round   Aberdeen v Mid-Annandale
These teams arranged to play off their tie at Dunblane. The weather was of the worst description, the rain coming down in torrents and the wind blowing hard. Both teams stripped and were on the field, but when the run was examined by the referee that functionary declared it unplayable. The Mid-Annandale team were, in spite of the referee's decision, wishing the game to proceed, but the Aberdeen men were quite well pleased to postpone the match for a week.
Ref 1891023

5th December 1891
F.S. First Round   Aberdeen 2-6 Mid-Annandale
At Stirling in wretched weather these teams played their undecided tie. Key, unfortunately, was absent from the Chanonry team, and Ramsay filled the vacant position. Play was in favour of the south team throughout the first half, and four goals were scored against Aberdeen. It was more by force than good football that the Mid-Annandale gained their points. Aberdeen scored early in the second half, but their opponents added another goal. Ritchie was in poor form, and ought to have saved three points against his side. Combined work enabled the north players to notch a second point, and often they were within an ace of further augmenting their total, but the heavy state of their ground caused erratic shooting. Ramsay scored both the Aberdeen goals and gave a good account of himself. A sixth goal fell to the Mid-Annandale before time, and the result was, Mid-Annandale, 6; Aberdeen 2. It was entirely impossible for the Aberdonians to play their usual game against the style adopted by the south club. Aberdeen have protested in consequence of the state of the ground and the rough play of their opponents.
Ref 1891024

28th November 1891
F.S. First Round   Monkcastle 3-4 Arbroath
On Saturday the Maroons travelled to Stirling to play off their tie with Monkcastle in the first round of the finals stage for the Scottish Cup. Arbroath is the only Forfarshire team

remaining in the Scottish ties, and much interest was taken in the match all over the district. The clubs are separated by more than one hundred miles, and accordingly they both had to travel. Arbroath made an effort by holding out considerable inducements, to bring Monkcastle to Dundee where a large gate would have undoubtedly been secured, but the coaxing process failed, Monkcastle not willing to throw away any advantage they might have on account of their previous experience of the Stirling ground.
Ref 1891025

12ᵗʰ December 1891
F.S. First Round   Cowlairs 3-1 Cambuslang
At Cowlairs there was a large turnout of spectators. Cambuslang had to start with ten men. Fully 15 minutes late the strangers kicked off against a strong wind, but Cowlairs at once took the lead, and Bishop, after a smart run, centred to Masterton, who defied Ross's power to stop. From a scrimmage Binks scored a second point. After 20 minutes' play Cambuslang were joined by Gourlay, which strengthened them considerably. A corner against Cambuslang brought forth a fine exhibition of play from Ross. Three times in encounters he saved out, and in the end the ball was sent over the bar. A rush and a rally, and M'Pherson put on the third point. Cambuslang appealed against it, but the referee declared it a goal. Half-time result – Cowlairs, 3; Cambuslang, 0. Cambuslang showed to more advantage when they got the wind with them, and M'Lelland had a little more to do than formerly. After ten minutes' confinement, Cowlairs got off and had a try or two at Ross, but none of them proved effective. Again the visitors got to close quarters, and from a throw-in a scrimmage followed, and Buchanan sent in a beauty which slipped through M'Lelland's fingers. Although the play continued hard to the end, no more scoring was done, and the game ended – Cowlairs, 3 goals; Cambuslang, 1 goal.
Ref 1891026

S.F.A.C.M. [Dec 15ᵗʰ]. A meeting of the Scottish Football Association was held last night to consider a protest from Cambuslang against their match with Cowlairs being considered a Cup Tie on account of the weather. It was unanimously agreed to dismiss the protest and retain the deposit.
Ref 1891027

11ᵗʰ December 1891
Miscellaneous   Broughty Football Club Notices
ALL Parties having Claims against the Broughty Football Club please send the same to Mr J. M. Forbes, 45 Fort Street, Broughty Ferry.
Ref 1891033

14ᵗʰ December 1891
We regret to hear that the Broughty Club is at present in a state of suspended animation. At present the Secretary has assumed the *role* of a trustee acting for a deceased person, and is anxious to be apprised of all debts due by the club.
Ref 1891028

6th February 1892
Semi-final　　　　　　**Celtic 5-3 Rangers**
At Parkhead, before 10,000 spectators. There was a change in each team. Madden was superceded by Cunningham in the Celtic team, and Law took Hugh M'Creadle's place in the Rangers. The Celtic started, and were at once at the Rangers' end. Henderson, of the Rangers, retired with a sprained wrist before five minutes. The Celtic were doing the pressing. The Rangers got away on the right and left, and a foul to them gave them a chance. Midfield play succeeded. Both goals were visited, but the Celtic were most confident. Law got a fine chance for the Rangers, but missed. In about a quarter of an hour Cunningham beat Haddow with a beauty. Play was desperately fast for the ground, and not unequal. The back play of Doyle, was splendid. The Rangers were now showing splendid attack, and keeping in their opponents they repeated their success. Out of a scrimmage M'Mahon got a fourth. At the interval the result was:- Celtic four goals; Rangers, nothing. The second half opened very much in favour of the Rangers, but after a chance or two the Celts took up the aggressive, and before five minutes scored a shady goal, which was allowed. The tide ebbed to the other end, and before ten minutes Low scored for the Rangers. The Rangers scored beautifully, but the referee disallowed. The game was as brisk as ever, and ruled very even. The Rangers had all the bad luck going. The Celts brightened up and put in some sharp attacks, but they were not capped with success. Five minutes before time the Rangers put on a third. The Rangers never lay down, and their form was wonderful. Result:- Celtic, five goals; Rangers, three goals.
Ref 1891029

13th February 1892
Semi-final　　　　　　**Renton 1-1 Queen's Park**
The "village" team again showed its pluck and skill in making a draw on Saturday at Renton, with the Queen's Park in the semi-final tie of the Scottish Association Cup. The day was a memorable one in "classic" Renton. The crowd of spectators was the largest which had ever assembled within the Tontine Park enclosure, and would number not less than 10000 people. The fine spring like weather tempted the supporters of the Q P to attend in such large numbers, that even the railway company at Queen Street Station were caught napping, and ran short of Renton tickets and had to extemporise. Two heavily laden trains were run. Renton committee erected extra stand accommodation, but unfortunately one of these erections gave way, and with it a crowd of occupants came tumbling down. One man, from Clydebank, got his leg fractured, and another his thigh. An elderly man from Jamestown got badly bruised. The ambulance van had to be called into requisition. A safety bicycle, which was below the erection, suffered in the wreckage. The arrangements made by the committee were in other respects creditable, and the crowd was very orderly.
Ref 1891030

12th March 1892
Final　　　　　　**Celtic 1-0 Queen's Park**
The final tie for the Scottish Cup has been played, but not yet won. The result was Celtic, 1; Queen's Park, nil, but the teams must meet again by Association decree. During the game there was doubt as to whether it was a Cup tie or not, as the crowd broke in. It was

reported that before half-time it was decided that the match should be a friendly one, and we think that this was the understanding, although the crowd didn't. Immense sums of money changed hands. Although the game was advertised to begin at four o'clock, the crowd began to mount the buses and cars at midday, and when the clock was striking the hour of four, quite forty thousand persons would be within the gates. A record crowd and no mistake! Never before was such a scene witnessed at a football match as that seen at Ibrox. The stands were crammed; the crowd was encroaching on the field, and mounted police were sent for.

Record crowd breakdown:

In the three stands ...6,000

On terracing behind west goal, and up to west end of north and south grand stands 15,200

On terracing behind east goal, and up to pavilion on one side and east end of south grand stand on the other, 10,150

On terracing in front of south grand stand, 8,350

Ref 1891031

9ᵗʰ April 1892
Final Replay   **Celtic 5-1 Queen's Park**

The protested final tie between the Celtic and the Queen's Park was played off on Saturday at Ibrox Park, the attendance being immense. It is idle to make a calculation how many would enter the gates. The Queen's Park were in a quandary up to the last minute, and when they entered the field they were minus Smellie and Arnott. Sellars, the forward to the former's place, and Sillars the latter's. Johnny Lambie occupied the gap in the Queen's front rank through Sellars going to back. The Queen's, winning the toss, played with a strong east wind at their backs, but they had to face a bright sun. At the outset the Queen's had the better of the match, the ball for the first five minutes never being away from the Celtic's twenty-five yards' flag. The Celtic played very erratic; they did not keep their places; but before one could speculate, the Glasgow Irishmen had the ball over the Queen's bar. The cry was, "Celts have scored!" but they hadn't. Robertson, of the Queen's, ducked and somersaulted a Celt. A free kick was the penalty. The Queen's citadel was again in danger, but a moment after the globe was in midfield. A dash at the Queen's goal again. Ah the ball is swishing away with the breeze, but the Celts' right back interposes. Do what they can, the Celts never get the ball past midfield. The Queen's are doing something unusual for them. They are playing a rough game. The Queen's pressed. The ball was kicked out. Sillars sent the leather spinning into goalmouth; a struggle ensued, and - and what? - the ball went past. It was another corner for the Queen's. The corner was abortive. However, in a little Waddel put in a surprise shot and scored for the Queen's. The cheering was immense from the grand stands. At the kick-off the Queen's again assumed the aggressive, and almost scored another. The breeze was still strong. A breakaway for the Celts. It is fruitless! If ever a club had hard lines it was the Celtic now. They had the ball every place but through their opponents' goal. The ball slipped past the post. Again the ball is over the Queen's lines. In a moment or two the sphere is at the Celt's goal, and the shout is "The Queen's have scored again;" but they hadn't. Now the Queen's had hard lines. Half-time - Queen's, 1; Celtic, nil. The second period was inaugurated by the Celts having the ball twice on the Queen's Park bar, and in a moment afterwards M'Mahon scored for the Celts amidst deafening cheers. Game three minutes old in the second half. A foul against the Queen's. At the kick-off Campbell scored a second goal for the Celts. The kick-off was followed up by the Celts,

who had the ball over their opponents' lines. Dowds banged in the ball, which the Queen's custodian saved in time. He bagged it in again, but the globe went past. The Queen's are not in it now. Lost ball! Ball over grand stand. A new one is supplied from the pavilion. Queen's had a run. Hamilton almost scored for Queen's. Another flier put into Celts' goal, which the keeper saved. Celts' custodian saved again. Match was faster and more exciting than ever. In a minute M'Mahon scored a third for the Celts. Sellars, of the Queen's now came forward and played on the wing. The Celtic supporters were very jubilant. Their team had matters now their own way, Dowds put in a surprise shot, and scored the fourth goal. Just a minute from time, M'Mahon scored a fifth for the Celts. So ended the final tie for this season - Celtic, 5; Queen's Park, 1.
Ref 1891032

3rd September 1892
P.S. First Round   **Arbroath 15-0 Brechin**
These teams met at Gayfield Park, Arbroath, on Saturday in the first round of the Scottish Cup ties before a poor turnout of spectators. The maroons losing the toss, Johnston kicked off against the wind. After some give-and-take play, Findlay registered the first point for Arbroath. From the kick-off the strangers invaded the home territory, but relief was got by Milne kicking strongly. From a throw-in the Arbroath rushed down the field, but the strangers' backs saved. Arbroath still keeping up the pressure, Johnston scored their second goal. The city men broke away, and gave the Arbroath defence an anxious time, but relief was got by the ball going behind. A foul fell to the Arbroath, and, Johnston securing the leather, again scored. The maroons would not be shaken off, and Hutton again added another point, and immediately after Robertson scored a fifth. The home team secured another two points before half-time, the scores standing - Arbroath, 7; Brechin, 0. On restarting, the maroons immediately scored, Suttie sending in a splendid shot. The strangers played up better, and had a shy at the home goal, but were driven back. Returning to the attack, they were awarded with a foul, but the Arbroath backs cleared. The maroons made a rush to the city goal, and were granted a corner, but it came to nothing. Play was confined chiefly to the Brechin goal, but Hendry saved his charge splendidly, fisting out some grand shots. The Brechin occasionally broke away, but were easily repulsed, and the Arbroath returning to the attack, had matters all their own way, and scored goal after goal till the whistle sounded. A very uninteresting game ended in favour of the maroons by 15 goals to 0.
Ref 1892001

3rd September 1892
P.S. First Round   **Glasgow Perthshire 2-17 Wishaw Thistle**
Wishaw Thistle had practically a walk over in their tie with Glasgow Perthshire on Kelburne Park. During the whole game the Wishaw custodian got only some three or four shots to negotiate. Not as the Perthshire keeper, who stopped numerous tries, besides the seventeen he failed to get a glimpse of. The Wishaw team all played well, but the weak play of their opponents made their victory a very easy thing.
Ref 1892002

The first half ended in favour of the Thistle by 6 goals to 2
Ref 1892003

The Glasgow Perthshire have greatly improved and altered their ground since last season. The Wishaw all round are a very capable eleven and should they improve a little with time, will take some shifting in the ties.
Ref 1892004

3rd September 1892
P.S. First Round   Whitefield v Summerton Athletic
These clubs were drawn together to play at Govan, but as both are defunct, no match took place.
Ref 1892003

Footnote
Whitefield had a revival and were drawn in the Second Round but scratched to Motherwell.

3rd September 1892
P.S. First Round   Vale of Gala 0-10 Kirkcaldy
Played at Hollybank, Galashiels, before a good attendance of spectators. A strong wind blew from goal to goal, and rendered accurate kicking almost impossible. The strangers were about 40 minutes late in taking the field. Kirkcaldy kicked off, and the ball travelled from end to end - a good chance being missed by the Vale for scoring a goal immediately after the start. After a time the strangers managed to score a goal, the ball going through off the goalkeeper's hand, and Walker almost immediately added another. Give-and-take play followed until the half-time whistle blew. In the second half the strangers had all the best of it, and managed to put on eight more goals. When the whistle sounded the score was - Kirkcaldy, 10 goals; Vale of Gala, 0.
Ref 1892003

10th September 1892
P.S. First Round   Motherwell 3-2 Hamilton Academical
[HT 2-1] On resuming, the Acas. broke away, and Sneddon's goal narrowly escaped downfall. Play became very slack for a time, both teams showing signs of fatigue. Dykes, who was playing a good game for the visitors, at last found an opening, and the score was again equalised. The shouting and cheering at this time was terrific, and as the game proceeded it could easily be seen that the players themselves were labouring under great excitement. The game looked as if it would again end in a draw, as the second half was pretty far gone. But it was not to be. Motherwell secured a corner, and Cowan placed the ball nicely into the goal mouth. Galloway, in endeavouring to head it through, was deliberately tripped, and a penalty kick fell to Motherwell. This proved fatal to the Acas., as Watson sent the ball beautifully through. The Acas. made strenuous efforts to equalise. It was all in vain, and they had thus to retire defeated by 3 goals to 2.
Mr Wright, of Cowlairs F.C., who acted as referee in the absence of Mr M'Leod, who was indisposed, gave every satisfaction.
The Acas. protested on the ground that no tie can be played unless the appointed referee turns up.
We have not done with the Hamilton Acas., their protest was sustained by a meeting of the Scottish Association held on Tuesday evening, and we are promised another ninety minutes of excitement and - well the pleasure of seeing the Acas. thrashed into oblivion. Protested due to absence of appointed referee.
Ref 1892007

24th September 1892
P.S. Second Round   Levendale 4-1 Bathgate Rovers
S.F.A.C.M. [4th Oct]. John Bryce, Bathgate Rovers, was severely censured for interfering with the referee in a match with Levendale.
Ref 1892008

24th September 1892
P.S. Second Round   Laurieston 1-5 King's Park
SERIOUS ACCIDENT - At Laurieston. In the first half play was very even. King's Park scored the first goal in a scrimmage after twenty minutes' play. Shortly afterwards a serious accident occurred to Ferguson, the King's Park goalkeeper, that player during a scrimmage having his right leg broken. He had to be carried off the field, and a doctor and the ambulance waggon sent for. No blame is attached to any player, and the game was remarkably free from roughness. King's Park were thus left to finish the game with ten men, and crossed over with the score one goal each. In the second half Gray, Johnston, D. M'Innes, and Gray scored goals in the order named for King's Park, who thus won by five goals to one.
Ref 1892009

24th September 1892
P.S. Second Round   Vale of Ruthven 3-3 Strathmore Athletic
Owing to Rule V, as regards private ground, the Dundee Strathmore Athletic had to travel to Auchterarder. Neither team were at their best, as the Strathmore wanted one or two of their ordinary team, while it was the Vale of Ruthven's first match for the season. A hard game resulted in a draw of 3 goals each.
Ref 1892010

24th September 1892
P.S. Second Round   Motherwell v Whitefield
Whitefield came to Motherwell with a team in which were several juniors who refused to take part in a Scottish tie, and scratched. The game was played as a friendly and the home team added another victory to their season's record.
Motherwell won the toss and with it the advantages of a stiff wind. They were repeatedly at goal in the first half, and had hard lines in only scoring twice. The visitors' goal-keeper was a crack hand and throughout the whole game his abilities were taxed to the uttermost, but his display was good, nevertheless. The teams crossed over with the home score at 2 and the visitors a similar number of points down. The Whitefield made nothing of the wind in the second half. They failed to score, while their opponents counted once, Watson banging the leather to the tune of "John Macpherson." Motherwell won by three goals to nil.
Ref 1892011

24th September 1892

P.S. Second Round   Carfin Shamrock 4-1 Airdriehill

Teams - Carfin - Sweeney, E. Pearson, D. Pearson, B. Breslin, White, P. Mitchell, J. Breslin, Hughes, James Breslin, Peter Mitchell, Mooney. Airdriehill - Devlin, P. Devlin, Duschy, Brady, Kane, O'Brien, Rice, Quinn, Summers, J. Rice, Derry.

The ground was in a terrible condition, the players often having to dash through pools of water to fish out the ball. Carfin won the toss and the Airdriehill kicked off. For a short time they made it hot for the home team, but they were driven back by the wind, aided by P. Mitchell (half). Carfin were slowly but surely gaining the upper hand, and Peter Mitchell scored after 15 minutes play. Mooney followed suit later on with a champion shot. Airdriehill, evidently expected to do wonders with the wind. And everybody laughed. This was when J. Rice attempted to take a corner, but failed to lift the heavy, wet ball, which rolled harmlessly over the goal line, leaving his partners round Sweeney like knotless threads, and causing D. Pearson to smile a bland No. 9 smile. Frowns - nay, imprecations - took the place of these blandishments, as Carfin saw Peter Mitchell miss a splendid chance of scoring bringing down on his shining pate the growls of the bystanders. Peter, however, made things all serene again by scoring. Proud of his success, he shook hands all round, and Jamie Breslin beamed benignly. No more scoring took place in this half.

With the re-start of the game, Airdriehill bore down on the home custodian, and secured a foul right in front of goal, J. Rice took the kick, and scored the first and only goal for his team. Carfin had the best of this half also, and put on one goal, making the score stand - Carfin Shamrock, 4; Airdriehill, 1.

Ref 1892011

26th September 1892

Miscellaneous   Football Forbidden by Acts of the Scottish Parliament, 1424-1491

It may not be generally known that the game of football and golf, now so popular, were prohibited by consecutive Acts of the Scottish Parliament by King James I., James II., James III., and James IV., as unprofitable sports, and that in their place weapon-schawinges were to be held, "all men to busk themselves to be archeree frae they be twelve years of age." In the first Parliament of King James I., held at Perth on the 26th day of May, 1424, it was ordained in quaint but concise terms "That na man play at the fute-ball. It is statute and the King forbiddis that na man play at the fute-ball, under the paine of fiftie schillinges as aft as he be tainted." In the fourteenth Parliament of James II., 1457, "It was decreeted and ordained that the weapon-schawinges be halden be the Lords and Barones, spiritual and temporal, four times in the year, and that the fute-ball and the golfe be utterly cryed downe, and not to be used, and that the bow-markes be made at ilk parish kirk a pair of Buttes and schutting be used, and that ilk man schutte six schotts at the least, under the paine to be raised upon them that comes not, at the least twa pennies to be given to them that comes to the bow-markes to drink." In the seventh Parliament of James III., 1474, it was again ordained "that fute-ball and golfe be abused in all time cumming, and that Zeaman that cannot deal with the bow that he have ane gude axe and targe of ledder, to resist the schott of the English." In the third Parliament of James IV., 1491, fute-ball and golfe was again forbidden, and the last Act appoints men to use shooting and archery. "It is statute and ordained that in na place of the Realme

there be used fute-ball, golfe, or uther sik unprofitable sportes under the paine of fourtie shillinges to be raised be the Scherrife."
Ref 1892009

24th September 1892
P.S. Second Round   Johnstone Wanderers 3a3 Harp (Dundee)
Mr Williamson, Edinburgh, refereed. Harp arrived late and the game started under protest. With the wind in their favour, the Wanderers pressed and Aitken shot through. Keeping up the aggressive they had some fine runs, and were successful in adding other two points, while the Harp, although they had one or two looks in, failed to count. Towards the close of the first half the crowd broke through the lines, and one of the stripes was carried off the field, play meantime being stopped. At the opening of the second period the Harp at once commenced to make up leeway, and were successful in equalising before time was up. Evidently displeased with one of the decisions, the spectators again began to encroach, whereupon the umpire sounded his whistle, and play ended with the figures standing:- Johnstone Wanderers, 3; Harp 3.

The cup tie at Clepington Park between Wanderers and Harp was not a pleasant exhibition. In the 80 odd minutes played such an amount of coarse play and noisy wrangling has not been seen for some time, and the sudden disappearance of the referee and consequent termination of the game was a fitting climax to a rough and disagreeable match. Flesh and blood could not stand 22 men trying to emphasise 22 different views at one time, and little surprise was expressed when he turned and fled.
Ref 1892014

4th October 1892
Miscellaneous   Bogus Clubs
S.F.A.C.M. [4th Oct]. Mr Crombie, Albion Rovers, called attention to the great number of clubs which scratched in the first round of the cup ties. He suspected that there were many combinations merely bogus clubs, who kept their membership with the Association in order that when they were drawn against a good club they might get money to scratch, such money being used for individual purposes. He moved that the Business Committee inquire into the question. - Agreed.
Ref 1892015

15th October 1892
P.S. Third Round   Arbroath 16-0 Strathmore Athletic
These teams played on the ground of the former at Gayfield on Saturday in the third round of the Scottish Cup ties. The teams were as follows:- Arbroath - Murray; Drummond and Milne; Rennie, Storrier, and Rae; Suttie, Findlay, Johnstone, Hutton, and Wishart. Strathmore Athletic - Malone; Stewart and Anderson; Dickson, Gray, and M'Nair; M'Nicoll, Mackersie, Dewar, Davie, and Wood.
There was good attendance of spectators, and a strong wind prevailed throughout the game. Arbroath winning the toss, the strangers put the ball in motion with the wind in their favour. Findlay soon put on the first point for the maroons, Arbroath kept up the

attack, and missed two opportunities at scoring, the ball in each case being sent behind. Findlay again smartly secured the second goal for the home team. Another goal soon fell to the maroons, and Hutton, within a short space of time, added other two goals to the Arbroath score. Before crossing over Johnstone scored once more for Arbroath. The scores at half-time stood:- Arbroath, 6 ; Strathmore Athletic, 0. The second half of the game was wholly in the favour of the home team, who raised the score by ten goals in the course of the second half. The result of the hollow game was:- Arbroath, 16; Strathmore Athletic, 0.
Ref 1892016

22nd October 1892

P.S. Third Round Rply   Aberdeen 4-2 Orion
S.F.A.C.M. [15th Nov]. The referee in the Cup-tie, Aberdeen and Orion, at Aberdeen, reported that he had ordered Walter Baird, of the Orion, off the field for kicking an opponent. Baird, in a letter, admitted the offence, but said it was for tripping not kicking. The offence, he urged, was done in the heat of a very exciting game, and being surrounded by a most demonstrative crowd, he could not restrain himself. He hoped for leniency on the ground of indignity already suffered in being ordered off the field. The Chairman said that in the circumstance, the ends of justice would be met by conveying censure. This was agreed to unanimously.
Ref 1892017

26th November 1892

F.S. First Round   Cowlairs v Queen's Park
These teams met at Cowlairs to play their tie, but the referee failed to turn up, and a friendly was played.
Result:- Queen's Park, 5 goals; Cowlairs, 2 goals.
Ref 1892018

S.F.A.C.M. [20th Dec]. [Owing to the oft postponement of the tie due to playing conditions] The question of changing the venue of the Queen's Park and Cowlairs tie was considered, but it was decided that the tie should be played on Cowlairs ground on Saturday first.
Ref 1892019

26th November 1892

F.S. First Round   Clyde v Dumbarton
These teams met on the ground of the Clyde to play off their tie on the first round of the final stage of the national cup competition. The ground was covered with water, and it was agreed to play a friendly game only. Result:- Clyde, 4 goals; Dumbarton, 1 goal.
Ref 1892018

17th December 1892

F.S. First Round   Clyde 1a6 Dumbarton
Played on Barrowfield Park before a very moderate crowd. Dumbarton were without Hartley (who had gone to England) and Millar. The referee's decisions did not give

satisfaction, and when in the second period Stevenson met with an accident, it was the signal for a break in by the crowd. It originated from the stand. Play was immediately stopped, and players sought refuge in the pavilion. The field was cleared in a few minutes, but the teams showed no anxiety to come out. The referee was injured, and refused to proceed with the game, which was therefore terminated. Several of the players were also cut. Result:- Dumbarton, six goals; Clyde, one goal.
Ref 1892021

S.F.A.C.M. [20th Dec]. The protested tie, Clyde v Dumbarton, was awarded to the latter club, who will now play the Rangers on Saturday first at Boghead.
Ref 1892019

26th November 1892
F.S. First Round   Motherwell 9-2 Campsie
From first appearances it looked as if the game were to be a hard tussle. The "Glen" boys rushed the leather, and had the honour of opening the day's scoring. (They had also the honour of closing it; but, alas, Motherwell sandwiched these two points too profusely with well taken goals). The visitors shot well when they got into close proximity to Sneddon, and the grand old custodian had plenty of work in the first twenty minutes. The home forwards made several raids on their opponents' goal. Campsie, however, hung tenaciously on to these individuals, and their work was for a time ineffectual. Latterly, however, Cowan found an opening and scored. From this till half-time goals fell fast and thick to Motherwell's lot, and at the cross over they had equalised and had half-a-dozen to spare. The second half was almost uninteresting. Motherwell, resting on their oars, only scored twice, while their opponents, who were fagged, added but another to their scanty total.
The visitors got disgusted towards the close, and it was shortly after someone advised his comrades to "give it up" that Quigley, centre-half, left the field "with a strained ankle" Imphm.
Ref 1892022

Campsie protested - bad ground.

S.F.A.C.M. [6th Dec]. The tie between Campsie and Motherwell was ordered to be replayed at Motherwell.

17th December 1892
F.S. First Round   Motherwell 6-4 Campsie
Campsie were defeated a month ago by nine goals to two, but protested. The tie was ordered to be replayed on the 10th inst., but was postponed, the field being in the iron grip of the Norse king.
Immediately the ball was kicked off, Motherwell rushed it up field, and Cowan brought himself quickly into favour by sending through the first goal of the game in magnificent style. Campsie were dumfounded. They had barely shrugged their shoulders and collected their wits when Steel made a brilliant onslaught on their citadel. The leather flew straight from the foot of the home centre, but was miraculously kicked out by M'Farlane. A minute later Cowan struck the under side of M'Vey's cross-bar, and it was

cleared by Quigley. The excellent combination of the home team had, however, its fatal results shortly. Campsie had now a spell of luck. They had a splendid opportunity, but a corner was all they secured. Pattison took the kick, and, not-withstanding that he placed the sphere well, it was cleared by Govan. Smith, however, notched Campsie's first point. Unfortunately, Motherwell missed with an open goal while M'Vey was on the ground in front of his sticks, and the opponents having again sent through, the teams crossed over each with two goals to their credit.

The teams changed ends and resumed play without leaving the field. Immediately Steel scored in rare style, and Denholm and Galloway added a fourth and fifth respectively for Motherwell. The home team were now having the game too much in their own hands. They fell into their too common habit of slackening down. Campsie saw an opportunity, and availing themselves of it, increased their score by two points, but not before Steel had defeated M'Vey and increased Motherwell's total to half-a-dozen, at which it remained, the game ending in favour of the home team by 6 goals to 4.

The ground was in bad condition.

The forwards carried off the honours of the day as regards both teams.

There was a large gate, and the stand was fully occupied.

Ref 1892023

25th February 1893

Final   **Celtic 1-0 Queen's Park**

Probably no match of the year arouses such widespread interest as the final tie in the Scottish National Cup competition when the combatants are well matched; but when, as is the case this year, the competing teams come together for the first time in the season, additional importance attaches to the game. The attraction afforded by the meeting of two such clubs as the Queen's Park and Celtic was fully attested last year on the occasion of the first meeting of the teams in the final of the same competition, when a record gate was established. In all respects, therefore, Saturday's game was looked forward to as one of the first magnitude. On the one hand it was looked upon as a contest of League v. Anti-League, and on the other as a trial of skill between professional and amateur talent; while the match also was not devoid of an international element; the members of the one team being of Irish nationality, and the other of Scottish. It was all the more to be regretted, therefore, in view of these circumstances, that the weather, as it has so often done this season with other matches of interest, proved so unpropitious, more especially in view of the large crowd which turned out to witness the struggle. A hard frost setting in on Friday night, the ground at Ibrox Park, the scene of the contest, on the forenoon of Saturday was found to be as hard as iron and everything pointed to a postponement of the tie. Notwithstanding the ominous outlook, however, the officials along with the referee, apparently did not deem it to be their duty to come to a prompt decision, and make the decision known to the public, but allowed the expectant spectators to make their way to and throng into the ground in their thousands in the hope of the referee's decision, after an inspection just prior to the start, being favourable to the playing of the tie. Naturally, once the ground was packed with a crowd numbering 30,000 people, it was deemed unwise, for fear of consequences, to make it known that the inspection had shown it to be impossible to proceed with the tie, and those present, save a few that they were to witness only a friendly match. Still, once the teams took the field, the difficulty which the players experienced in keeping control over the ball and maintaining their

equilibrium on the hard and slippery ground - in spite of a liberal sprinkling of sand and hay seed over the greatest part of its surface - could not escape notice, and with no official declaration on the subject having been made known, a feeling of doubt and uncertainty as to the nature of the contest prevailed, which was discreditable to the officials of the Association, inconsiderate to the members of the public, and detrimental to the best interests of the game. As the play proceeded, however, the apathy and unconcern with which the players proceeded about their work made the true state of the case apparent to most, and the feeling soon spread to the spectators, whose bearing was a most undemonstrative one for a crowd of such dimensions. By half-time the secret could no longer be kept, and ere the second period was well under way the news had spread rapidly round the enclosure that the clubs were expending their energy and the spectators their patience over a friendly game. When this came to be fully known expressions of dissatisfaction were heard on all hands at the action of the officials in not making the fact known early in the day, as might easily have been done, that the ground was too hard for the Cup contest to proceed and thus have saved thousands needless trouble and expense. In the circumstances, considering the game will require to be played over again on an early date, though this has not been fixed, it is needless to enter into any detailed description of Saturday's game. The only alteration on the teams previously announced was that Gillespie took Macfarlanes's place in the Queen's Park ranks. As an exhibition of football by two such teams the game was a poor one, as could only have been expected on ground so hard, and bearing in mind also the fact that none of the players cared to risk much. The Celts certainly adapted themselves better to the unfavourable conditions, but at half-time the teams still stood level, without scoring. In the second period some better and more spirited play was seen, and the Celtic, by the aid of Towie, put through a goal, ultimately retiring victors by one goal to nil.
Ref 1892024

11th March 1893
Final **Celtic 1-2 Queen's Park**
Death on the field
The final tie for the Scottish Cup was the all-absorbing topic in football circles, and eighteen thousand persons gathered at Ibrox Park to see the great game. The finalists were the same as last year - viz., Queen's Park and Celtic. Both teams were trained to the hour. The Celtic had gone through their preparations at Millport, a favourite Clyde watering-place, but the Queen's found their own ground at Hampden all that was necessary. The Celts were out to a man; not so with the Queen's. They wanted Robertson at half-back by force of circumstances, and Arnott at back by choice. The leaving out of Arnott was condemned, as he is a splendid man for the Irishmen's tactics. However, as to the game. The Queen's won by 2 goals to 1, which gives a real idea of the play. Winning the toss, the Queen's opened with fast play, and frequent shots just missed the goal by inches. In ten minutes Hamilton brought up the ball, which he banged into the goal. The keeper and Reynolds stopped it, and while they wavered what to do next Sellars rushed from the left and put the leather through. The cheering was deafening. Keeping at it, the Queen's should have scored often and well, but the Celtic defence was grand. Queen's then fell away, and with only fifteen minutes of the first half to go, and with the strong wind, the Queen's chances were fast dropping. However, just on half-time a second goal fell to the "Spiders," the ball being rushed through. Half-time saw the Queen's 2 up, and a gale of wind to face. The second half started all in favour of the

Irishmen, who scored a well-earned goal in nine minutes. So concerted was the Celtic play at this stage that it merely looked a matter of goals. However, the Queen's not only defended nobly, but were frequently dangerous. With ten minutes to go, Doyle went from back position into the centre. This "gallery" play was received with derision, and instead of his doing any good, the move enabled the Queen's to get within shooting distance often. The last ten minutes was a terrible struggle, the Queen's showing brilliantly. The Celtic could not score, and were therefore, to the delight of the large proportion of the spectators, beaten and robbed of the cup which they won last year. The Rangers also defeated them in the Glasgow Cup final tie this season. The Irishmen were disappointed, and the Queen's supporters jubilant that the Irish Catholic faction should have been put aside. Strangely enough all the injuries were on the Celtic side. The gate money was £620. When the Queen's scored their second goal, an elderly man, near the northern stand, dropped dead from excitement.
Ref 1892025

20ᵗʰ June 1893
Miscellaneous   Dundee Football Club
The twelve gentlemen appointed by the East End and Our Boys football clubs to constitute the ruling body of the new club known as Dundee, met in Mathers' Hotel on Tuesday evening – Mr A. Buttars presiding. The first business was the election of officebearers, and the appointments were as follows :- President, Mr J. Petrie; vice-president, Mr A. Buttars; business secretary, Mr Wm. Black; match secretary, Mr A. Williamson; joint treasurers, Messrs J. Forbes and W. M'Lean; members of Committee, Messrs M'Vicar, J. M'Intosh, Saunders, Charles, Spalding, T. M'Kee, W. K. Murray, and E. Fleming. Arrangements were then made for at once proceeding to select players and complete all the preliminary work necessary to the proper organisation of the club. East End meet Our Boys on Monday evening, the match taking the form of a benefit for the widow and family of one of the oldest members in connection with both clubs. This may justly be called the final of all local finals, as it is the last match between the old enemies, now fast friends. The match was at one time intended to be the new club Dundee *versus* the returned prof., but Mr Alcock, the English secretary, sent word that it was against a very strict rule of the English Association to play football in the close season. However, the Harp very kindly offered their ground and stand free, and the match will take place upon their ground. Kick-off, 7.15. All true footballers in Dundee, and especially all old Our Boys and East End members will turn out to witness this last match between the old rivals.
Ref 1892027

Footnote
Our Boys and East End resigned from the Northern League on the 24ᵗʰ June.

22nd August 1893
Miscellaneous   **Report on First Round Draw**
                                     East End v Dundee
                                     Our Boys (Dundee) - bye

No explanation is given in the telegram as to the obvious mistake in failing to recognise the amalgamation of the East End and the Our Boys.
Ref 1893001

Footnote
East End and Our Boys had amalgamated to form Dundee F.C. on the 20th June.

30th August 1893
P.S. First Round   **Brechin 4-6 Harp (Dundee)**
This, the first of the season's Scottish Cup ties, was played last night on Montrose Street Park, Brechin, by arrangement with the above Clubs, before a fair turnout of spectators, and in excellent weather. Brechin kicked off, and the Harp were down on goal but shot past. A few minutes later a shot from the left lowered the Brechin colours. Not to be behind, Brechin had a shy at the strangers, but it proved abortive. The Harp again assumed the upper hand, and a second goal was registered for the "jerseys." The Brechin seemed nettled at this, and forced a throw-in, from which Johnston scored with a splendid header. Equal play followed for some time, but at last the strangers got in the vicinity of the home team's goal, and from a scrimmage they registered their third goal. Following this up, the Harp tried Owler with several good shots, but he fisted out in capital style, and the Brechin forwards getting possession of the ball, it was rushed through the strangers' goal, amidst loud cheering. From the kick-off M'Farlane made off, but Falconer checked his progress, and play once more reigned in mid-field. Shortly after this half-time was called, the game standing - Harp, 3; Brechin, 2. On resuming, Harp began to show up, and after a few minutes registered their fourth goal. The home team appeared to be playing very loosely, until the "green jerseys," redoubling their efforts, secured their fifth goal. After this reverse the home team were seen to great advantage, and a combined run ended in a third goal for them. The Harp was now kept busy defending their goal, but at last it fell for a fourth time. It was now looking as if the home team were to equalise, the ball being kept wholly in the strangers' territory. However, they broke away, and were awarded a goal for a shot which went a foot over the bar. The home team demurred at this, but after a little wrangle they ultimately gave in. A few seconds later the game ended in darkness, it being impossible to follow the play. Result :- Harp, 6; Brechin, 4. The game was hard and fast, and it is to be regretted that the last goal claimed by the Harp, which went about a foot over the bar, should have been allowed by the referee, as it gave dissatisfaction, which need not be wondered at. Mr Bryan, President of the Arbroath Club, was referee.
Ref 1893002

Sep-04 Our Brechin correspondent writes:- "I was surprised to see Mr Diamond's letter in your issue of 2d September upholding Mr Bryan's decision in giving the Harp the sixth goal. Had I not been a witness to it I would not venture to give an opinion, and I still maintain that the ball went over the bar instead of under, and being behind the goal

I was in a good position to see, which the referee was not, as he was between 30 and 40 yards down the field, and owing to the light at the time he could not have seen it. Referees are human, and liable to err, seeing that the game ended at 7.50."
Ref 1893003

2nd September 1893
Friendly   **Falkirk v Clydebank**
At Falkirk - a friendly instead of Scottish tie, as some of the Clydebank refused to play. From the start Falkirk had the game in hand, and at half-time stood 6 to Clydebank's 0. Hamilton had 3 points and M'Laren 2, while one was scrimmaged. Clydebank made a better show in the beginning of the second period, but fell away miserably. Falkirk scoring other 4 goals, the game resulted - Falkirk, 10; Clydebank, 0.
Ref 1893004

2nd September 1893
Friendly   **Alloa Athletic v Clackmannan**
ROWDYISM AT ALLOA. Some disorderly scenes were witnessed during the course of the match between Alloa Athletic and Clackmannan at Alloa. Towards the close of the first half, when the ground team were pressing hard, Morris the Clackmannan goalkeeper, caught up the ball in his hands. M'Keil rushed in an endeavoured to "take the feet" from Morris. This the Clackmannan goalkeeper resented, and struck M'Keil a blow on the face. Blows were returned, and a fight ensued upon which the spectators broke in, and a scene of wild disorder prevailed. At lengths, through the efforts of the committee and the police, the fighting was stopped, and the ground cleared. The referee (Mr Murphy, Camelon) ordered Morris and M'Keil off the field, thus leaving the man on each side. The Athletic came into the field to play the remainder of the game with ten men, but Clackmannan refused to do so, and so the match ended with no scoring on either side. Disorderly scenes afterwards prevailed, and some excited Clackmannan spectators threatened to carry off the pay box because their admission money was not returned or the game fully played out.
Ref 1893005

Footnote
Due to Vale of Leven scratching to Clackmannan and Alloa Athletic having received a bye in the First Round, the above 'friendly' was arranged between the two clubs.

2nd September 1893
P.S. First Round   **Girvan Athletic v Pollockshaws**
This match of the Scottish Cup competition was to have been played at Girvan, but as there was no communication from the Pollockshaws Club the match did not take place.
Ref 1893005

S.F.A.C.M. [12th Sep]. The committee decided that the Pollockshaws and Girvan play off their tie on the former's ground on Saturday first. It was stated that the Pollockshaws had travelled to Girvan to play their tie, but found that the Girvan had gone off to

Maybole thinking the Shaws men were not to turn up. The Girvan players expected the strangers at two o'clock. They did not reach Girvan till about four o'clock.
Ref 1893007

A dispute between the Girvan and Pollockshaws provided a vast amount of amusement to the meeting. The tie should have been played at Girvan, but the ground club wrote to the Association saying they could get no information from Pollockshaws, and concluded that they were to get a walk-over. Pollockshaws wrote saying they travelled to Girvan, a distance of 66 miles, at a cost of £4, but found no ground, and no team to meet them. Thomas Cunningham, the captain of the 'Shaws, stated the case for his club, rattling off his story with an assurance seldom found in a witness. He presented a very plausible case, and though Mr. M'Lean put in some special pleading for Girvan, the Association ordered the tie to be replayed at Pollockshaws on Saturday. After this decision Thomas left the meeting jubilant, one of the very few men who leave happy.
Ref 1893008

2nd September 1893

P.S. First Round   Cowlairs 11-1 Carfin Hibernian
S.F.A.C.M. [12th Sep]. The Committee decided that the Cowlairs and Carfin Hibs, when they played each other on the 2d of September on the Cowlairs' ground, played a cup tie. The result was - Cowlairs, 11; Carfin Hibs, 1. The dispute at issue was - Were the Cowlairs to pay the Hibs £6 that they had guaranteed them? The Committee agreed that the Cowlairs would require to pay the £6. It should be explained that the Cowlairs also complained that some members of the Hibs played in their ordinary attire.
Ref 1893007

2nd September 1893

Miscellaneous   Action Against the Scottish Football Association
Sheriff Guthrie heard proof at Glasgow yesterday in an action raised a considerable time ago against the Scottish Football Association, and which arose out of a match which preceded the final cup tie played last year between the Queen's Park and the Celtic at Ibrox Park. The pursuer was Mr Robert Hamilton, Moore Street, Glasgow. It will probably be remembered that the Clubs met twice last year to decide the tie referred to. On the first occasion, however, the ground was found to be unplayable after the spectators had gathered, and what was termed a friendly unofficial game only was played. The pursuer was one of the spectators on that occasion, and in addition to paying 1s to get into the ground at Ibrox, he paid 2s more to get access to the stand. He pleads that as a cup tie was advertised, and that no intimation was given that, on account of the weather or otherwise, it had been arranged to play only a friendly game, he was defrauded. He therefore has raised the present action for damages. Mt Stuart Nicol appeared for the pursuer, and Mr Joseph Shaughnessy for the defender. Mr Shaughnessy reminded his Lordship that a long discussion took place upon the relevancy of the 10th April. He understood his friend's case was narrowed to this, that he was prepared to prove that the officials of the Association knew before the public were admitted to the ground that the game was to be a friendly one, and not cup tie. Mr M'Nicol said he could not admit that. His case was that the officials before the game commenced agreed secretly to have a friendly match only, and not to intimate the decision to the public until

half-time, and he did not think that they even did it then. Peter Kerr, an old football player, said it was the referee's duty to examine the ground two hours before the game commenced, to decide whether it was playable or not, and he was remiss in his duty if he did not do so. Mr Shaughnessy intimated that he was willing to admit that a cup tie was advertised, and that no notice was put up to the effect that the game was not to be a cup tie, and that the pursuer was present. John Brown gave evidence similar to that of the previous witness, Robert Hamilton, the pursuer, said he went to Ibrox Park to the final cup tie, and only saw a friendly game. The first intimation he got, was in the newspapers that it was not a cup-tie. He knew little or nothing about football. He did not raise this action for any pecuniary gain. He had offered to withdraw his claim if upon getting a promise that the money drawn at the gates would be sent to charities. John K. M'Dowall, Secretary to the Scottish Football Association, said that he knew that the referee was not on the ground two hours before the match commenced. Rule 15 stated that if there was doubt to the ground being playable, the referee should inspect the ground and give his decision as early as possible. He got no intimation from the referee. The Sheriff decided in favour of the Association without expenses.
Ref 1893010

23rd September 1893
P.S. Second Round   Q.O.S. Wanderers 15-1 Moffat
These teams played their tie in the second round of the contest for the Scottish Cup at the Recreation Grounds, on Saturday, in presence of a small attendance of spectators. The Wanderers, who were playing against a strong but somewhat fitful wind, assumed the aggressive immediately after ball had been set in motion, and ere five minutes of play had gone Little obtained their first point. Continuing to press, Glendinning shot just outside the posts, and Richardson sent over the top, and a minute later placed the leather between the uprights for a second time. Fairly roused by this, the visitors, playing with a dash they had hitherto failed to exhibit, bore down with a rush upon Mandell's keep, and from a shot by Steel secured their first, and what proved to be their only, goal. On the Wanderers once more getting the ball down the field, Little added a third with a nice high shot; and a little later the fourth was obtained by the forwards in concert rushing the ball up to the goal mouth and Richardson tipping it through. Another goal recorded by Sharpe a few minutes afterwards was disallowed on the plea of off-side ; but the home team still continued in the ascendancy, and Kennedy, with a shot from the touch line, placed a fifth goal to the credit of his team ; and when the half-time whistle blew the Wanderers had obtained seven goals - the last two being got by Sharpe and Little respectively - to the solitary point notched by their opponents. The second half of the game was too one-sided to call for description. The Wanderers' forwards, now fairly in their element, simply waltzed round their opponents, and launched through goal after goal ; while the Moffatonians succeeded in testing Mandell only once. When time was called the score was : Wanderers, 15 goals ; Moffat, 1. Three of the goals in the second period were registered by Kennedy, one by Little, one by Sharpe, two by Richardson, and one by Shankland. The only players among the Moffat eleven who made any effort to sustain the reputation of their club were Somers and Niven, the remainder being practically helpless; for, even when they did succeed in getting the ball, they were unable to use their opportunities. For the Wanderers, Richardson and Little were noticeable in the front rank ; the half-back division was as good as of old ; and in Kelly (of New

Cumnock), who played with the Wanderers for the first time on Saturday, the home team have secured a back whose services are very decidedly an acquisition.
Ref 1893011

14ᵗʰ October 1893
P.S. Third Round   Kilmarnock 3-3 Motherwell
... Two and a half minutes to go. Motherwell 3, Kilmarnock 1. An enthusiast for Motherwell jocularly observed - "It's all over but the shouting." Killie made another bold attempt, and Service scored goal number 2. Scarcely had the ball been kicked off when the home forwards collared it and had it between the posts. A few seconds afterwards the whistle sounded, an exciting and sensational game ending in a draw of 3 goals.
Ref 1893012

14ᵗʰ October 1893
P.S. Third Round   Kirkcaldy v Mossend Swifts
This Scottish Cup tie did not come off. The Mossend wired that they had lost the connection for Fife at Haymarket. The Kirkcaldy men have accordingly claimed the tie.
Ref 1893013

S.F.A.C.M. [24ᵗʰ Oct]. A letter was read from Kirkcaldy, claiming their tie against Mossend Swifts. The Edinburgh team failed to appear and telegraphed that they had missed the train connection at Haymarket. A certification was submitted from the stationmaster at West Calder to the effect that the Swifts could not have reached Kirkcaldy in time. It was agreed to replay the tie at Kirkcaldy on Saturday.
Ref 1893014

14ᵗʰ October 1893
P.S. Third Round   Cronberry Eglinton 1a3 Battlefield
S.F.A.C.M. [24ᵗʰ Oct]. The Battlefield protested against the Cronberry Eglinton. It seems that the referee ordered the game to be stopped 3 ¼ minutes from time owing to darkness. The game at that stage clearly showed a win for the Battlefield. Mr Robertson, the referee, said the darkness was such that he was forced to stop the match. The Committee decided that the tie was to be replayed at Cronberry on Saturday first.
Ref 1893015

14ᵗʰ October 1893
P.S. Third Round   Dunblane v Johnstone Wanderers
The Johnstone Wanderers ought to have played the Dunblane at Dunblane in the third round of the Scottish Cup ties, but, having scratched, succeeded in getting that team to come to Dundee to play a friendly encounter. The final result was:- Wanderers, 5; Dunblane, 3.
Ref 1893016

14th October 1893

P.S. Third Round   Strathmore (Dundee) 3-2 Arbroath

Unfortunately for the prospects of a good game, rain fell almost continuously for nearly the whole of Friday and Friday night, but it fortunately faired up on Saturday, but still the ground was very wet and sloppy, and nasty pools of water lay about. The match was billed to commence at 3.30, and by this time both teams, with about a thousand spectators, were in attendance, but at the last moment a telegram was received from the referee, Mr M'Lean, Ayr, intimating that he had lost the train, but would arrive about four o'clock. It was quarter past, however, when that gentleman made his appearance, and by this time the crowd and the players had become very impatient, as the afternoon was cloudy, and already the light was becoming bad.

.. the half-time whistle sounded, the scores standing three goals to nothing in favour of the Strathmore. When the second half started at ten minutes past five the light was beginning to fail and fog was beginning to make itself felt. The Maroons started the second period with a good deal of confidence, although immediately after the opening Collie was just in time in kicking out a good shot from Ireland. A foul against Rae for a "hand" did not improve matters. Milne caught the ball as it was almost through and drew it away with a splendid kick, and the Maroons forwards came away with one of their prettiest runs. Roberts kicked the ball out, and immediately afterwards handled it. Waterston sent the ball straight into the goal, and the Maroons backing up, scored the first goal for Arbroath. Away came the Maroons again, Hutton and Suttie going nicely together, but finding a grand back in Tosh. Willie Rae twice threw the ball half way across the field, and a terrific struggle took place. At one of the Strathie's uprights, the ball, to the disappointment of the Maroons, rolling behind. The Maroons were now straining their every nerve, the three halves lay close on the forwards, and with occasional drive now and then by the backs, proved quite sufficient to bottle up the Strathie forwards. A continuous bombardment was kept up, even Milne having his turn at shooting, and narrowly missing scoring. Arbroath's inability to score must remain a mystery. Time and again the ball was rushed in between the posts, only to be averted from its course by the Strathie defence, who blocked up the goal and kept the Maroons at bay by sheer weight. Corner after corner fell to the Maroons, and these were made the most of, but it seemed as if they were not to be able to score. The light was failing rapidly, and this told heavily against the Maroons, as their passing became very much a matter of random. However, a second goal was scored, by whom it was impossible to tell. Amid shouts of "Stop the game," the match was resumed, but as it soon became impossible to distinguish the players most of the spectators left the grounds. Still the struggle was kept up in front of the Strathie's goal, with now and then a confused struggling group under the cross-bar. The forms of the three Maroon halves could be seen flitting here and there, but at the far end only a shadowy outline told where Allan Mann was keeping guard. Close upon time the Maroons got the ball through again, but the Strathie goalkeeper disputed the point, and a corner was awarded. Suttie disappeared in the darkness and mist with the ball under his arm, and the usual struggle followed in front of goal. Immediately afterwards the whistle sounded, the scores being Strathmore 3 Arbroath 2. During the progress of the second half a protest was lodged by Willie Rae, captain of the Maroons, and at the conclusion of the match this was formally notified to the referee and the captain of the Strathmore.

Ref 1893017

S.F.A.C.M. [24th Oct]. The Arbroath lodged a protest against the Strathmore on the ground that darkness prevented the players from seeing the ball. The Arbroath's letter stated that the tie was advertised to begin at 3.30, but owing to the referee missing his train and not arriving till 4.17 the game did not start till then. The game proceeded satisfactorily until twenty-five minutes from time, when darkness set in. The Arbroath captain intimated a protest, but the match proceeded amidst shouts of disapprobation from the spectators. To show how great was the darkness, it was stated that the street lamps were lit. The Strathmore, on the other hand, admitted that the game was advertised to start at 3.30, but pointed out that Mr M'Lear, the referee, did not turn up till 4.15, and that the match started at that time. At half-time the Strathmore stood 3 to nil. In the second period the Arbroath with the wind score twice, and had the Strathmore not seen well, they could not have played such a splendid defence. The match ended in the Strathmore's favour by 3 to 2. The protest regarding the darkness was not lodged till after the match. The referee's report stated that the protest of Arbroath was lodged only three minutes from time. He had no difficulty in following the ball, and therefore he allowed the full time to be played. Mr Gray, the Arbroath captain, was called in. He stated that it was too dark near the close of the match to see the ball. In reply to the question as to how long it was dark ere the call of time, Mr Gray said twenty minutes. He lodged his protest fifteen minutes from time, and formally handed it to the referee at the close of the match. There was no representative from Strathmore present. Mr M'Lear, the referee, was called. A Member - Could you see the goal posts from the centre of the field? Mr M'Lear - I believe I could. The captain of the Arbroath lodged his protest with me three minutes from the call of time. Mr M'Culloch (Our Boys) - Could the two extreme wing men see each other? Mr M'Lear - I cannot answer for anybody's eyesight but my own. Mr M'Culloch - Is it possible to play the game when it is only problematical that you can *see* the goal posts? Mr Park moved and Mr Burnet seconded a motion that the protest be granted, and that the tie be replayed. Mr Martin moved and Mr Andrews seconded an amendment that the protest be dismissed. On a vote being taken it was decided that the two clubs play off their tie on Saturday. If the match prove a draw it was arranged that the clubs should play on the subsequent Saturday. Mr Fif thought the referee should be censured, for the whole difficulty was caused by him. The referee would try to laugh out of it, and say that he was able to see the game. It was not sufficient that he alone should see the game. He moved that Mr M'Lear, the referee, be spoken to from the chair. If he were a referee he should have turned up in time. He was the highest paid man on that occasion, and ought to have given his best services. The Chairman - as there is no seconder Mr Fif's motion falls to the ground.
Ref 1893015

25th November 1893
F.S. First Round   Orion 2-11 Leith Athletic
The Orion kicked off, and within five minutes Hislop [LA] scored the first goal. Fast play followed for about twenty minutes, when Fraser equalised. The visitors again took up the running, and Charles Henderson, by a neat low shot, placed his team one up. Equal play ensued for a considerable period, but ultimately the Athletic's forwards succeeded in bringing the leather within their opponents 25, and Wilson finding an opening sent in an effective shot. Fraser went away with a dribble, but was tackled before he got any distance. Shortly afterwards a foul was granted against the visitors, but nothing came of

it. The homesters were being hard pressed, but Mackay and Gray, who were in capital form, managed to keep their opponents at bay. Wight with a long kick sent the ball well up the field, and Leggat being in place carried it up the wing, and eventually scored a goal. The Athletic then returned to the charge, and twice in quick succession Gray had to fist it out. A goal-kick gave relief, and Carrie was the means of transferring the play to the visitor's quarters. At half-time the scores were - Leith Athletic, 3; Orion, 2. On a restart being made the Athletic commenced to press, and for some time the Orion had to play entirely on the defensive. Seven minutes from the restart J. Henderson sent in a very soft shot which Gray failed to fist out. The homesters now began to get disheartened, and several opportunities of scoring were lost through faulty shootings. A corner fell to the Orion, but Leggat failed to improve on it. The Orion got away the ball, but Young came to the relief, and by a smart pass to Lee the latter scored the fifth goal for the Athletic. The slippery condition of the ground was telling against the home eleven and every now and again some player fell and lost the ball. Lee got the leather at his toe, and by a soft tip sent it past Gray for the sixth time. The Orion seemed now quite done out, and the Athletics did pretty much as they liked. J. Henderson rushed the leather through, and thus scored the seventh goal. Ten minutes later Charles Henderson sent in an easy shot which Gray failed to negotiate. The Orion were by this time quite demoralised, and within five minutes the strangers score other three goals. The game ended - Leith Athletic 11, Orion 2.

Ref 1893019

16th December 1893

F.S. Second Round   Renton 2-2 Port Glasgow Athletic

S.F.A.C.M. [19th Dec]. ... for consideration of a protest from Renton against Port-Glasgow Athletic on account of the game being stopped 7½ minutes before time was up. The referee, Mr Bishop, admitted his mistake, and the committee decided that the tie must be played at Renton on Saturday first.

Ref 1893020

3rd April 1894

Miscellaneous   Suspensions and Admissions

S.F.A.C.M. [3rd Apr]. Harp F.C. (Dundee) were brought under the notice of the committee for not having paid to Renton £10, balance of guarantee due, and it was agreed to suspend the Harp until the money had been paid. Kilsyth Wanderers and Slamannan Rovers were also suspended until they had paid guarantees due Lochgelly United and Glengowan respectively. West End F.C. (Dundee) were admitted to the membership of the association.

Ref 1893021

21st August 1894
Miscellaneous   **East End's Amalgamation Overlooked Again**
S.F.A.C.M. The following East and North country clubs had, it was stated, failed to pay their subscriptions :- East End, Harp, and Our Boys (Blairgowrie). There were forty-five clubs in all who had failed to pay their subscriptions. The chairman moved that these clubs be struck off the roll. His motion was unanimously carried.
Ref 1894001

1st September 1894
P.S. First Round   **Arthurlie 0-2 Kilmarnock Athletic**
Played at Barrhead. Arthurlie kicked off the ball and for a short time stubbornly held their own with the visitors, but it soon became apparent that the forward division of the home team was lacking both in judgment and combination. On the other hand the visitors with indomitable pluck and better combined effort succeeded in scoring two goals in quick succession towards the end of the first half of the game, while the home team failed to notch a point. The game ended in favour of the Athletic by two goals to nil. Towards the finish of the game the play became pretty rough, and the referee ordered two of the Arthurlie team and one of the Kilmarnock team off the field.
Ref 1894002

1st September 1894
P.S. First Round   **Motherwell v Glasgow Wanderers**
Motherwell has got a walk over in the first round of the Scottish ties, the Glasgow Wanderers being unable to raise a team. This is certainly very fortunate for Motherwell, as it was sure to be a failure financially.
Ref 1894003

1st September 1894
P.S. First Round   **Adventurers 2-2 2nd Battalion Black Watch**
This was the only Cup tie decided in the capital, the four big clubs having been exempted from the qualifying stage. There was a good crowd at Easter Road to witness the appearance of the Black Watch, who at present hold the Army Cup. All through play was of a most exciting description, and it ended in a draw of two goals each. In the closing stages the scene all round the enclosure was something phenomenal, the spectators having worked themselves into a fever of excitement.
Ref 1894005

1st September 1894
P.S. First Round   **Falkirk 7-0 Kilsyth Hibernian**
[26th Sep]. Kilsyth Hibs are a bit put out at their claim against Falkirk being dismissed by the Scottish Association Committee. The Hibs, were drawn against Falkirk in Scottish Cup ties, with choice of ground. Falkirk's secretary, it is alleged, wrote stating he would guarantee £4 and half-gate above £8 if the Hibs, would go to Falkirk. To this the Hibs agreed, but they only got half gate, and their claim for £4 has been dismissed by the S.F.A.. The Hibs also think they are entitled to a better explanation from Mr M'Dowell

than a post card, simply stating "Your claim against Falkirk F.C. has been dismissed." The Hibs have written for an explanation.
Ref 1894008

1st September 1894
P.S. First Round   Lochgelly United 1-3 Mossend Swifts
S.F.A.C.M. [11th Sep]. David Ellis, of Lochgelly United and Thom. Vail, of Mossend Swifts, were reported by the referee for kicking each other on the field. After evidence, the committee decided that Vail be suspended for one month, While Ellis be censured.
Ref 1894006

1st September 1894
P.S. First Round   Kilsyth Wanderers v Grangemouth
The above teams were to have played off their tie in the first round for the Scottish cup on Saturday at Garrell Garden Park, but on Saturday afternoon the Grangemouth secretary telegraphed to the Wanderers' secretary that they were unable to raise a team. The Wanderers therefore engaged in a practice game.
Ref 1894007

1st September 1894
P.S. First Round   Broxburn Shamrock 11-1 Loch Rangers
The Shamrock were assisted by Wilson (half-back) and M'Leod (forward) of the now defunct Broxburn club. Result:- Broxburn Shamrock, eleven goals; Loch Rangers, one goal.
Ref 1894002

1st September 1894
P.S. First Round   Burnbank Swifts 5-3 Hamilton Academical
S.F.A.C.M. [11th Sep]. Hamilton Academical protested against Burnbank Swifts for playing a professional named Walter Mackay without being registered. The Swifts admitted the error. The tie was ordered to be replayed on Saturday at Burnbank. Mackay was censured.
Ref 1894009

8th September 1894
P.S. First Round Rply   Grasshoppers 0-7 Slamannan Rovers
S.F.A.C.M. [11th Sep]. Grasshoppers protested against Slamannan Rovers for playing Patrick Fisher, a last year's registered professional of the Dundee Harp, without having been registered. It was explained that Fisher had returned to Slamannan before the end of last season, and played for the Rovers. Fisher at this stage was called in. He stated that he thought, seeing that the Dundee Harp was expelled from the Association, that he could become an amateur player again. The committee then decided that Fisher be censured. The match was declared null and void, and it was ordered to be replayed on Saturday first on the Slamannan's field. The Chairman explained to Fisher that if he

wished to play in Scotland for any club he would require to be registered.
Ref 1894009

15th Sep Bonnybridge Grasshoppers scratched to Slamannan Rovers in the protested Scottish tie, as they did not fancy a second visit to Slamannan.
Ref 1894012

8th September 1894
P.S. First Round   St Cuthbert Wanderers v 6th G.R.V.
The Scottish tie between Dalbeattie and St Cuthbert Wanderers did not come off, the former had very reluctantly to scratch but without a satisfactory reason.
Ref 1894010

11th September 1894
Miscellaneous   Referees' Expenses
Mr M'Laughlin proposed and Mr Chrichton seconded - "That amateur referees be paid third-class railway fare, and hotel expenses if necessary." The motion was carried by casting vote of the chairman. Mr J. M'Kechnie, of Port-Glasgow, gave notice of the following motion for next meeting – "That the remuneration of professional referees be 10s, and third class railway fare from station nearest to residence."
Ref 1894006

22nd September 1894
P.S. Second Round   Mossend Swifts 2-0 Kilsyth Wanderers
S.F.A.C.M. [2nd Oct]. The protest by the Kilsyth Wanderers against the Mossend Swifts on the plea that the ground was dangerous and that the touch-line was not in conformity with rule was sustained, and the tie ordered to be replayed on the ground of the Mossend Swifts who are to bring their park into conformity with the rules.
Ref 1894014

22nd September 1894
P.S. Second Round   Vale of Ruthven 0-5 Lochee United
Played on the ground of the former at Auchterarder. Lochee United arrived without Oswald, who had lost the train, and had to consequently play with only ten men throughout. M'Leish and Reid, the backs of the suburban club, were also unable to get away from business. Winning the toss, the home team chose to play with wind and incline in their favour. The game started briskly, the home team causing the visitors to fall back on their own lines. A fine defence was maintained by Lochee, however, and they repelled all attacks of the home forwards to score. Increasing the pace, the United's quartette of forwards sent in some deadly shots, which were for a time negotiated by the home defence, the left back shining prominently. At length, Reid at centre half sent in a lovely shot, which was returned to that player, who with another beauty scored the first point for United. This was all the scoring done in the first half. On restarting, the Lochee men played all they were worth, and M'Intosh soon added a second goal, which was shortly after augmented by M'Laren scoring No. 3. United now had all the play, and

fairly toyed with their opponents. Murray and M'Intosh added the fourth and fifth goals, and no further scoring took place. Result - Lochee United, 5 goals; Vale of Ruthven, 0.
Ref 1894013

24th November 1894

F.S. First Round   Abercorn 1-5 Leith Athletic

S.F.A.C.M. [4th Dec]. Abercorn protested against the Leith Athletic getting the tie, on the ground that they played a man (Fraser) who had infringed the professional rules. The Leith Athletic representative admitted that the man had played in close season, but the club were unaware of that fact. It was agreed that the game be replayed at Paisley on Saturday.
Ref 1894015

24th November 1894

F.S. First Round   St Mirren 5-0 Battlefield

A protest was made by Battlefield against St Mirren for playing an ineligible man (Patrick), and the tie was ordered to be replayed at Paisley on Saturday.
Ref 1894015

24th November 1894

F.S. First Round   Raith Rovers 6-3 5th K.R.V.

Played at Kirkcaldy. The game was well contested all through. In the first half the visitors had the advantage, crossing over leading by a goal. In the second half the Rovers retaliated, and put on five goals to their opponent's one. Result:- Raith Rovers, six goals; 5th K.R.V. three.
Ref 1894017

S.F.A.C.M. [4th Dec]. The 5th K.R.V. claimed their tie with Raith Rovers be replayed at Dumfries, as the latter club had no goal nets. Raith Rovers stated that the nets had been ordered but were delayed in transit by railway. The tie was ordered to be replayed at Dumfries on Saturday.
Ref 1894018

24th November 1894

F.S. First Round   St Bernard's 4-2 Airdrieonians

S.F.A.C.M. [4th Dec]. A protest by Airdrieonians against the tie being awarded to St Bernard's was considered. Airdrieonians alleged that the referee infringed the rules by awarding a foul when it should have been a penalty kick. Mr Bishop, the referee, stated that one of the St Bernard's team intentionally kicked an Airdrieonian player, but the latter did not fall, and he did not consider that a penalty kick should have been awarded. By ten votes to five the protest was dismissed. The Airdrieonian representative intimated that he would protest to the general meeting of the Association.
Ref 1894018

24th November 1894
F.S. First Round   **Slamannan Rovers 2a3 Renton**
The Rovers kicked off. The visitors made a good run, and succeeded in scoring. This caused the playing to be afterwards very exciting, and the home team maintained their position well, although hard pressed. A few minutes before half time the Rovers scored, and no more goals were secured before the whistle was blown for half time. Two members of each team had at this stage to cease playing. In the second half Rovers scored in a short time, but the visitors pressed hard, and managed to pass the ball and again scored. Play was now very rough, and about six minutes before time was up the crowd broke in amongst the players, and the game stood unfinished. Result:- Renton, 3 goals, Rovers, 2 goals.
Ref 1894020

S.F.A.C.M. [4th Dec]. Renton claimed their tie with the Slamannan Rovers, despite the fact that the game stopped six minutes from time. They stated that the crowd broke onto the field of play and severely handled their players when they were leading by 3 goals to 2. Slamannan Rovers, on the other hand, said that their players in no way interfered with Renton, although they received provocation, one of the Renton men challenging anyone to a fight for £5. The referee said the game was a very rough one, and he had ordered two players off the field. The game was stopped by the crowd breaking in, and it was impossible to bring the match to a close before dark. M'Coll, of Renton, received severe treatment. He was convinced that one of the Rovers was the cause of the row. Mr Wotherspoon, secretary of the Renton said Renton would have been willing to continue the game, but the ground could not be cleared. The representative of the Rovers said that one of their players was injured, and being long in coming round, the crowd broke into see what was up. Ultimately on the casting vote of the chairman it was agreed that the tie be replayed at Renton.
Ref 1894015

8th December 1894
F.S. First Round Rply   **Renton 4-0 Slamannan Rovers**
In this undecided Scottish Cup tie, played at Tontine Park, Renton the home team got the better of Slamannan by 4 goals to 0. Renton's play was worth a bigger score, but the exceptionally brilliant goalkeeping of Bell for a time almost defied Renton's attack. Minus the goalkeeping Slamannan's play was poor.
Ref 1894022

8th December 1894
Miscellaneous   **Inverness Football Accident**
On Saturday afternoon a young man name Macdonnell, residing in Muirtown Street, got a leg badly broken while playing a football match at Telford Ground. The game was stopped, medical aid summoned, and the lad was afterwards carried to the infirmary. Amputation will probably be necessary. No fault attached to any of the players.
*Ref 1894023**

15th December 1894
F.S. Second Round   Hibernian 2-0 Celtic
S.F.A.C.M. [25th Dec]. The Celtic protested against the Hibernians on the ground that two of the Hibs team were ineligible to take part in the recent tie. After evidence, Mr M'Lean (Ayr), seconded by Mr Brown (Third Lanark), moved that the tie be replayed at Easter Road, Edinburgh, on Saturday first, on the ground that Neil and M. Murray had violated the professional rules. Mr Williamson (Mossend Swifts), seconded by Mr Smith (Hearts) moved as an amendment that the tie be awarded to the Hibernians. On a division, 3 voted for the amendment and 12 for the motion, so the tie will be replayed.
Ref 1894024

2nd February 1895
Semi-final   Clyde v St Bernard's
Intimation was given early on Saturday that the postponed Scottish Cup tie between St Bernards and Clyde would be played – the ground, on inspection by an official from the Scottish Football Association, having been declared in a fit state. By the hour appointed for the kick-off, however, the thaw had melted the coating of snow with which the ground was covered in the morning, and left such a treacherously hard and, in some parts, icy surface, that the referee at once pronounced it unplayable. A "friendly" was agreed on, and this the St Bernard's won by the score of six goals to two.
Ref 1894025

23rd February 1895
Semi-final   Clyde 1-2 St Bernard's
Barrowfield presented a patched up appearance on Saturday afternoon, but the committee were determined to leave no doubt as to the playing ability of the ground, and with the aid of tan bark, sand and fine ashes the surface was made tolerably good.
Ref 1894026

23rd February 1895
Semi-final Replay   Renton 3-3 Dundee
This tie was played by consent of the clubs on the Queen's Park ground, Hampden Park. Tremendous interest was evinced in the match, and the pressure of was so great that the spectators broke the barricades, and hundreds obtained free admission, while the field of play was sometimes encroached on. It is estimated that 25,000 spectators were present.
Ref 1894026

31ˢᵗ August 1895
Q.C. First Round   **Kilsyth Hibernian v Slamannan Rovers**
The Rovers failed to turn up, and the referee awarded the tie to the Hibernians.
Ref 1895001

31ˢᵗ August 1895
Q.C. First Round   **Lochee United 1-2 Hibernian (Dundee)**
The Dundee Hibs were the visitors at South Road park on Saturday, when they met the Lochee United in the qualifying stage for the Scottish Cup. The teams were:- Hibernians - Coupar; Murphy, Malloch; Kiddie, Donnachie, Calligan; MacMahon, Leggat, Colville, Kinsella, Brannan. Lochee United - Soutar; Robertson, Rollo; Vigrow, Millar, Burgess, Nisbet, Scott, MacLaren, W. Reid, Macintosh. Hibs kicked off, and at once invaded Lochee territory, but Soutar was on his guard, and saved several well-directed shots from the Irish forwards. Hibs., however, continued to press, and Brannan scored. Matters after this stage of the game grew somewhat interesting, the Lochee men making determined efforts to score, but Hibs. again getting possession of the globe, Brannan scored a second time. Half-time result - Hibs., 2; Lochee United, 0. On resuming, play became rough and reckless, but Lochee, from a fine shot by Scott, notched a point, and when the whistle blew Hibs had gained a meritorious victory by 2 goals to 1.
Ref 1895002

31ˢᵗ August 1895
Q.C. First Round   **Albion Rovers 1-0 Dykehead**
Crippled Dykehead supplied Albion Rovers with quite a stiff puzzle; in fact, it took the Coatbridge club all its time to win by the narrow majority of 1 goal to 0.
Ref 1895003

31ˢᵗ August 1895
Q.C. First Round   **Wishaw Thistle v Battlefield**
S.F.A.C.M. [3ʳᵈ Sep].   The Battlefield protested against the Wishaw Thistle on the ground of professional irregularities, and the tie ordered to be replayed in Glasgow on Saturday first.
Ref 1895004

3ʳᵈ September 1895
Miscellaneous   **Qualifying Cup Trophy**
S.F.A.C.M. [3ʳᵈ Sep].   The question of purchasing a cup for the Qualifying Competition was gone into, and it was ultimately agreed to remit the matter to a sub-committee, who will get designs and submit a short list of three to the General Committee for final choice, and on a vote being taken, £50 was decided on as the price to be paid for the trophy.
Ref 1895004

14th September 1895
Q.C. Second Round   Airdrieonians 1-0 Partick Thistle
S.F.A.C.M. [17th Sep]. Partick Thistle protested against Airdrieonians being awarded the tie in the second round of the qualifying cup competition, in consequence of three of the Airdrie players - Henderson, Friar, and Thomson - having contravened the professional rules. The protest was sustained in as far as it applied to the latter two players, and the tie was ordered to be replayed at Partick.
Ref 1895006

S.F.A.C.M. [17th Sep]. Mr M'Intyre, referee of the Partick Thistle and Airdrieonians match, reported P. Smith of the former team, for having struck him on the lip, and cut it. The committee suspended Smith till the 31st of May, 1896.
Ref 1895007

21st September 1895
Q.C. Second Rnd Rply   Partick Thistle 5-1 Airdrieonians
S.F.A.C.M. [1st Oct]. A protest from Airdrieonians v Partick Thistle on the ground of professional irregularities was dismissed.
Ref 1895008

14th September 1895
Q.C. Second Round   King's Park 3-2 Mossend Swifts
At Stirling. The visitors had the best of play in the first half, and crossed over leading by two goals to nil, both points having been secured in the opening minutes of the game. On resuming the home men played better, and scored three times, winning somewhat luckily by three goals to two.
Ref 1895009

14th September 1895
Q.C. Second Round   Rob Roy 2-2 Fair City Athletic
S.F.A.C.M. [17th Sep]. Rob Roy protested in regard to their tie with Fair City Athletic (Perth), who, they alleged, played an ineligible man - John R. Neilson, who was registered for Notts County last season. The protest was sustained, and the tie ordered to be replayed at Callander.
Ref 1895006

21st September 1895
Q.C. Second Rnd Rply   Rob Roy v Fair City Athletic
The Athletic scratched to the Callander club.

Fair City Athletics did not go to Callander on Saturday to play off their undecided Scottish Cup tie with the Rob Roy, and more is likely to be heard of the matter.
Ref 1895011

S.F.A.C.M. [1st Oct]. The Fair City Athletic appealed against the Scottish Football Association's decision, in ordering them to play their tie over again, with the Rob Roy. After hearing the correspondence read, the Chairman said it was not denied by either club that the player J.R. Neilson, was registered for Notts County, and that his

engagement expired on 30th April. It was not denied that he was not reinstated as an amateur, nor that he was registered for another club before playing. Mr M'Laughlan (Celtic) moved that the appeal be dismissed, and the tie awarded to the Rob Roy. Mr Hood seconded. Mr M'Lean moved an amendment that the teams play the tie. His amendment got no seconder. On a vote being taken, it was decided that the appeal be dismissed. The deposit from the Fair City Athletic was returned.
Ref 1895012

In the case of the protest awarded against them by the Scottish Association, the Perth club considers it has been unjustly treated, and it is said that an appeal will be made for a re-hearing of the case, the Neilson who was declared ineligible being, it is alleged, the victim of mistaken identity.
*Ref 1895013**

17th September 1895
Miscellaneous   Dundee Hibernians Case
S.F.A.C.M. The Dundee Hibs again asked that the committee should permit them to alter their name to that of the Harp. Mr Birrell, of the Forfarshire Association, hoped that Hibs.' request would be granted. He could assure the meeting that the Hibs. had no connection with the old Harp. Their gates, he believed, would be bigger were the club called the Harp instead of the Hibs.. Were they called the Harp they might become like the old Harp Club, which had been almost a terror to the Western teams. (Laughter) Mr M'Laughlan, of the Celtic, seconded Mr Birrell's motion. Mr Fairlie, of Renton, moved an amendment that they do not permit the Hibs. to change their name to Harp. The Harp in its day had not an enviable reputation. ("Oh.") His amendment found no seconder, and the committee agreed that Dundee Hibs. after this should be known as the Harp.
Ref 1895014

28th September 1895
Q.C. Second Round   Wishaw Thistle 1-1 Albion Rovers
These teams met at Wishaw in the Scottish Qualifying Cup Competition. Fifteen minutes from time the game was stopped for a period on account of a general break-in by the spectators. Play was resumed, but no change was made in the score, the result being a draw - one goal each.
Ref 1895015

S.F.A.C.M. [1st Oct]. Albion Rovers v Wishaw Thistle tie ordered to be replayed at Coatbridge on Saturday first.
Ref 1895008

12th October 1895
Q.C. Fourth Round   Alloa Athletic 5-4 Partick Thistle
S.F.A.C.M. [29th Oct]. The Secretary stated that a protest had been lodged by the Partick Thistle against the Alloa Athletic, and he accordingly stopped the match which had been arranged to take place between the Alloa Athletic and the Abercorn pending the decision of the committee. The Partick Thistle withdrew their protest, stating that they had failed

to get adequate information against the Alloa Athletic. He had two claims - one from the Abercorn and one from the Alloa Athletic. The two clubs had arranged to play a match, and, of course, as already hinted, they were stopped by the Scottish Football Association from doing so. The Alloa stated that their expenses amounted to £1 2s 1d, and the Abercorn intimated that they had been out £1 17s 6d. It was decided that the Partick Thistle pay the expenses the Abercorn and Alloa Athletic had incurred.
Ref 1895017

26th October 1895
Q.C. Fifth Round   St Johnstone 2-6 King's Park
The last hope of Perthshire in the Qualifying Cup competition - St Johnstone - went under very softly and also unexpectedly on Saturday, getting the biggest beating of any of the sixteen clubs engaged in the ties. Judged by form and physical superiority, they ought to have accounted for King's Park, but the boot was on the other leg, and the Stirling club, on the day's play, deserved their victory. In Stirling, as well as in Perth, the result was unexpected. King's Park have been doing badly for some time. King's Park were highly delighted with their treatment on and off the field by St Johnstone, but they don't think much of Perth spectators. The Stirling linesman was struck on the head on Saturday with a "dander," and the referee stopped the game and compelled St Johnstone to place two of their committee inside the ropes.
Ref 1895017

29th October 1895
Miscellaneous   The Qualifying Cup Trophy
S.F.A.C.M. The sub-committee showed three designs for the Qualifying Cup. The first was from Mr Brown, Kilmarnock ; the second from Mr Latimer, Edinburgh ; and the third from Mr Russell, Glasgow. The vote took place between Mr Latimer's cup and Mr Brown's. The vote was 16 for Mr Latimer's design and 4 for Mr Brown's. The cup will cost £50.
Ref 1895017

26th October 1895
Q.C. Fifth Round   Lochgelly United 2-1 Raith Rovers
S.F.A.C.M. [29th Oct]. A protest was lodged by the Raith Rovers against the Lochgelly United, on the ground that the latter club had played in their tie three men who had been guilty of professional irregularity. The men's names were Thomas Greenhorn, David Smith, and Alex Vail. It was asserted by the Raith Rovers that these three men had taken part in a five-a-side competition at Strathmiglo on July 20th, which was witnessed by persons who had paid to see the game. As it was proved that Greenhorn and Vail were amateurs, the Association considered only the case of David Smith. A Lochgelly United representative, who was invited in, said he could swear that none of the three men mentioned had been guilty of professional irregularity. Mr Birrell, of Kirkcaldy, said that he saw Smith play in the five-a-side competition at Strathmiglo. The two Vails took part in the match, one of them having gone to Dundee. Several witnesses identified Smith as one who had played at Strathmiglo, and it decided that the tie be replayed on the Raith Rovers' ground on Saturday first. David Smith was suspended for a month.

Ref 1895017

2nd November 1895

Q.C. Fifth Round Rply   Raith Rovers 2-1 Lochgelly United

This tie in the fifth round of the Scottish Qualifying Cup competition was played on Saturday at Stark's Park. The incidents of the tie being replayed are now so well known that it is useless to recapitulate them here; suffice it to say, that the greatest enthusiasm was manifest in the game, the recent meetings of the teams having engendered a strong feeling of rivalry. This, added to the fact that Lochgelly had a record to maintain, all went to increase the interest in Saturday's game. It was not surprising, therefore, to find a large concourse of spectators - nearly two thousand - present. The Rovers' quintette up to the last was a matter of uncertainty, but the appearance of Smith, "Wright," and "Goodman" somewhat raised the hopes of the home team's supporters. The Rovers were the first to appear, and were accorded a hearty reception. The Lochgelly United followed soon after, and were also accorded a warm reception, and it was soon evident that the miners had a large following of their supporters present. Mr James M'Pherson, Cowlairs, acted as referee. The teams lined up as follows:- Lochgelly United - Greenhorne; Bird and Robb; Vail, J. White, and J. Millar; Nisbet and Eadie; Millar; Wilson, and C. White. Raith Rovers - Cairns; Kay and Oag; Moodie, Lambert, and Blyth; Eckford and "Goodman;" Suttie; "Wright" and Smith. The visitors at once forced the pace, and it was sometime before the Rovers settled down. Moodie was making some bad misses, which kept Kay on the look-out. Both he and Oag, however, were safe. A smart shot from Whyte was as smartly cleared by Cairns. "Wright" was early conspicuous, and over and over again he gave Bird and Vail the slip. Smith partnered him well. A fine piece of play by Whyte and Wilson ended in Cairns foolishly leaving his goal. He, however, managed to punt out the ball, but before he could recover his equilibrium Miller sent in a shot, which Oag kicked out, but the verdict of the referee was a goal, and it seemed to be quite a fair decision, the ball being through before it was returned by Oag. Nothing daunted, the Rovers resumed and seemed to pull better together. A brilliant piece of play by Eckford outwitted two of his opponents, and finished up with a shot which Greenhorne could not save. The game, being now level, excitement increased ten fold, and the teams were urged by their followers to "play up" and secure the leading point. Strive as they liked, however, this was not forthcoming at half-time, and at that time the scores stood level one goal each. The play was resumed amidst a buzz of excitement. The visitors were first dangerous, and but for Whyte slipping in front of goal they must have received the coveted point. Eckford was playing a grand game. He, however, had a grand chance, with nothing before him but Greenhorne, but he tantalisingly shot the ball over the bar. It was quite evident that the Rovers were now showing improved form. Moodie and Blyth were tackling better, while the whole of the quintette were playing with more judgment. The Lochgelly were now indulging in the rushing game, and from one of those they all but scored. A foul well in on the Rovers' goal looked dangerous, but "Wright" emerged from the scrimmage with the ball at his foot, and in conjunction with Smith it was carried well up the field. Whyte intervened, but he fouled the ball. The foul was well placed by Suttie, "Goodman" headed in, and in striking one of the Lochgelly men's head it bounded into the net beyond the reach of Greenhorne. The excitement and hilarity of the home followers was now unbounded. However, the game was anybody's yet, and the Lochgelly forwards sweep down on the Rovers' goal, but it miraculously escaped. The game continued very fast, and hard knocks were the order of the day. The

forcibleness gradually increased, and in respect of a misdemeanor one of the Lochgelly United men was ordered off the field. Darkness began to set in, but up to the close the excitement never died, as both teams stubbornly contested the position up to the close. Despite all their efforts however, no further goals were put on, and the game resulted:- Raith Rovers, 2 goals; Lochgelly United, 1 goal.
Ref 1895021

7th December 1895

Q.C. Final   **East Stirlingshire 1-3 Annbank**

The final in the competitions for the new trophy in Scottish Football - the Qualifying Cup - was played at Paisley on Saturday, and the fairly large attendance of spectators justified the decision of the committee in having the final decided at Paisley. The providing of this handsome cup (the cost being 50 guineas) for those who engage in the preliminary Scottish ties was a very judicious action on the part of the Scottish Association. Hitherto the clubs who appeared in the preliminary ties had nothing to contend for beyond the hope of a chance of getting drawn against one or other of the crack teams in the closing stages for the Scottish Cup. But the Qualifying Cup has now given the preliminary competitors something tangible to struggle for, and it has further been the means of greatly popularising the winter pastime in the various towns and villages which may be regarded as outwith the influence of the League and other leading clubs.
Ref 1895022

Played at the Abercorn ground at Paisley. Annbank lodged a protest against Watson playing for East Stirlingshire. With the kick-off Annbank commenced to press, and opened the scoring. Fish, for East Stirlingshire, however, equalised, and the teams crossed over. Annbank having added another point to their score. Led on by Fisher and Alexander, East Stirlingshire made a splendid attack on Annbank's goal as soon as the second half was resumed; but Bowman, Dunlop, and Gourlay bustled the Stirlingshire men back in a forcible manner. Play now became very fast. Goal after goal was assailed. Fraser, Alexander, and Fisher playing grandly for the Eastern men. The chances of the game, however, were with the Annbank, and Donnelly secured their third goal. This dispirited the Stirlingshire team, who lay back on defence. Right up to the close East Stirlingshire fought bravely, but were really unlucky. Result:- Annbank, 3 goals; East Stirlingshire, 1.
Ref 1895023

11th January 1896

First Round   **Lochgelly United 2-1 Raith Rovers**

At Lochgelly. Suttie scored first for the Rovers. Nisbet, with a grand shot, equalised matters amidst great enthusiasm. Half-time score was 1 goal each. In the second half a well-timed pass was accepted by Millar from Kinnel, who shot the leather past Cairns, thus scoring the leading point for Lochgelly. Result:- United, 2 goals; Rovers, 1.
Ref 1895024

S.F.A.C.M. [28th Jan]. The Raith Rovers lodged a protest against the Lochgelly United on the ground of false registration. The player they complained of was David Anderson,

of Lochgelly, who, they held, was David M'Laren. That player, they maintained, had played for Lochee United against Dundee Hibs, in the first round of the ties. Lochgelly, in their reply, stated that the protest was informally lodged. The secretary of the Lochgelly was invited into the meeting. He said that his club had now discovered that David Anderson and David M'Laren was the same man. They knew the disputed player as Anderson, and he had promised to get another player for the tie, whose name he gave to them as David M'Laren. The following declaration was handed to the chairman:- "Declaration. 209 Lochee Road, Dundee. - I, the undersigned, do hereby declare that on the 11th day of January, 1896, I played for Lochgelly United Football Club in the Scottish Cup tie under the name and designation of 'David Anderson, 17 Mid Street, Lochgelly,' - DAVID A. M'LAREN. David Lambert, Links Street, Kirkcaldy, witness; Thomas Keeler, Alexandra Street, Kirkcaldy, witness." Mr M'Culloch of Dundee, said it was clear that Anderson and M'Laren was one and the same man. It was decided that the tie be replayed on Saturday first on the ground of the Kirkcaldy Club. David A. M'Laren was suspended from playing football this season.
Ref 1895025

11th January 1896
First Round Replay   Raith Rovers 5-2 Lochgelly United
Amongst the notable ties in the Scottish Cup competition this season is the one between the Raith Rovers and Lochgelly United which occupies a prominent position. The frequencies of the meeting, and the grounds on which the protests have been founded, has led to considerable feeling, with all its attendant excitement. Newton Park was the venue selected for the deciding of the tie. The gate must have cheered the hearts of the officials of both teams, as fully 2000 surrounded the track, the stands also being well filled. The ground was soft, but the weather was mild. The United first showed the way, and they were recorded a good reception. The Rovers followed suit, and so far as physique was concerned stood in conspicuous contrast to their opponents. Before the game began there was a council of war in the middle of the field between the teams and the referee. It seems the consultation was with regard to several of the United players whom the Rovers alleged were not eligible. Ultimately, the game was got under amidst considerable excitement.
... The half-time whistle sounded with the game standing Rovers, Two goals; Lochgelly, Two goals.
On resuming it seemed as if the fast pace of the first half in no way upset the staying power of both teams. The Rovers were first dangerous, and for the first few minutes kept up a complete fusillade on Greenhorn's charge, but they could not get the ball through. Millar and Vail were responsible for letting Millar off, but Lambert pulled him up. Passing on to Neilson, the latter player had a clever run down the field. He finished it off by sending across a very swift shot, which Eckford caught and sent it bang into the net. The point was well taken. The hopes of the local men began to rise. The visitors tried the banging game, but they soon spent themselves, as the Rovers' defence was as steady as a rock, while the forwards were always on the alert for any chance. Suttie and Neilson again got off with the leather, and as results of a bout with Bird, he was forced to save at the expense of a corner. Neilson sent in a beauty, and Lambert, getting the ball, sent it past Greenhorn. It was now evident that the game was lost and won. Still the United never lost heart, and they came away once or twice in irresistible force. Cairns, however, redeemed himself, and twice he saved smartly. On a third occasion he had only time to

scoop the ball past and save at the expense of a corner, which proved abortive. After this, however, the sting was taken out of their play, and some very forcible tactics were resorted to. A foul from midfield was well placed by Lambert. Bird saved, but Neilson fastening on the ball again landed it in the mouth of the goal. From the scrimmage Suttie gained the mastery, and netted the ball for the fifth time. The result of the game after this was a foregone conclusion, and excitement waned. Shortly afterwards the whistle sounded, and the game resulted - Raith Rovers, 5; Lochgelly United, 2.
Ref 1895026

Footnote
Raith Rovers and Lochgelly United were drawn together in the First Round having also played each other in the Qualifying Cup Fifth Round this season.

11ᵗʰ January 1896
First Round   Blantyre 1-12 Heart of Midlothian
At Blantyre, before 500 spectators. The Hearts left immediately took up the running, Walls scoring in two minutes. Immediately on the restart, Robertson had to save two hard shots from Walls, while Walker had a grand run on the left for the Hearts, and a second goal was scrimmaged through in five minutes. The Hearts still pressed, Robertson saving grandly in Blantyre goal. From a corner Walls scored a third goal for the Hearts. Play opened out somewhat, and a long drive by Powers was missed by M'Cartney, but M'Callum, lying handily, scored the first goal for Blantyre. A foul was given against Michael for a trip, and Kelly had a grand opening, Mirk relieved. Play for the most part was confined to the Blantyre quarters, Walker scoring a fourth goal, Michael a fifth, and Walker a sixth. The Hearts had matters all their own way in the second period and won by twelve goals to one.
Ref 1895027

4th August 1896
Miscellaneous   Cup Draw Exemption
Edinburgh University were granted exemption from the third round of the preliminary ties, but it was decided that they must play on the 10th October.
Ref 1896001

Footnote
S.F.A.C.M. [29th Sep]. Fourth, Fifth & Sixth Rounds drawn, the first two to accommodate Edinburgh University.

Fourth Round
Inverness Thistle v Edinburgh University
All others byes
Fifth Round
Duncrub Park v Inverness Thistle or Edinburgh University
All others byes

Edinburgh University scratched to Inverness Thistle

29th August 1896
Friendly   Ayr Parkhouse v Kilbirnie
At Beresford Park, Ayr. Kilbirnie scratched before the start of the game, and a friendly was played, which resulted in favour of Parkhouse by 9 goals to 3.
Ref 1896002

28th August 1896
Q.C. First Round   Glengowan v Motherwell
Motherwell should have played Glengowan away in the first round of the Qualifying Cup ties tomorrow, but the latter have scratched. £6 did it.
Ref 1896003

29th August 1896
Q.C. First Round   Monkcastle 1-1 Dalry
S.F.A.C.M. [1st Sep]. These clubs drew in the first round of the ties last Saturday at Kilwinning. It appears that Dalry had choice of ground for that match, but having no private park was forced to go to Kilwinning. Last night they informed the committee that they had secured private ground, and asked the replay there. It was agreed that this was not according to custom, and the application was refused. The tie therefore takes place at Kilwinning on Saturday.
Ref 1896004

29th August 1896
Q.C. First Round   Duncrub Park 2-2 Vale of Atholl
The Vale kicked off against the wind. Within ten minutes of starting the Vale scored, and within the half hour of starting the Duncrub Park scored twice, the second goal being secured within four minutes of their first, and in each case the ball was splendidly shot

through by Dewar. Up till half-time no further scoring took place. In the second half the Vale scored once, and the game ended in a draw – 2 goals each.
Ref 1896002

5th September 1896
S.F.A.C.M. [1st Sep]. In connection with the Vale of Atholl v Duncrub Park, the former club asserted that the latter failed to comply with Rule 12 of the ties, which held that opposing clubs under that rule should forward to each other on the Wednesday preceding the match a list of players, with their postal addresses. The neglect of observing the rule rendered the Vale of Atholl unable to make any inquiries previous to the match as to the eligibility of several new players included in their team, of whom they were rather doubtful. They wished the tie to be replayed. The Secretary said that the referee's communication bore that no protest had been made to him. The Chairman held, if the Vale of Atholl had read Rule 12 to the finish, they would have seen there was no violation of the rule. The club could have protested afterwards. The protest was dismissed.
Ref 1896007

1st September 1896
Miscellaneous   Qualifying Cup Second Round - Dundee Harp
S.F.A.C.M.   A communication was read from the Dundee Harp, stating that by an overlook they had omitted to send their subscription money to the Association. The committee of the Harp were under the impression that the money had been paid, and they regretted that the club in consequence had been struck off the roll. They wished the Harp admitted into the second round of the ties. The Secretary said, in reply to the communication, he could not say whether the Harp would get into the second round or not. In the event of their not getting into the second round they wished their application withdrawn. It was decided to admit the Harp into the Association. Mr M'Culloch, Dundee, proposed that they be allowed to take part in the second round of the ties. Mr Wylie, Aberdeen, seconded. Mr Dove, Alloa, moved the previous question. In other words he said he moved that the Harp be not allowed to take part in the second round. To permit them would be establishing a most dangerous precedent. Mr M'Gregor, Perth, supported the motion. For the amendment, that the Harp be not allowed to take part in the second round, there voted 6, and that they be allowed 7.
Ref 1896005

5th September 1896
Q.C. First Round Rply   Camelon 2-7 Falkirk
S.F.A.C.M. [15th Sep].   Camelon protested against the Falkirk because of the non-eligibility of Turnbull and M'Lauchlin, whom they declared played in a five-a-side competition at Bo'ness on June 27th. Mr Muirhead (Camelon) produced a programme of the sports at which the men were alleged to have played. They were Falkirk professionals at the time, and he alleged that in a five-a-side competition they played under the name of "The Unknown," (Laughter.) They were drawn against "Lipton's Select." (Laughter.) To his knowledge, "The Unknown" (Kay, of Stenhousemuir) had been suspended for a month at last meeting for playing at the same time. The Falkirk representative, on the contrary, declared that the club known as "The Unknown" did not play. After two ties had been played in the competition, the Falkirk players, who had went to Bo'ness as it

was a holiday in Falkirk, along with other two men, were allowed to play in the semi-final under the name of "Falkirk." He produced newspaper cuttings to show that Falkirk competed. The secretary of the sports bore out this statement. A controversy arose as to whether the newspaper reports of the matches should be allowed as evidence. A member said they had no evidence that the report was accurate; it might have been supplied by interested parties. The Chairman said he had always been against accepting such evidence. By 10 votes to 9 it was decided that in the first round "Falkirk" received a bye. Mr J. Bell, secretary of the Bo'ness sports, was examined, and generally confirmed the defence set up by Falkirk, whose entry, he remarked, was accepted on the field simply to make an even semi-final. An attempt was made to disprove that a Falkirk team took part in the competition, owing to the Bo'ness officials refusing on the day of the sports to take entries from Camelon and Falkirk, but Mr Bell explained that it was simply owing to the absentees that Falkirk were asked at the last minute to compete. Mr Mackenzie (Rangers) thought that the newspaper report threw a valuable light on the matter. That was printed at a time when no protest was thought of, and there was no reason why they should doubt its accuracy. The protest was a most flimsy one, and he moved that it be dismissed, and the deposit forfeited. Mr Brown (Stirlingshire) moved that the protest be granted. The evidence, he thought, clearly showed that the paper report could not be relied upon. It was strange that Falkirk should be allowed to enter the competition after two ties had been played. By twelve votes to ten the protest was dismissed.
Ref 1896008

12th September 1896
Q.C. Second Round   Wanderers (Dundee) 1-1 Lochee United
These teams met at Clepington Park on Saturday, before a large attendance of spectators. At the outset play was somewhat tame, but subsequently a little more life was infused into the game, both teams making several swift shots for goal. Peat, of the Wanderers, had runs along the entire field, and had the other players backed up his efforts to score a different result might have followed. For a time most of the play was in the vicinity of the Wanderers' goal, but Stewart, the Wanderers' goalkeeper, kept out the ball. A foul was given the Wanderers, and Watson, with a well-directed kick, landed the leather in the net. This success was the means of putting both elevens on their mettle, and after the ball was again set in motion Burgess was fortunate in equalising. Half-time sounded shortly thereafter with the scores standing - Wanderers, 1 goal; Lochee United, 1 goal. The second period was opened in spirited fashion. A well-saved shot was sent in by the Clepington goalkeeper, who sent the ball down to Williamson, and Peat kicked the leather out of play. A quarrel ensued at this stage between Rattray, of the Lochee, and Taylor, of the Wanderers, both players being ordered off the field by M'Farlane, the referee. Nothing of interest transpired during the rest of the game, the scores remaining unchanged. The tie will be replayed on Saturday.
Ref 1896010

12th September 1896
Q.C. Second Round   Kilsyth Wanderers 0-2 King's Park
King's Park defeated the Kilsyth Wanderers in the second round of the Scottish Qualifying Cup by 2 goals to 0. The Stirling team have on several occasions been drawn against the Kilsyth club in cup ties, and the latter have always been fortunate enough to have choice of ground. Mainly on that account the Stirling club have not been able to put a victory to their credit; but last Saturday's result broke the record. Neish headed the only goal for K.P. in the first half, though both teams should have counted. Stirling scored for the K.P. in the second half. Over-anxiety and the splendid defence opposed to them, however, spoiled all their efforts to score, and only once could they get the ball between the posts, but the referee disallowed it for off-side. The game was a hard one, the most prominent feature being the Stirling team's defensive work. A Kilsyth player was ordered off the field by the referee, five minutes before the close of the game, and as he did not appear at the Scottish Association on Tuesday evening, he has been suspended from playing until he does so.
Ref 1896008

12th September 1896
Q.C. Second Round   Fair City Athletic 0-1 Huntingtower
On Saturday, Huntingtower met the Fair City Athletics at Balhousie Park, Perth in the second round of the Qualifying Cup ties. Owing to the referee being late, it was half-an-hour behind time before a start was made. The strangers were the first to press, but were soon sent back. They again began to press, but Arnott fisted the ball out. The homesters now attacked the strangers' goal, but the goalkeeper cleverly held the ball. The strangers again pressed, and in a scrimmage at goal the ball was knocked through. Half-time scores - Huntingtower, 1; Fair City, 0. In the second half there was no scoring.
Ref 1896010

12th September 1896
Q.C. Second Round   Newton Stewart Athletic 1a1 6th G.R.V.
S.F.A.C.M. [15th Sep]. The G.R.V. stated that as their sports were to take place on Saturday the ordering of the tie to be replayed at Newton Stewart would mean their scratching. The Association decided that, according to the rules, the tie must be replayed on Saturday first at Newton Stewart.
Ref 1896012

The 6th G.R.V. were not satisfied with Mr Hendry stopping their tie with Newton-Stewart Athletic seven minutes from time, and were prepared to send "conscientious eye-witnesses" to prove that the light had not failed. Besides, on Saturday they had sports, "at which are to be Scotland's best athletes," and the team naturally wish to see these, but they must forego the pleasure, as the referee reported that the 6th G.R.V. had themselves to blame through not arriving in time, and that the Athletic had protested on darkness fourteen minutes from time. The 6th G.R.V. must travel again.
Ref 1896013

Footnote
6th G.R.V. scratched.

12th September 1896
Q.C. Second Round   Victoria United 2-5 Orion
A match between these Aberdeen clubs took place on Saturday on Victoria Bridge Grounds. As both teams had not lost a match this season the interest manifested in the game was very keen. Thom scored first for the Orion. Thom, Duncan, and Low subsequently had a goal each to their credit for the Orion. The Vics. only scored one goal in the first half, Tomin putting it through. The game resulted - Orion, 5; Vics., 2. During the latter part of the game the United played only nine men.
Ref 1896014

26th September 1896
Q.C. Third Round   East Stirlingshire 2-2 Falkirk
S.F.A.C.M. [29th Sep]. In the tie East Stirlingshire v Falkirk, the former protested against two players, named Turnbull and M'Lachlan, playing for the latter club, on the ground that they had contravened the professional rules by taking part in a five-a-side competition at Bo'ness in June last. The protest was dismissed, but it was decided to return the half-sovereign lodged by the protesting club, a member remarking that there was something altogether wrong in the evidence.
Ref 1896015

27th October 1896
Miscellaneous   Q.C. Seventh Round Draw
S.F.A.C.M. A proposal that the clubs left in the tie be divided into two lots and draws was defeated.
Ref 1896016

21st November 1896
Q.C. Semi-final   Kilmarnock 2-0 Dunblane
This semi-final tie for the Scottish Qualifying Cup was played at Kilmarnock on Saturday. Twenty minutes late Kilmarnock, having lost the toss, opened the game against a strong wind, but they did not make much headway. The visitors came away strongly, and, showing fine football, hemmed their opponents in; but they could not open the scoring. The Kilmarnock forwards got into their stride, but they confined themselves too much to the close passing game, with the result that they were seldom dangerous. Even against the play of the Killie forwards the opposing defence showed up well, and time and again sent them to the right about. Play became more even, although it was disappointingly dull. After a brief innings by the visitors, the Kilmarnock forwards broke away, and Watson, with a clever overhead kick, scored the first goal. Half-time result:- Kilmarnock, 1; Dunblane, 0. The second half was started much livelier than the former portion, and both teams showed slightly improved form. Still, there was a lack of style in the efforts of all. Do as they would, the Dunblane could not get beyond midfield, and the opposing halves kept shooting at a long range. A penalty was awarded Kilmarnock, but Cochrane turned the shot aside at the expense of a corner. Kilmarnock returned to the attack and Watson easily added another point. Excitement began to rise as the visitors

romped down the field, but Ralston saved nimbly. Kilmarnock continued to have the better of the play, and won a poor game by 2 goals to 0. At the close Dunblane lodged a protest on the grounds that the game was finished in darkness, and that full time was not played.
*Ref 1896017**

S.F.A.C.M. [24th Nov]. Dunblane's protest against Kilmarnock was on the ground of darkness and short time being played. The referee stated that the game lasted 90 minutes, and that he had no difficulty in following the play to the end. The committee accordingly dismissed the appeal.
Ref 1896018

21st November 1896
Q.C. Semi-final   Falkirk 4-1 Motherwell
S.F.A.C.M. [24th Nov]. Motherwell protested against Falkirk on the ground that Thomas Turnbull, of Falkirk, had broken the professional rules by playing for Falkirk while unregistered. Falkirk admitted the fault, and the committee unanimously decided that the tie be replayed at Falkirk on Saturday first.
Ref 1896018

28th November 1896
Q.C. Semi-final Replay   Falkirk 2a4 Motherwell
S.F.A.C.M. [1st Dec]. In the replayed semi-final tie at Falkirk on Saturday the crowd broke in nine minutes from the close of the game, at which stage Motherwell were leading by four goals to two. Falkirk sought a replay of the tie on the ground that the game was unfinished, and that the club had done everything in its powers to restore order, and to prevent the unseemly disturbance. Mr W. Crichton occupied the chair, and there was a full house. Evidence was led at considerable length. On behalf of the protestors, Mr Stevenson stated that Falkirk had all the available police that could be secured, six men in uniform and seven in plain clothes doing duty. On his opinion, the break-in was entirely caused by the conduct of one of the Motherwell players, who irritated the local spectators throughout by nagging on the field, by rough play, and slang talk to the crowd. This began when the game was only eight minutes in progress, and never ceased till the break-in took place. Falkirk led by two goals to one when "Jones" commenced these tactics. Mr Stevenson said he had not come before the committee with a cock and bull story, and that "Jones" had misbehaved throughout the game in a disgraceful manner. When the break in occurred a policeman who was escorting that player to the pavilion was also subjected to abuse. Mr Stevenson stated emphatically that the break-in was a general one, and that Motherwell supporters invaded the field of play, so that the stoppage of the game was not entirely caused by the Falkirk supporters. In the course of a long cross-examination, it was apparent that the ground club had done everything possible to restore order, both officials and police appealing to the spectators to allow the tie to proceed to a finish. The Motherwell linesman, who was also examined, attributed the stoppage of the game entirely to the action of the local crowd. As customary in all such cases, the principal evidence was tendered by the referee. In the course of a long cross-examination, Mr Wallace stated that he had occasion to award several free kicks against the player "Jones," mainly owing to his habit of putting his arms on his opponents' shoulders in heading the ball. There was, however, nothing

abusive in "Jones'" play. No fighting occurred on the field, although in the heat of the game one or two players had raised their hands in a threatening attitude. Asked if there was any incident in the play to account for the break-in, Mr Wallace answered in the negative, stating that the player was at the other end of the field, and that those who encroached did not seem to know exactly what to do next. Pressed by Mr M'Laughlin for an opinion, the referee said the object was to stop the game. He saw the captain of the Motherwell team assaulted, but the party who committed the assault appeared to be intoxicated. In moving that the tie be awarded to Motherwell, Mr M'Laughlin said that a deliberate attempt had been made by the spectators to stop this game, and it was ridiculous to suppose for a moment that a club in Motherwell's position - leading by four goals to two - would be parties to any organised break-in. Mr W. Sellar seconded the motion. An amendment, tabled by Mr J. Brown, found a ready seconder in Mr R. Smith. A heated discussion followed. Mr W.T. M'Culloch took the initiative, contending that the Association should not depart from the usual custom, and order a replay. An attempt had been made to fix the onus on a particular club, but evidence had been given to indicate that the one individual had been playing an unfair game, and it was well for the game that spectators should resent such conduct. Then it had been proved that Falkirk officials had done everything in their powers to cope with all emergencies, including the safety of players and referee. Mr Kirkwood supported the motion, stating that the evidence of the referee entirely put Falkirk out of court. He appealed to members to put sentiment aside in the matter. Mr Hutton, who was a spectator, was proceeding to give his knowledge of the circumstances when he was ruled out of order. Messrs M'Lean, Duff, Brown, Smith, Crichton, and M'Laughlin continued the debate, and on a division 11 voted for the amendment and 11 for the motion. The Chairman gave his casting vote in favour of Motherwell, who were thus awarded the tie.

Ref 1896020

9th January 1897

First Round   Duncrub Park 1-10 Hibernian

At Perth, in wintry weather, and before a small crowd. Pryce for the strangers, scored five minutes after the start. The Hibernians who were favoured with a strong wind, pressed, and added a second goal fifteen minutes later. The game became more open, and Duncrub had an occasional look in. The Hibernians, however, showed their superiority, their forward rank being conspicuous by their fine combination, Howie notched a third goal, and a few minutes later Breslin, after a nice dribble, contributed a fourth. The game was in favour of the Hibernians, who played their opponents with the greatest ease. Half-time:- Hibernians, seven goals; Duncrub, one goal. The game had no sooner been resumed than the Edinburgh men had once more the ball in the net. Duncrub were sorely pressed, but after a time they infused still greater energy into their play, and once, or twice carried the ball to the Hibernians' uprights. They were, however, immediately repulsed, and again the Hibernians gave the Duncrub players plenty of work to do. A ninth goal was in course of time registered, and followed by a tenth. The Hibernians surrounded their opponents' goal, and though apparently not eager to score, gave a splendid exhibition game. Pryce, the centre, did a lot of useful work. Final result:- Hibernians, ten goals; Duncrub, one goal.

Ref 1896021

9th January 1897
First Round **Arthurlie 4-2 Celtic**
At Barrhead. The Arthurlie team was the strongest that could be produced while that of the Celtic was composed of seven first-eleven players and four reserves. The home team kicked off, and for a little the Celtic looked rather dangerous; but the pressure being relieved, the Arthurlie had then a good run up the field, and Hannigan placed the ball between the uprights amidst great cheering. The Celtic then succeeded in breaking away, and after a brilliant run down to the Arthurlie goal the home custodian cleverly stopped a well directed ball from going through. Celtic, continuing to press their opponents hard, next succeeded in putting on an equalising point, which was loudly cheered by their followers. Again assuming the aggressive, the strangers made a hot attack on the Arthurlie goal, but the danger was soon averted, and after some give-and-take play in mid-field the Arthurlie had a look in at the Celtic goal. And Hannigan again sent the ball through, giving Arthurlie again the lead. On the resumption of the second half of the game, the Arthurlie continued to show their supremacy, and within 20 minutes succeeded in increasing their previous score by other two goals. Nothing daunted, the Celtic played up most determinedly, and were ultimately rewarded with a goal just a few minutes from the finish. In the remaining few minutes the game was stubbornly fought, but no further scoring was made on either side, the game, which was one of the hardest ever played at Barrhead, ending in the defeat of the Celtic by four goals to two goals.
Ref 1896021

23rd January 1897
Second Round **Arthurlie v Greenock Morton**
The ground was declared unplayable by the referee for the Cup tie, and it was agreed to play a friendly game. There were about 2000 spectators. Both teams were well represented. Result:- Morton, two goals; Arthurlie, none.
Ref 1896023

S.F.A.C.M. [25th Jan]. The Greenock Morton claimed their tie with Arthurlie on the ground that they had failed to comply with rule 16, which held that it was the duty of the ground team to advise the visiting team as to the playable condition of the field at least two hours previous to the time for the kick-off. The Arthurlie denied the breach of Rule 16, and explained that they had not delayed the advising the Greenock club. On the vote the tie was ordered to be played at Barrhead on Saturday first.
Ref 1896024

23rd January 1897
Second Round **Kilmarnock 3-1 Falkirk**
S.F.A.C.M. [25th Jan]. The Falkirk claimed that their tie with Kilmarnock should be no tie, as the ground was not properly marked off according to the rule. It was explained that the playing pitch was three inches at some parts above the cinder track. Mr Donald said he was the referee, and the protest was properly lodged. There was no line drawn, but he had no difficulty in deciding when the ball was out. The playing pitch was on average two inches above the cinder track.
Ref 1896024

The field was exactly in the same position as when the Welsh International was played upon it. Mr Smith (Hearts) moved that the tie be replayed at Kilmarnock, and that proper lines be put down. Mr Mackenzie (Rangers) moved that the result of the match be sustained. By 11 votes to 9 the protest was sustained, and the match ordered to be replayed at Kilmarnock.
Ref 1896026

23ʳᵈ January 1897
Second Round   **Dundee v King's Park**
These clubs should have met at Carolina Port on Saturday in the second round of the Scottish Cup ties, but, unfortunately, towards the latter part of the week severe frost set in, and on an inspection of the ground on Saturday morning it was declared unfit for such an important tie. Both clubs, however, agreed to play a friendly, and although many enthusiasts did not enter through the turnstiles when it became known that a friendly was the only outlook, nevertheless a goodly crowd turned out to gauge the form of the Stirling team. Scores - Dundee, 4; King's Park, 2.
Ref 1896027

30ᵗʰ January 1897
Second Round   **St Bernard's 5-0 St Mirren**
S.F.A.C.M. [9ᵗʰ Feb]. A protest by St Mirren against the St Bernard's being awarded their tie, on the ground that the touch lines were obliterated by the snow, was dismissed.
Ref 1896028

16ᵗʰ February 1897
Miscellaneous   **Emergency Committee Meeting**
The Emergency Committee of the Scottish Football Association met in the rooms at Carlton Place last night. It was intimated that Dumbarton and Leith Athletic had drawn twice, and the tie must therefore be decided on neutral ground. The clubs concerned could not agree, and asked the committee to appoint a ground. It was decided to order the clubs to play on the ground of the Motherwell Club on Saturday first, and in the event of another draw, to play 30 minutes extra. Mr D. R. Dickson (Wishaw Thistle) was appointed referee.
Ref 1896029

13ᵗʰ March 1897
Semi-final   **Dumbarton 4-3 Kilmarnock**
At Boghead, before 6000 spectators, in the semi-final of the Scottish Cup. For the first quarter the game was very fast, each of the uprights being visited in turn. A splendid chance for Dumbarton was frustrated by a foul, and a penalty kick was awarded, which was converted into a goal. Kilmarnock made strenuous endeavours to get an equalising goal, but the home men played with great determination. Half-time:- Dumbarton, one goal; Kilmarnock, one goal. The second half started in a sensational manner, Hendry netting the ball for Dumbarton. Dumbarton continued to hem in the visitors, and again scored by Thomson. Mackie followed with another goal immediately after. Kilmarnock

scored twenty minutes from time, and again scored shortly after. The game finished:-
Dumbarton, four goals, Kilmarnock, three goals.
Ref 1896030

16th March 1897
Miscellaneous   **Kilmarnock Protest**
S.F.A.C.M. The Scottish Football Association Committee held a special meeting last
night to consider a protest from the Kilmarnock Club against Dumbarton being awarded
the semi-final tie played on Saturday last at Dumbarton. Mr Walter Crichton was in the
chair. The protesting club stated that Dumbarton played in dark blue, whereas their
registered colours were black and gold. This they considered an infringement of rule,
more especially as Kilmarnock's colours were royal blue, and the distinction between
the two was not very pronounced. Dumbarton proved they had not registered any
particular colours this season, and affirmed that they had played in dark blue since last
August. The referee said he had no difficulty in distinguishing the different colours, and
after an exhaustive discussion, the protest was dismissed by 13 votes to 9. This decision
allows the final tie between Rangers and Dumbarton to be brought off at Hampden Park
on Saturday first, as arranged.
Ref 1896031

3rd August 1897
Miscellaneous   **Season Extension**
S.F.A.C.M. At the annual meeting of the association it was unanimously decided to shorten the playing season by one month - to begin in September and end in April. At last night's meeting there were 25 applications by clubs wishing the committee to grant them permission to commence the season on the 16th August.

The Chairman thought that such applications were entirely out of order, as the members of the association had passed the new rule unanimously at the annual meeting. To grant the applications of these 25 clubs would simply be to leave themselves open for a shoal of similar applications. He moved that the applications be not granted.

Mr Borke moved an amendment that the applications be granted, and Mr J.H. M'Laughlin seconded.

On a vote the motion was carried by 14 votes to 5 for the amendment.
Ref 1897001

11th September 1897
Q.C. First Round   Hearts of Beath 3-1 Dunfermline Athletic
S.F.A.C.M. [14th Sep]. Dunfermline Athletic protested against the Hearts of Beath on account of their not having goal nets, and, after discussion, the protest was sustained and the tie ordered to be replayed at Hill of Beath on Saturday.
Ref 1897002

11th September 1897
Q.C. First Round   Forfar Athletic v Arbroath Wanderers
Such treatment as was meted out to Forfar Athletic by Arbroath Wanderers on Saturday cannot be too strongly condemned. A large crowd had turned up at the station in expectation of seeing the Cup tie, and, after the receipt of a telegram from Arbroath stating that the team had lost the train, waited patiently for the arrival of the next train. About four o'clock, however, another telegram was received which revealed the true state of matters, the cause of the non-appearance of Wanderers being their inability to raise a team. The action of the Arbroath men was severely commented on by the disappointed spectators ; and surely a Club should be in a position to say if a team can be raised for such an important fixture before the crowd has assembled to witness the match. The failure of the Wanderers to turn up means a considerable monetary loss to the Athletic, as, in addition to the loss of the "gate," the cost of advertising and other expenses falls on them.
Ref 1897003

11th September 1897
Q.C. First Round   Dykehead 3-0 Linthouse
S.F.A.C.M. [14th Sep]. Linthouse protested against Dykehead, on account of their having worn metal buckles on their shin guards, and after a lengthy and heated discussion it was dismissed, but the protest money was returned to Linthouse.
Ref 1897002

25th September 1897
Q.C. Second Round   Alloa Athletic 3a2 Camelon
In the first minute of the game Alloa ran down and scored. Keeping up the pressure, another goal resulted from a foul. Camelon were confined to their own half, and at close quarters Cairns added a third. Half-time :- Athletic, 3; Camelon, 0. Camelon commenced to make up the leeway after ends had been changed, and the score stood at three goals to two in favour of Alloa about ten minutes before the finish, when one of the Camelon players struck the referee for giving a penalty kick to Alloa. Immediately after this the spectators rushed to midfield, and the referee (M'Lean, Alexandria), had to be escorted to the pavilion. The ball was shortly afterwards put on the field, but Camelon refused to play.
Ref 1897005

S.F.A.C.M. [28th Sep]. Mr Allan M'Lean, Alexandria, gave in a report as to the disturbance at Alloa which caused the stoppage of the Qualifying Cup tie between Alloa Athletic and Camelon. Mr M'Lean said the disturbance was a disgraceful one. He had awarded a penalty kick for an infringement by one of the Camelon backs, who rushed and caught him by the throat. This action caused the crowd to break in, and the tie, in consequence, was stopped. Alloa was leading by three goals to two and a penalty kick to go at the time the row occurred. The tie was unanimously awarded to Alloa, and, on the casting vote of the chairman, M. Burns, the player in question, was suspended for the remainder of the season.
Ref 1897006

It is to be hoped that the verdict and sentence in this instance will be a lesson to clubs and players in general to restrain their feelings a little when they cannot see eye to eye with the referee. I have always sympathy with these much maligned individuals, though I must admit that some of them undertake duties for which they are not qualified.
Ref 1897007

25th September 1897
Q.C. Second Round   Kilsyth Wanderers 4a5 East Stirlingshire
At Kilsyth on Saturday last before about 1500 spectators, of whom about 600 were conveyed from Falkirk by special train.
Teams:- *East Stirlingshire* - Shields; Johnston and Steel; M'Call, Fish, and Prentice; Murray; and M'Donald; M'Kee; Alexander and Nicholls.
Kilsyth Wanderers - Thompson; Heenan, and Black; Aitken, Drummond, and M'Laren; Pattison and Dunlop; Hamilton; Stirling and Black.
East Stirlingshire lost the toss, and kicked off against a strong wind. Play was for some time in the front of Shields, but the ball was ultimately shot past. From the goal-kick, the 'Shire took up the running, and the Wanderers' goal had some narrow escapes, M'Kee notching the first point from a scrimmage in front of the goal. After some give-and-take play, the 'Shire again returned to the attack, and for some time the home backs and goalkeeper had rather more than their share of work in repelling the 'Shire forwards, who returned again and again. Finally Alexander, accepting a pass from M'Kee, netted a second goal for the 'Shire, getting possession of the ball, carried it rapidly towards the home goal, play being mostly in the Wanderers' territory until the interval. Half-time score: East Stirlingshire, 2; Kilsyth Wanderers, 0. From the kick-off, the 'Shire once

more carried the ball towards the home goal, and Alexander, with a beautiful shot, scored the third point for the 'Shire within three minutes. A complete change now came over the game. The Wanderers, wakening up, rattled on four goals within 15 minutes. The 'Shire seemed to be played out, but after some mediocre play in midfield they recovered themselves, and within a minute or two they put a materially different complexion on the game by scoring twice in that remarkably short period of time, M'Kee and M'Call being responsible for them. The Wanderers' supporters, who had been in a state of unrest all the afternoon, and had threatened to break in on the playing pitch several times, now interfered, and rushed on to the field of play. A disgraceful scene ensued, free fights being engaged in all over the field. One of the 'Shire players, seizing hold of the ball, endeavoured to make for the centre of the field with it, but the attempt was frustrated, and the ball torn from his hands and carried into the pavilion. As there were no indications of the mob leaving the pitch, the game had to be abandoned. East Stirlingshire claimed the tie, while the Kilsyth Wanderers lodged a protest with the referee on account of the encroachment of spectators.
Ref 1897007

S.F.A.C.M. [28th Sep]. The game between Kilsyth Wanderers and East Stirlingshire, at the former's ground, had also to be stopped owing to the interference of the spectators, and both clubs claimed the tie, each throwing the responsibility for the scene on the supporters of the other. The referee stated that the first break-in was due to an East Stirlingshire player assaulting a spectator for kicking the ball out of the field. It was decided that the match should be replayed on neutral ground at Stenhousemuir.
Ref 1897008

25th September 1897
Q.C. Second Round   Penicuik 3a3 West Calder
S.F.A.C.M. [28th Sep]. It was reported that the game between Penicuik and West Calder had to be stopped, as the custodian of the latter, whether accidentally or intentionally, the referee was unable to say, broke the crossbar, and the game, which then stood three goals each, had to be stopped. Although the bar was subsequently repaired, West Calder refused to resume. Evidence having been heard, the committee decided, by a large majority, to award the tie to Penicuik.
Ref 1897008

9th October 1897
Q.C. Third Round   Stenhousemuir 3-3 East Stirlingshire
S.F.A.C.M. [12th Oct]. Stenhousemuir protested against the East Stirlingshire on the ground of professional irregularities. After evidence the protest was sustained, and the tie was ordered to be replayed on the ground of Stenhousemuir. One of the East Stirlingshire players, who it was said to have been guilty of a close season infringement, was suspended for a month.
Ref 1897011

23rd October 1897
Q.C. Fourth Round   6th G.R.V. 4-2 Dumfries Hibernian
Dumfries Hibs were quite outplayed at every part of the game on Saturday. Dalbeattie played a strong game from the start, putting on 3 goals in twelve minutes, and half-time came with the scores – 6th G.R.V. 3 goals, Hibs 1. The second half was more evenly contested, each team managing to secure a goal. 6th G.R.V. had a penalty-kick, but Thom shot high over. A regrettable incident took place when Gordon was ordered off the field. This was hard lines on Dalbeattie who were compelled to play the last 23 minutes with ten men.
Ref 1897012

6th November 1897
Q.C. Fourth Round   Cartvale 1-1 Port Glasgow Athletic
A disgraceful scene took place at the Port-Glasgow Athletic v. Cartvale match at Busby. Up to within a few minutes from the close the Cartvale were leading by a goal. The Athletics were awarded a corner, and in the bustle which ensued one of the SPECTATORS LEFT THE ROPES and struck Ward. He was immediately put off the field, and Referee Robertson (5th K.R.V.) allowed the corner kick over again. From it Carson put on the equaliser. The Cartvale players refused to resume, and standing on the field the remaining minute and a half with the Port players ready the referee on the expiry of that time declared the game finished at a draw - one goal each. There was a great scene at the close, free fights ruled all over, and it was possible that more will be heard of the matter at the next Association meeting. It may be mentioned that keen rivalry exists between the supporters of both Clubs.
Ref 1897013

S.F.A.C.M. [9th Nov]. It was decided that, on the ground of interference of spectators, the tie between Cartvale and Port-Glasgow Athletic be replayed on Saturday first on Cathkin Park.
Ref 1897014

20th November 1897
Q.C. Semi-final   Ayr Parkhouse 1-2 Port-Glasgow Athletic
S.F.A.C.M. [23rd Nov]. Ayr Parkhouse protested that their qualifying tie with Port Glasgow Athletic should be re-played on the ground of the referee awarding a penalty-kick, which, in the opinion of the Parkhouse, should not have been given. The protest was sustained, and the tie ordered to be re-played at Port-Glasgow.
Ref 1897015

26th March 1898
Final   Rangers 2-0 Kilmarnock
The final tie in the competition for the Scottish Cup was played on Hampden Park before an attendance which greatly exceeded expectations. The weather was dry, and the ground in fine condition, but there was a bitterly cold north-easterly breeze, which greatly interfered with the play. The sum drawn at the gates was £642, and the stands £104 - a total of £746, which would have been greatly increased had the weather been more

favourable. This, under the circumstances, must be regarded as one of the best gates drawn in the competition, as it was never anticipated that with a Second League club in the final the drawings would reach anything like this figure. The teams were:-
Kilmarnock - M'Allan; Busby and Brown; M'Pherson, Anderson, and Johnstone; Muir and Maitland; Campbell; Reid and Findlay.
Rangers - Dickie; N. Smith and Drummond; Gibson, Neil, and Mitchell; Miller and M'Pherson; Hamilton; Hyslop and A. Smith.
Referee - Mr Colville, Inverness.

The country men won the toss, and sharp on time Hamilton started for the Ibrox eleven against a slanting breeze. The Rangers' front rank got in at the start, but the attack was loose, and Campbell, Reid and Findlay got well past Smith, only, however, to finish weakly. A timely pass of Hamilton's at the other end let Miller away, and Smith headed through from the cross shot, but Brown had previously been penalised for upsetting Miller, and the point went for nothing. M'Allan saved from the free kick, and Kilmarnock went to the other end, unsteadiness spoiling them in front of Dickie. Macpherson and Miller dallied too much, and consequently made little progress towards M'Allan. Campbell nicely beat Mitchell, but Gibson intercepted the rush, and a free kick helped the provincials. Nothing came of it, however, and play ruled hard and fairly even. First Gibson and then Smith concede corners to the provincials, but the first was sent behind, and Dickie kicked away from the second. The county forwards came back with the aid of a free kick, but Smith and Drummond were safe, and the men were far too eager to score. The Killie forwards took some stopping, and with the wind were playing a hard, if unprofitable, game. At half-time there was no scoring. Kilmarnock resumed against the wind, and at once M'Allan had enough to do to get away a fine try of A. Smith's, and then, after a fine run from Findlay and Reid, Muir shot over. Hyslop was brought up for over-zeal, but nothing came of the free kick, and as little against Campbell for similar work, the ball going behind. Hyslop who was lame, exchanged places with Miller, but the change worked no wonders. Campbell was pulled up for attention to Findlay and from the free kick one of the Light Blues gave his own colleague a nasty shot to clear. Twenty-four minutes from the resumption A. Smith opened the scoring for Ibrox with a fine shot amidst loud cheers. The Rangers forwards were now a little like themselves, and J. Macpherson had a grand try, which just grazed the bar. Four minutes from the scoring of the first point Hamilton ran clean through the Kilmarnock defence, and raised the Ibrox total to two, almost raising the record to three a minute later. Until the close the Light Blues pressed, but could not score. Miller hit the post, and A. Smith shot past, and nothing subsequently of any accuracy troubled M'Allan. It was not a great final by any means, but Kilmarnock made all over a first-rate display, and to lose only two goals against the best scoring team in Scotland speaks well for them.
The result was - Rangers, 2; Kilmarnock, 0.
Ref 1897016

9th September 1898
Miscellaneous   **Pit Explosion Near Ayr**
A lamentable pit explosion, resulting in the death of four men and the injury of a number of others, took place in Drumley pit, near Annbank, five miles from Ayr, yesterday [September 9th] afternoon. The pit, which is situated close to Annbank Station, and belongs to Messrs George Taylor & Co, Annbank, has only been working for about five months. It is 154 fathoms deep, and there are three separate seams of coal - one the hard coal at the above depth, the diamond coal at about 140 fathoms, and the soft coal at 120 fathoms. It was the middle seam where the explosion occurred.
Ref 1898001

The number of men in the pit was about 100, but fortunately only 20 of these were in the diamond section. The seam was being worked on what is known as the long wall system. There were 16 men working at the face and three drawers, while the foreman, David Murdoch, had just come from the lower seam three minutes before the explosion occurred. He states that he was talking to the man James M'Carrol, who was working there, when suddenly there was a loud report, and their lights went out. They went to the pit bottom, about 30 yards away, got lights, and began to examine the place. They first came across Walter Dunlop, who is well known as a member of the Annbank Football Club. He was frightfully injured. He had been thrown against the wall, and, besides being burned, had his leg broken.
Ref 1898002

10th September 1898
Q.C. First Round   **Victoria United 5-3 Aberdeen**
S.F.A.C.M. [13th Sep]. Aberdeen protested against the Victoria United on account of their having played a man who took part in a close-season competition, and the tie was ordered to be replayed on Saturday first. A protest by Alloa Athletic against East Stirlingshire for a somewhat similar reason was dismissed.
Ref 1898003

10th September 1898
Q.C. First Round   **Duncrub Park 1-5 Morrisonians**
During the course of the first half of the match in the Qualifying Scottish Cup Ties, Duncrub Park v Morrisonians (Crieff), played on the ground of the former at Dunning on Saturday, Andrew Dougall, slater, son of Mr James Dougall, master slater and builder, Captain of the Duncrub Park team, sustained a severe fall, coming down on his right arm, which was completely broken immediately above the wrist. Dr Donaldson had his injuries attended to. In the latter half, James M'Cathie also came to grief, receiving a severe knock on the chest from the shoulder of one of the opponents (Crieff) and lay on the field for some time in an unconscious condition, the match meanwhile being suspended. On recovering M'Cathie, after a short rest, again resumed play.
*Ref 1898004**

10th September 1898
Q.C. First Round   Denny Athletic v Dunipace
Played at Denny, and ended in a draw – 1 goal each.
Ref 1898005

Denny Athletic scratched to the Dunipace, although they played a game last Saturday which ended in a draw. J. Gillespie, who once figured in the ranks of St Mirren and Sunderland, is once more playing for his old team, Denny Athletic.
Ref 1898006

17th September 1898
Q.C. Second Round   Beith 3-3 Annbank
On account of the disastrous explosion at Annbank this event was postponed till Saturday [17th], when a rattling good game resulted. Annbank led by 2 to 1 at half-time, and added another immediately on resumption. Then one of their team was hurt, and Beith made up their leeway easily. The tie ended in a draw - three each.
Ref 1898007

S.F.A.C.M. [20th Sep]. Beith protested against the referee not permitting the Beith to take a penalty kick against Annbank, in their tie played at Beith on Saturday. He only gave a free-kick for a foul within the penalty line, stating that he had discretionary power. Beith said that the decision was contrary to Rule 14. Annbank stated that only a verbal protest was lodged with them on Saturday evening. Mr Wallace, referee, said he did not hear of the protest until notified by the Association Secretary. The foul kick did not come under the penalty rule. The match finished 3 goals each. Beith held that the penalty kick would have given them the match, and that they had lodged the protest on the field. The protest was dismissed as being informally lodged.
*Ref 1898008**

5th November 1898
Q.C. Fifth Round   Kilsyth Wanderers v Wishaw Thistle
The unplayability of Garrel Garden Park was the cause of Wishaw Thistle having to postpone their tie with the Kilsyth Wanderers. As a special train had brought a large number of spectators from Wishaw, it was decided to play a friendly game. If it can be taken as any criterion of the respective merits of the teams. Kilsyth Wanderers should enter on the struggle to-day with stout hearts, as they score two goals in each half, and won by four goals to nil, but possibly the Thistle were reserving themselves.
Ref 1898009

12th November 1898
Q.C. Fifth Round   Kilsyth Wanderers 1a4 Wishaw Thistle
This postponed cup tie took place on Garrell Garden Park, the ground of the Wanderers. Wishaw, having lost the toss, kicked off, and forced a corner, but latterly the ball went past. The Wanderers retaliated strongly, but were beaten back, owing to a foul against Dunlop. From the free-kick the visitors rushed down, and Ferguson scored. The homesters tried hard to make appreciable progress, but of no avail, too well were the visitors playing. With great determination, however, they almost scored through White.

Broadley rescued his side with a great save. Even play followed for a while, and then Wishaw again pressed. A penalty was rightly awarded against M'Laren for deliberately fisting out, and a goal resulted. As time wore on the game became more even, the homesters especially improving greatly on their display of the first fifteen minutes. More than once they looked like scoring, but the opposing defence was too good. Following on some good forward play by the homesters, Boyd just missed scoring. Broadley left his goal, and if there had been a capable shot in the home eleven, a goal would inevitably have resulted. Both teams played bustling, go-a-head football, but sadly lacked decision at goal. Black, at right back, earned a round of applause for a fine piece of tackling and clearing at a critical moment, the visitors' left wing being well set for goal. Half-time - Wishaw Thistle, 2; Kilsyth Wanderers, 0. The homesters, after a raid on their goal by the visitors, on resuming, tried hard to get on an equal footing with their opponents. Their play, however, sadly lacked judgment, and consequently many good openings were carelessly thrown away. Brown once had a clear field, but he lacked speed, M'Lean out-sprinting him and returning the ball. After almost 15 minutes' play the homesters, by rushing tactics, nearly obtained a point, but Broadley saved well. The game was stopped five minutes from time owing to darkness. Result:- Wishaw Thistle, 4; Kilsyth Wanderers, 1.
Ref 1898010

19th November 1898

Q.C. Sixth Round   Annbank 2-2 Renton

S.F.A.C.M. [6th Dec]. Assaults on Referees. Mr Thomas Wallace, who refereed the Annbank v Renton tie at Annbank, reported that during the game and at the finish he had been attacked by a furious mob. After he left the field he was stoned, and had to be escorted to the village by the police, who were unable to keep the mob back. One of the stones - a piece of road metal - struck him on the back of the head and stunned him. An Annbank representative said that the officials of the club did their level best to protect the referee from abuse. The stone-throwing was carried out by a number of boys, who followed Mr Wallace into the village. The meeting decided to close Annbank's ground for 14 days.
Ref 1898011

14th January 1899

First Round   Rangers 4-1 Heart of Midlothian

S.F.A.C.M. [17th Jan]. The Hearts lodged a protest against awarding Saturday's tie to the Rangers on the following grounds:- (1) That within three minutes from the start the referee awarded the Rangers a goal that should not have been given; (2) that the referee awarded the Rangers a penalty-kick, which, in their opinion, was an unfair decision; and (3) that it was an error of judgment that led Hogg to be ordered off the field, but they were prepared to acknowledge the right to send Begbie off. All the same, Begbie, in the opinion of the Hearts, had received great provocation from one of the Rangers' team. The Hearts further were of opinion that the referee was either biased or incapable.

The captain of the Rangers' team was called in, and he stated that no protest was lodged with him, either on or off the ground.

Begbie, the captain of the Hearts, said that when he was ordered off the field he appointed Allan, the centre forward, to act in his place. In his absence Allan lodged a protest with the referee on the field.

The Chairman, seconded by Mr Stevenson, moved that the protest be dismissed, as not being formally lodged.

This was agreed to, and the protest money, 10s, was retained.

THE SCENE AT IBROX - SUSPENSION OF BEGBIE

The referee at the recent tie between the Rangers and the Hearts at Ibrox reported that he had occasion to order Hogg and Begbie, of the Hearts, off the field. Hogg, the referee added, was rough and foul in his play, and he had cautioned him twice before sending him off. Hogg at first refused to leave the field, in consequence of which the game was stopped for several minutes. The reason that Begbie was ordered off the field was, the referee said, for viciously kicking M'Pherson of the Rangers. Begbie had been playing a very rough game up to this time, and he had repeatedly penalised him and cautioned him twice before he sent him off the field.

In answer to Mr Lawrence, the referee said he had cautioned M'Pherson and Gibson, of the Rangers.

Hogg, on being called into the meeting, said he did not know what he had been ordered off the field for. He had been cautioned once previous to being ordered off the field.

Begbie said he supposed he tripped M'Pherson. He denied inviting any of his team to come off the field.

Mr Alex Hamilton, one of the members of the committee, said he had witnessed the tie, and he regretted to say a rougher exhibition on the part of two players he never saw. Had they been ordered off the field earlier the referee would only have done his duty. With regard to Begbie, it was without doubt the roughest exhibition he ever saw, and he hoped for the sake of football they would never see the like of it again.

Several other members of committee who had seen the match gave testimony. Mr Kirkwood said there was no doubt about the necessity of ordering Begbie off the field. Had that been done after the first ten minutes the game might have gone on all right. It was a mistake to order Hogg off the field at the time he was told to go. Mr Williamson said Begbie was very bad, but in the case of Hogg he thought the referee had made a mistake. Others gave similar evidence.

Mr Christie moved that Begbie be suspended for the remainder of the season. He regretted to move such a motion in the case of an old player, but brutality on the football field should be put down most stringently. Mr Hay seconded.

Mr Smith, seconded by Mr Boyle, moved as an amendment that Begbie be suspended for two months only, and, on a division, this was carried by 15 votes to 8.

It was moved that Hogg receive one month's suspension, but this was lost by 14 votes to 9.

Ref 1898012

4ᵗʰ February 1899

Second Round   **Clyde 3-1 Arbroath**

Notwithstanding that the grounds in the West were at the end of last week quite as frost-bound - if not more dangerous for play - as they were the previous week, Arbroath received word that they had to make their journey to Glasgow to play the Clyde in the second round of the Scottish Cup.

Great interest was taken locally in the game while in Glasgow - where so many Arbroathians are resident - the enthusiasm over the visit of the Maroons was unbounded, and, as was expected, the spectators present included a large number of Red Lichties - in fact, in one section of the spectators alone, there was estimated to be over 100 Arbroathians, who at times during the afternoon did not forget to use their lungs to some purpose.

Previous to starting the game the Arbroath Captain lodged a protest owing to the hard and dangerous condition of the pitch. The protest will be considered at Tuesday's S.F.A. meeting.

Clyde won the toss, and J. Brown [Arbroath] started the game. Arbroath were first to press, but in their anxiety sent the leather behind. Play was very fast, and a rattling good game it promised to be. Arbroath were moving about in a smart fashion, and a nimble play of the forwards and sturdy defence of the backs and half-backs were often applauded, while Harris was often seen to advantage in goal.

Arbroath swept down on Hendry, and Watson had to use his best efforts to clear the attack. Dour and determined in their work, the Maroons were awarded a free kick off a Clyde player, only, however, to be beaten by Coulter.

For a considerable time Clyde kept Arbroath pinned into their own quarters, and indeed a most anxious time was given them, on one occasion Harris standing alone between the sticks and Campbell.

A sensational piece of play was witnessed at the Arbroath end. A rush was made for goal by Clyde, and Harris ran out of his citadel to save - but Jebosaphat! He missed the ball, and an open goal was presented to Campbell, who almost under the post had nothing else to do but put it through. The situation staggered Campbell too, however, and trying to score with a terrific shot he sent the ball clean over the top of the net.

Cargill performed a splendid piece of dribbling, and carried the leather well down the field and passed it over to the left, but Leuchars lost a good opportunity of scoring.

Clyde received a free kick a few yards beyond the penalty line, and a corner was also got by them. From the latter, an opportunity was afforded Nash of scoring, and that he, quickly appropriated.

Hardly had the ball been set agoing than Clyde were up to Harris's charge, and the defence of the visitors had to grant Clyde another corner, Moran took the kick and landing the ball beautifully into goal, M'Donald, lying close to the left post, cutely headed it past Harris. This success was greeted with loud applause.

It was a grand game throughout and the Maroons were congratulated on their plucky play. A little luck might easily have given them the victory.

Play continued hard and interesting until the end of the first half, which soon came, and the teams crossed over with Clyde leading by 2 goals to 0.

The Maroons kept up strong play, and a shot was sent bang in by James Brown to the custodian, who caught the ball, and in attempting to throw it out put it into the net. The success of the visitors was warmly applauded.

The Maroons tried hard to equalise, but Moran sent through a third point for Clyde, and the finish arrived with the Clyde victorious by 3 goals to 1.

Arbroath protested against the Clyde being awarded last Saturday a tie, on the ground that Shawfield Park was not in a fit condition for play, being frost-bound and dangerous. The referee reported that he considered the ground playable, and the committee, by a large majority, affirmed this opinion and dismissed the protest.

Ref 1898013

18th February 1899

Third Round　　　　　**Queen's Park 2a4 Celtic**

... and half-time arrived with the score standing Queen's, two goals; Celtic, two goals. The Celtic again began strongly. A foul was given against the Queen's, and from the resulting free kick the visitors were again put on the lead. They maintained the pressure and once more a foul was given against Gillespie, and again a goal resulted. The Queen's made another effort and forced a corner from Storrier, but the Celtic cleared and mid-field play followed. Darkness was now settling down, and the ball was hardly visible from the Press-box. The Queen's scored a soft goal, but it was disallowed for off side, and another smart shot just missed the net. The darkness now made it impossible to follow the game, and the referee stopped play a quarter of an hour from time. Some excitement was manifested at the decision, the crowd breaking in and gathering in front of the pavilion cheering and hooting. Result:- Celtic, four goals; Queen's Park, two.

Ref 1898014

22nd April 1899

Final　　　　　**Celtic 2-0 Rangers**

The final for the Scottish Cup took place on Saturday at Hampden Park, in presence of over 30,000 spectators. Hamilton kicked off for the Rangers prompt to the scheduled time, and at once the Celtic got possession of the ball and made towards Dickie's quarters. Play from the outset was of the most exciting character, and it was evident that both teams meant to make the pace a hot one. Celtic were awarded a foul a few minutes after the start near midfield, but, although well placed, nothing came of it. From the return the Rangers got down the field, and M'Arthur was called upon to save a stiff shot from the left wing. After this play ruled pretty evenly between the two goals, both of which were assailed in turn. If anything, the Rangers' forwards showed to more advantages at close quarters, the Celts spoiling some chances. The Celtic defence, however, were in a working mood, and cleared their lines time and again in brilliant form. As the game progressed the players settled down to their work, and the play on both sides was greatly improved. A foul kick, well placed by Welford, let the Celtic in, but the forwards foozled the chance which was presented to them. Returning to the attack once more, Bell sent in a high shot, which, after bobbing about the goalmouth, was put into the net by Gibson in making an attempt to kick it over his head. The point was disallowed, however, Nick Smith having been previously fouled. The Celtic at this stage were certainly attacking more frequently than their *vis-a-vis*, and several pretty chances were thrown away by them. Fouls were frequent on both sides, the Rangers perhaps being the worst offenders in respect of the questionable tactics employed. There was no scoring up to half-time. Half-time result:- Rangers, nil; Celtic, nil. There was no signs of any slackening in the play when the game was resumed after a short adjournment. The Celtic were early the more prominent team, and twice within a short period Dickie saved from difficult positions. The pressure on the Rangers' goal was only relieved by Battles shooting over the bar. A spirited sprint by Hamilton seemed likely to be of some use to the Rangers, but Storrier relieved the lanky centre of the ball. The game was interrupted for a few minutes on account of an injury to Bell, whose leg was badly sprained, with the result that the popular Celt was rendered practically useless. The Rangers were successful at last in getting the ball into the net, but the point was disallowed on the score of offside. A minute later Celtic scored the first goal of the match, M'Mahon heading into the net after some scrambling work in front of Dickie. This Celtic success, which came after some fifteen minutes' play, added vigour to the game, which had certainly not been lacking in vim hitherto. The second goal in the match was also gained by Celtic, for which a bad mistake on the part of Crawford was responsible. The Rangers after this fell away badly, and they seemed to be able to do nothing right. Final result:- Celtic, 2; Rangers, nil.

Ref 1898015

22nd April 1899

Miscellaneous   Fatal Accident at Govan

Shortly before eight o'clock last night, while a football match was being played in a park off Summerton Road, Govan, between 2d Moorpark and Lilybank, Joseph Scuffle (17) a labourer, residing at 21 Albert Street, Govan, who was keeping goal for the Lilybank, was struck on the stomach by the ball, which had been shot into him. He cleared the ball and threw it out, and afterwards fell. He was carried home, but died before medical aid arrived. Dr Barras, who examined the body, is of opinion that death was due to shock.

Ref 1898016

1899
Miscellaneous   S.F.A. Annual Report
The membership is in a highly satisfactory state numerically, an increase having to be recorded.
A special place is given to rough play and rowdyism, and the means taken by the committee to cope with these evils is recounted. The opinion is expressed that the proper means of dealing with such things be in the hands of the police authorities, and the Association has been at no little pains to put this view before the various Scottish Chief Constables. Despite the theory regarding the ruinous tendency of professionalism, it seems to flourish, the increase being apparent in both clubs and players. But one thing will require to be legislated for and that is the present loose system of transfer. We are behind other countries in this respect, and it should not be open to wealthy organisations to buy for a time the services of a player to defeat its less endowed brother.
*Ref 1899001**

12th September 1899
Miscellaneous   Player Suspension
S.F.A.C.M. Campbell (Camelon) was suspended for one month for using bad language on the field and threatening the referee, and M'Farlane of the same club, was censured for refusing to leave the field at the request of the referee. The chairman added that the committee were determined at all costs to put down bad language on the field.
Ref 1899002

16th September 1899
Q.C. First Round   Vale of Leven 4-0 Clydebank
S.F.A.C.M. [26th Sep]. Clydebank protested against the Vale of Leven on account of the want of distinction between the colours of the teams and also alleging that the referee was incompetent. It was unanimously decided to dismiss the protest.
Ref 1899003

23rd September 1899
Q.C. Second Round   Wanderers (Dundee) 5-6 Forfar Athletic
These two clubs met on Clepington Park on Saturday in the second round of the Qualifying Cup. The weather conditions and the Dundee St Bernard's match were largely responsible for the poor attendance. Wanderers won the toss, and elected to play with the wind, Forfar kicking off towards the west goal. The strangers were early prominent, and the home defenders had an anxious time of it. With the strong wind in their favour the locals made things hum in their opponents' territory, and Mackay notched the first point. The Wanderers did most of the pressing, and Neave had the credit of again beating Soutar, after some fine play on the part of the homesters' front rank. Meanwhile the "county town" representatives were making good headway, but failed to score. The Wanderers took the game in hand, and for a time were always on the offensive, and Soutar was kept on the alert. Bett sent in a beauty, which rebounded off the bar, and M'Inroy, catching on, promptly netted the sphere. A corner was forced, which M'Inroy converted, Soutar failing to get away the ball. Still the homesters pressed, and half-time sounded with the scores :- Wanderers, 4; Forfar, 0. On resuming, it was

thought the Wanderers were pretty safe with four goals to the good, but the spirited display of the strangers soon caused anxiety to the home supporters. Forfar came away with a rush, and Ross had some difficulty in disposing of a low shot. Now the tables were turned, and Wanderers were on the defensive, but Boath scored the first point for Forfar. Shortly after this same player again did the needful. The homesters tried to break away, but were rather easily dispossessed, and seldom got within shooting distance. Prophet had the third goal for the strangers, and not many minutes after Shepherd put on the equaliser. Nettled at this reverse, the homesters, spurred on by the encouraging shouts of their supporters, made a determined onslaught on their opponents' goal, with the result that Graham secured the leading point. Forfar retaliated, and scored two goals inside a few minutes from the feet of Rodger and Prophet, a rather exciting game ending:- Forfar Athletic, 6; Wanderers, 5.
Ref 1899004

26th September 1899

Miscellaneous   Edinburgh University

S.F.A.C.M. At the first meeting of the Association this season, Edinburgh University were given three byes, but as it was found this would put the club into the Scottish cup competition proper without playing a tie, it was agreed to draw them in the third round.
Ref 1899003

30th September 1899

Q.C. Second Round   Bo'ness v Selkirk

Selkirk journeyed to Bo'ness on Saturday to play the team of that town in the undecided Scottish Qualifying Cup tie, the teams having drawn at Selkirk the previous Saturday. The weather was of the worst possible description, and on arrival at the field the referee, Mr Nisbet, Edinburgh, at once declared the ground unplayable for a cup tie. It was therefore agreed to play a friendly game. Result:- Bo'ness, two goals; Selkirk, nil. Rain fell in torrents all the time the match was in progress.
Ref 1899006

30th September 1899

Q.C. Second Round   Cowdenbeath v Mossend Swifts

S.F.A.C.M. [3rd Oct]. Mossend Swifts and Cowdenbeath were unable to play their tie at Cowdenbeath on Saturday last owing to the referee missing his train connection, and the Mossend Swifts asked that the Association should in some way recompense them for their outlay. The tie was ordered to be replayed on Saturday first at Cowdenbeath, while the Mossend Swifts' request was held over.
*Ref 1899007**

S.F.A.C.M. [7th Nov]. A letter was read from Mossend Swifts stating they had lost £13 through the failure of the referee to turn up in time. A motion was made to make some compensation, but on a vote being taken this was defeated by an amendment by the Chairman to take no action, the meeting being of the opinion that it would be a bad precedent were the club to receive money from the association to make up the deficit.
Ref 1899008

30th September 1899
Q.C. Second Rnd Rply   Stranraer 4-2 Douglas Wanderers
S.F.A.C.M. [10th Oct]. Douglas Wanderers and Stranraer were ordered to replay their tie at Stranraer on Saturday first, the previous match having been a friendly owing to the clubs not agreeing to the selection of an official referee.
Ref 1899009

23rd September 1899
Q.C. Second Round   Elgin City 2a3 Forres Mechanics
These teams met on Saturday afternoon at Milnfield Park in the second round of the above [Scottish Qualifying Cup] competition. The ground was rather heavy after the recent rains, but the weather kept fair during the game. Owing to the late arrival of the Forres team, the game was greatly delayed in starting. The referee appointed to conduct the game was unable to be present, and it was agreed to play the tie with Mr W. Macpherson as referee. The Forres won the toss, and played with a slight wind in their favour. The game started amid great excitement. Both goalkeepers got a lot of work at the start, and the City on several occasions had hard lines not scoring. The visitors, however, were more lucky, and at half time stood two goals up. The second half opened with the City pressing, but they were unable to beat the Forres defence. From a good run on the Forres left they again scored. After this reverse the City played splendidly. Fraser opened the scoring, and a few minutes later Milne added a second point. Darkness had now set in and the referee was unable to follow the game, and shortly before time the match was stopped with the score standing – Mechanics 3, City 2. It is expected the tie will be replayed on Milnfield Park on Saturday first, and, judging by last Saturday's play, the game will be a fast and exciting one.
Ref 1899010

30th September 1899
Q.C. Second Round   Elgin City 0-4 Forres Mechanics
S.F.A.C.M. [26th Sep]. Elgin City and Forres Mechanics were ordered to replay their unfinished tie at Elgin on Saturday first.
Ref 1899011

These teams met at Elgin to replay the match in the second round of the Scottish Qualifying Cup competition, which had been stopped on the previous Saturday on account of darkness. Rain fell during the whole game, and a strong gale blew down the field. The Mechanics had the wind and rain in their faces in the first half, but played a fine game, and scored three goals. In the second half the City played a defensive game, and only allowed the Mechanics to score once. The Mechanics held the City completely at bay, and they retired without notching a single goal, the visitors winning easily by four goals to nil. The City only played nine men in the second half, J. Haig and Milne both having been hurt. The first-named player played only about five minutes. Mr D. Grant, Forres, was referee. The Mechanics now meet the Inverness Caledonian at Inverness on Saturday.
Ref 1899012

30th September 1899
Q.C. Second Round   Dumbarton 2a3 Vale of Leven
Two once famous Clubs met at Dumbarton. To see the local team and Vale of Leven battling against each other reminded one of olden days. When the score stood Vale 3 Dumbarton 2 the crowd took the game in hand, and prevented the match being finished. At 26 minutes to go the spectators rushed on the field, and, landing on the net, brought the whole thing down, breaking the goal bar. It was found impossible to continue the game further. The circumstance will be duly reported to the Scottish Association, who, it is hoped, will deal firmly with such rowdyism.
Ref 1899013

S.F.A.C.M. [10th Oct]. Referee M'Leod (Cowlairs), who acted as referee in the cup tie between the Vale of Leven and Dumbarton, at the latter's ground, reported that he stopped the game while there was still twenty-six minutes to go, on account of a spectator having fallen foul of the goal net and brought down the cross-bar and one of the side posts. The game at that point stood at three goals to two in favour of Vale of Leven. The secretary of the Vale stated that the spectator who pulled down the net had used very threatening language towards their goalkeeper. The goalkeeper said that the spectator attempted to kick him from the outside of the net. After further evidence had been heard, it was decided that the match be replayed on Dumbarton's ground on Saturday first.
Ref 1899009

7th October 1899
Q.C. Second Rnd 2nd Rply Carfin Emmet 2-3 Motherwell
The play was greatly interfered with by the ball which was used. Shortly after the game started the ball got into an egg-shape, and although another ball was offered, Palmer [Carfin goalkeeper] declined to take it, and the game had to be played to a finish with the original ball, with the result that the players could not use the same judgment as with a round ball.
Hamilton Academicals were granted 10 per cent of the drawings (£57) for the use of their field.
Ref 1899015

21st October 1899
Q.C. Fourth Round   Bo'ness 2-2 Raith Rovers
At Bo'ness. Bo'ness played with the wind. M'Neill opened the scoring for the Rovers. After half an hour's play Porteous equalised for Bo'ness. Keeping up the pressure, Porteous scored another offside goal. Half-time - 1 goal each. On resuming, the Rovers made a determined attack on the Bo'ness goal, and Baillie fisted out some dangerous shots. Some rough play resulted in a break in, but play was resumed, and Kerr scored for Bo'ness, who pressed to the finish. Result - A draw, 2 goals each.
Ref 1899016

4ᵗʰ November 1899
Q.C. Fifth Round   Orion 3-5 Arbroath
This was the principal game in Aberdeen, and it was witnessed by a large turnout of spectators. Orion opened the game in spirited fashion, and with a quick rush drew first blood. A moment later, however, they were on the defensive, and failed to check an equally vigorous onslaught, which Leuchars [A] completed by heading through. Once more the ground team began to press, the ball being brought down smartly to Hogg, who slipped in a second goal for his side. Before half-time Orion had secured a third as the result of a penalty, the scorer being Livingstone. During the remaining half the strangers made strenuous efforts to turn the tide of the game, and in this, by hard work, they were successful. There was no further scoring on the part of the ground eleven, but Arbroath added other four goals to their total, and won by two up. The third goal for the visitors was got by Brown, and the fourth and fifth by Connell. During the last fifteen minutes darkness had suddenly settled down, and Orion lodged a protest on the account, the referee having refused to stop the game before time. Result Arbroath, 5; Orion, 3.
Ref 1899017

The whole team worked a will and each player was in his best form. It was certainly unfortunate that the Orion captain should think it necessary to protest against the failing light when so heavy a score stood against then at the time of appealing and so few minutes then to go.

Orion's protest withdrawn.
Ref 1899018

27ᵗʰ January 1900
Second Round   Rangers 12-0 Maybole
Played at Ibrox Park before 3000 spectators. It was early manifest that the Ayrshire men were no match for their more experienced opponents, who, although they made no great effort to put on a record score, led at the interval by 4 goals to 0. The second half was a repetition of what had taken place during the first moiety, and before time was called the Rangers had totalled 12 goals. Maybole seldom got over mid-field, and when they did they were never really dangerous. The Rangers were in a generous mood, else the score against Maybole would have been larger. Result:- Rangers, 12 goals; Maybole, 0.
Ref 1899019

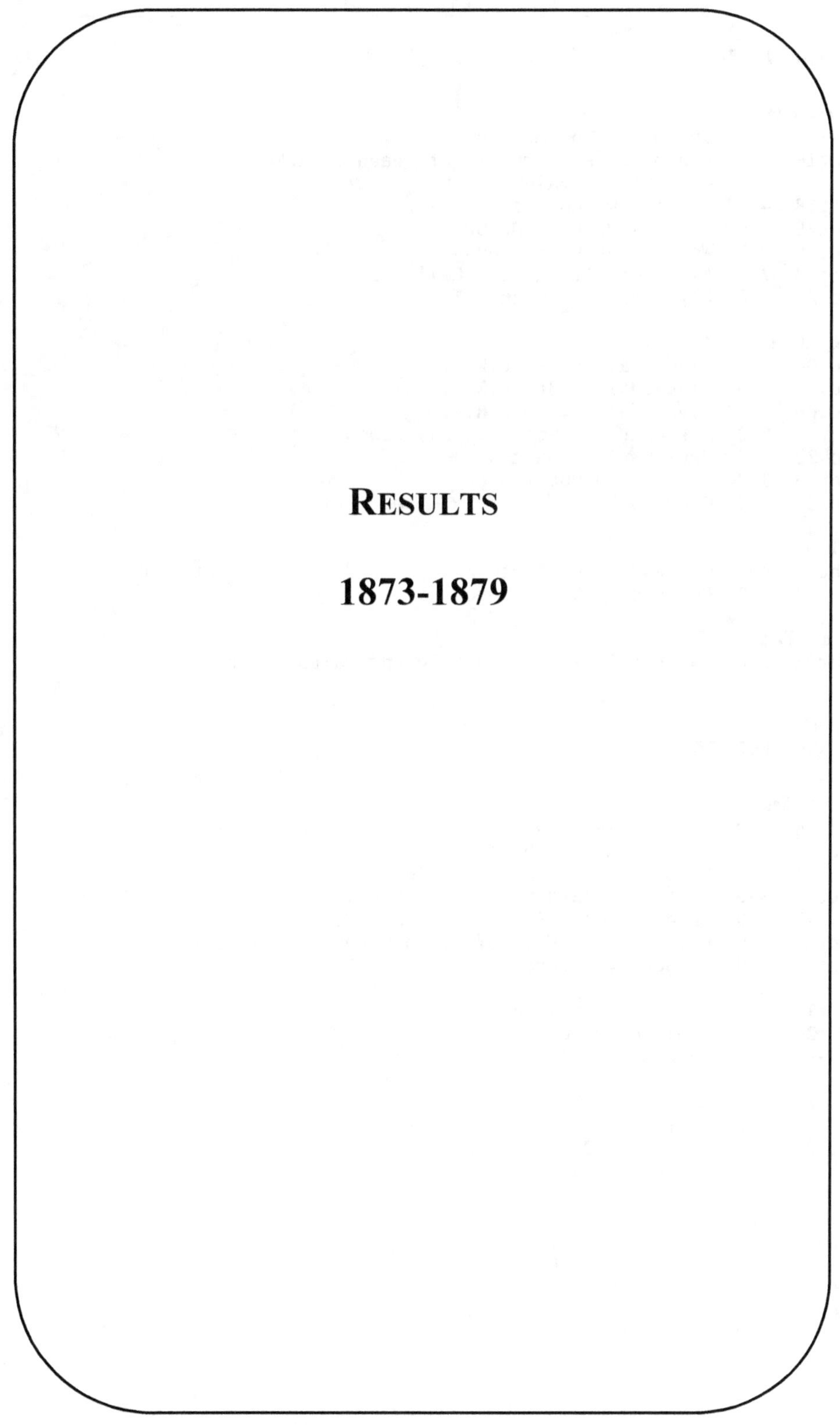

RESULTS

1873-1879

Season 1873-74

First Ties
```
-----  w/o  3rd L.R.V. v Southern - scr.
Oct18  2-0  Renton v* Kilmarnock  at Queen's Park
-----  w/o  Dumbarton v Vale of Leven - scr.
Oct18  4-0  Eastern v* Rovers
Oct25  7-0  Queen's Park v* Dumbreck
Oct25  0-1  Western v* Blythswood
Oct18  2-0  Alexandra Athletic v Callander
Oct25  6-0  Clydesdale v* Granville
```

Second Ties
```
Nov08  1-1  Clydesdale v 3rd L.R.V.
Nov15  0-0  Clydesdale v 3rd L.R.V.
Dec06  2-0  Clydesdale v 3rd L.R.V.
Nov22  0-2  Alexandra Athletic v* Blythswood
Nov22  0-0  Renton v* Dumbarton
Nov29  1-0  Renton v Dumbarton
Nov22  1a0  Queen's Park v Eastern - abd. 80mins darkness
```

Third Ties
```
Dec20  4a0  Clydesdale v* Blythswood  - abd. darkness at Kinning Park
Dec13  2-0  Queen's Park v* Renton  at Hampden Park
```

Final Ties
```
Mar21  2-0  Queen's Park v Clydesdale  at Hampden Park
```

Season 1874-75

First Ties
```
Oct24  0-0  Clydesdale v Vale of Leven - V. disqualified
Oct17  2-0  Dumbarton v Arthurlie
Oct24  5-1  Dumbreck v Alexandra Athletic
Oct17  3-0  Eastern v 23rd Renfrewshire R.V.
Oct17  3-0  Helensburgh v 3rd Edinburgh R.V.  at Glasgow
Oct17  4-0  Kilmarnock v Vale of Leven Rovers (Alexandria)
Oct10  2-0  Rangers v Oxford
-----  w/o  Renton v Blythswood - scr.
Oct17  1-1  Rovers v Hamilton
Oct24  0-0  Hamilton v Rovers
-----  w/o  Rovers v Hamilton - scr.
Oct17  0-0  3rd L.R.V. v Barrhead
Oct24  0-1  Barrhead v 3rd L.R.V.
Oct24  3-0  West End (Cowlairs) v Star of Leven
Oct24  0-1  Western v Queen's Park
       bye  Standard
```

Second Ties
```
Nov21  7-0  Queen's Park v West End (Cowlairs)
Nov21  1-0  Clydesdale v Dumbreck
Nov21  0-0  3rd L.R.V. v Standard
Nov28  0-2  Standard v 3rd L.R.V.
Nov21  0-3  Kilmarnock v* Eastern
Nov28  0-0  Rangers v* Dumbarton
```

```
Dec12  1-0  Dumbarton v Rangers
Nov21  2-0  Renton v Helensburgh
       bye  Rovers
```

Third Ties
```
Jan30  1-0  Dumbarton v 3rd L.R.V.
-----  w/o  Queen's Park v Rovers - scr.
Dec26  1-0  Renton v Eastern
       bye  Clydesdale
```

Fourth Ties
```
Mar20  0-0  Clydesdale v Queen's Park  at Kinning Park
Mar27  2-2  Queen's Park v Clydesdale  at Hampden Park
Apr03  0-1  Clydesdale v Queen's Park  at Kinning Park
Mar06  0-1  Dumbarton v Renton  - prot.  at Dumbarton
Mar27  1-1  Renton v Dumbarton  at Alexandria
Apr03  0-1  Dumbarton v Renton  at Dumbarton
```

Final Tie
```
Apr10  3-0  Queen's Park v Renton  at Hampden Park
```

Season 1875-76

First Ties
Edinburgh
```
Oct16  0-0  Heart of Midlothian v 3rd Edinburgh R.V.
Oct23  0-0  3rd Edinburgh R.V. v Heart of Midlothian - both qualified
       bye  Thistle (Edinburgh)
```
Dumbartonshire
```
Oct09  2-2  Lennox v* Dumbarton
Oct16  1-0  Dumbarton v Lennox
Oct16  0-1  Alclutha v* Renton
-----  scr  Vale of Leven Rovers (Alexandria) v Vale of Leven - w/o
Oct16  1-0  Helensburgh v* Star of Leven
```
Glasgow and Suburbs
```
Oct16  1-0  Clydesdale v Eastern
Oct16  2-0  3rd L.R.V. v Havelock
Oct23  0-0  Caledonian (Glasgow) v* Western
Oct30  0-3  Caledonian (Glasgow) v Western
Oct02  1-1  Partick v*  West End (Cowlairs)
Oct16  1-1  West End (Cowlairs) v Partick - both qualified
-----  scr  Queen's Park Juniors v Renton Thistle - w/o
-----  w/o  Dumbreck v Vale of Leven Rovers (Glasgow) - scr.
Oct16  2-0  Towerhill v Lancelot
-----  w/o  Rovers v Oxford - scr.
Oct16  4-0  Northern v* Ramblers
Oct16  3-0  Queen's Park v* Alexandra Athletic
Oct16  3-0  St Andrew's (Glasgow) v* Telegraphists
```
Renfrewshire
```
Oct09  0-0  23rd Renfrewshire R.V. v* Sandyford
Oct16  0-0  Sandyford v 23rd Renfrewshire R.V. - both qualified
```
Lanarkshire
```
Oct16  7-0  Rangers v 1st Lanarkshire R.V.
Oct16  0-0  Hamilton v Airdrie
Oct23  0-1  Airdrie v Hamilton
Oct09  0-0  Arthurlie v* Levern
```

```
Oct16  4-0  Levern v Arthurlie
Oct16  0-0  Drumpellier v Barrhead
Oct23  0-1  Barrhead v Drumpellier
```
Ayrshire
```
-----  scr  Ardrossan v Mauchline - w/o
Oct16  1-0  Kilbirnie v Ayr Thistle
Oct09  8-0  Kilmarnock v Ayr Eglinton
```

Second Ties
Lanarkshire
```
Nov13  3-0  Levern v Hamilton
```
Edinburgh
```
Nov06  0a0  Thistle (Edinburgh) v 3rd Edinburgh R.V. - abd. 65mins rain
Nov13  1-0  3rd Edinburgh R.V. v Thistle (Edinburgh)
Oct30  2-0  Drumpellier v Heart of Midlothian
```
Ayrshire
```
Nov06  0-0  Kilbirnie v Mauchline
-----  w/o  Mauchline v Kilbirnie - scr.
```
Glasgow and Suburbs
```
Nov06  6-0  Clydesdale v Kilmarnock
Nov06  2-0  Dumbreck v St Andrew's (Glasgow)
Nov06  2-0  Partick v Towerhill
Nov06  5-0  Queen's Park v Northern
Oct30  0-1  3rd L.R.V. v Rangers - prot.
Nov13  1a2  Rangers v 3rd L.R.V. - abd. 83mins darkness
Nov06  0-6  West End (Cowlairs) v Rovers
Nov06  3-0  Western v Sandyford
```
Dumbartonshire
```
Nov13  3-0  Vale of Leven v Renton
Nov06  2-1  Dumbarton v Renton Thistle
```
Renfrewshire
```
Nov13  0-1  23rd Renfrewshire R.V. v Helensburgh
```

Third Ties
```
Nov27  4-0  Rovers v* 3rd Edinburgh R.V.
Nov27  0-5  Partick v Dumbreck
Nov27  3-0  Western v Helensburgh
Nov27  2-0  Queen's Park v Clydesdale
Nov27  1-5  Drumpellier v* Dumbarton
Nov27  0-6  Mauchline v* Vale of Leven  at Victoria Park
Nov27  0-3  Levern v 3rd L.R.V.
```

Fourth Ties
```
Dec18  2-0  Queen's Park v Dumbreck
Dec18  5-0  3rd L.R.V. v Western
Dec18  2a0  Vale of Leven v Rovers - abd. darkness
       bye  Dumbarton
```

Fifth Ties
```
Jan08  2-1  Queen's Park v Vale of Leven  at Hampden Park
Jan08  1-1  3rd L.R.V. v Dumbarton  at Cathkin Park
Jan15  1-1  Dumbarton v 3rd L.R.V.  at Dumbarton
Jan22  3-0  3rd L.R.V. v Dumbarton  at Cathkin Park
```

Final Tie
```
Mar11  1-1  Queen's Park v 3rd L.R.V.  at Hamilton Crescent
Mar18  2-0  Queen's Park v 3rd L.R.V.  at Hamilton Crescent
```

Season 1876-77

First Ties
Ayrshire
Sep30   1-0   Ayr Thistle v Beith
Sep30   1-2   Cumnock v Portland
Sep30   3-2   Girvan v Dean   at Ayr Eglinton
Sep23   5-0   Kilbirnie v Maybole Carrick
Sep30   5-0   Mauchline v Winton
Sep30   1-1   St Andrew's (Kilmarnock) v Ayr Eglinton
-----   w/o   St Andrew's (Kilmarnock) v Ayr Eglinton - scr.
-----   w/o   Q.O.S. Wanderers v Ardrossan - scr.
-----   bye   Kilmarnock
Glasgow and Suburbs
Sep30   0-1   1st Lanarkshire R.V. v South Western
Sep30   1-2   Possilpark v Blythswood
Sep30   2-1   Caledonian (Glasgow) v Standard
Oct07   6-0   Clydesdale v Craigpark
Sep30   1-2   Hyde Park Locomotive Works v Crosshill
Sep30   3-1   Dumbreck v Dennistoun
Sep30   1-1   Alexandra Athletic v Eastern
Oct07   2-0   Eastern v Alexandra Athletic - prot.
Oct14   1-0   Alexandra Athletic v Eastern
-----   w/o   Govan v Western - scr.
Sep30   0-2   Parkgrove v Lancefield
Sep30 12-0   Northern v Telegraphists
Sep23   3-1   Partick v Havelock
Sep30   7-0   Queen's Park v Sandyford
Sep30   4-1   Rangers v Queen's Park Juniors
Sep30   2-1   Towerhill v Rovers
Sep30   6-0   3rd L.R.V. v Ramblers
Sep30   2-0   West End (Cowlairs) v 4th Renfrewshire R.V.
Renfrewshire
Sep30   1-1   23rd Renfrewshire R.V. v Thornliebank
Oct07   0-2   Thornliebank v 23rd Renfrewshire R.V.
Sep30   2-0   Busby v Renfrew
Lanarkshire
Sep30   3-0   Arthurlie v Drumpellier
Oct07   0-4   Hamilton Academical v Barrhead
Sep30   2-0   Hamilton v Thornhill
Sep30   0-1   Levern v Airdrie
Sep30   3-0   Stonelaw v Shotts
Dumbartonshire
Sep30   1-1   Dumbarton v Renton
Oct07   0-2   Renton v Dumbarton
Oct07   3-0   Lennox v Alclutha
Sep30   0-0   Renton Thistle v Vale of Leven Rovers (Alexandria)
Oct07   1-1   Vale of Leven Rovers (Alexandria) v Renton Thistle - both
              qualified
Sep30+ 4-0   Star of Leven v 10th Dumbartonshire R.V.
Sep30   1-0   Vale of Leven v Helensburgh
Edinburgh and East
-----   w/o   Dunfermline v Heart of Midlothian - scr.
Sep30   1-0   St Andrew's (Edinburgh) v Grasshoppers
Sep30   1-2   Lenzie v Edinburgh Swifts
Sep30   5-0   Thistle (Edinburgh) v Hanover
Sep30   1-0   St Clement v 3rd Edinburgh R.V.   at Kirkcaldy

Second Ties
Glasgow District
Oct21+ 0-2   South Western v Dumbreck
Oct21   0-8   Towerhill v* Rangers
Oct28   0-7   Caledonian (Glasgow) v* Queen's Park
Oct21   2-2   West End (Cowlairs) v Govan
Oct28   0-1   Govan v West End (Cowlairs)
Oct21   0-0   3rd L.R.V. v Clydesdale
Oct28   0-4   Clydesdale v 3rd L.R.V.
Oct21   5-1   Partick v Blythswood
Oct21   0-0   Crosshill v Lancefield
Oct28   2-0   Lancefield v Crosshill
Oct21   4-0   Northern v* Alexandra Athletic
Dumbartonshire
Oct21   7-0   Vale of Leven v Vale of Leven Rovers (Alexandria)
Oct21   0-4   Star of Leven v Dumbarton
Oct28   5-1   Lennox v Renton Thistle
Edinburgh District
Oct21   1-2   St Andrew's (Edinburgh) v St Clement at Kirkcaldy
Oct21   1-0   Edinburgh Swifts v* Thistle (Edinburgh)
Oct21+ 1-2   Dunfermline v Hamilton
Lanarkshire
Oct21   4-0   Barrhead v* Airdrie
Oct21   0-4   Stonelaw v* Arthurlie
Renfrewshire
Oct21   1-0   Busby v 23rd Renfrewshire R.V.
Ayrshire
Oct21   1-2   Kilmarnock v Mauchline
Oct21   2-0   Portland v St Andrew's (Kilmarnock)
Oct21   0-1   Kilbirnie v Ayr Thistle
Oct28   4-0   Girvan v Q.O.S. Wanderers at Newton Stewart

Third Ties
Nov18   1-0   Ayr Thistle v Dumbreck
Nov11   3-0   Lancefield v Girvan at Ayr
Nov11   7-0   Mauchline v Portland
Nov18   1-1   Edinburgh Swifts v West End (Cowlairs) - W. disqualified
Nov11   0-0   Hamilton v Busby
Nov18   0-0   Busby v Hamilton - both qualified
Nov18   1-0   Lennox v Dumbarton
Nov11   1-2   St Clement v Northern
Nov18   2-0   Partick v Barrhead
Nov18   7-0   Queen's Park v Arthurlie
Nov18   1-0   Vale of Leven v 3rd L.R.V.
        bye   Rangers

Fourth Ties
Dec09   1-1   Ayr Thistle v Partick - P. disqualified
Dec09   0-3   Mauchline v Rangers
Dec02   2-0   Lancefield v Hamilton
Dec02   0-4   Edinburgh Swifts v Lennox
Dec02   4-0   Queen's Park v Northern
Dec02   4-0   Vale of Leven v Busby

Fifth Ties
Dec23   2-2   Lancefield v Ayr Thistle
Dec30   1-0   Ayr Thistle v Lancefield
Dec30   1-2   Queen's Park v Vale of Leven

Dec30   0-3   Lennox v Rangers

Sixth Ties
Jan13   9-0   Vale of Leven v Ayr Thistle   at Kinning Park
        bye   Rangers

Final Tie
Mar17   1-1   Rangers v Vale of Leven   at Hamilton Crescent
Apr07   1-1   Rangers v Vale of Leven - aet. 1-1   at Hamilton Crescent
Apr13   2-3   Rangers v Vale of Leven   at Hampden Park

Season 1877-78

First Ties
Glasgow and District
Sep29   8-0   South Western v Our Boys (Glasgow)
Sep29   6-0   Govan v* Albatross
-----   w/o   Parkgrove v* Winton - scr.
Sep29   0-1   Clyde v 3rd L.R.V.
Sep29   0-1   Ramblers v* Stonefield
-----   w/o   Derby v Dumbreck - scr.
Sep29   3-0   Northern v* Pollockshields Athletic
Oct06   2-3   Shaftesbury v Rosslyn
-----   w/o   Blackfriars v Hyde Park Locomotive Works - scr.
Sep29   2-3   Petershill v* Kelvinbank
Sep22   0-1   Oxford v* Sandyford
Sep29   5-1   Strathclyde v West End (Cowlairs)
Oct06 13-0   Rangers v* Possilpark
Sep29   2-0   Lenzie v Ailsa
Sep29   2-0   Alexandra Athletic v Lancefield
Sep29   3-0   Clydesdale v* Dennistoun
Sep22   2-0   Partick v* Union (Glasgow)
Sep29   1-0   1st Lanarkshire R.V. v Blythswood
Sep29   1-0   Telegraphists v* 4th Renfrewshire R.V.
Sep29   6-0   Havelock v* Craigpark
Sep29   0-0   Rovers v John Elder
Oct06   2-2   John Elder v Rovers - both qualified
Sep29   9-0   Queen's Park v Whiteinch
Sep22   1-0   Jordanhill v Queen's Park Juniors
        bye   Caledonian (Glasgow)
Renfrewshire
Sep29   2-0   Glenkilloch v Wellington Park
Sep29   0-0   Renfrew v Pollockshaws Athletic
Oct06   0-2   Pollockshaws Athletic v Renfrew
Sep29   1-0   23rd Renfrewshire R.V. v* Levern
Sep29   7-0   Barrhead v Greenock Morton
Sep29   3-0   Arthurlie v Busby
Sep29   1-0   Thornliebank v Port Glasgow
        bye   17th Renfrewshire R.V.
Lanarkshire
Oct06   1-0   Hamilton v Avondale (Strathaven)
Sep22   1-3   Newmains v Uddingston
Oct06   2-3   Shotts v Drumpellier
Sep29   1-1   Stonelaw v Airdrie
Oct13   0-2   Airdrie v Stonelaw
Sep29+ 2-1   Glengowan v Mount Vernon

Dumbartonshire
```
-----  w/o  Renton v* Vale of Leven Rovers (Alexandria) - scr.
Oct06  0-2  Helensburgh v* Lennox
Oct06  1-0  Renton Thistle v* Alclutha
Sep29  0-2  Alexandria v* Milngavie
Sep29  1-0  10th Dumbartonshire R.V. v* Star of Leven
-----  w/o  Vale of Leven v Kilmaronock Thistle - scr.
Sep29  4-0  Dumbarton v* Waverley
```
Ayrshire
```
Sep29  4-0  Kilmarnock C&FC v* Maybole Thistle
Sep29  0-6  Girvan v Mauchline
Sep29  0-1  Catrine v* Beith
Sep29  0-1  Cumnock v* Portland
Sep29  1-1  Maybole Carrick v Tarbolton
Oct06  1-3  Tarbolton v Maybole Carrick
-----  w/o  Ayr Thistle v* St Andrew's (Kilmarnock) - scr.
Sep29  5-1  Kilmarnock v* Hurlford
Sep29  6-0  Kilbirnie v Dean
Sep29  4-1  Ayr Academicals v* Vale of Calder
```
Edinburgh District
```
Sep29  0-0  Heart of Midlothian v Hibernian
Oct06  2-1  Hibernian v Heart of Midlothian
Sep29  0-0  3rd Edinburgh R.V. v* Edinburgh Swifts
Oct06  1-2  3rd Edinburgh R.V. v Edinburgh Swifts
Sep29  1-0  Hanover v Thistle (Edinburgh)
```
Forfarshire
```
-----  w/o  St Clement v Dunfermline - scr.
       bye  Dunmore
```
Galloway
```
Oct06  6-0  Q.O.S. Wanderers v Stranraer
```
Stirlingshire
```
Sep29  1-2  Shaughraun v Clifton and Strathfillan
       bye  Grasshoppers
```

Second Ties
Ayrshire and Dumfriesshire
```
Oct20  1-0  Ayr Academicals v Kilmarnock
Oct20  0-0  Ayr Thistle v Kilbirnie
Oct27  3-1  Kilbirnie v Ayr Thistle
Oct27  1-0  Beith v Portland
Oct27  1-0  Mauchline v Kilmarnock C&FC
Oct27  2-0  Maybole Carrick v Q.O.S. Wanderers
```
Forfarshire
```
Oct27  3-0  St Clement v Dunmore
```
Dumbartonshire
```
Oct20  9-0  Lennox v Milngavie
Oct20  3-0  Renton v 10th Dumbartonshire R.V.
Oct20  1-1  Dumbarton v Vale of Leven
Oct27  4-1  Vale of Leven v Dumbarton
       bye  Renton Thistle
```
Renfrewshire
```
Oct20  1-0  Arthurlie v 17th Renfrewshire R.V.
Oct27  0-4  Glenkilloch v Renfrew
Oct20  0-1  23rd Renfrewshire R.V. v* Thornliebank
       bye  Barrhead
```
Edinburgh
```
Oct20  1-1  Hanover v Hibernian
Oct27  3-0  Hibernian v Hanover
       bye  Edinburgh Swifts
```

Glasgow and Suburbs
```
Oct20   4-0   1st Lanarkshire R.V. v Telegraphists
Oct20   2-2   Rovers v Blackfriars
Oct27   0-0   Blackfriars v Rovers - both qualified
Oct20   1-0   Caledonian (Glasgow) v Rosslyn
Oct20   0-2   Clydesdale v Queen's Park
Oct20   1-0   Govan v John Elder
Oct20   2-1   Jordanhill v Lenzie
Oct20   2-1   Parkgrove v Kelvinbank
Oct20   8-1   Partick v Strathclyde
Oct27   8-0   Rangers v Alexandra Athletic
Oct20   1-2   Northern v Sandyford
Oct20   2-2   Havelock v South Western
Oct27   2-0   South Western v Havelock
Oct27  11-0   3rd L.R.V. v Derby
        bye   Stonefield
```
Lanarkshire
```
Oct20   3-1   Glengowan v Stonelaw
Oct20   0-3   Hamilton v Uddingston
        bye   Drumpellier
```
Stirlingshire
```
Oct20   3-0   Grasshoppers v Clifton and Strathfillan
```

Third Ties
Glasgow and Suburbs
```
Nov10   5-2   Govan v* Stonefield
Nov10   4-0   South Western v* 1st Lanarkshire R.V.
Nov10   1-0   3rd L.R.V. v* Queen's Park
Nov10   3-2   Parkgrove v* Sandyford
Nov03   1-1   Blackfriars v* Rovers
Nov10   2-0   Rovers v Blackfriars
Nov10   4-0   Jordanhill v Grasshoppers
Nov17   0-3   Caledonian (Glasgow) v Partick
```
Lanarkshire
```
Nov10  13-0   Rangers v Uddingston
Nov10   2-2   Drumpellier v Glengowan
Nov17   0-0   Glengowan v Drumpellier - both qualified
```
Renfrewshire
```
Nov10   1-2   Renfrew v Barrhead - B. disq. 4th Ties R. reinstated
Nov10   0-0   Arthurlie v Thornliebank
Nov17   2-0   Thornliebank v Arthurlie
```
Dumbartonshire
```
Nov17   2-0   Renton v* Renton Thistle
Nov10   3-0   Vale of Leven v* Lennox
```
Ayrshire
```
Nov10   1-3   Ayr Academicals v Mauchline
Nov10   3-0   Beith v* Maybole Carrick
        bye   Kilbirnie
```
Edinburgh
```
Nov10   2-0   Hibernian v* Edinburgh Swifts
        bye   St Clement
```

Fourth Ties
```
Dec01   1-2   Kilbirnie v* Mauchline
Dec01   3-1   Parkgrove v Drumpellier
Dec01   0a0   Barrhead v* Partick - abd. 25mins accident
Dec08   1-0   Barrhead v Partick - B. disqualified P. reinstated
-----   w/o   Beith v St Clement - scr.
Dec01   7-0   3rd L.R.V. v* Govan
```

Dec01 5-0 South Western v Glengowan
Dec01 0-0 Rangers v Vale of Leven
Dec15 5-0 Vale of Leven v Rangers
Dec08 4-0 Renton v Rovers
Dec01 1-2 Thornliebank v* Hibernian - prot.
Dec08 2-2 Hibernian v Thornliebank - both qualified
       bye Jordanhill

Fifth Ties
Dec22 10-0 Vale of Leven v* Jordanhill
Jan05 0-4 Beith v* 3rd L.R.V.
Dec29 1-1 Parkgrove v* Partick
Jan05 1-2 Partick v Parkgrove
Dec29 1-3 Hibernian v South Western
Dec29 2-0 Renton v* Thornliebank
Jan05 0-2 Renfrew v Mauchline

Sixth Ties
Jan19 3-1 Renton v Mauchline
Jan12 1-0 South Western v 3rd L.R.V. - prot.
Jan19 1-2 South Western v 3rd L.R.V.
Jan19 5-0 Vale of Leven v Parkgrove

Seventh Ties
Feb16 1-3 Renton v 3rd L.R.V. - prot. at Renton
Mar09 1-1 Renton v 3rd L.R.V. - aet. 1-1 at Renton
Mar16 1-0 3rd L.R.V. v Renton at Cathkin Park
       bye Vale of Leven

Final Tie
Mar30 0-1 3rd L.R.V. v Vale of Leven at Hampden Park

Season 1878-79

First Ties
Dumfriesshire
Oct05 0-3 Annan v Q.O.S. Wanderers
Wigtownshire
----- w/o Cree Rovers v Stranraer - scr.
Ayrshire
Sep28 4-1 Ayr Academicals v Cumnock
Sep28 0-2 Auchinleck Boswell v Ayr Thistle
Sep28 1-0 Beith v Hurlford
----- w/o Catrine v Girvan - scr.
Sep28 0-2 Kilmarnock v Kilbirnie
Sep28 2-2 Lanemark v Kilmarnock Athletic
Oct05 4-0 Kilmarnock Athletic v Lanemark
----- w/o Mauchline v Maybole Carrick - scr.
Oct05 3-0 Maybole Ladywell v Tarbolton
Sep21 9-0 Portland v Dean
Glasgow and Suburbs
Sep28 0-0 1st Lanarkshire R.V. v Parkgrove
Oct05 6-2 Parkgrove v 1st Lanarkshire R.V.
Sep28 3-1 Alexandra Athletic v Jordanhill
Oct05 2-0 South Western v Caledonian (Glasgow)
----- w/o Clyde v Blythswood - scr.

```
-----  scr   Clydesdale v Dennistoun - scr.
Sep28  7-0   Govan v Ailsa
Sep28  w/o   Wellpark v Govanhill - scr.
Sep28  1-7   Havelock v 3rd L.R.V.
Sep28  0-7   Blackfriars v John Elder
Sep28  0-0   Derby v Oxford
Oct05  1-1   Oxford v Derby - both qualified
Sep28  2-2   Northern v Partick
Oct05  2-0   Partick v Northern
Sep28  4-2   Petershill v Albatross
Sep21  8-0   Possil Blue Bell v 19th Lanarkshire R.V.
Sep21  8-0   Queen's Park v Kelvinbank
Sep28  3-0   Rangers v Shaftesbury
-----  w/o   Stonefield v 4th Renfrewshire R.V. - scr.
Sep21  2-0   Thistle (Glasgow) v Possilpark
Sep28  0-1   Rosslyn v Union (Glasgow
Sep28  3-3   Pollockshields Athletic v Whiteinch
Oct05  3-3   Whiteinch v Pollockshields Athletic - both qualified
Sep28 10-0   Whitefield v Telegraphists
       bye   Partick Burnside
       bye   Glasgow University
```

Edinburgh
```
Sep28  3-1   3rd Edinburgh R.V. v Brunswick
Sep28  2-1   Thistle (Edinburgh) v Hanover
Sep21  3-1   Heart of Midlothian v Edinburgh Swifts
Sep28  5-2   Hibernian v Dunfermline
       bye   Edinburgh University
```

Dumbartonshire
```
Sep28  2-2   Alexandria v Renton Thistle
Oct05  1-1   Renton Thistle v Alexandria - both qualified
Sep28  8-1   Dumbarton v 10th Dumbartonshire R.V.
Oct05  4-0   Helensburgh v Kilmaronock Thistle
Sep21  3-1   Jamestown v Lennox
-----  w/o   Renton v Star of Leven - scr.
Sep21  6-0   Vale of Leven v Alclutha
```

Lanarkshire
```
Sep28+ 7-0   Airdrie v Avondale (Strathaven)
Sep28+ 4-3   Glengowan v Mount Vernon
Sep28  0-0   Hamilton Academical v Uddingston
Oct05  3-1   Hamilton Academical v Uddingston
Oct05  3-0   Shotts v Drumpellier
Oct05  4-0   Stonelaw v East Kilbride
Sep28  0-12  Newmains v Upper Clydesdale
       bye   Clarkston
```

Renfrewshire
```
Sep28  1-4   Cartvale v Arthurlie
Sep28  3-1   Busby v Greenock Morton
Sep28  1-1   Levern v 23rd Renfrewshire R.V.
Oct05  0-1   23rd Renfrewshire R.V. v Levern
Sep28  1-1   Renfrew v 17th Renfrewshire R.V.
Oct05  1-2   17th Renfrewshire R.V. v Renfrew
Sep28  3-0   Thornliebank v Glenkilloch
-----  w/o   Port Glasgow v Pollockshaws Athletic - disbanded
Sep21  2-0   Barrhead v Wellington Park
```

Stirlingshire
```
Sep28  2-0   Falkirk v* Campsie Glen
Oct05  8-1   Strathblane v Grasshoppers
Sep28  3-0   Lenzie v Thistle Athletic
```

```
        bye  Shaughraun
Forfarshire
Sep28  3-0  Arbroath v* Our Boys (Dundee)
        bye  St Clement
Perthshire
Oct05  1-0  Rob Roy v Coupar Angus  at North Inch, Perth
Oct05  0-1  Clifton and Strathfillan v Vale of Teith
```

Second Ties
Glasgow and Suburbs
```
Oct19  3-0  Alexandra Athletic v* Partick Burnside
Oct19  5-0  South Western v* Petershill - prot.
Oct26  8-0  South Western v Petershill
Oct19  2-1  Partick v* Possil Blue Bell
Oct12  2-1  Govan v* Oxford
Oct19  6-1  Rangers v Whitefield
Oct19  1-4  Clyde v* Thistle (Glasgow)
Oct19  1-3  Whiteinch v* Derby
Oct19  1-0  Parkgrove v Union (Glasgow)
Oct19  4-0  John Elder v Stonefield
Oct19  8-1  3rd L.R.V. v Wellpark
Oct19  6-0  Queen's Park v* Pollockshields Athletic
        bye  Glasgow University
```
Ayrshire
```
Oct19  3-1  Beith v Ayr Thistle
Oct19  3-1  Catrine v Maybole Ladywell
Oct19  0-2  Kilbirnie v Kilmarnock Athletic
Oct19  1-5  Ayr Academicals v* Mauchline
```
Renfrewshire
```
Oct19  4-1  Portland v Thornliebank
Oct19  3-1  Arthurlie v Busby
Oct19  1-2  Levern v Renfrew
Oct19  6-2  Barrhead v Port Glasgow
```
Lanarkshire
```
Oct19  1-1  Shotts v* Clarkston
-----  w/o  Clarkston v Shotts - scr.
Oct19  2-0  Stonelaw v Hamilton Academical
Oct26  2-1  Glengowan v* Airdrie - G. disqualified
```
Edinburgh
```
Oct19  3a0  Hibernian v 3rd Edinburgh R.V. - abd. 30mins conceded
Oct19  1-0  Heart of Midlothian v Thistle (Edinburgh)
        bye  Edinburgh University
```
Dumbartonshire
```
Oct19  1-6  Renton v* Dumbarton
Oct26 11-0  Vale of Leven v Renton Thistle
Oct19  4-1  Helensburgh v* Alexandria
Oct19  7-0  Jamestown v Upper Clydesdale
```
Stirlingshire
```
Oct19  1-0  Strathblane v Falkirk
Oct19  1-0  Shaughraun v Lenzie
```
Forfarshire
```
-----  w/o  Arbroath v St Clement - scr.
```
Perthshire
```
Oct26  3-1  Rob Roy v Vale of Teith
```
Wigtownshire and Dumfriesshire
```
Oct26  0-3  Cree Rovers v* Q.O.S. Wanderers
```

Third Ties
Glasgow and Suburbs
Nov09   8-2   Rangers v Parkgrove
Nov02   2-1   3rd L.R.V. v* South Western
Nov09   2-0   Alexandra Athletic v John Elder
Nov09   4-0   Govan v* Derby
-----   w/o   Queen's Park v Glasgow University - scr.
Nov16   1-2   Partick v* Thistle (Glasgow) - T. disqualified P. reinstated
Ayrshire, Dumfriesshire and Renfrewshire
Nov09   0-3   Catrine v* Portland
Nov16   5-0   Kilmarnock Athletic v Q.O.S. Wanderers
Nov09   7-1   Beith v* Barrhead
Nov09   4-1   Mauchline v* Arthurlie
        bye   Renfrew
Lanarkshire, Dumbartonshire, Stirlingshire and Perthshire
Nov09   1-0   Stonelaw v* Clarkston
Nov09   2-0   Helensburgh v* Shaughraun
Nov09   5-0   Dumbarton v* Strathblane
Nov09 15-0   Vale of Leven v Jamestown
        bye   Rob Roy
Edinburgh and Forfarshire
Nov16   2-5   Edinburgh University v* Hibernian
Nov09   2-1   Heart of Midlothian v Arbroath

Fourth Ties
Dec07   9-0   Hibernian v Rob Roy
Nov30   0-4   Renfrew v* 3rd L.R.V.
Nov30 11-1   Vale of Leven v Govan
Nov30   5-0   Queen's Park v Mauchline
Nov30   2-1   Thistle (Glasgow) v* Stonelaw - T. disqualif'd S. Reinstated
Nov30   1-1   Portland v Dumbarton
Dec07   6-1   Dumbarton v Portland
Nov30   3-0   Rangers v Alexandra Athletic
Nov30   2-1   Helensburgh v* Heart of Midlothian - prot.
Nov30   9-1   Beith v* Kilmarnock Athletic
        bye   Partick - P. reinstated

Fifth Ties
Mar08   6-1   Vale of Leven v Beith
Mar08   1-9   Stonelaw v Dumbarton
Mar08   1-2   Hibernian v Helensburgh
Mar08   5-0   Queen's Park v 3rd L.R.V.
Mar08   4-0   Rangers v Partick

Sixth Ties
Mar22   0-1   Queen's Park v Rangers
Mar22   3-1   Vale of Leven v Dumbarton
        bye   Helensburgh

Seventh Ties
Mar29   0-3   Helensburgh v Vale of Leven   at Helensburgh
        bye   Rangers

Final Tie
Apr19   1-1   Rangers v Vale of Leven   at Hampden Park
Apr26   npl   Rangers v Vale of Leven   at Hampden Park - R. failed to
              appear. Cup awarded to Vale of Leven

Season 1879-80

First Ties
Glasgow and Suburbs
```
-----  w/o  Havelock v 4th Renfrewshire R.V. - disbanded
-----  dbd  Union (Glasgow) v 3rd L.R.V. - w/o
Sep20  2-1  Jordanhill v* Kelvinbank
-----  w/o  John Elder v Derby - disbanded
-----  w/o  Parkgrove v Clydesdale - scr.
Sep27  2-0  Partick v* Petershill
-----  dbd  Whiteinch v South Western - w/o
Sep20  0-0  Rangers v Queen's Park
Sep27  5-1  Queen's Park v Rangers
-----  dbd  Stonefield v Harmonic Good Templars - w/o
-----  dbd  Telegraphists v Possil Blue Bell - w/o
-----  w/o  Athole v Blythswood - disbanded
-----  dbd  Wellpark v 19th Lanarkshire R.V. - w/o
-----  scr  1st Lanarkshire R.V. v Clyde - w/o
Sep20  2-1  Govan v* Caledonian (Glasgow)
Sep27  7-0  Whitefield v* Govanhill Lacrosse
-----  dbd  Partick Burnside v Ailsa - w/o
Sep20  1-1  City v Possilpark
Sep27  3-1  Possilpark v City
Sep20  2-2  Pollockshields Athletic v Oxford
Sep27  0-4  Oxford v Pollockshields Athletic
Sep20  4-0  Alexandra Athletic v Albatross
Sep20  3-0  Northern v Thistle (Glasgow)
-----  dbd  Blackfriars v Rosslyn - w/o
       bye  Glasgow University
```
Dumbartonshire
```
-----  w/o  Lennox v Renton Thistle - disbanded
Sep20  4-3  Dumbarton v Vale of Leven
Sep20  4-2  Helensburgh v* Alclutha
Sep20  2-1  Jamestown v* Star of Leven - J. later disqualified
Sep20  2-2  Renton v* Kilmaronock Thistle
Sep27  0-8  Kilmaronock Thistle v Renton
       bye  Kirkintilloch Athletic
```
Lanarkshire
```
Sep20  2-1  Clarkston v* Stonelaw
-----  scr  Uddingston v Cambuslang - w/o
Sep20  1-2  Clydebank v* Excelsior
Sep20  0-1  East Kilbride v* Airdrie
Sep27  2-1  Shotts v Drumpellier
-----  dbd  Mount Vernon v Upper Clydesdale - w/o
Sep20  2-0  Hamilton Academical v* Glengowan
-----  dbd  Avondale (Strathaven) v Newmains - w/o
```
Edinburgh and East
```
-----  w/o  Heart of Midlothian v 3rd Edinburgh R.V. - who were now St
                  Bernard's
Sep20  5-1  Hibernian v* Hanover
Sep20  5-0  Brunswick v Edinburgh Swifts
Sep20  2-0  Dunfermline v* Thistle (Edinburgh)
       bye  Edinburgh University
```
Ayrshire
```
-----  w/o  Cumnock v Irvine - I. disqualified
Sep27  0-2  Catrine v* Hurlford
Sep06  2-2  Beith v* Kilbirnie
Sep27  2-2  Kilbirnie v Beith - both qualified
```

```
Sep20  0-6  Ayr v* Kilmarnock Athletic
Sep27  0-2  Auchinleck Boswell v* Maybole Ladywell
Sep20  1-3  Dean v* Mauchline
-----  w/o  Maybole Carrick v Girvan - scr.
-----  scr  Lanemark v Portland - w/o
-----  w/o  Kilmarnock v Ayr Academicals - A.A. amalgamated
       bye  Tarbolton
```

Renfrewshire
```
-----  dbd  23rd Renfrewshire R.V. v Renfrew Ramblers - w/o
-----  dbd  Port Glasgow v Johnstone Athletic - w/o
Sep27  0-3  Busby v Arthurlie
Sep20  5-2  Cartvale v Wellington Park
Sep20  0-5  Barrhead v Renfrew
Sep20  2-2  Netherlee v* Greenock Morton
Sep27  7-4  Greenock Morton v Netherlee
Sep20  4-1  17th Renfrewshire R.V. v* Levern
Sep20  2-1  Kennishead v* Glenkilloch
Sep20  4-0  Thornliebank v Yoker
```

Stirlingshire
```
Sep20  3-1  Milton of Campsie v King's Park
Sep27  4-1  Campsie Glen v Milngavie Thistle - prot.
Oct04  4-0  Campsie Glen v Milngavie Thistle  at Kennyhill Park
Sep27  1-0  Strathblane v* Lenzie
Sep27  4-2  Falkirk v Grasshoppers
```

Perthshire
```
-----  w/o  Vale of Teith v Clifton and Strathfillan - disbanded
Sep27  1-2  Coupar Angus v* Rob Roy
```

Forfarshire
```
Sep20  5-1  Arbroath v Our Boys (Dundee)
       bye  St Clement
```

Dumfriesshire
```
-----  w/o  Q.O.S. Wanderers v Annan - disbanded
```

Wigtownshire
```
Sep20  0-2  Cree Rovers v Stranraer
```

Second Ties
Glasgow and Suburbs
```
Oct18  3-1  Ailsa v Rosslyn
Oct11  3-1  Whitefield v Northern - prot.
Oct25  w/o  Northern v Whitefield - scr.
Oct11  0-0  3rd L.R.V. v* Possil Blue Bell
Oct18  1-0  3rd L.R.V. v Possil Blue Bell
Oct11 14-1  Queen's Park v 19th Lanarkshire R.V.
Oct11  3-1  Partick v Havelock
Oct11  9-0  South Western v* Athole
Oct11  2-1  Clyde v Govan
Oct11  5-0  Alexandra Athletic v* Harmonic Good Templars
Oct18  4-1  Possilpark v* High School - H.S. admitted Second Ties
Oct11  5-1  Pollockshields Athletic v* Dennistoun - D. admitted into
              Second Ties
Oct11  1-0  John Elder v* Jordanhill - prot.
Oct25  1-2  Jordanhill v John Elder
       bye  Parkgrove
       bye  Glasgow University
```

Ayrshire
```
Oct04  1-1  Kilmarnock Athletic v Kilbirnie
Oct18  1-0  Kilbirnie v Kilmarnock Athletic
Oct18  2-1  Portland v Beith
Oct11  6-2  Mauchline v* Kilmarnock
```

```
-----   w/o   Cumnock v Tarbolton - scr.
Oct11   6-1   Maybole Ladywell v Stewarton Cunninghame - S.C. admitted
                 into Second Ties
Oct11   1-8   Maybole Carrick v* Hurlford
```
Renfrewshire
```
Oct11   1-2   Renfrew Ramblers v Barrhead Rangers - B.R. admitted into
                 Second Ties
Oct11   5-0   Kennishead v Cartside - C. admitted Second Ties
Oct11   6-0   Johnstone Athletic v Cartvale
Oct11   1-6   17th Renfrewshire R.V. v Thornliebank
Oct11   9-3   Arthurlie v* Greenock Morton
        bye   Renfrew
```
Lanarkshire
```
Oct11+  2-0   Plains Blue Bell v Newmains - P.B.B. admitted Second Ties
Oct11+  1-4   Airdrie v Cambuslang
Oct11   0-2   Shotts v* Clarkston
Oct11   3-0   Hamilton Academical v* Upper Clydesdale
Oct11   2-1   Excelsior v Bellshill - B. admitted Second Ties
```
Dumbartonshire
```
Oct11   1-1   Renton v Lennox
Oct18   1-1   Lennox v Renton - both qualified
Oct11   0-1   Kirkintilloch Athletic v Jamestown - J. disqualified K.A.
                 reinstated
Oct11   7-0   Dumbarton v* Helensburgh
```
Edinburgh
```
Oct18   3-2   Heart of Midlothian v Brunswick
Oct11   0-4   Dunfermline v Hibernian
        bye   Edinburgh University
```
Stirlingshire
```
Oct11   0-4   Milton of Campsie v* Campsie Glen
Oct11   1-0   Strathblane v* Falkirk
```
Perthshire
```
Oct18   3-0   Rob Roy v Vale of Teith
```
Forfarshire
```
-----   w/o   Strathmore (Dundee) v St Clement - scr.
        bye   Arbroath
```
Wigtownshire and Dumfriesshire
```
Oct18   6-0   Q.O.S. Wanderers v* Stranraer
```

Third Ties
Glasgow and Suburbs
```
Nov01   6-2   Parkgrove v* Alexandra Athletic
Nov01   5-1   Queen's Park v* Partick
Nov01   6-0   Clyde v Ailsa
Nov01   2-1   South Western v John Elder
Nov01   2-1   Pollockshields Athletic v* Northern
Nov08   1-1   3rd L.R.V. v* Glasgow University
Nov15   6-0   3rd L.R.V. v Glasgow University
        bye   Possilpark
```
Ayrshire
```
-----   scr   Maybole Ladywell v Kilbirnie - w/o
Nov01   0-0   Mauchline v* Portland
Nov08   0-1   Portland v Mauchline
Nov08   0-1   Cumnock v Hurlford
```
Renfrewshire
```
Nov01   1-2   Arthurlie v* Renfrew
Nov01   3-1   Johnstone Athletic v Kennishead
Nov01   1-0   Thornliebank v Barrhead Rangers
```
Lanarkshire and Dumfriesshire

```
Nov08  7-1  Hamilton Academical v Excelsior
Nov01  4-2  Cambuslang v Clarkston
-----  w/o  Plains Blue Bell v Q.O.S. Wanderers - scr.
```
Dumbartonshire
```
Nov01  5-0  Dumbarton v* Renton
Nov01  5-1  Jamestown v* Lennox - J. disqualified
```
Edinburgh and Perthshire
```
Nov15  2-1  Hibernian v* Heart of Midlothian
Nov08  1-0  Rob Roy v Edinburgh University
```
Stirlingshire
```
Nov01  2-1  Strathblane v* Campsie Glen
```
Forfarshire
```
Nov01  6-1  Arbroath v* Strathmore (Dundee) - S. admitted Second Ties
```

Fourth Ties
```
Nov22  2-2  Hibernian v* Parkgrove
Nov29  2-2  Parkgrove v Hibernian - both qualified
Nov22  4-0  South Western v* Arbroath
Nov22  2-1  Pollockshields Athletic v Renfrew
Nov22  1a1  Kilbirnie v Hurlford - abd. 75mins darkness
Nov29  1-1  Hurlford v Kilbirnie - both qualified
Nov22 11-0  Dumbarton v Clyde
Nov15  5-2  Kirkintilloch Athletic v Star of Leven  - K.A. & S.o.L.
                reinstated
Nov22  6-2  Kirkintilloch Athletic v Lennox - L. reinstated
Nov29  5-1  3rd L.R.V. v Kirkintilloch Athletic
Nov22  4-2  Rob Roy v* Johnstone Athletic
Nov22 12-0  Thornliebank v Possilpark
Nov29  0-2  Hamilton Academical v* Mauchline
Nov29  3-0  Cambuslang v Plains Blue Bell
Nov22 10-1  Queen's Park v* Strathblane
```

Fifth Ties
```
Dec20  0-1  Parkgrove v South Western  - prot.
Dec27  2-3  Parkgrove v South Western
Dec20  6-2  Dumbarton v* Kilbirnie
Dec20 15-1  Queen's Park v* Hurlford
Dec20 12-0  Thornliebank v Rob Roy
Dec20  0-4  Cambuslang v Pollockshields Athletic
Dec20  0-2  Mauchline v* Hibernian
       bye  3rd L.R.V.
```

Sixth Ties
```
Dec27  0a2  Thornliebank v* 3rd L.R.V. - abd. 35mins weather
Jan03  1-1  3rd L.R.V. v Thornliebank
Jan10  2-1  Thornliebank v 3rd L.R.V. - aet. 1-1
Jan03  6-1  Pollockshields Athletic v* South Western
Jan03  6-2  Dumbarton v Hibernian
       bye  Queen's Park
```

Seventh Ties
```
Jan17  1-0  Queen's Park v Dumbarton  at Hampden Park
Jan17  2-1  Thornliebank v Pollockshields Athletic  at Deacon's Bank
```

Final Tie
```
Feb21  3-0  Queen's Park v Thornliebank  at Cathkin Park
```

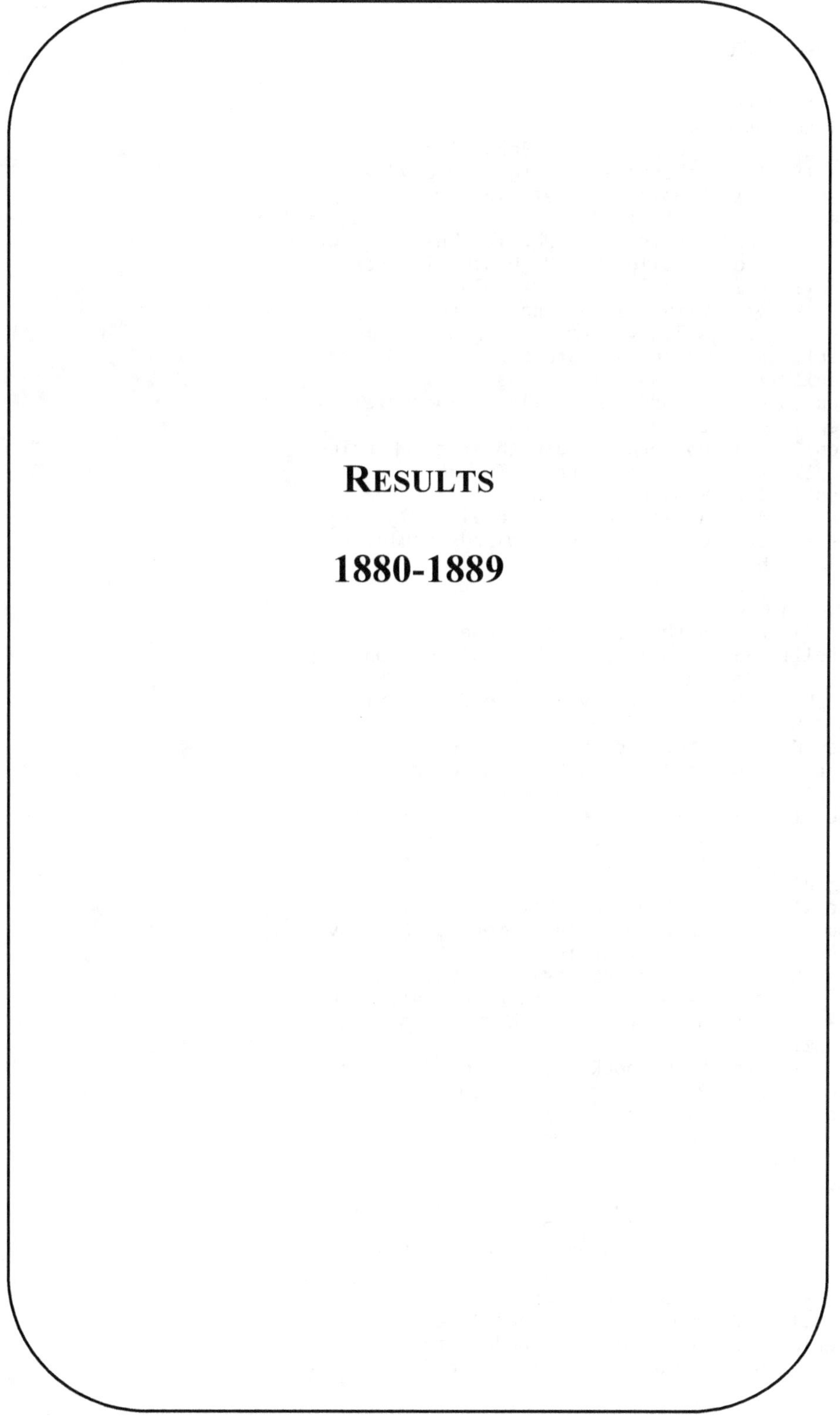

RESULTS

1880-1889

Season 1880-81

First Round
Glasgow and Suburbs
```
Sep11   7-0   Queen's Park v John Elder
Sep18   1-2   Caledonian (Glasgow) v Clyde
Sep11   1-1   Athole v Whitefield - void
Sep25   1-2   Whitefield v Athole - aet. 1-1  at Ibrox Park
-----   scr   Dennistoun v Partick Thistle - w/o
-----   w/o   Possilpark v High School - scr.
Sep18   4-2   Pilgrims v Lancefield
-----   w/o   City v 19th Lanarkshire R.V. - scr.
-----   scr   Ailsa v Harmonic - w/o
Sep11   3-1   Northern v 3rd L.R.V.
Sep11   1-0   Jordanhill v Windsor
Sep11   6-0   Oxford v Maxwell (Pollockshields)
Sep04   4-3   Cowlairs v Petershill
Sep11   0-4   Pollockshields Athletic v Partick
Sep11   7-0   South Western v* Ingram
Sep11   4-1   Rangers v Govan
Sep18   4-1   Alexandra Athletic v Kelvinbank
-----   scr   Clydesdale v Shawlands Athletic - w/o
        bye   Possil Blue Bell
        bye   Glasgow University
```
Renfrewshire
```
Sep04   2-0   Arthurlie v Johnstone
Sep11+  2-3   Glenkilloch v Greenock Morton
-----   w/o   Cartvale v Levern - scr.
Sep04   3-0   St Mirren v Johnstone Athletic
Sep18   6-2   Cartside v Kennishead
Sep18   3-0   Thornliebank v Renfrew
Sep04   5-0   Pollock v Johnstone Rovers
Sep18   7-1   Abercorn v* Barrhead
Sep11   6-1   17th Renfrewshire R.V. v Wellington Park
-----   scr   Renfrew Ramblers v Yoker - w/o
-----   w/o   Netherlee v Oakfield - disbanded
```
Ayrshire
```
Sep11+  -     Rankinston v Maybole - prot.
Sep30   3-1   Maybole v Rankinston  at Springvale Park
Sep11   4-1   Beith v Irvine
Sep18   1-7   Auchinleck Boswell v Cumnock
-----   scr   Girvan v Kilmarnock Athletic - w/o
-----   bye   Hurlford v Ayr Thistle - A.T. amalgamated
Sep11   0-2   Catrine v Ayr
-----   w/o   Kilmarnock v Stewarton Cunninghame - scr.
Sep11   8-0   Portland v Coylton Coila
Sep18   3-0   Kilbirnie v Lanemark
-----   w/o   Mauchline v Dean - scr.
```
Lanarkshire
```
Sep11+  3-0   Airdrie v Bellshill
-----   w/o   Airdriehill v Airdrie Bluebell - disbanded
Sep11   3-0   Excelsior v* Drumpellier
Sep04   1-0   Clarkston v* Plains Blue Bell
Sep11   0-5   Tollcross Athletic v Thistle (Lanark)
-----   w/o   Cambuslang v Upper Clydesdale - scr.
Sep11   2-2   Uddingston v Royal Albert
Sep18   5-0   Royal Albert v Uddingston
-----   scr   Stonelaw v Hamilton Academical - w/o
```

Sep11   4-0   Shotts v Lanark
        bye   Glengowan
Dumbartonshire
Sep11   1-2   Lennox v* Helensburgh - prot.
Sep25   8-1   Helensburgh v Lennox
Sep11   7-0   Dumbarton v Victoria (Helensburgh)
-----   w/o   Renton v Kilmaronock Thistle - scr.
Sep11   6-0   Jamestown v Alclutha
Sep18   3-2   Star of Leven v Kirkintilloch Athletic
        bye   Vale of Leven
Stirlingshire
Sep18   2-0   Campsie Central v Bridge of Allan
Sep11   w/o   Lenzie v Thistle Athletic - scr.
Sep11   1-0   King's Park v Strathblane
Sep11   w/o   Falkirk v Campsie Athletic - scr.
Sep04   1-2   Grasshoppers v Milton of Campsie
Perthshire and Forfarshire
Sep11   2-1   Rob Roy v Our Boys (Dundee)
-----   scr   St Clement v Dunkeld - w/o
-----   scr   Vale of Teith v Arbroath - w/o
Sep18   4-1   Coupar Angus v Strathmore (Dundee)
Edinburghshire and Fifeshire
Sep18   3-5   Hanover v Dunfermline
Sep11   3-1   Heart of Midlothian v Brunswick
        bye   Hibernian
        bye   Edinburgh University
Wigtownshire and Dumfriesshire
Sep11   3-0   Stranraer v Q.O.S. Wanderers
-----   w/o   5th K.R.V. v Cree Rovers - scr.

Second Round
Glasgow and Suburbs
-----   scr   Possil Blue Bell v Shawlands Athletic - w/o
Oct02   0-1   Northern v Rangers
Oct02   1-0   Alexandra Athletic v Athole
Oct09   2-0   South Western v Partick
Oct09   7-0   Pilgrims v City
Oct02   0-1   Jordanhill v Partick Thistle
Oct09   4-3   Cowlairs v Oxford
Oct02   5-0   Queen's Park v Possilpark
Oct02   1-1   Harmonic v Clyde
Oct09   1-0   Clyde v Harmonic
        bye   Glasgow University
Renfrewshire
Oct02   0-2   Netherlee v Yoker
Oct02   3-2   St Mirren v* 17th Renfrewshire R.V.
Oct02   4-2   Abercorn v Greenock Morton
Oct02   1-1   Arthurlie v Cartvale
Oct09   1-2   Cartvale v Arthurlie
Oct02   3-1   Pollock v Thornliebank
        bye   Cartside
Ayrshire
Oct02   2-1   Hurlford v Cumnock
Oct02   3a0   Kilbirnie v Kilmarnock Athletic - abd. 55min K.A. left the
                 field. prot.
Oct16   2-1   Kilbirnie v Kilmarnock Athletic
Oct09   6-3   Kilmarnock v Ayr
Oct09   6-1   Mauchline v Maybole
Oct02   0-1   Portland v Beith

Lanarkshire
Oct02 1-1 Glengowan v Thistle (Lanark)
Oct09 6-1 Thistle (Lanark) v Glengowan
Oct09 1-3 Hamilton Academical v Cambuslang
Oct02 2-3 Excelsior v Airdrie
Oct02 2-1 Clarkston v Airdriehill
Oct02 1-0 Royal Albert v Shotts
Dumbartonshire
Oct09 0-1 Renton v Vale of Leven
Oct02 2-1 Dumbarton v Jamestown
Oct02 5-1 Helensburgh v Star of Leven
Stirlingshire
Oct02 2-1 Falkirk v King's Park
Oct02 5-5 Campsie Central v Milton of Campsie
Oct09 1-3 Milton of Campsie v Campsie Central
       bye Lenzie
Perthshire and Forfarshire
Oct02 0-4 Dunkeld v Rob Roy
Oct02 1-2 Coupar Angus v Arbroath
Edinburgh District
Oct09 3-1 Hibernian v Dunfermline
       bye Heart of Midlothian
       bye Edinburgh University
Kirkcudbrightshire and Wigtownshire
Oct09 4-3 5th K.R.V. v Stranraer

Third Round
Glasgow and Suburbs
Oct23 2-1 Cowlairs v Alexandra Athletic - prot.
Nov06 2-1 Cowlairs v Alexandra Athletic
Oct23 3-0 Rangers v* Partick Thistle
Oct23 4-0 Clyde v Shawlands Athletic
Oct23 8-1 Queen's Park v* Pilgrims
       bye South Western
       bye Glasgow University
Renfrewshire
Oct30 4-3 Cartside v Yoker - prot.
Nov06 2-2 Yoker v Cartside
Nov13 4-3 Cartside v Yoker
Oct23 1-4 Abercorn v St Mirren
Oct23 2-0 Arthurlie v Pollock
Ayrshire and Kirkcudbrightshire
Oct23 17-2 Beith v 5th K.R.V.
Oct23 2-1 Mauchline v Kilmarnock - prot.
Nov06 3a3 Mauchline v Kilmarnock - abd. 60mins darkness
Nov13 0-3 Kilmarnock v Mauchline
Oct30 0-2 Kilbirnie v Hurlford
Lanarkshire
----- w/o Thistle (Lanark) v Airdrie - scr.
Oct23 0-5 Royal Albert v Cambuslang
       bye Clarkston

Dumbartonshire and Stirlingshire
Oct23 1-4 Helensburgh v Vale of Leven
Oct23 1-6 Falkirk v Dumbarton
Oct30 6-1 Campsie Central v* Lenzie
Perthshire, Forfarshire and Edinburgh District
Oct23 2-1 Arbroath v Rob Roy
Oct23 5-3 Heart of Midlothian v Hibernian

```
        bye  Edinburgh University
```

Fourth Round
```
Nov13   3-0  Heart of Midlothian v* Cambuslang
-----   awa  Mauchline v* Clarkston - awarded to M. after dispute
Nov20   1-3  Cartside v Hurlford
Nov13   0-1  Edinburgh University v Campsie Central
Nov13   4-3  Arthurlie v South Western - prot.
Nov27   2-1  Arthurlie v South Western - aet. 1-1
Nov13   w/o  Vale of Leven v Arbroath - scr.
Nov13   9-0  Dumbarton v* Glasgow University
Nov13  11-0  Rangers v Clyde
Nov13  11-2  Queen's Park v Beith
Nov13   1-0  St Mirren v Cowlairs
        bye  Thistle (Lanark)
```

Fifth Round
```
Dec04   7-1  Vale of Leven v* Thistle (Lanark)
Dec04   1-5  St Mirren v Dumbarton
Dec18   0-3  Hurlford v Rangers
Dec11   4-0  Arthurlie v Heart of Midlothian
Dec11   0-2  Mauchline v Queen's Park
        bye  Campsie Central
```

Sixth Round
```
Dec25  0-10  Campsie Central v Queen's Park
Dec25   1-3  Rangers v Dumbarton
Dec25   0-2  Arthurlie v Vale of Leven
```

Seventh Round
```
Feb05   0-2  Vale of Leven v Dumbarton  at Alexandria
        bye  Queen's Park
```
Final
```
Mar26   1-2  Dumbarton v Queen's Park  at Kinning Park - prot.
Apr09   1-3  Dumbarton v Queen's Park  at Kinning Park
```

Season 1881-82

First Round
Glasgow and Suburbs
```
Sep17   0-7  1st Lanarkshire R.V. v Cowlairs
-----   w/o  Harmonic v Govan - disbanded
-----   w/o  South Western v Jordanhill - scr.
Sep10   2-1  Rangers v 3rd L.R.V.
-----   w/o  John Elder v Shawlands Athletic - disbanded
-----   dbd  Windsor v Whitefield - w/o
-----   b/d  Athole v Ingram - both disbanded
Sep17  14-0  Queen's Park v Caledonian (Glasgow)
-----   scr  Clydesdale v Clyde - w/o
-----   w/o  Alexandra Athletic v Possil Blue Bell - disbanded
-----   b/d  Dennistoun v City - both disbanded
Sep17   5-1  Partick v Possilpark
-----   dbd  Oxford v Pilgrims - w/o
Sep10   1-3  Mavisbank v Partick Thistle
Sep10   1-3  Pollockshields Athletic v Petershill
-----   scr  Kelvinbank v Kinning Park Athletic - w/o
```

```
Sep10   1-1   Annfield  v Eastern Athletic
-----   w/o   Eastern Athletic v Annfield - disbanded
Sep10   1-3   Battlefield v Northern
        bye   Luton
        bye   Glasgow University
```

Renfrewshire
```
Sep17   6-1   Paisley Athletic v Port Glasgow Athletic
Sep10   8-1   Kilbarchan v Ladyburn
Sep10   9-1   Johnstone v* Greenock Southern
Sep03   5-1   St Mirren v Johnstone Rovers
Sep10   5-0   Thornliebank v Johnstone Athletic
Sep10+  1-4   Netherlee v Wellington Park
Sep17   4-2   Cartvale v Renfrew
Sep10   4-2   Levern v Greenock Morton
-----   dbd   Kennishead v Yoker - w/o
-----   dbd   Cartside v Pollock - w/o
Sep10   3-3   Abercorn v Arthurlie
Sep17   4-0   Arthurlie v Abercorn
Sep10   0-2   Barrhead v Glenkilloch
```

Ayrshire
```
Sep17   7-1   Kilmarnock Athletic v Ayr
Sep17   7-0   Maybole v Rankinston
-----   npl   Largs v Girvan
Sep10   3-0   Lugar Boswell v Lanemark
-----   dbd   Irvine v Hurlford - w/o
-----   scr   Coylton Coila v Beith - w/o
-----   dbd   Dean v Auchinleck Boswell - w/o
Sep10   6-0   Kilmarnock v Largs Athletic
Sep17   0-10  Stewarton Cunninghame v Portland
Sep10   1-1   Cumnock v Mauchline
Sep17   5-1   Mauchline v Cumnock
-----   w/o   Kilbirnie v Catrine - disbanded
        bye   Annbank
```

Dumbartonshire
```
-----   w/o   Star of Leven v Kirkintilloch Athletic - disbanded
Sep10   2-6   Kilmaronock Thistle v Helensburgh
-----   scr   Renton v Jamestown - w/o
Sep10   5-1   Shotts v Drumpellier
Sep10   9-1   Dumbarton v Alclutha
-----   scr   Lennox v Vale of Leven - w/o
        bye   Victoria (Helensburgh)
```

Stirlingshire
```
Sep17   1-1   Bridge of Allan v Thistle Athletic - aet. 1-1
Oct01   8-0   Thistle Athletic v Bridge of Allan
Sep10   3-0   Falkirk v King's Park
Oct01   7-0   Strathblane v Dunipace
-----   w/o   Grasshoppers v Campsie Central - disbanded
-----   dbd   Campsie Athletic v Lenzie - w/o
Sep10   0-3   Southfield v Milton of Campsie
```

Lanarkshire
```
-----   scr   Lanark v Clarkston - w/o
Sep10+  2-4   Glengowan v West Benhar
Sep10   5-0   Cambuslang v Royal Albert
-----   scr   Upper Clydesdale v Uddingston - w/o
-----   w/o   Thistle (Lanark) v Stonelaw - disbanded
-----   w/o   Airdrie v Tollcross - scr.
-----   w/o   Airdriehill v Bellshill - disbanded
Sep10   1-0   Hamilton Academical v Plains Blue Bell
```

```
       bye  Airdrieonians
Edinburgh
Aug27  7-0  Hibernian v Addiewell
Sep10  1-0  St Bernard's v Heart of Midlothian
Sep10  2-3  Hanover v Brunswick  at Tynecastle Park
Sep17  5-1  West Calder v Kinleith
       bye  Dunfermline
       bye  Edinburgh University
Perthshire
Sep10  0-4  Blairgowrie v Coupar Angus
-----  scr  Dunkeld v Rob Roy - w/o
-----  w/o  Vale of Teith v Aberfeldy - scr.
Forfarshire
-----  w/o  Strathmore (Dundee) v St Clement - disbanded
Sep10  1-2  Arbroath v Our Boys (Dundee)
       bye  Harp (Dundee)
Wigtownshire
-----  w/o  Stranraer v Cree Rovers - disbanded
Dumfriesshire
Sep17  3-2  5th K.R.V. v Moffat - aet. 2-2
       bye  Q.O.S. Wanderers
```

Second Round
Glasgow and Suburbs
```
Oct01  1-9  Luton v Northern
Oct08  2-2  Queen's Park v Cowlairs
Oct15  9-0  Queen's Park v Cowlairs
Oct01  3-0  Partick v Kinning Park Athletic
-----  w/o  Rangers v Harmonic - scr.
-----  scr  Eastern Athletic v South Western - w/o
-----  scr  John Elder v Clyde - w/o
Oct01  4-1  Alexandra Athletic v Whitefield
Oct01  3-1  Partick Thistle v Pilgrims  - prot.
Oct15  7-1  Partick Thistle v Pilgrims
       bye  Petershill
       bye  Glasgow University
```
Renfrewshire
```
Oct08  3-1  Paisley Athletic v St Mirren
Oct08  3-4  Wellington Park v Kilbarchan
Oct01  3-0  Arthurlie v Pollock
Oct01  3-4  Levern v Thornliebank
Oct08  2-0  Glenkilloch v Yoker
       bye  Johnstone
       bye  Cartvale
```
Ayrshire
```
Oct08  3-1  Lugar Boswell v Annbank
Oct08  1-1  Mauchline v Portland
Oct15  1-5  Portland v* Mauchline
Oct01  5-0  Kilmarnock Athletic v Maybole
Oct08  7-1  Kilmarnock v Auchinleck Boswell
Oct01  3-3  Beith v Hurlford
Oct08  4-4  Hurlford v Beith - both qualified
       bye  Kilbirnie
```
Lanarkshire
```
Oct01   6-2  Cambuslang v Airdrieonians
Oct01  10-0  Thistle (Lanark) v Uddingston
Oct01   1-1  Airdrie v Airdriehill - prot.
Oct22   2-3  Airdriehill v Airdrie
Oct08   2-1  Shotts v Hamilton Academical
```

Oct01 1-2 Clarkston v West Benhar
Stirlingshire
Oct08 0-5 Grasshoppers v Falkirk
Oct08 3-1 Milton of Campsie v Lenzie - prot.
Oct15 2-0 Milton of Campsie v Lenzie
Oct08 3-2 Thistle Athletic v Strathblane
Dumbartonshire
----- w/o Helensburgh v Victoria (Helensburgh) - scr.
Oct01 0-2 Vale of Leven v Dumbarton
Oct08 5-0 Jamestown v Star of Leven
Edinburghshire
----- w/o West Calder v Dunfermline - scr.
Oct08 2-1 Hibernian v St Bernard's
       bye Brunswick
       bye Edinburgh University
Perthshire
Oct08 2-6 Dunblane Wanderers v Vale of Teith – D.W. omitted in R1
Oct01 3-1 Rob Roy v Coupar Angus
Forfarshire
Oct08 1-1 Harp (Dundee) v Our Boys (Dundee)
Oct15 5-2 Our Boys (Dundee) v Harp (Dundee)
       bye Strathmore (Dundee)
Dumfriesshire
Oct08 1-2 5th K.R.V. v Q.O.S. Wanderers - aet. 1-1
Wigtownshire
       bye Stranraer

Third Round
Glasgow and Suburbs
Oct22 2-2 Petershill v Partick Thistle
Oct29 2-0 Partick Thistle v Petershill - prot.
Nov05 3-2 Partick Thistle v Petershill - aet. 2-2
Oct22 3-1 Rangers v Alexandra Athletic
Oct22 1-2 Northern v Clyde
Oct22 1-2 Partick v South Western - prot.
Nov05 1a0 South Western v Partick - abd. first half
       bye Queen's Park
       bye Glasgow University
Renfrewshire
Oct29 2-1 Kilbarchan v Johnstone - prot.
Nov05 2-2 Kilbarchan v Johnstone - aet. of 20mins 2-2
Nov12 3-0 Johnstone v Kilbarchan
Oct29 0-3 Glenkilloch v Cartvale
Oct29 7-1 Arthurlie v Paisley Athletic
       bye Thornliebank
Lanarkshire
Oct29 4-4 Airdrie v Shotts
Nov05 5-0 Shotts v Airdrie
Oct22 4-2 Cambuslang v West Benhar - prot.
Nov05 3-2 West Benhar v Cambuslang
       bye Thistle (Lanark)
Ayrshire
Oct22 2a0 Kilmarnock v Kilbirnie - abd. 70mins Kilb. left the field
Oct22 0-0 Hurlford v Mauchline
Oct29 2-0 Mauchline v Hurlford
Oct22 0-1 Lugar Boswell v Beith
       bye Kilmarnock Athletic
Stirlingshire
Oct22 0-2 Thistle Athletic v Falkirk

```
         bye   Milton of Campsie
Dumbartonshire
Oct22   5-0   Dumbarton v Jamestown
         bye   Helensburgh
Edinburgh
Oct22   4-1   West Calder v Brunswick
         bye   Hibernian
         bye   Edinburgh University
Perthshire
Oct22   1-6   Rob Roy v Vale of Teith
Forfarshire
Oct29   1-4   Strathmore (Dundee) v Our Boys (Dundee)
Dumfriesshire
Oct22   4a1   Stranraer v Q.O.S. Wanderers - abd. 83mins QOSW left the
               field
```

Fourth Round
```
Nov12   3-1   Falkirk v Milton of Campsie
Nov12   1-1   Helensburgh v Arthurlie
Nov19   1-0   Arthurlie v Helensburgh
Nov12   0-2   Thornliebank v Rangers
Nov12   2-3   Edinburgh University v Clyde
Nov19   3-1   Queen's Park v Johnstone
Nov12   2-3   Mauchline v Kilmarnock Athletic
Nov12   0-1   Thistle (Lanark) v Partick Thistle
Nov19   4-5   Glasgow University v Cartvale
Nov19   4-4   West Benhar v Hibernian
Nov26   8-0   Hibernian v West Benhar
Nov12   9-2   Kilmarnock v Our Boys (Dundee)
-----   w/o   West Calder v Stranraer - scr.
         bye   South Western
         bye   Dumbarton
         bye   Beith
         bye   Vale of Teith
         bye   Shotts
```

Fifth Round
```
Dec10   4-1   Arthurlie v Kilmarnock
Dec10   4-2   West Calder v Falkirk
Dec03  10-0   Queen's Park v Partick Thistle
Dec03   0-5   Vale of Teith v Shotts
Dec03   2-0   Kilmarnock Athletic v Beith
Dec03   4-5   Clyde v Cartvale
Dec03   2-6   Hibernian v Dumbarton - prot.
Dec24   2-6   Hibernian v Dumbarton
Dec03   1-2   South Western v Rangers - prot.
Dec24   4-0   Rangers v South Western
```

Sixth Round
```
Jan07  15-0   Queen's Park v* Shotts
Jan14   5-2   Kilmarnock Athletic v Arthurlie
Jan28   2-1   Dumbarton v Rangers - prot.
Feb04   5-1   Dumbarton v Rangers
Dec31   3-5   West Calder v Cartvale
```

Seventh Round
```
Feb18   3-2   Queen's Park v Kilmarnock Athletic  at Hampden Park
Feb18  11-2   Dumbarton v Cartvale  at Dumbarton
```

Final
```
Mar18   2-2   Dumbarton v Queen's Park   at Cathkin Park
Apr01   4-1   Queen's Park v Dumbarton   at Cathkin Park
```

Season 1882-83

First Round
Glasgow and Suburbs
```
Sep09    2-4   Battlefield v Partick Thistle
Sep09    0-4   Jordanhill v Rangers
Sep09    6-5   Pollockshields Athletic v Alexandra Athletic
Sep09   12-1   Queen's Park v Thistle (Glasgow)
Sep09    0-3   South Western v 3rd L.R.V.
Sep09    4-1   Cowlairs v Whitefield
Sep16    0-4   1st Lanarkshire R.V. v Northern
Sep09    3-1   Mavisbank v Granton
Sep09    0-6   Possilpark v Pilgrims
Sep16    5-0   Partick v Petershill
Sep09    4-0   Clyde v Luton
         bye   Apsley
         bye   Glasgow University
```
Ayrshire
```
Sep16    7-0   Annbank v Largs Athletic
Sep09    4-1   Lugar Boswell v Kilbirnie
Sep16    0-2   Mauchline v Kilmarnock
Sep09    1-1   Portland v Hurlford
Sep16    3-2   Hurlford v Portland
Sep16    3-5   Stewarton Cunninghame v Ayr
-----    w/o   Maybole v Rankinston - scr.
Sep09    4-2   Beith v Beith Thistle
Sep09    2-1   Kilmarnock Athletic v* Cumnock
```
Lanarkshire
```
Sep16    2-0   Wishaw v Holytown
Sep09    1-2   Bellshill v West Benhar
Sep09    3-3   Airdrieonians v Royal Albert
Sep16    3-3   Royal Albert v Airdrieonians - both qualified
Sep16    4-3   Drumpellier v Clarkston - prot.
Sep23    2-5   Drumpellier v Clarkston
Sep16    0-5   Hamilton Academical v Cambuslang
Sep16    0-7   Airdriehill v Shotts
Sep09    5-1   Airdrie v Plains Blue Bell
```
Stirlingshire
```
Sep16    1-5   Dunipace v Falkirk
Sep09    2-1   Milngavie v East Stirlingshire
Sep16    0-1   Lenzie v Strathblane
-----    w/o   Southfield v Aberfeldy Breadalbane - scr.
         bye   King's Park
```
Forfarshire
```
Sep09    7-2   Harp (Dundee) v Perseverance
Sep09    4-3   Arbroath v East End
Sep09    1-2   Angus v Balgay
Sep16    0-1   Strathmore (Dundee) v West End (Dundee)
Sep09    5-1   Our Boys (Dundee) v* Hibernian (Dundee)
```
Renfrewshire
```
Sep09   10-1   Abercorn v* Ladyburn
```

```
Sep16   0-3   Johnstone Athletic v Cartvale
Sep09   1-1   Woodland v Sir John Maxwell
Sep16   5-3   Sir John Maxwell v Woodland
Sep16   7-1   Thornliebank v Greenock Southern
Sep09   7-0   Arthurlie v Bute Rangers
Sep09   8-0   St Mirren v Yoker
Sep09   2-3   Clippens v Glenpatrick
Sep16   3-2   Pollock v Renfrew
Sep16   0-6   Woodside v Kilbarchan
Sep09   6-2   Johnstone v Paisley Athletic
Sep09   3-2   Port Glasgow Athletic v Lochwinnoch
Sep09   2-1   Greenock Morton v Johnstone Rovers
```

Dumbartonshire
```
Sep09+  1-3   Alclutha v Renton
-----   scr   Kilmaronock Thistle v Dumbarton - w/o
Sep09   7-1   Jamestown v Vale of Leven Hibernian
        bye   Vale of Leven
```

Edinburgh
```
Sep09   w/o   West Calder v Kinleith - scr.
Sep09   1-1   Heart of Midlothian v St Bernard's
Sep16   3-4   St Bernard's v Heart of Midlothian
Sep16   8-0   Hibernian v Brunswick
-----   w/o   Addiewell v Dunfermline - scr.
        bye   Edinburgh University
```

Perthshire
```
Sep16   0-1   Vale of Atholl v Vale of Teith
Sep16   1-3   Coupar Angus v Dunblane - prot.
Sep23   1-6   Coupar Angus v Dunblane
```

Southern Counties
```
-----   w/o   1ˢᵗ Dumfries R.V. v Dumfries Academicals - scr.
-----   w/o   Q.O.S. Wanderers v Lochmaben - scr.
Sep16   9-0   Moffat v East End Rovers
Sep16   8-0   5ᵗʰ K.R.V. v Drumlanrig Rangers
```

Second Round
Glasgow and Suburbs
```
Sep30  13-0   Cowlairs v* Apsley
Sep30   0-0   Northern v Pollockshields Athletic
Oct07   4-0   Pollockshields Athletic v Northern
Sep30   2-1   Partick v* Pilgrims
Sep30  14-2   Partick Thistle v* Mavisbank
Sep30   3-2   Queen's Park v Rangers
Sep30   2-0   3ʳᵈ L.R.V. v Clyde - prot.
Oct07   3-0   3ʳᵈ L.R.V. v Clyde
        bye   Glasgow University
```

Ayrshire
```
Oct07   4-5   Annbank v Kilmarnock Athletic
Oct07   6-3   Maybole v Ayr
Sep30   6-1   Lugar Boswell v Beith
Sep30   2-6   Kilmarnock v Hurlford
```

Lanarkshire
```
Oct07   1-3   Airdrieonians v Cambuslang
Oct07   6-2   Airdrie v Wishaw
Oct07  10-1   West Benhar v Shotts
Sep30   3-5   Royal Albert v Clarkston
```

Dumbartonshire and Stirlingshire
```
Sep30   8-0   Dumbarton v King's Park
Sep30  16-0   Vale of Leven v Milngavie
Sep30   1-14  Southfield v Renton
```

Oct07 12-1   Jamestown v Strathblane
       bye   Falkirk
Forfarshire and Perthshire
Oct07 1-4   Aberdeen v Harp (Dundee) - A. admitted Second Round
Sep30 3-1   Dunblane v Arbroath
Sep30 5-3   Our Boys (Dundee) v Balgay
Sep30 5-1   Vale of Teith v West End (Dundee)
Renfrewshire
Sep30 0-7   Kilbarchan v Johnstone
Sep30 2-2   Abercorn v Pollock
Oct07 2-2   Pollock v Abercorn - both qualified
Sep30 5-1   Greenock Morton v St Mirren
Sep30 7-0   Thornliebank v Glenpatrick
Sep30 5-3   Sir John Maxwell v Port Glasgow Athletic - prot.
Oct07 2-6   Sir John Maxwell v Port Glasgow Athletic
Sep30 2-1   Cartvale v Arthurlie - prot.
Oct07 1-3   Cartvale v Arthurlie
Edinburgh
Oct07 0-14 Addiewell v Heart of Midlothian
Oct07 2-3   West Calder v Hibernian
       bye   Edinburgh University
Southern Counties
Oct07 5-3   Q.O.S. Wanderers v 1st Dumfries R.V.
Sep30 5-3   5th K.R.V. v Moffat

Third Round
Glasgow and Lanarkshire
Oct21 3-0   Pollockshields Athletic v West Benhar
Oct21 13-0   Queen's Park v Clarkston
Oct21 3-3   Cambuslang v Partick Thistle
Oct28 3-3   Partick Thistle v Cambuslang - both qualified
Oct21 4-0   Partick v Cowlairs
Oct21 3-0   3rd L.R.V. v Airdrie
       bye   Glasgow University
Ayrshire and Renfrewshire
Oct28 2-5   Port Glasgow Athletic v Kilmarnock Athletic
Oct21 1-0   Arthurlie v Thornliebank - prot.
Oct28 0-0   Arthurlie v Thornliebank
Nov04 0-0   Thornliebank v Arthurlie - both qualified
Oct21 6-0   Lugar Boswell v Pollock
Oct28 8-0   Abercorn v Maybole
Oct28 2-1   Johnstone v* Greenock Morton
       bye   Hurlford
Stirlingshire, Dumbartonshire and Edinburgh
Oct21 2-2   Falkirk v Renton
Oct28 4-1   Renton v Falkirk
Oct21 8-1   Vale of Leven v Heart of Midlothian
Oct21 8-1   Dumbarton v Jamestown
       bye   Hibernian
       bye   Edinburgh University
Forfarshire and Perthshire
Oct21 0-5   Harp (Dundee) v Dunblane
Oct28 6-4   Vale of Teith v Our Boys (Dundee)
Dumfriesshire
Oct28 3-2   Q.O.S. Wanderers v 5th K.R.V.

Fourth Round
Nov11 2-3   Vale of Teith v Hurlford

```
Nov11   2-2   Hibernian v Partick
Nov18   1-4   Partick v Hibernian
Nov25   0-2   Edinburgh University v Vale of Leven
Nov18   3-1   Arthurlie v Q.O.S. Wanderers
-----   scr   Glasgow University v Partick Thistle - w/o
Nov11   5-0   Queen's Park v* Cambuslang
Nov11   3-5   Renton v Lugar Boswell
Nov11   1-7   Dunblane v 3rd L.R.V.
Nov11   5-2   Kilmarnock Athletic v Abercorn
Nov11   1-3   Johnstone v Pollockshields Athletic
Nov11   0-3   Thornliebank v Dumbarton
```

Fifth Round
```
Dec02   1-1   Lugar Boswell v Vale of Leven
Dec23   5-1   Vale of Leven v Lugar Boswell
Dec23   7-2   Queen's Park v Hurlford
Dec02   3-4   Hibernian v Arthurlie - prot.
Dec23   6-0   Arthurlie v Hibernian  at Kinning Park
        bye   3rd L.R.V.
        bye   Dumbarton
        bye   Kilmarnock Athletic
        bye   Partick Thistle
        bye   Pollockshields Athletic
```

Sixth Round
```
Feb10   0-4   Partick Thistle v Vale of Leven
Dec30   1-1   Arthurlie v Kilmarnock Athletic
Feb03   1-2   Kilmarnock Athletic v Arthurlie - prot.
Feb10   1-1   Arthurlie v Kilmarnock Athletic  at Cathkin Park
Feb17   0-1   Arthurlie v Kilmarnock Athletic  at Cathkin Park
Feb03   3-1   Dumbarton v Queen's Park
Dec23   1-1   3rd L.R.V. v Pollockshields Athletic
Feb03   5-2   Pollockshields Athletic v 3rd L.R.V.
```

Semi-finals
```
Feb24   1-1   Vale of Leven v Kilmarnock Athletic  at Alexandria
Mar17   0-2   Kilmarnock Athletic v Vale of Leven  at Holm Quarry
Feb24   0-1   Pollockshields Athletic v Dumbarton - prot.  at Hampden Park
Mar17   5-0   Dumbarton v Pollockshields Athletic  at Boghead Park
```

Final
```
Mar31   2-2   Dumbarton v Vale of Leven  at Hampden Park
Apr07   2-1   Dumbarton v Vale of Leven  at Hampden Park
```

Season 1883-84

First Round
Glasgow and District
```
Sep08   2-4   Possilpark v Orchard
Sep08   1-2   Dean Park v Mavisbank
-----   scr   Luton v Whitefield - w/o
Sep08   4-1   Pollockshields Athletic v Thistle (Glasgow)
Sep08   5-2   3rd L.R.V. v Clyde
Sep08   0-1   Northern v Rangers
-----   w/o   Partick Thistle v* Pilgrims - scr
Sep08   3-1   Whitehill v Alexandra Athletic
```

```
Sep08   0-8   Partick v* Queen's Park
Sep08   8-1   Battlefield v South Western
Sep08   3-1   Granton v Glencairn
        bye   Cowlairs
```

Renfrewshire
```
Sep08   7-0   Abercorn v Levern
Sep08   3-4   Kilbarchan v Paisley Athletic
Sep08   3-0   Arthurlie v Pollock
Sep08   6-0   St Mirren v* Caledonian (Glasgow)
Sep08   3-4   Johnstone v Thornliebank
Sep08   1-4   Linwood v Woodland
Sep08   npl   Glenpatrick v Bute Rangers - G. disqualified
-----   scr   Lochwinnoch v Port Glasgow Athletic - w/o
Sep08   5-3   Greenock Northern v Sir John Maxwell
Sep08   2-5   Netherlee v Greenock Southern
Sep08   2-4   Lyle Athletic v Johnstone Rovers
Sep08   1-0   Greenock Morton v Renfrew
Sep08   3-2   Clippens v Johnstone Athletic
Sep08   8-0   Cartvale v* West End Athletic
Sep08   0-2   Yoker v Olympic
```

Ayrshire
```
Sep08   w/o   Kilmarnock Athletic v Beith - B. failed to appear
-----   w/o   Kilmarnock v Kilbirnie - scr.
Sep08   1-3   Annbank v Mauchline
-----   dbd   Portland v Stewarton Cunninghame - w/o
-----   scr   Beith Thistle v Hurlford - w/o
Sep08   0-4   Maybole v* Cumnock
Sep08   3-1   Lugar Boswell v Ayr
```

Dumbartonshire
```
Sep08  12-0   Vale of Leven v Levendale
Sep08   2-1   Renton v Dumbarton
-----   scr   Kilmaronock Thistle v Jamestown - w/o
Sep08   1-1   Vale of Leven Wanderers v Dunbritton
Sep15   4-0   Dunbritton v Vale of Leven Wanderers
```

Lanarkshire
```
Sep08   2-2   Drumpellier v West Benhar
Sep15  12-0   West Benhar v Drumpellier
-----   w/o   Clarkston v Plains Blue Bell - scr.
Sep08   4-1   Hamilton Academical v Airdrieonians
Sep08   8-0   Royal Albert v Shettleston
Sep08   1-0   Airdrie v Tollcross - prot.
Sep22   4-3   Tollcross v Airdrie - aet. 3-3
Sep08   8-0   Cambuslang v Bellshill
        bye   Vale of Avon
```

Stirlingshire
```
Sep08   2-1   Dunipace v* Campsie
Sep08   3-2   Stenhousemuir v* Strathblane
Sep08   0-5   Alloa Athletic v Falkirk
Sep15  11-0   King's Park v* Lenzie
Sep08   3-0   East Stirlingshire v* Tayavalla
```

Edinburghshire
```
Sep08   2-1   Edina v Kinleith - prot.
Sep22   4-0   Edina v Kinleith
Sep08   5-0   Hibernian v West Calder
Sep15   1-13  Dunfermline v St Bernard's
Sep08   8-0   Heart of Midlothian v Brunswick
        bye   Newcastleton
        bye   Edinburgh University
```

Northern Counties
```
Sep08   9-0   Harp (Dundee) v* Angus
Sep08   2-2   Balgay v Strathmore (Arbroath)
Sep15   1-1   Strathmore (Arbroath) v Balgay  at Gayfield Park - both
                 qualified
Sep08   2-3   West End (Dundee) v Our Boys (Dundee)
Sep08   2-2   Perseverance v Hibernian (Dundee)
Sep15   3-4   Hibernian (Dundee) v Perseverance  at West Craigie Park
Sep08   3-3   Arbroath v Aberdeen
Sep15   7-0   Arbroath v Aberdeen
Sep08   0-1   East End v Strathmore (Dundee)
        bye   Coupar Angus
```
Perthshire
```
Sep08   2-1   Dunblane v Vale of Teith
-----   w/o   Vale of Athole v Aberfeldy Breadalbane - scr.
```
Southern Counties
```
Sep08   2-4   Vale of Nith v Moffat
-----   w/o   East End Rovers v Newton Stewart Athletic - scr.
Sep08   7-7   Q.O.S. Wanderers v 5th K.R.V.
Sep15   3-1   5th K.R.V. v Q.O.S. Wanderers
        bye   Drumlanrig Rangers
```

Second Round
Glasgow and District
```
Sep29   3-2   Cowlairs v Granton
Sep29   7-2   Battlefield v Whitefield
Sep29   6-2   Pollockshields Athletic v Mavisbank
Sep29   2-4   3rd L.R.V. v Queen's Park
Sep29  14-2   Rangers v Whitehill
Sep29   8-1   Partick Thistle v Orchard
```
Renfrewshire
```
Sep29   6-2   Cartvale v Greenock Southern
Sep29   1-3   Port Glasgow Athletic v Arthurlie
Sep29   5-0   Olympic v Clippens
Sep29   2-0   Abercorn v Paisley Athletic
Sep29  14a0   Thornliebank v Bute Rangers - mutually stopped 75mins
Sep29   7-0   St Mirren v* Woodland
Sep29   6-1   Johnstone Rovers v Greenock Northern
        bye   Greenock Morton
```
Ayrshire
```
Sep29   3-0   Kilmarnock v Hurlford
Sep29   9-1   Kilmarnock Athletic v Stewarton Cunninghame
Sep29   1-3   Lugar Boswell v Mauchline
        bye   Cumnock
```
Dumbartonshire and Stirlingshire
```
Sep29   6-1   Renton v King's Park
Sep29   9-1   Falkirk v Stenhousemuir
Sep29   7-1   Jamestown v Dunbritton
Sep29   2-2   East Stirlingshire v Dunipace
Oct06   1-2   Dunipace v East Stirlingshire
        bye   Vale of Leven
```
Lanarkshire
```
-----   w/o   West Benhar v Vale of Avon - scr.
Sep29   7-0   Cambuslang v Tollcross
Sep29   8-1   Royal Albert v Clarkston
        bye   Hamilton Academical
```
Edinburghshire
```
Sep29   1-4   Newcastleton v Heart of Midlothian
Oct06  10-0   Hibernian v Edina
```

```
        bye  St Bernard's
        bye  Edinburgh University
```
Perthshire and Northern Counties
```
Sep29   4-1  Dunblane v Coupar Angus
Sep29   3-1  Strathmore (Dundee) v* Balgay
-----   w/o  Harp (Dundee) v Vale of Athole - scr.
Sep29   2-0  Our Boys (Dundee) v Strathmore (Arbroath)
-----   scr  Perseverance v Arbroath - w/o
```
Southern Counties
```
Sep29   2-3  Drumlanrig Rangers v East End Rovers
Sep29   2-3  Moffat v 5th K.R.V.
```

Third Round
Northern Counties and Perthshire
```
Oct20   1-1  Arbroath v Harp (Dundee)
Oct27   2-1  Harp (Dundee) v Arbroath
Oct20   2-2  Strathmore (Dundee) v Our Boys (Dundee)
Oct27   5-1  Our Boys (Dundee) v Strathmore (Dundee)
        bye  Dunblane
```
Glasgow and Suburbs, Stirlingshire and Dumbartonshire
```
Oct20   6-0  Partick Thistle v East Stirlingshire
Oct20   5-2  Rangers v Falkirk
Oct20   2-4  Jamestown v Battlefield
Oct20   0-5  Cowlairs v Queen's Park
Oct20   4-1  Vale of Leven v Renton
        bye  Pollockshields Athletic
```
Edinburgh and Lanarkshire
```
Oct20   1-4  Heart of Midlothian v Hibernian
Oct20   7-0  St Bernard's v West Benhar
Oct20   6-0  Cambuslang v Hamilton Academical
        bye  Royal Albert
        bye  Edinburgh University
```
Southern Counties
```
Oct20   1-6  East End Rovers v 5th K.R.V.
```
Renfrewshire and Ayrshire
```
Oct20   1-2  Greenock Morton v Kilmarnock Athletic - prot.
Nov03   0-4  Greenock Morton v Kilmarnock Athletic
Oct20   0-5  Olympic v Mauchline
Oct20   4-1  Cartvale v Cumnock
Oct20   7-0  Abercorn v Johnstone Rovers
Oct20   3-1  Arthurlie v St Mirren
Oct20   1-0  Thornliebank v Kilmarnock  - prot.
Nov03   2-1  Thornliebank v Kilmarnock
```

Fourth Round
```
Nov10   1-8  5th K.R.V. v Hibernian
-----   w/o  Battlefield v Edinburgh University - scr.
Nov10   4-2  Cartvale v Abercorn
Nov10   1-6  Dunblane v Rangers
Nov10   2-3  Kilmarnock Athletic v Cambuslang
Nov10   4-0  Mauchline v Royal Albert
Nov10   0-4  Partick Thistle v Queen's Park
Nov10  11-0  Pollockshields Athletic v Our Boys (Dundee)
Nov10   2-0  St Bernard's v Thornliebank
Nov10   6-0  Vale of Leven v Harp (Dundee)
        bye  Arthurlie
```

Fifth Round

```
Dec01   0-0   Arthurlie v Vale of Leven
Dec08   3-1   Vale of Leven v Arthurlie
Dec01   2-3   Mauchline v Pollockshields Athletic
Dec01   0-3   St Bernard's v Rangers
        bye   Cartvale
        bye   Cambuslang
        bye   Hibernian
        bye   Battlefield
        bye   Queen's Park
```

Sixth Round
```
Dec22   1-5   Cambuslang v Rangers
Dec22   6-1   Hibernian v Battlefield
Dec22   6-1   Queen's Park v Cartvale
Dec22   4-2   Vale of Leven v Pollockshields Athletic
```

Semi-finals
```
Feb02   1-5   Hibernian v Queen's Park   at Easter Road
Jan19   3-0   Vale of Leven v Rangers   at Alexandria
```

Final
```
Feb23    -    Queen's Park v Vale of Leven   - V. didn't appear Q. awarded
                 cup
```

Season 1884-85

First Round
Glasgow and District
```
Sep13   3-3   Whitefield v Thistle (Glasgow)
Sep20   3-1   Thistle (Glasgow) v Whitefield
Sep13   7-0   Possilpark v Cyrus
Sep13   6-4   Northern v* Glasgow University YMCA AC
Sep13   1-2   Clyde v Cowlairs
Sep13   3-2   3rd L.R.V. v Partick Thistle
Sep13   9-1   Partick v Eastern Athletic
Sep13   0-1   Shawlands v Granton
Sep13   4-0   Queen's Park v Pollockshields   at Copeland Park
Sep13   6-2   Pollockshields Athletic v Pilgrims
Sep13   8-0   Battlefield v Kinning Park Athletic
Sep13  11-0   Rangers v* Whitehill
-----   scr   Orchard v Springburn Hibernian - w/o
-----   bye   Dean Park
```
Renfrewshire
```
Sep13   1-0   Renfrew v Johnstone Rovers
Sep13   3-1   Clippens v Greenock Rovers
Sep13   2-0   Arthurlie v Olympic
Sep13   4-3   St Mirren v Neilston - prot.
Sep27   1-4   Neilston v St Mirren
Sep13   6-0   Thornliebank v Greenock Northern
Sep13   2-2   Greenock Morton v Abercorn
Sep20   3-4   Abercorn v Greenock Morton - prot.
Sep27   2-2   Abercorn v Greenock Morton - both qualified
Sep13  12-1   Cartvale v Greenock Rangers
Sep13   2-3   Paisley Athletic v Greenock Southern
Sep13   6-1   Port Glasgow Athletic v* 1st Renfrewshire R.V.
-----   scr   Kilbarchan v Pollockshaws - w/o
```

```
Sep13   9-1   Johnstone v* Lyle Athletic
```
Ayrshire
```
Sep13   3-2   Cumnock v Mauchline
Sep13   3-7   Dalry v Annbank
Sep20  14-0   Kilmarnock Athletic v Stewarton Cunninghame
Sep20   6-1   Kilmarnock v Hurlford  - prot.
Sep27   3-1   Hurlford v Kilmarnock - H. disqualified
Sep13   4-1   Ayr v Lugar Boswell
        bye   Maybole
```
Dumbartonshire
```
Sep13   2-1   Renton v Vale of Leven Wanderers
-----   scr   Lenzie v Dumbarton Athletic - w/o
Sep13   1-1   Jamestown v Vale of Leven
Sep20   4-1   Vale of Leven v Jamestown
-----   w/o   Dumbarton v Levendale - scr.
Sep13   0-2   Rock v Yoker
-----   w/o   Albion v Dunbritton - scr.
```
Lanarkshire
```
Sep13   1-8   Chryston v West Benhar
Sep13   1-4   Clarkston v Hamilton Academical
Sep13   4-6   Airdrie v Shettleston
Sep13   2-6   Tollcross v Westburn
Sep13   1-4   Royal Albert v Cambuslang
-----   w/o   Airdriehill v Vale of Avon - scr.
Sep13   0-6   Drumpellier v Airdrieonians
Sep13   2-1   Wishaw Swifts v Dykehead  - prot.
Sep27   2-5   Dykehead v Wishaw Swifts
Sep13   1-2   Albion Rovers v Glengowan
```
Stirlingshire
```
Sep13   1-2   Stenhousemuir v Tayavalla
Sep13   4-0   Grasshoppers v Dunipace
Sep13   0-4   Alloa Athletic v King's Park
Sep13   4-2   East Stirlingshire v Campsie
-----   w/o   Falkirk v Strathblane - scr.
-----   bye   Campsie Central
```
Edinburghshire
```
Sep13   0-2   Bo'ness v Hibernian
Sep13  10-2   Dunfermline v Newcastleton
Sep13   6-0   St Bernard's v Edina
Sep13   3-0   West Calder v Norton Park
        bye   Heart of Midlothian
```
Perthshire
```
Sep13   8-0   Dunblane v Crieff Juniors
Sep13   scr   Aberfeldy Breadalbane v Vale of Teith - w/o
```
Northern Counties
```
Sep13   1-4   Lindertis v Aberdeen
Sep13   1-5   Angus v Strathmore (Dundee)
Sep13   1-4   Strathmore (Arbroath) v Our Boys (Dundee)
Sep13   3-2   Arbroath v Harp (Dundee)
-----   w/o   West End (Dundee) v Perseverance - scr.
Sep13   8-1   East End v Coupar Angus  at Rollo's Pier
```
Southern Counties
```
Sep13   0-13  Thornhill v Q.O.S. Wanderers
Sep13   2-5   Moffat v 5th K.R.V.
Sep13   1-4   Volunteer Athletic (Newton Stewart) v Vale of Nith
```

Second Round
Glasgow and District

```
Oct04   2-0   Dean Park v Springburn Hibernian
Oct04   1-2   Cowlairs v Pollockshields Athletic
Oct04   2-2   3rd L.R.V. v Rangers
Oct11   0-0   Rangers v 3rd L.R.V. - both qualified
Oct04   0-3   Possilpark v Battlefield
Oct04   1-3   Granton v Northern
Oct04   1-4   Thistle (Glasgow) v Queen's Park
        bye   Partick
```

Renfrewshire
```
Oct04   1-0   Arthurlie v Abercorn
Oct04   2-2   Greenock Southern v Pollockshaws
Oct11   3-3   Pollockshaws v Greenock Southern - both qualified
Oct04   1-0   Thornliebank v Port Glasgow Athletic - prot.
Oct18   2-2   Port Glasgow Athletic v Thornliebank
Oct25   2-1   Thornliebank v Port Glasgow Athletic
Oct04   1-7   Clippens v Renfrew
Oct04   3-0   St Mirren v Johnstone
        bye   Cartvale
        bye   Greenock Morton
```

Ayrshire
```
Oct04   1-4   Maybole v Kilmarnock Athletic
Oct04   4-1   Annbank v Kilmarnock
Oct04   5-0   Ayr v Cumnock
```

Dumbartonshire and Stirlingshire
```
Oct04  14-0   Vale of Leven v Campsie Central
Oct04  17-0   Yoker v Tayavalla
Oct04   3-1   Dumbarton Athletic v King's Park
Oct04   2-10  East Stirlingshire v Renton
Oct04   2-0   Dumbarton v* Albion
Oct04   1-4   Grasshoppers v Falkirk
```

Lanarkshire
```
Oct04   9-1   West Benhar v Shettleston - prot.
Oct18   4-1   West Benhar v Shettleston  at Airdrie
Oct04   2-2   Airdrieonians v Cambuslang
Oct11  10-2   Cambuslang v Airdrieonians
Oct04   4-1   Glengowan v Westburn
Oct04   8-2   Wishaw Swifts v Airdriehill
        bye   Hamilton Academical
```

Edinburghshire and Perthshire
```
Oct04   1-11  Dunfermline v Heart of Midlothian - H.o.M. disqualified
Oct04   5-1   Hibernian v Vale of Teith
Oct04   0-1   West Calder v Dunblane
        bye   St Bernard's
```

Northern Counties
```
Oct04   8-1   Our Boys (Dundee) v West End (Dundee)
Oct04   1-1   Strathmore (Dundee) v East End
Oct11   2a5   East End v Strathmore (Dundee) - abd. 70mins conceded
Oct04   1-7   Aberdeen v Arbroath
```

Southern Counties
```
Oct04   3-4   5th K.R.V. v Q.O.S. Wanderers
        bye   Vale of Nith
```

Third Round

Glasgow and District, Dumbartonshire and Stirlingshire
```
Oct25   4-1   Pollockshields Athletic v Dumbarton
Oct25   9-2   Renton v Northern
Oct25   2-2   Dean Park v Dumbarton Athletic - prot.  at Copeland Park
Nov01   0-3   Dean Park v Dumbarton Athletic
```

```
Oct25   4-1   Vale of Leven v Yoker
Oct25   0-3   3rd L.R.V. v Rangers
Oct25   2-3   Queen's Park v* Battlefield
Oct25   4-2   Partick v Falkirk
```
Renfrewshire and Ayrshire
```
Oct25   5-0   Greenock Morton v Greenock Southern
Oct25   3-0   Arthurlie v Cartvale
Oct25   1-0   St Mirren v Renfrew - prot.
Nov08   3a0   St Mirren v Renfrew - prot. - abd. 45mins
Nov13   6-3   St Mirren v Renfrew
Nov01   4-0   Thornliebank v Pollockshaws
Oct25   4-2   Ayr v Kilmarnock Athletic
        bye   Annbank
```
Edinburghshire and Lanarkshire
```
Oct25   5-1   Hibernian v Glengowan
Nov01   7-1   Wishaw Swifts  v Dunfermline
Oct25   5-1   West Benhar v St Bernard's
Oct25   3-0   Cambuslang v Hamilton Academical
```
Forfarshire and Perthshire
```
Oct25   2-4   Dunblane v Arbroath
Oct25   5-1   Our Boys (Dundee) v Strathmore (Dundee)
```
Southern Counties
```
Oct25   0-6   Vale of Nith v Q.O.S. Wanderers
```

Fourth Round
```
Nov15   5-1   Hibernian v Ayr
Nov15   0-3   Pollockshields Athletic v Battlefield
Nov15   2-2   Our Boys (Dundee) v West Benhar
Nov22   8-3   West Benhar v Our Boys (Dundee)
Nov15   5-2   Annbank v Q.O.S. Wanderers
Nov15   4-3   Arbroath v Rangers - prot.
Dec20   1-8   Arbroath v Rangers
Nov15   1-2   Wishaw Swifts v Greenock Morton
Nov15   2-2   Cambuslang v Thornliebank
Nov22   0-0   Thornliebank v Cambuslang - both qualified
Nov15   6-3   Dumbarton Athletic v Partick
Nov15   1-2   Arthurlie v Vale of Leven
Nov15   2-1   Renton v St Mirren
```

Fifth Round
```
Dec06   1-4   Dumbarton Athletic v Cambuslang
Dec06   5-1   Annbank v West Benhar
Dec06   4-0   Hibernian v Greenock Morton
        bye   Renton
        bye   Battlefield
        bye   Rangers
        bye   Vale of Leven
        bye   Thornliebank
```

Sixth Round
```
Dec27   npl   Battlefield v Cambuslang  at Kinning Park B. did not appear
Jan10   3-1   Cambuslang v* Battlefield
Dec27   5-0   Hibernian v Annbank
Dec27   5-3   Renton v Rangers
Dec27   3-4   Thornliebank v Vale of Leven
```

Semi-finals
```
Jan31   0-0   Vale of Leven v Cambuslang  at Alexandria
```

Feb07   1-3   Cambuslang v Vale of Leven   at Cambuslang
Jan24   2-3   Hibernian v Renton   at Easter Road

Final
Feb21   0-0   Renton v Vale of Leven   at Hampden Park
Feb28   3-1   Renton v Vale of Leven   at Hampden Park

Season 1885-86

First Round
Glasgow and Suburbs
Sep12   3-1   Cambridge v Southern Athletic - prot.
Sep26   1-2   Southern Athletic v Cambridge
Sep12   1-0   Clyde v Rangers
Sep12   3-1   Whitefield v Dennistoun Athletic
-----   w/o   Glasgow University YMCA AC v Eastern - scr.
-----   w/o   Pollockshields Athletic v Partick - scr.
Sep12   9-1   3rd L.R.V. v Shawlands
Sep12 11-0   Thistle (Glasgow) v* Westbourne
Sep12   0-2   Battlefield v Cowlairs   at Kinning Park
-----   w/o   St Andrew's (Pollockshields) v 10th Lanarkshire R.V. - scr.
Aug29 16-0   Queen's Park v St Peter's
Sep12 11-0   Partick Thistle v* Granton
Sep12   4-1   Northern v* Linthouse
        bye   Pilgrims
Renfrewshire
Sep12   5-1   Johnstone v Greenock Rangers – G. walked off in the 2ⁿᵈ half
Sep12   2-3   Mearns Athletic v Woodvale
Sep19   2-0   Abercorn v St Mirren
Sep12   2-1   Cartvale v Greenock Morton
-----   w/o   Arthurlie v Olympic - scr.
Sep12   1-0   Renfrew v Greenock Northern
Sep12   1-11 Greenock Southern v Neilston
Sep12   4-1   Port Glasgow Athletic v 1st Renfrewshire R.V.
Sep12   2-2   Paisley Hibernian v Thornliebank
Sep19   2-0   Thornliebank v Paisley Hibernian
Ayrshire
Sep12   7-0   Ayr v Maybole
Sep12   4-1   Lanemark v Monkcastle - prot.
Sep26   2-0   Monkcastle v Lanemark
Sep12   0-8   Ayr Rovers v Dalry
Sep12   5-1   Hurlford v Cumnock
Sep12   7-1   Kilmarnock v Annbank
Sep12   2-3   Mauchline v Lugar Boswell
Dumbartonshire
Sep12   1-1   Lenzie v Bonhill
Sep19   6-0   Bonhill v Lenzie
Sep19   3-1   Dumbarton v Vale of Leven Wanderers
Sep12   4-4   Albion v Jamestown
Sep19   0-1   Jamestown v Albion
-----   w/o   Vale of Leven v Dunbritton - scr.
-----   scr   Levendale v Rock - w/o
Sep12   5-1   Yoker v Union (Dumbarton) - prot.
Sep26   1-0   Union (Dumbarton) v Yoker
Sep12   0-14 Kirkintilloch Athletic v Renton
Sep12   npl   Helensburgh v Dumbarton Athletic - prot. goal post height

Sep26 2-3 Helensburgh v Dumbarton Athletic
Edinburghshire
----- w/o West Calder v Newcastleton - scr.
Sep05 9-0 Hibernian v* Edina
Sep12 1-1 Broxburn Shamrock v Bo'ness
Sep19 5-1 Bo'ness v Broxburn Shamrock
Sep12 6-2 Norton Park v Glencairn
Sep12 5-2 Heart of Midlothian v St Bernard's - prot.
Sep26 1-0 Heart of Midlothian v St Bernard's
Stirlingshire
Sep12 6-1 East Stirlingshire v Campsie
Sep12 1-3 Camelon v Falkirk
Sep12 3-1 King's Park v Avondale (Campsie)
Sep12 2-2 Grasshoppers v* Grahamston
Sep19 2-4 Grahamston v Grasshoppers
Sep12 4-2 Dunipace v Campsie Central
       bye Alloa Athletic
Lanarkshire
Sep12 6-8 Alpha v Cambuslang Hibernian
Sep12 2-4 Clydesdale (Lanarkshire) v Tollcross
----- w/o Hamilton Academical v West Benhar - scr.
Sep12 0-2 Rutherglen v Wishaw Swifts
Sep12 1-7 Shettleston v Cambuslang
Sep26 4-2 Airdrieonians v Royal Albert
Sep12 6-2 Albion Rovers v Drumpellier
       bye Dykehead
Northern Counties
Sep12 3-1 Forfar Athletic v Angus
Sep12 36-0 Arbroath v* Bon Accord
Sep12 35-0 Harp (Dundee) v Aberdeen Rovers
Sep05 7-0 Strathmore (Arbroath) v* Aberdeen
Sep12 3-3 West End (Dundee) v Broughty
Sep19 3-3 Broughty v West End (Dundee) - both qualified
Sep12 3-3 East End v Strathmore (Dundee)
Sep19 1-4 Strathmore (Dundee) v East End
Sep12 4-2 Our Boys (Dundee) v* Coupar Angus
Fifeshire and Perthshire
Sep12 9-1 Vale of Teith v Oban
----- w/o Cowdenbeath v Aberfeldy Breadalbane - scr.
----- w/o Dunblane v Dunfermline - scr.
Sep12 0-7 Crieff v Dunfermline Athletic
Southern Counties
Sep12 4-0 5th K.R.V. v Vale of Nith
----- w/o Thornhill v Moffat - scr.
       bye Q.O.S. Wanderers

Second Round
Glasgow and Suburbs
Oct03 1-0 Queen's Park v Pilgrims
Oct03 3-2 Cowlairs v Pollockshields Athletic
Oct03 2-3 Clyde v Thistle (Glasgow)
Oct03 6-0 St Andrew's (Pollockshields) v Cambridge
Oct03 7-2 Northern v Whitefield
Oct03 1-8 Glasgow University YMCA AC v 3rd L.R.V.
       bye Partick Thistle
Renfrewshire
Oct03 0-3 Renfrew v Abercorn
Oct03 1-2 Johnstone v Thornliebank
Oct03 2-0 Arthurlie v Woodvale

Oct03   1-1   Port Glasgow Athletic v Neilston
Oct10   0-2   Neilston v Port Glasgow Athletic
        bye   Cartvale
Ayrshire
Oct03   2-4   Monkcastle v Ayr
Oct03   6-2   Dalry v Lugar Boswell
Oct03   3-4   Kilmarnock v Hurlford - prot.
Oct17   1-1   Kilmarnock v Hurlford
Oct24   npl   Kilmarnock v Hurlford - K. failed to appear
Oct31   1a1   Hurlford v Kilmarnock - abd. 80mins crowd at Springvale
              Park
Nov07   2-2   Hurlford v Kilmarnock - aet. 2-2
Nov14   1-5   Kilmarnock v Hurlford at Rugby Park
Dumbartonshire
Oct03   7-0   Dumbarton v Union (Dumbarton)
Oct03   2-7   Dumbarton Athletic v Renton
-----   scr   Rock v Albion - w/o
Oct03 10-0   Vale of Leven v Bonhill
Edinburghshire
Oct03   7-1   Bo'ness v Norton Park
Oct03   2-1   Hibernian v Heart of Midlothian
        bye   West Calder
Stirlingshire
Oct03   1-6   Grasshoppers v East Stirlingshire
Oct03   7-1   King's Park v Dunipace
Oct03   0-4   Falkirk v Alloa Athletic
Lanarkshire
Oct03   2-2   Albion Rovers v Wishaw Swifts
Oct10   5-0   Wishaw Swifts v Albion Rovers
Oct03 15-2   Airdrieonians v Cambuslang Hibernian
Oct03   scr   Hamilton Academical v Cambuslang - w/o
Oct03   3-1   Dykehead v Tollcross - D. disqualified
Northern Counties
Oct03   4-5   West End (Dundee) v Strathmore (Arbroath)
Oct03   9-1   Arbroath v Forfar Athletic
Oct03   4-1   Harp (Dundee) v Our Boys (Dundee)
Oct03   2-2   East End v Broughty
Oct10   3-8   Broughty v East End - prot.
Oct17   1-2   Broughty v East End
Fifeshire and Perthshire
-----   w/o   Vale of Teith v Cowdenbeath - scr.
Oct03 10-0   Dunblane v Dunfermline Athletic
Southern Counties
Oct03   3-1   5th K.R.V. v Q.O.S. Wanderers - prot.
Oct17   4-3   Q.O.S. Wanderers v 5th K.R.V.
        bye   Thornhill

Third Round
Glasgow and Suburbs, Dumbartonshire and Stirlingshire
Oct24   0-12 Alloa Athletic v Partick Thistle
Oct24   2-1   Cowlairs v Northern
Oct24   0-3   East Stirlingshire v Queen's Park
Oct24   3-0   Dumbarton v Thistle (Glasgow)
Oct31 11-0   3rd L.R.V. v St Andrew's (Pollockshields)
Oct24   0-1   Albion v Renton
-----   w/o   Vale of Leven v King's Park - scr.
Renfrewshire and Ayrshire
Oct24   1-1   Cartvale v Port Glasgow Athletic
Oct31   4-2   Port Glasgow Athletic v Cartvale

```
Nov21  5-0  Arthurlie v Hurlford
Oct24  1-6  Dalry v Ayr
Oct24  1-5  Thornliebank v Abercorn
```
Lanarkshire and Edinburghshire
```
Oct24  3-0  Wishaw Swifts v West Calder
Oct24  6-0  Hibernian v Bo'ness
Oct24  8-2  Airdrieonians v Tollcross
       bye  Cambuslang
```
Northern Counties, Fifeshire and Perthshire
```
Oct24  3-1  Strathmore (Arbroath) v Dunblane
Oct24  7-1  Arbroath v East End
Oct24  8-1  Harp (Dundee) v Vale of Teith
```
Southern Counties
```
Oct24  8-0  Q.O.S. Wanderers v Thornhill
```

Fourth Round
```
Nov14  3-0  Dumbarton v Partick Thistle
Nov28  1-3  Q.O.S. Wanderers v Arthurlie
Nov14  9-0  Cambuslang v Wishaw Swifts
Nov14  5-3  Hibernian v Arbroath
Nov14  4-0  Renton v Cowlairs
Nov14  1-0  Queen's Park v Airdrieonians
Nov14  3-2  3rd L.R.V. v Ayr - prot.
Nov28  3-3  Ayr v 3rd L.R.V.
Dec05  5-1  3rd L.R.V. v Ayr
Nov14  7-2  Abercorn v Strathmore (Arbroath)
Nov14  6-0  Vale of Leven v Harp (Dundee)
       bye  Port Glasgow Athletic
```

Fifth Round
```
Dec05  2-2  Renton v Vale of Leven
Dec12  0-3  Vale of Leven v Renton
Dec12  1-1  3rd L.R.V. v Port Glasgow Athletic
Dec19  1-1  Port Glasgow Athletic v 3rd L.R.V.
Dec26  4-1  3rd L.R.V. v Port Glasgow Athletic  at Cathkin Park
Dec05  1-2  Arthurlie v Queen's Park
Dec05  0-1  Abercorn v Cambuslang
Dec05  2-2  Dumbarton v Hibernian
Dec12  4-3  Hibernian v Dumbarton
```

Sixth Round
```
Jan16  3-2  Hibernian v Cambuslang
       bye  3rd L.R.V.
       bye  Renton
       bye  Queen's Park
```

Semi-finals
```
Jan23  0-2  Hibernian v Renton  at Easter Road
Jan16  0a4  3rd L.R.V. v Queen's Park  at Cathkin Park - abd. Just after
            half-time
```

Final
```
Feb13  3-1  Queen's Park v Renton  at Cathkin Park
```

Season 1886-87

First Round
Glasgow and District
Sep11   2-1   Pollockshields Athletic v St Andrew's (Pollockshields) –
              prot.
Sep25   4-1   St Andrew's (Pollockshields) v Pollockshields Athletic
Sep11   9-1   Rangers v Govan Athletic
Sep11   0-2   Battlefield v Cowlairs
Sep11   2-3   Partick Thistle v Queen's Park
Sep11 13-0   Thistle (Glasgow) v Blairvaddich
Sep11   0-2   Carrick (Partick) v Westbourne
Sep11   4-0   Linthouse v Southern Athletic
Sep11   1-4   Northern v 3rd L.R.V.
Sep11   1-2   Kelvinside Athletic v Whitefield
Sep11   5-1   Clyde v* St Peter's
Renfrewshire
Sep11   0-6   Lochwinnoch v Greenock Morton
Sep11   6-2   Johnstone v Cartvale
Sep11   3-0   St Mirren v Arthurlie - friendly
Sep18   5-3   St Mirren v Arthurlie
Sep11   3-4   Greenock Rangers v 1st Renfrewshire R.V. - 1st. R.R.V.
               disqualified
Sep11   3-2   Thornliebank v Neilston
-----   scr   Woodvale v Pollockshaws – w/o
Sep11   3-3   Renfrew v Abercorn
Sep18   9-0   Abercorn v Renfrew
Sep11 10-1   Port Glasgow Athletic v Johnstone Harp
Ayrshire
Sep11   2-3   Ayr v Hurlford
Sep11   5-2   Dalry v Ayr Rovers
Sep11   3-4   Annbank v Kilbirnie
Sep11   w/o   Kilmarnock v Cumnock - scr.
-----   w/o   Lugar Boswell v Maybole
Sep11   1-3   Monkcastle v Lanemark
Dumbartonshire
Sep11   8a0   Dumbarton Athletic v Duntocher - abd. 75mins Dun. gave up
Sep11   w/o   Renton v Kirkintilloch Harp - scr.
Sep11   scr   Dunbritton v Lenzie – w/o
Sep11   9-0   Vale of Leven v Kirkintilloch Athletic
Sep11   6-3   Vale of Leven Wanderers v Jamestown - V.o.L.W. disqualified
Sep11   4-2   Yoker v Union (Dumbarton)
Sep11   5-0   Dumbarton v Vale of Leven Hibernian
Sep11   1-8   Kirkintilloch Central v Bonhill
Edinburghshire
Sep11   3-2   St Bernard's v Bo'ness
-----   w/o   Newcastleton v Norton Park - scr.
Sep11   2-2   Bellstane Birds v Broxburn Thistle
Sep18   4-1   Broxburn Thistle v Bellstane Birds
Sep11   1-3   West Calder v Armadale
Sep11   5-1   Hibernian v Durhamtown Rangers
Sep11   1-7   Edina v Heart of Midlothian
Sep11   1-2   Broxburn Shamrock v Mossend Swifts
Stirlingshire
Sep11   0-2   Grahamston v Laurieston
Sep11   6-3   East Stirlingshire v Camelon
Sep11   3-3   Thistle (Longcroft) v Vale of Bannock
Sep18   2-0   Vale of Bannock v Thistle (Longcroft)

Sep11 10-0 Campsie v Dunipace
Sep11 1-3 King's Park v Falkirk
Sep11 4-3 Slamannan v* Avondale (Campsie)
Fifeshire
Sep11 w/o Burntisland Thistle v Dunfermline - scr.
Sep11 4-8 Dunfermline Athletic v Alloa Athletic
       bye Cowdenbeath
Lanarkshire
Sep11 0-3 Tollcross v Royal Albert - R.A. disqualified
Sep11 2-0 Rutherglen v Drumpellier
Sep11 w/o Hamilton Academical v Wishaw Swifts - scr.
Sep11 5-0 Airdrieonians v Airdriehill
Sep11 1-5 Clydesdale (Lanarkshire) v Albion Rovers
Sep11 6-1 Cambuslang v Motherwell
Sep11 3-3 Shettleston v Carfin Shamrock
Sep18 3-0 Carfin Shamrock v Shettleston
       bye Cambuslang Hibernian
Perthshire
Sep11 w/o Coupar Angus v Fair City Athletic - scr.
Sep11 3-3 St Johnstone v Erin Rovers (Perth)
Sep18 7-1 Erin Rovers (Perth) v St Johnstone
Sep11 12-0 Dunblane v Crieff
Sep11 w/o Oban v Our Boys (Blairgowrie) - scr.
       bye Caledonian Rangers
Northern Counties
Sep11 scr Aberdeen v East End - w/o
Sep11 3-0 Strathmore (Arbroath) v Strathmore (Dundee)
Sep11 3-4 Lindertis v Harp (Dundee)
Sep11 20-0 Arbroath v Orion
Sep11 2-7 Dundee Wanderers v Broughty
Sep18 2-5 Our Boys (Dundee) v Forfar Athletic
Southern Counties
Sep11 w/o Q.O.S. Wanderers v Nithsdale - scr.
Sep11 w/o Vale of Nith v Vale of Annan - scr.
Sep11 w/o 5th K.R.V. v Thornhill - scr.
       bye Moffat

Second Round
Glasgow and Suburbs
Oct02 5-2 Rangers v Westbourne
Oct02 1-4 Linthouse v 3rd L.R.V.
Oct02 12-0 Thistle (Glasgow) v St Andrew's (Pollockshields)
Oct02 7-0 Queen's Park v Whitefield
Oct02 4-3 Clyde v Cowlairs
Edinburghshire
Oct02 1-2 Broxburn Thistle v Heart of Midlothian
Oct02 1-5 Newcastleton v Armadale
Oct02 1-1 Mossend Swifts v Hibernian
Oct09 3-0 Hibernian v Mossend Swifts
       bye St Bernard's
Stirlingshire
Oct02 0-3 Slamannan v Campsie
Oct02 1-3 Laurieston v Falkirk
----- w/o East Stirlingshire v Vale of Bannock - scr.
Renfrewshire
Oct02 8-2 Abercorn v Greenock Rangers
Oct02 4-0 Johnstone v Pollockshaws
Oct02 2-3 St Mirren v Port Glasgow Athletic
Oct02 0-2 Thornliebank v Greenock Morton

Ayrshire
Oct02   3-2   Lugar Boswell v Dalry   - prot.
Oct16   6-1   Lugar Boswell v Dalry
Oct02 10-2   Kilmarnock v Lanemark
Oct02   3-2   Hurlford v Kilbirnie
Dumbartonshire
Oct02   2-0   Renton v Dumbarton Athletic
Oct02   0-13 Lenzie v Vale of Leven
Oct02   1-2   Bonhill v Jamestown
Oct02   4-0   Dumbarton v Yoker
Fifeshire
Oct02   3-3   Burntisland Thistle v Cowdenbeath
Oct16   3-0   Cowdenbeath v Burntisland Thistle
        bye   Alloa Athletic
Lanarkshire
Oct02   3-2   Airdrieonians v Carfin Shamrock - A. disqualified
Oct02   1-1   Rutherglen v Cambuslang
Oct09   6-1   Cambuslang v Rutherglen
Oct02   7-0   Albion Rovers v Dykehead
Oct02   3-1   Cambuslang Hibernian v Hamilton Academical
        bye   Tollcross
Perthshire
Oct02   4-4   Caledonian Rangers v Erin Rovers (Perth)
Oct09   6-1   Erin Rovers (Perth) v Caledonian Rangers
Oct02   8-1   Dunblane v Oban
        bye   Coupar Angus
Northern Counties
Oct02   5-4   East End v Broughty
Oct02   3-3   Strathmore (Arbroath) v Harp (Dundee)
Oct09   3-3   Harp (Dundee) v Strathmore (Arbroath) - both qualified
Oct02   2-5   Forfar Athletic v Arbroath
Southern Counties
Oct02   3-5   Moffat v 5th K.R.V.
Oct02 12-2   Q.O.S. Wanderers v Vale of Nith

Third Round
Glasgow, Dumbartonshire, Stirlingshire and Lanarkshire
Oct23   5-1   Cambuslang Hibernian v Jamestown
Oct23   w/o   Dumbarton v Tollcross - scr.
Oct23   1-3   East Stirlingshire v Clyde
Oct23   3-8   Falkirk v Queen's Park
Oct23   3-1   3rd L.R.V. v Renton
Oct23   7-4   Vale of Leven v Campsie
Oct23   0-2   Rangers v Cambuslang
Oct23   4-2   Albion Rovers v Thistle (Glasgow)
        bye   Carfin Shamrock
Edinburghshire and Fifeshire
Oct23   5-2   St Bernard's v Armadale
Oct23   5-1   Hibernian v Heart of Midlothian
Oct23   6-1   Cowdenbeath v Alloa Athletic
Renfrewshire and Ayrshire
Oct23   0-5   Johnstone v Hurlford
Oct23   1-5   Abercorn v Port Glasgow Athletic
Oct23   7-2   Kilmarnock v Lugar Boswell
        bye   Greenock Morton
Perthshire and Northern Counties
Oct23   3-2   Erin Rovers (Perth) v Coupar Angus
Oct23   3-3   East End v Dunblane
Oct28   w/o   Dunblane v East End - scr.

Oct23 1-8 Strathmore (Arbroath) v Harp (Dundee)
       bye Arbroath
Southern Counties
Oct23 6-3 Q.O.S. Wanderers v 5th K.R.V.

Fourth Round
Nov13 1-6 Albion Rovers v Cambuslang
Nov13 8-2 Q.O.S. Wanderers v Arbroath
Nov13 5-1 St Bernard's v Erin Rovers (Perth)
Nov06 11-0 Greenock Morton v Carfin Shamrock
Nov13 0-3 Cowdenbeath v Cambuslang Hibernian
       bye Kilmarnock
       bye Hibernian, Clyde, Dunblane, Harp (Dundee)
       bye Vale of Leven, Dumbarton, Port Glasgow Athletic
       bye 3rd L.R.V., Hurlford, Queen's Park

Fifth Round
Dec04 7-3 Hibernian v Q.O.S. Wanderers
Nov27 2-0 Vale of Leven v Cambuslang Hibernian
Dec04 0-0 Clyde v 3rd L.R.V.
Dec11 4-2 3rd L.R.V. v Clyde
Dec04 1-1 Queen's Park v Cambuslang
Dec11 4-5 Cambuslang v Queen's Park
Dec04 5-1 Hurlford v Greenock Morton
Dec04 6-0 Kilmarnock v Dunblane
Dec04 6-2 Port Glasgow Athletic v St Bernard's
Dec04 w/o Dumbarton v Harp (Dundee) - scr.

Sixth Round
Dec25 1-3 Port Glasgow Athletic v Vale of Leven
Dec25 0-5 Kilmarnock v Queen's Park
Dec25 1-2 3rd L.R.V. v Hibernian
Dec25 0-0 Hurlford v Dumbarton
Jan08 1-2 Dumbarton v Hurlford - prot.
Jan22 3-1 Dumbarton v Hurlford

Semi-finals
Jan29 1-2 Queen's Park v Dumbarton at Hampden Park
Jan22 3-1 Hibernian v Vale of Leven at Easter Road

Final
Feb12 1-2 Dumbarton v Hibernian at Hampden Park

Season 1887-88

First Round
Glasgow and Suburbs
Sep03 10-0 Partick Thistle v Westbourne
Sep03 4-1 Pollockshields Athletic v United Abstainers
Sep03 4-1 Rangers v Battlefield
Sep03 6-3 Kelvinside Athletic v St Andrew's (Pollockshields)
Sep03 5-1 Northern v Govan Athletic
Sep03 3-3 Linthouse v Whitefield
Sep10 2-1 Whitefield v Linthouse
Sep03 1-2 3rd L.R.V. v Cowlairs - prot.
Sep17 1-4 3rd L.R.V. v Cowlairs

```
Sep03   0-7   Clyde v Queen's Park
Sep03   0-10  Carrick (Partick) v Thistle (Glasgow)
        bye   Southern Athletic
        bye   Glasgow University
```
Renfrewshire
```
Aug27  11-0   Port Glasgow Athletic v* Greenock Rangers
Sep03   5-1   Lochwinnoch v Pollockshaws
Sep03   scr   Paisley Athletic v Neilston - w/o
Sep03   0-4   Kilbarchan v Arthurlie
Sep03   5-2   Dykebar v Greenock Morton
Sep03   1-8   1st Renfrewshire R.V. v Renfrew
Sep03   9-0   Abercorn v* Johnstone Harp
Sep03   1-2   Thornliebank v St Mirren
```
Edinburghshire
```
Sep03   5-0   Hibernian v Broxburn Thistle
Sep03   5-0   Erin Rovers (Bathgate) v Bellstane Birds
Sep03   0-4   Broxburn Shamrock v Mossend Swifts - M.S. disqualified
Sep03   9-0   West Calder v* Athenians
Sep03   4-1   Heart of Midlothian v Norton Park
Sep03   4-1   Bo'ness v Leith Athletic
Sep03   3-2   St Bernard's v Armadale
```
Ayrshire
```
Sep03   w/o   Ayr v Monkcastle - scr.
Sep03   3-3   Maybole v 2nd Ayrshire R.V.
Sep10   4-6   2nd Ayrshire R.V. v Maybole
Sep03   w/o   Hurlford v Annbank - scr.
Sep03   9-0   Lugar Boswell v Dalry
-----   w/o   Kilbirnie v Lanemark - scr.
Sep03   8-2   Kilmarnock v Ayr Thistle
        bye   Mauchline
```
Dumbartonshire
```
Sep03   3-2   Jamestown v Vale of Leven Hibernian - prot.
Sep17   2-2   Vale of Leven Hibernian v Jamestown
Sep24   3-1   Jamestown v Vale of Leven Hibernian
Sep03   w/o   Vale of Leven v Kirkintilloch Harp - scr.
Sep01  10-0   Dumbarton v Dunbritton
Sep03   0-6   Union (Dumbarton) v Renton
Sep03   1-6   Bonhill v Dumbarton Athletic
Sep03   5-1   Kirkintilloch Athletic v Kirkintilloch Central
Sep03   7-2   Vale of Leven Wanderers v Methlan Park
```
Lanarkshire
```
Sep03   6-4   Cambuslang Hibernian v Hamilton Hibernian
Sep03  12-0   Albion Rovers v Airdriehill
Sep03   4-1   Rutherglen v* Clydesdale (Lanarkshire)
Sep03   4-0   Carfin Shamrock v Shettleston
Sep03   2-5   Uddingston v Royal Albert
Sep03   w/o   Plains v Tollcross - scr.
Sep03   2-3   Drumpellier v Motherwell
Sep03   scr   Hamilton Academical v Cambuslang - w/o
Sep03   8-0   Airdrieonians v Dykehead
```
Stirlingshire
```
Sep03   4-1   Falkirk v Kilsyth Wanderers
Sep03   1-5   King's Park v Camelon
Sep03   4-3   Grahamston v Redding Athletic - G. disqualified
Sep03   2-5   Grangemouth v East Stirlingshire
Sep03   3-4   Vale of Bannock v Campsie
Sep03   5-4   Slamannan v Laurieston
```
Fifeshire

```
Sep03   6-2   Alloa Athletic v Cowdenbeath
Sep03   4-2   Burntisland Thistle v Dunfermline Athletic - B.T.
                 disqualified
Sep03   3-2   Dunfermline v Lassodie - D. disqualified
```
Northern Counties
```
Sep03   6-3   Strathmore (Dundee) v Forfar Athletic
Sep03   7-0   Dundee Wanderers v Lochee
Sep03   5-7   Broughty v Montrose
Sep03   1-13  Strathmore (Arbroath) v East End
Sep03   1-2   Lindertis v Harp (Dundee) - H. disqualified
Sep03  18-0   Arbroath v Orion
Sep03   4-9   Aberdeen v Our Boys (Dundee)
        bye   Aberdeen Rovers
```
Perthshire
```
Sep03   3-9   Erin Rovers (Perth) v St Johnstone
Sep03   1-7   Caledonian Rangers v Crieff
Sep03   2-3   Dunblane v Fair City Athletic
Sep03   9-2   Coupar Angus v Our Boys (Blairgowrie)
```
Argyllshire
```
Sep03   1-9   Lochgilphead v Oban
```
Southern Counties
```
Sep03   6-0   Q.O.S. Wanderers v Vale of Nith
Sep03   7-1   Moffat v Newcastleton
Sep03   5-0   5th K.R.V. v Thornhill
        bye   Nithsdale
```

Second Round
Glasgow and District
```
Sep24   9-1   Cowlairs v Southern Athletic
Sep24   2-1   Partick Thistle v Rangers
Sep24   9-0   Queen's Park v Kelvinside Athletic
Sep24   6-0   Thistle (Glasgow) v Glasgow University
Sep24   2-0   Whitefield v Pollockshields Athletic
Sep24   6-3   Northern v Shettleston - S. reinstated
```
Renfrewshire
```
Sep24   6-0   Abercorn v Neilston
Sep24   3-3   Arthurlie v St Mirren
Oct01   4-1   St Mirren v Arthurlie
Sep24   2-5   Lochwinnoch v Dykebar
Sep24   3-3   Renfrew v Port Glasgow Athletic
Oct01   5-3   Port Glasgow Athletic v Renfrew
```
Edinburghshire
```
Sep24   0-6   Erin Rovers (Bathgate) v Hibernian
Sep24   5-1   Bo'ness v West Calder
Sep24   1-1   St Bernard's v Broxburn Shamrock
Oct01   1-4   Broxburn Shamrock v St Bernard's
        bye   Heart of Midlothian
```
Dumbartonshire
```
Sep24   1-5   Dumbarton v Vale of Leven
Oct01   7-1   Jamestown v Kirkintilloch Athletic
Sep24   4-2   Renton v Dumbarton Athletic
        bye   Vale of Leven Wanderers
```
Ayrshire
```
Sep24   3-0   Kilbirnie v Mauchline
Sep24   0-13  Maybole v Ayr
Sep24   9-1   Hurlford v Lugar Boswell
        bye   Kilmarnock
```
Lanarkshire
```
Sep24   3-1   Carfin Shamrock v Motherwell
```

```
Sep24   3-6   Rutherglen v Albion Rovers
Sep24   2-0   Cambuslang v Royal Albert
Sep24   3-0   Airdrieonians v Cambuslang Hibernian
        bye   Plains
```
Stirlingshire
```
Sep24   2-2   Falkirk v Campsie
Oct01   2-2   Campsie v Falkirk - both qualified
Sep24   0-17  Redding Athletic v Camelon
Sep24   1-6   Slamannan v East Stirlingshire
```
Fifeshire
```
Sep24   0-1   Alloa Athletic v Dunfermline Athletic
        bye   Lassodie
```
Northern Counties
```
Sep24  10-0   Dundee Wanderers v* Aberdeen Rovers
Sep24   3-2   Lindertis v East End
Sep24   5-3   Our Boys (Dundee) v Montrose
Sep24   3-1   Arbroath v Strathmore (Dundee)
```
Perthshire and Argyllshire
```
Sep24   3-0   Fair City Athletic v St Johnstone
Sep24   w/o   Coupar Angus v Crieff - scr.
        bye   Oban
```
Southern Counties
```
Sep24   4-4   Moffat v Q.O.S. Wanderers
Oct01   7-4   Q.O.S. Wanderers v Moffat
Sep24   2-9   Nithsdale v 5th K.R.V.
```

Third Round
Glasgow and District, Dumbartonshire, Stirlingshire and Lanarkshire
```
Oct15   2-2   Falkirk v Carfin Shamrock
Oct22   3-0   Carfin Shamrock v Falkirk
Oct15   9-0   Vale of Leven Wanderers v Plains
Oct15   3-0   Queen's Park v Jamestown
Oct15   0-8   Camelon v Renton
Oct15   8-1   Cowlairs v Campsie
Oct15   3-0   Vale of Leven v Airdrieonians
Oct15   2-0   Thistle (Glasgow) v Whitefield
Oct15   0-0   East Stirlingshire v Cambuslang
Oct22   4-2   Cambuslang v East Stirlingshire
Oct15   3-4   Northern v Albion Rovers
        bye   Partick Thistle
```
Edinburgh and Fifeshire
```
Oct15   1-1   Heart of Midlothian v Hibernian
Oct22   1-3   Hibernian v Heart of Midlothian
Oct15   w/o   St Bernard's v Dunfermline Athletic - scr.
Oct15   1-3   Lassodie v Bo'ness
```
Ayrshire and Renfrewshire
```
Oct15   1-3   Kilbirnie v Abercorn
Oct15   2-4   Hurlford v St Mirren
Oct15   4-0   Ayr v Port Glasgow Athletic
Oct15   2-2   Dykebar v Kilmarnock
Oct22   9-1   Kilmarnock v Dykebar
```
Perthshire and Northern Counties
```
Oct15   1-5   Oban v Arbroath
Oct15   8-0   Dundee Wanderers v Coupar Angus
Oct15   0-5   Fair City Athletic v Our Boys (Dundee)
        bye   Lindertis
```
Southern Counties
```
Oct15   2-6   5th K.R.V. v Q.O.S. Wanderers
```

Fourth Round
Nov05 3-2 Ayr v Vale of Leven
Nov05 2-2 Partick Thistle v Kilmarnock
Nov12 1-4 Kilmarnock v Partick Thistle
Nov05 1-13 Lindertis v Renton
Nov05 1-1 Heart of Midlothian v St Mirren
Nov12 2-2 St Mirren v Heart of Midlothian
Nov19 2-2 Heart of Midlothian v St Mirren at Merchiston Park
Nov26 2-4 Heart of Midlothian v St Mirren at Cathkin Park
Nov05 2-0 Vale of Leven Wanderers v Bo'ness
Nov05 4-3 Dundee Wanderers v Q.O.S. Wanderers
       bye Cambuslang, Carfin Shamrock, Our Boys (Dundee)
       bye Arbroath, Cowlairs, Albion Rovers, Abercorn
       bye St Bernard's, Thistle (Glasgow), Queen's Park

Fifth Round
Nov26 4a1 Our Boys (Dundee) v Albion Rovers – abd. 85mins A.R. refused
              to play
Nov26 0-2 Partick Thistle v Queen's Park
Nov26 5-1 Arbroath v Cowlairs
Nov26 9-0 Abercorn v St Bernard's
Nov26 10-0 Cambuslang v Ayr
Dec03 2-3 St Mirren v Renton
Nov26 2-9 Thistle (Glasgow) v Vale of Leven Wanderers
Nov26 5-2 Dundee Wanderers v Carfin Shamrock

Sixth Round
Dec17 3-1 Abercorn v Arbroath
Dec17 5-1 Renton v Dundee Wanderers
Dec17 6-0 Cambuslang v Our Boys (Dundee)
Dec17 7-1 Queen's Park v Vale of Leven Wanderers

Semi-finals
Jan14 3-1 Renton v Queen's Park at Renton
Jan14 1-1 Abercorn v Cambuslang at Blackstoun Park
Jan21 10-1 Cambuslang v Abercorn at Whitefield Park

Final
Feb04 1-6 Cambuslang v Renton at Hampden Park

Season 1888-89

First Round
Ayrshire
----- scr Ayr Thistle v 2nd Ayrshire R.V. – w/o
----- w/o Maybole v Kilmarnock Thistle – scr.
Sep01 npl Annbank v Darnconner Britannia
Sep08 5-1 Annbank v Darnconner Britannia
Sep01 0-5 Lugar Boswell v Kilmarnock
Sep01 4-3 Stewarton Cunninghame v* Rosebank
Sep01 7-0 Hurlford v Ayr
Sep01 7-0 Lanemark v Stevenston Thistle
Sep01 3-1 Kilbirnie v Dalry
Sep01 2-3 Beith v Irvine
Renfrewshire
Sep01 npl Kilbarchan v Abercorn – K. refused to play

```
Sep01 14-0  Pollockshaws v Carlton
Sep01  scr  Paisley Athletic v Thornliebank - w/o
Sep01  scr  Greenock Rangers v Pollockshaws Harp - w/o
Sep01  4-5  Johnstone Harp v Woodvale
Sep01  0-5  Lochwinnoch v Dykebar
Sep01  3-4  Neilston v St Mirren
Sep01  0-0  Renfrew v Arthurlie
Sep08  3-1  Arthurlie v Renfrew
Sep01  3-7  Port Glasgow Athletic v Greenock Morton
       bye  1st Renfrewshire R.V.
```

Dumbartonshire

```
Sep01  8-0  Renton v Bowling
Sep01 13-1  Dumbarton v Kirkintilloch Central
Sep01  1-6  Jamestown v* Vale of Leven Hibernian
Sep01  3-4  Clydebank v Vale of Leven Wanderers
Sep01  5-0  Methlan Park v Kirkintilloch Athletic
Sep01 15-0  Dumbarton Athletic v Union (Dumbarton)
       bye  Vale of Leven
```

Edinburghshire

```
Sep01  2-1  Mossend Swifts v Hibernian
Sep01 12-0  Armadale v Champfleurie
Sep01  2-3  Bellstane Birds v Norton Park
Sep01  7-0  St Bernard's v Leith Athletic
Sep01  2-6  Linlithgow Athletic v Adventurers
Sep01  3-2  Broxburn Shamrock v West Calder - void referee did not
              appear
Sep08  npl  Broxburn Shamrock v West Calder - prot.
Sep15  2-1  West Calder v Broxburn Shamrock
Sep01  6-0  Erin Rovers (Bathgate) v Leith Harp
Sep01  0-1  Bo'ness v Heart of Midlothian
       bye  Broxburn
```

Fifeshire

```
Sep01  3-1  Cowdenbeath v Lassodie
-----  w/o  Dunfermline Athletic v Dunfermline - scr.
Sep01  3-0  Kirkcaldy Wanderers v Townhill
```

Lanarkshire

```
Sep01  6-1  Carfin Shamrock v Whifflet Shamrock
Sep01  1-1  Clydesdale (Lanarkshire) v Rutherglen
Sep08  2-2  Rutherglen v Clydesdale (Lanarkshire) - both qualified
Sep01  w/o  Albion Rovers v Bellshill - scr.
Sep01  2-4  Wishaw Thistle v Cambuslang
Sep01  5-0  Hamilton Academical v Airdrieonians
Sep01  5-0  Cambuslang Hibernian v Coatbridge
Sep01  3-3  Motherwell v Royal Albert
Sep08  1-2  Royal Albert v Motherwell
       bye  Uddingston
```

Stirlingshire

```
Sep01  5-3  Slamannan v* Grangemouth
Sep01  3-2  Vale of Bannock v Laurieston
Sep01  4-3  King's Park v Alloa Athletic
Sep01  scr  Redding Athletic v Gairdoch - w/o fm.
Sep01  6-2  Alva v Kilsyth Wanderers
Sep01 10-1  East Stirlingshire v Stenhousemuir
Sep01  5-1  Campsie v Camelon
Sep01  5-0  Falkirk v Dunipace
```

Northern Counties

```
Sep01  w/o  Dundee Wanderers v Aberdeen Rovers
Sep01  5-4  Our Boys (Dundee) v East End
```

```
Sep01  1-8   Brechin v Montrose
Sep01  3-4   Aberdeen v Arbroath
Sep01 14-1   Forfar Athletic v Lindertis
Sep01  4-3   Harp (Dundee) v Strathmore (Dundee)
Sep08  2-3   Orion v Lochee
       bye   Broughty
```
Perthshire
```
Sep01  6-3   Dunblane v St Johnstone
Sep01 10-2   Crieff v Vale of Atholl
Sep01  8-2   Erin Rovers (Perth) v Our Boys (Blairgowrie)
Sep01  1-6   Bridgend Athletic v Coupar Angus
Sep01  5-0   Fair City Athletic v Caledonian Rangers
```
Argyllshire
```
-----  w/o   Oban v Campbeltown Athletic - scr.
Sep01 15-1   Lochgilphead v Balaclava Rangers
```
Southern Counties
```
Sep01  9-4   Q.O.S. Wanderers v 5th K.R.V.
Sep01 13-0   Newton Stewart Athletic v Nithsdale
Sep01  2a2   Thornhill v Vale of Nith - abd. 80mins - prot.
Sep15  w/o   Vale of Nith v Thornhill - T. failed to appear
-----  w/o   Mid-Annandale v Moffat - scr.
```
Glasgow and District
```
Sep01  4-2   Rangers v Partick Thistle
Sep01  2-4   Linthouse v Clyde
Sep01 16-0   Kelvinside Athletic v Govan Athletic
Sep01  w/o   3rd L.R.V. v* Whitefield - scr fm.
Sep08  2-3   Northern v Queen's Park
Sep01  3-1   Thistle (Glasgow) v Maryhill
Sep01  5-1   Celtic v Shettleston
Sep01  9-1   Battlefield v* Southern Athletic
Sep01  2-1   United Abstainers v Pollockshields Athletic
Sep01 18-2   Cowlairs v Temperance Athletic
       bye   Glasgow University
```

Second Round
Ayrshire
```
Sep22  2-0   Lanemark v Stewarton Cunninghame
Sep29  5-4   Annbank v* Hurlford - prot.
Oct06  2-2   Hurlford v Annbank
Oct13  2-3   Annbank v Hurlford  - aet. 2-2
Sep22  4-4   2nd Ayrshire R.V. v Maybole
Sep29  6-2   Maybole v 2nd Ayrshire R.V.
Sep22  1-3   Kilmarnock v Kilbirnie
       bye   Irvine
```
Renfrewshire
```
Sep22  3-2   Woodvale v 1st Renfrewshire R.V.  at Thornliebank's ground
Oct06  w/o   1st Renfrewshire R.V. v Woodvale - scr fm.
Sep22  1-4   Greenock Morton v Abercorn
Sep22  1-6   Dykebar v St Mirren
Sep22  2-5   Pollockshaws Harp v Thornliebank
Sep22  3-2   Arthurlie v Pollockshaws
```
Lanarkshire
```
Sep22  5-1   Uddingston v Clydesdale (Lanarkshire)
Sep22  9-1   Albion Rovers v Rutherglen
Sep22  4-2   Cambuslang v Carfin Shamrock
Sep22  5-1   Motherwell v Hamilton Academical
       bye   Cambuslang Hibernian
```
Glasgow and District
```
Sep22  8-0   3rd L.R.V. v* Kelvinside Athletic
```

```
Sep22 11-0  Battlefield v United Abstainers
Sep22  8-0  Celtic v Cowlairs
Sep22  6-0  Queen's Park v Thistle (Glasgow)
Sep22  2-2  Clyde v Rangers
Sep29  0-3  Rangers v Clyde
       bye  Glasgow University
```

Edinburgh District
```
Sep22  9-3  Broxburn v Adventurers
Sep22  4-0  Heart of Midlothian v Erin Rovers (Bathgate)
Sep29  3-1  St Bernard's v* Norton Park
Sep22  1-6  West Calder v Mossend Swifts
       bye  Armadale
```

Fifeshire
```
Sep22  2-4  Cowdenbeath v Dunfermline Athletic
       bye  Kirkcaldy Wanderers
```

Dumbartonshire
```
Sep22  4-2  Dumbarton Athletic v Vale of Leven
Sep22  2-10 Vale of Leven Wanderers v Renton
Sep22  1-3  Vale of Leven Hibernian v Methlan Park
       bye  Dumbarton
```

Stirlingshire
```
Sep22  3-3  Slamannan v King's Park
Sep29 13-1  King's Park v Slamannan
Sep22  0-6  Alva v Campsie
Sep22 11-2  East Stirlingshire v Vale of Bannock
Sep22  8-3  Falkirk v Gairdoch
```

Northern Counties
```
Sep22  2-4  Broughty v Harp (Dundee)
Sep22  6-5  Forfar Athletic v Dundee Wanderers
Sep22  6-2  Arbroath v Montrose
Sep22  4-2  Our Boys (Dundee) v Lochee
```

Argyllshire
```
Sep22  4-2  Oban v Lochgilphead
```

Perthshire
```
Sep22  1-3  Coupar Angus v Erin Rovers (Perth)
Sep22  7-1  Fair City Athletic v Crieff
       bye  Dunblane
```

Southern Counties
```
Sep22  3-0  Vale of Nith v Mid-Annandale
Sep22 14-2  Q.O.S. Wanderers v Newton Stewart Athletic
```

Third Round

Glasgow and District, Lanarkshire and Dumbartonshire
```
Oct13  2-6  Motherwell v Dumbarton
Oct13  w/o  Uddingston v Glasgow University - scr.
Oct13  0-4  Cambuslang Hibernian v Clyde
Oct13  4-1  Renton v Cambuslang
Oct13  1-3  Battlefield v Dumbarton Athletic
Oct13  4-1  Celtic v Albion Rovers
Oct13  2-1  3rd L.R.V. v Queen's Park - prot.
Oct27  4-2  3rd L.R.V. v Queen's Park
       bye  Methlan Park
```

East of Scotland and Fifeshire
```
Oct13  1-2  Kirkcaldy Wanderers v St Bernard's
Oct13  2-2  Broxburn v Heart of Midlothian
Oct20  2-0  Heart of Midlothian v Broxburn
Oct13  5-2  Mossend Swifts v Armadale
       bye  Dunfermline Athletic
```

Stirlingshire and Argyllshire
Oct13   2-2   Falkirk v Campsie
Oct20   2-2   Campsie v Falkirk - both qualified
Oct13   4-0   East Stirlingshire v King's Park
        bye   Oban
Renfrewshire and Ayrshire
Oct13   4-2   Lanemark v Maybole
Oct13   0-8   Thornliebank v Abercorn
Oct13   0-7   Arthurlie v St Mirren
Oct13   3-4   1st Renfrewshire R.V. v Kilbirnie
Oct20   4-2   Hurlford v Irvine
Southern Counties
Oct13 11-1   Q.O.S. Wanderers v* Vale of Nith
Northern Counties and Perthshire
Oct13   4-4   Dunblane v Erin Rovers (Perth)
Oct13   1-2   Forfar Athletic v Arbroath
Oct20   0-6   Erin Rovers (Perth) v Dunblane
Oct13   2-1   Our Boys (Dundee) v Harp (Dundee)
        bye   Fair City Athletic

Fourth Round
Nov03   3-1   Campsie v Heart of Midlothian
Nov03 11-1   Abercorn v Our Boys (Dundee)
Nov03   7-1   3rd L.R.V. v Hurlford
Nov03   1-3   Fair City Athletic v Arbroath
Nov03   1-4   St Bernard's v Celtic
Nov03   0-6   Oban v Clyde
Nov03 10-2   Q.O.S. Wanderers v Falkirk
Nov03   1-4   Uddingston v Mossend Swifts
Nov03   0-8   Lanemark v Renton
Nov03   4-4   Dunblane v East Stirlingshire
Nov10   4-0   East Stirlingshire v Dunblane
Nov03   1-6   Kilbirnie v St Mirren
Nov03   w/o   Dumbarton Athletic v Dunfermline Athletic
Nov03   9-0   Dumbarton v Methlan Park

Fifth Round
Dec01   3-1   Dumbarton v Mossend Swifts
Nov24   3-3   Arbroath v Renton
Dec01   4-0   Renton v Arbroath
Nov24   5-4   3rd L.R.V. v Abercorn - prot.
Dec08   2-2   3rd L.R.V. v Abercorn
Dec15   2-2   Abercorn v 3rd L.R.V.
Dec22   1-3   Abercorn v 3rd L.R.V. at Ibrox Park
Nov24   3-1   St Mirren v Q.O.S. Wanderers
Nov24   0-1   Celtic v Clyde - prot.
Dec08   9-2   Celtic v Clyde
        bye   Dumbarton Athletic
        bye   East Stirlingshire
        bye   Campsie

Sixth Round
Dec29   6-1   3rd L.R.V. v Campsie
Dec15   1-2   Dumbarton Athletic v Renton
Dec15   2-2   Dumbarton v St Mirren
Dec22   2-2   St Mirren v Dumbarton
Dec29   3-1   Dumbarton v St Mirren at Ibrox Park
Dec15   1-2   East Stirlingshire v Celtic

Semi-finals
Jan12   1-4   Dumbarton v Celtic   at Boghead Park
Jan12   2-0   3rd L.R.V. v Renton   at Cathkin Park

Final
Feb02   0-3   Celtic v 3rd L.R.V.   at Hampden Park - friendly
Feb09   1-2   Celtic v 3rd L.R.V.   at Hampden Park

Season 1889-90

First Round
Ayrshire
Sep07   3-3   Dalry v Kilbirnie
Sep14   5-2   Kilbirnie v Dalry
Sep07   6-6   Maybole v Ayr Athletic
Sep14   3-1   Ayr Athletic v Maybole
Sep07   1-4   Mauchline v Newmilns
Sep07   4-1   Stevenston Thistle v Kilmarnock Athletic
Sep07   16-0   Ayr v Beith
Sep07   0-5   Stewarton Cunninghame v Hurlford
Sep07   2-2   Irvine v Lugar Boswell
Sep14   8-0   Lugar Boswell v Irvine
Sep07   2-3   Kilmarnock v Annbank
         bye   Lanemark
Dumbartonshire
Sep07   1-8   Bowling v Renton
Sep07   0-0   Vale of Leven v Dumbarton
Sep14   1-1   Dumbarton v Vale of Leven - both qualified
Sep07   2-4   Jamestown v Methlan Park
Sep07   5-0   Duntocher Harp v Smithston Hibernians
Sep07   scr   Clydebank v Vale of Leven Wanderers - w/o
Sep07   1-7   Old Kirkpatrick v Union (Dumbarton)
         bye   Kirkintilloch Athletic
East of Scotland
Sep07   3-3   Bathgate Rovers v Champfleurie
-----   w/o   Champfleurie v Bathgate Rovers - scr.
Sep07   6-0   Mossend Swifts v Bo'ness
Sep07   6-3   Bellstane Birds v Norton Park
Sep07   0-3   St Bernard's v Heart of Midlothian
Sep07   6-2   Leith Athletic v Adventurers
Aug31   2-9   West Calder v Broxburn
Sep07   2-3   Armadale v Hibernian
         bye   Edinburgh University
Fifeshire
Sep07   3-2   Lassodie v Burntisland Thistle
Sep07   1-2   Raith Rovers v Dunfermline Athletic
Sep07   8-0   Cowdenbeath v Kirkcaldy Wanderers
         bye   Dunfermline
Renfrewshire
Sep07   2-4   Arthurlie v St Mirren
Sep07   7-1   1st Renfrewshire R.V. v* Pollockshaws Harp
Sep07   1-2   Bute Rangers v Kilbarchan
Sep07   scr   Renfrew v Greenock Abstainers - scr.
Sep07   3-1   Pollockshaws v Dykebar
Sep07   8-0   Greenock Morton v Carlton
Sep07   2-1   Port Glasgow Athletic v Neilston

Aug31 10-1 Abercorn v* Lochwinnoch
Sep07 w/o Thornliebank v Johnstone Harp - scr.
Glasgow and District
Sep07 6-2 Rangers v United Abstainers
Sep07 w/o Kelvinside Athletic v Southern Athletic - scr.
Sep07 scr Temperance Athletic v Summerton Athletic - w/o
Sep07 3-2 3rd L.R.V. v Partick Thistle
Sep07 1-7 Shettleston v Battlefield
Sep07 0-5 Whitefield v Northern
Sep07 7-2 Linthouse v Fairfield
Sep07 1-3 Glasgow Hibernian v Thistle (Glasgow)
Sep07 0-0 Celtic v Queen's Park - declared no cup tie after 75mins
Sep14 2-1 Queen's Park v Celtic
Sep07 0-3 Carrington v Maryhill
Sep07 21-1 Cowlairs v* Victoria (Glasgow)
       bye Clyde
Lanarkshire
Sep07 0-5 Hamilton Academical v Wishaw Thistle
Sep07 scr Cambuslang St Brides v Airdrieonians - w/o
Sep07 2-8 Rutherglen v Uddingston
Sep07 4-0 Carfin Shamrock v Albion Rovers
Sep07 12-0 Royal Albert v Whifflet Shamrock
Sep07 5-6 Airdriehill v Motherwell
Sep07 1-6 Clydesdale (Lanarkshire) v Cambuslang
Forfarshire
Sep07 2-4 Montrose v Forfar Athletic
Sep07 6-3 Our Boys (Dundee) v Strathmore (Dundee)
Sep07 0-5 Lindertis v Dundee Wanderers
Sep07 3-5 Arbroath v Harp (Dundee)
Sep07 4-1 Lochee v Brechin
Sep07 1-6 Broughty v East End
Northern Counties
----- scr Portland Lybster v Aberdeen - w/o
Sep07 3-1 Orion v Victoria United
Stirlingshire
Sep07 5-1 Kilsyth Wanderers v Stenhousemuir
Sep07 0-7 Gairdoch v East Stirlingshire
Sep07 3-6 Vale of Bannock v Campsie
Sep07 11-1 Falkirk v* Tillicoultry
Sep07 0-8 Slamannan v Grangemouth
Sep07 3-6 Alva v King's Park
Sep07 5-1 Alloa Athletic v Denny
Sep07 2-3 Dunipace v Laurieston
       bye Camelon
Perthshire
----- w/o Vale of Athole v Crieff - scr.
Sep07 8-0 Fair City Athletic v Coupar Angus
Sep07 3a5 Our Boys (Blairgowrie) v St Johnstone - abd. 75 mins
Sep07 4-1 Dunblane v Caledonian Rangers
Argyllshire
Sep07 5-2 Oban v Rangers (Oban)
       bye Lochgilphead
Southern Counties
Sep07 3-4 Newton Stewart Athletic v Q.O.S. Wanderers
Sep07 8-0 Moffat v Dumfries
Sep07 3-11 Mid-Annandale v 5th K.R.V.
       bye Dumfries Harp

Second Round
Ayrshire
```
Sep28   2-1   Lanemark v Hurlford
Sep28   3-2   Stevenston Thistle v Annbank
Sep28   5-0   Kilbirnie v Newmilns
Sep28   0-2   Lugar Boswell v Ayr
        bye   Ayr Athletic
```

Dumbartonshire
```
Sep28   5-2   Union (Dumbarton) v Kirkintilloch Athletic
Sep28   1-2   Renton v Dumbarton
Sep28   4-1   Vale of Leven v Methlan Park
Sep28   3-4   Duntocher Harp v Vale of Leven Wanderers
```
East of Scotland
```
Sep28   1-4   Bellstane Birds v Heart of Midlothian
Sep28   2-2   Broxburn v Leith Athletic
Oct05   2-1   Leith Athletic v Broxburn
Sep28   4-3   Hibernian v Mossend Swifts
        bye   Champfleurie
        bye   Edinburgh University
```
Fifeshire
```
-----   w/o   Dunfermline Athletic v Dunfermline
Sep28   3-3   Lassodie v Cowdenbeath - prot.
        w/o   Cowdenbeath v Lassodie - L. disqualified
```
Renfrewshire
```
Sep28  10-1   Abercorn v Thornliebank
Sep28   6-0   St Mirren v Kilbarchan
Sep28   8-0   Port Glasgow Athletic v Greenock Abstainers
Sep28   2-10  1st Renfrewshire R.V. v Greenock Morton
        bye   Pollockshaws
```
Glasgow and District
```
Sep28   1-2   Clyde v Northern
Sep28   0-2   Battlefield v Thistle (Glasgow)
Sep28   0-11  Summerton Athletic v Queen's Park
Sep28   9-3   3rd L.R.V. v Maryhill
Sep28   1-1   Cowlairs v Linthouse
Oct05   3-2   Linthouse v Cowlairs
Sep28   0-13  Kelvinside Athletic v Rangers
```
Lanarkshire
```
Sep28   6-2   Carfin Shamrock v Motherwell
Sep28   1-1   Royal Albert v Cambuslang
Oct05   4-1   Cambuslang v Royal Albert
Sep28   5-2   Airdrieonians v Uddingston
        bye   Wishaw Thistle
```
Forfarshire
```
Sep28   1-7   Lochee v Forfar Athletic
Sep28   0-2   Dundee Wanderers v East End
Sep28   5-6   Harp (Dundee) v Our Boys (Dundee)
```
Northern Counties
```
Sep28   2-1   Aberdeen v Orion
```
Stirlingshire
```
Sep28   4-4   Camelon v Grangemouth
Oct05   7-2   Grangemouth v Camelon
Sep28   3-7   Campsie v Alloa Athletic
Sep28   5-2   Falkirk v King's Park
Sep28   1-4   Laurieston v East Stirlingshire
        bye   Kilsyth Wanderers
```

Perthshire
Sep28   4-9   Vale of Athole v Dunblane
Sep28   2-2   St Johnstone v Fair City Athletic
Oct05   3-2   Fair City Athletic v St Johnstone

Argyllshire
-----   w/o   Oban v Lochgilphead - scr.
Southern Counties
Sep28   4-1   Moffat v 5th K.R.V.
Sep28   1-5   Dumfries Harp v Q.O.S. Wanderers

Third Round
Glasgow, Dumbartonshire and Lanarkshire
Oct19   2-2   Thistle (Glasgow) v Airdrieonians
Oct26   3-1   Airdrieonians v Thistle (Glasgow)
Oct19   1-2   Union (Dumbarton) v Cambuslang - prot.
Nov02   6-0   Cambuslang v Union (Dumbarton)
Oct19   2a1   Northern v Carfin Shamrock - abd. second half crowd
Nov02   3-4   Northern v Carfin Shamrock at Ibrox Park
Oct19   8-0   Queen's Park v Vale of Leven Wanderers
Oct19   1-1   Dumbarton v 3rd L.R.V.
Oct19   5-8   Wishaw Thistle v Linthouse
Oct26   1-0   3rd L.R.V. v Dumbarton
Oct19   0-0   Rangers v Vale of Leven
Oct26   3-2   Vale of Leven v Rangers
Renfrewshire and Ayrshire
Oct19   3-4   Port Glasgow Athletic v Kilbirnie
Oct19   4-3   Lanemark v Ayr Athletic
Oct19   5-2   Abercorn v Stevenston Thistle
Oct19   5-1   St Mirren v Pollockshaws
Oct19   1-4   Greenock Morton v Ayr
Forfarshire and Northern Counties
Oct19   2-3   Our Boys (Dundee) v East End
Oct19   5-3   Aberdeen v Forfar Athletic
Perthshire
Oct19   3-0   Dunblane v Fair City Athletic
Edinburghshire and Fifeshire
Oct19   1-9   Edinburgh University v Leith Athletic
Oct19   0-5   Champfleurie v Heart of Midlothian
Oct19   4-4   Dunfermline Athletic v Hibernian
Oct26 11-1   Hibernian v Dunfermline Athletic
         bye   Cowdenbeath
Stirlingshire and Argyllshire
Oct19   3-0   Alloa Athletic v Oban
Oct19   2-2   Grangemouth v Kilsyth Wanderers
Oct26   0-1   Kilsyth Wanderers v Grangemouth
Oct19   1-6   Falkirk v East Stirlingshire
Southern Counties
Oct19   4-4   Moffat v Q.O.S. Wanderers
Oct26   5-5   Q.O.S. Wanderers v Moffat - both qualified

Fourth Round
Nov09   8-2   St Mirren v* Lanemark
Nov09   4-6   Dunblane v Cowdenbeath
Nov09   3-7   Q.O.S. Wanderers v Hibernian
Nov09   2-0   3rd L.R.V. v Linthouse
Nov09   5-2   Kilbirnie v East Stirlingshire
Nov09   2-3   Airdrieonians v Abercorn
Nov09   9-1   Heart of Midlothian v Alloa Athletic

```
Nov09   2-2   Ayr v Leith Athletic
Nov16   4-1   Leith Athletic v Ayr
Nov09   1-7   Grangemouth v Vale of Leven
Nov09   3-2   East End v Cambuslang - prot.  at East Dock Street Park
Nov23   3-2   East End v Cambuslang  at Rollo's Pier
Nov09   4-2   Moffat v Carfin Shamrock
Nov09   1-13  Aberdeen v Queen's Park
```

Fifth Round
```
Nov30   2-8   Cowdenbeath v Abercorn
Nov30   1-0   Queen's Park v St Mirren
Nov30   3-1   Vale of Leven v Heart of Midlothian
Nov30   2-2   Moffat v East End
Dec07   5-1   East End v Moffat
        bye   Hibernian, 3rd L.R.V., Kilbirnie
        bye   Leith Athletic
```

Sixth Round
```
Dec21   4-0   Vale of Leven v East End
Dec21   6-2   Abercorn v Hibernian
Dec21   1-4   Kilbirnie v 3rd L.R.V.
Dec21   1-0   Queen's Park v Leith Athletic
```

Semi-finals
```
Jan18   2-0   Queen's Park v Abercorn  at Hampden Park
Jan18   3-0   Vale of Leven v 3rd L.R.V.  at Alexandria
```

Final
```
Feb15   1-1   Queen's Park v Vale of Leven  at Ibrox Park
Feb22   2-1   Queen's Park v Vale of Leven  at Ibrox Park
```

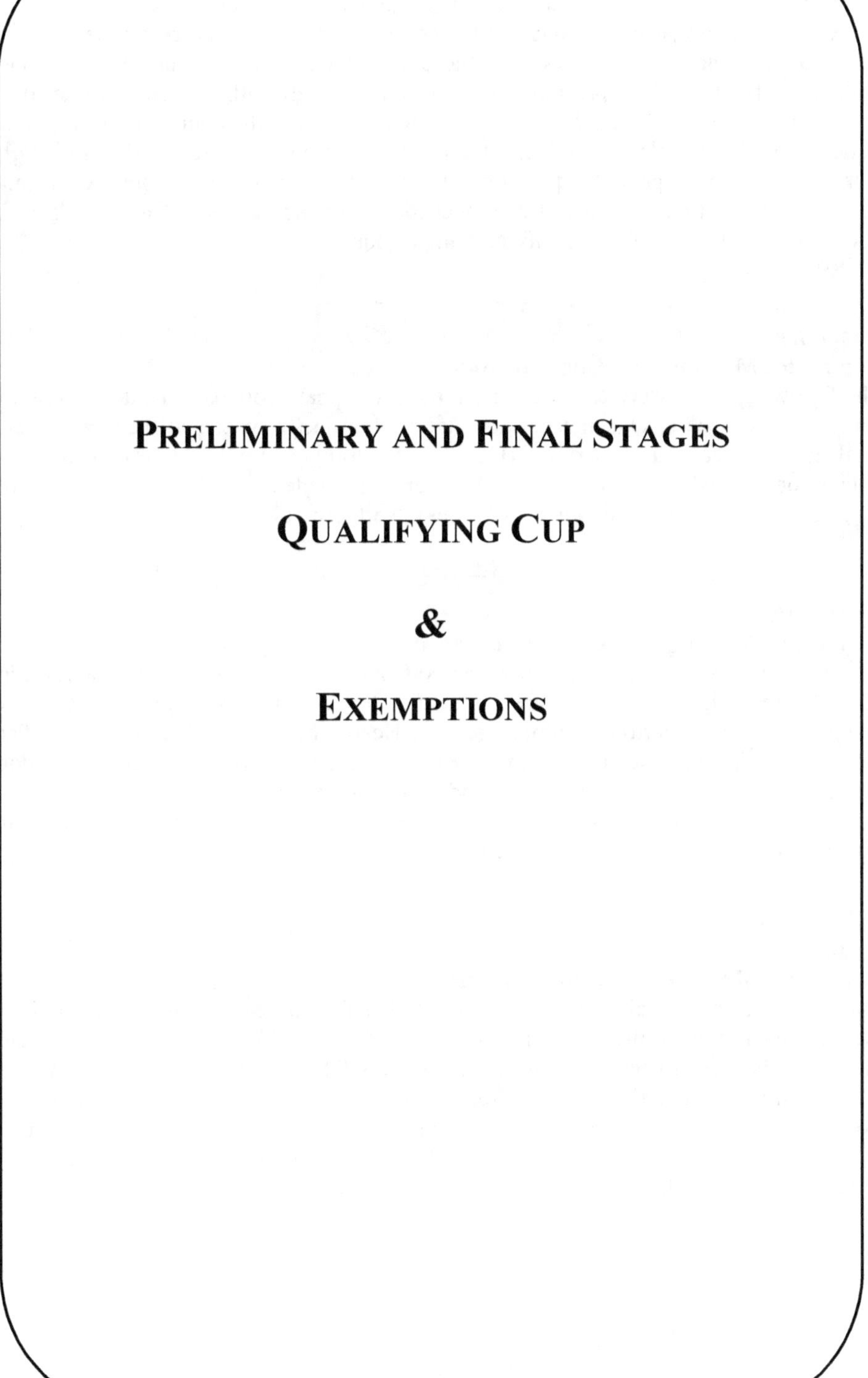

PRELIMINARY AND FINAL STAGES

QUALIFYING CUP

&

EXEMPTIONS

12th May 1891

S.F.A.A.G.M.   **Preliminary & Final Stages Proposal**

Mr Kennedy, Dumbarton, moved that the competition for the cup be divided into two parts – a preliminary and a final stage – the Committee to select sixteen clubs, composed of the semi-finalists of the preceding season, and the twelve other clubs they consider to be next in merit to be exempted for the preliminary stage of the competition should they so desire. Mr Maclachlan seconded. Mr Gardner, Airdrieonians, seconded by Mr Martin, Northern, moved the previous question. After an interesting debate a vote was taken, 54 voting for the motion, and a similar number for the amendment. The Chairman gave his casting vote in favour of the qualifying competitions.

Ref 1890043

31st May 1892

Committee Meeting   **Cup Exemptions**

The following clubs were exempted from the preliminary rounds of next season's Cup competition:- Celtic, Queen's Park, Rangers, Renton (by virtue of their being semi-finalists last year), Dumbarton, Heart of Midlothian, Leith Athletic (18 votes), Kilmarnock, Clyde, Third Lanark, Abercorn (17 votes), St Bernards, St Mirren, Cambuslang (13 votes), Linthouse (12 votes), Northern (11 votes).

Ref 1891034

30th May 1893

Committee Meeting   **Cup Exemptions**

At the first meeting of the newly-elected Scottish F.A. Committee on Tuesday evening, the following eighteen clubs were nominated for exemptions from the preliminary competition :- Dumbarton, Renton, Rangers, Hearts, St Mirren, Thistle, King's Park, Abercorn, Leith Athletic, Third Lanark, Linthouse, Clyde, Airdrieonians, Kilmarnock, Partick Thistle, Annbank, Our Boys, and Morton. The first twelve were elected, and together with Queen's Park, Celtic, St Bernard, and Broxburn Shamrock, the semi-finalists of last season, form the envied "sixteen."

Ref 1892026

29th May 1894

Committee Meeting   **Cup Exemptions**

The committee next decided as to the clubs which should be exempted from playing in the preliminary ties for the Scottish Challenge Cup. The Chairman said that the Rangers, the Celtic, the Queen's Park, and the Third Lanark fell to be exempted from their position on the semi-final and final ties last season. There remained twelve other clubs to be exempted. The vote was taken by ballot, with the result that the following twelve clubs were also exempted:- Heart of Midlothian, Dumbarton, Dundee, St Bernards, St Mirrens, Hibernians, Leith Athletic, Clyde, Renton, East Stirlingshire, Battlefield, and Abercorn.

Ref 1893022

7ᵗʰ May 1895

S.F.A.A.G.M.   **Qualifying Cup Proposal**

The Scottish Committee proposed that a qualifying cup should be instituted. Mr Sliman said it would be a stimulus to the young Clubs, and would be for the good of football generally. Mr M'Lean (Ayr Parkhouse), seconded the proposal, as it frequently happened that the exempted Clubs snuffed out at the first attempt the qualifying Clubs left in. Mr Hood (Ayrshire), was against the exemption rule altogether. He moved accordingly. Mr M'Culloch pointed out that the country Clubs had a double chance. It was agreed by 28 to 23 to have the qualifying cup.

Ref 1894027

6ᵗʰ June 1895

Committee Meeting   Cup Exemptions

The selection of the sixteen clubs to be exempted from the preliminary stage of the National Cup competition next season was considered. In addition to the semi-finalists in the last competition, St Bernard, Renton, Hearts, and Dundee, it was agreed to exempt the Queen's Park and the seven remaining clubs in the first division of the League – Celtic, Rangers, Third Lanark, St Mirren, Clyde, Dumbarton, and Hibernians. For the last four places six clubs were nominated, and the result of the ballot was that the following four were successful:- Leith Athletic, 16 votes; Kilmarnock, 16; Port-Glasgow Athletic,15 votes; and Morton, 12 votes. The unsuccessful clubs were:- Motherwell, 11 votes; and Abercorn, 5 votes.

Ref 1894028

2ⁿᵈ June 1896

Committee Meeting   Cup Exemptions

The following Clubs were exempted from playing in the preliminary stage of the Scottish Cup ties next season:- Heart of Mid-Lothian, St Bernards, Hibernians, and Renton (the semi-finalists of last season); and St Mirren, Dundee, Celtic, Rangers, Clyde, Third Lanark (22 votes), Abercorn, Queen's Park (20 votes), Leith Athletic (16 votes), Greenock Morton (15 votes), Dumbarton and Ayr Parkhouse (14 votes). The unsuccessful candidates were Port-Glasgow Athletic and Airdrieonians (12 votes), and Motherwell (9 votes).

Ref 1895028

1ˢᵗ June 1897

Committee Meeting   Cup Exemptions

By virtue of their being semi-finalists, Dumbarton, Rangers, Kilmarnock and Greenock Morton were exempted without a vote being taken. The other Clubs proposed for exemption were – Queen's [Park], Celtic, Third Lanark, Heart of Midlothian, Dundee, Clyde, St Bernard, Leith Athletic, Port-Glasgow Athletic, Hibernians, Abercorn, Partick Thistle, St Mirren, Airdrieonians, Motherwell, and Renton. Upon a ballot the following 12 clubs were selected to form the 16 Clubs exempted:- Queen's Park, 20 votes; Celtic, 20; Third Lanark, 20; Dundee, 20; Hibernians, 20; St Bernard, 20; Heart of Midlothian, 19; St Mirren, 18; Partick Thistle, 17; Clyde, 15; Leith Athletic, 11; Abercorn, 9. The Renton and Port-Glasgow Athletic also had 9 votes, but the Chairman gave his casting vote to the Paisley Club [Abercorn]. The other votes were – Airdrieonians, 7; Motherwell, 6.

Ref 1896032

31ˢᵗ May 1898

Committee Meeting   Cup Exemptions

A meeting of the newly-elected Scottish Football Association Committee was held in Glasgow on Tuesday night. The main business was the selection of the sixteen clubs who are exempted from taking part in the Qualifying Cup competition. Rangers, Kilmarnock, Third Lanark, and Dundee, as the Scottish Cup semi-finalists, were exempted. Other fourteen clubs proposed for twelves places, and a ballot became necessary, the result being that Dumbarton and Abercorn were struck off the list. The sixteen exempted clubs are :- Rangers, Kilmarnock Third Lanark, Dundee, Celtic Queen's Park, Hearts, Hibs., Clyde, St Bernard, St Mirren, Leith Athletic, Morton, Airdrieonians, Partick Thistle, and Port-Glasgow Athletic.

Ref 1897017

23ʳᵈ May 1899

Committee Meeting   Cup Exemptions

After several applications for extensions of the playing season for charity matches had been disposed of, a ballot was taken as to which clubs should be exempted from the Qualifying Cup Competition. The following clubs were nominated:- Celtic, Rangers, Port Glasgow, St Mirren, [semi-finalists] Heart of Midlothian, St Bernards, Clyde, Hibernians, Queen's Park, Third Lanark, Greenock Morton, Dundee, Kilmarnock, Leith Athletic, Partick Thistle, Airdrieonians, East Stirlingshire, Raith Rovers, and Abercorn. Upon the ballot papers being adjudged it was found that the leading Scotch clubs had received 19 votes; Kilmarnock, Leith Athletic, and Partick Thistle, 13; that Airdrieonians and East Stirlingshire had tied for twelfth place on the list; and that Raith Rovers and Abercorn had been balloted out of the exempted lot. The chairman gave his casting vote to the Airdrieonians, and East Stirlingshire was therefore added to the refusal list.

Ref 1898017

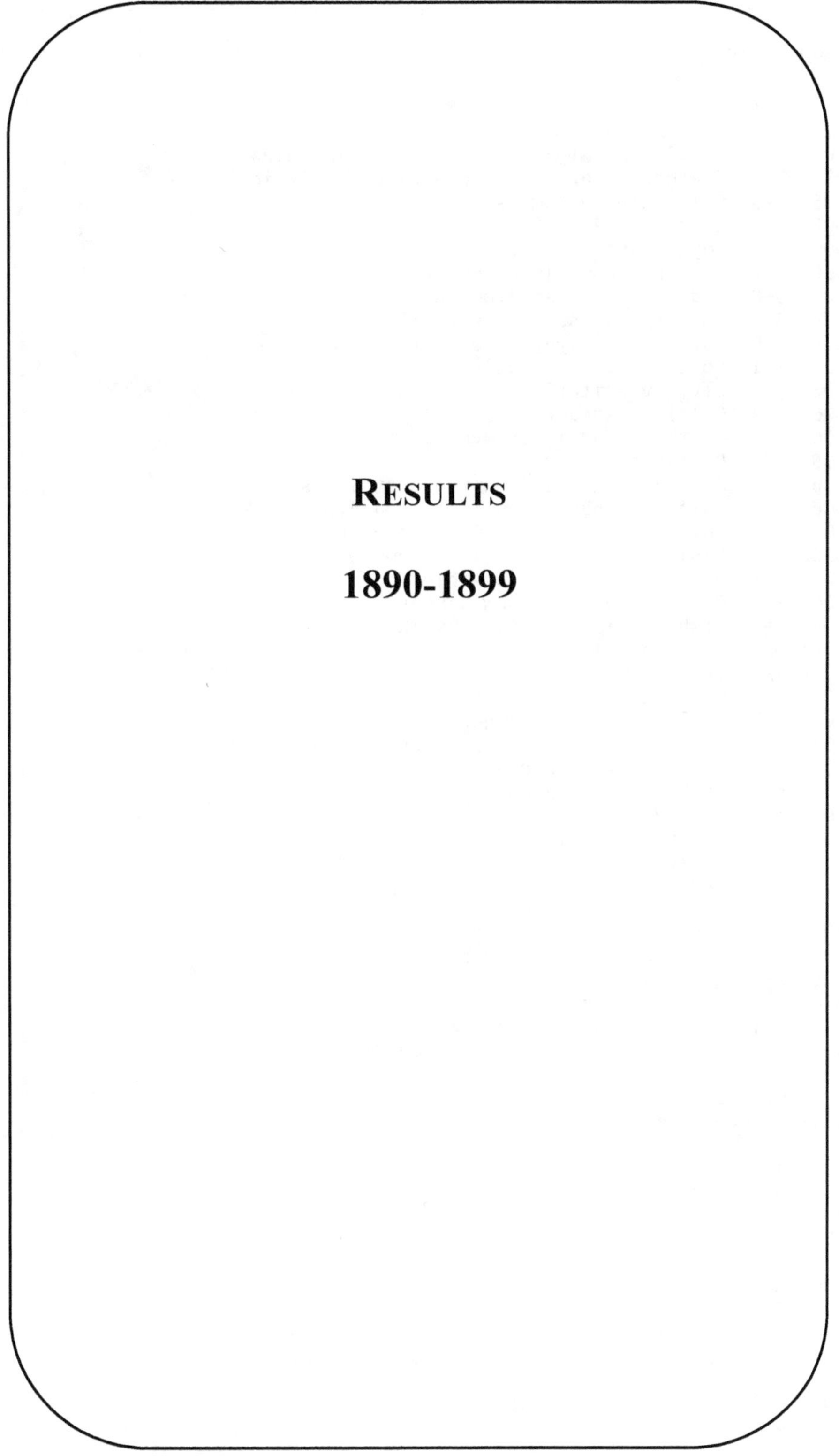

RESULTS

1890-1899

Season 1890-91

First Round
Glasgow and Lanarkshire
```
Sep06   1-1   Kelvinside Athletic v Glasgow Hibernian
Sep13   5-1   Glasgow Hibernian v Kelvinside Athletic
Sep06   6-0   Rutherglen v Cambuslang St Brides
Sep06   3-1   Airdrieonians v* Cowlairs
Sep06   5-4   Royal Albert v Motherwell
Sep06   1-2   Carrington v Albion Rovers
Sep06   6-0   Uddingston v Hamilton Harp
Sep06   3-7   Motherwell Shamrock v Fairfield
Sep06   5-0   Northern v Clydesdale - prot.
Sep20   7-1   Northern v Clydesdale
Sep06   7-2   Clyde v Whitefield
Sep06   1-0   Celtic v Rangers
Sep06   scr   Cartha v Carfin Shamrock - w/o
Sep06   1-4   Battlefield v 3rd L.R.V.
Sep06  13-0   Burnbank Swifts v United Abstainers
Sep06   scr   Whifflet Shamrock v Summerton Athletic - w/o
Sep06   3-5   Thistle (Glasgow) v Queen's Park
Sep06   0-8   Hamilton Academical v Linthouse
Sep06   4-1   Maryhill v Southern Athletic
Sep06   3-1   Cambuslang v Glasgow Wanderers
Sep06   3-2   Wishaw Thistle v Partick Thistle
```
Renfrewshire, Ayrshire and Buteshire
```
Sep06   w/o   Carlton v Lugar Boswell - scr.
Sep06   7-2   Greenock Morton v Ayr Athletic
Sep06   7-3   Neilston v Bute Rangers
Sep06   9-2   Stevenston Thistle v Stewarton Cunninghame
Sep06   4-4   Kilmarnock v Annbank
Sep13   6-2   Annbank v Kilmarnock
Sep06   w/o   Lanemark v Dykebar - scr fm.
Sep06   3-4   Maybole v Hurlford
Sep06   4-3   Saltcoats Victoria v Lochwinnoch
Sep06   5-3   Cathcart v Pollockshaws Harp
Sep06   5-2   Dalry v Pollockshaws
Sep06   1-3   Mauchline v Kilmarnock Athletic
Sep06   w/o   Ayr v Kilbarchan - scr.
Sep06   2-5   Arthurlie v St Mirren
Sep06   6-1   Ayr Parkhouse v Kilbirnie
Sep06   0-13  Greenock Abstainers v Newmilns
Sep06   0-2   Port Glasgow Athletic v Monkcastle
Sep06   8-0   Abercorn v Irvine
        bye   Beith
```
Dumbartonshire and Stirlingshire
```
Sep06   0-4   Denny v Alva
Sep06   4-1   Campsie v Laurieston
Sep06   6-2   Slamannan v Gairdoch
Sep06   8-2   Dumbarton v* Smithston Hibernians
Sep06   2-2   Kirkintilloch Athletic v Clydebank
Sep13   4-3   Clydebank v Kirkintilloch Athletic
Sep06   1-6   Old Kilpatrick v Jamestown
Sep06   9-0   Clackmannan v Milton of Campsie
Sep06   scr   Dunipace v Vale of Leven Wanderers - w/o
Sep06   3-6   Campsie Hibernian v Clydebank Athletic
Sep06   1-6   Tillicoultry v Dalmuir Thistle
Sep06   4-3   Camelon v Alloa Athletic
```

Sep06 2-1   Kilsyth Wanderers v Renton
Sep06 scr   Stenhousemuir v Vale of Leven - w/o
Sep06 12-1 Union (Dumbarton) v Grasshoppers
Sep06 1-0   Methlan Park v King's Park
Sep06 7-2   Bridge of Allan v Southfield Rangers
Sep06 scr   Vale of Bannock v Falkirk - w/o
Sep06 8-2   East Stirlingshire v Grangemouth

East of Scotland and Fifeshire
Sep06 w/o   Mossend Swifts v Lassodie - scr.
Sep06 3-2   Bathgate Rovers v Dunfermline Athletic
Sep06 3-4   Kirkcaldy Wanderers v Hibernian
Sep06 7-2   Heart of Midlothian v Raith Rovers
Sep06 4-2   Burntisland Thistle v Bonnyrigg Rose
Sep06 10-1 Cowdenbeath v Linlithgow Athletic
Sep06 7-0   St Bernard's v Adventurers - St B. disqualified
Sep06 w/o   Bo'ness v Blairadam - scr.
Sep06 3-2   Leith Athletic v Armadale
Sep06 w/o   Broxburn v West Calder - scr.
Sep06 5-3   Penicuik Athletic v Champfleurie
       bye   Bellstane Birds
       bye   Edinburgh University

Forfarshire
Sep06 w/o   Harp (Dundee) v* Lochee - scr fm.
Sep06 2-7   Forfar Athletic v Our Boys (Dundee)
Sep06 3-3   Dundee Wanderers v Arbroath
Sep13 4-1   Arbroath v Dundee Wanderers
Sep06 7-1   Montrose v Broughty
Sep06 3-4   Brechin v Kirriemuir
Sep06 scr   Strathmore (Dundee) v East End - w/o

Perthshire
Sep06 2a2   St Johnstone v Coupar Angus - abd. dispute - C.A. disqualified
Sep06 7-3   Fair City Athletic v Dunblane
Sep06 w/o   Crieff v Vale of Atholl - scr.

Aberdeenshire
Sep06 2-1   Caledonian (Aberdeen) v Victoria United
Sep06 1-5   Orion v Aberdeen

Northern Counties
Sep06 2-4   Inverness Thistle v Inverness Caledonian
       bye   Portland Lybster

Southern Counties
Sep06 2-8   Annan v Dumfries Wanderers
Sep06 16-1 Mid-Annandale v Rising Thistle
Sep06 0-5   Douglas Rovers v 5th K.R.V.
Sep06 9-0   Dumfries v* Newton Stewart
Sep06 w/o   Stranraer v Moffat - scr.

Argyllshire
Sep06 4-1   Inveraray v Lochgilphead
Sep06 3-0   Oban v Rangers (Oban)

Second Round
East of Scotland, Fifeshire, Dumbartonshire and Stirlingshire
Oct11 7-0   Bo'ness v Bellstane Birds
Sep27 5-3   Broxburn v Clackmannan
Sep27 2-1   Camelon v Alva
Sep27 1-5   Bridge of Allan v Vale of Leven
Sep27 3-5   Clydebank Athletic v Kilsyth Wanderers
Sep27 5-7   Dalmuir Thistle v Cowdenbeath
Sep27 4-4   Campsie v East Stirlingshire
Oct04 3-1   East Stirlingshire v Campsie

```
Sep27   2-5   Jamestown v Mossend Swifts
Sep27   5-2   Slamannan v Clydebank - prot.
Oct11   5-2   Clydebank v Slamannan
Sep27   1-9   Hibernian v Dumbarton
Sep27   7-2   Leith Athletic v Falkirk
Sep27   3-4   Penicuik Athletic v Methlan Park
Sep27   w/o   Heart of Midlothian v Burntisland Thistle - scr.
Sep27   6-2   Bathgate Rovers v Union (Dumbarton)
-----   awa   Adventurers v Vale of Leven Wanderers - V.o.L.W.
                 disqualified
        bye   Edinburgh University
```

Glasgow, Lanarkshire, Renfrewshire and Ayrshire
```
Sep27   scr   Carlton v Glengowan - w/o
Sep27   2-4   Beith v Cambuslang
Sep27   2-2   Celtic v Carfin Shamrock
Oct04   1-3   Carfin Shamrock v Celtic
Sep27   2-5   Fairfield v Royal Albert
Sep27   5-1   St Mirren v Albion Rovers
Sep27   5-1   Queen's Park v Northern
Sep27   2-2   Newmilns v Uddingston
Oct04   5-1   Uddingston v Newmilns
Sep27   2-1   Burnbank Swifts v Stevenston Thistle - prot.
Oct11   3-0   Burnbank Swifts v Stevenston Thistle
Sep27   7-2   Linthouse v Maryhill
Sep27   3-2   Greenock Morton v Neilston
Sep27   4-3   Clyde v Hurlford
Sep27   1-3   Rutherglen v Ayr
Sep27   4-1   Wishaw Thistle v Glasgow Hibernian
Sep27   3-2   Saltcoats Victoria v Lanemark
Sep27   8-1   3rd L.R.V. v Kilmarnock Athletic
Sep27   1-2   Ayr Parkhouse v Summerton Athletic
Sep27   4-2   Monkcastle v Dalry
Sep27   3-1   Airdrieonians v Annbank
Sep27  12-0   Abercorn v Cathcart
```

Forfarshire and Perthshire
```
Sep27   0-11  Crieff v Fair City Athletic
Sep27   0-3   Kirriemuir v Montrose
Sep27   4-2   East End v St Johnstone
Sep27   1-5   Harp (Dundee) v Arbroath
        bye   Our Boys (Dundee)
```

Aberdeenshire
```
Sep27   8-0   Aberdeen v Caledonian (Aberdeen)
```

Northern Counties
```
Sep27   w/o   Inverness Caledonian v Portland Lybster - scr.
```

Southern Counties
```
Sep27   9a1   5th K.R.V. v Mid-Annandale - abd. MA walked off in protest
Sep27   6-5   Dumfries Wanderers v Dumfries
        bye   Stranraer
```

Argyllshire
```
Sep27   4-2   Inveraray v Oban
```

Third Round

Glasgow and Suburbs, Lanarkshire, Ayrshire, Renfrewshire and Argyllshire
```
Oct18   8-0   Airdrieonians v Glengowan
Oct18   3-4   Linthouse v Abercorn
Oct18   1-7   Monkcastle v Burnbank Swifts
Oct18   6-0   Queen's Park v Uddingston
Oct18   8-1   3rd L.R.V. v Summerton Athletic
```

Oct18 10-0 Greenock Morton v Inveraray
Oct18 6-2 Royal Albert v Saltcoats Victoria
Oct18 2-6 Wishaw Thistle v Celtic
Oct18 1-2 Cambuslang v St Mirren
Oct18 3-4 Clyde v Ayr

East of Scotland, Stirlingshire, Dumbartonshire and Fifeshire
Oct18 3-2 Edinburgh University v Cowdenbeath
Oct18 6-0 Dumbarton v Clydebank
Oct18 0-8 Kilsyth Wanderers v Vale of Leven
Oct18 3-0 Heart of Midlothian v* Methlan Park at International
               Exhibition
Oct18 12-0 Leith Athletic v Adventurers
Oct18 6-0 Bathgate Rovers v Broxburn
Oct18 3-3 East Stirlingshire v Camelon
Oct25 6-10 Camelon v East Stirlingshire
Oct18 1-1 Bo'ness v Mossend Swifts
Oct25 9-1 Mossend Swifts v Bo'ness

Forfarshire and Perthshire
Oct18 4-0 Our Boys (Dundee) v East End
Oct18 4-1 Montrose v Fair City Athletic
       bye Arbroath

Northern Counties
Oct18 6-2 Inverness Caledonian v Aberdeen

Southern Counties
Oct18 w/o Dumfries Wanderers v Stranraer - scr.
       bye 5th K.R.V.

Fourth Round
Nov08 0-7 Edinburgh University v Queen's Park at Tynecastle Park
Nov08 6-2 5th K.R.V. v Arbroath
Nov08 0-3 Montrose v 3rd L.R.V.
Nov08 1-3 Our Boys (Dundee) v Celtic
Nov08 3-4 Ayr v Heart of Midlothian
Nov08 1-2 Airdrieonians v St Mirren
Nov08 8-0 Abercorn v Bathgate Rovers
Nov08 7-3 Dumbarton v Mossend Swifts
Nov08 6-4 Greenock Morton v Dumfries Wanderers
Nov08 1-0 Royal Albert v Burnbank Swifts
Nov08 3-1 Leith Athletic v Vale of Leven
Nov08 2-0 East Stirlingshire v Inverness Caledonian

Fifth Round
Dec06 8-0 Dumbarton v 5th K.R.V.
Nov29 5-1 Heart of Midlothian v Greenock Morton
Nov29 2-2 Celtic v Royal Albert
Dec06 0a4 Royal Albert v Celtic - abd. 78mins crowd
Dec13 2-0 Celtic v Royal Albert at Ibrox Park
Dec06 2-3 St Mirren v Queen's Park
       bye Abercorn
       bye East Stirlingshire
       bye Leith Athletic
       bye 3rd L.R.V.

Sixth Round
Dec20 2-3 Leith Athletic v Abercorn
Dec20 3-0 Dumbarton v Celtic
Jan10 1-1 3rd L.R.V. v Queen's Park
Jan17 2-2 Queen's Park v 3rd L.R.V.

Jan24 1-4 Queen's Park v 3rd L.R.V. at Hampden Park
Dec20 1-3 East Stirlingshire v Heart of Midlothian

Semi-finals
Jan17 3-1 Dumbarton v Abercorn at Boghead Park
Jan31 1-4 3rd L.R.V. v Heart of Midlothian at Cathkin Park

Final
Feb07 0-1 Dumbarton v Heart of Midlothian at Hampden Park

Season 1891-92

Preliminary Stage First Round
Glasgow and Lanarkshire
Sep05 scr Cambuslang St Brides v Carrington - w/o
Sep05 5-1 Burnbank Swifts v Hamilton Harp
Sep05 w/o Kelvinside Athletic v Uddingston - scr.
Sep05 6-1 Thistle (Glasgow) v Shettleston Swifts
Sep05 w/o Glengowan v Summerton Athletic - S. failed to appear
Sep05 scr Fairfield v Whifflet Shamrock - w/o
Sep05 12-0 Linthouse v Carfin Hibernian
Sep05 7-3 Wishaw Thistle v Albion Rovers
Sep05 1-4 Motherwell v Cowlairs
Sep05 w/o Battlefield v United Abstainers - scr.
Sep05 scr Maryhill v Airdrieonians - w/o
Sep05 1-2 Glasgow Wanderers v Partick Thistle
Sep05 1-6 Southern Athletic v Royal Albert
Sep05 2-4 Hamilton Academical v 21st Royal Scots Fusiliers
Sep05 2-2 Clydesdale v Whitefield
Sep12 7-0 Whitefield v Clydesdale
       bye Rutherglen
Renfrewshire and Ayrshire
Sep05 w/o Mauchline v Maybole - scr.
Sep05 6-3 Port Glasgow Athletic v Lanemark
Sep05 5-2 Stevenston Thistle v Galston
Sep05 1-3 Cathcart v Ayr Athletic
Sep05 20-1 Johnstone v Greenock Abstainers
Sep05 10-0 Kilbarchan v 1st Argyll R.V.
Sep05 3-4 Dalry v Catrine Thistle - friendly ref. did not appear
Sep12 5-0 Dalry v Catrine Thistle
Sep05 12-0 Ayr v Pollockshaws
Sep05 3-4 Bute Rangers v Monkcastle
Sep05 2-2 Beith v Arthurlie
Sep12 3-1 Arthurlie v Beith
Sep05 1-7 Newmilns v Dykebar
Sep05 2-4 Cronberry Eglinton v Hurlford
Sep05 6-3 Saltcoats Victoria v Lochwinnoch
Sep05 2-2 Kilbirnie v Greenock Morton
Sep12 8-1 Greenock Morton v Kilbirnie
Sep05 3-2 Stewarton Cunninghame v Irvine
Sep05 8-3 Annbank v Ayr Parkhouse
Sep05 3-6 Neilston v Kilmarnock Athletic
Dumbartonshire, Stirlingshire and Clackmannanshire
Sep05 2-4 Laurieston v Denny
Sep05 1-0 Alva v Stenhousemuir
Sep05 w/o Falkirk v Tillicoultry - scr.

```
Sep05  1-3  Camelon v Dalmuir Thistle
Sep05  7-3  Campsie v Kilsyth Wanderers
Sep05  5-3  King's Park v Clydebank Athletic
Sep05  2-4  Gairdoch v Grangemouth
Sep05  1-3  Methlan Park v Slamannan Rovers
Sep05  6-3  Smithston Hibernians v Alloa Athletic
Sep05  5-3  Vale of Bannock v Slamannan
Sep05  3-4  Kilsyth Standard v Dunipace
Sep05  8-2  East Stirlingshire v Jamestown
Sep05  0-3  Old Kilpatrick v Kirkintilloch Athletic
Sep05  7-2  Bridge of Allan v Union (Dumbarton)
Sep05  7-1  Clydebank v Grasshoppers
       bye  Clackmannan
```

East of Scotland and Fifeshire
```
Sep05  1-6  Bonnyrigg Rose v Penicuik Athletic
Sep05  0-3  Lassodie v Cowdenbeath
Sep05  2-3  Kirkcaldy Wanderers v Polton Vale
Sep05  3-3  Armadale v Bathgate Rovers
Sep12  3-0  Bathgate Rovers v Armadale
Sep05  w/o  Broxburn Shamrock v Lochgelly United - scr.
Sep05  4-6  Burntisland Thistle v Linlithgow Athletic
Sep05  1-7  Muirhouse Rovers v Mossend Swifts
Sep05  4-0  Dunfermline Athletic v Bo'ness
Sep05  2-1  Broxburn v Raith Rovers
Sep05  0-5  Adventurers v St Bernard's
       bye  Edinburgh University
```

Forfarshire
```
Sep05  3-3  Harp (Dundee) v Our Boys (Dundee)
Sep12  0-2  Our Boys (Dundee) v Harp (Dundee)
Sep05  3-3  Broughty v Montrose
Sep12  5-1  Montrose v Broughty
Sep05  1-3  Forfar Athletic v East End
Sep05  0a1  Arbroath v Brechin - prot. - abd. 87mins crowd
Sep19  3-9  Brechin v Arbroath
Sep05  3-4  Lochee United v Johnstone Wanderers
Sep05  3-7  Strathmore (Dundee) v Kirriemuir
```

Perthshire
```
Sep05  0-5  Our Boys (Blairgowrie) v Dunblane
Sep05  2-3  St Johnstone v Fair City Athletic
Sep05  1-6  Vale of Ruthven v Coupar Angus
       bye  Vale of Atholl
```

Argyllshire
```
Sep05  w/o  Rangers (Oban) v Lochgilphead - scr.
Sep05  3-2  Inveraray v Oban
```

Aberdeenshire and Kincardineshire
```
Sep05  0-0  Victoria United v Orion
Sep12  5-1  Orion v Victoria United
Sep05  w/o  Aberdeen v Caledonian (Aberdeen) - scr.
Sep05  0-8  Stonehaven v Bon Accord
```

Northern Counties
```
Sep05  w/o  Fort William v Inverness Union - scr.
Sep05  w/o  Inverness Thistle v Wick Rovers - scr.
Sep05  0-5  Clachnacuddin v Inverness Caledonian
```

Selkirkshire
```
Sep05  3-4  Vale of Gala v Selkirk
```

Southern Counties
```
Sep05  2-2  Newton Stewart v Annan
-----  w/o  Annan v Newton Stewart - scr.
```

```
Sep05   2-3   Stranraer v 5th K.R.V.
Sep05   5-4   Mid-Annandale v Dumfries
Sep05   w/o   Newton Stewart Athletic v Rising Thistle - scr.
Sep05  14-0   Q.O.S. Wanderers v* Douglas Rovers
        bye   Moffat
```

Preliminary Stage Second Round

East of Scotland, Fifeshire, Dumbartonshire and Stirlingshire
```
Sep26   3-0   Bridge of Allan v Clackmannan
Sep26   3-9   Alva v Mossend Swifts
Sep26   3a0   East Stirlingshire v King's Park - abd. 42mins blizzard
Oct03   7-2   East Stirlingshire v King's Park
Sep26   4-2   Kirkintilloch Athletic v Polton Vale
Sep26   2-1   Denny v Dunfermline Athletic
Sep26   2-3   Penicuik Athletic v Dalmuir Thistle
Sep26   0-7   Vale of Bannock v Clydebank
Sep26   7-1   St Bernard's v Dunipace
Sep26  11-1   Smithston Hibernians v Linlithgow Athletic
Sep26   6-4   Broxburn Shamrock v Campsie - prot.
Oct10   3-1   Broxburn Shamrock v Campsie
Sep26   0-2   Grangemouth v Falkirk
Sep26   8-1   Bathgate Rovers v Slamannan Rovers
Sep26   4-2   Duntocher Harp v Broxburn
        bye   Cowdenbeath
        bye   Edinburgh University
```
Glasgow, Lanarkshire, Renfrewshire and Ayrshire
```
Sep26   4-0   Annbank v Rutherglen
Sep26   9-0   Dalry v Stewarton Cunninghame
Sep26   2-8   Carrington v Burnbank Swifts
Sep26   0-3   Partick Thistle v Hurlford
Sep26   5-2   Wishaw Thistle v Arthurlie
Sep26   3-1   Greenock Morton v Airdrieonians
Sep26   3-3   Ayr v 21st Royal Scots Fusiliers
Oct03   1-2   21st Royal Scots Fusiliers v Ayr
Sep26   6-6   Royal Albert v Cowlairs
Oct03   4-4   Cowlairs v Royal Albert - both qualified
Sep26   1-4   Dykebar v Mauchline
Sep26   4-7   Johnstone v Thistle (Glasgow)
Sep26   3-3   Ayr Athletic v Kilbarchan
Oct03   4-1   Kilbarchan v Ayr Athletic
Sep26   3-3   Stevenston Thistle v Kilmarnock Athletic
Oct03   2-2   Kilmarnock Athletic v Stevenston Thistle - both qualified
Sep26   9-0   Battlefield v Whitefield
-----   scr   Kelvinside Athletic v Monkcastle - w/o
Sep26   4-1   Port Glasgow Athletic v Glengowan
-----   w/o   Linthouse v Whifflet Shamrock - scr.
        bye   Saltcoats Victoria
```
Forfarshire and Perthshire
```
Sep26   1-7   Vale of Athole v East End
Sep26   7-1   Arbroath v Fair City Athletic
Sep26   5-2   Harp (Dundee) v Johnstone Wanderers
Sep26   4-0   Coupar Angus v Montrose
Sep26   1-8   Kirriemuir v Dunblane
```
Argyllshire
```
Sep26   4-2   Inveraray v Rangers (Oban)
```
Aberdeenshire
```
Sep26   2-5   Bon Accord v Aberdeen
        bye   Orion
```

Northern Counties
```
-----  w/o  Inverness Thistle v Fort William - scr.
       bye  Inverness Caledonian
```
Southern Counties and Selkirkshire
```
Sep26  6-1  Q.O.S. Wanderers v Moffat
Sep26  1-1  Newton Stewart Athletic v Mid-Annandale
Oct03  w/o  Mid-Annandale v Newton Stewart Athletic - scr.
Sep26  w/o  5th K.R.V. v Selkirk - scr.
       bye  Annan
```

Preliminary Stage Third Round
Glasgow, Lanarkshire, Renfrewshire, Ayrshire and Argyllshire
```
Oct17  1-7  Saltcoats Victoria v Linthouse
Oct17  4-2  Monkcastle v Greenock Morton
Oct17  5-0  Cowlairs v* Dalry
Oct17  6-1  Ayr v Inveraray
Oct17  2-0  Annbank v Hurlford
Oct17  5-0  Burnbank Swifts v Mauchline
Oct17  9-1  Thistle (Glasgow) v Kilbarchan
Oct17  5-4  Kilmarnock Athletic v Port Glasgow Athletic
Oct17  3-2  Wishaw Thistle v Royal Albert
Oct17  4-2  Battlefield v Stevenston Thistle
```
Dumbartonshire, Fifeshire, Stirlingshire and East of Scotland
```
Oct17  0-3  Cowdenbeath v Clydebank
Oct17  6-1  Denny v Edinburgh University
Oct17  4-2  Bridge of Allan v Duntocher Harp
Oct17  5-1  St Bernard's v Kirkintilloch Athletic
Oct17  5-5  Bathgate Rovers v Falkirk
Oct24  0-3  Falkirk v Bathgate Rovers
Oct17  5-4  East Stirlingshire v Mossend Swifts
Oct17  1-2  Smithston Hibernians v Broxburn Shamrock
       bye  Dalmuir Thistle
```
Forfarshire and Perthshire
```
Oct17  1-1  Harp (Dundee) v East End
Oct24  2-0  East End v Harp (Dundee)
Oct17  3-3  Coupar Angus v Dunblane
Oct24  w/o  Dunblane v Coupar Angus - scr.
       bye  Arbroath
```
Aberdeenshire
```
Oct17  1-3  Orion v Aberdeen
```
Northern Counties
```
Oct17  2-1  Inverness Thistle v Inverness Caledonian
```
Southern Counties
```
Oct17  4-7  Q.O.S. Wanderers v 5th K.R.V.
-----  w/o  Mid-Annandale v Annan - scr.
```

Preliminary Stage Fourth Round
```
Nov07   2-1  Aberdeen v* Dalmuir Thistle
Nov07  10-0  Arbroath v Denny
Nov07   8-2  Annbank v Wishaw Thistle
Nov07   0-1  Inverness Thistle v Battlefield  at Pitlochry
Nov07   5-1  Bathgate Rovers v Clydebank
Nov07   3-6  East End v Monkcastle  at Forthbank
Nov07   5-2  Thistle (Glasgow) v Burnbank Swifts
Nov07   9-3  Cowlairs v 5th K.R.V. - prot.
Dec05   7-3  Cowlairs v 5th K.R.V.
        bye  Linthouse, Ayr, Bridge of Allan, East Stirlingshire
        bye  Mid-Annandale, Dunblane, Broxburn Shamrock
        bye  St Bernard's, Kilmarnock Athletic
```

Final Stage First Round
Nov28   4-0   Dumbarton v Thistle (Glasgow)
Nov28   1-6   East Stirlingshire v Kilmarnock
Nov28   2-4   St Mirren v Celtic
Nov28   7-2   Broxburn Shamrock v Northern
Nov28   5-0   Leith Athletic v Dunblane
Nov28   3a1   Heart of Midlothian v Clyde - abd. 85mins darkness
Dec05   8-0   Heart of Midlothian v Clyde
Nov28   7-2   Kilmarnock Athletic v Bridge of Allan
Nov28   2-1   Annbank v Battlefield
Nov28   0-6   Linthouse v Bathgate Rovers
Dec12   3-1   Cowlairs v Cambuslang
Nov28   2-3   Abercorn v Queen's Park
Nov28   3-0   3rd L.R.V. v Vale of Leven
Nov28   5-1   Rangers v St Bernard's
Dec05   2-6   Aberdeen v Mid-Annandale at Forthbank Park
Nov28   3-4   Monkcastle v Arbroath at Forthbank Park
Nov28   7-4   Renton v Ayr

Final Stage Second Round
Dec19   1-3   3rd L.R.V. v Dumbarton
Dec19   4-5   Broxburn Shamrock v Heart of Midlothian
Dec19 11-2   Cowlairs v Mid-Annandale
Dec19   2-1   Annbank v Leith Athletic
Dec19   6-0   Queen's Park v Bathgate Rovers
Dec19   0-0   Rangers v Kilmarnock
Dec26   1-1   Kilmarnock v Rangers
Jan23   2-3   Kilmarnock v Rangers at Westmarch
Dec19   0-3   Arbroath v Renton at Carolina Port
Dec19   3-0   Celtic v Kilmarnock Athletic

Final Stage Third Round
Jan30   2-0   Rangers v Annbank
Jan23   4-1   Celtic v Cowlairs
Jan23   4-4   Renton v Heart of Midlothian
Jan30   2-2   Heart of Midlothian v Renton
Feb06   2-3   Heart of Midlothian v Renton at Hampden Park
Jan23   2-2   Dumbarton v Queen's Park
Jan30   4-1   Queen's Park v Dumbarton

Semi-finals
Feb13   1-1   Renton v Queen's Park at Tontine Park
Feb27   3-0   Queen's Park v Renton at Hampden Park
Feb06   5-3   Celtic v Rangers

Final
Mar12   1-0   Celtic v Queen's Park at Ibrox Park - decreed a friendly
Apr09   5-1   Celtic v Queen's Park at Ibrox Park

Season 1892-93

Preliminary Stage First Round
Glasgow and Lanarkshire
Sep03   w/o   Royal Albert v Fairfield - scr.
Sep03   5-0   Airdriehill v Burnbank Swifts
Sep03   w/o   Partick Thistle v Maryhill - scr.

```
Sep03  b/d   Whitefield v Summerton Athletic - both defunct
Sep03  5-5   Hamilton Academical v Motherwell
Sep10  3-2   Motherwell v Hamilton Academical - prot.
Sep17  5-2   Motherwell v Hamilton Academical
Sep03  scr   Kelvinside Athletic v Glengowan - w/o
Sep03  7-0   Cowlairs v Battlefield
Sep03  scr   Southern Athletic v Airdrieonians - w/o
Sep03  w/o   Cartha Hibernian v Whifflet Shamrock
Sep03  2-17  Glasgow Perthshire v Wishaw Thistle
Sep03  9-1   Albion Rovers v Shettleston Swifts
Sep03  scr   United Abstainers v Glasgow Wanderers - w/o
Sep03  3-2   Carrington v Dykehead
Sep03  2-4   Thistle (Glasgow) v Carfin Shamrock
Sep03  2-1   Pollockshaws v Hamilton Harp
```

East of Scotland and Perthshire
```
Sep03  0-10  Vale of Gala v Kirkcaldy
Sep03  1-4   Dunfermline Athletic v Armadale
Sep03  7-1   Bathgate Rovers v Adventurers
Sep03  2-1   Mossend Swifts v Broxburn
Sep03  0-5   Lassodie v Cowdenbeath
Sep03  4-1   Linlithgow Athletic v Muirhouse Rovers
Sep03  5-0   Broxburn Shamrock v Bonnyrigg Rose
Sep03  3-4   Bo'ness v Polton Vale
Sep03  2-2   Penicuik Athletic v Lochgelly United
Sep10  7-1   Lochgelly United v Penicuik Athletic
       bye   Raith Rovers
       bye   Edinburgh University
```

Renfrewshire and Ayrshire
```
Sep03  0-7   Dalry v Kilbarchan
Sep02  w/o   Galston v Lochwinnoch - scr.
Sep03  7-1   Greenock Morton v 1st Argyll R.V.
Sep03  4-6   Irvine v Stevenston Thistle
Sep03  scr   Ayr Athletic v Monkcastle - w/o
Sep03  1-1   Cumnock Springbank v Kilbirnie
Sep10  5-1   Kilbirnie v Cumnock Springbank
Sep03  4-0   Ayr Parkhouse v Lanemark
Sep03  5-1   Saltcoats Victoria v Mauchline
Sep03  11-2  Annbank v Cronberry Eglinton
Sep03  3-1   Ayr v Beith
Sep03  5-0   Port Glasgow Athletic v Kilmarnock Athletic
Sep03  w/o   Girvan Athletic v Newmains - scr.
Sep03  1-0   Johnstone v Hurlford
Sep03  0-2   Dykebar v Arthurlie
Sep03  w/o   Bute Rangers v Lugar Boswell - scr.
       bye   Neilston
```

Dumbartonshire, Stirlingshire and Clackmannanshire
```
Sep03  7-0   Smithston Hibernians v Alloa Athletic
Sep03  9-1   King's Park v Tillicoultry
Sep03  4-6   Slamannan Rovers v Vale of Leven
Sep03  5-1   Falkirk v Vale of Bannock
Sep03  2-4   Dalmuir Thistle v Gairdoch
Sep03  scr   Old Kilpatrick v Kilsyth Standard - w/o
Sep03  1-0   Stenhousemuir v Dunipace
Sep03  4-0   Kilsyth Wanderers v Alva
Sep03  3-3   Grasshoppers v Denny
Sep10  1-1   Denny v Grasshoppers - both qualified
Sep03  w/o   Campsie v Clydebank Athletic - scr.
Sep03  w/o   Laurieston v Jamestown - scr.
```

```
Sep03  w/o  Grangemouth v Methlan Park - scr.
Sep03  2-2  Kirkintilloch Athletic v Union (Dumbarton)
Sep10  6-1  Union (Dumbarton) v Kirkintilloch Athletic
Sep03  1-1  Levendale v Camelon
Sep10  2-2  Camelon v Levendale - both qualified
Sep03  7-1  East Stirlingshire v Slamannan
Sep03  4-1  Clackmannan v Clydebank
Sep03  w/o  Duntocher Harp v Vale of Leven Wanderers - scr.
       bye  Bridge of Allan
```

Forfarshire
```
Sep03  4-3  Harp (Dundee) v Montrose
Sep03  4-1  East End v Arbroath Wanderers
Sep03  4-3  Our Boys (Dundee) v Lochee United
Sep03 15-0  Arbroath v* Brechin
Sep03  3-4  Strathmore (Dundee) v Strathmore Athletic
Sep03  0-10 Kirriemuir v Forfar Athletic
       bye  Johnstone Wanderers
```

Aberdeenshire
```
Sep03  2-7  Victoria United v Orion  at Chanonry
Sep03  w/o  Peterhead v Stonehaven - scr.
       bye  Aberdeen
```

Northern Counties
```
Sep03  4-1  Inverness Caledonian v Inverness Thistle
Sep03  4-1  Inverness Union v Clachnacuddin
```

Perthshire
```
Sep03  0-3  Fair City Athletic v St Johnstone
Sep03  3-7  Vale of Atholl v Dunblane
Sep03  5-2  Our Boys (Blairgowrie) v Coupar Angus
       bye  Vale of Ruthven
```

Argyllshire
```
Sep03  6-2  Inveraray v Lochgilphead
Sep03  4-3  Oban v Rangers (Oban)
```

Southern Counties
```
Sep03  w/o  St Cuthbert Wanderers v Rangers (Sanquhar) - scr.
Sep03 14-2  Q.O.S. Wanderers v Gladstonians
Sep03  1-6  Newton Stewart Athletic v 5th K.R.V.
Sep03  w/o  Stranraer v Mid-Annandale - defunct
Sep10  2-6  Rising Thistle v Douglas Rovers
Sep03  scr  St John's (Dumfries) v Moffat - w/o
       bye  Annan
```

Preliminary Stage Second Round
Glasgow, Lanarkshire, Renfrewshire and Ayrshire
```
Sep24  6-0  Wishaw Thistle v Ayr
Sep24  w/o  Motherwell v* Whitefield - scr fm.
Sep24  4-4  Bute Rangers v Neilston
Oct01  w/o  Neilston v Bute Rangers - scr.
Sep24  7-1  Port Glasgow Athletic v Saltcoats Victoria
Sep24  9-2  Pollockshaws v Glasgow Wanderers
Sep24 10-3  Annbank v Carrington
Sep24  2-2  Arthurlie v Airdrieonians
Oct01  6-3  Airdrieonians v Arthurlie
Sep24  2-0  Ayr Parkhouse v Greenock Morton
Sep24  4-1  Carfin Shamrock v Airdriehill
Sep24  3-1  Partick Thistle v Johnstone
Sep24  2-3  Kilbirnie v Cowlairs
Sep24 16-0  Stevenston Thistle v Girvan Athletic
Sep24  w/o  Royal Albert v Glengowan - scr.
```

```
Sep24   5-2   Galston v Kilbarchan
Sep24  10-0   Albion Rovers v Carfin Hibernian
        bye   Monkcastle
```
East of Scotland, Dumbartonshire, Fifeshire and Stirlingshire
```
Sep24   w/o   Broxburn Shamrock v Bridge of Allan - scr.
Sep24   1-3   Raith Rovers v Smithston Hibernians
Sep24   4-1   Levendale v Bathgate Rovers
Sep24   6-0   Union (Dumbarton) v Grasshoppers
Sep24   3-6   Vale of Leven v East Stirlingshire
Sep24   2-2   Polton Vale v Grangemouth
Oct01   3-3   Grangemouth v Polton Vale
Sep24   1-5   Laurieston v King's Park
Sep24   4-3   Clackmannan v Armadale
Sep24   0-1   Denny v Kilsyth Wanderers
Sep24   6-2   Cowdenbeath v Kirkcaldy
Sep24   2-1   Duntocher Harp v Mossend Swifts
Sep24   3-3   Linlithgow Athletic v Gairdoch
Oct01   6-0   Gairdoch v Linlithgow Athletic
Sep24   6-1   Stenhousemuir v Lochgelly United
Sep24   3-1   Campsie v Falkirk
Sep24   0-6   Kilsyth Standard v Camelon
        bye   Edinburgh University
```
Forfarshire and Perthshire
```
Sep24   3-3   Vale of Ruthven v* Strathmore Athletic
Oct01   0-4   Vale of Ruthven v Strathmore Athletic
Sep24   3a3   Johnstone Wanderers v Harp (Dundee) - abd. 80mins referee
Oct01   3-2   Harp (Dundee) v Johnstone Wanderers
Sep24   2-5   Our Boys (Blairgowrie) v Arbroath
Sep24   2-0   Dunblane v St Johnstone
Sep24   2-3   East End v Forfar Athletic
        bye   Our Boys (Dundee)
```
Argyllshire
```
Sep24   w/o   Inveraray v Oban - scr.
```
Aberdeenshire
```
Sep24   9-2   Aberdeen v Peterhead
        bye   Orion
```
Northern Counties
```
Sep24   1-2   Inverness Union v Inverness Caledonian
```
Southern Counties
```
Sep24   2-2   Douglas Rovers v Annan
Oct01   w/o   Annan v Douglas Rovers - scr.
Sep24   3-10  Stranraer v Q.O.S. Wanderers
Sep24   6-4   St Cuthbert Wanderers v Moffat
        bye   5th K.R.V.
```

Preliminary Stage Third Round
Glasgow, Lanarkshire, Renfrewshire, Ayrshire and Argyllshire
```
Oct15   6-0   Royal Albert v Stevenston Thistle
Oct15   5-0   Monkcastle v Neilston
Oct15   4-2   Airdrieonians v Carfin Shamrock
Oct15   2-2   Cowlairs v Galston
Oct22   0-2   Galston v Cowlairs
Oct15   4-2   Albion Rovers v Port Glasgow Athletic
Oct15   w/o   Annbank v Inveraray - scr.
Oct15   4-2   Pollockshaws v Wishaw Thistle
Oct15   2-2   Partick Thistle v Motherwell
Oct22   3-3   Motherwell v Partick Thistle - both qualified
        bye   Ayr Parkhouse
```
East of Scotland, Dumbartonshire, Fifeshire, Stirlingshire and Clackmannanshire

```
Oct15   4-0   Gairdoch v Polton Vale
Oct15   3-1   Broxburn Shamrock v East Stirlingshire
Oct15   3-3   Campsie v Grangemouth
Oct22   2-4   Grangemouth v Campsie
Oct15   3-3   Cowdenbeath v Stenhousemuir
Oct22   7-2   Stenhousemuir v Cowdenbeath
Oct15   4-1   Camelon v Kilsyth Wanderers
Oct15   4-2   Levendale v Duntocher Harp
Oct15   2-3   Union (Dumbarton) v Clackmannan
Oct15   1-2   Smithston Hibernians v King's Park
        bye   Edinburgh University
```

Forfarshire and Perthshire
```
Oct15   2-2   Our Boys (Dundee) v Dunblane
Oct22   5-2   Dunblane v Our Boys (Dundee)
Oct15  16-0   Arbroath v* Strathmore Athletic
Oct15   2-2   Harp (Dundee) v Forfar Athletic
Oct22   3-2   Forfar Athletic v Harp (Dundee)
```

Southern Counties
```
Oct15   1-9   St Cuthbert Wanderers v 5th K.R.V.
Oct15   1-3   Annan v Q.O.S. Wanderers
```

Northern Counties and Aberdeenshire
```
Oct15   3-3   Orion v Aberdeen
Oct22   4-2   Aberdeen v Orion
        bye   Inverness Caledonian
```

Preliminary Stage Fourth Round
```
Nov05   2-5   Inverness Caledonian v Aberdeen
Nov05   1-2   Pollockshaws v Albion Rovers
Nov05   w/o   Monkcastle v Edinburgh University - scr.
Nov05   6-3   Campsie v Arbroath
Nov05   6-2   5th K.R.V. v Ayr Parkhouse
Nov05   4-1   Motherwell v Levendale
Nov05   8-3   Stenhousemuir v Forfar Athletic
Nov05   4-3   Broxburn Shamrock v Partick Thistle
Nov05   4-2   Q.O.S. Wanderers v Clackmannan  at Holm Quarry
Nov05   1-3   Gairdoch v King's Park
        bye   Annbank, Cowlairs, Camelon, Airdrieonians
        bye   Dunblane, Royal Albert
```

Final Stage First Round
```
Nov26   3-1   Celtic v Linthouse
Nov26   3-6   Airdrieonians v 3rd L.R.V.
Jan21   1-4   Cowlairs v Queen's Park
Dec17   1a6   Clyde v Dumbarton - abd. 65mins crowd
Nov26   9-2   Motherwell v Campsie - prot.
Dec17   6-4   Motherwell v Campsie
Nov26   4-6   Aberdeen v* St Mirren
Nov26   0-3   Dunblane v Broxburn Shamrock
Nov26   1-1   Stenhousemuir v Heart of Midlothian
Dec17   8-0   Heart of Midlothian v Stenhousemuir
Nov26   1-3   Northern v Leith Athletic
Nov26   6-1   Royal Albert v Cambuslang
Nov26   6-0   Abercorn v Renton
Nov26   1-2   Albion Rovers v Kilmarnock
Nov26   5-1   St Bernard's v Q.O.S. Wanderers
Nov26   7-0   Rangers v Annbank
Nov26   6-1   King's Park v Monkcastle
Nov26   5-3   5th K.R.V. v Camelon
```

Final Stage Second Round
Jan21 0-1 Dumbarton v Rangers
Dec17 0-2 Leith Athletic v St Mirren
Jan28 0-8 Kilmarnock v Queen's Park
Dec24 2-4 Motherwell v Heart of Midlothian
Dec17 7-0 Celtic v 5th K.R.V.
Dec17 1-1 Royal Albert v St Bernard's
Dec24 5-2 St Bernard's v Royal Albert
Dec17 4-5 Abercorn v 3rd L.R.V.
Dec17 3-0 Broxburn Shamrock v King's Park

Final Stage Third Round
Feb04 1-1 Heart of Midlothian v Queen's Park
Feb11 5-2 Queen's Park v Heart of Midlothian
Jan21 4-3 Broxburn Shamrock v St Mirren
Jan28 3-2 St Bernard's v Rangers
Jan21 5-1 Celtic v 3rd L.R.V.

Semi-finals
Feb18 4-2 Queen's Park v Broxburn Shamrock at Hampden Park
Feb04 5-0 Celtic v St Bernard's at Celtic Park

Final
Mar11 1-2 Celtic v Queen's Park at Ibrox Park

Season 1893-94

Preliminary Stage First Round
Glasgow and Lanarkshire
Sep02 scr   Southern Athletic v 2nd Battalion Black Watch - w/o
Sep02 scr   Maryhill v Royal Albert - w/o
Sep02 scr   Kelvinside Athletic v Hamilton Academical - w/o
Sep02 1-3   Shettleston Swifts v 4th VBSR (Cameronians)
Sep02 0-5   Airdriehill v Motherwell
Sep02 0-3   Northern v Wishaw Thistle
Sep02 3-3   Partick Thistle v Airdrieonians
Sep09 3-1   Airdrieonians v Partick Thistle
Sep02 6-1   Cambuslang v Carrington
Sep02 scr   Whitefield v Albion Rovers - scr.
Sep02 2-3   Glengowan v Burnbank Swifts
Sep02 w/o   Hamilton Harp v Fairfield - scr.
Sep02 0-2   Glasgow Wanderers v Dykehead
Sep02 11-1 Cowlairs v* Carfin Hibernian
Sep02 w/o   Carfin Shamrock v Whifflet Shamrock - scr.
Sep02 w/o   Battlefield v United Abstainers - scr.
Renfrewshire and Ayrshire
Sep02 3-4   Bute Rangers v Neilston
Sep02 3-3   Hurlford v Kilbirnie
Sep09 2-3   Kilbirnie v Hurlford
Sep02 2-5   Lochwinnoch v Cronberry Eglinton
Sep02 4-0   Galston v Kilwinning Eglinton
Sep02 w/o   Port Glasgow Athletic v Bridge of Weir - scr.
Sep02 4-3   Beith v Kilbarchan
Sep02 12-2 Newmilns v Cumnock Springbank
Sep02 4-2   Ayr v Ayr Parkhouse
Sep02 scr   Paisley Academicals v Annbank - scr.

```
Sep02   4-1   Paisley Celtic v Dykebar
Sep02   npl   Girvan Athletic v Pollockshaws
Sep16   w/o   Pollockshaws v Girvan Athletic - scr.
Sep02   3-2   Johnstone v Kilmarnock Athletic
Sep02   3-3   Lanemark v Cathcart Volunteers
Sep09   3-4   Cathcart Volunteers v Lanemark
Sep02   6-0   Cartvale v 1st Argyll R.V.
Sep02   5-3   Kilmarnock v Greenock Morton
Sep02   w/o   Monkcastle v Mauchline - scr.
Sep02   5-3   Stevenston Thistle v Thornliebank
Sep02   5-3   Saltcoats Victoria v Arthurlie
Sep02   5-2   Irvine v Dalry
```

East of Scotland and Fifeshire
```
Sep02   5-0   Selkirk v Vale of Gala
Sep02   1-2   Cowdenbeath v Hibernian
Sep02   8-1   Armadale v 1st Argyll and Sutherland Highlanders
Sep02   2-5   Uphall v Polton Vale
Sep02   9-0   Mossend Swifts v Adventurers
Sep02   0-0   Bathgate v Kirkcaldy
Sep09   3-2   Kirkcaldy v Bathgate
Sep02   6-2   Muirhouse Rovers v Penicuik Athletic
Sep02   8-0   Raith Rovers v Dunfermline Athletic
Sep02   w/o   Lochgelly United v Linlithgow Athletic - scr.
Sep02   4-3   Bonnyrigg Rose v Bo'ness
        bye   Broxburn
        bye   Edinburgh University
```

Dumbartonshire, Stirlingshire and Clackmannanshire
```
Sep02   w/o   Duntocher Harp v Union (Dumbarton) - scr.
Sep02   scr   Campsie v Camelon - w/o
Sep02   0-2   Kirkintilloch Athletic v Slamannan Rovers
Sep02   8-0   Denny v Bridge of Allan
Sep02   2-3   Kilsyth Hibernian v Vale of Leven
Sep02   w/o   Falkirk v* Clydebank - scr fm.
Sep02   scr   Vale of Leven Wanderers v Clackmannan - w/o
Sep02   5-1   Kilsyth Wanderers v Dunipace
Sep02   3-2   Gairdoch v Stenhousemuir
Sep02   w/o   Laurieston v Vale of Bannock - scr.
Sep02   2-1   Dalmuir Thistle v Slamannan
Sep02   4-0   Grangemouth v Grasshoppers
Sep02   scr   Levendale v Methlan Park - w/o
Sep02   8-1   East Stirlingshire v Alva
        bye   Alloa Athletic
```

Forfarshire
```
Aug30   4-6   Brechin v Harp (Dundee)
Sep02   1-6   Forfar Athletic v Strathmore (Dundee)
Sep02   7-1   Arbroath v Arbroath Wanderers
Sep02   6-2   Johnstone Wanderers v Lochee United
Sep02   2-3   Kirriemuir v Montrose
        bye   Dundee v* East End - not in existence
        bye   Our Boys (Dundee)
```

Aberdeenshire
```
Sep02    9-1   Orion v Hawthorn
Sep02   11-1   Aberdeen v Fraserburgh Wanderers
Sep02    2-3   Peterhead v Victoria United
```

Northern Counties
```
Sep02   1-3   Inverness Union v Clachnacuddin
Sep02   6-2   Inverness Thistle v Inverness Caledonian
```

Perthshire
Sep02 4-4   Dunblane v St Johnstone
Sep09 3-5   St.Johnstone v Dunblane
Sep02 5-0   Fair City Athletic v Vale of Atholl
Sep02 1-7   Vale of Ruthven v Our Boys (Blairgowrie)
Argyllshire
Sep02 w/o   Inveraray v Fort William - scr.
Sep02 1-4   Rangers (Oban) v Dunach
Dumfriesshire
Sep02 scr   6ᵗʰ G.R.V. v St Cuthbert Wanderers – w/o
Sep02 2-3   Newton Stewart Athletic v Q.O.S. Wanderers
Sep02 0-9   Thistle (Lochmaben) v 5th K.R.V.
Sep02 w/o   Annan v Douglas Rovers - scr.
Sep02 w/o   Moffat v Barholm Rovers - scr.

Preliminary Stage Second Round
Glasgow, Lanarkshire, Renfrewshire and Ayrshire
Sep23 6-2   Saltcoats Victoria v Royal Albert
Sep23 6-1   Motherwell v Burnbank Swifts
Sep23 w/o   Port Glasgow Athletic v Pollockshaws - scr.
Sep23 1-7   Hamilton Academical v Airdrieonians
Sep23 1-3   Beith v Hurlford
Sep23 1-0   Kilmarnock v Newmilns
Sep23 4-3   Cambuslang v Paisley Celtic
Sep23 2-3   Hamilton Harp v* 2ⁿᵈ Battalion Black Watch
Sep23 w/o   Cronberry Eglinton v Monkcastle - scr.
Sep23 5-3   Neilston v Stevenston Thistle
Sep23 5-1   Cowlairs v 4ᵗʰ VBSR (Cameronians)
Sep23 4-3   Battlefield v Wishaw Thistle
Sep23 5-1   Albion Rovers v Dykehead
Sep23 3-0   Galston v Irvine
Sep23 4-2   Cartvale v Annbank
Sep23 w/o   Carfin Shamrock v Lanemark - scr.
Sep23 0-1   Ayr v Johnstone
East of Scotland, Fifeshire, Dumbartonshire, Stirlingshire and Clackmannanshire
Sep23 6-2   Alloa Athletic v Bonnyrigg Rose
Sep23 5-0   Hibernian v Broxburn
Sep23 w/o   Kilsyth Wanderers v Methlan Park - scr.
Sep23 w/o   Polton Vale v Clackmannan - scr.
Sep23 3-3   Denny v Vale of Leven
Sep30 w/o   Vale of Leven v Denny - scr.
Sep23 w/o   Lochgelly United v Selkirk - scr.
Sep23 1-12 Laurieston v Falkirk
Sep23 5-0   Slamannan Rovers v Muirhouse Rovers
Sep23 0-2   Dalmuir Thistle v East Stirlingshire
Sep23 2-3   Raith Rovers v Gairdoch
Sep23 6-2   Grangemouth v Armadale
Sep23 3-5   Camelon v Kirkcaldy
Sep23 2-5   Duntocher Harp v Mossend Swifts
       bye   Edinburgh University
Forfarshire and Perthshire
----- bye   Arbroath v* Our Boys (Dundee) - not in existence
Sep23 4-2   Strathmore (Dundee) v Dundee A
Sep23 4-2   Dunblane v Fair City Athletic
Sep23 1-3   Montrose v Harp (Dundee)
Sep23 9-1   Johnstone Wanderers v Our Boys (Blairgowrie)
Argyllshire
Sep23 1-3   Dunach v Inveraray
Aberdeenshire

```
Sep23   8-0   Victoria United v Aberdeen
        bye   Orion
```
Northern Counties
```
Sep23   4-3   Inverness Thistle v Clachnacuddin
```
Southern Counties
```
Sep23   5-0   5ᵗʰ K.R.V. v Annan
Sep23  15-1   Q.O.S. Wanderers v Moffat
        bye   St Cuthbert Wanderers
```

Preliminary Stage Third Round
Glasgow, Lanarkshire, Renfrewshire, Ayrshire and Argyllshire
```
Oct14   7-0   Albion Rovers v Neilston
Oct14   2-2   Galston v Cambuslang
Oct21   2-2   Cambuslang v Galston - both qualified
Oct14   1a3   Cronberry Eglinton v Battlefield - abd. 86mins darkness
Oct28   1-5   Cronberry Eglinton v Battlefield
Oct14   3-3   Cowlairs v 2nd Battalion Black Watch
Oct21   1-1   Cowlairs v 2nd Battalion Black Watch - both qualified
Oct14   scr   Inveraray v Port Glasgow Athletic - w/o
Oct14   3-0   Hurlford v Johnstone
Oct14   4-2   Lanemark v Saltcoats Victoria
Oct14   1-3   Cartvale v Airdrieonians
Oct14   3-3   Kilmarnock v Motherwell
Oct21   1-3   Motherwell v Kilmarnock
```
Southern Counties
```
Oct14   2-2   St Cuthbert Wanderers v 5ᵗʰ K.R.V.
Oct21   9-0   5ᵗʰ K.R.V. v St Cuthbert Wanderers
        bye   Q.O.S. Wanderers
```
Dumbartonshire, Clackmannanshire, Fifeshire, Stirlingshire and East of Scotland
```
Oct14   4-5   Alloa Athletic v Falkirk
Oct14   3-1   Gairdoch v Polton Vale
Oct14   1-4   Lochgelly United v Kilsyth Wanderers
Oct14   npl   Kirkcaldy v Mossend Swifts  - M. missed the train
Oct28   3-3   Kirkcaldy v Mossend Swifts
-----   w/o   Mossend Swifts v Kirkcaldy - scr.
Oct14   1-0   Vale of Leven v Hibernian
Oct14   3-0   Grangemouth v Slamannan Rovers
        bye   East Stirlingshire
        bye   Edinburgh University
```
Aberdeen and Northern Counties
```
Oct14   1-6   Victoria United v Orion
        bye   Inverness Thistle
```
Forfarshire and Perthshire
```
Oct14   w/o   Dunblane v Johnstone Wanderers - scr.
Oct14   3-2   Strathmore (Dundee) v Arbroath - prot.
Oct28   3-3   Strathmore (Dundee) v Arbroath
Nov04   3-1   Arbroath v Strathmore (Dundee)
        bye   Harp (Dundee)
```

Preliminary Stage Fourth Round
```
Nov04   1-3   Harp (Dundee) v East Stirlingshire
Nov04   4-3   Inverness Thistle v* Q.O.S. Wanderers
Nov04   4-2   5ᵗʰ K.R.V. v Dunblane
Nov04   3-3   Edinburgh University v Hurlford
Nov11   8-1   Hurlford v Edinburgh University
Nov04   4-2   Orion v Kilsyth Wanderers
Nov04   7-0   Cambuslang v Gairdoch
Nov04   8-1   Battlefield v Lanemark
Nov04   3-3   Falkirk v Albion Rovers
```

```
Nov11   5-2   Albion Rovers v Falkirk
Nov04   2-2   Mossend Swifts v Port Glasgow Athletic
Nov11   9-3   Port Glasgow Athletic v Mossend Swifts
Nov04   3-1   Grangemouth v Galston
        bye   Kilmarnock, Arbroath, Airdrieonians
        bye   2nd Battalion Black Watch, Vale of Leven, Cowlairs
```

Final Stage First Round
```
Nov25   9-3    3rd L.R.V. v Inverness Thistle
Nov25   1-7    Grangemouth v Renton
Nov25   3-2    Cambuslang v East Stirlingshire
Nov25   1-0    St Mirren v Heart of Midlothian
Nov25   2-1    Abercorn v 5th K.R.V.
Nov25   1-3    Kilmarnock v St Bernard's
Nov25   6-0    Albion Rovers v 2nd Battalion Black Watch
Nov25   2-5    King's Park v Clyde
Nov25   1-5    Linthouse v Queen's Park
Nov25   1-3    Thistle (Glasgow) v Battlefield
Nov25   8-0    Rangers v Cowlairs
Nov25   2-11   Orion v Leith Athletic
Nov25   6-0    Celtic v Hurlford
Nov25   1-2    Vale of Leven v Dumbarton
Nov25   3-8    Broxburn Shamrock v Arbroath
Nov25   7-5    Port Glasgow Athletic v Airdrieonians
```

Final Stage Second Round
```
Dec16   6-0   Clyde v Cambuslang
Dec16   0-3   Arbroath v Queen's Park
Dec16   3-3   Battlefield v Abercorn
Dec23   3-0   Abercorn v Battlefield
Dec16   2-0   Rangers v Leith Athletic
Dec16   1-3   Dumbarton v St Bernard's
Dec16   2-2   Renton v Port Glasgow Athletic - prot.
Dec23   1-3   Renton v Port Glasgow Athletic
Dec16   3-2   3rd L.R.V. v St Mirren
Dec16   7-0   Celtic v Albion Rovers
```

Final Stage Third Round
```
Jan13   2-1   3rd L.R.V. v Port Glasgow Athletic
Jan13   3-3   Abercorn v Queen's Park
Jan20   3-3   Queen's Park v Abercorn
Jan27   0-2   Abercorn v Queen's Park  at Ibrox Park
Jan13   0-5   Clyde v Rangers
Jan13   8-1   Celtic v St Bernard's
```

Semi-finals
```
Feb03   1-1   Rangers v Queen's Park  at Ibrox Park
Feb10   1-3   Queen's Park v Rangers  at Hampden Park
Feb03   3-5   3rd L.R.V. v Celtic  at Cathkin Park
```

Final
```
Feb17   1-3   Celtic v Rangers  at Hampden Park
```

Season 1894-95

Preliminary Stage First Round
Glasgow and Lanarkshire
Sep01   4-4   Cowlairs v Dykehead
Sep08   1-1   Dykehead v Cowlairs
Sep15   1-2   Cowlairs v Dykehead   at Airdrie
Sep01   3-2   Airdriehill v Gaelic
Sep01   3-5   Albion Rovers v Carfin
Sep01   w/o   Motherwell v Glasgow Wanderers - scr.
Sep01   0-6   4th VBSR (Cameronians) v Airdrieonians
Sep01   6-1   Partick Thistle v Royal Albert
Sep01   1-3   Glengowan v Wishaw Thistle
Sep01   3-5   Cambuslang v Linthouse
Sep01   3-3   Northern v Gordon Highlanders
Sep08   4-1   Northern v Gordon Highlanders
Sep01   5-3   Burnbank Swifts v Hamilton Academical - prot.
Sep22   1-4   Hamilton Academical v Burnbank Swifts
        bye   Hamilton Harp

Renfrewshire, Ayrshire and Argyllshire
Sep01   4-1   Monkcastle v Neilston
Sep01   w/o   Girvan Athletic v Bridge of Weir - scr.
Sep01   5-6   Kilwinning Eglinton v Paisley Celtic
Sep01   3-2   Ayr Parkhouse v Ayr
Sep01   scr   Pollockshaws v Kilmarnock - w/o
Sep01   w/o   Hurlford v Cathcart Volunteers - scr.
Sep01   3-1   Cartvale v Lochwinnoch
Sep01   4-6   Cronberry Eglinton v Paisley Academicals
Sep01   w/o   Thornliebank v Inveraray - scr.
Sep01   0-2   Arthurlie v Kilmarnock Athletic
Sep01   w/o   Galston v Bute Rangers - scr.
Sep01   1-7   Irvine v Annbank
Sep01   2-3   Kilbirnie v Lanemark
Sep01   1-4   Beith v Port Glasgow Athletic
Sep01   9-0   Greenock Morton v Saltcoats Victoria
Sep01   1-4   Dalry v Stevenston Thistle
Sep01   scr   Dykebar v Johnstone - w/o
        bye   Kilbarchan

East of Scotland, Fifeshire and Border Counties
Sep01   1-8   Selkirk v Raith Rovers
Sep01   3-3   Kirkcaldy v Polton Vale
Sep08   5-2   Polton Vale v Kirkcaldy
Sep01   0-5   Kelso v Uphall
Sep01   1-4   Bonnyrigg Rose v Bo'ness
Sep01   1-3   Lochgelly United v Mossend Swifts
Sep01   4-2   Penicuik Athletic v Casuals
Sep01   2-2   Adventurers v 2nd Battalion Black Watch
Sep08   2-5   2nd Battalion Black Watch v Adventurers
Sep01 11-1   Broxburn Shamrock v Loch Rangers
Sep01   4-1   Linlithgow Athletic v Bathgate
Sep01   2-4   Townhill v Cowdenbeath
        bye   Edinburgh University

Dumbartonshire, Stirlingshire and Clackmannanshire
Sep01   w/o   Camelon v Clydebank - scr.
Sep01   0-3   Dalmuir Thistle v Alloa Athletic
Sep01   5-3   Dunipace v Vale of Leven
Sep01   4-4   Slamannan Rovers v Grasshoppers
Sep08   0-7   Grasshoppers v Slamannan Rovers - prot.

Sep15 w/o Slamannan Rovers v Grasshoppers - scr.
Sep01 7-2 King's Park v Newtown Thistle
Sep01 3-2 Laurieston v Alva
Sep01 7-1 Stenhousemuir v* Slamannan
Sep01 7-0 Falkirk v* Kilsyth Hibernian
Sep01 2-4 Duntocher Harp v Clackmannan
Sep01 w/o Kilsyth Wanderers v Grangemouth - scr.
       bye Gairdoch

Forfarshire
Sep01 w/o Forfar Athletic v West End (Dundee) - scr.
Sep01 0-7 Kirriemuir v Lochee United
Sep01 11-0 Dundee Wanderers v* Arbroath Wanderers
Sep01 2-1 Arbroath v Montrose
       bye Brechin

Aberdeenshire
Sep01 3-3 Aberdeen v Orion
Sep08 5-1 Orion v Aberdeen
Sep01 8-1 Victoria United v Peterhead

Northern Counties
Sep01 2-0 Inverness Caledonian v Clachnacuddin
Sep01 3-1 Inverness Thistle v* Inverness Union

Perthshire
Sep01 3-5 Duncrub Park v Fair City Athletic
Sep01 1-3 St Johnstone v* Rob Roy
Sep01 4-3 Vale of Atholl v Dunblane
       bye Vale of Ruthven

Southern Counties
Sep01 w/o Mid-Annandale v Garlieston - scr.
Sep01 2-4 Annan v 5th K.R.V.
Sep01 3-5 Barholm Rovers v Newton Stewart Athletic
Sep08 w/o St Cuthbert Wanderers v 6th G.R.V. - scr.

Preliminary Stage Second Round
Glasgow, Lanarkshire, Ayrshire and Renfrewshire
Sep22 3-7 Kilbarchan v Ayr Parkhouse
Sep22 0-0 Hamilton Harp v Northern
Sep29 4-1 Northern v Hamilton Harp
Sep22 2-1 Linthouse v Burnbank Swifts
Sep22 1-3 Airdriehill v Motherwell
Sep22 5-3 Galston v Wishaw Thistle
Sep22 4-0 Stevenston Thistle v Monkcastle
Sep22 3-0 Annbank v Partick Thistle
Sep22 3-4 Paisley Celtic v Paisley Academicals
Sep22 6-0 Port Glasgow Athletic v Hurlford
Sep22 2-1 Lanemark v Kilmarnock Athletic
Sep22 scr Girvan Athletic v Airdrieonians - w/o
Sep22 4-2 Thornliebank v Johnstone
Sep22 4-4 Carfin v Kilmarnock
Sep29 4-2 Kilmarnock v Carfin
Sep22 4-2 Dykehead v Greenock Morton
       bye Cartvale

East of Scotland, Fifeshire, Dumbartonshire, Stirlingshire and Clackmannanshire
Sep22 4-0 Falkirk v Gairdoch
Sep22 3-1 Slamannan Rovers v Stenhousemuir
Sep22 4-1 Polton Vale v Penicuik Athletic
Sep22 2-0 Mossend Swifts v Kilsyth Wanderers - prot.
Oct05 5-0 Mossend Swifts v Kilsyth Wanderers
Sep22 w/o Clackmannan v Laurieston - scr.

```
Sep22   6-7   Alloa Athletic v Adventurers
Sep22   2-5   Linlithgow Athletic v Bo'ness
Sep22   3-1   Camelon v Broxburn Shamrock
Sep22   5-0   Cowdenbeath v Dunipace
Sep22   2-4   Uphall v Raith Rovers
        bye   King's Park
        bye   Edinburgh University
```
Forfarshire and Perthshire
```
Sep22   0-5   Vale of Ruthven v Lochee United
Sep22   4-1   Forfar Athletic v Brechin
Sep22   4-1   Vale of Atholl v Arbroath
Sep22   4-1   Fair City Athletic v* Rob Roy
        bye   Dundee Wanderers
```
Aberdeenshire
```
Sep22   4-4   Victoria United v Orion
Sep29   5-0   Orion v Victoria United
```
Northern Counties
```
Sep22   1-0   Inverness Thistle v Inverness Caledonian
```
Southern Counties
```
Sep22   2-1   St Cuthbert Wanderers v Mid-Annandale
Sep22  12-2   5th K.R.V. v Newton Stewart Athletic
```

Preliminary Stage Third Round
Glasgow, Lanarkshire. Ayrshire and Renfrewshire
```
Oct13   2-3   Cartvale v Annbank
Oct13   2-4   Thornliebank v Stevenston Thistle
Oct13   4-0   Galston v Port Glasgow Athletic
Oct13   4-2   Airdrieonians v Linthouse
Oct13   1-3   Dykehead v Kilmarnock
Oct13   3-7   Paisley Academicals v Motherwell
Oct13   2-5   Lanemark v Ayr Parkhouse
        bye   Northern
```
East of Scotland, Fifeshire, Dumbartonshire, Stirlingshire and Clackmannanshire
```
Oct13   3-2   King's Park v Camelon
Oct13   5-1   Slamannan Rovers v Adventurers
Oct13   8-2   Polton Vale v Falkirk
Oct13   1-3   Clackmannan v Mossend Swifts
Oct13   3-3   Cowdenbeath v Raith Rovers
Oct27   2-1   Raith Rovers v Cowdenbeath
        bye   Bo'ness
        bye   Edinburgh University
```
Forfarshire and Perthshire
```
Oct13   5-3   Forfar Athletic v Dundee Wanderers
Oct13   2-0   Lochee United v Vale of Atholl
        bye   Fair City Athletic
```
Aberdeenshire and Northern Counties
```
Oct13   3-1   Orion v Inverness Thistle
```
Southern Counties
```
Oct13   3-0   5th K.R.V. v St Cuthbert Wanderers
```

Preliminary Stage Fourth Round
```
Nov03   2-2   Bo'ness v Ayr Parkhouse
Nov17   6-1   Ayr Parkhouse v Bo'ness
Nov03   1-3   Fair City Athletic v Airdrieonians
Nov03   9-1   King's Park v* Edinburgh University
Nov03   4-0   Forfar Athletic v Northern
        bye   5th K.R.V., Annbank, Stevenston Thistle
        bye   Raith Rovers
        bye   Motherwell, Galston, Lochee United, Kilmarnock
```

```
bye  Slamannan Rovers, Polton Vale, Mossend Swifts
bye  Orion
```

Final Stage First Round
```
Nov24  2-1  Dumbarton v Galston
Nov24  5-3  Ayr Parkhouse v Polton Vale
Nov24  6-1  Hibernian v Forfar Athletic
Nov24  1-5  Orion v Dundee
Nov24  2-5  Lochee United v King's Park
Nov24  4-1  Celtic v Queen's Park
Nov24  6-3  Raith Rovers v 5th K.R.V. - prot.
Dec08  4-3  5th K.R.V. v Raith Rovers
Nov24  1-2  Rangers v Heart of Midlothian
Nov24  2a3  Slamannan Rovers v Renton - abd. 84mins darkness
Dec08  4-0  Renton v Slamannan Rovers
Nov24  7-2  Clyde v Stevenston Thistle
Nov24  1-2  Motherwell v Mossend Swifts
Nov24  5-4  Annbank v 3rd L.R.V.
Nov24  5-1  Kilmarnock v East Stirlingshire
Nov24  1-5  Abercorn v Leith Athletic - prot.
Dec08  4-1  Abercorn v Leith Athletic
Nov24  4-2  St Bernard's v Airdrieonians
Nov24  5-0  St Mirren v Battlefield  - prot.
Dec08  8-1  St Mirren v Battlefield
```

Final Stage Second Round
```
Dec15  2-1  King's Park v Dumbarton
Dec15  3-1  St Bernard's v Kilmarnock
Dec15  6-0  Renton v 5th K.R.V.
Dec15  2-0  Hibernian v Celtic - prot.
Dec29  0-2  Hibernian v Celtic
Dec15  2-0  Dundee v St Mirren
Dec15  1-6  Abercorn v Heart of Midlothian
Dec15  4-2  Clyde v Annbank
Dec15  3-1  Ayr Parkhouse v Mossend Swifts
```

Final Stage Third Round
```
Feb23  1-2  Clyde v St Bernard's
Jan19  1-0  Dundee v Celtic
Jan12  4-2  Heart of Midlothian v King's Park
Jan19  2-3  Ayr Parkhouse v Renton
```

Semi-finals
```
Feb16  1-1  Dundee v Renton  at Carolina Port
Feb23  3-3  Renton v Dundee  at Hampden Park
Mar09  0-3  Dundee v Renton  at Celtic Park
Mar09  0-0  Heart of Midlothian v St Bernard's  at Tynecastle Park
Mar16  1-0  St Bernard's v Heart of Midlothian  at Logie Green
```

Final
```
Apr20  1-2  Renton v St Bernard's
```

Season 1895-96

Qualifying Cup First Round
Renfrewshire and Ayrshire
```
Aug31  8-0  Galston v Johnstone
Aug31  4-0  Kilmarnock Athletic v Irvine
Aug31  3-1  Ayr Parkhouse v Saltcoats Victoria
Aug31  0-0  Beith v Kilbarchan
Sep07  1-4  Kilbarchan v Beith
Aug31  1-3  Kilbirnie v Ayr  at Milton Field
Aug31  w/o  Arthurlie v Lochwinnoch - scr.
Aug31  7-1  Lugar Boswell v Paisley Academicals
Aug31  1-0  Thornliebank v Neilston
Aug31  2-2  Stevenston Thistle v Monkcastle
Sep07  4-2  Monkcastle v Stevenston Thistle
Aug31  6-2  Abercorn v Cartvale
Aug31  4-3  Lanemark v Kilwinning Eglinton
Aug31  scr  Dalry v Paisley Celtic - w/o
Aug31  0-1  Hurlford v Annbank
```
East of Scotland, Fifeshire and Border Counties
```
Aug31  2-5  Uphall v Kirkcaldy
Aug31  2-2  Penicuik Athletic v Cowdenbeath
Sep07  8-1  Cowdenbeath v Penicuik Athletic
Aug31  4-3  Raith Rovers v Casuals
Aug31  5-1  Lochgelly United v Adventurers
Aug31  3-4  Selkirk v* 2ⁿᵈ Battalion Black Watch
Aug31  5-0  Bathgate v Linlithgow Athletic
Aug31  3-2  Polton Vale v Bonnyrigg Rose
Aug31  w/o  Bo'ness v Kelso - scr.
       bye  Mossend Swifts
```
Dumbartonshire, Stirlingshire and Clackmannanshire
```
Aug31  4-0  King's Park v* Duntocher Harp
Aug31  4-3  Clackmannan v Helensburgh Union
Aug31  2-1  Denny Athletic v Rumford Rovers
Aug31  w/o  Grasshoppers v Vale of Leven - scr.
Aug31  3-2  East Stirlingshire v Falkirk
Aug31  2-4  Gairdoch v Dunipace
Aug31  w/o  Kilsyth Hibernian v Slamannan Rovers - scr.
Aug31  3-3  Newtown Thistle v Camelon
Sep07  2-2  Camelon v Newtown Thistle
Sep14  4-3  Newtown Thistle v Camelon  at Barrowfield Park
Aug31  1-2  Kilsyth Wanderers v Alloa Athletic
       bye  Stenhousemuir
```
Glasgow and Lanarkshire
```
Aug31  1-1  Hamilton Academical v Airdrieonians
Sep07  4-1  Airdrieonians v Hamilton Academical
Aug31  2-2  Linthouse v* Gordon Highlanders
Sep07  7-3  Linthouse v Gordon Highlanders
Aug31  4-1  Glengowan v Cambuslang
Aug31  0-10 4ᵗʰ VBSR (Cameronians) v Cowlairs
Aug31  8-0  Wishaw Thistle v Battlefield - prot.
Sep07  1-1  Battlefield v Wishaw Thistle
Sep14  1-1  Wishaw Thistle v Battlefield
Sep21  1-3  Battlefield v Wishaw Thistle  at Fir Park
Aug31  1-0  Albion Rovers v Dykehead
Aug31  2-6  Burnbank Swifts v Partick Thistle
Aug31  5-2  Hamilton Harp v Northern
Aug31  2-4  Airdriehill v Blantyre
```

```
Aug31   0-1   Royal Albert v Motherwell
        bye   Gaelic
```
Forfarshire
```
Aug31   5-0   Arbroath v Brechin
Aug31   9-3   Dundee Wanderers v Forfar Athletic
Aug31   3-0   Montrose v Arbroath Wanderers
Aug31   1-2   Lochee United v Hibernian (Dundee)
        bye   Kirriemuir
```
Aberdeenshire
```
Aug31   1-9   Aberdeen v Victoria United
Aug31   0-8   Culter v Orion
        bye   Peterhead
```
Inverness-shire
```
Aug31   1-1   Inverness Thistle v Inverness Caledonian
Sep07   3-1   Inverness Caledonian v Inverness Thistle
        bye   Clachnacuddin
```
Perthshire and Argyllshire
```
Aug31   9-1   St Johnstone v Vale of Ruthven
Aug31   w/o   Rob Roy v Dunkeld & Birnam - scr.
Aug31   w/o   Our Boys (Blairgowrie) v Vale of Atholl - scr.
Sep07   4-5   West End (Oban) v Duncrub Park
Aug31   scr   Comrie v Fair City Athletic - w/o
        bye   Dunblane
```
Southern Counties
```
Aug31   2-3   Garlieston v Newton Stewart Athletic
Aug31   w/o   St Cuthbert Wanderers v Barholm Rovers - scr.
        bye   5th K.R.V.
```

Qualifying Cup Second Round
Glasgow and Suburbs, Lanarkshire, Ayrshire and Renfrewshire
```
Sep14   scr   Gaelic v Kilmarnock Athletic - w/o
Sep28   1-1   Wishaw Thistle v Albion Rovers
Oct05   5-1   Albion Rovers v Wishaw Thistle
Sep14   3-2   Ayr Parkhouse v Glengowan
Sep14   1-3   Beith v Galston
Sep14   1-0   Airdrieonians v Partick Thistle - prot.
Sep21   5-1   Partick Thistle v Airdrieonians
Sep14   0-0   Thornliebank v Arthurlie
Sep21   1-0   Arthurlie v Thornliebank
Sep14   0-3   Monkcastle v Blantyre
Sep14   2-3   Motherwell v Abercorn
Sep14   6-2   Linthouse v Cowlairs
Sep14   5-1   Lanemark v Lugar Boswell
Sep14   3-0   Annbank v Hamilton Harp
Sep14   5-1   Ayr v Paisley Celtic
```

East of Scotland, Fifeshire, Dumbartonshire and Clackmannanshire
```
Sep14   3-2   King's Park v Mossend Swifts
Sep14   7-0   Stenhousemuir v Bathgate
Sep14   7-0   East Stirlingshire v 2nd Battalion Black Watch
Sep14   7-1   Polton Vale v Denny Athletic
Sep14   6-2   Raith Rovers v Dunipace
Sep14   4-0   Kirkcaldy v Bo'ness
Sep21   5-0   Clackmannan v Newtown Thistle
Sep14   2-2   Kilsyth Hibernian v Cowdenbeath
Sep21   w/o   Cowdenbeath v Kilsyth Hibernian - scr.
Sep14   4-1   Lochgelly United v Grasshoppers
        bye   Alloa Athletic
```
Forfarshire, Perthshire and Argyllshire

Sep14 3-3 Our Boys (Blairgowrie) v Arbroath
Sep21 w/o Arbroath v Our Boys (Blairgowrie) - scr.
Sep14 4-6 Kirriemuir v Dunblane
Sep14 4-2 Dundee Wanderers v Duncrub Park
Sep14 2-2 Rob Roy v Fair City Athletic - prot.
Sep21 awa Rob Roy v Fair City Athletic - did not appear
Sep14 4-2 St Johnstone v Hibernian (Dundee)
       bye Montrose
Aberdeenshire
Sep14 2-5 Peterhead v Orion
       bye Victoria United
Northern Counties
Sep14 5-2 Clachnacuddin v Inverness Caledonian
Southern Counties
Sep14 8-2 5th K.R.V. v St Cuthbert Wanderers
       bye Newton Stewart Athletic

Qualifying Cup Third Round

Sep28 1-2 Galston v Lochgelly United
Sep28 3-1 St Johnstone v Orion
Sep28 2-3 Newton Stewart Athletic v Alloa Athletic
Sep28 1-3 5th K.R.V. v Arbroath
Sep28 4-1 Dundee Wanderers v Lanemark
Sep28 3-2 Arthurlie v Stenhousemuir
Oct05 4-4 Rob Roy v Clackmannan
Oct12 3-3 Clackmannan v Rob Roy
Oct19 1-2 Rob Roy v Clackmannan at Stirling
Sep28 3-1 Polton Vale v Victoria United
Sep28 1-3 Kilmarnock Athletic v Blantyre
Sep28 3-1 Raith Rovers v Montrose
Sep28 2-3 Dunblane v Cowdenbeath
Sep28 7-1 Ayr v Clachnacuddin
Sep28 3-0 Annbank v Linthouse
Sep28 1-0 King's Park v Ayr Parkhouse
Sep28 3-0 Abercorn v Kirkcaldy
Oct12 0-2 Albion Rovers v East Stirlingshire
       bye Partick Thistle

Qualifying Cup Fourth Round

Oct12 5-4 Alloa Athletic v Partick Thistle
       bye Lochgelly United, St Johnstone, Arbroath
       bye Polton Vale, Cowdenbeath, King's Park, Arthurlie
       bye Blantyre, Ayr, Raith Rovers, Clackmannan
       bye Dundee Wanderers, Annbank, Abercorn
       bye East Stirlingshire

Qualifying Cup Fifth Round

Oct26 2-6 St Johnstone v King's Park
Oct12 6-4 Arthurlie v Cowdenbeath
Oct26 3-2 Arbroath v Polton Vale
Oct26 2-1 Lochgelly United v Raith Rovers - prot.
Nov02 2-1 Raith Rovers v Lochgelly United
Oct26 2-3 Blantyre v East Stirlingshire
Oct26 3-1 Clackmannan v Ayr
Oct26 0-3 Alloa Athletic v Abercorn
Oct26 0-3 Dundee Wanderers v Annbank

Qualifying Cup Sixth Round
Nov09 5-1 Annbank v Arthurlie
Nov09 2-1 Arbroath v Abercorn
Nov09 0-2 Clackmannan v East Stirlingshire
Nov16 1-4 Raith Rovers v King's Park

Qualifying Cup Semi-finals
Nov23 1-2 King's Park v East Stirlingshire
Nov23 0-0 Arbroath v Annbank
Nov30 4-2 Annbank v Arbroath

Qualifying Cup Final
Dec07 1-3 East Stirlingshire v Annbank at Underwood Park

First Round
Jan11 4-3 St Johnstone v Dundee Wanderers
Jan11 1-12 Blantyre v Heart of Midlothian
Jan11 2-3 East Stirlingshire v Hibernian
Jan11 0-3 Polton Vale v Clyde
Jan11 2-3 Greenock Morton v Dundee
Jan11 7-0 St Mirren v Alloa Athletic
Jan18 3-2 Ayr v Abercorn
Jan11 1-0 Renton v Cowdenbeath
Jan18 1-1 Dumbarton v Rangers
Jan25 3-1 Rangers v Dumbarton
Jan18 6-0 3rd L.R.V. v Leith Athletic
Jan11 5-0 Arbroath v King's Park
Jan18 3-2 Annbank v Kilmarnock
Jan11 8-1 St Bernard's v* Clackmannan
Jan18 2-4 Celtic v Queen's Park
Jan18 4-2 Port Glasgow Athletic v Arthurlie
Jan11 2-1 Lochgelly United v Raith Rovers - prot.
Feb01 5-2 Raith Rovers v Lochgelly United at Newton Park

Second Round
Jan25 2-1 Renton v Clyde
Jan25 3-1 Arbroath v St Johnstone
Feb01 5-0 Rangers v St Mirren
Feb01 1-5 Ayr v Heart of Midlothian
Jan25 4-1 3rd L.R.V. v Dundee
Feb08 6-1 Hibernian v Raith Rovers
Jan25 2-0 St Bernard's v Annbank
Jan25 8-1 Queen's Park v Port Glasgow Athletic

Third Round
Feb08 0-4 Arbroath v Heart of Midlothian
Feb08 3-3 3rd L.R.V. v Renton
Feb15 2-0 Renton v 3rd L.R.V.
Feb08 2-3 Queen's Park v St Bernard's
Feb15 2-3 Rangers v Hibernian

Semi-finals
Feb22 1-0 Heart of Midlothian v St Bernard's at Tynecastle Park
Feb22 2-1 Hibernian v Renton at Easter Road

Final
Mar14 3-1 Heart of Midlothian v Hibernian at Logie Green

Season 1896-97

Qualifying Cup First Round
Glasgow and Lanarkshire
```
Aug29  w/o  Cameronians v Hamilton Harp - scr.
Aug29  w/o  Hamilton Academical v Dykehead - scr.
Aug29  0-3  Cambuslang v Airdrieonians
Aug29  1-1  Blantyre v Battlefield
Sep05  1-2  Battlefield v Blantyre
Aug29  1-4  Albion Rovers v Royal Albert
Aug29 14-0  Linthouse v Airdriehill
Aug28  scr  Glengowan v Motherwell - w/o
Aug29  w/o  Wishaw Thistle v Northern - scr.
Aug29  w/o  Burnbank Swifts v Gordon Highlanders - scr.
       bye  Partick Thistle
```
Ayrshire
```
Aug29  3-3  Hurlford v Beith
Sep05  0-4  Beith v Hurlford
Aug29  8-0  Kilmarnock Athletic v Irvine
Aug29  1-1  Monkcastle v* Dalry
Sep05  2-2  Monkcastle v Dalry
Sep12  3-1  Monkcastle v Dalry
Aug29  2-6  Lugar Boswell v Kilmarnock
Aug29  w/o  Ayr Parkhouse v* Kilbirnie - scr
Aug29  7-1  Lanemark v Galston
Aug29  3-2  Annbank v Stevenston Thistle
Aug29  4-5  Girvan Athletic v Kilwinning Eglinton
Aug29  1-6  Maybole v Ayr
       bye  Saltcoats Victoria
```
Renfrewshire
```
Aug29  2-2  Johnstone v Cartvale
Sep05  0-0  Cartvale v Johnstone
Sep12  4-3  Johnstone v Cartvale - aet. 3-3  at Govan
Aug29  3-2  Thornliebank v Port Glasgow Athletic
Aug29  2-5  Bridge of Weir v Lochwinnoch
Aug29  scr  Paisley Celtic v Kilbarchan - w/o
Aug29  3-1  Neilston v Paisley Academicals
       bye  Arthurlie
```
Forfarshire
```
Aug29  5-0  Forfar Athletic v Montrose
Aug29  0-1  Arbroath Wanderers v Lochee United
Aug29  4-2  Dundee Wanderers v Arbroath
```
East of Scotland, Fifeshire and Border Counties
```
Aug29  3-1  Armadale Volunteers v Broxburn Shamrock
Aug29  w/o  Bathgate v West Calder - scr.
Aug29  0-7  Benburb v Cowdenbeath
Aug29  2-2  Adventurers v Dunfermline Athletic  at Easter Road
Sep05  3-1  Dunfermline Athletic v Adventurers
Aug29  w/o  Penicuik Athletic v Linlithgow Athletic - scr.
Aug29  w/o  Lochgelly United v Bo'ness - scr.
Aug29  1-2  Mossend Swifts v Raith Rovers
Aug29  3-2  Polton Vale v Kirkcaldy
Aug29  w/o  Selkirk v Bonnyrigg Rose - scr.
       bye  Kelso
       bye  Edinburgh University
```
Dumbartonshire and Argyllshire
```
Aug29  4-4  Helensburgh v Duntocher Harp
Sep05  6-0  Duntocher Harp v Helensburgh
```

Aug29 w/o Newtown Thistle v West End (Oban) - scr.
Aug29 w/o Vale of Leven v Clydebank United - scr.
Stirlingshire and Clackmannanshire
Aug29 0-1 Dunipace v Stenhousemuir
Aug29 2-1 Kilsyth Hibernian v Denny Athletic
Aug29 2-0 King's Park v Clackmannan
Aug29 0-4 Grasshoppers v East Stirlingshire
Aug29 3-3 Falkirk v Camelon
Sep05 2-7 Camelon v Falkirk
Aug29 scr Gairdoch v Alloa Athletic - w/o
       bye Kilsyth Wanderers
Aberdeenshire
Aug29 8-0 Victoria United v* Culter
Aug29 6-2 Peterhead v Aberdeen
       bye Orion
Northern Counties
Aug29 1-1 Clachnacuddin v Inverness Caledonian
Sep05 2-0 Inverness Caledonian v Clachnacuddin
       bye Inverness Thistle
Perthshire
Aug22 2-1 Fair City Athletic v* Our Boys (Blairgowrie)
Aug29 2-4 Dunkeld & Birnam v Huntingtower
Aug29 13-1 Dunblane v Vale of Ruthven
Aug29 7-3 St Johnstone v Rob Roy
Aug29 2-2 Duncrub Park v Vale of Atholl
Sep05 4-6 Vale of Atholl v Duncrub Park
Southern Counties
Aug29 w/o St Cuthbert Wanderers v Barholm Rovers - scr.
Aug29 5-0 Newton Stewart Athletic v 5ᵗʰ K.R.V.
Aug29 6-0 6ᵗʰ G.R.V. v Douglas Wanderers

Qualifying Cup Second Round
Glasgow, Lanarkshire and Dumbartonshire
Sep12 1-1 Partick Thistle v Linthouse
Sep19 3-5 Linthouse v Partick Thistle
Sep12 8-2 Royal Albert v Duntocher Harp
Sep12 w/o Wishaw Thistle v Burnbank Swifts - scr.
Sep12 2-3 Newtown Thistle v Blantyre
Sep12 4-2 Motherwell v Airdrieonians
Sep12 5-0 Vale of Leven v Hamilton Academical
       bye Cameronians
Ayrshire
Sep12 13-2 Kilmarnock v* Saltcoats Victoria
Sep19 6-0 Annbank v Monkcastle
Sep12 4-1 Kilmarnock Athletic v Lanemark
Sep12 1-1 Ayr v Ayr Parkhouse
Sep19 0-1 Ayr Parkhouse v Ayr
Sep12 5-0 Hurlford v Kilwinning Eglinton
Renfrewshire
Sep12 0-1 Thornliebank v Arthurlie
Sep19 1-4 Lochwinnoch v Johnstone
Sep12 0-2 Neilston v Kilbarchan
Forfarshire
Sep12 1-3 Harp (Dundee) v Forfar Athletic
Sep12 1-1 Dundee Wanderers v* Lochee United
Sep19 0-1 Dundee Wanderers v Lochee United
East of Scotland, Fifeshire and Border Counties
Sep12 w/o Lochgelly United v Kelso - scr.
Sep12 2-1 Raith Rovers v Cowdenbeath

```
Sep12  w/o  Bathgate v Selkirk - scr.
Sep12  4-4  Polton Vale v Dunfermline Athletic
Sep19  3-1  Dunfermline Athletic v Polton Vale
Sep12  4-0  Penicuik Athletic v Armadale Volunteers
       bye  Edinburgh University
```

Stirlingshire and Clackmannanshire
```
Sep12  0-2  Kilsyth Wanderers v King's Park
Sep19  5-1  Falkirk v Alloa Athletic
Sep08  6-2  Stenhousemuir v Kilsyth Hibernian
       bye  East Stirlingshire
```

Aberdeenshire
```
Sep12  2-5  Victoria United v Orion
       bye  Peterhead
```

Northern Counties
```
Sep12  4-5  Inverness Caledonian v Inverness Thistle
```

Southern Counties
```
Sep12  1a1  Newton Stewart Athletic v 6ᵗʰ G.R.V. - abd. 83mins bad light
-----  w/o  Newton Stewart Athletic v 6ᵗʰ G.R.V. - scr.
       bye  St Cuthbert Wanderers
```

Perthshire
```
Sep12  0-1  Fair City Athletic v* Huntingtower
Sep12  6-2  Dunblane v St Johnstone
       bye  Duncrub Park
```

Qualifying Cup Third Round

Glasgow, Dumbartonshire and Lanarkshire
```
Sep26  1-2  Dunfermline Athletic v Blantyre
Sep26  6-2  Bathgate v Cameronians
Sep26  1-0  Raith Rovers v Vale of Leven
Sep26  0-2  Penicuik Athletic v King's Park
Sep26  2-4  Stenhousemuir v Lochgelly United
Sep26  2-2  East Stirlingshire v Falkirk
Oct03  1-1  Falkirk v East Stirlingshire
Oct10  2-0  Falkirk v East Stirlingshire  at Brockville Park
Sep26  3-5  Wishaw Thistle v Motherwell
Sep26  2-0  Partick Thistle v Royal Albert
       bye  Edinburgh University
```

Ayrshire and Renfrewshire
```
Sep26  0-1  Kilbarchan v Johnstone
Sep26  2-1  Arthurlie v Kilmarnock Athletic
Sep26  4-1  Hurlford v Annbank
Sep26  7-1  Kilmarnock v Ayr
```

Forfarshire, Aberdeenshire, Northern Counties and Perthshire
```
Sep26  7-0  Orion v Peterhead
Sep26  2-7  Huntingtower v Duncrub Park
Sep26  4-1  Dunblane v Forfar Athletic
Sep26  3-2  Inverness Thistle v Lochee United
```

Southern Counties
```
Sep26  2-6  St Cuthbert Wanderers v Newton Stewart Athletic
```

Qualifying Cup Fourth Round
```
Oct10  w/o  Inverness Thistle v Edinburgh University - scr.
       bye  Arthurlie, Bathgate, Blantyre, Dunblane
       bye  Duncrub Park, Falkirk, Hurlford
       bye  Inverness Thistle, Johnstone, Kilmarnock
       bye  King's Park, Lochgelly United, Motherwell
       bye  Newton Stewart Athletic, Orion
       bye  Partick Thistle, Raith Rovers
```

Qualifying Cup Fifth Round
```
Oct17 10-1  Inverness Thistle v* Duncrub Park
       bye  Arthurlie, Bathgate, Blantyre, Dunblane
       bye  Falkirk, Hurlford, Johnstone, Kilmarnock
       bye  King's Park, Lochgelly United, Motherwell
       bye  Newton Stewart Athletic, Orion
       bye  Partick Thistle, Raith Rovers
```

Qualifying Cup Sixth Round
```
Oct24  3-0  Motherwell v Johnstone
Oct24  4-2  Kilmarnock v Hurlford
Oct24  3-2  Arthurlie v Blantyre
Oct24  9-2  Partick Thistle v* Newton Stewart Athletic
Oct24  5-1  Orion v Bathgate
Oct24  0-3  Lochgelly United v Dunblane
Oct24  3-2  King's Park v Raith Rovers
Oct24  1-4  Inverness Thistle v Falkirk
```

Qualifying Cup Seventh Round
```
Nov07  1-3  Orion v Motherwell
Nov07  2-5  Partick Thistle v Kilmarnock
Nov07  8-2  Falkirk v Arthurlie
Nov07  3-2  Dunblane v King's Park
```

Qualifying Cup Semi-finals
```
Nov21  2-0  Kilmarnock v Dunblane
Nov21  4-1  Falkirk v Motherwell - prot.
Nov28  2a4  Falkirk v Motherwell - abd. 81mins crowd
```

Qualifying Cup Final
```
Dec05  4-1  Kilmarnock v Motherwell  at Hampden Park
```

First Round
```
Jan09  2-1  St Bernard's v Queen's Park
Jan09  4-2  Arthurlie v Celtic
Jan09  2-1  Dumbarton v Raith Rovers
Jan09  1-10 Duncrub Park v Hibernian
Jan09  5-1  St Mirren v Renton
Jan09  2-0  Falkirk v Orion
Jan09  4-0  Abercorn v Hurlford
Jan09  3-1  Greenock Morton v Johnstone
Jan09  7-1  Dundee v* Inverness Thistle
Jan09  5-1  Leith Athletic v* Dunblane
Jan09  1-2  Lochgelly v King's Park
Jan09  5-0  Blantyre v Bathgate
Jan09  2-0  Heart of Midlothian v Clyde
Jan09  3-3  Motherwell v Kilmarnock
Jan16  5-2  Kilmarnock v Motherwell
Jan09  2-4  Partick Thistle v Rangers
Jan09  8-1  3rd L.R.V. v* Newton Stewart Athletic
```

Second Round
```
Feb06  5-2  3rd L.R.V. v Heart of Midlothian
Jan23  3-0  Rangers v Hibernian
Jan30  5-0  Dundee v* King's Park
Jan23  3-1  Kilmarnock v Falkirk - prot.
Feb06  7-3  Kilmarnock v Falkirk
Feb13  1-5  Arthurlie v Greenock Morton
```

Feb06 4-4 Dumbarton v Leith Athletic
Feb13 3-3 Leith Athletic v Dumbarton
Feb20 3-2 Dumbarton v Leith Athletic at Fir Park
Jan23 4-1 Abercorn v* Blantyre
Jan30 5-0 St Bernard's v St Mirren

Third Round
Feb27 2-0 Dumbarton v St Bernard's
Feb13 3-1 Kilmarnock v 3rd L.R.V.
Feb13 0-4 Dundee v Rangers
Feb20 2-2 Greenock Morton v Abercorn
Feb27 2-3 Abercorn v Greenock Morton

Semi-finals
Mar13 2-7 Greenock Morton v Rangers at Cappielow Park
Mar13 4-3 Dumbarton v Kilmarnock at Boghead Park

Final
Mar20 1-5 Dumbarton v Rangers at Hampden Park

Season 1897-98

Qualifying Cup First Round
Lanarkshire and Glasgow
Sep11 3-1 Longriggend v 1st Argyll and Sutherland Highlanders
Sep11 3-4 Carfin v Albion Rovers
Sep11 w/o Royal Albert v Airdriehill - scr.
Sep11 3-4 Hamilton Academical v Motherwell
Sep11 5-0 Wishaw Thistle v Blantyre
Sep11 3-0 Dykehead v Linthouse
Sep11 scr Battlefield v Airdrieonians - w/o
Sep11 w/o Cameronians v Burnbank Swifts - scr.
Ayrshire
Sep11 1-2 Galston v Stevenston Thistle
Sep11 3-1 Monkcastle v Irvine
Sep11 1-2 Maybole v Kilmarnock Athletic
Sep11 1-3 Lugar Boswell v Hurlford
Sep11 w/o Lanemark v Girvan Athletic - scr.
Sep11 3-1 Ayr Parkhouse v Ayr
Sep11 w/o Kilwinning Eglinton v Saltcoats Victoria - scr.
Sep11 6-0 Annbank v Beith
Renfrewshire
Sep11 7-0 Johnstone v Lochwinnoch
Sep11 2-2 Paisley Academicals v Arthurlie
Sep18 4-0 Arthurlie v Paisley Academicals
Sep11 2-2 Neilston v Port Glasgow Athletic
Sep18 4-1 Port Glasgow Athletic v Neilston
Sep11 1-3 Kilbarchan v Cartvale
Sep11 scr Bridge of Weir v Thornliebank - w/o
East of Scotland and Border Counties
Sep11 0-2 Adventurers v Polton Vale
Sep11 w/o Trinity v Benburb - scr.
Sep11 2-3 Selkirk v* Broxburn Shamrock
Sep11 w/o Penicuik v Kelso - scr.
Sep11 4-0 West Calder v Armadale Volunteers
Sep11 8-1 Bathgate v Vale of Leithen

Sep11 1-4 Mossend Swifts v Bo'ness
Fifeshire
Sep11 3-1 Hearts of Beath v Dunfermline Athletic - prot.
Sep18 4-2 Dunfermline Athletic v Hearts of Beath
Sep11 4-0 Cowdenbeath v Kirkcaldy
Sep11 1-2 Lochgelly United v Raith Rovers
Stirlingshire
Sep11 3-1 Alloa Athletic v* Dunipace
Sep11 3-4 Falkirk v Camelon
Sep11 2-0 King's Park v Denny Athletic
Sep11 2-0 Kilsyth Wanderers v Grasshoppers
Sep11 1-6 Clackmannan v Stenhousemuir
Sep11 7-0 East Stirlingshire v Falkirk Amateurs
Dumbartonshire and Argyllshire
Sep11 6-1 Renton v* Newtown Thistle
Sep11 9-0 Vale of Leven v* West End (Oban)
Perthshire
Sep11 11-2 Dunblane v Duncrub Park
Sep11 w/o St Johnstone v Rob Roy - scr.
Sep11 3-0 Fair City Athletic v* Vale of Atholl
Sep11 w/o Huntingtower v Our Boys (Blairgowrie) - scr.
Forfarshire
Sep11 4-1 Lochee United v Montrose
Sep11 2-1 Dundee Wanderers v Arbroath
Sep11 w/o Forfar Athletic v* Arbroath Wanderers - scr.
Aberdeenshire
Sep11 2-4 Peterhead v Orion
Sep11 2-1 Victoria United v Aberdeen
Northern Counties
Sep11 4-4 Forres Mechanics v Clachnacuddin
Sep18 7-1 Clachnacuddin v Forres Mechanics
Sep11 3-0 Inverness Caledonian v Inverness Thistle
Southern Counties
Sep11 5-0 Nithsdale v St Cuthbert Wanderers at Cresswell
Sep11 2-5 Thornhill v 6th G.R.V.
Sep11 0-5 Barholm Rovers v Dumfries
Sep11 w/o Tarff Rovers v Glenarnott Athletic - scr.
Sep11 7-2 Dumfries Hibernian v Newton Stewart Athletic
       bye Douglas Wanderers

Qualifying Cup Second Round
Glasgow, Lanarkshire and Dumbartonshire
Sep25 3-0 Albion Rovers v Longriggend
Sep25 3-1 Vale of Leven v Wishaw Thistle
Sep25 2-2 Royal Albert v Airdrieonians
Oct02 2-1 Airdrieonians v Royal Albert
Sep25 1-3 Cameronians v Dykehead
Sep25 0-3 Renton v Motherwell
Ayrshire
Sep25 5-1 Ayr Parkhouse v Kilwinning Eglinton
Sep25 3-0 Kilmarnock Athletic v Stevenston Thistle
Sep25 5-0 Hurlford v Monkcastle
Sep25 3-3 Annbank v Lanemark
Oct02 1-4 Lanemark v Annbank
Renfrewshire
Sep25 4-1 Cartvale v Johnstone
Sep25 0-2 Thornliebank v Arthurlie
       bye Port Glasgow Athletic
Forfarshire

```
Sep25  3-0  Dundee Wanderers v Forfar Athletic
       bye  Lochee United
```
East of Scotland and Border Counties
```
Sep25  3a3  Penicuik v West Calder - abd. W.C. refused to play on. Awarded
                                     to P.
Sep25  w/o  Bo'ness v Broxburn Shamrock - scr.
Sep25  w/o  Bathgate v Trinity - scr.
       bye  Polton Vale
```
Fifeshire
```
Sep25  1-2  Dunfermline Athletic v Raith Rovers
       bye  Cowdenbeath
```
Stirlingshire and Clackmannanshire
```
Sep25  4a5  Kilsyth Wanderers v East Stirlingshire - abd. crowd
Oct02  5-0  East Stirlingshire v Kilsyth Wanderers  at Ochilview Park
Sep25  6-0  Stenhousemuir v King's Park
Sep25  3a2  Alloa Athletic v Camelon - abd. 80mins crowd
```
Aberdeenshire
```
Sep25  4-2  Orion v Victoria United
```
Northern Counties
```
Sep25  2-1  Inverness Caledonian v Clachnacuddin
```
Perthshire
```
Sep25  1-2  Fair City Athletic v Dunblane
Sep25  1-2  St Johnstone v Huntingtower
```
Southern Counties
```
Sep25  w/o  Douglas Wanderers v Tarff Rovers - scr.
Sep25  2-4  Dumfries v 6th G.R.V.
Sep25  2-4  Nithsdale v Dumfries Hibernian
```

Qualifying Cup Third Round
```
Oct09  2-4   Douglas Wanderers v Dumfries Hibernian
Oct09  6-3   Kilmarnock Athletic v Hurlford
Oct09  3-3   Annbank v Ayr Parkhouse
Oct16  6-1   Ayr Parkhouse v Annbank
Oct09  0-2   Inverness Caledonian v Orion
Oct09  3-0   Lochee United v Huntingtower
Oct09  4-0   Dundee Wanderers v Dunblane
Oct09  4-2   Cartvale v Dykehead
Oct09  4-0   Motherwell v Vale of Leven
Oct09  2-4   Albion Rovers v Port Glasgow Athletic
Oct09  4-2   Arthurlie v Airdrieonians
Oct09  0-1   Alloa Athletic v Raith Rovers
Oct09  3-0   Polton Vale v Cowdenbeath
Oct09  3-3   Stenhousemuir v East Stirlingshire
Oct16  2-1   East Stirlingshire v Stenhousemuir
Oct09  1-0   Bo'ness v Penicuik
       bye   6th G.R.V., Bathgate
```

Qualifying Cup Fourth Round
```
Oct23   3-2   Cartvale v Arthurlie
Oct23   2-2   Motherwell v Port Glasgow Athletic
Oct30   3-2   Port Glasgow Athletic v Motherwell
Oct23   1-2   Kilmarnock Athletic v Ayr Parkhouse
Oct23   4-2   6th G.R.V. v Dumfries Hibernian
Oct23  10-1   Orion v Lochee United
Oct23   1-2   Dundee Wanderers v Raith Rovers
Oct23   7-0   Polton Vale v Bathgate
Oct30   2-2   Bo'ness v East Stirlingshire
Nov06   6-2   East Stirlingshire v Bo'ness
```

Qualifying Cup Fifth Round
Nov06   1-3   6th G.R.V. v* Ayr Parkhouse
Nov06   1-1   Cartvale v Port Glasgow Athletic – C. didn't finish match
Nov13   4-2   Port Glasgow Athletic v Cartvale   at Cathkin Park
Nov13   1-0   East Stirlingshire v Raith Rovers
Nov06   5-0   Orion v Polton Vale

Qualifying Cup Semi-finals
Nov27   3-4   Orion v East Stirlingshire
Nov20   1-2   Ayr Parkhouse v Port Glasgow Athletic
Nov27   2-1   Port Glasgow Athletic v Ayr Parkhouse

Qualifying Cup Final
Dec18   2-4   East Stirlingshire v Port Glasgow Athletic   at Hampden Park

First Round
Jan08   8-0   Rangers v* Polton Vale
Jan08   0-8   Lochee United v Heart of Midlothian
Jan08   2-4   Raith Rovers v East Stirlingshire
Jan08   0-6   Bo'ness v Queen's Park
Jan08   2-0   Leith Athletic v Port Glasgow Athletic
Jan08   7-1   Greenock Morton v Motherwell
Jan08   1-1   St Bernard's v Dumbarton
Jan15   1-3   Dumbarton v St Bernard's
Jan08   0-7   Arthurlie v Celtic
Jan08   2-7   Dumfries Hibernian v St Mirren
Jan08   2-1   Dundee v Partick Thistle
Jan08   2-1   Ayr Parkhouse v Kilmarnock Athletic
Jan08   1-1   Abercorn v Hibernian
Jan15   7-1   Hibernian v Abercorn
Jan15   1-3   Clyde v 3rd L.R.V.
Jan08   2-4   Bathgate v Cartvale
Jan08   3-1   Dundee Wanderers v Orion
Jan08   5-1   Kilmarnock v 6th G.R.V.

Second Round
Jan22   3-1   Hibernian v East Stirlingshire
Jan22   12-0   Rangers v Cartvale
Jan22   4-1   Heart of Midlothian v Greenock Morton
Jan22   9-2   Kilmarnock v Leith Athletic
Jan22   3-2   3rd L.R.V. v Celtic
Jan22   3-6   Dundee Wanderers v Ayr Parkhouse
Jan22   2-0   Dundee v St Mirren
Jan22   0-5   St Bernard's v Queen's Park

Third Round
Feb05   2-0   3rd L.R.V. v Hibernian
Feb05   3-0   Dundee v Heart of Midlothian
Feb05   2-7   Ayr Parkhouse v Kilmarnock
Feb05   1-3   Queen's Park v Rangers

Semi-finals
Feb19   1-1   Rangers v 3rd L.R.V.   at Ibrox Park
Feb26   2-2   3rd L.R.V. v Rangers   at Cathkin Park
Mar12   0-2   3rd L.R.V. v Rangers   at Cathkin Park
Feb19   3-2   Kilmarnock v Dundee   at Rugby Park

Final
Mar26 0-2 Kilmarnock v Rangers   at Hampden Park

Season 1898-99

Qualifying Cup First Round
Glasgow and Lanarkshire
Sep10 scr Airdriehill v Royal Albert - w/o
Sep10 2-4 Dykehead v Albion Rovers
Sep10 scr Blantyre v Carfin - w/o
Sep10 w/o Uddingston v Longriggend - scr.
Sep10 6-2 Linthouse v East Lanarkshire
Sep10 3-1 Wishaw Thistle v Motherwell
Sep10 2-1 Cameronians v Glengowan
       bye Hamilton Academical
       bye Glasgow University
Ayrshire
Sep10 5-0 Maybole v Lanemark
Sep10 w/o Stevenston Thistle v Lugar Boswell - scr.
Sep10 1-3 Hurlford v Irvine
Sep17 3-3 Beith v Annbank
Oct01 3-2 Annbank v Beith
Sep10 4-3 Monkcastle v Girvan Athletic
Sep10 5-0 Ayr Parkhouse v Galston
Sep10 0-4 Kilwinning Eglinton v Ayr
       bye Kilmarnock Athletic
Renfrewshire
Sep10 1-3 Neilston v Paisley Academicals
Sep10 w/o Thornliebank v Lochwinnoch - scr.
Sep10 2-4 Kilbarchan v Arthurlie
Sep10 4-3 Abercorn v Cartvale
Sep10 6-1 Johnstone v Bridge of Weir
East of Scotland and Border Counties
Sep10 1-1 Penicuik v Bathgate
Sep17 2-2 Bathgate v Penicuik
Oct01 3-0 Penicuik v Bathgate   at Easter Road
Sep10 4-1 Polton Vale v Armadale Volunteers
Sep10 w/o Bo'ness v Selkirk - scr.
Sep10 8-1 West Calder v Mossend Swifts
Sep10 scr Broxburn Shamrock v Vale of Leithen - w/o
       bye Adventurers
Fifeshire
Sep10 2-1 Hearts of Beath v Kirkcaldy
Sep10 1-0 Lochgelly United v Raith Rovers
       bye Cowdenbeath
Stirlingshire and Clackmannanshire
Sep10 7-1 East Stirlingshire v Alloa Athletic
Sep10 w/o Stenhousemuir v Rumford Rovers - scr.
Sep10 4-4 King's Park v Kilsyth Wanderers
Sep17 7-1 Kilsyth Wanderers v King's Park
Sep10 2-3 Grasshoppers v Clackmannan
Sep10 0-2 Falkirk Amateurs v Camelon
Sep10 1-1 Denny Athletic v* Dunipace
----- w/o Dunipace v Denny Athletic - D.A. scratched
       bye Falkirk
Dumbartonshire

Sep10 0-0 Renton v Jamestown
Sep17 0-3 Jamestown v Renton
Sep10 w/o Vale of Leven v Newtown Thistle - scr.
       bye Dumbarton
Perthshire
Sep10 1-5 Duncrub Park v Crieff Morrisonians
Sep10 3-0 Dunblane v Fair City Athletic
Sep10 4-2 St Johnstone v Stanley
Sep10 3-5 Tulloch v Huntingtower
Sep17 0-5 Rob Roy v Vale of Atholl
Forfarshire
Sep10 2-0 Montrose v Dundee Wanderers
Sep10 1-1 Arbroath v Lochee United
Sep17 1-2 Lochee United v Arbroath
       bye Forfar Athletic
Aberdeenshire
Sep10 0-4 Peterhead v Orion
Sep10 5-3 Victoria United v Aberdeen - prot.
Sep17 1-3 Victoria United v Aberdeen
Northern Counties
Sep10 2-2 Inverness Thistle v Elgin City
Sep17 4-1 Elgin City v Inverness Thistle
Sep10 2-3 Clachnacuddin v Inverness Caledonian
       bye Forres Mechanics
Dumfriesshire
Sep10 2-1 Dumfries v Dumfries Hibernian
Sep10 3-2 Annan v Nithsdale
       bye Thornhill
Galloway
Sep10 w/o Douglas Wanderers v Garlieston - scr.
Sep10 w/o 6th G.R.V. v Barholm Rovers - scr.
Sep10 scr Glenarnott Athletic v St Cuthbert Wanderers - w/o
Sep10 3-0 Wigtown v Newton Stewart Athletic

Qualifying Cup Second Round
Glasgow, Lanarkshire and Dumbartonshire
Sep24 6-2 Dumbarton v Linthouse
Sep24 1-4 Hamilton Academical v Wishaw Thistle
Sep24 4-2 Albion Rovers v Vale of Leven
Sep24 2-1 Royal Albert v Cameronians
Sep24 2-1 Carfin v Uddingston
       bye Renton
       bye Glasgow University
Ayrshire
Sep24 5-3 Irvine v Kilmarnock Athletic
Oct08 1-3 Monkcastle v Annbank
Sep24 4-2 Maybole v Stevenston Thistle
Sep24 1-1 Ayr Parkhouse v Ayr
Oct01 1-1 Ayr v Ayr Parkhouse
Oct08 2-4 Ayr v Ayr Parkhouse
Renfrewshire
Sep24 3-2 Johnstone v Abercorn
Sep24 5-0 Arthurlie v Paisley Academicals
       bye Thornliebank
Forfarshire
Sep24 5-1 Forfar Athletic v Montrose
       bye Arbroath
East of Scotland and Border Counties
Sep24 0-3 Adventurers v Bo'ness at Hawkhill

```
Sep24   w/o   West Calder v Vale of Leithen - scr.
Oct08   2-0   Polton Vale v Penicuik
```
Fifeshire
```
Sep24   5-0   Cowdenbeath v Hearts of Beath
        bye   Lochgelly United
```
Stirlingshire and Clackmannanshire
```
Sep24   0-3   Falkirk v Kilsyth Wanderers
Sep24   1-4   Camelon v East Stirlingshire
Sep24   1-2   Stenhousemuir v Clackmannan
        bye   Dunipace
```
Aberdeenshire
```
Sep24   2-5   Aberdeen v Orion
```
Perthshire
```
Sep24   1-5   Crieff Morrisonians v Dunblane
Sep24   2-4   Vale of Atholl v St Johnstone
        bye   Huntingtower
```
Northern Counties
```
Sep24   5-1   Forres Mechanics v Inverness Caledonian
        bye   Elgin City
```
Southern Counties
```
Sep24   1-11  Thornhill v 6th G.R.V.
Sep24   3-6   Annan v Wigtown
Sep24   5-1   Dumfries v Douglas Wanderers
        bye   St Cuthbert Wanderers
```

Qualifying Cup Third Round
Ayrshire and Southern Counties
```
Oct15   w/o   Annbank v St Cuthbert Wanderers - scr.
Oct08   2-0   Irvine v Wigtown
Oct08   3-1   6th G.R.V. v Dumfries
Oct15   2-4   Maybole v Ayr Parkhouse
```
Northern Counties and Aberdeenshire
```
Oct08   6-0   Elgin City v Forres Mechanics
        bye   Orion
```
Perthshire and Forfarshire
```
Oct08   5-1   Forfar Athletic v Huntingtower
Oct08   0-4   St Johnstone v Arbroath
        bye   Dunblane
```
Lanarkshire, Dumbartonshire and Renfrewshire
```
Oct08   2-4   Thornliebank v Dumbarton
Oct08   2-1   Renton v Carfin
Oct08   4-2   Arthurlie v Johnstone
Oct08   5-1   Wishaw Thistle v Albion Rovers
        bye   Royal Albert
        bye   Glasgow University
```
East of Scotland, Fifeshire and Stirlingshire
```
Oct15   3-2   Bo'ness v Polton Vale
Oct08   6-2   Kilsyth Wanderers v Lochgelly United
Oct08   2-1   Cowdenbeath v Dunipace
Oct08   1-2   Clackmannan v West Calder
        bye   East Stirlingshire
```

Qualifying Cup Fourth Round
```
Oct22   6-1   Dumbarton v* Glasgow University
Oct22   4-1   Royal Albert v Cowdenbeath
Oct22   3-0   Forfar Athletic v Dunblane
Oct22   3-4   Elgin City v Arbroath
        bye   Renton, East Stirlingshire, Annbank
        bye   6th G.R.V., Irvine, Wishaw Thistle, Arthurlie
```

```
        bye  Kilsyth Wanderers, Ayr Parkhouse
        bye  West Calder, Orion, Bo'ness, Polton Vale
```

Qualifying Cup Fifth Round
North and East
```
Nov05  3-2  Bo'ness v Forfar Athletic
Nov05  0-1  Orion v Arbroath
Nov05  3-1  East Stirlingshire v West Calder
```
South and West
```
Nov12  1a4  Kilsyth Wanderers v Wishaw Thistle - abd. 85mins darkness
Nov19  3-2  Wishaw Thistle v Kilsyth Wanderers  at Celtic Park
Nov05  0-2  6th G.R.V. v Royal Albert
Nov12  2-0  Annbank v Irvine
Nov05  3-2  Renton v Dumbarton
Nov05  2-2  Ayr Parkhouse v Arthurlie
Nov12  4-1  Arthurlie v Ayr Parkhouse
```

Qualifying Cup Sixth Round
```
Nov19  2-2  Arbroath v Bo'ness
Nov26  1-2  Bo'ness v Arbroath
Dec03  1-5  Wishaw Thistle v East Stirlingshire
Nov19  2-2  Annbank v Renton
Nov26  1-0  Renton v Annbank
Nov19  0-2  Royal Albert v Arthurlie
```

Qualifying Cup Semi-finals
```
Dec10  3-1 East Stirlingshire v Renton
Dec03  5-0 Arthurlie v Arbroath
```

Qualifying Cup Final
```
Dec17  4-1 East Stirlingshire v Arthurlie   at Hampden Park
```

First Round
```
Jan14  7-1  St Mirren v Leith Athletic
Jan14  3-1  Ayr Parkhouse v Dundee
Jan14  3-2  Port Glasgow Athletic v Renton
Jan14  4-1  East Stirlingshire v Dumbarton
Jan14  3-3  Bo'ness v St Bernard's
Jan21  4-2  St Bernard's v Bo'ness
Jan14  4-1  3rd L.R.V. v Arthurlie
Jan14  3-1  Greenock Morton v Annbank
Jan14  1-8  6th G.R.V. v Celtic
Jan14  4-0  Queen's Park v* Kilsyth Wanderers
Jan14  2-1  Hibernian v Royal Albert
Jan14  4-5  Forfar Athletic v West Calder
Jan14  0-2  Orion v Kilmarnock
Jan14  5-0  Partick Thistle v Irvine
Jan14  3-3  Airdrieonians v Arbroath
Jan21  3-2  Arbroath v Airdrieonians
Jan14  4-1  Rangers v Heart of Midlothian
Jan14  3-0  Clyde v Wishaw Thistle
```

Second Round
```
Feb11  2-2  Partick Thistle v Greenock Morton
Feb18  1-2  Greenock Morton v Partick Thistle
Feb04  3-1  Port Glasgow Athletic v West Calder
Feb11  1-2  3rd L.R.V. v St Mirren
Feb11  1-4  Ayr Parkhouse v Rangers
Feb04  3-0  Celtic v St Bernard's
```

```
Feb11   5-1   Queen's Park v Hibernian
Feb11   1-1   East Stirlingshire v Kilmarnock
Feb18   0-0   Kilmarnock v East Stirlingshire
Feb25   2-4   East Stirlingshire v Kilmarnock   at Cathkin Park
Feb04   3-1   Clyde v Arbroath
```

Third Round
```
Feb18   4-0   Rangers v Clyde
Mar11   1-2   Kilmarnock v St Mirren
Feb25   7-3   Port Glasgow Athletic v Partick Thistle
Feb18   2a4   Queen's Park v Celtic - abd. 75mins darkness
Feb25   2-1   Celtic v Queen's Park
```

Semi-finals
```
Apr15   1-2   St Mirren v Rangers   at Love Street
Mar11   4-2   Celtic v Port Glasgow Athletic   at Celtic Park
```

Final
```
Apr22   2-0   Celtic v Rangers   at Hampden Park
```

Season 1899-00

Qualifying Cup First Round
Glasgow and Lanarkshire
```
Sep09   1-7   Glengowan v Uddingston
Sep09   0-1   Wishaw Thistle v Wishaw
Sep09   3-1   Carfin Emmet v Albion Rovers
Sep09   5-1   Motherwell v Linthouse
Sep09   3-0   Hamilton Academical v* Cameronians
Sep09   scr   Carfin v Royal Albert - w/o
Sep09   1-4   Glasgow University v Longriggend
Sep09   2-0   East Lanarkshire v Dykehead
```
Ayrshire
```
Sep09   4-2   Monkcastle v Annbank
Sep09   4-1   Kilwinning Eglinton v Lugar Boswell
Sep09   1-2   Ayr v Beith
Sep09   2-6   Girvan Athletic v Ayr Parkhouse
Sep09   0-1   Lanemark v Galston
Sep09   w/o   Stevenston Thistle v Kilmarnock Athletic - scr.
Sep09   w/o   Maybole v Irvine - scr.
        bye   Hurlford
```
Renfrewshire
```
Sep09   2-3   Johnstone v Thornliebank
Sep09   scr   Bridge of Weir v Cartvale - w/o
Sep09   2-1   Paisley Academicals v* Neilston
Sep09   0-4   Arthurlie v Abercorn
        bye   Kilbarchan
```
East of Scotland
```
Sep09   w/o   Selkirk v Penicuik - scr.
Sep09   scr   Armadale Volunteers v Mossend Swifts - w/o
Sep09   7-1   West Calder v Vale of Leithen
Sep09   1-4   Adventurers v Polton Vale
Sep09   4-1   Bo'ness v Bathgate
        bye   Edinburgh University
```
Fifeshire
```
Sep09   3-0   Cowdenbeath v Lochgelly United
```

```
Sep09   1-2   Dunfermline Athletic v Raith Rovers
Sep09   1-2   Kirkcaldy v Hearts of Beath
```
Stirlingshire
```
Sep09   5-1   Stenhousemuir v Dunipace
Sep09   0-6   Grasshoppers v Falkirk
Sep09   1-6   King's Park v East Stirlingshire
Sep09   scr   Slamannan v Falkirk Amateurs - w/o
Sep09   0-3   Alloa Athletic v Camelon
Sep09   1-2   Clackmannan v Kilsyth Wanderers
```
Perthshire
```
Sep09   3-3   Duncrub Park v Dunblane
Sep16   6-0   Dunblane v Duncrub Park
Sep09   3-2   Fair City Athletic v Vale of Atholl
Sep09  12-0   St Johnstone v Huntingtower
Sep09   5-1   Scone v Tulloch
Sep09   3-2   Stanley v Crieff Morrisonians
```
Forfarshire
```
Sep09   2-2   Montrose v Dundee Wanderers
Sep16   2-0   Dundee Wanderers v Montrose
Sep09   4-1   Forfar Athletic v Lochee United
        bye   Arbroath
```
Aberdeenshire
```
Sep09   6-3   Orion v* Peterhead
Sep09   0-1   Aberdeen v Victoria United
```
Northern Counties
```
Sep09   1-2   Clachnacuddin v Inverness Caledonian
Sep09   2-1   Forres Mechanics v Inverness Thistle
        bye   Elgin City
```
Dumbartonshire
```
Sep09   1-2   Renton v Dumbarton
Sep09   1-1   Clydebank v Vale of Leven
Sep16   4-0   Vale of Leven v Clydebank
        bye   Jamestown
```
Dumfriesshire
```
Sep09   3-0   Annan v Dumfries Hibernian
Sep09   7-1   Dumfries v Thornhill
```
Galloway
```
Sep09   0-0   Newton Stewart Athletic v St Cuthbert Wanderers
Sep16   0-3   St Cuthbert Wanderers v Newton Stewart Athletic
Sep09   8-1   Stranraer v Barholm Rovers
Sep09   1-6   6ᵗʰ G.R.V. v Douglas Wanderers
```

Qualifying Cup Second Round
Glasgow and Lanarkshire
```
Sep23   3-1   Wishaw v Uddingston
Sep23   2-1   Longriggend v East Lanarkshire
Sep23   1-1   Carfin Emmet v Motherwell
Sep30   3-3   Motherwell v Carfin Emmet
Oct07   2-3   Carfin Emmet v Motherwell   at Douglas Park
Sep23   1-2   Royal Albert v Hamilton Academical
```
Dumbartonshire
```
Sep23   4-2   Thornliebank v Cartvale
Sep23   scr   Jamestown v Kilbarchan - w/o
Sep30   2a3   Dumbarton v Vale of Leven - abd. 64mins crossbar
Oct14   1-4   Dumbarton v Vale of Leven
Sep23   1-1   Paisley Academicals v Abercorn
Sep30   1-1   Abercorn v Paisley Academicals
Oct07   0-3   Paisley Academicals v Abercorn   at Cathkin Park
```
Ayrshire

Sep23 5-1 Galston v Kilwinning Eglinton
Sep23 4-2 Monkcastle v Hurlford
Sep23 2-0 Maybole v Beith
Sep23 3-1 Ayr Parkhouse v Stevenston Thistle
Perthshire and Forfarshire
Sep23 8-2 Arbroath v Scone
Sep23 5-6 Dundee Wanderers v Forfar Athletic
Sep23 0-4 Stanley v Dunblane
Sep23 2-1 St Johnstone v Fair City Athletic
East of Scotland, Border Counties and Fifeshire
Sep23 0-1 West Calder v Raith Rovers
Oct07 2-0 Cowdenbeath v Mossend Swifts
Sep23 1-2 Polton Vale v Hearts of Beath
Sep23 1-1 Selkirk v Bo'ness
Sep30 npl Bo'ness v Selkirk – friendly, not playable for cup tie
Oct07 4-0 Bo'ness v Selkirk
       bye Edinburgh University
Stirlingshire
Sep23 3-3 Kilsyth Wanderers v Camelon
Oct07 2-0 Camelon v Kilsyth Wanderers
Sep23 3-0 East Stirlingshire v Falkirk Amateurs
Sep23 0-2 Stenhousemuir v Falkirk
Northern Counties
Sep23 1-1 Orion v Victoria United
Oct07 0-3 Victoria United v Orion
Sep23 2a3 Elgin City v Forres Mechanics – abd. 83mins darkness
Sep30 0-4 Elgin City v Forres Mechanics
       bye Inverness Caledonian
Dumfriesshire
Sep23 6-3 Dumfries v Annan
Galloway
Sep23 2-2 Douglas Wanderers v Stranraer
Sep30 4-2 Stranraer v Douglas Wanderers – deemed a friendly
Oct14 3-4 Stranraer v Douglas Wanderers
       bye Newton Stewart

Qualifying Cup Third Round
Lanarkshire, Dumbartonshire and Renfrewshire
Oct21 1-2 Vale of Leven v Hamilton Academical
Oct14 5-2 Abercorn v Thornliebank
Oct07 1-0 Wishaw v Longriggend
Oct14 2-5 Kilbarchan v Motherwell
East of Scotland, Fifeshire, Border Counties and Stirlingshire
Oct14 2-3 Camelon v Raith Rovers
Oct14 4-0 Falkirk v Cowdenbeath
Oct14 5-2 Bo'ness v Hearts of Beath
Oct07 w/o East Stirlingshire v Edinburgh University – scr.
Perthshire and Forfarshire
Oct07 4-4 Dunblane v Arbroath
Oct14 2-2 Arbroath v Dunblane
Oct21 1-2 Dunblane v Arbroath at Kirkcaldy
Oct07 6-0 Forfar Athletic v St Johnstone
Northern Counties and Aberdeenshire
Oct07 0-1 Inverness Caledonian v Forres Mechanics
       bye Orion
Ayrshire and Southern Counties
Oct21 3-3 Newton Stewart Athletic v Douglas Wanderers
Oct28 2-1 Douglas Wanderers v Newton Stewart Athletic
Oct07 1-8 Monkcastle v Ayr Parkhouse

```
Oct07   2-5   Dumfries v Galston
        bye   Maybole
```

Qualifying Cup Fourth Round
```
Oct21   2-2   Bo'ness v Raith Rovers
Oct28   3-1   Raith Rovers v Bo'ness
Oct21   4-2   East Stirlingshire  v Falkirk
Oct28   0-3   Forfar Athletic v Arbroath
Oct21   3-2   Orion v Forres Mechanics
Nov04   2-2   Douglas Wanderers v Maybole
Nov11   6-2   Maybole v Douglas Wanderers
Oct21   1-4   Ayr Parkhouse v Galston
Oct28   2-4   Motherwell v Hamilton Academical
Oct21   5-0   Abercorn v Wishaw
```

Qualifying Cup Fifth Round
```
Nov04   3-1   Raith Rovers v East Stirlingshire
Nov04   3-5   Orion v Arbroath
Nov18   1-4   Maybole v Galston
Nov18   2-0   Hamilton Academical v Abercorn
```

Qualifying Cup Semi-finals
North
```
Nov18   3-1   Arbroath v Raith Rovers
```
South
```
Nov25   5-2   Galston v Hamilton Academical
```

Qualifying Cup Final
```
Dec16   5-2   Galston v Arbroath   at Hampden Park
```

First Round
```
Jan13   3-4   Forfar Athletic v Motherwell
Jan13   3-0   Queen's Park v Leith Athletic
Jan13   1-1   Forres Mechanics v Orion
Jan20   4-1   Orion v Forres Mechanics
Jan13   0-0   Heart of Midlothian v St Mirren
Jan20   0-3   St Mirren v Heart of Midlothian
Jan13   7-1   Celtic v* Bo'ness
Jan13   7-1   Port Glasgow Athletic v Falkirk
Jan13   5-1   3rd L.R.V. v Raith Rovers
Jan13   8-0   Dundee v Douglas Wanderers
Jan13   4-2   Maybole v Wishaw Thistle
Jan13   5-2   Abercorn v Ayr Parkhouse
Jan13   4-2   Rangers v Greenock Morton
Jan13   1-2   Galston v Partick Thistle
Jan13   1-0   St Bernard's v Arbroath
Jan13   0-1   Airdrieonians v Clyde
Jan13   2-0   Kilmarnock v East Stirlingshire
Jan13   3-2   Hibernian v Hamilton Academical
```

Second Round
```
Jan27    1-1   Heart of Midlothian v Hibernian
Feb03    1-2   Hibernian v Heart of Midlothian
Jan27   10-0   Kilmarnock v Orion
Jan27    5-1   Queen's Park v Abercorn
Jan27    3-3   Dundee v Clyde
Feb17    0-3   Clyde v Dundee
Jan27    2-1   Partick Thistle v St Bernard's
Jan27   12-0   Rangers v Maybole
```

```
Jan27   1-5   Port Glasgow Athletic v Celtic
Jan27   2-1   3rd L.R.V. v Motherwell
```

Third Round
```
Feb17   1-6   Partick Thistle v Rangers
Feb10   1-2   3rd L.R.V. v Heart of Midlothian
Feb17   4-0   Celtic v Kilmarnock
Feb24   1-0   Queen's Park v Dundee
```

Semi-finals
```
Mar10   2-1   Queen's Park v Heart of Midlothian   at Hampden Park
Feb24   2-2   Rangers v Celtic   at Ibrox Park
Mar10   4-0   Celtic v Rangers   at Celtic Park
```

Final
```
Apr14   3-4   Queen's Park v Celtic   at Ibrox Park
```

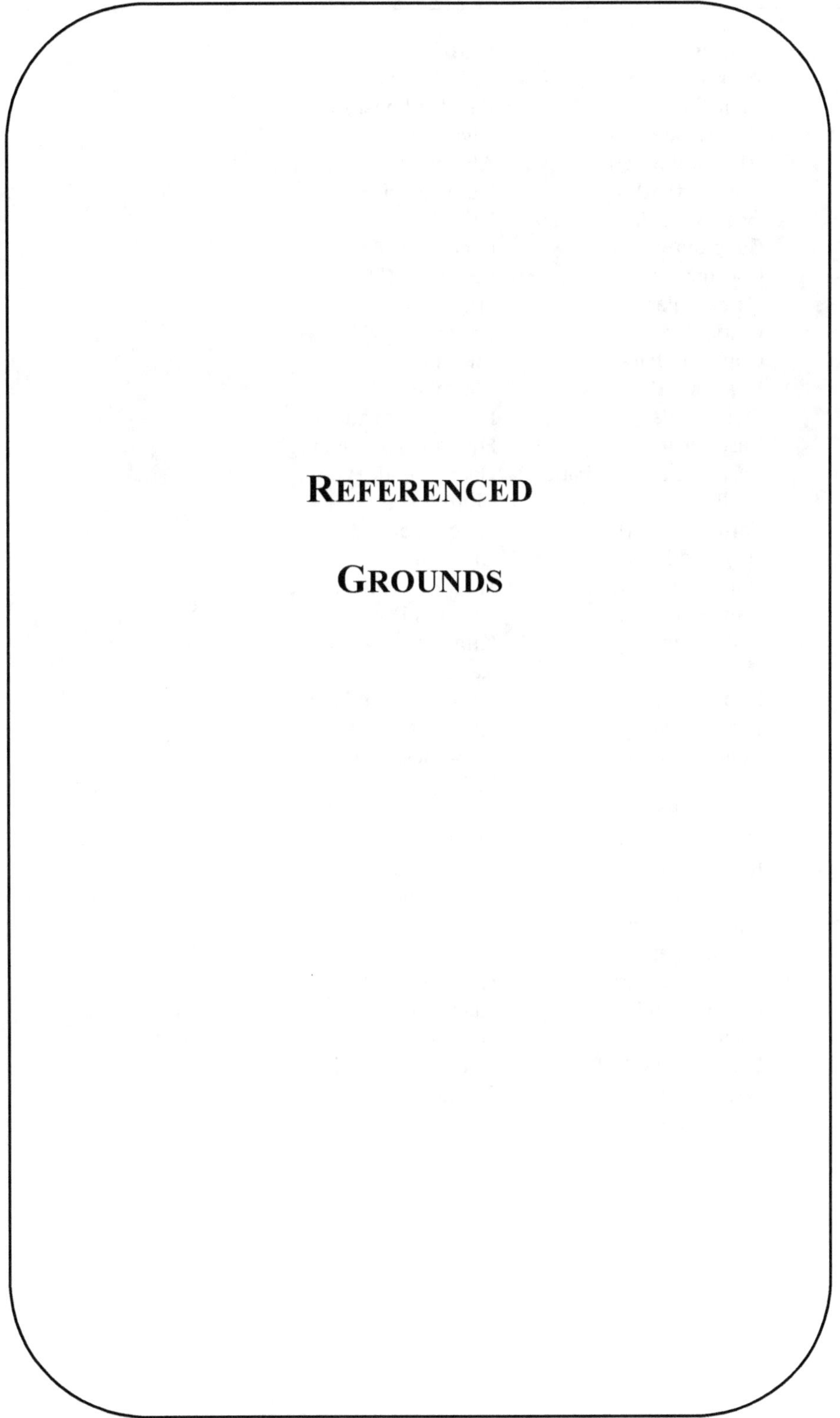

REFERENCED

GROUNDS

Ground	Club
Alexandria	Vale of Leven
Bainsford	East Stirlingshire
Barrowfield Park	Clyde
Blackstoun Park	Abercorn
Boghead Park	Dumbarton
Brockville Park	Falkirk
Cappielow Park	Greenock Morton
Carolina Port	East End (Dundee)
Cathkin Park	3rd L.R.V.
Celtic Park	Celtic
Copeland Park	Pilgrims
Deacon's Bank	Thornliebank
Douglas Park	Hamilton Academical
Easter Road	Hibernian (Edinburgh)
East Dock Street Park	Harp (Dundee)
Fir Park	Motherwell
Forthbank Park	King's Park
Gayfield Park	Arbroath
Hamilton Crescent	West of Scotland C.C.
Hampden Park	Queen's Park
Holm Quarry	Kilmarnock Athletic
Ibrox Park	Rangers
Kennyhill Park	Alexandra Athletic
Kinning Park	Clydesdale
Logie Green	St Bernard's
Love Street	St Mirren
Newton Park	Kirkcaldy
Ochilview Park	Stenhousemuir
Rollo's Pier	Strathmore (Dundee)
Rugby Park	Kilmarnock
Springvale Park	Ayr
Tontine Park	Renton
Tynecastle Park	Heart of Midlothian
Underwood Park	Abercorn
Victoria Park	3rd L.R.V.
West Craigie Park	Our Boys (Dundee)
Westmarch	St Mirren
Whitefield Park	Cambuslang

Early Laws

of the

Game

THE FOOTBALL ASSOCIATION 1863

The fourth meeting of the members of this recently formed association was held on Tuesday evening, Dec 1, at seven o'clock, at the Freemasons' Tavern, Great Queen-street, Lincoln's Innfields, for the further consideration of the laws, and perfecting generally the working arrangements of the association.

LAWS

1. The maximum length of the ground shall be 200 yards, the maximum breadth shall be 100 yards, the length and breadth shall be marked off with flags; and the goal shall be defined by two upright posts, eight yards apart, without any tape or bar across them.

2. A toss for goals shall take place, and the game shall be commenced by a place kick from the centre of the ground by the side losing the toss for goals; the other side shall not approach within 10 yards of the ball until it is kicked off.

3. After a goal is won, the losing side shall be entitled to kick off, and the two sides shall change goals after each goal is won.

4. A goal shall be won when the ball passes between the goal-posts or over the space between the goal-posts (at whatever height), not being thrown, knocked on, or carried.

5. When the ball is in touch, the first player who touches it shall throw it from the point on the boundary line where it left the ground in a direction at right angles with the boundary line, and the ball shall not be in play until it has touched the ground.

6. When a player has kicked the ball, any one of the same side who is nearer to the opponent's goal line is out of play, and may not touch the ball himself, nor in any way whatever prevent any other player from doing so, until he is in play; but no player is out of play when the ball is kicked off from behind the goal line.

7. In case the ball goes behind the goal line, if a player on the side to whom the goal belongs first touches the ball, one of his side shall be entitled to a free kick from the goal line at the point opposite the place where the ball shall be touched. If a player of the opposite side first touches the ball, one of his side shall be entitled to a free kick at the goal only from a point 15 yards outside the goal line, opposite the place where the ball is touched, the opposing side standing within their goal line until he has his kick.

8. If a player makes a fair catch, he shall be entitled to a free kick, providing he claims it by making a mark with his heel at once; and in order to take such kick he may go back as far as he pleases, and no player on the opposite side shall advance beyond his mark until he has kicked.

9. No player shall run with the ball.

10. Neither tripping nor hacking shall be allowed, and no player shall use his hands to hold or push his adversary.

11. A player shall not be allowed to throw the ball or pass it to another with his hands.

12. No player shall be allowed to take the ball from the ground with his hands under any pretence whatever while it is in play.

13. No player shall be allowed to wear projecting nails, iron plates, or gutta percha on the soles or heels of his boots.

DEFINITION OF TERMS

A **PLACE KICK** - Is a kick at the ball while it is on the ground, in any position which the kicker may choose to place it.

A **FREE KICK** – Is the privilege of kicking the ball, without obstruction, in such a manner as the kicker may think fit.

A **FAIR CATCH** – Is when the ball has been kicked or knocked on by an adversary, and before it has touched the ground or one of the side catching it; but if the ball is kicked behind goal-line, a fair catch cannot be made.

HACKING – Is kicking an adversary.

TRIPPING – Is throwing an adversary by use of the legs.

KNOCKING ON - Is when a player strikes or propels the ball with his hands, arms, or body without kicking or throwing it.

HOLDING – Includes the obstruction of a player by the hand or any part of the arm below the elbow.

TOUCH – Is that part of the field, on either side of the ground, which is beyond the line of flags.

Ref 1863001

THE SCOTTISH FOOTBALL ASSOCIATION 1875

LAWS OF THE GAME

1. The limits of the ground shall be: maximum length, 200 yards; minimum length, 100 yards; maximum breadth, 100 yards; minimum breadth, 50 yards. The length and breadth shall be marked off with flags; and the goals shall be upright posts, 8 yards apart, with a tape or bar across them, 8 feet from the ground.

2. The winners of the toss shall have the option of kick-off or choice of goals. The game shall be commenced by a place-kick from the centre of the ground; the other side shall not approach within ten yards of the ball until it is kicked off, nor shall any player on either side pass the centre of the ground in the direction of his opponents' goal until the ball is kicked off.

3. Ends shall only be changed at half-time. After a goal is won, the losing side shall kick-off, but after the change of ends at half-time, the ball shall be kicked off by the opposite side from that which originally did so; and always as provided in Law 2.

4. A goal shall be won when the ball passes between the goal-posts under the tape or bar, not being thrown, knocked or carried. The ball hitting the goal, or boundary posts, or goal bar, or tape, and rebounding into play, is considered in play.

5. When the ball is in touch a player of the opposite side to that which kicked it out, shall throw it from the point on the boundary-line where it left the ground in a direction at right angles with the boundary-line, at least six yards, and it shall not be in play until it has touched the ground, and the player throwing it in shall not play it until it has been played by another player.

6. When a player kicks the ball, any one of the same side who at such moment of kicking is nearer to the opponents' goal-line is out of play, and may not touch the ball himself, nor in any way whatever prevent any other player from doing so until the ball has been played, unless there are at least three of his opponents nearer their own goal-line; but no player is out of play when the ball is kicked from the goal-line.

7. When the ball is kicked behind the goal-line by one of the opposite side, it shall be kicked off by one of the players behind whose goal-line it went, within six yards of the nearest goal-post; but if kicked behind by any one of the side whose goal-line it is, a player of the opposite side shall kick it from within one yard of the nearest corner flag-post. In either case no other players shall be allowed within six yards of the ball until it is kicked off.

8. No player shall carry or knock on the ball, and handling the ball, under any pretence whatever, shall be prohibited, except in the case of the goal-keeper, who shall be allowed to use his hands in defence of his goal, either by knocking on or throwing, but shall not carry the ball. The goal-keeper may be changed during the game, but not more than one player shall act as goal-keeper at the same time, and no second player shall step in and act during any period in which the regular goal keeper may have vacated his position.

9. Neither tripping nor hacking shall be allowed, and no player shall use his hands to hold or push his adversary nor charge him from behind.

10. No player shall wear any nails, excepting such as have their heads driven in flush with the leather, nor iron plates or gutta-percha, on the soles or heels of his boots.

11. In the event of any infringement of Rules 6, 8 or 9, a free kick shall be forfeited to the opposite side from the spot where the infringement took place.

12. In no case shall a goal be scored from any free kick, nor shall the ball be again played by the kicker until it has been played by another player. The kick-off and corner-flag kick shall be free kicks within the meaning of this rule.

13. That in the event of any supposed infringement of Rules 6, 8, 9 or 10, the ball be in play until the decision of the Umpire on his being appealed to, shall have been given.

DEFINITION OF TERMS.

A **PLACE KICK** is a kick at the ball while it is on the ground, in any position in which the kicker may choose to place it.

HACKING is kicking an adversary intentionally.

TRIPPING is throwing an adversary by use of the legs.

KNOCKING ON is when a player strikes or propels the ball with his hands or arms.

HOLDING includes the obstruction of a player by the hand or any part of the arm below the elbow.

TOUCH is that part of the field, on either side of the ground, which is beyond the line of flags.

A **FREE KICK** is a kick at the ball in any way the kicker pleases, when it is lying on the ground; none of the kicker's opponents being allowed within six yards of the ball, but in no case can a player be forced to stand behind his own goal-line.

HANDLING is understood to be playing the ball with the hand or arm.

Ref 18750037

6th December 1882

Law Changes   **International Football Conference**

MANCHESTER, Wednesday night – A conference of the representatives of the National Football Association of England, Wales, Scotland, and Ireland was held… The object of the conference was to assimilate the rules of the respective National Associations for application to International matches … The 5th rule was remodelled as follows:-

"When the ball is in touch, a player of the opposite side to that which kicked it out should throw it in from the point of the boundary line where it left the ground. The thrower, facing the field of play, shall hold the ball above his head and throw it with both hands in any direction, and it shall be in play when thrown in. The player throwing it in shall, not play it until it has been played by another player."

The 6th rule was altered so as to read in harmony with the rule of the English Association, and the 8th and 9th were made to correspond with these of the Scotch Association, with the following addition to the 9th :-

"A player with his back towards his opponent's goal cannot claim the protection of this rule when charged from behind, provided, in the opinion of the umpires or referee, he is in this position willfully impeding his opponent."

The 10th rule was made to read according to the English rule, with the addition of the words:-

"Any player discovered infringing this rule shall be prohibited from taking any further part in the game."

Some minor differences in the rules of the respective Associations were also adjusted. The chief alterations recommended by the conference, therefore, consist in the adoption

for international matches of the Scotch rule as to throwing in from "touch," and of the English rule of "side."
Ref 1882037

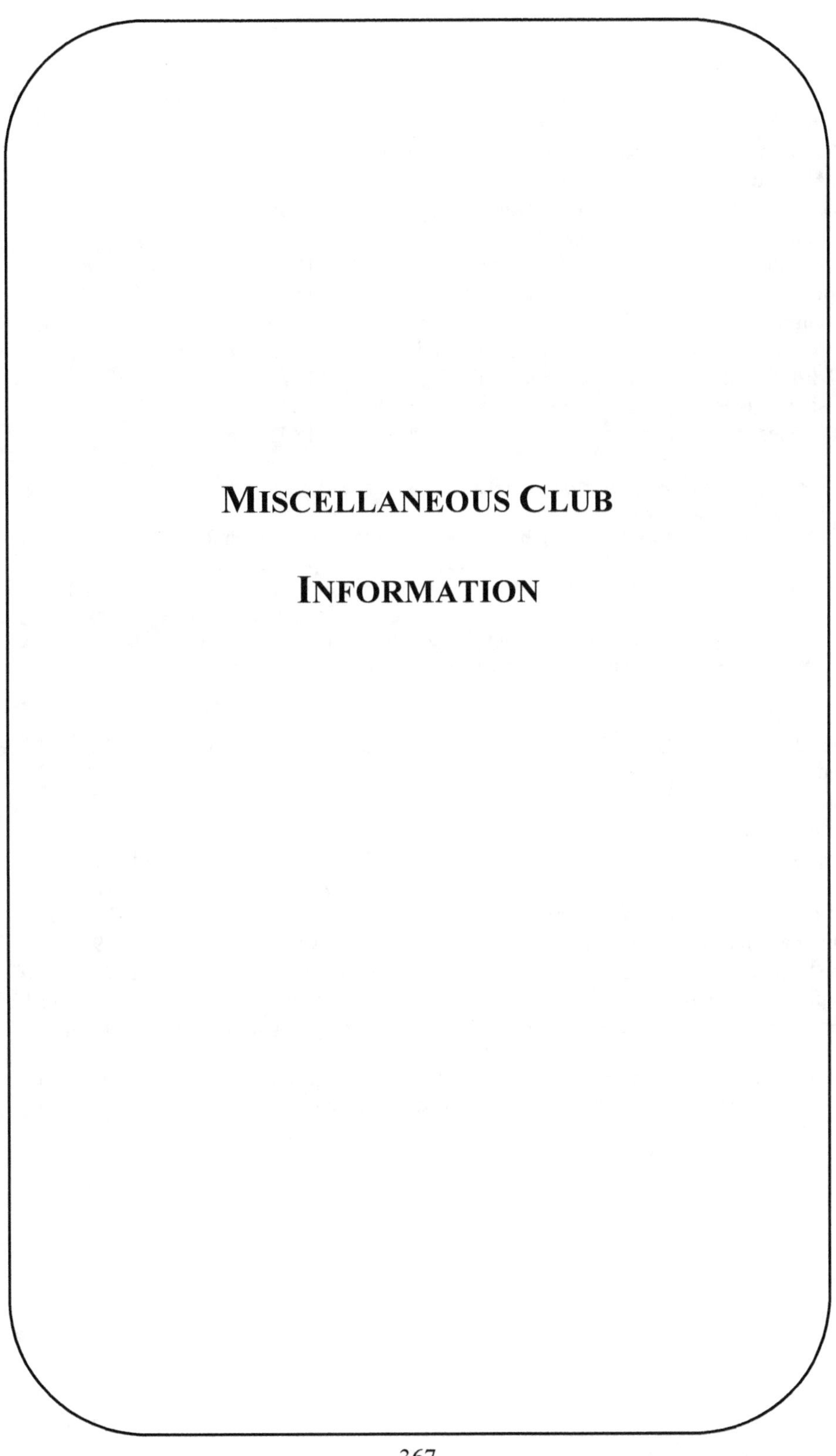

Miscellaneous Club Information

Name Changes

From	To	Date
Kilmarnock C&FC [I]	Kilmarnock Athletic	1878
10th Dumbartonshire R.V.	Kirkintilloch Athletic	1879
Shawfield	Derby	1876
2nd Ayrshire R.V.	Newmilns	1889
Alclutha	Dunbritton	1883
Excelsior	Airdrieonians	1881
Lochee	Lochee United	1890 Sep
Shaughraun	Milton of Campsie	1879
Hibernian (Dundee)	Harp (Dundee) [II]	1895 Sep 17th
3rd Edinburgh R.V.	St Bernard's [III]	1878
Rising Thistle	Thistle (Lochmaben)	1893
Dumfries Wanderers	Q.O.S. Wanderers [IV]	1891 Jun 11th

[I] - name was changed owing to its similarity to Kilmarnock F.C.

[II] - formed 28th July 1879

[III] - St Bernard's were a footballing breakaway from the 3rd Edinburgh Rifle Volunteers

[IV] - the previous "Q.O.S. Wanderers" were permanently suspended from the Association for professionalism on 19th November 1889 and later reformed under the name of Leafield Swifts. A new club Dumfries Wanderers then leased Cresswell Park, before being given approval by the S.F.A. the following year, to rename to Q.O.S. Wanderers. Dumfries Wanderers played their first match on 16th August 1890.

Black Watch

The 2nd Battalion Black Watch were based in Glasgow in seasons 1892-93 & 1893-94 and in Edinburgh in season 1894-95.

Amalgamations

Teams	New Team	Date
Ayr Academy & Ayr Eglinton	Ayr Academicals	1876 Oct 19th
Ayr Academicals & Ayr Thistle	Ayr	1879 Apr 7th [II]
Dumbarton & Dumbarton Atheltic	Dumbarton	1889 Aug 5th [III]
East End and Our Boys	Dundee	1893 Jun 20th
Alpha & Glencairn	Motherwell	1886 May 17th
Johnstone Wanderers & Strathmore (Dundee) [I]	Dundee Wanderers	1894 Jun

[I] - Johnstone Wanderers and Strathmore amalgamated to form the Dundonians Club in January 1894 but in June changed their name to Dundee Wanderers.

[II] - probable date based on research.

[III] - announced in the newspapers

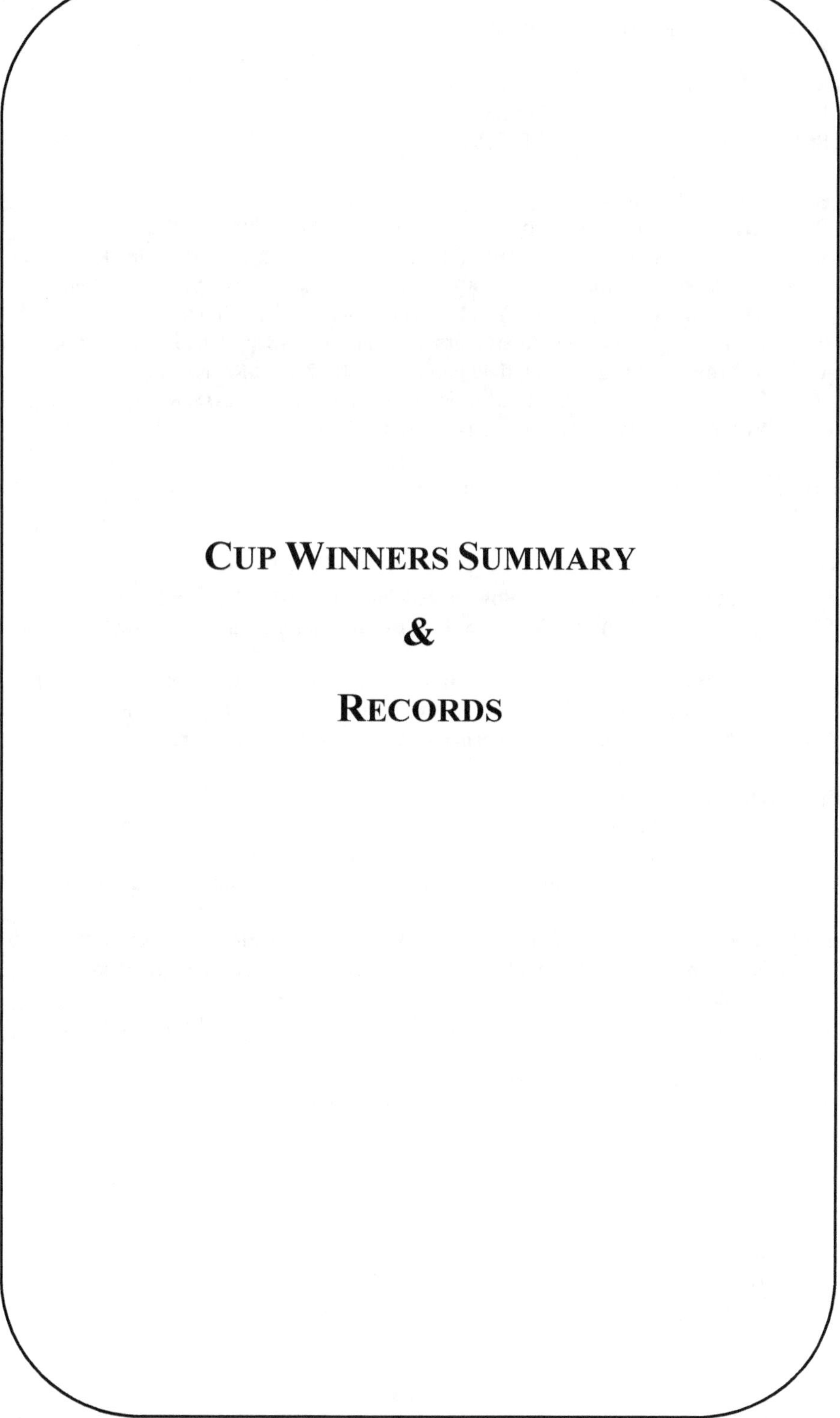

CUP WINNERS SUMMARY

&

RECORDS

Cup Winners Summary 1874-1900

10 Queen's Park	3 Celtic	3 Rangers
3 Vale of Leven	2 Heart of Midlothian	2 Renton
1 Dumbarton	1 Hibernian	
1 St Bernard's	1 3rd L.R.V.	

Record Scores - Home Wins

36-0	**Arbroath** v Bon Accord	at Gayfield Park, 12-Sep-1885, First Round
35-0	**Harp** [1] v Rovers (Aberdeen)	at East Dock Street, 12-Sep-1885, First Round
21-1	**Cowlairs** v Victoria (Glasgow)	at Gourlay Park, 7-Sep-1889, First Round
20-0	**Arbroath** v Orion	at Gayfield Park, 11-Sep-1886, First Round
20-1	**Johntone** v Greenock Abstainers	at Johnstone, 5-Sep-1891, P.S. First Round
18-0	**Arbroath** v Orion	at Gayfield Park, 3-Sep-1887, First Round
18-2	**Cowlairs** v Temperance Athletic	at Gourlay Park 1-Sep-1888, First Round
17-0	**Yoker** v Tayavalla	at Yoker, 4-Oct-1884, Second Round

[1] - Harp held the scoring record for 5 minutes, having kicked their match off earlier than Arbroath's.

Record Scores - Away Wins

0-17	Redding Athletic v **Camelon**	at Redding, 24-Sep-1887, Second Round
2-17	Glasgow Perthshire v **Wishaw Thistle**	at Kelburne Park, 3-Sep-1892, P.S. First Round
0-14	Addiewell v **Heart of Midlothian**	at West Calder , 7-Oct-1882, First Round
0-14	Kirkintilloch Athletic v **Renton**	at Townhead Park, 12-Sep-1885, First Round
1-14	Southfield v **Renton**	at Slamannan, 30-Sep-1882, Second Round

Record Scores - Draws

7-7	Q.O.S. Wanderers v 5th K.R.V.	at Nunholm North, 8-Sep-1883, First Round
6-6	Maybole v Ayr Athletic	at Maybole, 7-Sep-1889, First Round
6-6	Royal Albert v Cowlairs	at Larkhall, 26-Sep-1891, Preliminary Stage First Round

Most Matches in a Tie – 6 Kilmarnock v Hurlford 1885-86 Second Round

3-4	Kilmarnock v Hurlford	at Rugby Park, 3-Oct-1885 Protested registration
1-1	Kilmarnock v Hurlford	at Rugby Park, 17-Oct-1885
npl	Kilmarnock v Hurlford	at Beresford Park, 24-Oct-1885, Kilmarnock did not appear
1-1	Kilmarnock v Hurlford	at Springvale Park, 31-Oct-1885
2-2	Hurlford v Kilmarnock	at Hurlford, 7-Nov-1885
1-5	Kilmarnock v Hurlford	at Rugby Park, 14-Nov-1885

Most Individual Goals in a Match

13	**John Petrie** for Arbroath v Bon Accord	at Gayfield Park, 12-Sep-1885, First Round
10	**Michael D'Arcy Jun.** for Harp v Rovers (Aberdeen)	at East Dock Street, 12-Sep-1885, First Round

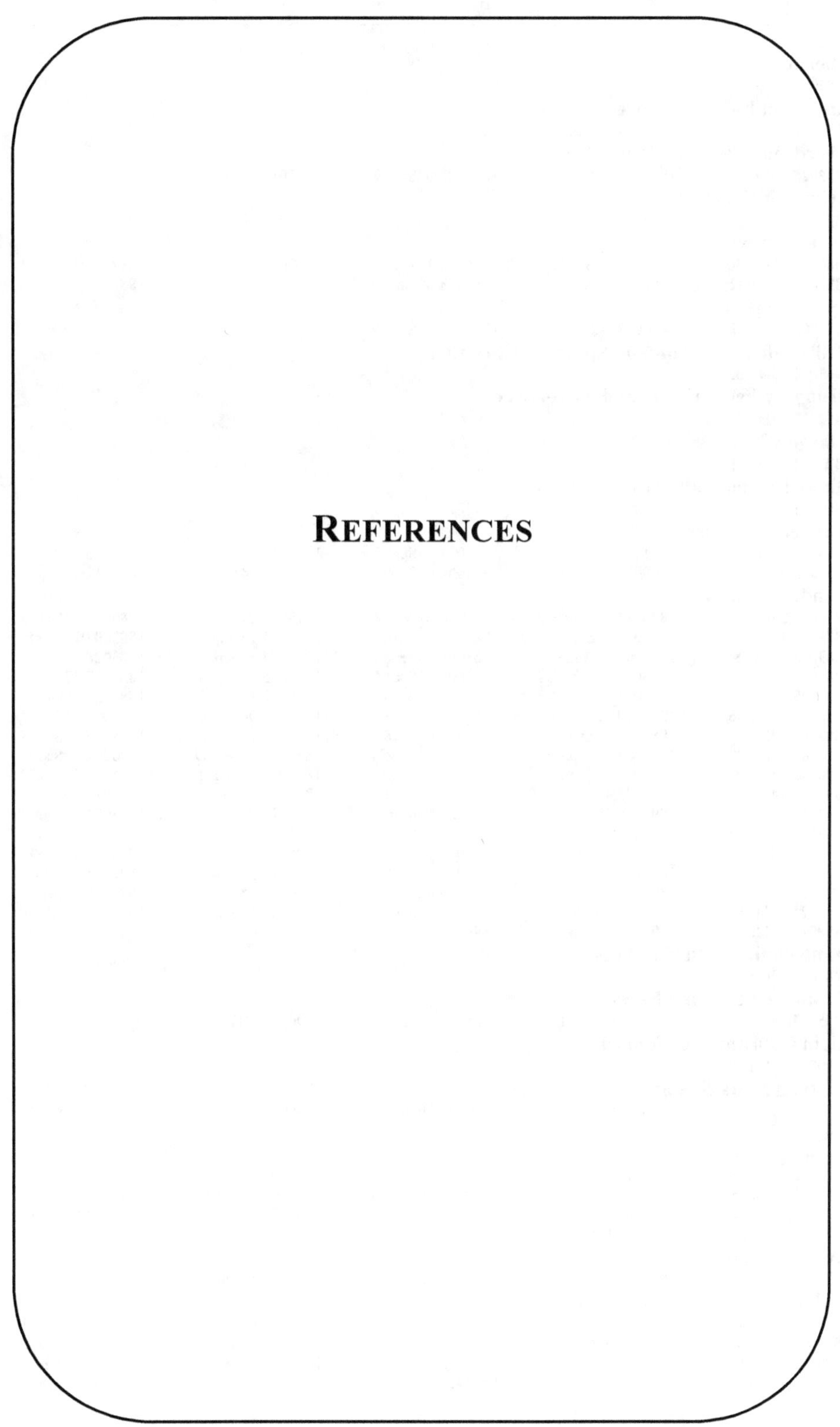# References

Aberdeen Free Press
1885002:31Aug85

Aberdeen Evening Express
1886007:13Sep86   1891024:07Dec91

Aberdeen Press and Journal
1882022:09Oct82   1886003:13Sep86   1889028:09Sep89   1891019:09Nov91

Arbroath Herald
1891025:03Dec91   1893017:19Oct93   1898013:09Feb99   1899018:09Nov99

Athletic News
1880034:01Dec80   1880038:01Sep80   1881042:11Jan82   1882010:04Oct82   1882017:11Oct82
1882019:04Oct82   1882027:01Nov82   1882028:08Nov82   1883012:12Sep83   1886024:12Oct86

Ayr Advertiser
1883005:06Sep83   1891003:10Sep91   1891004:17Sep91

Bell's Life in London and Sporting Chronicle
1863001:05Dec63

Broughty Ferry Guide and Advertiser
1891033:11Dec91

Glasgow News
1873004:20Oct73

Dumfries and Galloway Standard
1890003:10Sep90   1891005:09Sep91   1893011:27Sep93

Dundee Advertiser
1879003:22Sep79   1881018:17Oct81   1884001:15Sep84   1884016:14Oct84   1885013:14Sep85
1885025:20Oct85   1889020:20Nov89   1893004:04Sep93   1895028:04Jun96   1896012:16Sep96

Dundee Courier
1876006:23Oct76   1876014:13Nov76   1877034:01Apr78   1879012:04Nov79   1880021:25Oct80
1881016:11Oct81   1882004:11Sep82   1882021:09Oct82   1883001:13Aug83   1883002:21Aug83
1883003:27Aug83   1883004:29Aug83   1883009:20Sep83   1883024:18Sep83   1883028:01Oct83
1883032:29Oct83   1883036:25Feb84   1884003:15Sep84   1884035:15Sep84   1884027:17Nov84
1884029:26Nov84   1884031:22Dec84   1885014:14Sep85   1885022:19Oct85   1885023:14Oct85
1886004:13Sep86   1886009:22Sep86   1886022:13Oct86   1886031:06Sep86   1887007:05Sep87
1887008:14Sep87   1887014:13Sep87   1887022:05Oct87   1887034:28Nov87   1888005:03Sep88
1889001:09Sep89   1889005:18Sep89   1889019:11Nov89   1889021:25Nov89   1890002:08Sep90
1890043:13May91   1891001:19Aug91   1891008:07Sep91   1891009:16Sep91   1891028:14Dec91
1891031:14Mar92   1891032:11Apr92   1891034:02Jun92   1892001:05Sep92   1892014:26Sep92
1892015:05Oct92   1892016:17Oct92   1892025:13Mar93   1892027:23Jun93   1893001:23Aug93
1893007:13Sep93   1893015:25Oct93   1893016:16Oct93   1893022:30May94   1894001:22Aug94
1894005:03Sep94   1894009:12Sep94   1894013:24Sep94   1895002:02Sep95   1895007:18Sep95
1895011:23Sep95   1895012:02Oct95   1895014:18Sep95   1895017:30Oct85   1895023:09Dec95
1895024:13Jan96   1895025:29Jan95   1896005:02Sep96   1896007:16Sep96   1896010:14Sep96
1896024:27Jan97   1896027:25Jan97   1896014:14Sep96   1897003:13Sep97   1898015:24Apr99
1898017:24May99   1899004:25Sep99   1899016:23Oct99   1899017:06Nov99

Dunfermline Saturday Press
1887030:22Oct87

Edinburgh Evening News
1875007:15Nov75   1883018:24Sep83   1885003:23Sep85   1890034: 01Dec90

Elgin Courant and Courier
1899010:26Sep99

Evening News & Star
1877032:11Mar78   1878027:11Dec80   1879027:29Dec79   1880006:11Sep80   1880029:24Nov80
1880031:27Nov80   1882008:20Sep82

Evening Telegraph
1878037:28Oct78   1880010:20Sep80   1880013:04Oct80   1882002:11Sep82   1884034:05Sep84
1884037:07Jan85   1886030:29Oct86   1889025:20Nov89   1890007:24Sep90   1890036:08Dec90
1893002:31Aug93   1893003:04Sep93   1893010:02Sep93   1894027:08May95   1896032:02Jun97
1897013:08Nov97   1899013:02Oct99

Evening Times
1877002:12Sep77   1877003:01Oct77   1877022:05Dec77   1877033:18Mar78   1878020:30Oct78

Falkirk Herald and Linlithgow Journal
1878007:05Oct78   1879007:04Oct79   1880022:30Oct80   1880032:02Dec80   1882024:28Oct82
1884024:25Oct84   1885024:17Oct85   1887029:01Oct87   1888001:08Sep88   1888006:15Sep88
1888025:21Sep88   1890014:13Sep90   1890033:29Oct90   1891014:30Sep91   1892026:03Jun93
1894007:15Sep94   1894008:26Sep94   1894012:22Sep94   1895001:04Sep95   1896008:19Sep96

1896020:05Dec96	1897006:02Oct97	1897007:29Sep97	1897017:04Jun98	1898005:14Sep98
1898006:17Sep98	1898009:12Nov98	1898010:19Nov98	1899011:29Sep99	

Fife Free Press

1895021:09Nov95	1895026:08Feb96			

Glasgow Herald

1869001:01Jun69	1869002:10Aug69	1870001:27Jun70	1870002:12Jul70	1870003:22Sep70
1870004:27Sep70	1870005:01Nov70	1873001:18Mar73	1873101:15Apr73	1873002:10Oct73
1873003:20Oct73	1873006:27Oct73	1873011:24Nov73	1873012 25Nov73	1873013:01Dec73
1873016:26Mar74	1873017:25Aug74	1874007:26Oct74	1874010:09Mar75	1874011:29Mar75
1875009:08Nov75	1875011:29Nov75	1875013:20Dec75	1876004:09Oct76	1876007:23Oct76
1876008:30Oct76	1877004:01Oct77	1877005:02Oct77	1877008:08Oct77	1877028:22Jan78
1878002:04Sep78	1878005:23Sep78	1878017:21Oct78	1878001:28Oct78	1878035:15Apr78
1878034:28Apr79	1878035:30Apr79	1879002:22Sep79	1879019:27Sep79	1879005:29Sep79
1879009:22Oct79	1879010:27Oct79	1879017:17Nov79	1879018:12Nov79	1879022:03Dec79
1879024:22Dec79	1879026:29Dec79	1879028:23Feb80	1879029:29Apr80	1880008:22Sep80
1880026:25Oct80	1880027:15Nov80	1880036:28Mar81	1880037:11Apr81	1881002:12Sep81
1881003:19Sep81	1881010:03Oct81	1881013:12Oct81	1881022:24Oct81	1881023:02Nov81
1881024:07Nov81	1881029:31Oct81	1881032:14Nov81	1881034:21Nov81	1881038:19Dec81
1881041:09Jan82	1881045:20Feb82	1881046:27Apr82	1882001:11Sep82	1882011:05Oct82
1882013:02Oct82	1882014:09Sep82	1882031:04Dec82	1882039:25Dec82	1882038:09Apr83
1883007:10Sep83	1883025:24Sep83	1883033:12Nov83	1883037:03Mar84	1884007:24Sep84
1884009:01Oct84	1884017:27Oct84	1884020:10Nov84	1884021:12Nov84	1884022:14Nov84
1884030:17Dec84	1884036:29Dec84	1885001:26Aug85	1885008:14Sep85	1885020:19Oct85
1885033:25Nov85	1885034:18Jan86	1885036:08Feb86	1886002:25Aug86	1886006:13Sep86
1886017:20Sep86	1886023:04Oct86	1886026:13Oct86	1886033:12Jan87	1886034:11May87
1887001:29Aug87	1887002:05Sep87	1887004:14Sep87	1887019:19Sep87	1887020:26Sep87
1887021:05Oct87	1887037:04Jun88	1888002:03Sep88	1888043:04Feb89	1888045:06Feb89
1889007:09Sep89	1889010:09Oct89	1889012:21Oct89	1889013:30Oct89	1889023:11Dec89
1890001:08Sep90	1890015:17Sep90	1890024:29Sep90	1890031:13Oct90	1890035:08Dec90
1890037:22Dec90	1890040:03Jun91	1890041:08Jun91	1891006:07Sep91	1891011:28Sep91
1891016:05Oct91	1891017:15Sep90	1891018:26Oct91	1891022:03Dec91	1891023:30Nov91
1891026:14Dec91	1891027:16Dec91	1891030:15Feb92	1892003:05Sep92	1892008:05Oct92
1892018:28Nov92	1893012:16Oct93	1893020:20Dec93	1893021:04Apr94	1894006:12Sep94
1894014:03Oct94	1894015:05Dec94	1894020:26Nov94	1894022:10Dec94	1894024:26Dec94
1894026:25Feb95	1895004:04Sep95	1895008:02Oct95	1895015:30Sep95	1895022:09Dec95
1896001:05Aug96	1896002:31Aug96	1896016:28Oct96	1896018:25Nov96	1896028:10Feb97
1896029:17Feb97	1896031:17Mar97	1897001:04Aug97	1897002:15Sep97	1897005:29Sep97
1897011:13Oct97	1897014:10Nov97	1897015:24Nov97	1897016:28Mar98	1898002:10Sep98
1898003:14Sep98	1898007:19Sep98	1898011:07Dec98	1898012:18Jan99	1899002:13Sep99
1899003:27Sep99	1899008:08Nov99	1899019:29Jan00		

Kilmarnock Standard

1883030:xxNov83	1883031:xxNov83			

Lennox Herald

1877031:23Feb78	1882012:07Oct82	1885007:19Sep85		

Motherwell Times

1885004:19Sep85	1886027:16Oct86	1890042 13Jun91	1892007:17Sep92	1892011:01Oct92
1892022:03Dec92	1892023:24Dec92	1894003:01Sep94	1896003:28Aug96	1899015:13Oct99

North British Daily Mail

1873005:27Oct73	1873009:17Nov73	1874003:26Oct74	1874006:09Nov74	1876003:02Oct76
1877012:22Oct77	1878006:23Sep78	1878019:28Oct78	1878021:30Oct78	1882006:11Sep82
1882009:18Sep82	1888037:15Oct88			

Scotsman

1873002:13Oct73	1873007:27Oct73	1873010:17Nov73	1873014:22Dec73	1873015:23Mar74
1874002:19Oct74	1874005:26Oct74	1874008:30Nov74	1874012:12Apr75	1875001:03Sep75
1875002:22Sep75	1875004:18Oct75	1875006:15Nov75	1875008:17Nov75	1875010:08Nov75
1875012:29Nov75	1875015:24Jan76	1876001:25Sep76	1876018:01Jan77	1877011:18Oct77
1877015:03Dec77	1876019:15Dec76	1877018:06Dec77	1877019:10Dec77	1877027:14Jan78
1877029:21Jan78	1877036:22Oct77	1878003:04Sep78	1878004:23Sep78	1878008:30Sep78
1878028:02Dec78	1878029:12Dec78	1878031:23Dec78	1878036:01May79	1879011:20Oct79
1879013:12Nov79	1879014:03Nov79	1879015:10Nov79	1879016:12Nov79	1879025:24Dec79
1880012:04Oct80	1880018:03Nov80	1880028:24Nov80	1881001:12Sep81	1881036:05Dec81
1881039:26Dec81	1882020:02Oct82	1882023:09Oct82	1882025:23Oct82	1882029:06Nov82
1882032:04Dec82	1882037:07Dec82	1883022:10Sep83	1883023:17Sep83	1883035:23Feb84
1883038:31Mar84	1884019:06Nov84	1884025:30Oct84	1885018:05Oct85	1885035:22Jan86
1886028:25Oct86	1886032:10Jan87	1887013:14Sep87	1887031:14Nov87	1887036:21May88
1888003:03Sep88	1888010:12Sep88	1888020:17Sep88	1888026:24Sep88	1888038:26Nov88

1888039:05Dec88	1888040:10Dec88	1888044:04Feb89	1889002:09Sep89	1889017:21Oct89
1889027:09Sep89	1889024:07Jun90	1890005:17Sep90	1890008:22Sep90	1890010:08Sep90
1890020:29Sep90	1890022:08Oct90	1890023:13Oct90	1890026:08Oct90	1890032:20Oct90
1891002:07Oct91	1891021:18Nov91	1891029:08Feb92	1892009:26Sep92	1892019:21Dec92
1892024:27Feb93	1892021:19Dec92	1893005:04Sep93	1893013:16Oct93	1893014:25Oct93
1894002:03Sep94	1894017:26Nov94	1894018:05Dec94	1894025:04Feb95	1894028:07Jun95
1895006:18Sep95	1895009:16Sep95	1895027:13Jan96	1896015:30Sep96	1896021:11Jan97
1896023:25Jan97	1896026:27Jan97	1896030:15Mar97	1897008:29Sep97	1898001:10Sep98
1898014:20Feb99	1898016:15May99	1899009:11Oct99		

Scottish Athletic Journal

1878033:29Feb84	1883026:05Oct83	1883034:22Feb84	1888036:16Oct88	1889003:20Sep89

Scottish Football Annual 1875

1875003:14Oct75

S.F.A. Minutes

1880030:23Nov80	1881007:20Sep81	1881014:04Oct81	1881015:11Oct81	1881037:13Dec81
1883016:18Sep83	1887018:13Sep87	1888021:17Sep88	1888030:02Oct88	

Scottish Football Reminiscences and Sketches – D.D. Bone 1890

1880035

Scottish Referee

1892004:05Sep92	1896004:04Sep96	1897012:25Oct97

Scottish Sport

1889004:13Sep89	1892002:06Sep92	1892010:27Sep92	1893008:15Sep93	1894010:11Sep94
1895003:03Sep95	1896013:18Sep96			

Southern Reporter

1899006:05Oct99

Stirling Journal

1881006:23Sep81

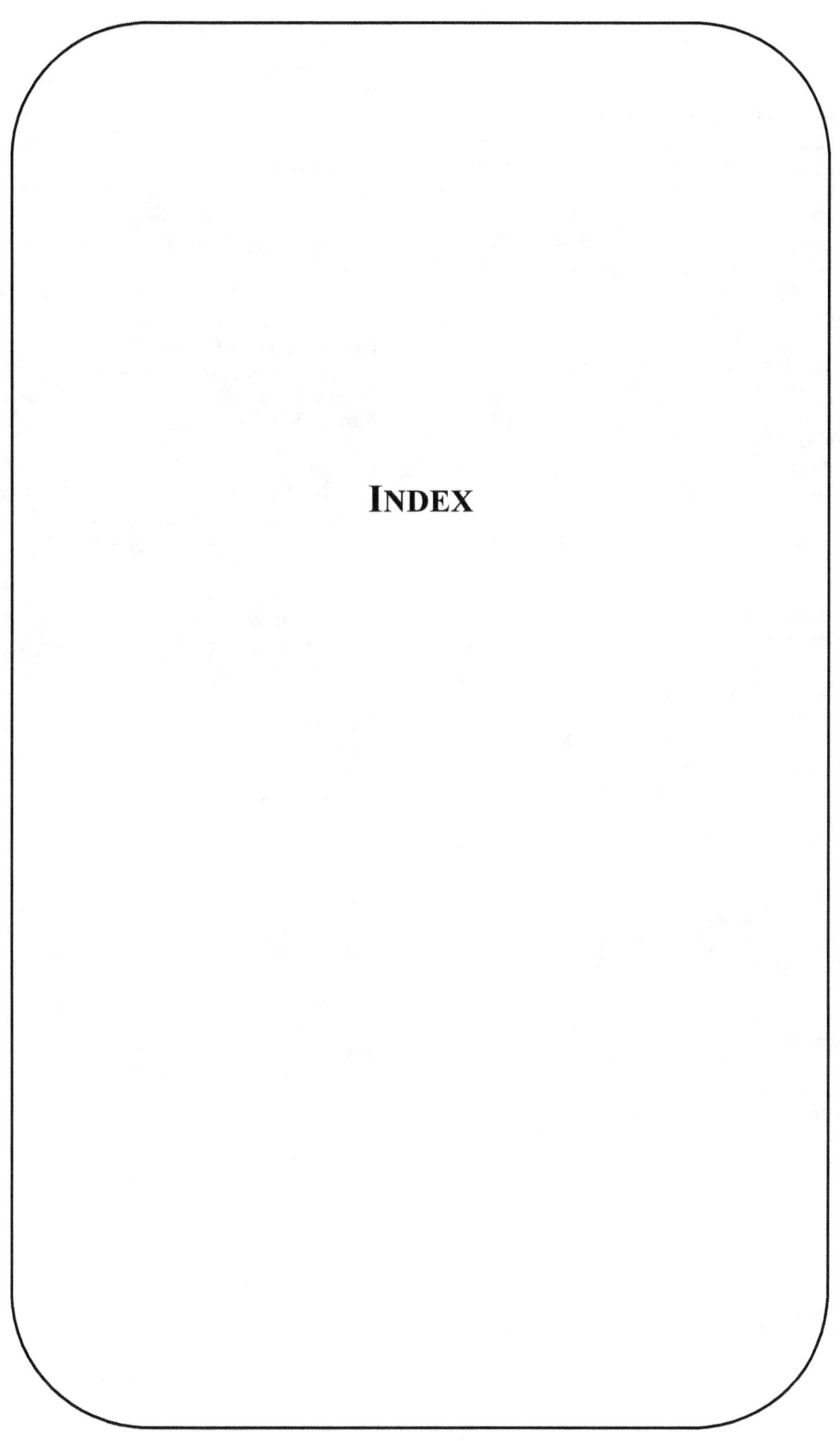

INDEX

A

abandoned *see Match Incidents*
Abercorn 58, 105, 151, 158, 213, 360
Aberdeen 88, 113, 127, 140, 185, 187, 197, 239
Aberfeldy Breadalbane 104, 127
abuse *see Spectators & Match Officials*
accidents 28, 31, 32, 39, 40, 69, 77, 94, 109, 120,
    136, 163, 178, 183, 184, 186, 194, 197, 214,
    236, 245
Acts of Parliament 195
Addiewell 89
admissions *see Committee Meetings*
Adventurers 170, 175, 210
Ailsa 28
Airdrie 2, 3 , 41, 60, 73, 100, 113
Airdriehill 58, 73, 113, 127, 195
Airdrieonians 72, 126, 132, 162, 179, 213, 217,
    368
Albatross 28
Albion 127
Albion Rovers 145, 149, 216, 218
Alclutha 368
Alexandra Athletic 8, 15, 19, 24, 62, 360
Alexandria 28
Alloa Athletic 142, 203, 218, 235
Alpha 113, 368
amalgamations 23, 47, 202, 210, 368
ambulance *see Emergency Services*
amendments *see Committee Meetings*
amputations *see Injuries*
amusement 67, 79, 96, 159, 204
anger *see Spectators*
Angus 83, 127
ankle *see Injuries*
Annbank 74, 97, 112, 136, 152, 155, 165, 184,
    186, 221, 240, 241
Annfield 69
Apsley 85
Arbroath 40, 42, 47, 51, 61, 62, 94, 102, 110,
    111, 117, 129, 137, 182, 187, 192, 196, 207,
    243, 250, 360
Arbroath Wanderers 234
Armadale 127, 132
Arthurlie 14, 30, 64, 65, 86, 90, 91, 92, 131, 154,
    210, 231
Athole 59
attacked *see Match Officials, Players*
Auchinleck Boswell 60
Avondale 28, 113
awarded cup 45, 103
awarded tie 96, 98, 107, 129, 130, 149, 157,
    175, 216, 230, 235
Ayr 47, 124, 136, 164, 167, 182, 360, 368

Ayr Academicals 47, 368
Ayr Academy 368
Ayr Athletic 166
Ayr Eglinton 23, 368
Ayr Parkhouse 224, 237
Ayr Rovers 113
Ayr Thistle 26, 30, 47, 368
2nd Ayrshire R.V. 153, 368

B

bad language *see Players*
bad light *see Playing Conditions*
Balgay 83, 99, 100
Barrhead 31, 38, 48
Barrhead Rangers 49
Bathgate 65
Bathgate Rovers 194
2nd Battalion Black Watch 210, 368
Battlefield 102, 108, 112, 206, 213, 216
beautiful dribbling game 3
Beith 33, 95, 163, 240
Bellshill 49, 149
Bellstane Birds 127, 174
Blackburn Rovers 103
Blackfriars 28
Blairvaddick 127
Blantyre 223
blood *see Injuries*
Blythswood 9, 12
Bon Accord 113, 117, 127
Bonhill 113
Bo'ness 106, 174, 247, 249
boots *see Equipment*
break-ins *see Spectators*
Brechin 182, 192, 202
bribe 133
brick *see Spectators*
Bridge of Allan 58, 71, 72
broken bones *see Injuries*
brothers 30, 32
Broughty 113, 119, 128, 188
Broxburn 176
Broxburn Shamrock 113, 139, 152, 184, 211
Broxburn Thistle 127
bruises *see Injuries*
Brunswick 51
brutality *see Match Incidents*
Burnbank Swifts 174, 175, 211
Burntisland Thistle 127, 137, 142
Busby 24
Bute Rangers 98, 100
bye-law *see Rules and Regulations*